lonely planet

New York City

"All you've got to do is decide to go and the hardest part is over.

So go!"

TONY WHEELER, COFOUNDER – LONELY PLANET

ALI LEMER, ANITA ISALSKA, MASOVAIDA MORGAN, KEVIN RAUB

Contents

Plan Your Trip 4

Explore New York City 58

Understand New York City 347

Survival Guide 379

New York City Maps 403

AUGUSTO VITALE/SHUTTERSTOCK ©

COVID-19

We have re-checked every business in this book before publication to ensure that it is still open following the COVID-19 outbreak. However, the economic and social impacts of COVID-19 will continue to be felt long after the outbreak has been contained, and many businesses, services and events referenced in this guide may experience ongoing restrictions. Some businesses may be temporarily closed, have changed their opening hours and services, or require bookings; some unfortunately could have closed permanently. We suggest you check with venues before visiting for the latest information.

(left) Flatiron Building (p167)

(right) Sphinx, Temple of Dendur, Metropolitan Museum of Art (p214)

ITZAVU/SHUTTERSTOCK ©

Right: Bryant Park (p191)

WELCOME TO New York City

Life in NYC can be both thrilling and maddening. It's not the easiest place to live, but the dizzying array of rewards here – restaurants, live music and theatre, museums, shopping, beautiful parks, a breathtaking skyline – makes most other cities pale in comparison. But best of all is the indefatigable spirit of the people. When the pandemic hit, New Yorkers came together to figure out ways to help each other survive, from mutual-aid groups delivering groceries to musicians playing outside to entertain during lockdown. Tough times never last, but New Yorkers do – and so does NYC.

by Ali Lemer, Writer
For more about our writers, see p448

New York City's Top Experiences

1 SKYLINE VIEWS

If anything can make even the most cynical heart thrill, it's the sheer breadth of the unforgettable New York City skyline. Get the best views by heading up or heading east. And there's never a bad time: glass facades mirror azure skies by day and pink-streaked clouds at dawn and sunset; by night, a million windows sparkle with light against the dark expanse.

H GO/GETTY IMAGES ©

SEAN PAVONE/SHUTTERSTOCK ©

Empire State Building

The striking art-deco skyscraper may no longer be NYC's tallest, but it remains one of its most recognizable icons and still offers one of the best views in town – particularly around sunset when the twinkling lights of the city and New Jersey switch on. p180

Right: Empire State Building

F11PHOTO/SHUTTERSTOCK ©

DROP OF LIGHT/SHUTTERSTOCK ©

One World Observatory

One World Trade Center, the Western Hemisphere's tallest building, looms like a beacon above Lower Manhattan. Take a high-speed elevator ride to the 102nd floor for fabulous views over the city and several surrounding states. There's also a virtual time-lapse showing the skyline's evolution from the 1600s to the present. p71

Above: One World Observatory

Brooklyn Waterfront

Don't like heights? Head east to Brooklyn, where a string of riverfront locations offer stunning skyline-and-bridge views: the Brooklyn Heights Promenade, Brooklyn Bridge Park in Dumbo, or East River State Park in Williamsburg. p266

Above: Brooklyn Heights Promenade

2 GREEN SPACES

Breaking up all those concrete canyons are the hundreds of parks spread throughout the five boroughs. Some are pocket-sized, while others range for acres, providing New Yorkers with crucial outlets for some fresh air, green grass underfoot, and a chance to relax in nature.

GAGLIARDIPHOTOGRAPHY/SHUTTERSTOCK ©

Central Park

One of the world's most renowned green spaces (and the USA's most-visited park), this urban oasis boasts 843 acres of landscaped greenery, boulder-studded outcrops, elm-lined walkways, European-style gardens and a central lake and reservoir. Head to the forested North Woods to forget you're even in NYC. p228

Left: Autumn boaters,Central Park

Below: Great Lawn, Central Park

TETRA IMAGES/GETTY IMAGES ©

SIVAN ASKAYO/LONELY PLANET ©

QUIGGYT4/SHUTTERSTOCK ©

Prospect Park

This green jewel at the center of Brooklyn is where locals come to play, filling its meadows for picnics, taking boats out onto the lake; running and cycling its shaded loop road; and ambling with their kids and dogs amid beautifully landscaped scenery. p264

Left: Brooklyn Botanic Garden (p270), Prospect Park

Brooklyn Bridge Park

One of NYC's best-sited parks, strung along over a mile of Brooklyn's western shoreline, has revitalized a derelict waterfront to provide sports fields, playgrounds, a carousel, walking paths, lush lawns and absolutely jaw-dropping views of Lower Manhattan framed by the Brooklyn and Manhattan Bridges. p263

Above: Brooklyn Bridge Park

3 HIGH ART & BIG STAGES

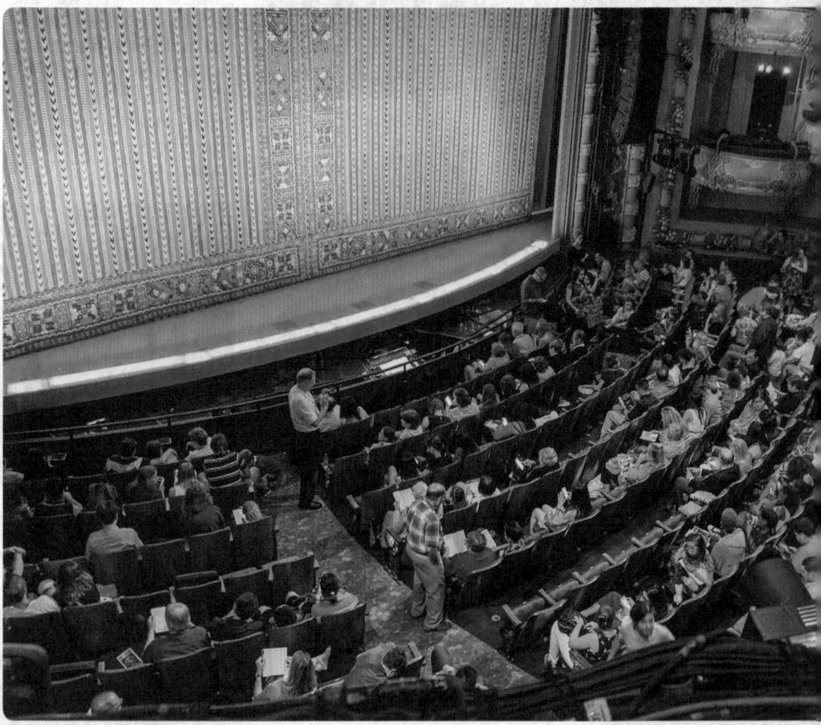

Befitting its status as one of the world's supreme culture capitals, New York City is stuffed with museums and performance venues featuring the best and brightest in their fields. But don't just stop at the stately temples of art and the top Broadway theaters – you'll find fantastic art and photography and talented actors, musicians and dancers in smaller venues all over town, too.

Above: New Amsterdam Theatre (p178)
Right: Museum of Modern Art (MoMA; p182)

STUDIO BARCELONA/SHUTTERSTOCK ©

PIT STOCK/SHUTTERSTOCK ©

Metropolitan Museum of Art

The country's most encyclopedic museum is packed with dazzling sights: an Egyptian temple, chiseled sculptures from ancient Greece, medieval armor, exquisite Islamic art and European Old Masters. p214

Left: Metropolitan Museum of Art

Museum of Modern Art (MoMA)

A trove like few others, where you can see icons from Van Gogh's *The Starry Night* to Warhol's *Campbell's Soup Cans*. Leave time for Chagall, Krasner and Haring – and a vino in the Sculpture Garden. p182

Broadway Shows

Set around the electrifying energy of Times Square, the stages of Broadway are NYC's dream factory, where romance, betrayal and triumph come with dazzling choreography and stirring songs. p179

Below: Ambassador Theatre (p208)

MIKECPHOTO/SHUTTERSTOCK ©

EQROY/SHUTTERSTOCK ©

4 NEIGHBORHOOD RAMBLING

The best way to see New York is on foot, popping in and out of shops or cafes as your fancy takes you and delighting at moments when street scenes mirror the New York you know from TV. A walker's delight, this is a city that invites endless wandering. One of the USA's oldest cities, New York has layers upon layers of human habitat SoHo & Chinatown ion starting with the Lenape people, who inhabited these lands for untold centuries before the Dutch arrived in 1624. Get a sense of the countless millions who have called this place home at these historic sites.

Chinatown

It's all about sensory stimuli here. Listen for the prayer gong in a Buddhist temple, follow the aroma of freshly roast duck, and melt into the flow of everyday life on the streets of this bustling neighborhood. p88

Below: Chinatown

GUILLAUME GAUDET/LONELY PLANET ©

RBLFMR/SHUTTERSTOCK ©

RYAN DEBERARDINIS/SHUTTERSTOCK ©

East Village & Lower East Side

Wander the streets of these historic 'hoods to catch glimpses of the different cultures that have called it home, reflected in its international restaurants, vintage shops, art-punk bars and Hispanic community gardens dotted throughout. p107

Above left: Cargo bike rider, East Village

Greenwich Village

Predating Manhattan's organized street grid, 'the Village' and neighboring Meatpacking District form a picturesque labyrinth of cobblestone streets dotted with pocket-sized boutiques, narrow sidewalk cafes and quaint restaurants. p140

Above right: Outdoor dining, Greenwich Village

5 EXPLORING BROOKLYN

Manhattanites don't like to admit it, but you can have a stellar NYC experience entirely in this one borough, which almost feels like its own town. Brooklyn offers street-art-splashed live-music venues, knowingly hip coffee shops, postindustrial reinvention into arts and shopping precincts, waterside parks, retro cocktail lounges and exemplary restaurants dishing out everything from vegan comfort food to Michelin-starred gastronomy.

GUILLAUME GAUDET/LONELY PLANET ©

SOLEPSIZM/SHUTTERSTOCK ©

Williamsburg

Browse thrift stores, artists markets and boutiques, followed by dinner at an eclectic restaurant and cocktails with a view at a rooftop bar. p140

Top left: Williamsburg retailer

Park Slope

Stroll past 19th-century brownstones and beaux-art row houses, then down buzzy main drag Fifth Avem before a perusal of historic Green-Wood Cemetery. p270

Bottom left: Park Slope streetscape

Brooklyn Heights & Dumbo

Cross the Brooklyn Bridge, grab a picnic lunch at historic Empire Stores and catch cutting-edge theater at St Ann's Warehouse. p266

Above: Brooklyn Flea (p299), Dumbo

6 AMAZING ARCHITECTURE

MEUNIERD/SHUTTERSTOCK ©

ROMAN TIRASPOLSKY/SHUTTERSTOCK ©

NIELSKLIIM/SHUTTERSTOCK ©

Skyscrapers may have been invented in Chicago, but they were perfected in New York. With buildings here going back to the 17th century, you can see architecture across a range of styles: from stately Federal to exuberant Beaux Arts to brutalist postmodern, all the way up to contemporary projects from international 'starchitects'.

Chrysler Building

William Van Alen's 1930 art-deco masterpiece is one of the world's most famous buildings, with one of NYC's most beautiful lobbies. Its lit-up triangular spire windows are an unforgettable feature of the NYC skyline. p186

Left: Chrysler Building

Grand Central Terminal

Conceived as a temple to transportation, this 1913 Beaux-Arts beauty is stunning both outside and in – especially the painted constellations on the ceiling of its marbled main concourse. p184

Left: Grand Central Terminal

Cathedral Church of St John the Divine

Begun in 1892 and still not completely finished, this uptown cathedral is a towering melange of architectural styles, with elements of Romanesque, Gothic and neo-Gothic design. p247

7 STEP BACK IN TIME

One of the USA's oldest cities, New York has layers upon layers of human habitation starting with the Lenape people, who inhabited these lands for untold centuries before the Dutch arrived in 1624. Get a sense of the countless millions who have called this place home at these historical sites.

Lower East Side Tenement Museum

Gain insight into how 19th-century immigrants lived on an eye-opening tour of the cramped, two-room apartments inside a preserved tenement building, or on one of the museum's neighborhood walking tours. p109

Below right: Lower East Side Tenement Museum

/SHUTTERSTOCK ©

Ellis Island & Statue of Liberty

Migrant gateway Ellis Island is home to one of the city's most moving museums. Nearby Lady Liberty has symbolized new-world hope since her unveiling in 1886. p64

Above: Statue of Liberty

Merchant's House Museum

Tour this lovingly preserved 1832 townhouse of the upper-middle-class Tredwells, with all of its original furniture and decorations intact. p91

Right: Servants' room, Merchant's House Museum

8 SAVE YOUR WALLET

When you figure in the cost of a hotel room, three meals per day, entertainment tickets, transport and souvenir shopping, a trip to NYC can definitely set you back a chunk of change. Thankfully there's plenty you can do around town without spending a nickel.

High Line

One of New York's best examples of urban renewal, the linear park on this former elevated rail track is perfect for strolling, sitting and picnicking 30ft above the city, with fabulous Hudson River views. p134

Staten Island Ferry

The best free boat ride in town offers fresh sea air and the closest views of the Statue of Liberty without actually visiting it. The Financial District looks amazing on the return trip, especially at sunset. p85

National September 11 Memorial

Two reflecting pools weep like dark, elegant waterfalls. Framing them are the names of those who lost their lives here in 2001 and in the 1993 World Trade Center bombing. p68

Above: National September 11 Memorial; designers Michael Arad and Peter Walker

What's New

After a tough year battling the pandemic, New York City has rebounded thanks to vigorous vaccination efforts. Outdoor attractions and activities are booming, bars and restaurants have reopened with COVID-safe protocols, and indoor live performances are welcoming audiences back with proof of vaccination.

Little Island

The newest piece of real estate in town is this 2.4-acre artificial **island park** (www.littleisland.org) perched above the Hudson on flower-like concrete pilings. It's free and open to the public, with a variety of events and performances at low or no cost.

Poster House

One of NYC's newest museums, **Poster House** (www.posterhouse.org) is the world's only museum dedicated exclusively to the humble poster, both as means of visual communication and as historical documents.

The High Line

NYC's famed elevated linear park, the High Line (p134) completed its final extension phase in 2019. Running from Gansevoort St to W 34th, it offers 360-degree city views, generous seating and monumental art.

Museum of Modern Art (MoMA)

An ambitious 2019 expansion project for this bold modern-art museum (p182) added 40,000 sq ft of gallery space, purpose-built performance spaces, free street-level galleries and a redesigned shop.

LOCAL KNOWLEDGE

WHAT'S HAPPENING IN NYC

Ali Lemer, Lonely Planet writer

You can't keep a good city down. After an incredibly tough year battling COVID-19, New York City is back, though not without changes that offer a stark reminder that the pandemic is far from over. People are riding the subways again; restaurants have indoor dining (though the outdoor patios remain popular); museums offer timed ticket slots to limit guest capacity; Coney Island amusement parks have reopened; and Broadway shows are raising their curtains. Outdoor life has boomed like never before, with locals flocking to parks, streets blocked off to traffic and outdoor bars to enjoy well-ventilated activities in the sunshine.

But as the delta variant spread widely in summer 2021, even vaccinated New Yorkers were asked to wear masks indoors again, and Mayor De Blasio declared that proof of vaccination would be required to patronize restaurants, bars, nightclubs, gyms and entertainment venues, the first initiative of its kind in the US. Life continues to find a way here – if a bit more cautiously than before.

Empire State Building

Millions of dollars went into a redesign (p180) promising shorter queues, a flash new museum exhibit and knee-trembling views through floor-to-ceiling glass windows on the 102nd floor.

Airport Concept Hotel

Famed architect Eero Saarinen's iconic 1962 TWA Flight Center at JFK has been reimagined as a time-capsule of a hotel (p346) – and maybe NYC's coolest rooftop pool.

Bronx Night Market

Benefiting from its open-air location in a newly reopened NYC, the Bronx Night Market (p254) takes place every Saturday from May to October, featuring some 50 local food and drink vendors, plus live music.

Harlem Supper Club

Noted for pioneering San Francisco's underground supper club scene, California chef Russell Jackson makes his NYC debut at Harlem's Reverence (p255) with a five-course tasting menu.

The Bronx's New Bookstore

Two years after the Bronx's only bookstore (a Barnes and Noble) closed in 2017, native Noëlle Santos launched Lit. Bar (p254), an indie shop-meets-wine-bar emphasizing minority-authored titles.

Art at Chelsea Market

A departure from the neighborhood's typical white-cube gallery scene, Artechouse (p141) brings modern, hallucinatory innovations in experiential art to the previously unused, 6000-sq-ft boiler room space beneath historic Chelsea Market.

LISTEN, WATCH & FOLLOW

For inspiration and up-to-date news, visit www.lonelyplanet.com.

@TimeOutNewYork The weekly mag tweets the latest about happenings around town.

Eater NY (http://ny.eater.com) New openings and reviews from New York's ever-changing restaurant and bar scenes.

The Bowery Boys (www.boweryboyshistory.com) Biweekly podcast dives deep into New York's long and fascinating history.

Tracy's New York Life (www.tracysnewyorklife.com) Local lifestyle writer's blog with NYC travel tips, shopping, nightlife, day trips, eating and more.

Humans of New York (www.humansofnewyork.com) Meet the locals through the poignant interviews of this acclaimed photoblog.

FAST FACTS

Food trend Streetside dining
Languages spoken 637
Annual tourists 65.1 million (2018)
Population 8.8 million

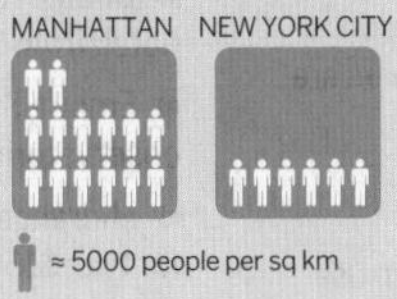

NYC by Ferry

Ferry services (p384) linking the boroughs by water continue to expand, with new routes to Coney Island, Staten Island (from Midtown West) and the Bronx on the way.

For more recommendations and reviews, see lonelyplanet.com/new-york-city

Need to Know

For more information, see Survival Guide (p379)

Currency
US dollar (US$)

Language
English

Visas
The US Visa Waiver Program allows nationals of 38 countries to enter the US without a visa, but you must fill out an ESTA application before departing.

Money
ATMs widely available; credit cards accepted at most hotels, stores and restaurants. Farmers markets and some food trucks, restaurants and bars are cash-only.

Cell Phones
International travelers can use local SIM cards in a smartphone, provided it is unlocked. Alternatively, you can buy a cheap US phone and load it with prepaid minutes. Some phone carriers also offer free international data roaming so check your package before leaving home.

Time
Eastern Standard Time (GMT/UTC minus five hours)

Tourist Information
NYC Information Center (p390)

Daily Costs

Budget: Less than $250
- Dorm bed: $40–70
- Slice of pizza: around $4
- Food-truck taco: from $3
- Happy-hour glass of wine: $10
- Bus or subway ride: less than $3

Midrange: $250–500
- Double room in a midrange hotel: from $200
- Empire State Building dual observatories ticket: $58
- Midrange restaurant dinner for two: $150
- Craft cocktail: $15–19
- Discount Broadway tickets: around $80

Top end: More than $500
- One night at opulent Greenwich Hotel: from $650
- Upscale tasting menu: $90–315
- One-hour massage at Great Jones Spa: $150
- Metropolitan Opera orchestra seats: $85–445

Advance Planning

Two months before Reserve accommodation – prices increase closer to check-in. Snag tickets to Broadway blockbusters and request a free Big Apple Greeters tour.

One month before Most high-end restaurants release bookings four weeks ahead so reserve your table for that blow-out meal.

One week before Surf the web and scan blogs and Twitter for the latest restaurant and bar openings, music, comedy and art events.

Useful Websites

NYC: The Official Guide (www.nycgo.com) New York City's official tourism portal.

Explore Brooklyn (www.explorebk.com) Brooklyn-specific events and listings.

Free Williamsburg (www.freewilliamsburg.com), **Brokelyn** (www.brokelyn.com) and **Brooklyn Based** (www.brooklynbased.com) Keep tabs on the latest borough news, music gigs, art openings and more.

Gothamist (https://gothamist.com) Light-hearted NYC news, local gossip and entertainment listings.

Lonely Planet (www.lonelyplanet.com/usa/new-york-city) Destination information, hotel reviews, traveler forum and more.

WHEN TO GO

Summer can be scorchingly hot, but brings a packed lineup of events. Winter sometimes brings blizzards, but festive fun draws crowds. Spring or fall offer the best weather for exploring.

New York City

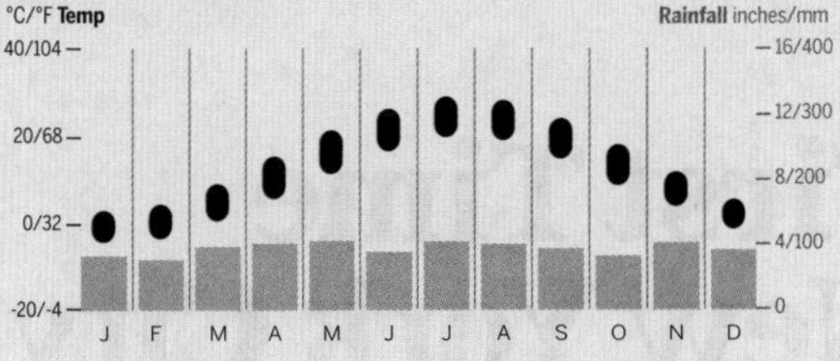

Arriving in New York City

John F Kennedy International Airport The AirTrain ($5) links to the subway ($2.75), which makes the one-hour journey into Manhattan. Express buses to Grand Central or Port Authority cost $19. Taxis cost a flat $52, excluding tolls, tip and rush-hour surcharge.

LaGuardia Airport The closest airport to Manhattan but the least accessible by public transportation: take the Q70 express bus from the airport to the 74th St–Broadway subway station. Express buses to Midtown cost $16. Taxis range from $35 to $55, excluding tolls and tip.

Newark Liberty International Airport Take the AirTrain ($5.50) to Newark Airport train station, and board any train bound for New York's Penn Station ($13). Taxis range from $50 to $70 (plus $15 toll and tip). Allow 45 minutes to one hour of travel time.

For much more on **arrival** see p380

Getting Around

Check the Metropolitan Transportation Authority website (www.mta.info) for bus and subway information. Delays have increased as ridership has expanded.

Subway Inexpensive, somewhat efficient and operates around the clock, though navigating lines can be confusing. A single ride is $2.75 with a MetroCard (or the expanding OMNY contactless system).

Buses Convenient during off hours – especially between the city's eastern and western sides (most subway lines run north to south). Uses MetroCard (and, eventually, OMNY); same price as the subway.

Taxi Meters start at $2.50, increasing 50¢ per 0.2 miles (with an additional 50¢ night surcharge). Congestion surcharge adds $2.50. See www.nyc.gov/taxi.

Bicycle Bike-share program Citi Bike (www.citibikenyc.com; 24-hour pass $12) is very popular. BYO helmet.

Inter-borough ferries The ferry (www.ferry.nyc) is handy between waterside stops in Manhattan, Brooklyn and Queens.

For much more on **getting around** see p383

Sleeping

Expect high prices and small spaces. Rates waver by availability, not by high-season or low-season rules. You'll pay dearly during holidays. Accommodations fill quickly, especially in summer and December, and range from cookie-cutter chains to stylish boutiques.

Brooklyn and Queens offer better value; Long Island City has a few bargain designer hotels, and Staten Island has affordable B&Bs if you don't mind a ferry ride. A few hostels are scattered throughout NYC.

Useful Websites

NYC (www.nycgo.com/hotels) Loads of listings from the NYC Official Guide.

Lonely Planet (lonelyplanet.com/usa/new-york-city/hotels) Find independent reviews as well as recommendations on the best places to stay.

For much more on **sleeping** see p330

First Time New York City

For more information, see Survival Guide (p379)

Checklist

- Ensure your passport is valid for at least six months past your arrival date.
- Check you meet all requirements for travel to the US and apply for an ESTA.
- Check airline baggage restrictions.
- Arrange for appropriate travel insurance.
- Inform your credit-/debit-card company of your travels.
- Book popular restaurants, shows and accommodations well in advance.

What to Pack

- Good walking shoes – NYC is best seen on foot, so make sure your shoes are super comfy.
- Dress shoes and a stylish outfit for smart restaurants and bars.
- If you take medications, bring enough for your entire trip.
- US electrical adapter.
- Hand sanitizer...trust us.

Top Tips for Your Trip

- Subway lines run both local and express trains. Local trains stop at all stations; express trains do not.
- MetroCards are valid on subways, buses and the tramway to Roosevelt Island. If staying awhile, buy a 7-Day Unlimited Pass. The touch-and-go OMNY service, gradually rolling out across the city, is making transport even snappier.
- If the number on a taxi's top light is lit, it's available. Note that green Boro taxis can't make pick-ups in Manhattan south of W 110th St and E 96th St.
- When giving an address, always include the nearest cross street/s (eg 700 Sixth Ave *at* 22nd St).
- Ferry tickets can be purchased at dockside machines or through the website (www.ferry.nyc) or app.
- The TKTS Booth in Times Square (p179) sells half-price, same-day tickets to selected shows and musicals. The South Street Seaport (p63) branch also sells next-day matinee tickets.

What to Wear

If visiting during New York's hot, humid summer, pack light, breathable garments (though higher-end restaurants and bars often call for more stylish attire, so bring at least one evening dress or long-sleeved shirt, pair of pants and dress shoes). Fluctuating temperatures in spring and fall call for layers. New York winters can be brutally cold, requiring gloves, scarf, hat, insulated jacket and waterproof boots.

Be Forewarned

NYC is one of the USA's safest cities, and violent-crime statistics have declined for the 28th straight year. Still, keep your wits about you.

- Don't walk alone at night in unfamiliar, sparsely populated areas.
- Beware pickpockets, particularly in mobbed areas like Times Square or Penn Station.
- While it's generally safe to ride the subway after midnight, you may want to take a taxi, especially when alone (ride in the back).

Tackling Crowds

Avoid the ire of millions of harried New Yorkers by following some basic rules. When catching the subway, have your payment card ready as you enter the station (a MetroCard's black stripe faces inwards for scanning at turnstiles). If carrying a backpack, take it off on crowded trains or wear it in front. When walking on busy sidewalks, keep to the right. If you need to stop or slow down, move to the side to let others pass.

Taxes & Refunds

Restaurants and retailers never include the sales tax – 8.875% – in their prices, so beware of ordering the $14.99 lunch special when you only have $15 to your name. Hotel rooms in New York City are subject to a 14.75% tax, plus a flat $3.50 occupancy tax per night. Since the US has no nationwide value-added tax (VAT), foreign visitors cannot make 'tax-free' purchases.

Tipping

Tipping is *not* optional.

Restaurant servers 18–20%

Bartenders Minimum per drink $1, $2 per specialty cocktail or 15–20% overall

Taxi drivers 10–15%, rounded up to the next dollar

Airport & hotel porters $2 per bag, minimum per cart $5

Hotel maids $2–4 per night; envelope or card may be provided

BLACKMAC/SHUTTERSTOCK ©

Taxis outside Grand Central Terminal (p184)

Etiquette

Politeness It's common courtesy to greet nearby staff when entering or leaving a shop, cafe or restaurant.

Greetings Shake hands with men and women when meeting for the first time and when saying goodbye. A single (air) kiss is common between friends.

Seating System When entering a restaurant (and some upscale bars), hover until you are seated by waitstaff. Coffee places and casual bars are self-service; cafes can be either.

Lively Debate Politics is loudly discussed by New Yorkers, and like religion it's a topic that can quickly reveal allies...or enemies.

Transport Allow passengers to exit the subway car before entering; don't block the doors.

Common Scams & Tourist Traps

➡ Avoid persistent street vendors selling tickets for tours or shows. You'll overpay or possibly fall victim to a scam.

➡ Folks in Times Square wearing costumes and body paint will expect payment if you pose for a picture with them.

➡ Be cautious about pedicabs. Operators are required to disclose their price per minute in written form on their vehicle; if you can't see that, it may be an unscrupulous operator.

➡ Never agree to buy a stranger's subway card or transport ticket.

➡ Beware fake Buddhist monks offering beads and demanding payment.

Getting Around

For more information, see Transportation (p380)

Check the Metropolitan Transportation Authority website (www.mta.info) for bus and subway information. Delays have increased as the number of users has grown.

Subway Inexpensive, somewhat efficient and operates around the clock, though navigating lines can be confusing. A single ride is $2.75 with a MetroCard (or the expanding OMNY contactless system).

Buses Convenient during off hours – especially between the city's eastern and western sides (most subway lines run north to south). Uses MetroCard (and, eventually, OMNY); same price as the subway.

Taxi Meters start at $2.50, increasing 50¢ per 0.2 miles (with an additional 50¢ night surcharge). Congestion surcharge adds $2.50. See www.nyc.gov/taxi.

Bicycle Bike-share program Citi Bike (www.citibikenyc.com; 24-hour pass $12) is very popular. BYO helmet.

Inter-borough ferries The ferry (www.ferry.nyc) is handy between waterside stops in Manhattan, Brooklyn and Queens.

Key Phrases

Boro Taxi If you're north of 116th St in Manhattan or in the outer boroughs, you can hail these green taxis, which have metered rates identical to yellow cabs.

Car service You can phone a car service (often a black sedan) to pick you up. Useful on return trips to the airport or if needing outer-borough transport (where taxis are in short supply).

Citi Bike The ubiquitous blue bikes that are part of NYC's bike-sharing scheme, with hundreds of quick-hire kiosks around town.

Express train/local train Express subway trains make limited stops, skipping many stations; local trains stop at every station. To switch between the two, usually you just have to cross the platform.

LIRR The Long Island Rail Road, useful for speedy transport to JFK airport and for beach getaways.

MetroCard The flimsy yellow-and-blue card, which you load with credit, then swipe through for every ride on the subway or bus.

Uptown/Downtown Uptown means going north (Upper East Side, Harlem etc), downtown means going south (SoHo, Lower Manhattan etc).

Key Routes

Scenic views Take the J, M or Z line over the Williamsburg Bridge or the B, D, N or Q line over the Manhattan Bridge for great views of Manhattan. There's also the Roosevelt Island Tramway (p193) for stunning views of the East Side of Manhattan.

Uptown bound The 4, 5 and 6 lines go to the Upper East Side, as does the Second Ave Q line. For the Upper West Side take the B, C, 1, 2 or 3 trains.

How to Hail a Taxi

➡ To hail a yellow cab, look for one with its roof light lit (if it's not lit, the cab is taken).

➡ Stand in a prominent place on the side of the road and stick out your arm.

➡ Once inside the cab, tell them your destination (it's illegal for drivers to refuse you a ride).

➡ Pay your fare at the end, either with cash or credit card (via the touch screen in the back). Don't forget to tip 10% to 15%.

TOP TIPS

➡ Pay attention to 'Downtown' vs 'Uptown' subway station entrances. Sometimes there are separate entrances depending on which direction the train is going.

➡ Plan your route carefully. Sometimes walking a few blocks can get you to a faster or more direct subway line, which will save you time.

➡ Download a smartphone app like CityMapper, Transit or MyMTA for journey planning, maps and service updates.

When to Travel

➡ Rush hour is never just an hour! On weekdays, from 8am to 9:30am, and 4:30pm to 6:30pm, trains and buses are frustratingly packed, particularly in Manhattan.

➡ If it's not possible to avoid traveling at these peak times, allow extra time to get to places (particularly to/from the airport).

➡ Hailing a cab can be difficult on weekdays from 4pm to 5pm when many drivers change shifts. And when it's raining, finding an available taxi can seem a monumental challenge.

Traveling at Night

Huge numbers of New Yorkers ride the subway late at night without incident, but it's worth staying alert. Pickpockets (or worse) may target the distracted or sleepy. For safety, get on the conductor's car (in the middle of the platform). Many opt for taxis or ride-shares for late-night journeys; if summoning an Uber, Lyft or the like, always check the number plate and ride in the back seat.

Etiquette

➡ Have your MetroCard ready before you go through the gate. New Yorkers are skilled at moving through the ticket barriers without breaking stride.

➡ On subway platforms, stand to the side of the train doors and wait for passengers to exit before boarding.

➡ On escalators, stand on the right-hand side or use the left if you want to walk down/up.

➡ When walking on the sidewalk, think of yourself as a car on the street: don't stop short, pay attention to the speed limit, and pull off to the side if you need to look at a map or dig through your bag for an umbrella.

Transporting Children

Note that taking a stroller on the subway can be challenging, especially where there aren't any elevators. As an alternative, it's possible to book transfers and taxi rides in vehicles installed with seats for kids; try www.kidcar.com.

Tickets & Passes

➡ The yellow-and-blue MetroCards (www.mta.info/metrocard) are the swipe cards used for all of NYC's public transportation (though they're gradually being phased out by the contactless OMNY payment system). Purchase or add value at easy-to-use automated machines at any station. Each ride on the subway or bus (except for express buses) deducts $2.75 from the card.

➡ Purchase the MetroCard itself for $1 at machines in subway stations, and load it with credit ($22, which will give you eight rides, is a good start). If you plan to ride a lot, buy a 7-Day Unlimited Pass ($33). These cards are handy for visitors – particularly if you're jumping around town each day.

➡ The subway machines take credit or ATM cards (larger machines also take cash). To add more credit, just insert your card and follow the prompts. Many Manhattan stations also have staffed information kiosks where you can load your card using cash.

➡ Transfers from subway to bus, or bus to subway, are free. Just swipe/insert your card; no extra charge will be deducted.

For much more on **getting around** see p383

Perfect Days

Day One

Upper West Side & Central Park (p226)

Spend the morning exploring the wonders of **Central Park**, taking in the fortress-like walls of skyscrapers surrounding the green. Start at **Columbus Circle**, then head in the northeast direction passing the **Bethesda Fountain**, the **Conservatory Water** and **Strawberry Fields** on the western side. If you have kids in tow, check out the dinosaur skeletons at the **American Museum of Natural History**, then hit up the **Loeb Boathouse** to rent rowboats.

Lunch Pick up supplies at Zabar's (p243) for a picnic in Central Park.

Midtown (p175)

It's now time to uncover some of the city's architectural wonders: **Grand Central Terminal**, the **Chrysler Building**, the **New York Public Library** and **Rockefeller Center**. Round it off with a visit to the city's museum darling: **MoMA**.

Dinner Slurp oysters at Grand Central's Oyster Bar & Restaurant (p196).

Midtown (p175)

Before leaving Grand Central, have a cocktail at **The Campbell**. Afterwards, catch an electrifying jazz performance at **Birdland** or ahead-of-the-curve theater at **Playwrights Horizon**. Soak up the urban maelstrom of **Times Square**, then head to the **Top of the Rock** to bid the city goodnight.

Day Two

Upper East Side (p211)

Start at the staggering **Metropolitan Museum of Art**. Wander through the Egyptian and Roman collections, take in European masters, then head up to the rooftop (in summer) for a view over Central Park. If you aren't exhausted by its monumental galleries, visit the nearby **Neue Galerie** for a feast of German and Austrian art in a 1914 mansion.

Lunch Tuck into classic American comfort food at old-school diner EJ's Luncheonette (p220).

SoHo & Chinatown (p86)

Head down to SoHo for an afternoon of shopping along **Prince** and **Spring Streets** amid crowds of tourists seeking the best brands in the world. Wander over to Chinatown's **Mulberry Street**, which feels worlds away from mainstream consumerism, but is – in reality – only a few blocks over. Visit the **Museum of Chinese in America**, then stroll the streets for pork buns and durian ice cream. Head to **Madison Square Park** to admire the Flatiron Building before dinner in Gramercy Park.

Dinner Book ahead for farm-to-table food at Craft (p171).

Union Square, Flatiron District & Gramercy (p164)

Afterwards wet your whistle in classic New York watering hole **Pete's Tavern**, or enjoy some belly laughs at bustling comedy joint **Peoples Improv Theater**. Finish up with Italian wine at Eataly's gorgeous rooftop bar, **Serra**.

Rose Main Reading Room, New York Public Library (p191)

Skyline, Lower Manhattan (p62)

Day Three

Brooklyn (p260)

Catch the East River Ferry over to Dumbo, and admire the magnificent view of Manhattan from the expansive **Brooklyn Bridge Park**. Afterwards, stroll through the cobblestone streets of Dumbo, browsing bookshops, boutiques and cafes. Don't miss the vintage **Jane's Carousel** and more great views from the **Empire Fulton Ferry**.

Lunch Take a bite of classic New York pizza pie at Juliana's (p278).

Brooklyn (p260)

Jump on the subway south to the **Brooklyn Museum** for a look at fascinating works from Africa, the Americas and Ancient Egypt, plus cutting-edge temporary shows. Afterwards take a stroll in **Prospect Park**, pausing for refreshments at the scenic **LeFrak Center**. Jump in a Boro Taxi up to **Williamsburg**, on the northern side of the borough; **Bedford Avenue** is a colorful place to experience the unique boutiques and cafe culture.

Dinner Order a pound of smoky brisket at Brooklyn's best BBQ house, Fette Sau (p286).

Brooklyn (p260)

After dinner, have a bespoke cocktail at **Maison Premiere**. Head up to rooftop bar, **Berry Park**, for a fabulous view over the city. End the night two blocks southwest at the **Brooklyn Bowl**, with a side of bowling and some groovy musical acts.

Day Four

Lower Manhattan & Financial District (p62)

Catch the **Staten Island Ferry** in the early morning and watch the sun come up over Lower Manhattan. After gliding back from Staten, head skyward for a marvelous view from the **One World Observatory**. Afterwards, visit the moving **National September 11 Memorial and Museum**.

Lunch Munch on gourmet goodies at the food-loving Chelsea Market (p151).

West Village, Chelsea & the Meatpacking District (p132)

Head up to the Meatpacking District and visit the gorgeous **Whitney Museum of American Art**. Afterwards, take the nearby steps up to the **High Line** for a wander along a once-abandoned rail line. Along the way stop for snacks, coffee breaks and intriguing views over the streetscape.

Dinner Dine on creative Asian fusion at RedFarm (p147).

West Village, Chelsea & the Meatpacking District (p132)

Stroll the lovely, meandering streets of Greenwich Village and delve into its soul-filled roots for an evening of intimate live jazz at **Mezzrow**, **Smalls** or the **Village Vanguard**. Afterwards, stop by for a bit of wine and snacks at buzzing **Buvette**, then head over to **Tippler** beneath Chelsea Market for craft beer or cocktails.

Month By Month

TOP EVENTS

Tribeca Film Festival, April

Cherry Blossom Festival, April or May

SummerStage, May through October

Independence Day, July

Village Halloween Parade, October

January

The winter doldrums arrive following the buildup of Christmas and New Year's Eve. Despite the long nights, New Yorkers take advantage of the frosty weather, with outdoor ice skating and weekend ski trips to the Catskills.

New Year's Day Swim

There's no more invigorating way to begin the new year than an icy dip in the Atlantic! Brace yourself and join the Coney Island Polar Bear Club (www.polarbearclub.org) for a communal splash (and hasty retreat).

No Pants Subway Ride

On the second Sunday in January, around 4000 New Yorkers bare their legs on public transit), to add some surreality to their commute. Anyone can participate, and there's usually an after-party. Check the website for meeting times, details and COVID-19 status.

Winter Jazzfest

This week-long music festival (www.winterjazzfest.com) brings over 100 acts to nearly a dozen venues around the city, mostly around the West Village.

February

The odd blizzard and below-freezing temperatures make February a good time to stay indoors nursing a drink or a warm meal at a cozy bar or bistro.

Lunar (Chinese) New Year Festival

One of the biggest Chinese New Year celebrations in the country, this display of fireworks and dancing dragons draws mobs of thrill seekers into the streets of Chinatown. The date of Chinese New Year follows the lunar calendar, typically falling in late January or early February.

Winter Restaurant Week

From late January to early February, celebrate the dreary weather with slash-cut meal deals at some of the city's finest eating establishments during New York's Winter Restaurant Week (www.nycgo.com/restaurant-week), which actually runs for nearly three weeks. A two-course lunch costs around $26 ($42 for a three-course dinner).

March

After months of freezing temperatures and thick winter coats, the odd warm spring day appears and everyone rejoices – though it's usually followed by a week of subzero drear as winter lingers on.

St Patrick's Day Parade

A massive audience, rowdy and wobbly from cups of green beer, lines Fifth Ave on March 17 for this popular parade of bagpipe blowers, floats and clusters of Irish-lovin' politicians. The parade, which was first held here in 1762, is the city's oldest and largest.

Armory Show

New York's biggest contemporary art fair (www.thearmouryshow.com) sweeps into the city for one weekend in March, showcasing the works of thousands of artists from around the world on two piers that jut into the Hudson River.

April

Spring finally appears: optimistic alfresco joints have a sprinkling of street-side chairs as the city squares overflow with bright tulips and blossom-covered trees.

Tribeca Film Festival

Created in response to the tragic events of September 11, Robert De Niro's downtown film festival (p47) has quickly become a star in the indie-movie circuit. You'll have to make some tough choices: over 150 films are screened during the 10-day fest.

May

April showers bring May flowers in the form of brilliant bursts of blossoms adorning trees all around the city. The weather is warm and mild without the unpleasant humidity of summer.

Cherry Blossom Festival

Known in Japanese as Sakura Matsuri, this annual tradition, held on one weekend usually in late April or early May, celebrates the magnificent flowering of cherry trees in the Brooklyn Botanic Garden. It's complete with entertainment and activities, plus refreshments and, of course, beautiful blossoms.

Fleet Week

For one week in late May (www.fleetweeknewyork.com), Manhattan resembles a 1940s movie set as clusters of uniformed sailors go 'on the town', a celebration that's been going strong for more than 30 years. Their ships, docked in the Hudson River, invite the curious to hop aboard.

June

Summer's definitely here and locals crawl out of their office cubicles to relax in the city's green spaces. Parades roll down the busiest streets and portable movie screens are strung up in several parks.

SummerStage

Central Park's SummerStage (p242), which runs from May through October, features an incredible lineup of music and dance. Talib Kweli, Dinosaur Jr., B-52s and OMD are among recent standouts. Most events are free. There's also a SummerStage Kids program.

Bryant Park Summer Film Festival

Mid-June through August, Bryant Park hosts free Monday-night outdoor screenings (p191) of classic Hollywood films, which kick off after sundown. Arrive early (the lawn area opens at 5pm and folks line up by 4pm); films begin at sunset.

Puerto Rican Day Parade

The second Sunday in June attracts thousands of flag-waving revelers for the annual Puerto Rican Day Parade. Marching since 1958, it runs up Fifth Ave from 44th to 79th Sts with costumed floats and dancing attendees.

NYC Pride

Gay Pride Month culminates in a major march down Fifth Ave on the last Sunday of the month, attended by tens of thousands of people. NYC Pride (www.nycpride.org) is a five-hour spectacle of dancers, drag queens, gay police officers, leathermen, lesbian soccer-moms and representatives of every other queer scene under the rainbow.

Mermaid Parade

Celebrating sand, sea and summer is this wonderfully quirky afternoon parade (p35). It's a flash of glitter and glamour, as elaborately costumed folks display their fishy finery along the Coney Island boardwalk. Held on the Saturday closest to the summer solstice; all in costume are welcome.

River to River Festival

Performers bring theater, music, dance and film to downtown parks for two weeks in June. More than 100 free events (p36) take place at outdoor spaces in Lower Manhattan.

July

As the city swelters, locals flee to beachside escapes on Long Island. It's a busy month for tourism, however, as holidaying North Americans and Europeans fill the city.

☆ Shakespeare in the Park

For decades free Shakespeare in the Park (p242) performances in Central Park have paid tribute to the bard, though tickets are worth more than their weight in gold. Expect to endure long lines for tickets (or win them in the lottery). Tickets are given out at noon; arrive no later than 10am.

July Fourth Fireworks

America's Independence Day is celebrated on the 4th of July with fireworks over the East River, starting around 9pm. Good viewing spots include the waterfronts of the Lower East Side and Williamsburg, Brooklyn; high rooftops; or east-facing Manhattan apartments. Check online to scout viewing locations.

September

Labor Day officially marks the end of the Hamptons' share-house season as the blistering heat of summer fades to more tolerable levels. As locals return to work, the cultural calendar ramps up.

Feast of San Gennaro

Rowdy, loyal crowds descend on the narrow streets of Little Italy for carnival

(Top) Mermaid Parade (p35), Coney Island
(Bottom) Chinese dragon at the Lunar New Year Festival (p28)

ANOOP BALAKRISHNAN REMA/SHUTTERSTOCK ©

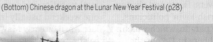

STEVE EDREFF/SHUTTERSTOCK ©

games, sausage-and-fried-pepper sandwiches, a meatball-eating contest and more Italian treats than you can ever hope to digest. Held over 11 days in mid-September, the San Gennaro Festival (p92) remains an old-world tradition, going for more than 90 years.

October

Brilliant bursts of color fill the trees as temperatures cool and alfresco cafes finally shutter their windows. Along with May, October is one of the most pleasant and scenic months to visit NYC.

BAM's Next Wave Festival

Running for around 12 weeks from October to mid-December at the Brooklyn Academy of Music, the Next Wave Festival (p294) offers the city's edgiest, most comprehensive survey of avant-garde music, theater, opera and dance.

Blessing of the Animals

In honor of the Feast Day of St Francis, which falls early in the month, pet owners flock to the grand Cathedral Church of St John the Divine for the annual Blessing of the Animals with their sidekicks – poodles, lizards, parrots, llamas, you name it.

Open House New York

The country's largest architecture and design event, the Open House New York (www.ohny.org) weekend features special architect-led tours, plus lectures, design workshops, studio visits and site-specific performances at more than 250 buildings all over the city.

Village Halloween Parade

On Halloween, New Yorkers don their wildest costumes for a night of revelry. See the most outrageous displays at the Village Halloween Parade (p35) that runs up Sixth Ave in the West Village. It's fun to watch, but even better to join in – there are 60,000 participants and millions more spectators.

November

As the leaves tumble, light jackets are replaced by wool and down. A headliner marathon is tucked into the final days of prehibernation weather; then families gather to give thanks.

New York Comedy Festival

Funny-makers take the city by storm during the New York Comedy Festival (p48) with stand-up sessions, improv nights and big-ticket shows hosted by the likes of Bill Maher, Trevor Noah and Tracy Morgan.

New York City Marathon

Held on the first Sunday of November, this annual 26-mile run (www.nycmarathon.org) draws thousands of athletes from around the world, and many more excited viewers line the streets to cheer the runners on.

Thanksgiving Day Parade

Massive helium-filled balloons soar overhead, high-school marching bands rattle their snares and millions of onlookers bundle up with scarves and coats to celebrate Thanksgiving (the fourth Thursday in November) with Macy's world-famous 2.5-mile-long parade.

December

Winter's definitely here, but there's plenty of holiday cheer to warm the spirit. Fairy lights adorn most buildings and Fifth Ave department stores (as well as Macy's) create elaborate worlds within their storefront windows.

Rockefeller Center Christmas Tree Lighting Ceremony

People flock around the massive spruce tree (p188) in Rockefeller Plaza to watch it come aglow with energy-efficient bulbs before it's taken down and recycled into lumber. It's a green Christmas! The lighting happens in late November or early December and the tree is taken down early in the new year.

New Year's Eve

The ultimate place to ring in the New Year, Times Square (www.timessquarenyc.org/nye) swarms with millions who come to stand squashed together like sardines, swig booze, freeze in subarctic temperatures, witness the annual dropping of the ball, and to chant the '10…9…8…' countdown in perfect unison.

With Kids

New York City has loads of activities for young ones, including imaginative playgrounds and leafy parks where kids can run free, plus lots of kid-friendly museums and sights. Other highs include carousel rides, puppet shows and noshing at markets around town.

LEE O/SHUTTERSTOCK ©

Heckscher playground (p33), Central Park

Attractions

For many kids, some of New York City's top attractions are a world of fun.

Wildlife

The city has a number of zoos. The best, by far, is the Bronx Zoo (p254), which is known for its well-designed habitats (the Asian Jungleworld is a stunner) and seasonal rides. Otherwise, if you're pressed for time, the zoos in Central Park and Prospect Park are great for short visits.

Statue of Liberty

The boat ride (p65) to Lady Liberty (p64) offers the chance to chug around New York Harbor and get up close to an icon that many kids only know from TV and books.

On Top of the World

A glass-roofed elevator leads to the Top of the Rock (p193), a lookout that offers glittering views of New York and fun coin-operated telescopes.

Coney Island

Hot dogs. Ice cream. Amusement-park rides. Coney Island (p275) is just the ticket if you're in need of some retro entertainment that might just remind parents of their own childhoods.

Best Museums

The American Museum of Natural History (p234), with its dinosaurs, marine world, planetarium and IMAX films, should not be missed. Nearly every big museum – including the Metropolitan Museum of Art (p214), the Museum of Modern Art (p182), Guggenheim Museum (p213), Museum of the City of New York (p219), and the Brooklyn Museum (p265) – has a kids' program, but many smaller institutions are even more appealing for young visitors. The Lower East Side Tenement Museum (p109) offers an interactive tour where kids can meet an immigrant (costumed interpreter) of centuries past.

Toddler Time

For tots aged one to five, hit the Children's Museum of the Arts (p90) in West SoHo and the interactive Brooklyn Children's

CITY TRAILS

For an insight into New York aimed directly at kids, pick up a copy of Lonely Planet's *City Trails: New York*. Perfect for children aged eight and up, it offers intriguing stories and fascinating facts about NYC's people, places, history and culture.

Museum (p271) in Crown Heights. Both have story times, art classes, craft hours and painting sessions.

Five & Over

Bigger kids can clamber on vintage subway cars at the New York Transit Museum (p266) or slide down a pole at the New York City Fire Museum (p90). The Brooklyn Children's Museum (p271) also has plenty of hands-on activities for kids up to 11. Out in Astoria, the Museum of the Moving Image (p306) has hands-on exhibits for kids. Budding fans of planes, submarines and space will love the excellent Intrepid Sea, Air & Space Museum (p194) of military relics docked at a Midtown pier. The Children's Museum of Manhattan (p234) has perennial favorites like the Talking Dragon, Dora the Explorer–themed rooms and an 8ft mural wall for fingerpainting.

Best Parks & Playgrounds

Central Park

More than 800 acres of green space, a lake that can be navigated by rowboat, a carousel, a zoo and a massive statue of Alice in Wonderland. Replete with swings, chutes and water features, Heckscher playground, near Seventh Ave and Central Park South, is the biggest and best of the 21 playgrounds in Central Park (p228); another good one is Ancient Playground (85th St and Fifth Ave).

Prospect Park

Brooklyn's hilly 585-acre Prospect Park (p264) has abundant amusements for kids, including a zoo, several playgrounds, a nature exploration area, and an ice-skating rink that becomes a roller rink and water-splash area in summer. Pedal boats and kayaks for Brooklyn's only lake and a variety of kid-friendly bikes are available at the LeFrak Center at Lakeside (p264) in the park.

Brooklyn Bridge Park

Check out the fun playgrounds at the park (p263), then hit the beach and boat rental at Pier 4 or water-filled play area on Pier 6 (bring swimsuits, all will get wet), followed by pizza at waterfront Fornino (p278). Pier 2 has shuffleboard and bocce courts and a roller rink that becomes an ice-skating rink in the winter. Further north are the grassy hills of Pier 1 and Jane's Carousel (p266).

Hudson River Park

Coursing along Manhattan's western side, this park (p139) offers loads of kiddy excitement, including mini-golf at Pier 25 (Tribeca), fun playgrounds at Piers 51 and 84, a carousel off W 22nd St, a water-splash play area at W 23rd & Eleventh Ave, and summertime movie screenings on Pier 46 (Greenwich Village).

Family Food

Markets around NYC are great snack spots, particularly Smorgasburg (p281), which has vendors selling everything from popsicles, doughnuts and pickles to tacos and pork sandwiches. The Chelsea Market (p151) also has many temptations – assemble a picnic, then head over to the Hudson River Park for a waterside nibble.

Need to Know

Car Seats Children under seven can ride on an adult's lap in a taxi or you can bring your own seat.

Strollers Not allowed on public buses unless folded, but permitted on the subway.

Free rides Children under 44in (112cm) ride free on the subway and buses.

Resources Check out Time Out New York Kids (www.timeout.com/new-york-kids) and Mommy Poppins (www.mommypoppins.com).

Like a Local

New Yorkers have developed winning strategies when it comes to nightlife, dining out and partaking of the city's staggering cultural calendar. From long weekend brunches to leisurely spring days in the park, there are plenty of appealing ways to go local – without having to pay those ridiculous rents.

ALAN SCHEIN PHOTOGRAPHY/GETTY IMAGES ©

Ice skating, Central Park (p228)

Dos & Don'ts: On the Street

Hailing a Cab

Only do this if the roof light is on. If it's not lit, the cab is taken, so put your arm down already!

Crossing the Street

New Yorkers don't always obey 'walk' signs, simply crossing when there isn't oncoming traffic. If you follow suit, look carefully!

Sidewalk Traffic

When negotiating pedestrian traffic on the sidewalk think of yourself as a vehicle – don't stop short, follow the speed of the crowd around you and pull off to the side if you need to take out your map or umbrella. Most New Yorkers are respectful of personal space, but they will bump into you – and not apologize – if you get in the way.

Boarding the Subway

Stand to the side of the doors to let disembarking passengers off first, then hop on (assertively, so the doors don't close in front of you).

Language

In New York you wait 'on line' instead of 'in line.' For telling time, you'll hear 'quarter of' rather than 'quarter to.' Oh, and Houston St is *How*-sten, not *Hugh*-sten, got it?

Eating & Drinking

The Culture of Brunch

Brunch in New York is deeply woven into the city's social fabric, much like teatime for British royals. It typically happens between 11am and 4pm on weekends (though some places, especially in Brooklyn, have begun serving brunch every day). The meal provides a perfect setting for friends to catch up on the week's events and the weekend's shenanigans over dishes anywhere between a light, superfood-laced breakfast and a hangover-busting, blowout lunch…with an indiscriminate mix of cocktails and coffees.

Weekends Are for Amateurs

New Yorkers tend to avoid the big clubs, packed bars and certain neighborhoods (East Village, Lower East Side) on the weekends when crowds are at their peak. Instead, weeknights can be great for going out – with fewer crowds, fewer tourists and drunken weekenders, and more creative folk who don't work the typical nine-to-five (actors, writers, artists). Plus, you'll be able to score happy-hour and early-in-the-week specials.

Bar Food

Many of New York's best bars blur the boundary between eating and drinking. Slide onto a bar stool, pick up a menu, and you'll often be faced with some enjoyably refined dining options. That could be oysters at the bar, small sharing plates (seared scallops, sliders, truffle-oil fries), cheese boards and charcuterie, or anything else – roasted-beet salads, gourmet sandwiches, braised artichokes, rack of lamb. When planning a meal, don't limit yourself to a sit-down restaurant – you can also eat and drink your way around a neighborhood by stopping in at gastropubs.

Joining In

Truth be told, watching a parade can be a pretty dull affair. It's much more fun to get in amongst the locals, whether it's dress-up events or community activities. Along those lines, there are many ways you can join in the action. Don an outrageous costume for the **Village Halloween Parade** (www.halloween-nyc.com; Sixth Ave; ⌚7-11pm Oct 31) or the summertime **Mermaid Parade** (www.coneyisland.com; ⌚late Jun) in Coney Island. Sign up for an organized race in the city (New York Road Runners stages dozens of annual runs). Take a rock-climbing class at Brooklyn Boulders (p300) or Cliffs (p318) in Queens. Polish up those old poems and take the stage at open-mic night at Nuyorican Poets Café (p129). Meanwhile, Brooklyn Brainery (p300) offers evening and weekend courses in all sorts of topics. Whatever your passion – chess, hip-hop, drawing, architecture, beer-making – you'll find it in NYC, and be surrounded by plenty of like minds.

NYC TWITTERATI

New Yorker (@NewYorker) Insightful commentary on politics and culture.

Guest of a Guest (@guestofaguest) A glimpse into NYC's elite parties, and social and fashion scenes.

Grubstreet (@grubstreet) Restaurant reviews, food trends and must-try dishes across the boroughs.

Gothamist (@gothamist) News and curiosities in NYC and beyond.

Hyperallergic (@Hyperallergic) Tweets from NYC's favorite art blogazine.

Seasonal Activities

Winter

Even dreary winter weather brings its delights – ice skating! Beginning in November or December, the city's skating rinks provide ample amusement (and a good prequel to fireside drinks in a toasty bar afterwards). Locals skip tourist-swarmed Rockefeller Center and Bryant Park and head to Central Park (p228), Prospect Park (p264) or Riverbank State Park for skating.

Spring

The city's blossoming parks are the places to be for spring picnics, sun-drenched strolls and lazy days lounging on the grass. Top spots for flower-gazing: the New York Botanical Garden (p254) and the Brooklyn Botanic Garden (p270). The latter hosts a lovely Cherry-Blossom Festival (p270), much adored by Brooklynites.

Summer

Summer is the time for free open-air events: film screenings in Bryant Park (p191), street festivals around town, and concerts in Central Park, Hudson River Park (p139), Prospect Park and other green spaces around the city.

Fall

In fall the cultural calendar ramps up again as the city's premier performing arts halls open their seasons (which run from September through May) and galleries kick off their new shows (Thursday night, incidentally, is when the art openings happen).

For Free

It will come as no surprise that the Big Apple isn't a cheap destination. Nevertheless, there are many ways to kick open the NYC treasure chest without spending a dime – free concerts, theater and film screenings, pay-what-you-wish nights at legendary museums, city festivals, free ferry rides and kayaking, plus loads of green space.

BRIAN LOGAN PHOTOGRAPHY/SHUTTERSTOCK ©

National Museum of the American Indian (p72)

Live Music, Theater & Dance

In summer there are scores of free events around town. From June through early September, SummerStage (p242) features over 100 free performances at 18 parks around the city, including Central Park. You'll have to be tenacious to get tickets to Shakespeare in the Park (p242), also held in Central Park, but it's well worth the effort. Top actors like Meryl Streep, Philip Seymour Hoffman and Al Pacino have taken to the stage in years past. Prospect Park has its own venerable open-air summer concert and events series, the Celebrate Brooklyn! Festival (p269).

Summertime also brings free film screenings and events to the water's edge during the **River to River Festival** (https://lmcc.net/river-to-river-festival; ⌚Jun) at various venues in Lower Manhattan. Another great option for film lovers is the free HBO Bryant Park Summer Film Festival (p191) screenings on Monday nights.

A few places offer free music throughout the year. BAM Café (p294) in Brooklyn has free concerts (world music, R&B, jazz, rock) on select Friday and Saturday nights. In Harlem, Marjorie Eliot (p258) opens her home for free jazz jams on Sunday afternoons.

Museums

Always Free

- National September 11 Memorial (p68)
- National Museum of the American Indian (p72)
- Museum at FIT (p194)
- Hamilton Grange (p252)
- American Folk Art Museum (p233)
- Nicholas Roerich Museum (p233)

Admission by Donation

- American Museum of Natural History (p234)
- Museum of the City of New York (p219)
- Brooklyn Historical Society (p266)

Free or Pay-What-You-Wish on Certain Days

MoMA (p182) 5:30–9pm Friday

Guggenheim Museum (p213) 5–8pm Saturday

Whitney Museum of American Art (p136) 7–10pm Friday

Neue Galerie (p218) 5–8pm first Friday of month

Frick Collection (p218) 2–6pm Wednesday & 6–9pm first Friday of month

New Museum of Contemporary Art (p110) 7–9pm Thursday

New-York Historical Society (p233) 6–8pm Friday

Jewish Museum (p219) 5–8pm Thursday, all day Saturday

Rubin Museum of Art (p141) 6–10pm Friday

Asia Society & Museum (p219) 6–9pm Friday, September to June

Japan Society (p191) 6–9pm Friday

Studio Museum in Harlem (p249) Sunday

MoMA PS1 (p303) Free with your MoMA ticket

National September 11 Memorial Museum (p68) 5–8pm Tuesday

Historic Richmond Town, Staten Island (p73) Wednesday

On the Water

The free Staten Island Ferry (p85) provides magical views of the Statue of Liberty, and you can enjoy them with a cold beer (available on the boat). While it's not free, for just $2.75 you can sail from Lower Manhattan across to Brooklyn, Queens or all the way out to Rockaway on the NYC Ferry (www.ferry.nyc) – a great alternative to the subway.

From May to October, you can also take a ferry (free on summer weekend mornings, $2 at other times) over to Governors Island (p76), a car-free oasis with priceless views.

For a bit more adventure, take out a free kayak (p54), available in the Hudson River Park, Brooklyn Bridge Park and Red Hook.

NEED TO KNOW

Handy websites for tracking down free and discounted events in the city include Club Free Time (www.clubfreetime.com) and the Skint (www.theskint.com). These have daily listings of free tours, concerts, workshops, talks, art openings, book readings and more.

TV Tapings

Some of America's top evening shows (p205) are taped in New York City. *The Late Show with Stephen Colbert, The Daily Show with Trevor Noah* and *The Tonight Show Starring Jimmy Fallon* all give out free tickets to their shows. Go online, well in advance, to reserve seats.

Walking Tours

One of the best ways to experience the city is to have a local show you around. The highly recommended Big Apple Greeter (p385) provides free tours by locals who love showing off their cities; prior booking (minimum four weeks) is required.

Wi-Fi

If you're out for the day and need to get online, you'll find free wi-fi in public parks such as the High Line, Bryant Park, Battery Park, Tompkins Square Park and Union Square Park. Most cafes and many restaurants also offer free wi-fi.

Under the Radar

Many come to New York to see Times Square, the Empire State Building and the Brooklyn Bridge, but there's so much more to be seen here than the big-ticket postcard sights. Take some time to seek out the NYC that's not buffed up for tourists and see the real New York.

GUILLAUME GAUDET/LONELY PLANET ©

Yankee Stadium (p254)

Explore the Boroughs

Manhattan is the physical and financial center of NYC, but it's by no means the only worthwhile place to visit. COVID-19 turned commercial and tourist-heavy areas like Midtown and SoHo into ghost towns of shuttered storefronts, while life bloomed in the boroughs, where New Yorkers working from home turned to hyperlocal pursuits.

Brooklyn is full of lively bars and restaurants, and offers unforgettable cityscape views from Brooklyn Bridge Park (p263); the bucolic jewels of Prospect Park (p264) and the Brooklyn Botanic Garden (p270) are perfect for strolling or picnicking. Queens boasts a patchwork quilt of diverse neighborhoods featuring cultures and cuisines from around the world, as well as notable art museums like MoMA PS1 (p303) and some of NYC's most popular beaches (p307). The Bronx has some top sights, such as the country's largest zoo (p254), a huge botanical garden (p254) and Yankee Stadium (p254), but also offers intriguing community enclaves such as **Arthur Avenue** (www.arthuravenuebronx.com; 2344 Arthur Ave, btwn 186th St & Crescent Ave; ⏲8am-7pm, individual stalls vary; SB/D to Fordham Rd, Metro-North to Fordham) and **City Island** (Bx29). Staten Island offers a glimpse into NYC's past at Historic Richmond Town (p73), plus the city's best free boat ride, the Staten Island Ferry (p85).

Buy Black-owned

Small businesses have had to compete with chains and franchises for years; when the pandemic hit they had less to fall back on, and many have struggled. Ensure your dollars support actual New Yorkers and their local neighborhoods by patronizing locally owned businesses. Check out Black-Owned Brooklyn (www.blackownedbrooklyn.com; @blackownedbklyn) for curated listings of Black-owned shops, restaurants and bars around Fort Greene, Bed-Stuy, Crown Heights and Prospect Lefferts Gardens. In the Bronx, visit local microbreweries and indie bookshop/wine bar Lit. Bar (p254). In Manhattan head north to Harlem for *haute cuisine* at Red Rooster (p256) or Maison Harlem (p255), followed by beer at Harlem Hops (p258).

Totto Ramen (p196)

Dining Out

From inspired iterations of world cuisine to quintessentially local nibbles, New York City's dining scene is infinite, all-consuming and a testament to its kaleidoscope of citizens. Even if you're not an obsessive foodie hitting the newest cult-chef openings and enclaves of global cuisine, an outstanding meal is always only a block away.

Market Munchies

Don't let the concrete streets and buildings fool you – New York City has a thriving greens scene that comes in many shapes and sizes. At the top of your list should be the Chelsea Market (p151), which is packed with gourmet goodies of all kinds – both shops (where you can assemble picnics) and food stands (where you can eat on site). Many other food halls offer equally diverse spreads, including Gansevoort Market (p142) in the Meatpacking District, a duo of food halls at Brookfield Place (p79) in Lower Manhattan, and gourmet picnic paradise Essex Market (p119), rehoused on the Lower East Side. Across the river, there's DeKalb Market Hall (p278) in downtown Brooklyn, plus small food hall and drinking den Berg'n (p284) out in Crown Heights.

Many neighborhoods in NYC have their own Greenmarket. One of the biggest is the Union Square Greenmarket (p167), open four days a week throughout the year. Check Grow NYC (www.grownyc.org/greenmarket) for a list of the other 50-plus markets around the city.

Out in Brooklyn, the best weekend markets for noshers (rather than cook-at-home

NEED TO KNOW

Opening Hours

Generally speaking, meal times often bleed together as New Yorkers march to the beat of their own drums: breakfast is served from 7am to noon, lunch from 11:30am to 3pm, and dinner stretches between 5pm and 11pm. The popular weekend brunch lasts from 11am until 3pm or 4pm.

Price Ranges

The following price ranges refer to a main dish, exclusive of tax and tip:

$	under $15
$$	$15–25
$$$	more than $25

Tipping

New Yorkers generally tip 18% to 20% of the final price of the meal. For takeout, it's polite to drop a few dollars in the tip jar (or add 10% to 15% through the app or website).

Reservations

Popular restaurants abide by one of two rules: either they take reservations and you need to plan in advance (weeks or months early for the real treasures); or they only seat patrons on a first-come basis, in which case you should arrive when they open and eat early, or risk a two-hour wait.

Useful Websites

Open Table (www.opentable.com) Click-and-book reservation service for many restaurants.

Tasting Table (www.tastingtable.com) Sign up for handy news blasts about the latest and greatest.

The Infatuation (www.theinfatuation.com/new-york) Searches reviews and guides to compile restaurant info.

types) are Smorgasburg (p281), with over 100 craft-food vendors, and the Brooklyn Flea Market (p299), which has dozens of stalls. The Time Out Market at Empire Stores (p267) has a smorgasbord of global eats plus river views.

Also popular are high-end market-cum-grocers like Eataly (p169) and Dean & DeLuca (temporarily closed at the time of research), where fresh produce and ready-made fare are given the five-star treatment.

Tours & Courses

There's no better way to engage with the city's infinite dining scene than to link up with a savvy local for a food tour or cooking class. Check out these rewarding gastronomic odysseys:

Institute of Culinary Education (p85) America's largest cooking school offers accessible, top-notch cooking courses, as well as foodie tours.

Urban Oyster (www.urbanoyster.com) High-quality, themed foodie tours mostly in Lower Manhattan and Brooklyn.

Scott's Pizza Tours (p279) Offbeat and always fun, Scott promises to unveil all of the secrets of the city's pizza-pie scene.

Nosh Walks (p385) Myra Alperson leads wide-ranging food tours focusing on NYC's rich ethnic cuisine.

Pizza A Casa (www.pizzaacasa.com) Much-loved pie school on the Lower East Side specializing in rolling and decorating dough.

Chopsticks & Marrow (www.chopsticksandmarrow.com) Fantastic Queens food blog written by local Joe DiStefano, who also runs food tours.

League of Kitchens (www.leagueofkitchens.com) Cooking classes taught by immigrant women in their own kitchens, in Brooklyn and Queens.

Meatless Meals

Though the city's herbivore scene has long lagged behind that of West Coast cities, and was for years mocked by serious foodies, many former naysayers are beginning to come around. That's thanks in part to the local-food movement, as well as a slew of new restaurants and cafes that have enticed skeptics by injecting big doses of cool ambience – and top-notch wine, liquor and dessert options – into the mix. Topping the list is Nix (p150), a brilliantly creative vegetarian restaurant that's earned rave reviews and a Michelin star. Brunch favorite Butcher's Daughter (p285) has locations in Brooklyn and Manhattan.

Eating by Neighborhood

Vegans have much to celebrate, too. Top choices include Modern Love (p286), which serves up comfort fare out in Williamsburg, Screamer's Pizza (p285) in Crown Heights, Champs Diner (p286) in East Williamsburg, and elegant Blossom (p152), with locations in Chelsea and elsewhere. Another icon is the soul food gem, Seasoned Vegan (p255), up in Harlem.

Top Local Dishes

Here are a few of our favorite dishes from NYC's always changing but ever-creative restaurant scene:

Omakase, Tanoshi (p221) The unbelievably good chef's selection of sushi changes daily at this tiny, well-worn joint in the Upper East Side.

Pork belly buns, Momofuku Noodle Bar (p116) The mouthwatering highlight of an oft-changing menu.

Pizza No. 2, Juliana's (p278) Pizza topping in harmonious simplicity: cherry tomatoes, mozzarella, garlic and sea salt.

Buttermilk-fried chicken on cheddar waffles, Buttermilk Channel (p280) Sweet-savory comfort food perfected.

Lonely Planet's Top Choices

Chefs Club (p95) Visiting chefs from around the globe showcase outstanding recipes.

Modern (p198) Mouthwatering Michelin-starred morsels beside MoMA's sculpture garden.

RedFarm (p147) Savvy Sino-fusion dishes boast bold flavors, but it doesn't take itself too seriously.

Uncle Boons (p94) Michelin-starred Thai with good-time vibes and Asian-inspired cocktails.

Jeffrey's Grocery (p147) Much-loved West Village neighborhood spot.

Tom's Restaurant (p284) Nostalgic Brooklyn diner with efficient service and big portions.

Best by Budget

$

Chelsea Market (p151) Foods from around the world served up in a sprawling converted factory.

Burger Joint (p196) Scruffy graffiti-scrawled bar with juicy patties in a hidden Midtown locale.

Mamoun's (p142) Famous, spicy shawarma sandwiches at rock-bottom prices.

$$

Upstate (p118) A seafood feast awaits in the East Village.

Ivan Ramen (p121) Sublime steaming bowls from a Long Islander by way of Tokyo.

Roberta's (p287) Hip Williamsburg pizza place with garden bar and weekend brunch.

$$$

Eleven Madison Park (p171) Arresting, cutting-edge cuisine laced with unexpected whimsy.

Blue Hill (p147) A West Village classic using ingredients sourced straight from the upstate farm.

Best by Cuisine

Asian

Zenkichi (p286) Candlelit culinary temple of exquisite sushi in Williamsburg.

Drunken Munkey (p221) Well spiced Indian curries in a lively neighborhood bistro setting.

Totto Ramen (p196) Hotly touted as the best ramen in NYC; sit at the bar and watch roast pork get blow-torched.

Italian

Il Buco Alimentari & Vineria (p95) Be transported to the old country in this Nolita standout.

Rosemary's (p150) A beautifully designed West Village spot with memorable cooking.

Charlie Bird (p95) Rustic, locavore-leaning dishes served up in slim SoHo digs.

Vegan

Blossom (p152) Tofu Benedict, shiitake risotto and other exemplary plant-based fare.

Modern Love (p286) Comfort-food classics in East Williamsburg with outstanding vegan plates.

Screamer's Pizza (p285) 100% vegan slices, topped with seasonal mushrooms, plant-based chorizo and more.

Best For Solo Diners

Essex Market (p119) Take Thai, Dominican, seafood or ice cream to the open-atrium seating.

Maman (p79) A large, communal table keeps diners convivial at this French-inflected bistro-cafe.

Best Bakeries

Dough (p281) Probably NYC's best doughnut, in Brooklyn.

Four & Twenty Blackbirds (p282) Heavenly slices of homemade pies in Gowanus.

Dominique Ansel Kitchen (p143) Sweet magnificence from NYC's most famous pastry chef in the West Village.

Best Old-School NYC

Barney Greengrass (p238) Perfect plates of smoked salmon and sturgeon for over 100 years in the Upper West Side.

Russ & Daughters (p130) A celebrated Jewish deli in the Lower East Side.

Zabar's (p243) Upper West Side store selling gourmet, kosher foods since the 1930s.

Margon (p196) Unfussy, unchanged Cuban lunch counter in Midtown.

Best For Brunch

Cookshop (p151) Great indoor-outdoor dining spot in west Chelsea.

BLVD Bistro (p255) Harlem outpost for down-home delights like fried catfish and grits.

Cafe Mogador (p116) An icon of the East Village brunch scene.

Big Daddy's (p169) Satisfying American diner food near Union Sq with breakfast burritos and, of course, fluffy pancakes.

House of Yes (p291)

Bar Open

You'll find all species of thirst-quenching venues here, from terminally hip cocktail lounges and historic dive bars to specialty taprooms and third-wave coffee shops. Then there's the legendary club scene, spanning everything from upscale celebrity staples to gritty, indie hangouts. Head downtown or to Brooklyn for the parts of the city that, as they say, truly never sleep.

Historic Cocktails, Crafty Brews

Here in the land where the term 'cocktail' was born, mixed drinks are still stirred with the utmost gravitas. The city's top barkeeps create some of the world's most sophisticated and innovative libations. Often it's a case of history in a glass: New York's obsession with rediscovered recipes and Prohibition-era style continues to drive many a cocktail list.

The city's craft-beer culture is equally dynamic, with an ever-expanding bounty of breweries, bars and shops showcasing local artisanal brews. While Brooklyn may no longer be the major beer exporter of yesteryear, craft breweries like Brooklyn Brewery (p274) and Sixpoint (www.sixpoint.com) have put it back on the map. Other boroughs are also making amber waves, with start-ups including SingleCut Beersmiths (singlecut.com) and Big Alice Brewery (bigalicebrewing.com) in Queens, as well as Bronx Brewery (p254) and Gun Hill Brewing Co (www.gunhillbrewing.com) in the Bronx.

NEED TO KNOW

Websites

New York Magazine (http://nymag.com/tags/nightlife) Brilliant nightlife and insider news.

Thrillist (www.thrillist.com) What's hot or coming soon on the bar scene.

Urbandaddy (www.urbandaddy.com) Up-to-the-minute info and a 'hot right now' list.

Time Out (www.timeout.com/newyork/nightlife) On-the-ball listings of where to drink and dance.

partyearth (www.partyearth.com/newyork) Detailed club reviews from savvy party kids.

Opening Hours

Opening times vary. While some dive bars open as early as 8am, most drinking establishments get rolling around 5pm. Some bars stay open until 4am, while many others close around 1am early in the week and 2am from Thursday to Saturday. Clubs generally operate from 10pm to 4am or 5am.

Costs

Happy-hour beers typically start from $4; expect to pay about $7 or $8 for a regular draft, and more for imported bottles. Glasses of wine start at around $9. Specialty cocktails run from $12 to well over $20. Expect to pay between $5 and $30 to get into clubs.

Clubbing

New Yorkers are always looking for the next big thing, so the city's club scene changes faster than a New York minute. Promoters drag revelers around the city for weekly events held at all of the finest addresses, and when there's nothing on, it's time to hit the dance-floor stalwarts.

When clubbing it never hurts to plan ahead; having your name on a guest list can relieve unnecessary frustration and disappointment. If you're an uninitiated partyer, dress the part. If you're fed the 'private party' line, try to bluff – chances are high that you've been bounced. Also, don't forget a wad of cash as many nightspots (even the swankiest ones) often refuse credit cards, and in-house ATMs scam a fortune in fees.

The Coffee Revolution

A boom in specialty coffee roasters continues to raise New York's caffeine culture to ever-greater heights. More locals are cluing in to single-origin beans and different brewing techniques, with numerous roasters now offering cupping classes for curious drinkers. Many are transplants from A-list coffee cities, among them Portland's Stumptown (p201) and the Bay Area's Blue Bottle (p293). The Australian influence is especially notable, with antipodean mavericks including Little Collins (p200) and Bluestone Lane (p81).

Drinking & Nightlife by Neighborhood

Financial District & Lower Manhattan (p81) FiDi office slaves loosen their ties in everything from specialist beer and brandy bars to revered cocktail hot spots.

SoHo & Chinatown (p99) Swanky lounge bars, a sprinkling of dives and a few speakeasy-style standouts.

East Village & Lower East Side (p123) Proud home of the original-flavor dive bar, the East Village is brimming with options.

West Village, Chelsea & Meatpacking District (p152) Jet-setters flock here, with wine bars, backdoor lounges and gay hangouts.

Union Square, Flatiron District & Gramercy (p172) Vintage drinking dens, swinging cocktail bars and fun student hangouts – this trio spans all tastes.

Midtown (p200) Rooftop bars with skyline views, historic cocktail salons and rough-n-ready dive bars: welcome to Midtown.

Harlem & Upper Manhattan (p258) A burgeoning mix of fabulous live-music spots, speakeasy-style bars and old-school dives.

Brooklyn (p287) Everything on the nightlife spectrum, with Williamsburg as the heart and Bushwick a gritty up-and-comer.

Lonely Planet's Top Choices

House of Yes (p291) Unrivaled destination for a wild night out at a Bushwick warehouse space.

Silvana (p258) Hidden basement bar in Harlem with great live music every night of the week.

Apothéke (p99) An atmospheric lounge and former opium den with great cocktails hidden away in Chinatown.

Rue B (p123) An appealing little East Village venue with live jazz and a fun crowd.

Ear Inn (p101) Creaking old-school SoHo pub with jazz on Sundays and wooden tables.

Maison Premiere (p291) Absinthe, juleps and oysters shine bright at this Big Easy tribute in Williamsburg.

Best Cocktails

Bar Goto (p127) Lower East Side icon with New York's most famous mixologist at the helm.

Dead Rabbit (p81) Meticulously researched cocktails, punches and pop-inns – lightly hopped ales spiked with different flavors – in a snug FiDi den.

Employees Only (p152) Award-winning barkeeps and arresting libations in the timeless West Village.

Raines Law Room (p172) Well-composed cocktails from serious mixologists in a Prohibition-style den near Union Sq.

Best Beer

Spuyten Duyvil (p292) A much-loved Williamsburg spot serving high-quality crafts.

Harlem Hops (p258) Pair craft brews with spicy meat pies at Harlem's only 100% African American–owned beer bar.

Astoria Bier & Cheese (p315) Artisanal suds meet gourmet cheeses in Astoria, Queens.

Bronx Brewery (p254) Community-minded microbrewery with excellent brews and a creative events roster.

Proletariat (p126) Tiny East Village bar serving up extremely uncommon brews.

Best Wine Selection

Terroir Tribeca (p83) An enlightened, encyclopedic wine list in trendy Tribeca.

La Compagnie des Vins Surnaturels (p101) A love letter to Gallic wines steps away from Little Italy.

Buvette (p153) A buzzing, candlelit wine bar on a tree-lined West Village street.

Best Coffee

Stumptown Coffee Roasters (p201) Cool baristas serving Portland's favorite cup o' joe.

Bluestone Lane (p81) Aussie brewing prowess in the shadow of Wall St.

La Colombe (p81) Sucker-punch roasts for the downtown cognoscenti.

Little Collins (p200) A tribute to Melbourne coffee culture in Midtown East.

Best Classic Date Bars

Pegu Club Made-from-scratch concoctions in a Burma-inspired SoHo hideaway.

Hotel Delmano (p293) Old-school romance at a vintage bar serving seasonal cocktails.

The Campbell (p200) Gilded-age-style grandeur tucked away in Grand Central.

Best Dance Clubs & House DJs

Le Bain (p154) Well-dressed crowds still pack this favorite near the High Line.

Bossa Nova Civic Club (p293) A hip little Bushwick haunt for those craving off-the-radar thrills.

Berlin (p123) Yesteryear's free-spirited dance days live on at this concealed East Village bolt-hole.

Best Dive Bars

Sunny's (p290) A favorite Red Hook dive, near the Brooklyn waterfront.

Cowgirl SeaHorse (p83) Always a good time at this nautically themed drinkery in Lower Manhattan.

Ear Inn (p101) Expect friendly, diverse patrons and straightforward service at one of the oldest drinking establishments in NYC.

Best For Solo Travelers

Brandy Library (p81) A civilized Tribeca spot in which to take your time over top-shelf cognac, whiskey and brandy.

Spuyten Duyvil (p292) Low-key Brooklyn beer bar with an easygoing ambience.

Caledonia (p224) A long, comfortable bar staffed by folk who love to chat about whiskey, on the Upper East Side.

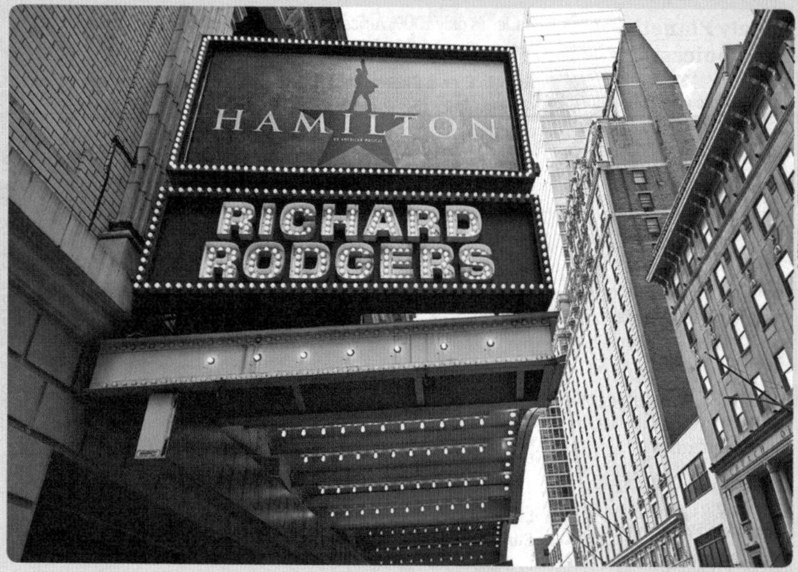

TIMOTHY A. CLARY/GETTY IMAGES ©

Richard Rodgers Theatre (p204)

Showtime

Actors, musicians, dancers and artists flock to the bright lights of the Big Apple, hoping to finally get that big break. The result? Audiences are spoiled by the continual influx of supremely talented, dedicated, boundary-pushing performers. Like the song goes: if you can make it here, you can make it anywhere.

Theater

From the legendary hit factories of Broadway to the scruffy black-box theaters that dot countless downtown blocks, NYC boasts the full gamut of theater experiences. The most celebrated scene is, of course, Broadway – nicknamed the Great White Way in 1902 for its bright billboard lights. There's something truly magical about sitting in one of the ornate Broadway theaters and letting the show take you to another world as the lights dim.

The term 'off Broadway' is not a geographical one – it simply refers to theaters that are smaller in size (200 to 500 seats) and usually have less of a glitzy production budget than the big hitters. 'Off Off Broadway' takes place in even smaller theaters, with shows that are often inexpensively produced and experimental in nature.

A few of the best non-Broadway venues are the Public Theater (p102), Performing Garage (home to experimental Wooster Group), Brooklyn's St Ann's Warehouse (p294) and the Brooklyn Academy of Music (p294). Otherwise, the highest concentration is in the East and West Villages.

Traditional theaters aside, another great place to catch a show is at Shakespeare in the Park (p242). Though the wait for tickets is long, you'll be rewarded with free seats to see star-studded performances in the open air in Central Park.

Live Music

NYC is the country's live-music capital, and just about every taste can be catered for here within a variety of wonderful venues spread throughout the boroughs. However, some of the highest-profile opera and classical music is performed at the Lincoln Center (p232); jazz greats and up-and-coming talents play at clubs throughout town, but especially in Harlem, Midtown and the Village.

Big-name indie rockers earn their stripes downtown, as well as in Brooklyn venues like National Sawdust (p294). Major acts play in stadiums like Madison Square Garden (p207) and the Barclays Center (p296), and summertime brings outdoor music festivals, notably several prominent hip-hop fests.

For current listings, check out *New York Magazine* and *Time Out.*

Film & TV

The movie scene in New York City is amplified far beyond blockbuster-at-the-multiplex standards. Film-going is an immersive pastime that draws in connoisseurs of silver-screen classics as well as indie, avant-garde, foreign and otherwise nonstandard fare.

Frequent film festivals, such as indie movie-focused **Tribeca Film Festival** (☎212-941-2400; www.tribecafilm.com; ⏲Apr-May), provide additional texture to the scene.

One of the least-known gems for films is the Museum of Modern Art (p182), which has a rich collection of movies spanning all genres and corners of the world. The Film Society of Lincoln Center (p241) stages an incredible array of documentary and art-house films.

Also worth checking out is the BAM Rose Cinemas (p294), which does similar fare as well as revivals, and indulgent full-service screenings at the Alamo Drafthouse (p295).

NEED TO KNOW

Listings & Reviews

➡ **Playbill** (www.playbill.com) The publisher of that happy little yellow-and-white program provided at Broadway plays also has an online version.

➡ **Talkin' Broadway** (www.talkingbroadway.com) Dishy reviews as well as a board for posting extra tickets to buy or sell.

➡ Traditional publications include the *New York Times, New York Magazine* and *Time Out.*

Buying Tickets

To purchase tickets for shows, you can either head directly to the venue's box office, or use one of several ticket agencies (most of which add a surcharge) to order by phone or online.

Ticket Agencies

Broadway Line (www.broadway.org) Good prices for shows on the Great White Way.

NYTIX (www.nytix.com) Discount Broadway tickets.

Telecharge (www.telecharge.com) Broadway and off-Broadway shows.

Theatermania (www.theatermania.com) Theater listings, reviews and ticketing.

Ticketmaster (www.ticketmaster.com) Tickets for every conceivable entertainment.

TKTS Booths Cut-price same-day Broadway tickets; locations in Midtown (p179) and South Street Seaport (p78).

A handful of TV shows (p205) are taped in Midtown Manhattan, including *Saturday Night Live* and *The Late Show with Stephen Colbert.* You can be an audience member by signing up online or trying for standby tickets.

Comedy

A good laugh is easy to find in the Big Apple, where comedians sharpen their stand-up and improv chops practising new material or hoping to get scouted by a producer or agent. Some of the best spots for chuckles are downtown, particularly around Chelsea and Greenwich Village.

Several festivals, including the **New York Comedy Festival** (www.nycomedyfestival.com; ⏲Nov), draw big names throughout the year. You can also snag seats to tapings of America's popular late-night variety shows.

Laughter continues across the river at Brooklyn's Eastville Comedy Club (p296), along with venues like Friends and Lovers (p291), which have occasional comedy nights.

Dance

Dance fans are spoiled for choice in this town, which is home to both the New York City Ballet (p241) and the American Ballet Theatre (p241). Another key venue dedicated to dance is the Joyce Theater (p159), which stages acclaimed contemporary productions by dance companies from every corner of the globe.

There are also modern dance companies galore, including those of masters Alvin Ailey, Paul Taylor, Merce Cunningham, Martha Graham, Bill T Jones, Mark Morris and a slew of up-and-comers, which often take to the stage downtown and at the Brooklyn Academy of Music (p294).

Opera & Classical Music

When thinking about opera, one name rules the roost: the Metropolitan Opera (p241), which stages lavish and exceptional productions. However, many other forms live within the city limits. The laudable company Amore Opera (p259) performs impressive works in the uptown Riverside Theatre. Other roving companies include Opera on Tap (www.operaontap.org/newyork), which stages performances not at grand theaters but bars around Brooklyn.

The choices for orchestras, chamber music and soloists are abundant, with the more cutting-edge options often stealing center stage. For all things traditional on a grand scale, don't miss Lincoln Center (p232) and the famously stunning Carnegie Hall (p204).

For something more cutting edge, check out the eclectic lineup at the Brooklyn Academy of Music (p294).

Radio City Music Hall (p193)

Entertainment by Neighborhood

Financial District & Lower Manhattan (p61) Tribeca is home to the Flea Theater and SoHo Rep, two venerable theater companies.

East Village & Lower East Side (p61) Experimental performance spaces, poetry slams and stand-up comics fill basements with laughter.

West Village, Chelsea & Meatpacking District (p61) Unofficial HQ of the world's jazz club scene, plus dance troupes galore in Chelsea.

Midtown (p206) Razzle-dazzle extravaganzas, fresh American theater, world-class jazz sessions and stand-up comedy blue bloods.

Upper West Side & Central Park (p243) Lincoln Center supplies an endless amount of high culture, while other venues provide more intimate settings.

Harlem (p61) Intimate jazz clubs, live-music bars and the venerable Apollo Theater make Harlem one of NYC's best music 'hoods.

Brooklyn (p260) A bit of everything, from classical offerings to indie rock bands to edgy comedy.

Lonely Planet's Top Choices

Richard Rodgers Theatre (p204) Home to one of Broadway's greatest hits: *Hamilton,* an American history lesson set to urban rhythms.

Brooklyn Academy of Music (p294) This hallowed theater hosts cutting-edge works, particularly during its celebrated Next Wave Festival.

Radio City Music Hall (p193) Midtown's gorgeous art-deco music hall hosts NYC's phenomenally popular Rockettes Christmas Spectacular.

Jazz at Lincoln Center (p204) Glittering evening views of Central Park and world-class musical acts.

Carnegie Hall (p204) Legendary concert hall, blessed with perfect acoustics; hosts everything from opera to jazz.

Best Broadway Shows

Harry Potter and the Cursed Child (p207) Broadway's highest grossing play of all time.

Book of Mormon (p206) Brilliantly funny, award-winning show by the creators of *South Park*.

Chicago (p208) One of the most scintillating shows on Broadway.

Hamilton (p204) If you can't get tickets, try standing in the cancellation line outside the theater.

Mean Girls (p207) The Tony-winning comedy musical has sharp wit and dazzling songs.

Best Off-Broadway Theater

Playwrights Horizons (p206) Showcase of inventively written plays.

Signature Theatre (p206) Stages works by some of the world's top playwrights.

Public Theate (p102)r Venerable downtown venue that launched many hit shows, including *Hamilton* back in 2015.

St Ann's Warehouse (p294) A creative dynamo based in beautiful post-industrial space near the Brooklyn waterfront.

Best For Film

Nitehawk Cinema (p295) Nibble great food and sip cocktails while watching first-run and foreign flicks in Williamsburg.

BAM Rose Cinemas (p294) A good mix of first-run and foreign films in a landmark Fort Greene building.

Film Forum (p102) Another downtown film innovator with an excellent indie repertoire.

Museum of Modern Art (p182) A must for film lovers, with a brilliantly curated film calendar.

Best Classical Music & Opera

Metropolitan Opera House (p241) Enchanting setting to see some of the world's best opera.

National Sawdust (p294) Cutting-edge contemporary composers who fuse classical, opera and global sounds against an illuminated backdrop.

Brooklyn Academy of Music (p294) Innovative works by Brooklyn's renowned hit-maker.

Bargemusic (p296) String quartets on a barge parked on the East River.

Best For Dance

Joyce Theater (p159) NY's best venue devoted solely to dance.

New York Live Arts (p158) Experimental performances by troupes from around the globe.

New York City Center (p208) Excellent lineup of dance companies and mini-festivals.

Brooklyn Academy of Music (p294) Catch Mark Morris Dance Group and many others.

Best For Jazz

Jazz at Lincoln Center (p204) Exceptional talent at nightly shows within three state-of-the-art venues.

Village Vanguard (p158) Legendary West Village jazz club.

Birdland (p205) Midtown lounge with big-band sounds, Afro-Cuban jazz and more.

Blue Note (p158) This West Village stalwart is one of NYC's most famous jazz clubs.

Best For Rock

Bowery Ballroom (p129) Celebrated downtown concert hall.

Music Hall of Williamsburg (p296) Indie rock galore out in Brooklyn.

Rockwood Music Hall (p128) Music all the time at this Lower East Side spot.

Bell House (p294) South Brooklyn charmer with an innovative lineup of indie and folk sounds.

Best For Laughs

Upright Citizens Brigade Theatre (p207) Hilarious comedy sketches and Sunday-night improv.

Comedy Cellar (p157) A well-loved basement comedy joint in Greenwich Village.

Caroline's on Broadway (p208) The go-to spot for seeing famous comics perform.

URBAN BY HABIT/SHUTTERSTOCK ©

Fishs Eddy (p173)

Treasure Hunt

Not surprisingly for a capital of commercialism, creativity and fashion, New York City is quite simply one of the best shopping destinations on the planet. Every niche is filled. From indie designer-driven boutiques to landmark department stores, thrift shops to haute couture, record stores to the Apple store, street eats to gourmet groceries, it's quite easy to blow one's budget.

A Homage to Luxury

One of the world's fashion capitals, NYC is ever setting trends for the rest of the country to follow. To check out the latest designs hitting the streets, it's worth browsing some of the best-loved boutiques around town – regardless of whether you intend to spend. A few favorites include Opening Ceremony (p105), Issey Miyake, Marc Jacobs, Rag & Bone (p106), John Varvatos (p130) and By Robert James.

If time is limited, or you simply want to browse a plethora of labels in one go, then head to those heady conglomerations known worldwide as department stores. New York has a special blend of alluring draws – in particular you could lose an entire afternoon in Bergdorf Goodman (p209), Macy's (p210) or Bloomingdale's (p209).

Local Icons

A few stores have cemented their status as NYC legends. This city just wouldn't quite be the same without them. For label hunters, Century 21 (p84) is a Big Apple institution, with wears by D&G, Prada, Marc Jacobs and many others at low prices. Book lovers of the world unite at the Strand (p161), the city's biggest and best bookseller. Run by Hassidic Jews and employing mechanized whimsy, B&H Photo Video (p210) thrills digital and audio geeks. For secondhand clothing, home furnishings and books, good-hearted Housing Works (p162), with many locations around town, is a perennial favorite.

Flea Markets & Vintage Adventures

As much as New Yorkers gravitate towards all that's shiny and new, it can be infinitely fun to riffle through unwanted wares and threads. The most popular flea market is the Brooklyn Flea (p299), found in different locations on different days, April through October. Another gem is Artists & Fleas (p299), with scores of vendors. The East Village is the city's go-to neighborhood for secondhand and vintage stores – the uniform of the unwavering legion of hipsters.

Sample Sales

While clothing sales happen year-round – usually when seasons change and old stock must be moved out – sample sales are held frequently, mostly in the huge warehouses in the Fashion District of Midtown or in SoHo. While the original sample sale was a way for designers to get rid of one-of-a-kind prototypes that weren't quite up to snuff, most sample sales these days are for high-end labels to get rid of overstock at wonderfully deep discounts. For the latest sample sales, consult Chicmi (www.chicmi.com/new-york/sample-sales). Consignment stores are another fine place to look for top (gently used) fashions at reduced prices; label hunters find the Upper East Side prime territory with standouts like Michael's (p225).

NEED TO KNOW

Useful Websites

New York Magazine (www.nymag.com) Trustworthy opinions on the Big Apple's best places to swipe your plastic.

The Glamourai (www.theglamourai.com) Glossy downtown fashion blog that's packed with cutting-edge style ideas.

Mimosas & Manhattan (www.mimosasmanhattan.com) Fashion and lifestyle blog with inspiration and beauty tips.

He Spoke Style (http://hespokestyle.com) Gentlemen's style resource with fashion tips from NYC-based writers.

Opening Hours

In general, most businesses are open from 10am to around 7pm on weekdays and 11am to around 8pm Saturdays. Sundays can be variable – some stores stay closed while others keep weekday hours. Stores tend to stay open later in the neighborhoods downtown. Small boutiques often have variable hours – many open at noon.

Sales Tax

Clothing and footwear that costs less than $110 is exempt from sales tax. For everything else, you'll pay 8.875% retail sales tax on every purchase.

Shopping by Neighborhood

Financial District & Lower Manhattan (p84) While not a shopping hot spot per se, Lower Manhattan serves up a trickle of gems.

SoHo & Chinatown (p102) West Broadway is a veritable outdoor mall of encyclopedic proportions. It's like the UN of retail.

East Village & Lower East Side (p129) Hip treasure trove of vintage wares and design goods.

West Village, Chelsea & Meatpacking District (p159) Bleecker St, running off Abingdon Sq, is lined with boutiques, with a handful on nearby W 4th St.

Midtown (p208) Epic department stores, global chains and the odd in-the-know treasure – window shoppers unite!

Upper East Side (p225) The country's most expensive boutiques are found along Madison Ave.

Upper West Side & Central Park (p242) Home to some great bookshops (new and used), along with some little stores.

Brooklyn (p296) A riveting mix of independent boutiques, art purveyors and thrift stores.

Lonely Planet's Top Choices

Bergdorf Goodman (p209) The most magical of NYC's legendary department stores, with stellar store displays.

Brooklyn Flea (p299) Brooklyn's collection of flea markets offers plenty of vintage furnishings, retro clothing and bric-a-brac.

ABC Carpet & Home (p174) Spread over seven levels like a museum, ABC is packed with treasures large and small.

MoMA Design & Book Store (p209) The perfect one-stop shop for coffee-table tomes, art prints and 'Where-did-you-get-that?' homewares.

Best Fashion Boutiques

Rag & Bone (p106) Beautifully tailored clothes for men and women, in SoHo and elsewhere.

John Varvatos (p130) Rugged but worldly wearables in a former downtown rock club.

Opening Ceremony (p105) Head-turning, cutting-edge threads and kicks for the fashion avant-garde in SoHo.

Best For Women

Galeria Melissa (p103) Stylish Brazilian-designed plastic footwear in a surreal SoHo concept store.

Resurrection (p103) Valhalla for lovers of designer vintage and friendly staff to help you.

Century 21 (p84) Discounted designers at a city institution.

Best For Men

Nepenthes New York (p210) Japanese collective selling covetable, in-the-know labels.

Odin (p161) Tiny downtown men's boutique for one-of-a-kind pieces.

New York Shaving Company (p106) Classic SoHo-inspired colognes and traditional shaving kit in a barbershop beloved by celebs.

Best For Children

FAO Schwarz (p209) New York institution with a new lease of life: nirvana for kids big and small.

Dinosaur Hill (p130) In the East Village, you'll find fun, creative toys, books and music to inspire young minds.

Yoya (p161) Small, pretty clothing store in the West Village.

Best Bookstores

Strand Book Store (p161) Hands-down NYC's best second-hand bookstore.

Housing Works Book Store (p105) Used books and a cafe in an atmospheric setting in Nolita.

McNally Jackson (p106) Great SoHo spot for book browsing and author readings.

Best Music Stores

Rough Trade (p299) Vinyl is far from dead at this sprawling music shop and concert space in Williamsburg.

A-1 Records (p130) Endless bins of records in the East Village.

Best Vintage Stores

Housing Works Thrift Shop (p162) Always a fun place to browse, with locations around the city.

Screaming Mimi's (p162) Lots of appealing clothes from decades past.

Beacon's Closet (p160) Get a new outfit without breaking the bank at this great vintage shop. In Brooklyn, too.

Best Homewares & Design Stores

Shinola (p84) Unusual accessories from a cutting-edge Detroit design house in Tribeca.

Fishs Eddy (p173) Tongue-in-cheek New York designs on all manner of useful homewares you'll want to own.

Guggenheim Store (p213) Modernist-inspired teapots, exhibition posters and statement decorative *objets d'art* inspired by artists on display.

Best NYC Souvenirs

New York Public Library (p191) Stationery, tote bags, library lion bookends and literary-minded graphic T-shirts.

CityStore (p85) *The* place for official NYC memorabilia such as NYPD baseball caps and subway station signs.

Lower East Side Tenement Museum (p109) Books, jewelry, bags, scarves and more from the museum shop.

Best Unique Souvenirs & Gifts

Obscura Antiques (p129) A cabinet of curiosities packed with strange and eerie objects.

Top Hat (p131) Lovely collectible objects from around the globe.

Philip Williams Posters (p84) A treasure trove of printed posters from around the world.

Active New York City

Although hailing cabs in New York City can feel like a blood sport, and waiting on subway platforms in summer heat is steamier than a sauna, New Yorkers still love to stay active in their spare time. Considering the city's reputation as a megalopolis of neck-craning skyscrapers, the range of outdoor activities is a terrific surprise.

Spectator Sports

Just because there's so much else going on in the city and it doesn't shut down during playoff games like other smaller, sports-mad cities, it doesn't mean New Yorkers are any less passionate about their home-town teams. With a total of 13 professional major sports franchises, both men's and women's, not to mention minor league teams, other comparably more obscure sports like lacrosse and innumerable amateur leagues for sports like cricket and roller derby, there's almost always a competition to take in somewhere.

The Yankees, who play baseball in the Bronx, are easily the most successful with 27 championships. Next are the National Football League New York Giants with eight, who play at **MetLife Stadium** (201-559-1500, box office 201-559-1300; www.metlifestadium.com; Meadowlands Sports Complex, East Rutherford; 351 from Port Authority, NJ Transit from Penn Station to Meadowlands) in East Rutherford, New Jersey, along with the New York Jets. The New York Knicks have been a woeful National Basketball Association team for many years now, and their cross-borough rival the Brooklyn Nets have been gradually clawing back from their dismal reputation.

Soccer (football to the rest of the world) has a growing fanbase in the NYC area, with two rival major-league teams in action: the New York Red Bulls, based in Harrison, New Jersey; and New York City FC, which currently play home games in Yankee Stadium.

If this all sounds a little testosterone-driven, the **Gotham Girls Roller Derby** (www.gothamgirlsrollerderby.com; tickets from $30; Mar-Aug;) has four borough-inspired home teams and their events are spirited, high-energy spectaculars. Women's hockey, baseball and football have active scenes, too, with games taking place in Central Park, Prospect Park and beyond.

If you can't see a game in person (though it's worth trying to catch at least one while in town), try a little neighborhood bar when a Knicks, Giants, Yankees or Mets game is on – they can really light up. Even if you don't understand American sports, you'll likely find some more-than-willing tutors.

The *New York Times* sports page has excellent analysis and reporting, while the *New York Daily News* and the *New York Post* are more no-holds barred with their boosterism and criticism.

Cycling

NYC has taken enormous strides in making the city more bike friendly, adding hundreds of miles of bike lanes in recent years. That said, we recommend that the uninitiated stick to the less hectic trails in the parks and along the waterways, such as Central Park, Prospect Park, the Manhattan Waterfront Greenway and the Brooklyn Waterfront Greenway.

With 750 automated bike-share stations, The Citi Bike (www.citibikenyc.com) program is handy for quick jaunts, but for longer rides,

NEED TO KNOW

Useful Websites

NYC Parks (www.nycgovparks.org) Details on park services, including free pools, playgrounds, basketball courts, plus borough biking maps.

New York Road Runners Club (www.nyrr.org) Organizes weekend runs and races citywide.

Central Park (www.centralparknyc.org) Lists myriad activities and events held at NYC's best-loved green space.

NYC (www.nycgo.com/sports) Lists all the major sporting events and activities happening in town.

Buying Game Tickets

With so many teams and overlapping seasons, a game is rarely a day away. Some teams' hotlines or box offices sell tickets directly (available under 'Tickets' on the relevant websites), but most go via Ticketmaster (www.ticketmaster.com). The other major buy/sell outlet is StubHub (www.stubhub.com).

you'll want a proper rental. Biking tours let you cover a lot of ground. Bike the Big Apple (p385) and Central Park Bike Tours (p244) are recommended.

Running

Central Park's loop roads are best during traffic-free hours, though you'll be in the company of many cyclists and in-line skaters. The 1.6-mile path surrounding the Jacqueline Kennedy Onassis Reservoir (where Jackie O used to run) is for runners and walkers only; access it between 86th and 96th Sts. Running along the Hudson River is a popular path, best from about 30th St to Battery Park in Lower Manhattan. The Upper East Side has a path that runs along FDR Dr and the East River (from 63rd St to 115th St).

Brooklyn's Prospect Park has plenty of paths (and a 3-mile loop), while 1.3-mile-long Brooklyn Bridge Park has incredible views of Manhattan (reach it via Brooklyn Bridge to up the mileage). The New York Road Runners Club (www.nyrr.org) organizes weekend runs citywide, including the New York City Marathon.

Street Sports

With all that concrete around, New York has embraced a number of sports and events played directly on the streets themselves. Those with hoop dreams will find pick-up basketball games all over the city, usually free and first-come, first-served. The most famous courts are the West 4th St Basketball Courts, known as 'the Cage.' Or try Holcombe Rucker Park up in Harlem – that's where many NBA bigshots cut their teeth. You'll also find pick-up games in Tompkins Square Park and Riverside Park. Hudson River Park has courts at Canal St and on 11th Ave at W 23rd St. Pier 2 in Brooklyn Bridge Park also has public courts.

Lesser-known handball and stickball are also popular in NYC – you'll find one-wall courts in outdoor parks all over the city. For stickball, link up with the Bronx-based Emperors Stickball League (www.facebook.com/groups/bxstickball) to check out its Sunday games during the warmer months.

Water Sports

Manhattan's an island, after all, and as such there are plenty of opportunities for getting out on the water. The Downtown Boathouse (p85) offers free 20-minute kayaking (including equipment) in the protected embayment of the Hudson River; it also has a **Governors Island** (Map p438; www.downtownboathouse.org/governors-island; ⏲11am-4pm Sat & Sun mid-Jun–mid-Sep) FREE location (summer only). The Manhattan Community Boathouse (p210) also has free kayaking on summer weekends, plus lessons. Over in Brooklyn, there's occasional free kayaking at Pier 2 of Brooklyn Bridge Park (p263) and down at Red Hook Boaters (p300).

In Central Park, Loeb Boathouse (p244) rents rowboats for romantic trysts, and even fills Venice-style gondolas in summer. For a sailing adventure, hop aboard the Schooner Adirondack (p163) at Chelsea Piers.

Surfers may be surprised to find a tight group of wave worshippers within city limits, at Queens' Rockaway Beach (p307) at 90th St, which is a 75-minute ride on the A train from Midtown.

Lonely Planet's Top Choices

Central Park (p228) The city's playground has rolling hills, forested paths, open green spaces and a beautiful lake.

Brooklyn Bridge Park (p263) This beautifully designed waterfront green space offers kayaking, basketball and plenty more.

Prospect Park (p264) Escape the crowds at Brooklyn's gorgeous park, with trails, hills, tennis courts, lake and meadows.

New York Spa Castle (p318) A bathing behemoth with wallet-friendly prices, inspired by ancient Korean traditions of wellness.

Manhattan Community Boathouse (p210) On summer weekends this volunteer-run boathouse offers free kayaking and lessons on the Hudson.

Best Spectator Sports

New York Yankees (p254) One of the country's most successful baseball teams.

New York Giants (p53) Football powerhouse that, despite the name, plays in New Jersey.

New York Knicks (p207) See the Knicks sink a few three-pointers at Madison Square Garden.

Brooklyn Nets (p296) Brooklyn's hot NBA team hold court in the high-tech Barclays Center.

Brooklyn Cyclones (p295) See a Minor League Baseball game near Coney Island's boardwalk.

New York Mets (p317) NYC's underdog baseball team play their games at Citi Field in Queens.

Best Urban Green Spaces

Governors Island (p74) Car-free, seasonal island only a quick ferry ride from Lower Manhattan or Brooklyn.

Bryant Park (p191) A small appealing oasis amid the skyscrapers of Midtown.

Madison Square Park (p167) A pretty little park between Midtown and downtown.

Fort Greene Park (p269) Historic intrigues and picnic potential at an atmospheric green space in Brooklyn.

Gantry Plaza State Park (p305) A lovely riverside spot to relax in Long Island City, Queens.

Inwood Hill Park (p253) Serene setting of forest and salt marsh in Upper Manhattan.

Queens County Farm Museum (p305) Get a taste of barnyard life without leaving the metropolis.

Best Indoor Activities

Cliffs (p318) Massive climbing center in Long Island City, Queens.

Brooklyn Boulders (p300) Another great spot for rock climbers.

Jivamukti Lavish yoga center near Union Square.

MNDFL (p163) Be rejuvenated with an enriching meditation class.

Best Spas

Great Jones Spa (p103) Book a massage, then enjoy the steam room, hot tub and rock sauna.

New York Spa Castle (p318) An enchanting wonderland of waterfalls and steam rooms far out in Queens.

Russian & Turkish Baths (p128) A grungy East Village icon since 1892 with steam baths and an icy plunge pool.

Best Bowling

Brooklyn Bowl (p300) A Williamsburg classic that's equal parts hip hangout, concert space and bowling alley.

Chelsea Piers Complex (p163) Knock down some pins at this waterfront sports center, then stroll along the Hudson.

Lucky Strike (p210) Midtown bowling fun, complete with drinks in the company of a fashion-conscious crowd.

Best Out-of-the-Box Activities

Royal Palms (p290) A palace for shuffleboard lovers, this lively place has courts, plus food trucks and microbrews.

New York Trapeze School (p163) Channel your inner circus star at this trapeze school with two locations.

Gotham Girls Roller Derby (p53) Watch one of the world's elite teams in a hard-hitting sport blazing through various locations.

Best Gardens

Brooklyn Botanic Garden (p270) Japanese gardens, native flora and photogenic springtime cherry blossoms.

New York Botanical Garden (p254) Fifty acres of old-growth forest up in the Bronx.

Met Cloisters (p252) Medicinal plants blooming next to a medieval-esque building.

LGBTIQ+ New York City

From hand-locked married couples leaving the City Clerk's office wearing matching Bride & Bride hats to a rainbow-hued Empire State Building at Pride, there's no doubt that New York City is one of the world's great cities for LGBTIQ+ travelers. Indeed, few places come close to matching the breadth and depth of queer offerings here, from cabarets and clubs to festivals and readings.

School Night Shenanigans

Here in the Big Apple, any night of the week is fair game to paint the town rouge – especially for the gay community, who attack the weekday social scene with gusto. Wednesday and Thursday nights roar with a steady stream of parties, and locals love raging on Sunday (especially in summer). While there's undoubtedly much fun to be had on Friday and Saturday nights, weekend parties tend to be more 'bridge and tunnel' (that is, swarming with partygoers from the 'burbs). Manhattanites often use these nonwork days to catch up with friends, check out new restaurants and attend house parties rather than hit the clubs.

RESOURCES & SUPPORT

One of the largest centers of its kind in the world, the **LGBT Community Center** (Map p416; ☎212-620-7310; www.gaycenter.org; 208 W 13th St, btwn Seventh & Greenwich Aves, West Village; ⏰9am-10pm Mon-Sat, to 9pm Sun; Ⓢ1/2/3 to 14th St, A/C/E, L to 8th Ave-14th St) provides a ton of regional publications about LGBTIQ+ events and nightlife, and hosts frequent special events – dance parties, art exhibits, Broadway-caliber performances, readings and political panels. Plus it's home to the National Archive for Lesbian, Gay, Bisexual & Transgender History (accessible to researchers by appointment); a community-oriented cafe; a small exhibition space; and a cyber center.

Party Promoters

One of the best ways to dial into the party hotline is to follow the various goings-on of your favorite promoter. Here are some to start you off:

BoiParty (www.boiparty.com)

Saint at Large (www.saintatlarge.com)

Daniel's Big Ideas (www.danielsbigideas.com)

LGBTIQ+ by Neighborhood

East Village & Lower East Side Slightly grittier, sweatier, grungier versions of the West Side haunts.

West Village, Chelsea & the Meatpacking District Classic bars and clubs in the Village, with a wilting scene in high-rent Chelsea.

Union Square, Flatiron District & Gramercy Hosts a small spillover of venues from the East Village, West Village and Chelsea.

Midtown Hell's Kitchen is the city's 21st-century gay epicenter, with a plethora of eateries, bars, clubs and shops for the LGBTIQ+ community.

Brooklyn Multineighborhood borough with gays of every ilk, and diverse watering holes peppered throughout.

Lonely Planet's Top Choices

NYC Pride (www.nycpride.org) Rainbow-clad pomp and circumstance at the world's largest LGBTIQ+ march.

Leslie-Lohman Museum of Gay & Lesbian Art (p91) The world's first LGBTIQ+ art museum.

Industry (p201) One of the best-loved bar-clubs in kicking Hell's Kitchen.

Marie's Crisis (p153) Sing your heart out at this fun show-tunes bar in the West Village.

Duplex (p159) Camp quips, smooth crooners and a riotously fun piano bar define this Village veteran.

Eagle NYC (p155) Love-it-or-loathe-it debauchery and plenty of leather.

Useful Websites

Get Out! (www.getoutmag.com) Online version of a print guide to all things queer in town.

Gayletter (www.gayletter.com) E-newsletter covering queer-related culture, musings and parties.

Gay City News (www.gaycitynews.nyc) News and current affairs with a queer bent, as well as arts and travel reviews.

Metrosource (www.metrosource.com) Bimonthly publication focusing on culture, design, entertainment and travel.

Best Places to Stay

Ink48 (p341) Skyline views and a hop away from Hell's Kitchen bars and clubs.

Standard East Village (p335) Crisp, fresh, boutique chic in the funky East Village.

Chelsea Pines Inn (p336) Hollywood posters, diva-moniker rooms and a Chelsea address.

Gansevoort Meatpacking NYC (p336) Jet-setter cool and a rooftop pool in the Meatpacking District.

Best For Women

Ginger's Bar (p291) Happy hour specials, karaoke and Sunday bingo pull the girls at Brooklyn's lesbian epicenter.

Cubbyhole (p155) No-attitude Village veteran with jukebox tunes and chatty regulars.

Henrietta Hudson (p155) A fun, classic dive packed with supercool rocker chicks.

Best Classic Hangouts

Marie's Crisis (p153) One-time dive bar turned Village show-tune piano bar.

Stonewall Inn (p155) Scene of rioting drag queens during the Stonewall riots of '69.

Julius' (p155) The oldest gay in the Village.

Cock (p126) Tongue-in-cheek sleaze in a former gay-punk hangout.

Best Daytime Scenes

Brunch on Ninth Avenue Pick a sidewalk table and do your bit for Neighborhood Watch, Hell's Kitchen–style.

Shopping in Chelsea (p159) Style-up at Nasty Pig and other queer-centric Chelsea boutiques.

Pier 45 (Christopher Street Pier) (p139) Butt-hugging trunks and loved-up couples make this a summertime sunbaking staple.

Fire Island Mingle with the hot and rich at this sand-dune-swept playground just off of Long Island.

Best For Weeknights

Therapy (p201) Evening music, drag and showbiz guests give school nights some much-needed razzle dazzle.

Flaming Saddles (p201) Boot-scootin' barmen pouring liquor down your throat – who said weeknights were boring?

Boxers NYC (p173) This sports bar sees dudes tackling the tighter ends on and off the field.

Duplex (p159) Nightly entertainment, like drag storytelling and comedy, plus 4pm to 8pm happy hours on weeknights.

Best For Dancing

Industry (p201) As night deepens, this Hell's Kitchen hit turns from buzzing bar to thumping club.

Monster (p155) Cheeky go-go boys and cheekier drag queens keep the punters purring in the basement.

Therapy (p201) Small fun dancefloor when you need a break from the mega clubs.

Best Events

NYC Pride (pwww.nycpride.org) A monthlong celebration in June, with parties, cultural events and the famous march down Fifth Ave.

NewFest (www.newfest.or) NYC's premier queer film fest, with a weeklong program of flicks in late October.

MIX New York Queer Experimental Film Festival (www.facebook.com/mixnyc) Six days of avant-garde and political queer cinema in March.

Explore New York City

View down 42nd St to Chrysler Building (p186)

NEW YORK CITY'S TOP EXPERIENCES

Neighborhoods at a Glance

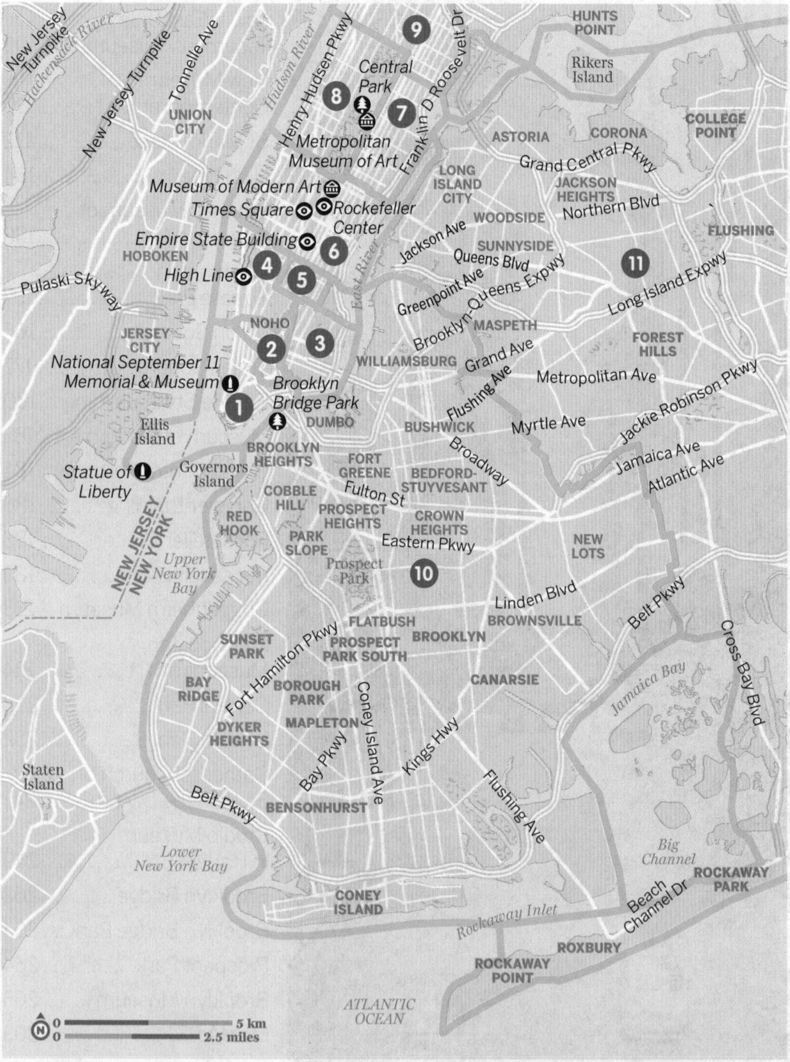

1 Lower Manhattan & the Financial District p62

Peppered with some big-hitting New York sights and purveyors of fine food and drink, Manhattan's Financial District is no longer strictly business. Prosperous Tribeca to the north offers upmarket restaurants and bars, art galleries and high-end retail.

2 SoHo & Chinatown p86

SoHo is one of Manhattan's trendiest 8eighborhoods, known for boutiques, bars and eateries. To the south, expanding Chinatown and a nostalgic sliver of Little Italy lure with idiosyncratic street life.

3 East Village & the Lower East Side p107

Once home to generations of immigrants, today the Lower East Side and East Village buzz with bohemian energy, offering some of NYC's finest bars and indie boutiques, seasoned with just a bit of vestigial grittiness.

4 West Village, Chelsea & the Meatpacking District p132

The West Village's twisting streets offer intimate spaces for dining, drinking and wandering. Manhattan's young professionals hit up the Meatpacking District to see and be seen in its many clubs and bars, while Chelsea offers art galleries and a vibrant gay scene.

5 Union Square, the Flatiron District & Gramercy p164

Though short on sights, Union Square bustles with New Yorkers of all stripes. To the north, Madison Square Park provides a verdant respite in the shadow of the Flatiron Building. Residential Gramercy offers more drinking and dining spots.

6 Midtown p175

Midtown is the NYC of postcards, home to icons such as Times Square, Broadway theaters, Grand Central Terminal, the Empire State Building, MoMA and the New York Public Library. Located nearby are the food-packed, gay-friendly streets of Hell's Kitchen.

7 Upper East Side p211

High-end boutiques line Madison Ave, while architecturally magnificent Fifth Ave, which runs parallel to the leafy realms of Central Park, is home to the so-called Museum Mile – one of the most cultured strips in New York (and possibly the world).

8 Upper West Side & Central Park p226

Cinematic rows of brownstones on quiet side streets feature in this noted family neighborhood dotted with artisan coffee shops and designer emporiums. Nearby is Central Park's verdant expanse; cultural anchors include Lincoln Center and the American Museum of Natural History.

9 Harlem & Upper Manhattan p245

Harlem is inextricably connected to the African American experience, and despite gentrification, remains packed with soulfood eateries and swinging jazz clubs. Columbia University sprawls through Morningside Heights and leafy Inwood hides medieval treasures.

10 Brooklyn p260

International buzzword for 'artsy cool', the real Brooklyn offers much more than hipster stereotypes, with some of NYC's most historic and culturally diverse neighborhoods and fantastic dining, drinking, shopping and entertainment options.

11 Queens p301

It's NYC's largest borough, and with nearly half of its residents foreign-born, Queens is truly an international melting pot. Gorge on ethnic eats, surf in Rockaway Beach and visit contemporary art centers.

Lower Manhattan & Financial District

FINANCIAL DISTRICT | NEW YORK HARBOR | BATTERY PARK CITY | EAST RIVER WATERFRONT | CITY HALL & CIVIC CENTER

Neighborhood Top Five

❶ **Statue of Liberty** (p64) Climbing up America's most famous statue, peering out from her crown and seeing the world's greatest city spread out before you.

❷ **National September 11 Memorial & Museum** (p68) Reflecting on loss, hope and resilience at New York City's beautifully transformed Ground Zero.

❸ **One World Trade Center** (p70) Zipping up to the top of the Western Hemisphere's tallest building for a knockout panorama of Manhattan and beyond at One World Observatory.

❹ **Staten Island Ferry** (p85) Taking in skyscrapers while crossing the harbor on one of New York City's floating (and free) icons.

❺ **Ellis Island** (p67) Exploring American immigration at the country's most historically significant point of entry.

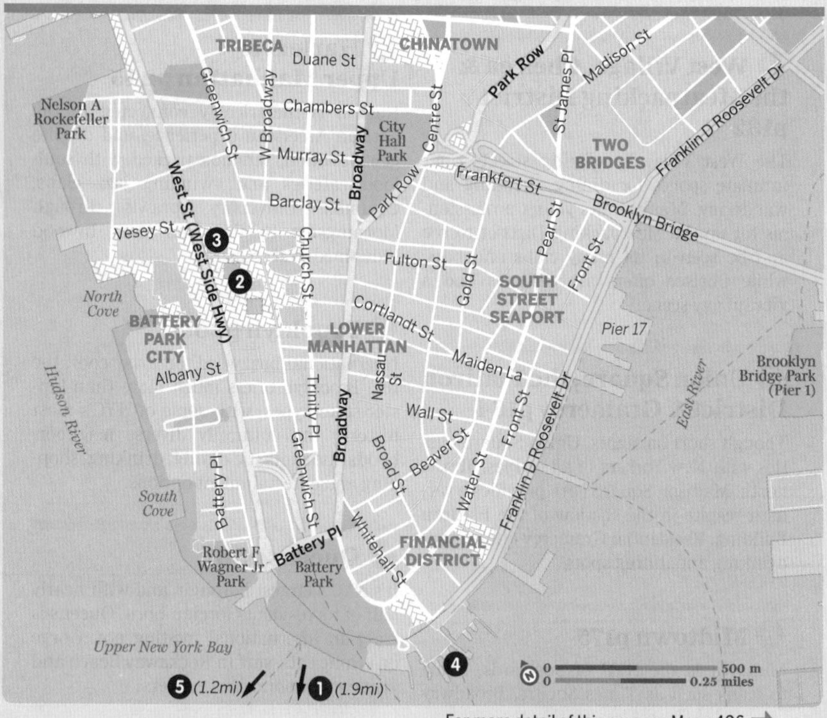

For more detail of this area see Map p406

Explore Financial District & Lower Manhattan

A little planning will save you a lot of time here. Book tickets online to the unmissable Ellis Island (p66) and Statue of Liberty (p64) (if you can, catch an early ferry and avoid weekends, especially in summer). Budget four or five hours to explore them properly, and you'll want to bring lunch (the food on-site is awful). Online ticket purchasing is also highly recommended for both the National September 11 Memorial Museum (p68) and the neighboring One World Observatory (p71).

Several museums around the southern tip of Manhattan, including the Skyscraper Museum (p75), Museum of Jewish Heritage (p75) and National Museum of the American Indian (p72), can easily fill a half a day. To experience the Financial District's intensity, go during business hours. But to calmly contemplate the area's Federal homes and early-modern skyscrapers, go after hours or on weekends.

In fine weather, soak up some rays and river views on Pier 17 (p78) at South Street Seaport, or walk across the Brooklyn Bridge for jaw-dropping views of Lower Manhattan. For an evening buzz, head to Tribeca's renowned eateries and drinking dens.

Local Life

- **Coffee** Ditch the corporate chains for in-the-know Bluestone Lane (p81) and La Colombe (p81).
- **Wine** Swill free vino on Saturday afternoons at Pasanella & Son (p85).
- **Shopping** Browse the aisles at Pearl River Mart (p84) for fun gifts with an Asian flair.
- **Escape** Cycle, relax and eye-up art on the summer oasis that is Governors Island (p74).

Getting There & Away

- **Subway** The A/C, J/Z, 2/3 and 4/5 all meet at the Lower Manhattan hub of Fulton St. The 1 terminates at South Ferry, from where the Staten Island Ferry departs.
- **Boat** The Staten Island Ferry Terminal (p85) is at the southern end of Whitehall St. Ferries to Governors Island (p74) leave from the adjacent Battery Maritime Building. Statue Cruises (p65) runs to Liberty and Ellis Islands from Battery Park. On summer weekends and holidays, **New York Beach Ferry** (www.newyorkbeachferry.com) runs from Pier 11 to Jacob Riis Beach Park in the Rockaways.

Lonely Planet's Top Tip

Looking for discounted tickets to Broadway shows? Skip the long lines at the TKTS Booth in Times Square for the much quieter **TKTS Booth** (www.tdf.org; cnr Front & John Sts; ⌚ 11am-6pm Mon-Sat, to 4pm Sun; **S** A/C, 2/3, 4/5, J/Z to Fulton St; R/W to Cortlandt St) at South Street Seaport. Queues usually move a little faster and you can also purchase tickets for next-day matinees (something you can't do at Times Square). The TKTS smartphone app offers real-time listings of what's on sale.

Best Places to Eat

- Locanda Verde (p80)
- Bâtard (p80)
- Maman (p79)
- Le District (p80)
- Two Hands (p79)

For reviews, see p78

Best Places to Drink

- Dead Rabbit (p81)
- Brandy Library (p81)
- Weather Up (p81)
- Smith & Mills (p81)
- Bluestone Lane (p81)

For reviews, see p81

Best Places to Shop

- Philip Williams Posters (p84)
- Pearl River Mart (p84)
- Century 21 (p84)
- Bowne & Co Stationers (p85)
- Pasanella & Son (p85)

For reviews, see p84

SANCHAI KUMAR/SHUTTERSTOCK ©

TOP EXPERIENCE
STATUE OF LIBERTY

Lady Liberty has been gazing sternly toward 'unenlightened Europe' since 1886. Dubbed the 'Mother of Exiles,' she's often interpreted as a symbolic admonishment to an unjust old world. Emma Lazarus' 1883 poem 'The New Colossus' articulates this challenge: 'Give me your tired, your poor, your huddled masses yearning to breathe free, the wretched refuse of your teeming shore.'

From the Suez to the City

It comes as a surprise to many that France's jumbo-size gift to America was not originally conceived with the US in mind. Indeed, when sculptor Frédéric-Auguste Bartholdi began planning the piece, his vision was for a colossal sculpture to guard the entrance to the Suez Canal in Egypt, one of France's greatest 19th-century engineering achievements. Bartholdi's ode to Gallic ingenuity would incorporate elements of two of the Seven Wonders of the Ancient World: the Colossus of Rhodes and the lighthouse of Alexandria. Despite its appeal to human vanity, the ambitious monument failed to attract serious funding from either France or Egypt, and Bartholdi's dream seemed destined for the scrap heap. Salvation came from Bartholdi's friend Édouard de Laboulaye. A French jurist, writer and anti-slavery activist, de Laboulaye proposed a gift to America as a symbol of the triumph of republicanism and of the democratic values that underpinned both France and the US. Seeing an opportunity too good to miss, Bartholdi quickly set to work, tweaking his vision and turning his Suez concept into 'Liberty Enlightening the World' – an immortal gift to commemorate America's centennial of the Declaration of Independence.

DID YOU KNOW?

The Statue of Liberty weighs 225 tons, and stretches 305ft and 1in from ground to torch tip (or about as tall as a 22-story building).

PRACTICALITIES

- Map p406, C8
- 212-363-3200, tickets 877-523-9849
- www.nps.gov/stli
- Liberty Island
- adult/child incl Ellis Island $18.50/9, incl crown $21.50/12
- 8:30am-6pm, hours vary by season
- to Liberty Island, S 1 to South Ferry, 4/5 to Bowling Green, then ferry

Creating the Lady

Bartholdi spent almost 20 years turning his dream – to create the hollow copper colossus and mount it in New York Harbor – into reality. Along the way the project was hindered by serious financial problems but helped in part by the fund-raising efforts of newspaper publisher Joseph Pulitzer. Lending a further hand was poet Emma Lazarus, whose ode to Lady Liberty was part of a fund-raising campaign for the statue's pedestal, designed by American architect Richard Morris Hunt. Bartholdi's work on the statue was also delayed by structural challenges – a problem resolved by the metal-framework mastery of railway engineer Gustave Eiffel (yes, of the famous tower). The work of art was finally completed in France in 1884, a bit behind schedule for the centennial. It was shipped to NYC as 350 pieces packed into 214 crates, reassembled over a span of four months and placed on the US-made granite pedestal. Its spectacular October 1886 dedication included New York's first ticker-tape parade and a flotilla of almost 300 vessels. The Lady was placed under the administration of the National Park Service in 1933; a restoration of her oxidized copper began in 1984, the same year she made it onto the UN's list of World Heritage Sites.

Liberty Today

Folks who reserve their tickets in advance are able to climb the (steep) 162 steps from the top of the pedestal level to Lady Liberty's crown, from where the city and harbor views are breathtaking. Be advised: crown access is extremely limited, and the only way in is to reserve your spot in advance; the further ahead you can do it, the better (a six-month lead time is allowed). Each customer can reserve a maximum of four crown tickets, and children must be at least 4ft tall to be admitted.

If you miss out on crown tickets, you may have better luck with tickets to the pedestal, which also offers commanding views. Like crown tickets, pedestal tickets are limited and should be reserved in advance, either online or by phone. Only crown- and pedestal-ticket holders have access to the **Statue of Liberty museum** in the pedestal.

If you don't have crown or pedestal tickets, don't fret. All ferry tickets to Liberty and Ellis Islands offer basic access to the grounds of Liberty Island, including guided ranger tours or self-guided audio tours. There's also a gift shop and cafeteria open to all. (Tip: bring your own nibbles and enjoy them by the water with the Manhattan skyline stretched out before you.)

TOP TIPS

To see both the Statue of Liberty and Ellis Island, get a ferry before the 2pm sailing.

Security at the ferry terminal is tight – don't take anything you wouldn't take on a plane, and allow for 90-minute waits in high season.

Don't believe any street sellers who tell you otherwise – official tickets are sold only through **Statue Cruises** (Map p406; ☎877-523-9849; www.statuecruises.com; Battery Park, Lower Manhattan; adult/child from $18.50/9; ⏲departures 8:30am-5pm, shorter hours winter). Buying tickets in advance online is strongly recommended.

The 162-step slog up tight, narrow steps to the crown is arduous and should not be undertaken by anyone with health conditions that might impair their ability to complete the climb.

TAKE A BREAK

For a picnic lunch – **Gourmet Garage** (☎212-571-5850; www.gourmetgarage.com; 366 Broadway, at Franklin St; ⏲7am-9pm; ✍; Ⓢ N/Q/R/W, 6 to Canal St) is a great option for fresh food to go.

TOP EXPERIENCE
ELLIS ISLAND

The most famous port of entry in the world, and a physical symbol of the American immigrant story, Ellis Island is now a National Monument. Operating only from 1892 to 1924, it nonetheless processed some 12 million new arrivals. An estimated 40% of Americans today descend from those millions, making this island central to the story of modern America.

Restoration

In 1990, following a long and expensive restoration, Ellis Island's dignified beaux-arts-style main building was reopened to the public as the Ellis Island Immigration Museum. Now anybody who rides the ferry to the island can experience a cleaned-up, modern version of the historic new-arrival experience, with the museum's interactive exhibits paying homage to the hope, jubilation and sometimes bitter disappointment of the millions who came here in search of a new beginning. Among them were Hungarian Erik Weisz (Harry Houdini), Italian Rodolfo Guglielmi (Rudolph Valentino), Frenchwoman Lily Chauchoin (Claudette Colbert) and Brit Archibald Alexander Leach (Cary Grant).

Immigration Museum Exhibits

The museum's exhibits are spread over three levels. To get the most out of your visit, opt for the 50-minute self-guided audio tour (free with ferry ticket, available from the museum lobby). Featuring narratives from a number of sources, including historians, architects and the immigrants themselves, the tour brings to life the museum's hefty collection of personal objects, official documents, photographs and film footage. It's an evocative experience to witness personal memories – both good and bad – in the very halls and corridors in which they occurred.

The collection is divided into permanent and temporary exhibitions. *Journeys: The Peopling of America 1550–1890* on the 1st floor is interesting, but the real focus begins on the 2nd floor, where you'll find the two most fascinating exhibitions. *Through America's Gate* examines the step-by-step process faced by the newly arrived (including the chalk-marking of those suspected of illness, a wince-inducing eye examination, and 29 questions) in the beautiful, vaulted Great Hall, while *Peak Immigration Years: 1880–1924* explores the motives behind the immigrants' journeys and the challenges they faced once free to begin their new American lives. Particularly interesting is the collection of old photographs, which offers intimate glimpses into the daily lives of these courageous new Americans.

For a history of the rise, fall and resurrection of the building itself, make time for the *Restoring a Landmark* exhibition on the 3rd floor; its assortment of trashed desks, chairs and other abandoned possessions is strangely eloquent. Best of all, the audio tour offers optional in-depth coverage for those who want to delve deeper into the collections and the island's history. If you don't feel like listening to the audio tour, you can always pick up one of the phones in each display area and hear the recorded, affecting memories of real Ellis Island immigrants, taped in the 1980s. Another option is the free 45-minute guided tour with a park ranger. If booked three weeks in advance by phone, the tour is also available in American Sign Language.

DON'T MISS

- Immigration Museum exhibits
- Great Hall
- American Immigrant Wall of Honor & Fort Gibson ruins

PRACTICALITIES

- Map p406, B8
- 212-363-3200, tickets 877-523-9849
- www.nps.gov/elis
- Ellis Island
- ferry incl Liberty Island adult/child $18.50/9
- 8:30am-6pm, hours vary by season
- to Ellis Island, S 1 to South Ferry, 4/5 to Bowling Green, then ferry

Main Building Architecture

With the Main Building, architects Edward Lippincott Tilton and William A Boring created a suitably impressive and imposing 'prologue' to America. The duo won the contract after the original wooden building burnt down in 1897. Having attended the École des Beaux-Arts in Paris, it's not surprising that they opted for a beaux-arts aesthetic for the project. The building evokes a grand train station, with majestic triple-arched entrances, decorative Flemish bond brickwork, and granite cornerstones and belvederes. Inside, it's the 338ft-long **Registry Room** on the 2nd floor that takes the breath away. Under its beautiful vaulted ceiling, the newly arrived lined up to have their documents checked (people such as polygamists, paupers, criminals and anarchists were turned back). The original plaster ceiling was severely damaged by an explosion of munition barges at nearby Black Tom Wharf. It was a blessing in disguise – the rebuilt version was adorned with striking herringbone-patterned tiles by Rafael Guastavino.

American Immigrant Wall of Honor & Fort Gibson Ruins

Accessible from the 1st-floor *Journeys: The Peopling of America 1550–1890* exhibit is the outdoor **American Immigrant Wall of Honor**, inscribed with the names of more than 700,000 immigrants. Believed to be the world's longest wall of names, it's a fundraising project, allowing any American to have an immigrant relative's name recorded in return for a donation. Construction of the wall in the 1990s uncovered the remains of the island's original structure, **Fort Gibson**. Built in 1808, the fortification was part of a harbor-defense system against the British that also included Castle Clinton in Battery Park and Castle Williams on Governors Island. During this time, Ellis Island measured 3.3 acres of sand and slush – between 1892 and 1934 the island expanded dramatically thanks to landfill brought in from the ballast of ships and construction of the city's subway system.

An Irish Debut

Ellis Island's very first immigrant was 17-year-old Anna 'Annie' Moore. After a 12-day journey in steerage from County Cork, Ireland, Annie arrived on January 1, 1892, accompanied by her brothers Phillip and Anthony; the three were headed to America to join their parents, who had migrated to New York City four years earlier. She later married German immigrant Joseph Augustus Schayer and gave birth to at least 11 children, only five of whom survived. Annie died on December 6, 1924, and was laid to rest at Calvary Cemetery, Queens.

HOSPITAL OF ALL NATIONS

At the turn of the 20th century, the hospital on Ellis Island (now defunct) was one of the world's largest. Consisting of 22 buildings and dubbed the 'Hospital of All Nations,' it was America's front line in the fight against 'imported' diseases. The institution's fascinating history is vividly relayed in writer-producer Lorie Conway's documentary and accompanying book *Forgotten Ellis Island.* A guided 'Hard Hat Tour' ($58.50) of the unrestored hospital can be booked when you reserve your ticket online.

TAKE A BREAK

The menu in the island's **cafe** is pretty uninspiring. Your best bet is to grab some prepared food from the food trucks north of Bowling Green station on your way to the ferry, or wait until you return to Manhattan and hit up the myriad options at Brookfield Place (p79).

PIT STOCK/SHUTTERSTOCK ©

TOP EXPERIENCE

NATIONAL SEPTEMBER 11 MEMORIAL & MUSEUM

The National September 11 Memorial and Museum is a dignified tribute to the victims of the worst terrorist attack to occur on American soil. Titled *Reflecting Absence,* the memorial's two massive reflecting pools feature the names of the thousands who lost their lives. Beside them stands the Memorial Museum, a striking, solemn space documenting that fateful day in 2001.

DON'T MISS

- *Reflecting Absence* pools
- Memorial Museum
- Santiago Calatrava's Oculus

PRACTICALITIES

- Map p406, B5
- www.911memorial.org
- 180 Greenwich St, Lower Manhattan
- admission free
- ⏲7:30am-9pm
- [S] E to World Trade Center, 2/3 to Park Pl, R/W to Cortlandt St

Reflecting Pools

Surrounded by a plaza planted with more than 400 white oak trees, the 9/11 Memorial's reflecting pools occupy the footprints of the ill-fated Twin Towers. From their rim, a cascade of water pours 30ft down toward a central void. The flow of the water is richly symbolic, beginning as thousands of smaller streams, merging into a massive torrent of collective confusion, and ending with a slow journey toward an abyss. Bronze panels frame the pools, inscribed with the names of those who died in the attacks of September 11, 2001, and in the World Trade Center (WTC) car bombing on February 26, 1993. Designed by Michael Arad and Peter Walker, the pools are both striking and deeply poignant.

Memorial Museum

The contemplative energy of the monument is further enhanced by the **National September 11 Memorial Museum** (☎212-312-8800; www.911memorial.org/museum; 180 Greenwich St, Lower Manhattan; memorial free, museum adult/child $26/15, 5-8pm Tue free; ⏲9am-8pm Sun-Thu, to 9pm Fri & Sat, last entry 2 hours before close; [S] E to World Trade Center, 2/3 to Park Pl, R/W to Cortlandt St). Standing between the reflective pools, the museum's glass entrance pavilion eerily evokes a toppled tower. Inside the entrance, an escalator leads down to the museum's subterranean main lobby. On the descent, visitors stand in the shadow of two **steel tridents**, originally embedded in the bedrock at the base of the North Tower. Each over 80ft tall and weighing 50 tons, they once provided the structural support that allowed the towers to soar over 1360ft into the sky. They remained standing in the subsequent sea of rubble, becoming immediate symbols of resilience.

The tridents are two of more than 10,300 objects in the museum's collection. Among these are the Vesey Street Stairs. Dubbed the **Survivors' Staircase**, they allowed hundreds of workers to flee the WTC site on the morning of 9/11. At the bottom of these stairs is the moving *In Memoriam* gallery, its walls lined with the photographs and names of those who perished. Interactive touch screens and a central reflection room shed light on the victims' lives. Their humanity is further fleshed out by the numerous **personal effects** on display. Among these is a dust-covered wallet belonging to Robert Joseph Gschaar, an insurance underwriter who worked on level 92 of the South Tower. The wallet's contents include a photograph of Gschaar's wife, Myrta, and a $2 bill: when he proposed, Gschaar gave her a $2 bill as a symbol of their second chance at happiness (theirs was a second marriage for them both); he kept another with him.

Around the corner from the *In Memoriam* gallery is the **NYC Fire Department's Engine Company 21**. One of the largest artifacts on display, its burnt-out cab is testament to the inferno faced by those at the scene. The fire engine stands at the entrance to the museum's main historical exhibition. Divided into three sections – *Events of the Day, Before 9/11* and *After 9/11* – its collection of videos, audio recordings, images, objects and testimonies provide a rich, meditative exploration of the tragedy, the events that preceded it (including the WTC bombing of 1993), and the stories of grief, resilience and hope that followed.

The historical exhibition spills into the monumental **Foundation Hall**, flanked by a massive section of the original slurry wall, built to hold back the waters of the Hudson River during the towers' construction. It's also home to the last steel column removed during the cleanup, adorned with the messages and mementos of recovery workers, first responders and loved ones of the victims.

Angel of 9/11

One of the Memorial Museum's most famous (and curious) artifacts is the so-called 'Angel of 9/11,' the eerie outline of a woman's anguished face on a twisted girder believed to originate from the point where American Airlines Flight 11 slammed into the North Tower. (Experts have a more prosaic explanation: natural corrosion and sheer coincidence.)

CALATRAVA'S ARCHITECTURE

The image of a flying dove allegedly inspired Santiago Calatrava's dramatic white Oculus above the new WTC Transportation Hub. Made from 36,500 tons of steel, the arresting structure streams natural light into the $3.9-billion transit center, which serves 250,000 train commuters daily. A whopping 2½ times bigger than Grand Central Terminal, it also features multiple levels of retail and dining space. Every year on September 11, the central skylight is opened for 102 minutes, the length of time from the first attack to the collapse of the second tower.

TAKE A BREAK

Escape the swarm of restaurants serving the lunching Wall St crowd and head to Tribeca for a variety of in-demand eateries, such as Locanda Verde (p80).

A good alternative for less-expensive dining is Two Hands (p79).

EO NAYA/SHUTTERSTOCK ©

TOP EXPERIENCE
ONE WORLD TRADE CENTER

Filling what was a sore and glaring gap in the Lower Manhattan skyline, One World Trade Center symbolizes rebirth, determination and resilience. More than just another supertall skyscraper, it's a richly symbolic giant, well aware of the past yet firmly focused on the future. For lovers of New York, it's also the city's highest stop for dizzying, unforgettable urban views.

The Building

Leaping from the northwestern corner of the World Trade Center site, the 104-floor tower is architect David M Childs' redesign of Daniel Libeskind's original 2002 concept. Not only the loftiest building in America, this tapered giant is currently the tallest building in the Western Hemisphere – not to mention the sixth tallest in the world by pinnacle height. The tower soars skywards with chamfered edges, resulting in a series of isosceles triangles that, seen from the building's base, reach to infinity. Crowning the structure is a 408ft cable-stayed spire. Co-designed by sculptor Kenneth Snelson, it brings the building's total height to 1776ft, a symbolic reference to the year of American independence.

Indeed, symbolism feeds several aspects of the building: the tower's footprint is equal to those of the original Twin Towers, while the observation decks match the heights of those in the old complex. Unlike the original towers, however, One WTC was built with a whole new level of safety in mind, its precautionary features including a 200ft-high blast-resistant base (clad in more than 2000 pieces of glimmering prismatic glass) and 39.4in-thick concrete walls encasing elevators, stairwells, and communication and safety systems.

Not only is the building one of the world's tallest, but it's also one of the most sustainable, winning LEED Gold certification for its various ecofriendly features. Almost half of the construction materials were made from postindustrial recycled content, and 87%

DON'T MISS

- A photo from the base looking up
- Sky Pod elevators
- Observatory views

PRACTICALITIES

- One WTC
- Map p406, B4
- www.onewtc.com
- cnr West & Vesey Sts, Lower Manhattan
- S E to World Trade Center, 2/3 to Park Pl, A/C, J/Z, 4/5 to Fulton St, R/W to Cortlandt St

of the construction waste was kept out of landfills. Rainwater is harvested for cooling machinery and irrigating greenery. Natural light reaches 90% of office areas, reducing electrical requirements, and low-consumption electrical and HVAC systems are programmed to adapt to occupancy levels to maximize efficiency.

One thing not foreseen by the architects and engineers, though, was the antenna's noisy disposition: the strong winds that race through its lattice design produce a haunting, howling sound known to keep some locals up at night.

One World Observatory

Not one to downplay its assets, the skyscraper is home to **One World Observatory** (212-602-4000; www.oneworldobservatory.com; adult/child/under-5s $35/29/free; 9am-9pm Sep-Apr, from 8am May-Aug), the city's loftiest observation deck. While the observatory spans levels 100 to 102, the experience begins at the ground-floor **Global Welcome Center**, where an electronic world map highlights the many homelands of the building's visitors (with data relayed from ticket scans). The bitter bickering that plagued much of the project's development is all but forgotten in the adjoining *Voices* exhibition, where architects and construction workers wax lyrical about the tower's formation on 144 video screens.

After a quick rundown of the site's geology, the real thrills begin as you step inside one of five **Sky Pod elevators**, among the fastest in the world. As the elevators begin their 1250ft skyward journey, LED wall panels kick into action. Suddenly you're in a veritable time machine, watching Manhattan's evolution from forested island to teeming concrete jungle. Forty-seven seconds (and 500 years) later, you're on level 102, where another short presentation ends with a spectacular reveal.

Skip the overpriced eateries on level 101 and continue down to the real highlight: level 100. Waiting for you is an **epic 360-degree panorama** guaranteed to keep you busy searching for landmarks, from the Brooklyn and Manhattan Bridges to Lady Liberty and the Woolworth, Empire State and Chrysler Buildings. If you need a hand, interactive mobile tablets programmed in eight languages are available for hire (included with the combo ticket for $10 more). As expected, the view is extraordinary – try to go on a clear day – taking in all five boroughs and three adjoining states. For a close-up view of the Midtown skyscrapers, however, you're better off scaling the Empire State Building or the Rockefeller Center's Top of the Rock.

FAMOUS RESIDENTS

VIP buildings demand VIP clients, and One World Trade Center delivers. Its most famous tenant is Condé Nast Publications, which made the move from 4 Times Square in 2014. The company's portfolio includes high-end magazines like *Vogue, Vanity Fair, GQ, Architectural Digest, Wired* and – aptly enough – *The New Yorker*. As is to be expected, the company's headquarters are nothing short of fabulous, complete with dramatic spiral staircase and a glamorous cafeteria with gourmet bites and a million-dollar view.

TAKE A BREAK

There are dining options on level 101, but, being aimed at tourists, they're wildly overpriced. You're better off holding on to your appetite until you're down, then walking a block west to Brookfield Place and grabbing a bite at Hudson Eats (p79) or Le District (p80).

SIGHTS

⊙ Financial District

Most of Lower Manhattan's must-see sights are in the Financial District, among them Colonial-era New York churches and the site of George Washington's first presidential inauguration. Modern history is documented in a string of commendable museums, including the unmissable National September 11 Memorial Museum.

★NATIONAL SEPTEMBER 11
MEMORIAL & MUSEUM MUSEUM
See p68.

NATIONAL SEPTEMBER 11
MEMORIAL MONUMENT
See p68.

ONE WORLD TRADE
CENTER NOTABLE BUILDING
See p70.

★ONE WORLD OBSERVATORY VIEWPOINT
See p71.

NATIONAL MUSEUM OF THE
AMERICAN INDIAN MUSEUM
Map p406 (☑212-514-3700; www.nmai.si.edu; 1 Bowling Green, Financial District; ⊙10am-5pm Fri-Wed, to 8pm Thu; ♿; ⑤4/5 to Bowling Green, R/W to Whitehall St) FREE An affiliate of the Smithsonian Institution, this elegant tribute to Native American culture occupies Cass Gilbert's spectacular 1907 **Custom House**, one of NYC's finest beaux-arts buildings. Beyond a vast elliptical rotunda capped by a 140-ton skylight, sleek galleries play host to changing exhibitions featuring Native American art, culture, life and beliefs. The museum's permanent collection includes stunning decorative arts, textiles and ceremonial objects that document the diverse native cultures across the Americas, while the **imagiNATIONS Activity Center** explores their technologies.

TRINITY CHURCH CHURCH
Map p406 (☑212-602-0800; www.trinitywallstreet.org; 75 Broadway, at Wall St, Lower Manhattan; ⊙7am-6pm, churchyard closes 6pm summer, dusk in winter; ⑤1, R/W to Rector St, 2/3, 4/5 to Wall St) New York City's tallest building upon consecration in 1846, Trinity Church features a 280ft-high bell tower and a richly colored stained-glass window over the altar. Famous residents of its serene cemetery include Founding Father and first secretary of the Treasury (and now Broadway superstar) Alexander Hamilton, while its excellent musical program includes organ-recital series Pipes at One (1pm Friday), and evening choral performances including new works co-commissioned by Trinity and an annual December rendition of Handel's *Messiah*.

FRAUNCES TAVERN MUSEUM MUSEUM
Map p406 (☑212-425-1778; www.frauncestavernmuseum.org; 54 Pearl St, btwn Broad St & Coenties Slip, Financial District; adult/6-18yr/under 6yr $7/4/free; ⊙noon-5pm Mon-Fri, 11am-5pm Sat & Sun; ⑤J/Z to Broad St; 4/5 to Bowling Green; R/W to Whitehall St; 1 to South Ferry) Combining five early-18th-century structures, this unique museum/restaurant/bar pays homage to the nation-shaping events of 1783, the momentous year in which the British officially relinquished control of New York following the end of the Revolutionary War, and General George Washington gave a farewell speech to the officers of the Continental Army in the 2nd-floor dining room before returning to his home at Mt Vernon.

FEDERAL HALL MUSEUM
Map p406 (☑212-825-6990; www.nps.gov/feha; 26 Wall St, Financial District; ⊙9am-5pm Mon-Fri year-round, plus 9am-5pm Sat Jul-Oct; ⑤J/Z to Broad St; 2/3, 4/5 to Wall St) FREE A Greek Revival masterpiece, Federal Hall houses a museum dedicated to postcolonial New York. Themes include George Washington's inauguration, Alexander Hamilton's relationship with the city, and the struggles of John Peter Zenger, a printer who on this site in 1734 was jailed, tried and eventually acquitted of libel for exposing government corruption in his newspaper. There's also a visitor information hall with city maps and brochures.

ST PAUL'S CHAPEL CHURCH
Map p406 (☑212-602-0800; www.trinitywallstreet.org; 209 Broadway, at Fulton St, Lower Manhattan; ⊙10am-6pm Mon-Sat, from 7am Sun, churchyard closes dusk; ⑤A/C, J/Z, 2/3, 4/5 to Fulton St, R/W to Cortlandt St) After his inauguration in 1789, George Washington worshipped at this Classical Revival brownstone chapel, built in 1766 and narrowly avoiding destruction in the fire of

WORTH A DETOUR

STATEN ISLAND

Caricatures of Staten Island abound, and there's a glimmer of truth in the tough-talking, Italian-food-guzzling stereotypes. But these 60 sq miles are also dotted with impressive historic sites, and a day trip to Staten Island offers some culture and good eating. Sights are dispersed, so be selective: either start early or stay overnight if you want to tour more than one or two cultural attractions.

Snug Harbor Cultural Center & Botanical Garden (718-425-3504; www.snug-harbor.org; 1000 Richmond Tce; galleries & Chinese Scholar's Garden adult/child $8/free, grounds free; grounds dawn-dusk daily, Chinese Scholar's Garden noon-5pm Tue-Fri, from 10am Sat & Sun Apr-Nov, shorter hours Dec-Mar, building hours vary, usually noon-5pm Thu-Sun; S40 to Snug Harbor) offers a tranquil sweep of gardens, heritage buildings and gallery spaces. Highlights include the artwork-packed Staten Island Museum, an ancient-style Chinese Scholar's Garden, an Italian garden and a fascinating maritime museum. It's 2 miles west of the ferry terminal. In the island's center, 100-acre **Historic Richmond Town** (718-351-1611; www.historicrichmondtown.org; 441 Clarke Ave; adult/child $8/5, Wed pay-as-you-wish; noon-5pm Wed-Sun; S74 to Arthur Kill Rd & Clarke Ave) includes famous buildings like the US's oldest schoolhouse. Guides lead tours (included with admission) at 2pm on weekdays and 1:30pm and 3pm on weekends. It's about 45 minutes from the ferry terminal by bus.

The harborside **Alice Austen House** (718-816-4506; www.aliceausten.org; 2 Hylan Blvd, at Edgewater St; $5; 1-5pm Tue-Fri, 11am-5pm Sat & Sun Mar-Dec, by appointment only Jan & Feb; S51 to Hylan Blvd & Bay St) explores the life and artistic legacy of the first notable female American photographer. It's a 15-minute bus ride from the ferry. A one-off among Staten Island's many scrap-metal yards, **Lenny's Creations** (718-759-7344; www.lennyscreation.com; 16 Rector St; suggested donation $5; hours vary, usually 11am-7pm; S40 to Richmond Ter/Clove Rd) is the work of visionary metalsmith Lenny Prince, who shapes old car parts into sculptures of Transformers, Chinese dragons, superheroes and armor-clad knights.

Near the ferry terminal, **Enoteca Maria** (718-447-2777; www.enotecamaria.com; 27 Hyatt St; mains $17-25; noon-8:30pm Thu-Sun) is a delightful, warmly lit Italian eatery that attracts foodies for its exquisite old-world recipes made with care by sweet, deeply knowledgeable *nonne* (grandmothers); cash only and reservations essential. Atmospheric **Lakruwana** (347-857-6619; http://lakruwana.com; 668 Bay St, at Broad St; mains $14-17; noon-3:30pm Tue-Thu, 5-10pm Tue-Fri, noon-10pm Sat & Sun; S51 to Oakwood Mill Rd) serves up mouthwatering curries, saffron-tinged rice and other delicacies from Sri Lanka. The weekend buffet offers a wide array of temptations. It's about 1.2 miles south of the ferry terminal. Don't miss the small museum nearby with Sri Lankan art and artifacts. For a casual veggie bowl or bagel sandwich, try the bookstore/cafe **Everything Goes** (718-447-8256; www.etgstores.com/bookcafe; 208 Bay St; noon-7pm Tue & Wed, to 9pm Thu, to 10pm Fri & Sat; S76 to Victory Blvd/Bay St).

Near the ferry terminal, **Flagship Brewing Company** (718-448-5284; www.flagshipbrewery.nyc; 40 Minthorne St; 2-10pm Tue & Wed, noon-midnight Thu-Sat, noon-8pm Sun) serves up craft brews in a sprawling taproom that also hosts live bands. In summer, stay for a game of minor-league baseball at the **Staten Island Yankees** (box office 718-720-9265; www.siyanks.com; Richmond County Bank Ballpark, 75 Richmond Tce; tickets from $12; ticket office 10am-5pm Mon-Fri, plus game days from 10am or noon; Staten Island), or take the S51 bus from the ferry to **Midland Beach** and **South Beach**, with great views of the Verrazzano–Narrows Bridge.

To get here, take the free Staten Island Ferry (p85), which runs around the clock from Lower Manhattan to St George on Staten Island's northern tip.

1776. It avoided disaster again on September 11, 2001, when the destruction of the World Trade Center a mere block away left the chapel untouched. Now famous as 'The Little Chapel That Stood,' St Paul's offered round-the-clock refuge, spiritual and emotional support, and food service to first responders and rescue workers.

WORTH A DETOUR

GOVERNORS ISLAND

Off-limits to the public for 200 years, former military outpost **Governors Island** (Map p438; www.govisland.com; ⌚10am-6pm Mon-Fri, to 7pm Sat & Sun May-Oct, later hours Fri Jun-Aug; 👪; Ⓢ4/5 to Bowling Green, 1 to South Ferry) FREE is now one of New York's most popular seasonal playgrounds. The 172-acre oasis is a short ferry ride away is threaded with cycling and walking trails and offers vistas of glinting skyscrapers across the water. You won't forget you're in NYC – but it's an invigorating interlude with historic sites and fun activity areas to explore, including art-studded **Liggett Terrace** and **Hammock Grove**, which has 50 hammocks for relaxing in.

In the northern corner, there's star-shaped **Fort Jay**, built in 1794 and rebuilt 15 years later, a failed attempt to prevent the British from invading Manhattan; **Colonels Row**, a collection of eight lovely 19th-century brick officers' quarters; and the red sandstone **Castle Williams**, a 19th-century fort with 8ft-thick walls, which was later converted to a military penitentiary. The building exteriors and courtyards are free to explore, though visitors will enjoy deeper historical insights with a ranger-led **guided tour** from the National Park Service (www.nps.gov/gois). **The Hills**, in the southwest part of the island, have flower-fringed walking trails up to panoramic views of Manhattan (from 70ft high); below is attractive **Picnic Point**, with grassy spaces and lounge chairs. Inspiring views are also on tap along the **Great Promenade**: running for 2.2 miles along the island's perimeter, the path takes in everything from Lower Manhattan and Brooklyn to Staten Island and New Jersey. On weekends **The Yard**, a 50,000-sq-ft space, opens up for family-friendly play.

Originally named 'Nut Island' (Paggank) by the indigenous Lenape people, the island was renamed first by the Dutch and then, when it became a military installation, dubbed Governors Island. Besides serving as a successful military fort in the Revolutionary War, the Union Army's central recruiting station during the Civil War, and the take-off point for Wilbur Wright's famous 1909 flight around the Statue of Liberty, Governors Island is where the 1988 Reagan/Gorbachev summit signaled the beginning of the end of the Cold War. You can visit the spot where that famous summit took place at the **Admiral's House**, a grand, colonnaded military residence completed in 1843 that's part of the elegant ghost-town area of **Nolan Park**.

Ferries (Map p406; www.govisland.com; Battery Maritime Bldg, 10 South St, Lower Manhattan; round-trip adult/child $3/free, before noon Sat & Sun free; ⌚departures 10am-4:15pm Mon-Fri, to 5:30pm Sat & Sun May-Oct, later hours Fri & Sat Jun-Aug; Ⓢ1 to South Ferry, R/W to Whitehall St, 4/5 to Bowling Green) travel to the island from Lower Manhattan and Brooklyn. The island is easily walkable but cycling is a very pleasant way to get around; rent wheels from **Blazing Saddles** (www.blazingsaddles.com, per day $25) or use one of three Citibike stations around the island. Liggett Terrace hosts food trucks, from tacos to ice pops, and an outpost of Brooklyn beer favorite Threes Brewing; weekends offer the biggest choice of refreshments. Since 2018, the island has hosted a seasonal glamping site by **Collective Retreats** (www.collectiveretreats.com); prices range from $149 to $549 per night and early bookings are recommended.

USCGC LILAC — SHIP

Map p406 (www.lilacpreservationproject.org; Pier 25, at N Moore St, Tribeca; ⌚2-6pm Sat & Sun late May-Oct; 👪; Ⓢ1 to Franklin St; A/C/E to Canal St) FREE Lovers of all things maritime can step aboard the US Coast Guard Cutter *Lilac,* the last existing steam-powered lighthouse tender in the US, which once brought supplies to lighthouses and their keepers before American lighthouses were automated. Launched in 1933, *Lilac* was decommissioned in 1972 and since 2011 has been berthed at Pier 25, undergoing restoration work and serving as an educational and community resource.

NEW YORK STOCK EXCHANGE — NOTABLE BUILDING

Map p406 (www.nyse.com; 11 Wall St, Financial District; ⌚closed to the public; ⓈJ/Z to Broad St; 2/3, 4/5 to Wall St) Home to the world's best-known stock exchange (the NYSE), Wall Street is an iconic symbol of US capitalism. Behind the portentous neoclassical facade, about one billion shares change hands daily, a sight no longer publicly viewable due to security concerns. Feel free to gawk outside the building, protected by barricades and police. Directly across the cobblestones of Broad St stands the renowned **Fearless Girl statue** by Kristen Visbal, which was moved here in 2018 from its original spot outside Bowling Green.

BOWLING GREEN PARK
Map p406 (cnr Broadway & State St, Financial District; S4/5 to Bowling Green; R/W to Whitehall St) New York's oldest public park is purportedly the spot where Dutch settler Peter Minuit paid Native Americans the equivalent of $24 to purchase Manhattan Island. At its northern edge stands Arturo Di Modica's 7000lb bronze *Charging Bull,* placed here permanently after it mysteriously appeared in front of the New York Stock Exchange in 1989, two years after a market crash.

⊙ New York Harbor

STATUE OF LIBERTY MONUMENT
See p64.

ELLIS ISLAND LANDMARK
See p66.

⊙ Battery Park City

MUSEUM OF
JEWISH HERITAGE MUSEUM
Map p406 (☑646-437-4202; www.mjhnyc.org; 36 Battery Pl, Financial District; adult/child $8/free, 4-9pm Wed & Thu free; ⊙10am-9pm Sun-Thu, to 5pm Fri mid-Mar–mid-Nov, to 3pm Fri rest of year; ⚹; S4/5 to Bowling Green, R/W to Whitehall St) This evocative waterfront museum explores all aspects of modern Jewish identity and culture, from religious traditions to artistic accomplishments. The museum's core exhibition covers three themed floors: *Jewish Life a Century Ago, Jewish Renewal* and *The War Against the Jews* – a detailed exploration of the Holocaust through thousands of personal artifacts, photographs, documentary films and survivor testimony. Also commemorating Holocaust victims is the external installation **Garden of Stones**, a narrow pathway of 18 boulders supporting living trees.

The building itself consists of six sides, symbolizing the Star of David and the six million Jews who perished in WWII. Exhibitions aside, the venue also hosts films, music concerts, lecture series and special holiday performances. Frequent, free workshops for families with children are also on offer, while on-site **LOX at Café Bergson** serves light food, including lox (smoked salmon) in intriguing flavors such as grapefruit and gin and pastrami spice (mains $13 to $16).

The museum is closed on Saturday and major Jewish holidays, so check the website's holiday schedule before visiting. Be aware that some temporary exhibitions require an extra admission ticket.

SKYSCRAPER MUSEUM MUSEUM
Map p406 (☑212-968-1961; www.skyscraper.org; 39 Battery Pl, Financial District; adult/child $5/2.50; ⊙noon-6pm Wed-Sun; S4/5 to Bowling Green; R/W to Whitehall) Fans of phallic architecture will appreciate this compact, high-gloss gallery, examining skyscrapers as objects of design, engineering and urban renewal. Temporary exhibitions dominate the space, with past exhibitions exploring everything from New York's new generation of superslim residential towers to the world's new breed of supertalls. Permanent fixtures include information on the design and construction of the Empire State Building and World Trade Center.

BATTERY PARK PARK
Map p406 (www.nycgovparks.org; Broadway, at Battery Pl, Financial District; ⊙6am-1am; S4/5 to Bowling Green, R/W to Whitehall St, 1 to South Ferry) Skirting the southern edge of Manhattan, this 12-acre oasis lures with public artworks, meandering walkways and perennial gardens. Its memorials include tributes to those who died in the Korean War and Italian navigator Giovanni da Verrazzano. The first Dutch settlement on Manhattan was founded here in 1625, and the city's first battery was later erected in its defense.

You'll also find the lovely **SeaGlass Carousel** (Map p406; ☑212-344-3491; www.seaglasscarousel.nyc; off State St; $5; ⊙10am-10pm), historic **Castle Clinton** (Map p406; ☑212-344-7220; www.nps.gov/cacl; ⊙7:45am-5pm) FREE and the ferry service to Ellis Island and the Statue of Liberty.

LUCKY-PHOTOGRAPHER/SHUTTERSTOCK ©

1. New York Stock Exchange (p74)
About one billion shares change hands daily at this historical Wall St institution.

2. Woolworth Building (p78)
Book a guided tour to walk beneath the exquisite mosaic ceiling in the building's lobby.

3. Bowling Green (p75)
New York City's oldest public park.

4. Oculus at World Trade Center (p69)
Designed by architect Santiago Calatrava, the Oculus skylight opens up on September 11 every year to allow light to enter the vast space.

3

MARIA_ERMOLENKO/SHUTTERSTOCK ©

East River Waterfront

SOUTH STREET SEAPORT MUSEUM MUSEUM

Map p406 (212-748-8600; www.southstreetseaportmuseum.org; 12 Fulton St, btwn Water & Front Sts, Lower Manhattan; exhibitions & ships adult/child $20/free, printing press & shop free; ships & visitor center 11am-5pm Wed-Sun, print shop 11am-7pm Tue-Sun; ; S 2/3, 4/5, A/C, J/Z to Fulton St) Opened in 1967, this museum dispersed amid the cobblestone streets of the **seaport district** (Map p406; www.seaportdistrict.nyc) consists of fascinating exhibitions relating to the city's maritime history, an 18th-century printing press and shop (p87), and a handful of mighty sailing ships to explore on Pier 16. Besides touring the moored 1885 *Wavertree* and the 1907 lightship *Ambrose,* in warmer months you can take a harbor cruise on the 1885 **Pioneer** (adult/child $42/28; hours vary) and the 1930 wooden tugboat **WO Decker** (adult/child over 10yr $35/29, 7pm cruise $25; 2pm & 7pm Wed-Fri, 1:30pm, 3pm, 4:30pm & 7pm Sat & Sun).

PIER 17 PIER

Map p406 (www.pier17ny.com; 89 South St, South Street Seaport, Lower Manhattan; S 2/3, 4/5, A/C, J/Z to Fulton St) Formerly a shopping center, this large pier off South Street Seaport has been redeveloped for dining and entertainment, with several upmarket restaurants and a rooftop bar and outdoor concert venue. The best reason to visit, however, is the expansive **Riverdeck**, which offers built-in wooden loungers right on the water, where you can revel in grand views of the Brooklyn and Manhattan Bridges, Governors Island and Brooklyn on the opposite shore, as ferries cheerily ply their routes to and fro.

City Hall & Civic Center

AFRICAN BURIAL GROUND NATIONAL MONUMENT MEMORIAL

Map p406 (212-637-2019; www.nps.gov/afbg; 290 Broadway, btwn Duane & Reade Sts, Lower Manhattan; 10am-4pm Tue-Sat; S J/Z to Chambers St, R/W to City Hall, 4/5/6 to Brooklyn Bridge-City Hall) FREE In 1991, construction workers here uncovered more than 400 stacked wooden caskets, just 16ft to 28ft below street level. The boxes contained the remains of both enslaved and free African Americans from the 17th and 18th centuries (from 1697, nearby Trinity Church refused them burial in its graveyard). Today, a poignant **memorial site** and a **visitor center** with four rooms of educational displays honor the estimated 15,000 men, women and children buried in America's largest and oldest African cemetery.

WOOLWORTH BUILDING NOTABLE BUILDING

Map p406 (203-966-9663; www.woolworthtours.com; 233 Broadway, at Park Pl, Lower Manhattan; 30/60/90min tours $20/30/45; S R/W to City Hall, 2/3 to Park Pl, 4/5/6 to Brooklyn Bridge-City Hall) The world's tallest building upon completion in 1913 (it was only surpassed in height by the Chrysler Building in 1930), Cass Gilbert's 60-story, 792ft-tall Woolworth Building is a neo-Gothic marvel, elegantly clad in masonry and terra-cotta. The breathtaking lobby – a spectacle of dazzling, Byzantine-like mosaics – is accessible only on prebooked guided tours, which also offer insight into the building's more curious original features, among them a subway entrance and a secret swimming pool. Check online for the status of the tours.

CITY HALL HISTORIC BUILDING

Map p406 (guided tours 212-788-2656; Park Row, City Hall Park, Lower Manhattan; guided tours noon Wed & 10am Thu; S 4/5/6 to Brooklyn Bridge-City Hall; R/W to City Hall; J/Z to Chambers St) FREE This Federal-style beauty has been home to NYC's government since 1812, and free guided tours of the building run twice weekly (you'll need to book a few weeks ahead online; search for 'city hall tours' on www.nyc.gov). Tours take in the building's elegant coffered rotunda, the City Council chamber, and the Governor's Room, which is where you'll see portraits by John Trumbull, George Washington's writing table and the remnants of a flag flown at the first president's 1789 inaugural ceremony.

EATING

The Financial District's food scene is enjoying new verve thanks to the myriad upmarket fast-casual options at Brookfield Place, and quirky pleasers such as South Street Seaport's Luchadores NYC. Further north, Tribeca is no stranger to cool, with a string of celeb-chef hot spots.

HUDSON EATS FOOD HALL $

Map p406 (212-978-1698; https://bfplny.com/directory/food; Brookfield Place, 225 Liberty St, at West St, Lower Manhattan; dishes from $7; 8am-9pm Mon-Sat, to 7pm Sun; ; SE to World Trade Center, 2/3 to Park Pl, R/W to Cortlandt St, 4/5 to Fulton St, A/C to Chambers St) Sleekly renovated office-and-retail complex Brookfield Place is home to Hudson Eats, a shiny, upmarket food hall. Decked out with terrazzo floors, marble countertops and floor-to-ceiling windows with expansive views of Jersey City and the Hudson River, it has a string of respected, chef-driven eateries, including Blue Ribbon Sushi, Fuku, Northern Tiger and Dos Toros Taqueria.

MAMAN CAFE $

Map p406 (www.mamannyc.com; 211 W Broadway, Tribeca; mains $13-16; 8am-4pm Mon-Fri, 9am-4pm Sat & Sun; S1 to Franklin St) With faded white paint, skylight windows and lavender in jars, this beloved local cafe combines the air of a Provençal farmhouse with an industrial-hip downtown space. The French-inflected menu features a host of richly designed salads, omelettes and sandwiches, as well as luscious nectarine buttermilk waffles and a daily quiche. A front counter offers coffee and pastries to go.

VAN LEEUWEN ICE CREAM $

Map p406 (917-261-6376; www.vanleeuwenicecream.com; 224 Front St, btwn Beekman St & Peck Slip, Lower Manhattan; ice-cream cones from $5.75; 11am-11pm Sun-Thu, to midnight Fri & Sat; ; S2/3, 4/5, A/C, J/Z to Fulton St) This stalwart of the Brooklyn artisanal food movement started with a truck and now boasts half a dozen stores across Manhattan and Brooklyn. More than two dozen delicious flavors range from standards (mint chip or pistachio) to gourmet concoctions (passion-fruit layer cake or peanut butter marshmallow crunch), and many are entirely vegan, made with coconut cream and cashews. No cash.

GOTAN CAFE $

Map p406 (212-431-5200; www.gotannyc.com; 130 Franklin St, btwn Varick St & W Broadway, Tribeca; sandwiches & salads $11-14; 7am-5pm Mon-Fri, 8am-5pm Sat & Sun; ; S1 to Franklin St) This buzzy, light-filled corner cafe is frequented by the downtown digerati, who make ample use of free wi-fi, thoughtfully placed power outlets and tabletop charging pads. The menu is light but filling, featuring sandwiches, salads and breakfast dishes with Mediterranean and Middle Eastern accents. Counter Culture coffee provides the beans; the skilled baristas do the rest.

LUCHADORES NYC MEXICAN $

Map p406 (917-409-3033; 87 South St, at John St, Lower Manhattan; tacos $5-7, burritos $10-12; noon-10pm; S2/3 to Wall St) On a nice day grab a seat in the tiny courtyard of this corner joint featuring fresh-made burritos, tacos and quesadillas made with short ribs, *carne asada* (charred beef), *pollo asado* (roasted chicken) or cajun shrimp. With a happy hour from 3pm to 6pm (nachos free with any two beers), it's a welcome alternative to less down-to-earth options around South Street Seaport.

DA MIKELE PIZZA $$

Map p406 (212-925-8800; www.luzzosgroup.com/about-us-damikele; 275 Church St, btwn White & Franklin Sts, Tribeca; pizzas $17-22; noon-11pm Sun-Thu, to midnight Fri & Sat; S1 to Franklin St; A/C/E, N/Q/R, J/Z, 6 to Canal St) An Italo-Tribeca hybrid where pressed tin and recycled wood meet retro Vespa, Da Mikele channels *la dolce vita* (the sweet life) with its weeknight *aperitivo* (5pm to 8pm), where your drink includes a complimentary spread of lip-smacking bar bites. However, pizzas are the specialty. We're talking light, beautifully charred revelations, simultaneously crisp and chewy, and good enough to make a Neapolitan weep.

BROOKFIELD PLACE FOOD HALL $$

Map p406 (212-978-1673; www.brookfieldplaceny.com; 230 Vesey St, at West St, Lower Manhattan; ; SE to World Trade Center, 2/3 to Park Pl, R/W to Cortlandt St, 4/5 to Fulton St, A/C to Chambers St) This polished, high-end office-and-retail complex offers two fabulous food halls. Francophile foodies should hit Le District (p80), a charming and mouthwatering marketplace with several stand-alone restaurants and counters selling everything from stinky cheese to steak-*frites*. One floor above is Hudson Eats, a fashionable enclave of upmarket fast bites, from sushi and tacos to salads and burgers.

TWO HANDS AUSTRALIAN $$

Map p406 (www.twohandsnyc.com; 251 Church St, btwn Franklin & Leonard Sts, Tribeca; lunch & brunch mains $14-19; 8am-5pm; ; S1 to Franklin St, N/Q/R/W, 6 to Canal St) An interior of whitewashed brick gives this modern

'Australian-style' cafe-restaurant an airy feel – and the local crowds love it. The menu offers light breakfast and lunch dishes such as a fully loaded acai bowl with berries and granola or a chicken sandwich with feta cream and olive tapenade. The coffee's top-notch, and there's happy hour from 2pm to 5pm.

GRAND BANKS — SEAFOOD $$

Map p406 (☎212-660-6312; www.grandbanks.nyc; Pier 25, near N Moore St, Tribeca; oysters $3-4, mains $19-29; ⏰11am-12:30am Mon-Fri, from 10am Sat & Sun late Apr–Oct; Ⓢ1 to Franklin St; A/C/E to Canal St) Chef Kerry Heffernan's menu features sustainably harvested seafood at this restaurant on the *Sherman Zwicker,* a 1942 schooner moored on the Hudson, with the spotlight on Atlantic Ocean oysters. Alternatively, try the ceviche, lobster rolls or soft-shell crab. It's mobbed with dressy crowds after work and on weekends; come for a late-dinner sundowner and enjoy the stupendous sunset views.

PARIS CAFE — FRENCH $$

Map p406 (☎212-240-9797; http://pariscafenyc.com; 119 South St, Lower Manhattan; mains $20-26; ⏰11am-4am; ⓈA/C, J/Z, 2/3, 4/5 to Fulton St) New York City is known for small, cramped restaurants, but the Paris Cafe (open since 1873) in the South Street Seaport revels in its high ceilings and ample floor space. The food is unpretentious and easy to enjoy, and there is a large bar at which you can delight in the generous happy hour, with drinks for $6.

★LOCANDA VERDE — ITALIAN $$$

Map p406 (☎212-925-3797; www.locandaverdenyc.com; 377 Greenwich St, at N Moore St, Tribeca; mains lunch $24-36, dinner $27-58; ⏰7am-11pm Mon-Thu, to 11:30pm Fri, 8am-11:30pm Sat, to 11pm Sun; Ⓢ1 to Franklin St, A/C/E to Canal St) Curbside at the Greenwich Hotel (p333) is this Italian fine diner by Andrew Carmellini, where velvet curtains part onto a scene of loosened button-downs, black dresses and slick bar staff. It's a place to see and be seen, but the food – perhaps grilled swordfish with farro salad, *orecchiette* with duck sausage, or rigatoni with white-veal Bolognese – is still the main event.

★TINY'S & THE BAR UPSTAIRS — AMERICAN $$$

Map p406 (☎212-374-1135; www.tinysnyc.com; 135 W Broadway, btwn Thomas & Duane Sts, Tribeca; mains lunch $13-19, dinner $25-34; ⏰8am-midnight; Ⓢ1 to Franklin St, A, C to Chambers St) The rustic interior of this 1810 Tribeca town house – antique wallpaper, salvaged wood paneling, original tin ceilings, pressed copper and marble bar tops, and handmade tiles – alone makes it worth a visit, but you won't regret staying for a meal or a cocktail. Food is modern American with French accents: perhaps seared duck with turnip and shallots or saffron mussels.

BÂTARD — EUROPEAN $$$

Map p406 (☎212-219-2777; www.batardtribeca.com; 239 W Broadway, btwn Walker & White Sts, Tribeca; 2/3/4 courses $65/89/99; ⏰5:30-10pm Mon-Wed, to 10:30pm Thu-Sat; Ⓢ1 to Franklin St, A/C/E to Canal St) Austrian chef Markus Glocker heads this warm, Michelin-starred hot spot, where a pared-back interior puts the focus squarely on the food.

Glocker's dishes are precise examples of classical French and Italian cooking: the prix-fixe menus hold rich delights such as striped bass with chanterelle mushrooms, or tagliatelle with roast lamb loin, olives and pecorino.

AUGUSTINE — FRENCH $$$

Map p406 (☎212-375-0010; www.augustineny.com; 5 Beekman St, btwn Park Row & Nassau St, Financial District; mains $27-43; ⏰7:30am-11pm Mon-Thu, to midnight Fri, 10am-midnight Sat, to 10pm Sun; Ⓢ4/5/6 to Brooklyn Bridge-City Hall) Augustine is a hip, upscale eatery from famed New York City restaurateur Keith McNally. The food combines classic French brasserie fare with an eye toward local seafood and vegetables, while the cocktails menu was created by world-renowned bartender Dale Degroff. All of this is served in a decadent, yet tasteful space complete with antique art nouveau tiling and light fixtures.

LE DISTRICT — FOOD HALL $$$

Map p406 (☎212-981-8588; www.ledistrict.com; Brookfield Place, 225 Liberty St, at West St, Lower Manhattan; market mains $12-30, Beaubourg dinner mains $19-36; ⏰Beaubourg 8am-10pm Mon, to 11pm Tue & Wed, to midnight Thu & Fri, 10am-midnight Sat, to 10pm Sun, other hours vary; 📶; ⓈE to World Trade Center, 2/3 to Park Pl, R/W to Cortlandt St, 4/5 to Fulton St, A/C to Chambers St) Paris on the Hudson reigns at this sprawling French food emporium selling everything from high-gloss pastries and pretty *tartines* to stinky cheese and savory steak-*frites*. Main restaurant **Beaubourg** does bistro classics such as *coq au vin,* but for a quick sit-down feed, head to the **Market District** counter for *frites* or the **Cafe District** for a savory crepe.

DRINKING & NIGHTLIFE

Corporate types don't always bolt for the 'burbs when 5pm hits: many loosen their ties in the wine bars and pubs around Stone St, Wall St and South Street Seaport. Tribeca keeps its cool with artisanal coffee shops and venerated cocktail dens.

DEAD RABBIT BAR

Map p406 (☎646-422-7906; www.deadrabbitnyc.com; 30 Water St, btwn Broad St & Coenties Slip, Financial District; ⏰Taproom 11am-4am Mon-Fri, 10am-3am Sat & Sun, Parlor 11am-3pm & 5pm-2am Mon-Sat, noon-midnight Sun; Ⓢ R/W to Whitehall St, 1 to South Ferry) Named for a feared 19th-century Irish American gang, this three-story drinking den is regularly voted one of the world's best bars. Hit the sawdust-sprinkled Taproom for specialty beers, historic punches and pop-inns (lightly soured ale spiked with different flavors). On the next floor there's the cozy Parlor, serving meticulously researched cocktails, and above that the reservation-only Occasional Room, 'for whiskey explorers.'

★**BLUESTONE LANE** COFFEE

Map p406 (☎718-374-6858; www.bluestonelaneny.com; 30 Broad St, Financial District; ⏰7am-5pm Mon-Fri, 8am-4pm Sat & Sun; Ⓢ J/Z to Broad St, 2/3, 4/5 to Wall St) The second installment in Bluestone Lane's booming US empire of Aussie-style coffee shops, this tiny outpost in the corner of an art deco office block is littered with Melbourne memorabilia. Alongside Wall St suits you'll find homesick antipodeans craving a decent, velvety flat white and a small selection of edibles, including the Australian cafe standard, smashed avocado on toast ($8).

BRANDY LIBRARY COCKTAIL BAR

Map p406 (☎212-226-5545; www.brandylibrary.com; 25 N Moore St, btwn Varick & Hudson Sts, Tribeca; ⏰5pm-1am Sun-Wed, 4pm-2am Thu, 4pm-4am Fri & Sat; Ⓢ 1 to Franklin St) This brandy-hued bastion of brown spirits is the place to go for top-shelf cognac, whiskey and brandy. Settle into handsome club chairs facing floor-to-ceiling, bottle-lined shelves and sip your tipple of choice, paired with nibbles such as Gruyère-cheese puffs, hand-cut steak tartare and foie gras. Saturday nights are generally quieter than weeknights, making it a civilized spot for a weekend tête-à-tête.

SMITH & MILLS COCKTAIL BAR

Map p406 (☎212-226-2515; www.smithandmills.com; 71 N Moore St, btwn Hudson & Greenwich Sts, Tribeca; ⏰11am-2am; Ⓢ 1 to Franklin St) Petite Smith & Mills ticks all the cool boxes: unmarked exterior, design-conscious industrial interior, and expertly crafted cocktails with a penchant for the classics. Space is limited, so head in early if you fancy kicking back on a banquette. A seasonal menu spans light snacks to a particularly notable burger bedecked with caramelized onions.

LA COLOMBE COFFEE

Map p406 (☎212-343-1515; www.lacolombe.com; 319 Church St, at Lispenard St, Tribeca; ⏰7:30am-6:30pm Mon-Fri, from 8:30am Sat & Sun; Ⓢ A/C/E to Canal St) Coffee and a few baked treats is all you'll get at this roaster but, man, are they good. Join cool kids and clued-in Continentals for dark, intense espresso and signature offerings like draft latte, a naturally sweet iced caffe latte. Also on tap is La Colombe's cold-pressed Pure Black Coffee, steeped in oxygen-free stainless steel wine tanks for 16 hours.

Take a moment to read the bronze plaque on the Lispenard wall – a previous building on this site was a 'station' on the 19th-century Underground Railroad, the network of secret routes and safe houses that helped thousands of enslaved African Americans escape to freedom; Frederick Douglass arrived here after fleeing north from Maryland.

WEATHER UP COCKTAIL BAR

Map p406 (☎212-766-3202; www.weatherupnyc.com; 159 Duane St, btwn Hudson St & W Broadway, Tribeca; ⏰5pm-midnight Mon-Thu, to 2am Fri & Sat; Ⓢ 1/2/3 to Chambers St) Simultaneously hip and classy: softly lit subway tiles, amiable and attractive barkeeps and seductive cocktails make for a bewitching trio at Weather Up. Sweet-talk the staff over a Fancy Free (bourbon, maraschino, orange and Angostura bitters). Failing that, comfort yourself with some satisfying bites like oysters and beef tartare. There's a Brooklyn branch in Prospect Heights (p291).

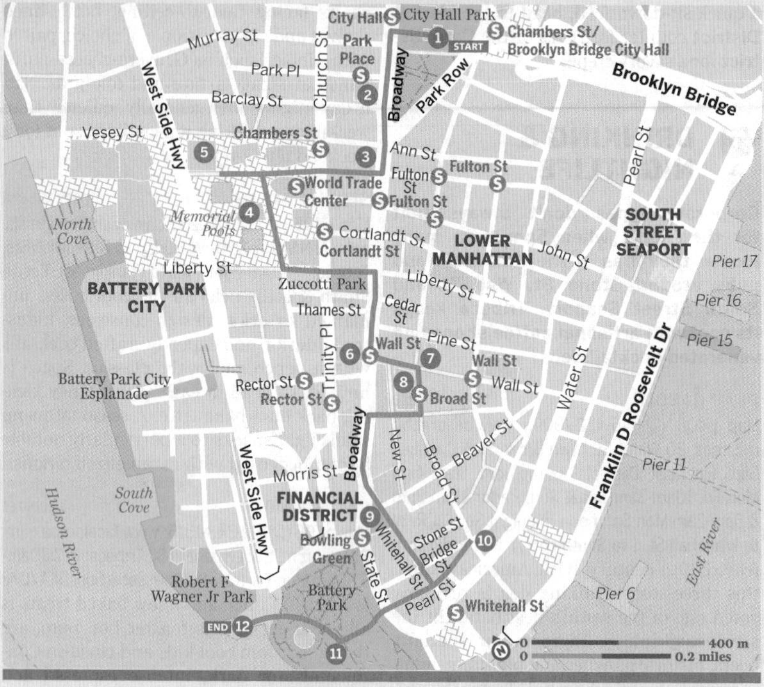

Neighborhood Walk Broadway to Battery

START CITY HALL
END PIER A HARBOR HOUSE
LENGTH 2 MILES; 1½ HOURS

As NYC's oldest neighborhood, Lower Manhattan is filled with narrow streets and historic buildings. Start at 1 **City Hall** (p78), seat of New York's municipal government since 1812. Across Broadway is the neo-Gothic 2 **Woolworth Building** (p78), the world's tallest skyscraper in 1913.

South is 3 **St Paul's Chapel** (p72), the city's only surviving pre–Revolutionary War church. Nearby is the World Trade Center site, where the two giant reflecting pools of the 4 **National September 11 Memorial** (p68) mark the footprints of the collapsed towers; the accompanying museum contains exhibits about the tragedy. Soaring above is the 1776ft 5 **One World Trade Center** (p70), whose observatory offers jaw-dropping views of the city.

Return to Broadway and continue to the 1846 6 **Trinity Church** (p72), itself once NYC's tallest building; buried here is American Founder (and Broadway star) Alexander Hamilton. Head east on Wall St to visit 7 **Federal Hall** (p72), where journalist John Peter Zenger was acquitted of libel in 1735, opening free press in America. Across is the 8 **New York Stock Exchange** (p74), where the *Fearless Girl* statue stands, flocked with photo-opping visitors.

Two blocks southwest is 9 **Bowling Green** (p75), NYC's oldest public park, and the adjacent *Charging Bull* statue. At Broad and Pearl Sts is historic 10 **Fraunces Tavern** (p72), where George Washington had a final dinner with his officers (including trusted aide Alexander Hamilton) before becoming president.

Double back on Pearl St to end up at 11 **Battery Park** (p75), a downtown oasis on the site of Manhattan's first Dutch settlement. Finish up with a well-earned meal of classic New York Harbor oysters at 12 **Pier A Harbor House** (p83).

MACAO TRADING CO
COCKTAIL BAR

Map p406 (212-431-8642; www.macaonyc.com; 311 Church St, btwn Lispenard & Walker Sts, Tribeca; bar 5pm-1:30am Mon-Wed, to 3:30am Thu-Sat, to 12:30am Sun; S A/C/E to Canal St) Though we love the 1940s-style 'gambling parlor' bar/restaurant, it's the downstairs 'opium den' (open Thursday to Saturday) that gets our hearts racing. A Chinese-Portuguese fusion of grub and liquor, both floors are solid locales for late-night sipping and snacking, especially if you have a soft spot for sizzle-on-the-tongue libations.

TERROIR TRIBECA
WINE BAR

Map p406 (212-625-9463; www.wineisterroir.com; 24 Harrison St, btwn Greenwich & Hudson Sts, Tribeca; 4pm-midnight Mon & Tue, to 1am Wed-Sat, to 11pm Sun; S 1 to Franklin St) This amiable wine bar gratifies oenophiles with its well-versed, well-priced wine list, including drops from the Old World and the New, among them natural wines and niche tipples from smaller producers. There's good knowledge behind the bar, a generous selection of wines by the glass and good French bistro food (mains $18 to $28). Offers early *and* late happy hours.

COWGIRL SEAHORSE
BAR

Map p406 (212-608-7873; www.cowgirlseahorse.com; 259 Front St, at Dover St, Lower Manhattan; 11am-2am Mon-Fri, 10am-1am Sat & Sun; S A/C, J/Z, 2/3, 4/5 to Fulton St) In an ocean of more serious bars and restaurants, Cowgirl SeaHorse is a party ship. Its ranch-meets-sea theme (wagon wheels and seahorses on the walls) and southern home cooking (blackened fish, oyster po'boy sliders, shrimp and grits etc) make it irresistibly fun. Live music on Monday, happy hour every day except Saturday and great frozen margaritas don't hurt, either.

PIER A HARBOR HOUSE
BAR

Map p406 (212-785-0153; www.piera.com; 22 Battery Pl, Battery Park, Financial District; Harbor House 11am-midnight Sun-Wed, to 2am Thu-Sat, BlackTail 5pm-2am; ; S 4/5 to Bowling Green, R/W to Whitehall St, 1 to South Ferry) Built in 1886 as the New York City Board of Dock Commissioners' Headquarters, Pier A is a superspacious casual eating and drinking house right on New York Harbor. Go for a seat on the waterside deck in warm weather – picnic benches, sun umbrellas and the New York skyline create a brilliant spot for sipping craft beers or on-tap house cocktails.

WARD III
COCKTAIL BAR

Map p406 (212-240-9194; www.ward3.com; 111 Reade St, btwn Church St & W Broadway, Tribeca; 4pm-2am Mon-Thu, to 4am Fri, 5pm-4am Sat, 3pm-midnight Sun; ; S A/C, 1/2/3 to Chambers St) Ward III channels old-school jauntiness with low-key lighting, a bustling atmosphere under high pressed-tin ceilings, elegant libations and a vintage vibe (including old Singer sewing machine tables behind the bar). Reminisce over a painstakingly made bespoke cocktail or sample their covetable collection of whiskeys. Upscale bar grub is served till late.

★ ENTERTAINMENT

★ FLEA THEATER
THEATER

Map p406 (tickets 212-226-0051; www.theflea.org; 20 Thomas St, btwn Timble Pl & Broadway, Tribeca; tickets from $10; ; S A/C, 1/2/3 to Chambers St, R/W to City Hall) One of NYC's top off-off-Broadway venues, Flea is famous for staging innovative and timely new works. It houses three performance spaces, including the 'Siggy,' named for co-founder Sigourney Weaver. The year-round program includes music and dance productions, as well as Sunday shows for young audiences (aged two and up) and SERIALS, a rollicking late-night competition series of 10-minute plays.

SOHO REP
THEATER

Map p406 (Soho Repertory Theatre; 212-941-8632; www.sohorep.org; 46 Walker St, btwn Church St & Broadway, Tribeca; S A/C/E to Canal St, 1 to Franklin St) This is one of New York's finest off-Broadway companies, wowing audiences and critics with its annual trio of sharp, innovative new works. Kathleen Turner, Allison Janney, Ed O'Neill and John C Reilly all made their professional debuts in this 65-seat theater, and the company's productions have garnered more than 20 Obie (Off-Broadway Theater) Awards. Check the website for current or upcoming shows.

CITY VINEYARD
LIVE MUSIC

Map p406 (www.citywinery.com; Pier 26, 233 West St, near N Moore St, Tribeca; S 1 to Franklin St; A/C/E to Canal St) This great waterside bar-restaurant has an intimate, 233-seat cabaret-style theater that features live music nightly. The calendar tends toward emerging singer-songwriters, along with folk superstars and occasionally indie rock bands; past performers include notables such as Suzanne Vega, Squirrel Nut Zippers, Shawn Colvin, Robyn Hitchcock, Los Lobos, Aimee Mann, Billy Bragg and Yo La Tengo.

SHOPPING

While the Financial District isn't a shopping destination per se, bargain-hunters flock here for cut-price fashion mecca Century 21. Further north in Tribeca, hit the lower end of Hudson and surrounding streets for high-end interior design, antiques and a handful of niche shops selling everything from local threads to handmade axes.

★PHILIP WILLIAMS POSTERS — VINTAGE

Map p406 (212-513-0313; www.postermuseum.com; 122 Chambers St, btwn Church St & W Broadway, Lower Manhattan; 10am-7pm Mon-Sat; S A/C, 1/2/3 to Chambers St) You'll find more than 100,000 posters dating back to 1870 in this cavernous treasure trove, from oversized French advertisements for perfume and cognac to Eastern European film posters and decorative Chinese *Nianhua* posters. Prices range from $15 for small reproductions to thousands of dollars for rare, showpiece originals like a Cassandre. There's a second entrance at 52 Warren St.

★CENTURY 21 — FASHION & ACCESSORIES

Map p406 (212-227-9092; www.c21stores.com; 22 Cortlandt St, btwn Church St & Broadway, Financial District; 7:45am-9pm Mon-Wed, to 9:30pm Thu & Fri, 10am-9pm Sat, 11am-8pm Sun; S A/C, J/Z, 2/3, 4/5 to Fulton St, R/W to Cortlandt St) For penny-pinching fashionistas, this giant cut-price department store is dangerously addictive. It's physically dangerous as well, considering the elbows you might have to throw to ward off the competition beelining for the same rack. Not everything is a knockout or a bargain, but persistence pays off. You'll also find bespoke tailoring, accessories, shoes, cosmetics, homewares and toys.

PEARL RIVER MART — DEPARTMENT STORE

Map p406 (212-431-4770; www.pearlriver.com; 395 Broadway, at Walker St, Tribeca; 10am-7:20pm; S N/Q/R/W, J/M/Z, 6 to Canal St) A local institution since 1971, Pearl River offers a dizzying array of Asian gifts, housewares, clothing and accessories: silk men's pajamas, cheongsam dresses, blue-and-white Japanese ceramic tableware, clever kitchen gadgets, paper lanterns, origami and calligraphy kits, bamboo plants and an abundance of lucky-cat figurines. The mezzanine art gallery features free rotating shows with work from Asian American artists and photographers.

BEST MADE COMPANY — FASHION & ACCESSORIES

Map p406 (646-478-7092; www.bestmadeco.com; 36 White St, at Church St, Tribeca; noon-7pm Mon-Fri, 11am-7pm Sat, to 6pm Sun; S A/C/E to Canal St; 1 to Franklin St) Give your next camping trip a Manhattan makeover at this store/design-studio hybrid. Pick up handcrafted axes, leather duffel bags, sunglasses, enamel camping mugs and even designer dartboards and first-aid kits, many emblazoned with their signature 'X' logo. A small, smart collection of men's threads includes designer flannel shirts and pullovers, sweatshirts and rugged knitwear from Portland's Dehen Knitting Mills.

MYSTERIOUS BOOKSHOP — BOOKS

Map p406 (212-587-1011; www.mysteriousbookshop.com; 58 Warren St, btwn W Broadway & Church St, Tribeca; 11am-7pm Mon-Sat; S 1/2/3, A/C to Chambers St) With more crime per square inch than any other corner of the city, this mystery-themed bookstore peddles everything from classic espionage and thrillers to contemporary Nordic crime fiction and literary criticism.

You'll find both new and secondhand titles, including rare first editions, signed copies, obscure magazines and picture books for budding sleuths. See the website for in-store events.

SHINOLA — FASHION & ACCESSORIES

Map p406 (917-728-3000; www.shinola.com; 177 Franklin St, btwn Greenwich & Hudson Sts, Tribeca; 11am-7pm Mon-Sat, noon-4pm Sun; S 1 to Franklin St) Well known for its coveted wristwatches, Detroit-based Shinola branches out with a supercool selection of Made-in-USA life props.

Bag anything from leather tablet cases and journal covers to jewelry, limited-edition bicycles with customized bags and even high-end turntables. Bonuses include complimentary monogramming of leather goods and stationery, and an in-house artisan watchmaker.

BOWNE & CO
STATIONERS
GIFTS & SOUVENIRS

Map p406 (☑646-628-2707; 211 Water St, btwn Beekman & Fulton Sts, Lower Manhattan; ⊙11am-7pm; ⑤2/3, 4/5, A/C, J/Z to Fulton St) Suitably set in cobbled South Street Seaport and affiliated with the attached South Street Seaport Museum (p78), this 18th-century veteran stocks reproduction-vintage New York posters and NYC-themed notepads, pencil cases, cards, stamps and even wrapping paper.

At the **printing workshop** you can order customized business cards or hone your printing skills in monthly **classes** (see the museum website's Events page).

PASANELLA & SON
WINE

Map p406 (☑212-233-8383; www.pasanellaandson.com; 115 South St, btwn Peck Slip & Beekman St, Lower Manhattan; ⊙noon-9pm Mon-Sat, to 7pm Sun; ⑤A/C, J/Z, 2/3, 4/5 to Fulton St; R/W to Cortlandt St) Oenophiles adore this savvy wine peddler, with its 400-plus drops both inspired and affordable. The focus is on small producers, with a number of biodynamic and organic winemakers in the mix. It offers an impressive choice of American whiskeys and free wine-tastings of the week's new arrivals on Saturdays (from 5pm to 7pm).

CITYSTORE
GIFTS & SOUVENIRS

Map p406 (☑212-386-0007; www.nyc.gov/citystore; North Plaza, Municipal Bldg, 1 Centre St, at Chambers St, Lower Manhattan; ⊙10am-5pm Mon-Fri; ⑤J/Z to Chambers St, 4/5/6 to Brooklyn Bridge-City Hall, R/W to City Hall) Score all manner of officially produced New York City memorabilia here, from authentic-looking taxi medallions, sewer-hole-cover coasters and borough-themed T-shirts to NYPD baseball caps, subway-station signs and books about NYC.

A curiosity, though less relevant for the average visitor, is the municipal building codes and other regulatory guides that are for sale.

🏃 SPORTS & ACTIVITIES

★STATEN ISLAND FERRY
CRUISE

Map p406 (www.siferry.com; Whitehall Terminal, 4 Whitehall St, at South St, Lower Manhattan; ⊙24hr; ⑤1 to South Ferry, R/W to Whitehall St, 4/5 to Bowling Green) **FREE** Staten Islanders know these hulking orange ferries as commuter vehicles, while Manhattanites think of them as their secret, romantic vessels for a spring-day escape. Yet many tourists are also wise to the charms of the Staten Island Ferry, whose 25-minute, 5.2-mile journey between Lower Manhattan and the Staten Island neighborhood of St George is one of NYC's finest free adventures.

INSTITUTE OF CULINARY
EDUCATION
COOKING

Map p406 (ICE; ☑212-847-0700; http://recreational.ice.edu; Brookfield Pl, 225 Liberty St, Lower Manhattan; courses from $75; ⑤E to World Trade Center; 4/5 to Fulton St; R/W to Cortlandt St) Release your inner Jean-Jacques with a cooking course at the Institute of Culinary Education, which runs the country's largest program of cooking, baking and wine-appreciation courses, from 90-minute classes to multiday sessions. Courses range from Tuscan cooking and American comfort food to knife skills and classic cocktails. Restless foodies can choose from numerous culinary tours of the city (from $90).

DOWNTOWN BOATHOUSE
KAYAKING

Map p406 (www.downtownboathouse.org; Pier 26, Hudson River Greenway, near N Moore St, Tribeca; ⊙9am-5pm Sat & Sun mid-May–mid-Oct, plus 5:30-7pm Tue-Thu mid-Jun–mid-Sep; 🚻; ⑤1 to Canal St) **FREE** This active public boathouse on Pier 26 offers free, walk-up, 20-minute kayaking sessions (including equipment) on the Hudson River on weekends and some weekday evenings. For more activities here and at Piers 84 and 96 – kayaking trips, stand-up paddle boarding and classes – check out www.hudsonriverpark.org. There are also free lessons on Wednesday evenings and a summer-only location on Governors Island (p74).

SoHo & Chinatown

SOHO, NOHO & NOLITA | CHINATOWN & LITTLE ITALY

Neighborhood Top Five

❶ **Shopping** (p102) Maxing out the credit cards on SoHo's big-name fashion streets, followed by cool-hunting lesser-known labels in the cognoscenti sidewalks of nearby Nolita and NoHo.

❷ **Chinatown** (p88) Slurping soup dumplings and haggling for designer wares of ambiguous authenticity amid the sizzling lights of Chinatown.

❸ **Little Italy** (p92) Getting your fix of rich sugo or a delicate tiramisu, while listening in on grandfathers sipping grappa and speaking in the mother tongue.

❹ **Merchant's House Museum** (p91) Snooping around this time-jarred, possibly haunted, museum, imagining NYC life in the wild and dusty 1800s.

❺ **Peking Duck House** (p99) Sharing a tender, succulent Peking duck in the quintessential spot to have it if you're not in Beijing.

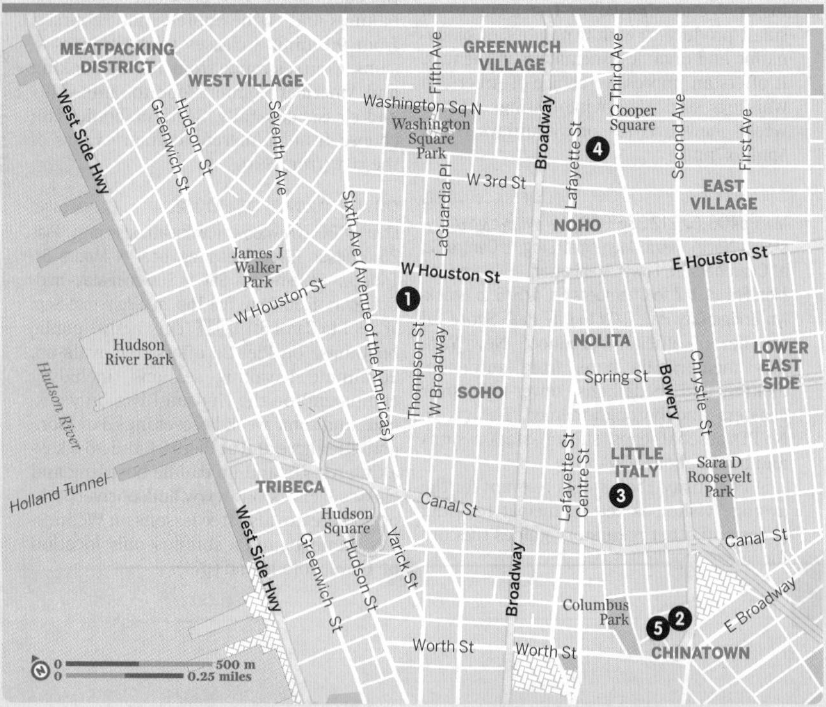

For more detail of this area see Map p408 and p411

Explore SoHo & Chinatown

Like a colorful quilt of subneighborhoods sewn together in mismatched patches, the areas around SoHo (SOuth of HOuston) feel like a string of mini republics. Style mavens boutique-hop in Nolita (NOrth of LIttle ITAly), Italian Americans channel Napoli in ever-shrinking Little Italy, and Chinese families chat over *xiao long bao* (soup dumplings) in hyperactive Chinatown.

Lower-rise buildings inject these streets with a cozy, village-like vibe (main drags Broadway and Canal St excepted). Celebrities, cast-iron lofts and A-list boutiques stud SoHo's cobbled side streets, while humbler 19th-century tenements and quirkier one-off boutiques flavor neighboring Nolita.

Chinatown has an 'anything goes' spirit, with bustling crowds and hawkers haggling under faded billboards. The best way to weave your way around here is on foot. And don't bother planning a route – just let your senses guide you. Whether you're following your nose down an alleyway for freshly baked pork buns, or your ears to a prayer gong in a heady Buddhist temple, unexpected surprises await.

Local Life

➡ **Family style** Hit Chinatown's bustling dining dens with a handful of friends and eat 'family style' (order a ton of dishes and sample spoonfuls of each). You'll think the waiter left a zero off the bill.

➡ **Side streets** The stretch of Broadway cutting through SoHo is reserved for the tourists – New Yorkers scour the one-of-a-kind boutiques on the side streets for idiosyncratic buys.

➡ **Cultural breaks** Explore the area's artistic legacy at the Drawing Center (p90) and the Leslie-Lohman Museum of Gay & Lesbian Art (p91), or just marvel at 140 tons of dirt at the New York Earth Room (p90).

Getting There & Away

➡ **Subway** The subway lines dump off along various points of Canal St (J/Z, N/Q/R/W and 6). Once you arrive, it's best to explore on foot. The neighborhood's downtown location makes it easy to access from Midtown and Brooklyn.

➡ **Bus & Taxi** Avoid taking cabs or buses – especially in Chinatown, as the traffic is full-on. For SoHo, have your taxi let you off along Broadway if you aren't fussed about your final destination. Don't take cabs south of Canal St if you're simply planning to wander around Chinatown. The area is so small that you'll make much better time on foot than waiting for lights to change.

Lonely Planet's Top Tip

Serious shopaholics should consult the city's in-the-know retail blogs (p51) before hitting SoHo and surrounds – there's always some sort of 'sample sale' or offer going on, not to mention the opening of yet another boutique stocking fresh, emerging design talent.

Best Places to Eat

- ➡ Wayan (p95)
- ➡ Uncle Boons (p94)
- ➡ Dutch (p95)
- ➡ Il Buco Alimentari & Vineria (p95)
- ➡ Prince Street Pizza (p94)
- ➡ Chefs Club (p95)

For reviews, see p93 ➡

Best Places to Drink

- ➡ Apothéke (p99)
- ➡ Spring Lounge (p101)
- ➡ Joe's Pub (p102)

For reviews, see p99 ➡

Best Places to Shop

- ➡ Glossier Flagship (p102)
- ➡ Opening Ceremony (p105)
- ➡ MiN New York (p103)
- ➡ Resurrection (p103)
- ➡ Galeria Melissa (p103)
- ➡ Saturdays (p103)

For reviews, see p102 ➡

TOP EXPERIENCE
CHINATOWN

America's biggest Chinatown is a feast for the senses: the scent of fresh fish melds with ripe persimmons, mah-jongg tiles clatter on makeshift tables, and duck roasts dangle in restaurant windows. Plus it's a delight for shopping treasures – score everything from 'faux-lex' watches and jade Buddha statues to tire irons and a pound of ground turmeric.

Museum of Chinese in America

The **Museum of Chinese in America** (Map p411; ☎212-619-4785; www.mocanyc.org; 215 Centre St, btwn Grand & Howard Sts; adult/child $12/8, 1st Thu of month free; ⏰11am-6pm Tue, Wed & Fri-Sun, to 9pm Thu), designed by Maya Lin (architect of Washington, DC's Vietnam Memorial) is a multifaceted space with exhibitions that illuminate Chinese American life, both past and present. Wind your way through multimedia exhibits and imbibe maps, timelines, photos, letters, films and artifacts. The museum's anchor exhibit, *With a Single Step: Stories in the Making of America,* offers a look into topics ranging from immigration to cultural identity and racial stereotyping.

Food, Glorious Food

The most rewarding experience for Chinatown visitors is to access this wild and wonderful world through their taste buds. More than any other area of Manhattan, Chinatown's menus sport wonderfully low prices, uninflated by ambience, hype or reputation. But more than cheap eats, the neighborhood is rife with family recipes passed across generations and continents. Food displays and preparation remain unchanged and untempered by American norms; it's not unusual to walk by storefronts sporting a tangled array of lacquered animals – chickens, rabbit and duck, in particular –

DON'T MISS

- Museum of Chinese in America
- Chinatown back alleys, like Mott and Mulberry Sts
- Mahayana Temple
- Nom Wah Tea Parlor
- Apothéke

PRACTICALITIES

- Map p411, C3
- www.explorechinatown.com
- south of Broome St & east of Broadway
- Ⓢ N/Q/R/W, J/Z, 6 to Canal St; B/D to Grand St; F to East Broadway

ready to be chopped up and served at a family banquet. Steaming street stalls clang down the sidewalk serving pork buns and other finger-friendly food.

Buddhist Temples

Chinatown is home to Buddhist temples large and small, public and obscure. They are easily stumbled upon during a stroll of the neighborhood, and at least two such temples are considered landmarks. The **Eastern States Buddhist Temple** (Map p411; 212-966-6229; 64 Mott St, btwn Bayard & Canal Sts; 8:30am-6pm) is filled with hundreds of Buddhas, while the **Mahayana Temple** (Map p414; 212-925-8787; http://en.mahayana.us; 133 Canal St, at Manhattan Bridge Plaza; 8:30am-6pm; B/D to Grand St; J/Z to Bowery; 6 to Canal St) holds one golden, 16ft-high Buddha, sitting on a lotus and edged with offerings of fresh oranges, apples and flowers. Mahayana is the largest Buddhist temple in Chinatown, and its entrance, which overlooks the frenzied vehicle entrance to the Manhattan Bridge, is guarded by two proud and handsome golden lions. Step inside and you'll find a simple interior of wooden floor and red paper lanterns, dramatically upstaged by the temple's magnificent Buddha, thought to be the largest in the city.

Canal, Mott & Mulberry Streets

Traditionally Canal St has been Chinatown's spine, but the relentless force of gentrification is coming and the first sure signs can be seen here. It's still busy as hell, where oncoming human and car traffic wait for nobody. You'll still see roasted ducks and pigs hanging by their skinny necks in windows, but it's also where you'll find persistent street vendors pushing knock-off Prada bags, and hipster design markets catering to an altogether different crowd. To find the true heart of Chinatown, find your way into the side streets: Mott and Mulberry are particularly evocative hunting grounds for treasures from the Far East. You'll pass stinky seafood stalls hawking slippery fish; mysterious herb shops peddling a witch's cauldron of roots and potions; storefront bakeries with steamy windows and 80¢ pork buns; and produce markets piled high with fresh lychees, bok choy and Asian pears.

History of Chinese Immigrants

The history of Chinese immigrants in New York City is a long and tumultuous one. The first Chinese people to arrive in America came to work under difficult conditions on the Central Pacific Railroad; others were lured to the West Coast in search of gold. When prospects dried up, many moved east to NYC to work in factory assembly lines and in the laundry houses of New Jersey.

IMMIGRATION PATTERNS

When New York City's Chinatown was founded in the mid-18th century, it was immigrants from Guandong (Canton Province) that built it. Many of the traditional shops hawking pork buns, and restaurants serving dim sum, are grounded in Cantonese culture. After the Vietnam War came Chinese groups from Vietnam, then the late 20th century brought a wave of Fujianese that caused tensions with the original community. Since then, Chinatown has become a hot pot of different Asian cultures, from Burmese to Filipino. Even Latin American flavor is creeping in down Canal St.

TAKE A BREAK

Dive into a dim sum feast at 1920s Nom Wah Tea Parlor (p98), where the decor is American diner but the flavors are finger-licking Cantonese.

If your visit extends into the evening, drink at Apothéke (p99), where 'chemists' mix up perfect potions to cure all ailments.

SIGHTS

SoHo is the NYC of incognito celebrities and prized cast-iron lofts. It's also home to a number of cultural assets, including an LGBTIQ+ art museum, ambitious installations by Walter De Maria, and New York's most authentic Federal-era abode. Chinatown harbors Buddhist temples and a museum dedicated to the Chinese-American experience.

SoHo, NoHo & Nolita

BROKEN KILOMETER GALLERY

Map p408 (212-989-5566; www.diaart.org; 393 W Broadway, btwn Spring & Broome Sts, SoHo; noon-3pm & 3:30-6pm Wed-Sun, closed mid-Jun–mid-Sep; S N/R to Prince St; C/E to Spring St) FREE Occupying a cavernous ground-floor space in SoHo is this 1979 installation by the late American artist Walter De Maria. The work consists of 500 solid brass rods, positioned in five parallel rows, with the space between the rods increasing by 5mm with each consecutive space, from front to back. The result: a playful subversion of spacial perception. The rods appear to be identically spaced, even though at the back they're almost 2ft apart. No photos allowed.

NEW YORK CITY FIRE MUSEUM MUSEUM

Map p408 (212-691-1303; www.nycfiremuseum.org; 278 Spring St, btwn Varick & Hudson Sts, SoHo; adult/child $10/8; 10am-5pm; S C/E to Spring St) In a grand old firehouse dating from 1904, this ode to firefighters includes a fantastic collection of historic equipment and artifacts. Eye up everything from horse-drawn firefighting carriages and early stovepipe firefighter hats to Chief, a four-legged firefighting hero from Brooklyn. Exhibits trace the development of the NYC firefighting system, and the museum's heavy equipment and friendly staff make this a great spot for kids.

The New York Fire Department (FDNY) lost half of its members in the collapse of the World Trade Center on September 11, 2001, and memorials and exhibits have become a permanent part of the collection – as well as the 2019 planting of a seedling from the Word Trade Center survivor tree out front. Fans can stock up on books about firefighting history and official FDNY clothing and patches in the gift shop.

NEW YORK EARTH ROOM GALLERY

Map p408 (212-989-5566; www.earthroom.org; 141 Wooster St, btwn Prince & W Houston Sts, SoHo; noon-3pm & 3:30-6pm Wed-Sun; S N/R to Prince St) FREE Since 1980 the oddity of the New York Earth Room, the work of artist Walter De Maria, has been wooing the curious with something not easily found in the city: dirt (250 cu yd, or 280,000lb, of it, to be exact). Walking into the small space is a heady experience, as the scent will make you feel like you've entered a wet forest; the sight of such beautiful, pure earth in the midst of this crazy city is surprisingly moving.

DONALD JUDD HOME STUDIO GALLERY

Map p408 (212-219-2747; http://juddfoundation.org; 101 Spring St, at Mercer St, SoHo; adult/student $24/11.50; by prebooked guided tour Tue-Sat; S N/R to Prince St; 6 to Spring St) The former home and studio of the late American artist Donald Judd offers a fascinating glimpse into the life and artistic practices of the minimalist maverick. Guided tours of the space run for approximately 90 minutes and must be booked online (tours often sell out a month in advance). The home studio also hosts drawing classes and art talks; see the website for details.

DRAWING CENTER GALLERY

Map p408 (212-219-2166; www.drawingcenter.org; 35 Wooster St, btwn Grand & Broome Sts, SoHo; noon-6pm Wed & Fri-Sun, to 8pm Thu; S A/C/E, 1, N/Q/R to Canal St) FREE America's only nonprofit institute focused solely on drawings, the Drawing Center uses work by masters as well as unknowns to juxtapose the medium's various styles. Historical exhibitions have included work by Michelangelo, James Ensor and Marcel Duchamp, while contemporary shows have showcased heavyweights such as Richard Serra, Ellsworth Kelly and Richard Tuttle. As to the themes themselves, expect anything from the whimsical to the politically controversial.

CHILDREN'S MUSEUM OF THE ARTS MUSEUM

Map p408 (212-274-0986; www.cmany.org; 103 Charlton St, btwn Greenwich & Hudson Sts, SoHo; $13, 4-6pm Thu by donation; noon-5pm Mon & Fri, to 6pm Thu, 10am-5pm Sat & Sun; ; S 1 to Houston St; C/E to Spring St) This small but worthy stop encourages kids aged 10 months to 15 years to view, make and share art. Rotating exhibitions aside, the center offers a vast program of daily activities for

TOP EXPERIENCE
MERCHANT'S HOUSE MUSEUM

Built in 1832 and purchased by merchant magnate Seabury Tredwell three years later, this red-brick mansion is the most authentic Federal-style house in town (of about 300). An antiquarian's dream, the Merchant's House is as much about the city's mercantile past as it is a showcase of high-end domestic furnishings from the 19th century. Everything in the house is testament to what money could buy, from the mahogany pocket doors, bronze gasoliers and marble mantelpieces, to the elegant parlor chairs, attributed to noted furniture designer Duncan Phyfe. Even the elaborate system of multilevel call bells for the servants works to this day.

Many believe that the ghost of Gertrude Tredwell – Seabury's youngest child and the building's last resident – haunts the place, making cameos late in the evening and at public events. Several attendees once witnessed the shadow of a woman walk up to the performers and take a seat in the parlor chairs at a Valentine's Day concert. Apropos, the museum offers ghost tours after dark (typically in late October), plus lectures, special events and historical walking tours of NoHo. Check the website for details.

DON'T MISS

- Chairs attributed to Duncan Phyfe
- Ghost tours

PRACTICALITIES

- Map p408, G2
- www.merchantshouse.org
- 29 E 4th St, btwn Lafayette St & Bowery, NoHo
- adult/child $15/free
- noon-5pm Fri-Mon, to 8pm Thu, guided tours 2pm Thu-Mon & 6:30pm Thu
- S 6 to Bleecker St; B/D/F/M to Broadway-Lafayette St

fledgling artists, from sculpture and collaborative mural painting, to songwriting and children's book design. It also runs movie nights and other special treats. See the website for upcoming offerings.

Chinatown & Little Italy

CHINATOWN AREA

See p88.

LESLIE-LOHMAN MUSEUM OF GAY & LESBIAN ART MUSEUM

Map p408 (212-431-2609; www.leslielohman.org; 26 Wooster St, btwn Grand & Canal Sts, Little Italy; suggested donation $10; noon-6pm Wed & Fri-Sun, to 8pm Thu; S A/C/E, N/Q/R, 1 to Canal St) FREE The world's first museum dedicated to LGBTIQ+ themes stages six to eight annual exhibitions of both homegrown and international art. Offerings have included solo-artist retrospectives as well as themed shows exploring the likes of 'art and sex along the New York waterfront.' Much of the work on display is from the museum's own collection, which consists of over 24,000 works. The space also hosts queer-centric lectures, readings, film screenings and performances; check the website for updates.

MULBERRY STREET STREET

Map p411 (Little Italy; S N/Q/R, J/Z, 6 to Canal St; B/D to Grand St) Named for the mulberry farms that once stood here, Mulberry St is now better known as the meat in Little Italy's sauce. It's an animated strip, packed with smooth-talking restaurant hawkers (especially between Hester and Grand Sts), wisecracking baristas and a healthy dose of kitschy souvenirs.

Despite the neighborhood's many changes over the years, history looms large. One block north stands fourth-generation **Alleva** (Map p411; 212-226-7990; 188 Grand St; 9am-7pm; S J/Z, N/Q/R, 6 to Canal St; B/D to Grand St), one of the city's original cheese shops and famed for its mozzarella. Across the street on Grand lies another veteran, Ferrara Cafe & Bakery (p99), celebrated for its classic Italian pastries and gelati. Back on Mulberry, old-time **Mulberry Street Bar** (Map p411; 212-226-9345; www.facebook.com/MulberryStBar; 176 Mulberry St, at Broome St; 11am-midnight

Sun-Thu, to 2am Fri & Sat; S B/D to Grand St; J/Z to Bowery) was a favorite haunt of the late Frank Sinatra; its own TV cameos include *Law & Order* and *The Sopranos*.

Alcohol was openly traded on the corner of Mulberry and Kenmare Sts during Prohibition, leading to its nickname, the 'Curb Exchange.' That police headquarters at the time were only a block away at 240 Centre St is testament to the power of good old-fashioned bribes. From this point north, the old-school delis and restaurants of Little Italy give way to the new-school boutiques, galleries and restaurants of Nolita. Take a gander at what was once the **Ravenite Social Club** (Map p408; 247 Mulberry St, Nolita; S 6 to Spring St; N/R to Prince St) to see how things have really changed around here. Now a designer shoe store, it was once a mobster hangout (originally known as the Alto Knights Social Club). Indeed, it was right here that big hitters such as John Gotti (as well as the FBI, which kept a watchful eye from the building across the street) logged time. Only the shop's tile floor remains from the day, the shop windows once an intimidating brick wall.

ARTISTS SPACE — GALLERY

Map p411 (212-226-3970; www.artistsspace.org; 80 White St, at Cortland Alley, Chinatown; noon-6pm Wed-Sun; S N/Q/R/W to Canal St) FREE One of the first alternative spaces in New York, Artists Space made its debut in 1972 with a mission to support contemporary artists working in the visual arts – from video, electronic media and performance to architecture and design. More than 40 years on, it remains a solid choice for those seeking crisp, provocative and experimental creativity. In late 2019 the venue moved to a new location with two floors of exhibition space.

COLUMBUS PARK — PARK

Map p411 (Mulberry & Bayard Sts, Chinatown; S J/Z, N/Q/R, 6 to Canal St) Mah-jongg meisters, slow-motion tai-chi practitioners and old aunties gossiping over homemade dumplings: it might feel like Shanghai, but this leafy oasis is core to NYC history. In the 19th century, this was part of the infamous Five Points neighborhood, the city's first tenement slums and the inspiration for Martin Scorsese's *Gangs of New York*.

TOP EXPERIENCE
LITTLE ITALY

In the last 50 years, New York's Little Italy has shrunk from a big, brash boot to an ultra-slim sandal. A mid-century exodus to Brooklyn and beyond has seen this neighborhood turn into a micro-pastiche of its former self. It's now little more than **Mulberry Street** (p91), a kitsch strip of gingham tablecloths, mandolin muzak and nostalgia for the old country.

Come late September, Mulberry St turns into a raucous, 11-day block party for the **San Gennaro Festival** (www.facebook.com/sangennaronyc), a celebration honoring the patron saint of Naples. It's a loud, convivial affair, with food and carnival stalls, free entertainment and more big hair than Jersey Shore.

If you're after an old-world-style Italian dinner, family-run **Da Nico** (Map p411; 212-343-1212; www.danicoristorante.com; 164 Mulberry St, btwn Grande & Broome Sts; mains $18-38; noon-10pm Sun-Thu, to 11pm Fri & Sat; S J/Z N/Q/R/W, 6 to Canal St) checks all the boxes. To satisfy your sweet tooth, head to **Ferrara Cafe & Bakery** (p99) for mouthwateringly good tiramisu, or tasty coffee.

DON'T MISS

- Mulberry St
- San Gennaro Festival in September
- Great tiramisu

PRACTICALITIES

- Map p411, B2
- S N/Q/R/W, J/Z, 6 to Canal St; B/D to Grand St

✖ EATING

SoHo, Chinatown and Little Italy provide the full spectrum for food lovers. The thrifty are spoiled for choice in Chinatown, where heaping portions are served up for just a few dollars. SoHo is a constantly evolving hunting ground for Instagram gourmands, with cult-status restaurants, fledgling food superstars and an increasingly upmarket drive. Little Italy has the good, the bad and the ugly: there's less authentic Italian food here than you might expect (though there's a couple of standouts), and the area is slowly homogenising, with hispanic and other European influences just as visible on menus.

✖ SoHo, NoHo & Nolita

TWO HANDS CAFE $

Map p411 (www.twohandsnyc.com; 164 Mott St, btwn Broome & Grand Sts, Nolita; dishes $11-16; ⊗8am-5pm; ✔; ⑤B/D to Grand St; J/Z to Bowery) Named after the crime-com film starring Heath Ledger, Two Hands encapsulates Australia's relaxed, sophisticated cafe culture. Dream of Byron Bay over small-batch specialty coffee and out-of-the-box grub, such as sweet-corn fritters ($14) with spinach, avocado, sour cream, pickled beets and chili, or a healthier-than-thou acai bowl.

LITTLE CUPCAKE BAKESHOP DESSERTS $

Map p408 (☎212-941-9100; www.littlecupcake bakeshop.com; 30 Prince St, at Mott St, Nolita; cakes from $4.50; ⊗7:30am-11pm Mon-Thu, to midnight Fri, 8am-midnight Sat, 8am-11pm Sun; ⑤6 to Spring St, R/W to Prince St) ✐ Famed for its version of the Brooklyn blackout cake, regularly called the best chocolate cake in the USA, this prim little bakeshop has plenty of other tricks up its sleeve. The four Italian brothers from Brooklyn who own the shop also ruin waistlines with homemade ice-cream flavors such as banana pudding, key lime pies and moist mini cupcakes.

LAN LARB THAI $

Map p411 (☎646-895-9264; 227 Centre St, at Grand St, SoHo; dishes $12-26; ⊗11:30am-10:30pm; ⑤N/Q/R/W, J/Z, 6 to Canal St) Food fiends flock to Lan Larb for cheap, flavor-packed Thai. It specializes in *larb*, a spicy, minced-meat salad from Thailand's north-

east Isan region (try the duck version; $14). Other top choices include sucker-punch *som tam* (green papaya salad; $11) and a delicate *kui teiw nam tok nuer* (dark noodle soup with beef, morning glory, scallion, cilantro and bean sprouts; $12).

DOMINIQUE ANSEL BAKERY BAKERY $

Map p408 (☎212-219-2773; www.dominique ansel.com; 189 Spring St, btwn Sullivan & Thompson Sts, SoHo; desserts $5-8; ⊗8am-7pm Mon-Sat, from 9am Sun; ⑤C/E to Spring St) One of NYC's best and most well-known patisseries has more to offer than just cronuts (its world-famous doughnut-croissant hybrid), including buttery *kouign-amman* (Breton cake), gleaming berry tarts, and the Paris-New York, a chocolate/caramel/peanut twist on the traditional Paris-Brest. If you insist on a cronut, head in by 7:30am on weekdays (earlier on weekends) to beat the 'sold out' sign.

TACOMBI FONDA NOLITA MEXICAN $

Map p408 (☎917-727-0179; www.tacombi.com; 267 Elizabeth St, btwn E Houston & Prince Sts, Nolita; tacos $4-9; ⊗11am-11pm Sun-Wed, to midnight Thu-Sat; ⑤F to 2nd Ave; 6 to Bleecker St) Festively strung lights, foldaway chairs and Mexican men flipping tacos in an old VW Kombi: if you can't make it to the Yucatan shore, here's your Plan B. Casual, convivial and ever-popular, Tacombi serves up fine, fresh tacos, including a *barbacoa* (roasted black Angus beef). Wash down the goodness with a pitcher of sangria and start plotting that south-of-the-border getaway.

CAFÉ GITANE MEDITERRANEAN $

Map p408 (☎212-334-9552; www.cafegitane nyc.com; 242 Mott St, at Prince St, Nolita; salads $10.50-18, mains $15-16; ⊗8:30am-midnight; ✔; ⑤N/R to Prince St; 6 to Spring St) Clear the Gauloise smoke from your eyes and blink twice if you think you're in Paris: bistro-esque Gitane has that kind of louche vibe. This is a classic see-and-be-seen haunt, popular with salad-picking models and the odd Hollywood regular. Join them for a nibble on the likes of heart-of-palm salad with grilled salmon or Moroccan couscous with merguez sausages.

MARCHÉ MAMAN BISTRO $

Map p411 (☎212-226-0700; www.mamannyc.com; 239 Centre St, Nolita; mains $12-16; ⊗bistro & takeaway 8am-4pm Mon-Fri, from 9am Sat & Sun, shop 10am-6pm; ⑤N/Q/R/W, J/Z, 6 to

Canal St) This clean French bistro, homewares store and 'secret garden' feels like it's been picked up and placed here from Provence. Enjoy quiche lorraine or beignets from the takeaway bar or sit for a meal on the other side of the shop, where tables and chairs are cleverly placed to show off the fanciful French country kitchenware and gorgeous kids accessories.

PRINCE STREET PIZZA PIZZA $

Map p408 (☎212-966-4100; 27 Prince St, btwn Mott & Elizabeth Sts, Nolita; pizza slices from $3.30; ⊙11:45am-11pm Sun-Thu, to 2am Fri & Sat; ⓢR/W to Prince St; 6 to Spring St) It's a miracle the oven door hasn't come off at this classic standing-room-only slice joint, its brick walls hung with shots of celebrity fans like Rebel Wilson, Usher and Kate Hudson. The sauces, mozzarella and ricotta are made in-house and New Yorkers go wild for the pepperoni square. The pizza is decent, but not dazzling enough to justify the queues.

MOONCAKE FOODS ASIAN $

Map p408 (☎212-219-8888; www.mooncakefoods.com; 28 Watts St, btwn Sullivan & Thompson Sts, SoHo; sandwiches from $12.50, mains from $14.95; ⊙11am-10pm Mon-Sat; ⓢ1 to Canal St; C/E to Spring St) This unpretentious family-run restaurant serves some of the best sandwiches in the neighborhood, nay, the city. Try the smoked white-fish salad sandwich or Vietnamese pork meatball hero; nothing is fried or greasy and all dishes contain high-quality ingredients. Cash or Venmo mobile app only.

★UNCLE BOONS THAI $$

Map p408 (☎646-370-6650; www.uncleboons.com; 7 Spring St, btwn Elizabeth St & Bowery, Nolita; small plates $15-18, large plates $25-31; ⊙5:30-11pm Sun-Thu, to midnight Fri & Sat; 📶; ⓢJ/Z to Bowery; 6 to Spring St) Michelin-star Thai is served up in a fun, tongue-in-cheek combo of retro wood-paneled dining room with Thai film posters and old family snaps. Spanning the old and the new, dishes are tangy, rich and creative. Standouts include the *kob woonsen* (garlic and soy marinated frogs legs), *koong* (grilled head-on prawns) and *kaduuk* (roasted bone marrow satay).

Cocktails are as exquisite as the food. A limited number of tables are released two weeks in advance for reservations, but the restaurant encourages walk-ins: arrive either before 6pm or after 10pm and prepare for a bit of a scrum as you wait to be called. It's extremely popular, but absolutely worth it. Tip: it's usually less of a wait if you're happy to eat at the bar.

ATLA MEXICAN $$

Map p408 (☎347-662-3522; www.atlanyc.com; 372 Lafayette St, at Great Jones St, NoHo; dishes $12-26; ⊙11am-10pm Sun-Wed, to 11pm Thu-Sat; ⓢ6 to Bleecker St, B/D/F/M to Broadway-Lafayette St) The Mexican dishes on ATLA's menu – enchiladas, quesadillas, tacos, *chilaquiles* – might sound like standard fare, but here they've been elevated to fine-dining level. Settle into the striking black-and-white dining hall with a mezcal negroni, and order a banquet of sharing dishes such as arctic char and farmer's cheese tostada, striped bass black *aguachile* or duck wings and scallions.

BUTCHER'S DAUGHTER VEGETARIAN $$

Map p408 (☎212-219-3434; www.thebutchersdaughter.com; 19 Kenmare St, at Elizabeth St, Nolita; salads & sandwiches $13-15, dinner mains $15-18; ⊙8am-10pm; 🌶; ⓢJ to Bowery; 6 to Spring St) The butcher's daughter certainly has rebelled, peddling nothing but fresh herbivorous fare in her whitewashed cafe. While healthy it is, boring it's not: everything from the soaked organic muesli to the spicy kale Caesar salad with almond Parmesan or the dinnertime Butcher's burger (vegetable and black-bean patty) is devilishly delish.

RUBIROSA PIZZA $$

Map p408 (☎212-965-0500; www.rubirosanyc.com; 235 Mulberry St, btwn Spring & Prince Sts, Nolita; pizzas $20-32, mains $13-34; ⊙11:30am-11pm Sun-Wed, to midnight Thu-Sat; ⓢN/R to Prince St; B/D/F/M to Broadway-Lafayette St; 6 to Spring St) Rubirosa's infallible family recipe for its whisper-thin pie crust lures a steady stream of patrons from all over the city. Shovel slices from the bar stools or grab a table amid cozy surrounds and make room for savory appetizers and antipasti. Other options include bowls of pasta (the 'small' portion should fill most bellies). Gluten-free diners have their own menu.

BOQUERIA SOHO TAPAS $$

Map p408 (☎212-343-4255; www.boquerianyc.com; 171 Spring St, btwn West Broadway & Thompson St, SoHo; tapas $6-18; ⊙11am-10:30pm Sun-Thu, to 11:30pm Fri & Sat; ⓢC/E to Spring St) Channeling Barcelona, this expansive, welcoming tapas joint serves both classic and classic-with-a-twist morsels, dexterously assembled in the open kitchen. Order a beer-and-pear sangria and feast on standouts such as *abondigas* (Colorado lamb meatballs with tomato sauce and sheep's milk cheese), mushroom and Serrano ham croquettes, and a fine selection of hard and soft cheeses.

★WAYAN BALINESE $$$

Map p408 (☎917-261-4388; www.wayan-nyc.com; 20 Spring St, Nolita; small plates $16-19, mains $22-66; ⏰11:30am-3:30pm & 5:30-10:30pm Mon, to 11pm Tue-Thu, to midnight Fri, 11am-3:30pm & 5:30pm-midnight Sat, to 10pm Sun; Ⓢ J/Z to Bowery; 4/6 to Spring St) In his first solo venture, chef Cédric Vongerichten – son of restaurant royalty, Jean-Georges – wields the flavors of Bali with a French flair at Wayan, which means first-born in Balinese. The sultry warmth of the Nolita space invites you to linger over plates of silky satays, Jimbaran-style clams with sweet onion and coconut, and the crowd-acclaimed buttered lobster noodles with Gruyère.

★CHEFS CLUB FUSION $$$

Map p408 (☎212-941-1100; www.chefsclub.com; 275 Mulberry St, Nolita; prix-fixe $85-125; ⏰5:30-10:30pm Mon-Sat; Ⓢ R/W to Prince St, B/D/F/M to Broadway-Lafayette St) In a building used in part for the show *Will & Grace*, Chefs Club sounds more like a discount warehouse than the spectacular dining spot it really is: visiting chefs prepare a menu for anywhere from three weeks to three months, offering their finest selections in menus that span the flavors of the globe.

The decor is industrial warehouse, with unique touches like a 1500lb block of pink Himalayan salt that hangs from a glass case above the bar. If you don't fancy what's cooking in the main restaurant, you could instead try the Chefs Club Counter – a fine offshoot on the corner of Spring and Lafayette Sts.

★IL BUCO ALIMENTARI & VINERIA ITALIAN $$$

Map p408 (☎212-837-2622; www.ilbucovineria.com; 53 Great Jones St, btwn Bowery & Lafayette St, NoHo; mains lunch $14-34, dinner $34-70; ⏰8am-11pm Mon-Thu, to midnight Fri, 9am-midnight Sat, 9am-11pm Sun; 📶; Ⓢ 6 to Bleecker St; B/D/F/M to Broadway-Lafayette St) Whether it's espresso at the front bar, cheese from the deli or long-and-lazy Italian feasting in the sunken dining room, Il Buco's trendier spin-off delivers the goods. Brickwork and giant industrial lamps set a hip, rustic tone, echoed in the menu. The lunchtime paninis are huge, decadent and divine: try the porchetta with fried eggs, salsa verde and arugula ($18).

CHARLIE BIRD ITALIAN $$$

Map p408 (☎212-235-7133; www.charliebirdnyc.com; 5 King St, entrance on Sixth Ave, SoHo; small plates $12-21, mains $21-36; ⏰noon-11pm Mon-Thu, to midnight Fri, 11:30am-midnight Sat, to 11pm Sun; Ⓢ C/E to Spring St; 1 to Houston St) Tweeting away on SoHo's western fringe, skinny Charlie Bird is all about local produce, rustic Italian know-how and clever homespun twists. Mingle at the marble bar, or slip into a hand-sewn leather chair for artful dishes, such as whole grilled branzino with salsa verde, or chicken liver with crab apple mostarda. Keeping company is a wine list laced with pleasant surprises.

DUTCH AMERICAN $$$

Map p408 (☎212-677-6200; www.thedutchnyc.com; 131 Sullivan St, at Prince St, SoHo; mains lunch $20-39, dinner $38-69; ⏰11:30am-3pm & 5:30-10:30pm Mon-Thu, to 11:30pm Fri, 10am-3pm & 5:30-11:30pm Sat, 5:30-10:30pm Sun; Ⓢ C/E to Spring St; R/W to Prince St; 1 to Houston St) Whether perched at the bar or dining snugly in the back room, you can always expect smart, farm-to-table comfort grub at this see-and-be-seen stalwart. Flavors traverse the globe, from wagyu steak tartare with béarnaise aioli to grilled rack of lamb with jerk sauce and roti pancake. Reservations are recommended, especially for dinner and all day on weekends.

BALTHAZAR FRENCH $$$

Map p408 (☎212-965-1414; www.balthazarny.com; 80 Spring St, btwn Broadway & Crosby St, SoHo; mains $22-45; ⏰7:30am-midnight Sun-Thu, to 1am Fri, 8am-1am Sat; Ⓢ 6 to Spring St; N/R to Prince St) Still the king of bistros after more than 20 years, bustling (OK, *loud*) Balthazar is never short of a mob. That's all thanks to three winning details: its location in SoHo's shopping-spree heartland; the uplifting Paris-meets-NYC ambience; and the something-for-everyone menu. Highlights include the outstanding raw bar, steak *frites*, Niçoise salad, as well as the roasted beet salad.

1
PRINCE ST.
PIZZA
OPEN
EXIT

MASSIMO BORCHI/ATLANTIDE PHOTOTRAVEL/GETTY IMAGES ©

CLAY WILLIAMS/CLAYWILLIAMSPHOTO.COM/GETTY IMAGES ©

1. Prince Street Pizza (p94)
Try the pepperoni square at this classic New York pizza joint.

2. Mahayana Temple (p89)
Pay your respects to the golden 16ft-high Buddha at Chinatown's largest Buddhist temple.

3. Nom Wah Tea Parlor (p98)
New York City's oldest dim-sum restaurant.

4. Mulberry Street (p91)
Discover the heart of Little Italy.

MAREMAGNUM/GETTY IMAGES ©

Chinatown & Little Italy

★NOM WAH TEA PARLOR CHINESE $

Map p411 (212-962-6047; www.nomwah.com; 13 Doyers St, Chinatown; dim sum from $4; 10:30am-10pm Sun-Wed, to 11pm Fri & Sat; J/Z to Chambers St; 4/5/6 to Brooklyn Bridge-City Hall) Hidden down a narrow lane, 1920s Nom Wah Tea Parlor might look like an American diner, but it's actually the oldest dim-sum place in town. Grab a seat at one of the red banquettes or counter stools and simply tick off what you want on the menu provided. Roast pork buns, Shanghainese soup dumplings, shrimp *siu mai*...it's all finger-licking good.

CANAL ST MARKET FOOD HALL $

Map p408 (www.canalstreet.market; 265 Canal St, btwn Broadway & Lafayette St; food 10am-10pm Mon-Sat, to 6pm Sun; retail 11am-7pm Mon-Sat, to 6pm Sun; 6, N/Q/R/W to Canal St) In the borderlands where Chinatown morphs into SoHo, this food and retail market unavoidably turns heads. The warehouse-like dining area is a world tour of food trends – Japanese shaved ice, ceviche, seasonal farm food etc. The shopping floor is the place to hunt for unusual indie gems such as vintage skateboards, K-pop clothing and locally made jewelry.

BAZ BAGELS JEWISH $

Map p411 (212-335-0609; www.bazbagel.com; 181 Grand St, btwn Baxter & Mulberry Sts, Little Italy; bagels $12-16; 7am-3pm Mon-Fri, 8am-4pm Sat & Sun; J/Z, N/Q/R, 6 to Canal St; B/D to Grand St) A shamelessly flamboyant combo of pink, palm prints and Dolly and Barbra portraits, New York's campest diner keeps things fabulous with its hand-rolled, kettle-boiled bagels. Star of the show is the Mooch ($16), a scrumptious concoction that's half Scottish salmon and half cold-smoked sable. Bagels aside, other standouts include blintzes and latkes, the latter made to the owner's grandmother's recipe.

XI'AN FAMOUS FOODS CHINESE $

Map p411 (212-786-2068; www.xianfoods.com; 45 Bayard St, btwn Elizabeth St & Bowery, Chinatown; dishes $4.70-12; 11:30am-9pm Sun-Thu, to 9:30pm Fri & Sat; N/Q/R/W, J/Z, 6 to Canal St, B/D to Grand St) Food bloggers hyperventilate at the mere mention of this small chain's hand-pulled noodles. The burgers are also menu stars: tender lamb sautéed with ground cumin and toasted chili seeds, or melt-in-the-mouth stewed pork. There are 13 other locations throughout the city.

DELUXE GREEN BO CHINESE $

Map p411 (212-625-2359; www.deluxegreenbo.com; 66 Bayard St, btwn Elizabeth & Mott Sts, Chinatown; mains $5.95-19.95; 11am-11pm Mon-Thu, to midnight Fri & Sat, to 10:30pm Sun; N/Q/R, J/Z, 6 to Canal St; B/D to Grand St) It's all about the food at this no-frills Chinese spot: gorgeous *xiao long bao* served in steaming drums, heaping portions of greasy noodles and gleaming plates of salubrious, sautéed spinach. Cash only.

BÁNH MÌ SAIGON BAKERY VIETNAMESE $

Map p411 (212-941-1541; 198 Grand St, btwn Mulberry & Mott Sts, Little Italy; sandwiches $7-8; 8am-7pm; N/Q/R, J/Z, 6 to Canal St) This no-frills storefront doles out some of the best banh mi in town – crisp, toasted baguettes generously stuffed with hot peppers, pickled carrots, daikon, cucumber, cilantro and your choice of meat. Top billing goes to the classic barbecue pork version. Tip: head in by 3pm as the banh mi sometimes sell out, upon which the place closes early. Cash only.

BUDDHA BODAI CHINESE $

Map p411 (212-566-8388; www.buddha-bodai.com; 5 Mott St, Chinatown; mains $9-22; 11am-9:30pm Mon-Fri, from 10am Sat & Sun; ; J/Z to Chambers St; 4/5/6 to Brooklyn Bridge-City Hall) Serves exquisite vegetarian and kosher cuisine with Cantonese flavors like a vegetarian duck noodle soup, spinach rice rolls and vegetarian 'roast pork' buns. Since another restaurant with the same name and similar menu opened a few blocks away in 2015, this restaurant (which opened in 2004) is referred to as the 'Original Buddha Bodai'. Dim sum is served until 4pm.

GOLDEN STEAMER CHINESE $

Map p411 (212-226-1886; 143a Mott St, btwn Grand & Hester Sts, Chinatown; buns 80¢-$1.75, 3 for $2.50; 7am-7pm; B/D to Grand St; N/Q/R, 6 to Canal St; J/Z to Bowery) Squeeze into this hole-in-the-wall for some of the fluffiest, tastiest *bao* (steamed buns) in Chinatown. Made on-site by bellowing Chinese cooks, fillings include succulent roast pork, Chinese sausage, salted egg and the crowd favorite – pumpkin. For something a little sweeter, try the egg custard tart. Come early for the best choice.

BIG WONG CHINESE $

Map p411 (☎212-964-0540; www.big-wong.com; 67 Mott St, btwn Canal & Bayard Sts, Chinatown; mains $5.50-16; ⏰7am-11pm; ⓈN/Q/R, J/Z, 6 to Canal St) A fast-moving favorite that's famous for its roast pork and BBQ-style chicken, duck and ribs, Big Wong also does a mean rice crepe for breakfast. You'll likely have to share a table, and the food (and your check) comes lightning quick, but it's a fun, communal (and affordable) experience. Cash only.

FERRARA CAFE & BAKERY BAKERY $

Map p411 (☎212-226-6150; www.ferraranyc.com; 195 Grand St, btwn Mulberry & Mott Sts, Little Italy; pastries $7-9; ⏰9am-11pm Sun-Thu, to midnight Fri & Sat; ⓈJ/Z, N/Q/R, 6 to Canal St; B/D to Grand St) Here since 1882, just a half block from Mulberry, is the legendary Ferrara Cafe & Bakery, brimming with classic Italian pastries and old-school ambience. The tiramisu, layers of espresso-dipped ladyfingers and rich marscarpone cheese with a lovely hint of vanilla, is heavenly.

ORIGINAL CHINATOWN ICE CREAM FACTORY ICE CREAM $

Map p411 (☎212-608-4170; www.chinatownicecreamfactory.com; 65 Bayard St, Chinatown; ice cream from $5; ⏰11am-10pm; ⓈN/Q/R, J/Z, 6 to Canal St) Chinatown's favorite ice-cream peddler keeps it local with flavors such as green tea, pandan, durian and lychee sorbet, all written on a whiteboard. The Factory also sells ridiculously cute, trademark T-shirts with an ice-cream-slurping happy dragon on them.

NYONYA MALAYSIAN $$

Map p411 (☎212-334-3669; www.ilovenyonya.com; 199 Grand St, btwn Mott & Mulberry Sts, Little Italy; mains $8-26; ⏰11am-11pm Sun-Thu, to midnight Fri & Sat; ⓈN/Q/R/W, J/Z, 6 to Canal St; B/D to Grand St) Take your palate to steamy Melaka at this bustling temple to Chinese-Malay cuisine. Savor the sweet, the sour and the spicy in classics such as tangy Assam fish-head casserole, rich beef *rendang* (spicy dry curry) and refreshing *rojak* (savory fruit salad tossed in a piquant tamarind dressing). Vegetarians, be warned: there's not much on the menu for you. Cash only.

AMAZING 66 CHINESE $$

Map p411 (☎212-334-0099; www.amazing66.com; 66 Mott St, btwn Canal & Bayard Sts, Chinatown; mains $12-36; ⏰11am-11pm; ⓈN/Q/R/W, J/Z, 6 to Canal St) One of the best places to chomp on Cantonese cuisine, bright, bustling Amazing 66 draws waves of local Chinese immigrants pining for a taste of home. Join them for standout dishes such as barbecued honey spare ribs, shrimp with black-bean sauce and salt-and-pepper chicken wings. Lunch specials start at $7.

PEKING DUCK HOUSE CHINESE $$$

Map p411 (☎212-227-1810; www.pekingduckhousenyc.com; 28 Mott St, Chinatown; Peking duck per person $35-56; ⏰11:30am-10:30pm Sun-Thu, to 11:30pm Fri & Sat; ⓈJ/Z to Chambers St; 6 to Canal St) Offering arguably the best Peking duck in the region, the eponymous restaurant has a variety of set menus that include the house specialty. The space is fancier than some Chinatown spots, making it great for a special occasion. Do have the duck: perfectly crispy skin and moist meat make the slices ideal for a pancake, scallion strips and sauce.

DRINKING & NIGHTLIFE

From reformed speakeasies to secretive cocktail dens and celebrity haunts, an air of history and mystique surrounds many of this neighborhood's drinking holes.

★APOTHÉKE COCKTAIL BAR

Map p411 (☎212-406-0400; www.apothekenyc.com; 9 Doyers St, Chinatown; ⏰6:30pm-2am Mon-Sat, from 8pm Sun; ⓈJ/Z to Chambers St; 4/5/6 to Brooklyn Bridge-City Hall) It takes a little effort to track down this former opium-den-turned-apothecary bar on Doyers St (look for the 'chemist' sign with a beaker illustration hanging above the doorway). Inside, skilled barkeeps work like careful chemists, using local, seasonal produce from Greenmarkets to concoct intense, flavorful 'prescriptions.' The pineapple-cilantro spiced Sitting Buddha is one of the best drinks on the menu.

The menu is just as much fun as sipping the drinks, divided into sections including 'aphrodisiacs', 'pain killers' and 'stress relievers.' Special nightly entertainment

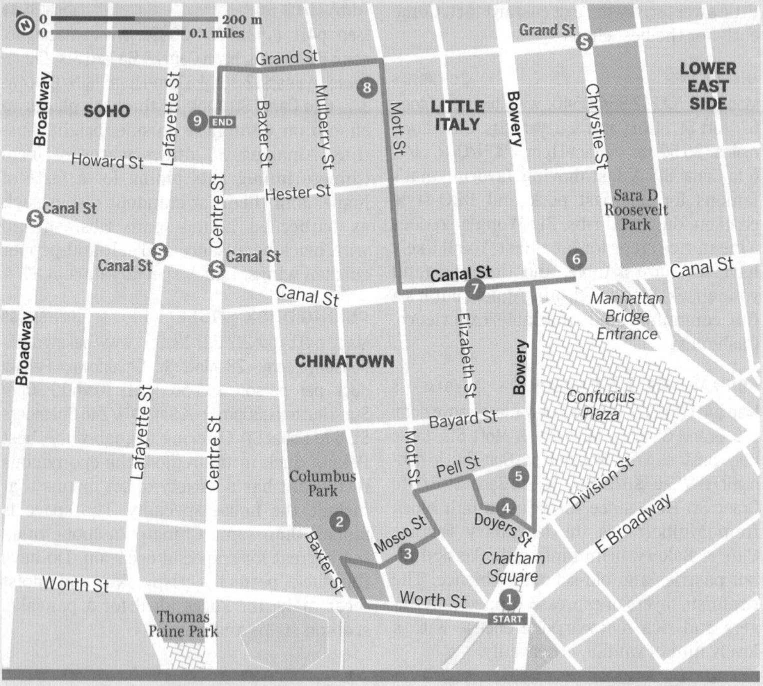

Neighborhood Walk Inside Chinatown

START CHATHAM SQ
END MUSEUM OF CHINESE IN AMERICA
LENGTH 0.9 MILES; 1½ HOURS

Begin exploring at 1 **Chatham Square**, home to the Kim Lau Memorial Arch, erected in 1962 to honor the Chinese Americans who have fallen in battle. There's also a statue of Lin Ze Xu, a Qing-dynasty scholar whose anti-drug trafficking stance largely led to the First Opium War in 1839.

From Chatham Sq head northwest on Worth St until you hit 2 **Columbus Park** (p92), Chinatown's unofficial living room. In the 19th century, this was NYC's notorious Five Points slum, famous for its debauchery. To the east, slip into 3 **Mosco Street**, known in the 19th century as Bandits Roost, a menacing hangout for Irish gangs. Turn left into Mott St, right into Pell St, then right into 4 **Doyers Street**, a crooked lane dubbed 'Barbers Row' for its bounty of hair snippers. The lane's popularity with feuding tongs (secret societies) early last century earned it the nickname Bloody Angle. American composer Irving Berlin practiced at number 10, while at number 12 stands the neighborhood's oldest Chinese restaurant, wokking since 1920.

Turn left into Bowery and head north. At the southwest corner of Pell St and Bowery stands 5 **Edward Mooney House**, NYC's oldest town house, built in 1785 by butcher Edward Mooney. This Georgian-Federal-style veteran has housed a store, a hotel, a billiards parlor and a Chinese social club; it's now a bank. Continue north on Bowery to Canal St, where you'll see Manhattan Bridge and, just beyond that, the 6 **Mahayana Temple** (p89). See the massive golden Buddha inside, then dive into 7 **Canal Street**, Chinatown's hyperactive spine and NYC's one-time Jewish Diamond District. Make a right on Mott St for superlative steamed *bao* (Chinese steamed bun, usually served as dim sum) at 8 **Golden Steamer** (p98). Turn left into Grand St and left again at Centre St, delving into the Chinese-American experience at the 9 **Museum of Chinese in America** (p88).

features the likes of a Prohibition-based theme on Wednesdays and 'Absinthe Minded' Sundays.

★EAR INN PUB

Map p408 (☎212-226-9060; www.earinn.com; 326 Spring St, btwn Washington & Greenwich Sts, SoHo; ⏰bar 11:30am-4am, kitchen to 2am; 📶; Ⓢ C/E to Spring St) Want to see what SoHo was like before the trendsetters and fashionistas? Come to the creaking old Ear Inn, proudly billed as one of the oldest drinking establishments in NYC. The house it occupies was built in the late 18th century for James Brown, an African aide to George Washington. Drinks are cheap and the crowd's eclectic.

Regulars come for late-night dinners at barebones wooden tables with paper tablecloths, crammed between walls drowning in old ad signs and Americana. Three nights a week, a corner of the bar is cleared for popular jazz ensembles (8pm to around 11:30pm). Check the calendar on the website for dates.

LA COMPAGNIE DES VINS SURNATURELS WINE BAR

Map p411 (☎212-343-3660; www.compagnienyc.com; 249 Centre St, btwn Broome & Grand Sts, Nolita; ⏰5pm-1am Mon-Wed, to 2am Thu & Fri, 3pm-2am Sat, noon-1am Sun; Ⓢ 6 to Spring St; R/W to Prince St) A snug melange of Gallic-themed decor, svelte armchairs and tea lights, La Compagnie des Vins Surnaturels is an offshoot of a Paris bar by the same name. Head sommelier Theo Lieberman steers an impressive, French-heavy wine list, with some 600 drops and no shortage of arresting labels by the glass. A short, sophisticated menu includes housemade charcuterie and duck buns.

The good-value happy hour (Monday to Friday from 5pm to 6pm; 3pm to 4pm on weekends) offers $5 snacks and all wines at a $5 discount. Try the mystery wine and you may win the bottle... you just have to identify which wine it is on the menu first. La Compagnie des Vins Surnaturels is a popular place to settle in with nibbles and a good bottle of plonk: reserve a table if you want a comfy spot.

SPRING LOUNGE BAR

Map p408 (☎212-965-1774; www.thespringlounge.com; 48 Spring St, at Mulberry St, Nolita; ⏰8am-4am Mon-Sat, from noon Sun; Ⓢ 6 to Spring St; R/W to Prince St) This neon-red rebel has never let anything get in the way of a good time. In Prohibition days, it peddled buckets of beer. In the '60s its basement was a gambling den. These days, it's best known for its kooky stuffed sharks, early-start regulars and come-one, come-all late-night revelry. Perfect last stop on a bar-hopping tour of the neighborhood.

Fueling the fun are cheap drinks and free grub (hot dogs on Wednesdays from 5pm, bagels on Sundays from noon, while they last). Bottoms up, baby!

GHOST DONKEY BAR

Map p408 (☎212-254-0350; www.ghostdonkey.com; 4 Bleecker St, NoHo; ⏰5pm-2am; Ⓢ 6 to Bleecker St; B/D/F/M to Broadway-Lafayette St) Rowdy meets trippy meets craft at this mezcal and tequila house, with vibes of Mexico, the Middle East and the Wild West. If the moon had a saloon, this place would fit right in. It's more than just a gimme-a-shot-and-lime stop. The extensive mezcal and tequila menu is organized by region and mezcal pours come with seasonal fruits and salts.

Or sink into a low, cushioned couch to sample the excellent craft cocktails beneath a star-lit sky of fairy lights (try the spicy frozen house margarita).

CAFÉ INTEGRAL CAFE

Map p408 (☎646-801-5747; www.cafeintegral.com; 149 Elizabeth St, btwn Broome & Kenmare Sts, Nolita; ⏰7am-5pm Mon-Fri, from 8am Sat & Sun; Ⓢ N/Q/R, J/Z, 6 to Canal St) Refuel with exceptional single-origin coffee at Café Integral, an airy spot with a crowd on Elizabeth St. Tasty pastries are another reason to stop by.

JIMMY COCKTAIL BAR

Map p408 (☎212-201-9118; www.jimmysoho.com; James New York, 15 Thompson St, at Grand St, SoHo; ⏰5pm-1am Mon-Wed, to 2am Thu & Fri, 3pm-2am Sat, 3pm-1am Sun; Ⓢ A/C/E, 1 to Canal St) Lofted atop the James New York hotel in SoHo, Jimmy is a sky-high hangout with sweeping views of the city below. The summer months teem with tipsy patrons who spill out onto the open deck; in cooler weather, drinks are slung indoors from the centrally anchored bar guarded by floor-to-ceiling windows. An outdoor pool adds to the fun.

RANDOLPH COCKTAIL BAR

Map p411 (☎646-383-3623; www.randolphnyc.com; 343 Broome St, btwn Bowery & Elizabeth St, Nolita; ⊙11am-midnight Mon-Wed, to 2am Fri & Sat, to 11pm Sun; ; ⓈJ/Z to Bowery) Randolph serves diverse, creative cocktails in an expansive, dark-wood spot that seems perfect for crowds. Afternoons are quiet, almost contemplative, the kind of place where writers might come with a laptop or an Underwood typewriter and write that perfect draft...while drinking draft. Happy hour runs daily to 8pm.

ENTERTAINMENT

JOE'S PUB LIVE MUSIC

Map p408 (☎212-539-8778, tickets 212-967-7555; www.joespub.com; Public Theater, 425 Lafayette St, btwn Astor Pl & 4th St, NoHo; Ⓢ6 to Astor Pl; R/W to 8th St-NYU) Part bar, part cabaret and performance venue, intimate Joe's serves up both emerging acts and top-shelf performers. Past entertainers have included Patti LuPone, Amy Schumer, the late Leonard Cohen and British songstress Adele. Entrance is through the Public Theater.

FILM FORUM CINEMA

Map p408 (☎212-727-8110; www.filmforum.org; 209 W Houston St, btwn Varick St & Sixth Ave, SoHo; adult/child $15/9; ⊙noon-midnight; Ⓢ1 to Houston St) This nonprofit cinema shows an astounding array of independent films, revivals and career retrospectives from greats such as Orson Welles. Showings often include director talks or other film-themed discussions for hardcore cinephiles. In 2018, the cinema upgraded its theaters to improve the seating, leg room and sight lines, and expanded to add a fourth screen.

PUBLIC THEATER LIVE PERFORMANCE

Map p408 (☎212-539-8500, tickets 212-967-7555; www.publictheater.org; 425 Lafayette St, btwn Astor Pl & 4th St, NoHo; Ⓢ6 to Astor Pl; R/W to 8th St-NYU) This legendary theater was founded as the Shakespeare Workshop back in 1954 and has launched some of New York's big hits, including *Hamilton* in 2015.

Today, you'll find a lineup of innovative programming as well as reimagined classics, with Shakespeare in heavy rotation. Speaking of the bard, the Public also stages star-studded Shakespeare in the Park (p242) performances during the summer.

SHOPPING

The area around SoHo bursts at its fashionable seams with stores big and small. With so many interesting independent shops in close proximity, it is hands-down one of the best retail areas in Manhattan. Broadway has the chain stores; head west or east of there for higher-end fashion, accessories and fragrances. Over on Lafayette, shops cater to the DJ and skate crowds. If indie-chic is your thing, continue east to Nolita. Mott St is best for browsing, followed by Mulberry and Elizabeth. For medicinal herbs, exotic Eastern fruits, woks and Chinese teapots, scour the frenetic streets of Chinatown.

★**GLOSSIER FLAGSHIP** COSMETICS

Map p408 (www.glossier.com; 123 Lafayette St, SoHo; ⊙11am-9pm Mon-Sat, to 8pm Sun; Ⓢ6; J/Z to Canal St) Initially an online beauty retailer, Glossier (franco-phonetically pronounced *glossy-eh*) now beckons fans to its brick-and-mortar flagship, where the queue regularly runs beyond the Lafayette St storefront. Once inside, ascend red quartz stairs to the rosy, high-sheen showroom awash with Insta-worthy aesthetics like diffuse light, polished concrete, pale-pink plaster and cushy banquette seating that resembles red lips.

Swoon over shades of makeup at cylindrical podiums with ribbed tops, then head to the 'wet bar,' where you can play with skincare testers displayed on cube shelves over dark slate sinks. The brand's 'cloud paint' cheek stain even has its own concept room, where you can snap selfies with human-sized sculptures of the product that playfully topple along the mirrored walls.

Place card-only orders with iPad-toting sales associates in blush-pink boiler suits, and pick them up about 10 minutes later at the counter on the way out. You'll see your swag descend from HQ upstairs via a space-age, vertical conveyor belt that drops a clear bag containing the brand's iconic, rosy-pink bubblewrap envelopes stuffed with your goodies.

GREAT JONES SPA

Don't skimp on the services at this downtown feng shui–designed **spa** (Map p408; ☎212-505-3185; www.gjspa.com; 29 Great Jones St, btwn Lafayette St & Bowery, NoHo; ⏰9am-10pm; Ⓢ6 to Bleecker St; B/D/F/M to Broadway-Lafayette St), whose offerings include blood-orange salt scrubs and stem-cell facials. If you spend over $100 per person (not difficult: hour-long massages/facials start at $150/135), you get access to the water lounge with thermal hot tub, sauna, steam room and cold plunge pool (swimwear required). There's even a three-story indoor waterfall.

★BULLETIN — CONCEPT STORE

Map p408 (☎646-928-0213; https://bulletin.co; 27 Prince St, Nolita; ⏰11am-8pm Mon-Sat, to 7pm Sun; ⓈN/Q/R/W to Prince St; 4/6 to Spring St) With beginnings as an online magazine from which readers could shop, Bulletin is now a brick-and-mortar wholesale marketplace decked with pink neon lights. Curated commodities from indie, women-owned enterprises run the gamut from edgy, ready-to-wear apparel, graphic tees and sweatshirts emblazoned with feminist slogans to small housewares, accessories and novelties like keychains engraved with phrases like 'Oprah for president'.

★GALERIA MELISSA — SHOES

Map p408 (☎212-775-1950; www.melissa.com.br/us/galerias/ny; 500 Broadway, btwn Broome & Spring Sts, SoHo; ⏰10am-7pm Mon-Fri, to 8pm Sat, 11am-7pm Sun; 🚻; Ⓢ6 to Spring St, R/W to Prince St) This Brazilian designer specializes in downpour-friendly plastic footwear. Recyclable, sustainable, stylish – women's and kids' shoes run the gamut from mod sandals to brogues, runners and, of course, boots.

Melissa's SoHo boutique is the only one in the USA and it's a lesson in the future of retail, with an Instagram room, a vertical rainforest plant wall, shoes displayed on plinths and prismatic mirror walls.

★MIN NEW YORK — COSMETICS

Map p408 (☎212-206-6366; www.min.com; 117 Crosby St, btwn Jersey & Prince Sts, SoHo; ⏰11am-7pm Tue-Sat, noon-6pm Sun & Mon; ⓈB/D/F/M to Broadway-Lafayette St; N/R to Prince St) This chic, library-like fragrance apothecary has exclusive perfumes, bath and grooming products, and scented candles. Look out for artisanal fragrance 'stories' from MiN's own line. Prices span affordable to astronomical (from $70), and the scents are divine. Unlike many places, here there's no pressure to buy.

★RESURRECTION — VINTAGE

Map p408 (☎212-625-1374; www.resurrectionvintage.com; 45 Great Jones St, btwn Lafayette & Bowery Sts, NoHo; ⏰10am-6pm Mon-Fri; Ⓢ6 to Spring St; N/R to Prince St) Resurrection gives new life to cutting-edge designs from past decades. Striking, mint-condition pieces cover the eras of mod, glam-rock and new-wave design, and design deities such as Marc Jacobs have dropped by for inspiration. Top picks include Halston dresses, Courrèges coats and Jack Boyd jewelry.

There's only a small number of men's pieces on display, but you can ask to see more from the storeroom.

3X1 — FASHION & ACCESSORIES

Map p408 (☎212-391-6969; www.3x1.us; 15 Mercer St, btwn Howard & Grand Sts, SoHo; ⏰11am-7pm Mon-Sat, noon-6pm Sun; ⓈN/Q/R/W, J/Z, 6 to Canal St) Design your most flattering pair of jeans at this bespoke denim factory/showroom, with three levels of service. Quick, on-the-spot 'ready-to-wear' lets you choose the hem for ready-to-wear denim (women's from $200, men's from $265); 'custom' has you choose the fabric and detailing for an existing fit ($625 to $1200); and 'full bespoke' ($1800) designs your perfect pair from scratch.

You can watch the jeans being painstakingly made (it can take two to four weeks for a single pair) in a glass-enclosed workshop. Also sells ready-to-go accessories, including totes, shirts and skirts.

SATURDAYS — FASHION & ACCESSORIES

Map p411 (☎212-966-7875; www.saturdaysnyc.com; 31 Crosby St, btwn Broome & Grand Sts, SoHo; ⏰store 10am-7pm, coffee bar 8am-7pm Mon-Fri, from 10am Sat & Sun; 📶; ⓈN/Q/R/W, J/Z to Canal St; 6 to Spring St) SoHo's version of a surf shop sees boards and wax paired up

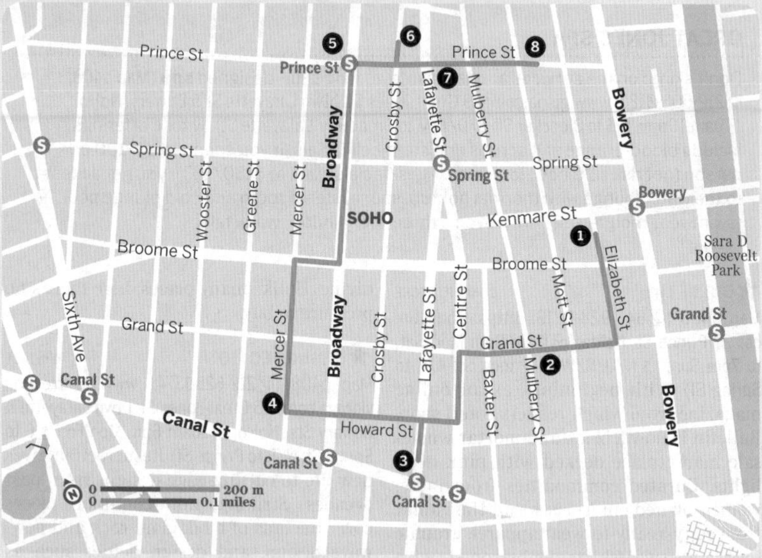

Local Life
An Artisanal Afternoon in SoHo

Shopaholics across the world lust for SoHo and its sharp, trendy whirlwind of flagship stores, coveted labels and strutting fashionistas. Look beyond the giant global brands, however, and you'll discover that talented artisans and independent, one-off enterprises keep things local, unique and utterly inspiring.

❶ A Shop with Single Origin
Charge up with a cup of single-origin coffee from Café Integral (p101), an airy spot on Elizabeth St. Add a great pastry or croissant and you're ready to take yourself outside.

❷ Top-notch Tiramisu
Ferrara Cafe & Bakery (p99) has a huge selection of goodies, but don't pass up the chance to indulge in a world-class tiramisu ($8.95).

❸ Cool-Girl Cosmetics
Around SoHo, you'll note a legion of it-babes toting giant, clear zipper bags containing pink bubblewrap envelopes stuffed with makeup and skincare products from Glossier Flagship (p102). With beginnings as a direct-to-consumer retailer, the cult-favorite company's HQ now features a pink-laden, Insta-worthy showroom with a queue that regularly winds down Lafayette St.

❹ Perfect Jeans
3x1 (p103) lets you design your perfect pair of jeans. Choose a hem for a ready-to-wear pair; customize fabric and detailing on existing cuts; or go all out and create your most flattering pair from scratch.

❺ Curbside Culture
The sidewalk engraving on the northwest corner of Prince St and Broadway is the work of Japanese-born sculptor Ken Hiratsuka, who has carved almost 40 sidewalks since moving to NYC in 1982. While this took about five hours of actual work, its completion took two years (1983–84), as Hiratsuka's illegal nighttime chiseling was often disrupted by pesky police patrols.

❻ Fragrance Flights
Drop into library-like apothecary MiN New York (p103) and request a free 'fragrance flight,' a guided exploration of the store's

DAN HERRICK/LONELY PLANET ©

Ferrara Cafe & Bakery (p99)

extraordinary collection of tantalizing 'stories' told in scent. The staff are welcoming and you may go home smelling like a rose, a spa, the surf or the sea.

7 Books & Conversation

If MiN ignites a passion for fragrance, scan the shelves at McNally Jackson (p108) for a title on the subject. This is one of the city's best-loved independent bookstores, stocked with cognoscenti magazines and books, and an in-house cafe for quality downtime and conversation. In short, a pleasing downtown epilogue.

8 Feminist Finds

Vibrant in both hues of pink and smash-the-patriarchy attitude, Bulletin (p103) features a curated collection of feminist wares from indie makers. The likes of ready-to-wear dresses, witty graphic tees, pop-culture figure altar candles and mantra-engraved keychains are a'glow amid plenty of neon signage in the narrow, lively space.

with designer grooming products, graphic art and surf tomes, and Saturdays' own line of high-quality, fashion-literate threads for dudes. There's a second branch in the West Village (p160).

Once you're styled up, grab a coffee from the in-house espresso bar, hang in the back garden and fish for some crazy, shark-dodging tales.

OPENING CEREMONY FASHION & ACCESSORIES

Map p408 (212-219-2688; www.openingceremony.com; 35 Howard St, btwn Broadway & Lafayette St, SoHo; 11am-8pm Mon-Sat, noon-7pm Sun; S N/Q/R/W, J/Z, 6 to Canal St) Opening Ceremony is famed for its never-boring edit of A-list indie and streetwear labels. It showcases a changing roster of names from across the globe, both established and emerging, for men, women and unisex; complementing them are Opening Ceremony's own avant-garde creations. No matter who's hanging on the racks, you can always expect showstopping, 'where-did-you-get-that?!' threads that are refreshingly unexpected.

For extra pizzazz, visit the customisation bar at the back of the shop.

HOUSING WORKS BOOKSTORE BOOKS

Map p408 (212-334-3324; www.housingworks.org/locations/bookstore-cafe; 126 Crosby St, btwn E Houston & Prince Sts, SoHo; 10am-9pm Mon-Thu, to 6pm Fri-Sun; ; S B/D/F/M to Broadway-Lafayette St; N/R to Prince St) Relaxed, earthy and featuring a great selection of secondhand books, vinyl, CDs and comics you can buy for a good cause (proceeds go to the city's HIV-positive and AIDS-infected homeless population), this creaky hideaway is a very local place to while away a few quiet afternoon hours browsing, sitting in the on-site cafe, or rummaging in its adjoining thrift store.

Check the website for regular events, which include highly entertaining Moth StorySLAM (www.themoth.org) storytelling competitions.

FONG ON FOOD

Map p411 (917-261-7222; 81 Division St, Chinatown; 11am-7pm Tue-Sun; S F to East Broadway) Shuttering after an 80-plus-year run, family-operated tofu purveyor Fong Inn Two recently got a reboot. Catering to both a new generation and devoted, longtime locals at the Eng family's original manufacturing location, son Paul has recreated beloved recipes for homemade tofu, soy milk, *bai tang gao* (a sweet, steamed rice cake) *dau fu fa* (a syrupy tofu pudding) and more.

NEW YORK SHAVING COMPANY
HEALTH & WELLNESS

Map p408 (212-334-9495; www.nyshavingcompany.com; 202b Elizabeth St, btwn Prince & Spring Sts, Nolita; 11am-8pm Mon-Fri, from 10am Sat, 11am-7pm Sun; S 6 to Spring St, J/Z to Bowery) This lovely male grooming shop was founded by John Scala, a Brooklyn-born Sicilian. Wooden cabinets display gorgeous traditional grooming products, like beard creams, shaving gels and razor kits, as well as a series of colognes – the classic Elizabeth St fragrance is said to be a favorite of Justin Timberlake.

The tonsorial parlor at the back of the shop has 1800s leather barbershop chairs and counts Leonardo DiCaprio among its clients; shaves come complete with whiskey shots.

INA MEN
VINTAGE

Map p408 (212-334-2210; www.inanyc.com; 19 Prince St, at Elizabeth St, Nolita; noon-8pm Mon-Sat, to 7pm Sun; S 6 to Spring St; N/R to Prince St) Male style-meisters love INA for pre-loved, luxury clothes, shoes and accessories. Edits are high quality across the board, with sought-after items, including the likes of Rag & Bone jeans, Alexander McQueen wool pants, Burberry shirts and Church's brogues. Next door is the **women's store** (Map p408; 212-334-9048; 21 Prince St, btwn Mott & Elizabeth Sts; noon-8pm Mon-Sat, to 7pm Sun).

RAG & BONE
FASHION & ACCESSORIES

Map p408 (212-219-2204; www.rag-bone.com; 117-119 Mercer St, btwn Prince & Spring Sts, SoHo; 11am-8pm Mon-Sat, to 7pm Sun; S R/W to Prince St) Downtown label Rag & Bone is a hit with many of New York's coolest, sharpest dressers – both men and women. Detail-oriented pieces range from clean-cut shirts and blazers and graphic tees to monochromatic sweaters, feather-light strappy dresses, leather goods and Rag & Bone's highly prized jeans (from $200). Accessories include shoes, hats, bags and wallets.

See the website for details of all its New York locations.

MCNALLY JACKSON
BOOKS

Map p408 (212-274-1160; www.mcnallyjackson.com; 52 Prince St, btwn Lafayette & Mulberry Sts, Nolita; 10am-10pm Mon-Sat, to 9pm Sun; S R/W to Prince St; 6 to Spring St) Bustling indie MJ stocks an excellent selection of magazines and books, covering contemporary fiction, food writing, architecture and design, art and history. If you can score a seat, the in-store cafe is a fine spot to settle in with some reading material or to catch one of the frequent readings and book signings held here.

East Village & Lower East Side

Neighborhood Top Five

1 New Museum of Contemporary Art (p110) Admiring the off-white webbing of the boxy facade of this museum, then wandering in to appreciate mind-bending iterations of art across myriad media.

2 Lower East Side Tenement Museum (p109) Witnessing the shockingly cramped conditions of 19th-century immigrants at this brilliantly curated museum.

3 St Marks Place (p112) Passing knickknack shops and sake bars on St Marks Place, then exploring neighboring streets for a quieter round of nibbling and boutique-ing.

4 Alphabet City (p115) Hitting up pubs and cocktail lounges, stopping for a bite to eat or to peek into a lush community garden.

5 Essex Market (p119) Sampling an array of international cuisines at this spacious new food hall and market.

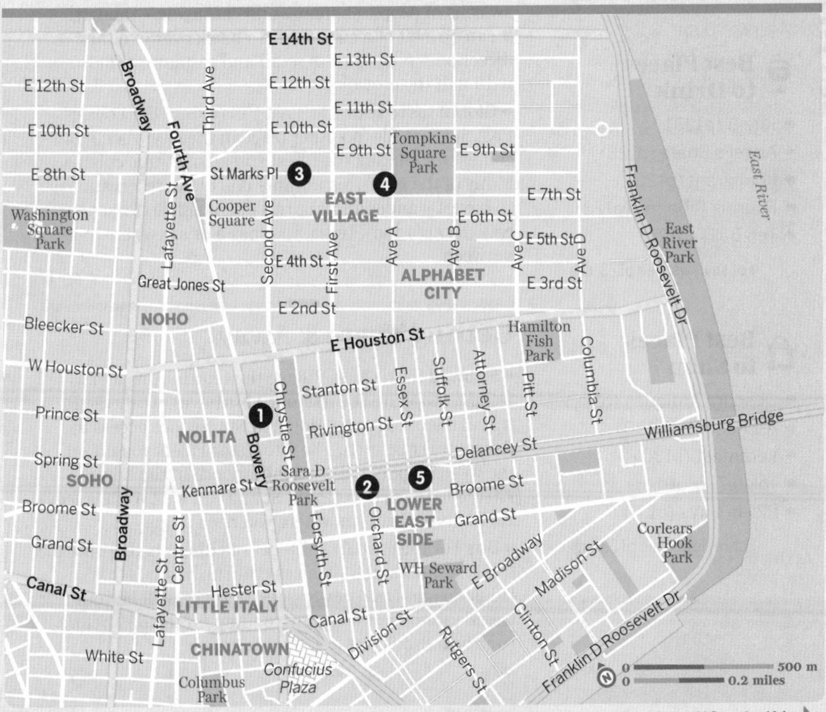

For more detail of this area see Map p412 and p414

Lonely Planet's Top Tip

A lot of the restaurants in this neck of the woods don't take reservations, so stop by the restaurant of your choosing in the early afternoon (2pm should do the trick) and place your name on the roster for the evening meal – chances are high that they'll take your name and you'll get seated right away when you return for dinner later on.

Best Places to Eat

- Veselka (p116)
- Momofuku Noodle Bar (p116)
- Essex Market (p119)
- Hearth (p119)
- Mamoun's (p115)

For reviews, see p115

Best Places to Drink

- Rue B (p123)
- Angel's Share (p123)
- Immigrant (p126)
- Pouring Ribbons (p123)
- Ten Bells (p127)

For reviews, see p123

Best Places to Shop

- Obscura Antiques (p129)
- A-1 Records (p130)
- Verameat (p130)
- Tokio 7 (p130)
- Pickle Guys (p131)

For reviews, see p129

Explore East Village & Lower East Side

If you've been dreaming of those quintessential New York City moments – graffiti on crimson brick; skyscrapers rising overhead; punks, grannies and financial-industry types walking side by side; cute cafes with rickety tables spilling out onto the sidewalks – then the East Village is your Holy Grail. Stick to the area around Tompkins Square Park (p114), and the lettered avenues (known as Alphabet City) to its east, for interesting little nooks in which to eat and drink – as well as a collection of great community gardens that provide leafy respite and the occasional live performance. The streets below Houston St and east of the Bowery are packed with cool boutiques and inventive restaurants, with the odd divey, grungy punk bar still surviving amid the trendy speakeasies. During the day, the vibe is relaxed, whereas at night, when the drinks are flowing, the hormones are pulsing and the crowds descend, it's a very different place. It's a mixed bag, indeed, and perhaps one of the most emblematic of today's city.

Local Life

One block over Famed St Marks Place (p112) draws swarms of people shopping and carousing – though it can be a bit of a circus. Hop a block over in either direction for some great retail and restaurant finds with half the crowds.

Global taste tour The East Village and the Lower East Side are like no other place in the city when it comes to sampling the finest spread of ethnic cuisine. Many of the area's restaurants don't take reservations, so have a wander and grab an open table to feast your way through Italy, India, Indonesia or anywhere in-between.

Getting There & Away

Subway In the East Village the L train runs along 14th St, stopping at First and Third Aves, while the F train at Second Ave at Houston St provides access to the southern stretch. The 6 to Astor Pl lets you off on the western side of the neighborhood. In the Lower East Side the B/D to Grand St and F, J/M/Z to Delancey-Essex Sts will get you where you need to go.

Bus For the eastern stretches of either neighborhood, the M14, M21 and B39 buses that run down 14th, Houston and Delancey Sts, respectively, will be your friend (although make sure to jump off the B39 before it runs into Brooklyn).

TOP EXPERIENCE
LOWER EAST SIDE TENEMENT MUSEUM

Spread across two 19th-century tenements in the gentrifying Lower East Side, this wonderful, immersive museum gives some sense of what life was like in the poorest parts of the world's greatest city in the 19th and early 20th centuries. For access, you must take one of numerous tours that illuminate particular aspects of the period, the people and the places.

103 Orchard St

The **visitor center** at 103 Orchard St (originally three tenements, built 1888) has an excellent museum shop and a small screening room that plays an original film about the history and influence of immigrants on the Lower East Side. Several evenings a month the museum hosts talks here, often relating to the present immigrant experience in America.

Inside the Tenement

A wide range of tenement tours lead visitors into the building where hundreds of immigrants lived and worked over the years. 'Hard Times,' one of the most popular tours, visits apartments from two periods – the 1870s and the 1930s. There you'll see the squalid conditions tenants faced – in the early days there was a wretched communal outhouse and no electricity or running water – and what life was like for the families who lived there. Recorded testimony from a surviving member of the Baldizzi family, who lived here during the Depression, makes it easier to relate to what you see. Other tours focus on Irish immigrants and the harsh discrimination they faced, sweatshop workers and 'shop life' (with a tour through a recreated 1870s German beer hall).

DON'T MISS

- Themed neighborhood walks
- The 'Hard Times' tour
- A prix-fixe meal called Tastings at the Tenement (6:30pm Thursday)
- The free 30-minute film shown in the visitor center

PRACTICALITIES

- Map p414, C4
- ☎877-975-3786
- www.tenement.org
- 103 Orchard St, btwn Broome & Delancey Sts, Lower East Side
- tours adult/student 6-17yr & senior $29/24
- ⌚visitor center 10am-6:30pm Fri-Wed, to 8:30pm Thu
- Ⓢ B/D to Grand St, F, J/M/Z to Delancey-Essex Sts

Meet Victoria

Travel back to 1916 and meet Victoria Confino, a 14-year-old girl from a Greek Sephardic family. Played by a costumed interpreter, Victoria 'lives' at 97 Orchard St, interacting with visitors and answering questions about what her life was like in those days. It's especially recommended for kids, as visitors are free to handle household objects. This one-hour tour is held on Saturday and Sunday year-round, daily during the summer.

Neighborhood Tours

A great way to understand the immigrant experience is on a walking tour around the neighborhood. These tours, ranging from 90 minutes to two hours, explore a variety of topics. 'Foods of the Lower East Side' looks at the ways traditional foods have shaped American cuisine; 'Outside the Home' and 'Building on the Lower East Side' look at life beyond the apartment – where immigrants stored (and lost) their life savings, the churches and synagogues so integral to community life, and the meeting halls where poorly paid workers gathered to fight for better conditions.

LEWIS TSE PUI LUNG/SHUTTERSTOCK ©

TOP EXPERIENCE

NEW MUSEUM OF CONTEMPORARY ART

The New Museum of Contemporary Art's Lower East Side avatar, designed by renowned Japanese architecture firm SANAA, is proof that it's not just what's inside a museum that makes it noteworthy. The street view of the museum alone manages to punctuate the neighborhood with something unique, and its cache of artistic work will dazzle just as much as its facade.

SANAA's Vision

While exhibits rotate through the museum, regularly changing the character of the space within, the shell – an inspired architectural gesture – remains a constant, acting as a unique structural element in the diverse cityscape, while simultaneously fading into the background and allowing the exhibits to shine.

The building's structure is the brainchild of hot Japanese firm SANAA – a partnership between two great minds, Kazuyo Sejima and Ryue Nishizawa. In 2010 SANAA won the coveted Pritzker Prize (think the Oscars of architecture) for its contributions to the world of design. Its trademark vanishing facades are known worldwide for abiding by a strict adherence to a form-follows-function design aesthetic, sometimes taking the land plot's footprint into the overall shape of the structure. The box-atop-box scheme provides a striking counterpoint to the clusters of crimson brick and iron fire escapes outside, while alluding to the geometric exhibition chasms within.

DON'T MISS

- The facade from across the street
- New Museum Cafe
- New Museum Store

PRACTICALITIES

- Map p414, A3
- ☎212-219-1222
- www.newmuseum.org
- 235 Bowery, btwn Stanton & Rivington Sts, Lower East Side
- adult/child $18/free, 7-9pm Thu by donation
- 11am-6pm Tue, Wed & Fri-Sun, to 9pm Thu
- S F to 2nd Ave, R/W to Prince St, J/Z to Bowery, 6 to Spring St

In Orbit

It's now been several years since the New Museum has taken hold, inspiring nearby structures to adopt similarly ethereal designs. Perhaps most interestingly, the museum has become somewhat of a magnetic force attracting a clutch of small workshops and creative spaces (p118) to its orbit.

A Museum with a Mission

Founded in 1977 by Marcia Tucker and housed in five different locations over the years, the museum's mission statement is simple: 'New art, new ideas.' The institution gave gallery space to artists Keith Haring, Jeff Koons, Joan Jonas, Mary Kelly and Andres Serrano at the beginning of their careers, and continues to show contemporary heavy-hitters. The city's sole museum dedicated to contemporary art has brought a steady menu of edgy works in new forms, such as seemingly random, discarded materials fused together and displayed in the middle of a vast room.

The museum also houses the New Museum Cafe, a great spot for sampling the gourmet goodies of NYC purveyors, including baked goods by Cafe Grumpy, teas by McNulty, coffee by Intelligentsia and sandwiches by Duck's Eatery.

In Orbit

If you aren't so keen on the current exhibits, it's still worth stopping by the museum's store to peruse some of the excellent coffee-table books – sometimes the take-homes include savvy collaborations with showcased artists. The shop has the same hours of operation as the museum.

First Saturdays for Families

On the first Saturday of the month, the New Museum hosts special events for budding artists, with hands-on crafts and activities for kids aged four to 15. Free museum admission is included for two adults (it's always free for kids).

PAY-WHAT-YOU-WISH THURSDAYS

To save cash, stop by on Thursday evening between 7pm and 9pm, when admission is 'pay what you wish.' Depending on the show, the crowds can be sizable. We recommend lining up by 6:45pm.

TAKE A BREAK

If nothing in the museum cafe tickles your fancy, Freemans (p122) is down the block and around the corner for lunch or an afternoon cocktail.

Round K (Map p414; www.roundk.com; 99 Allen St, btwn Delancey & Broome Sts, Lower East Side; ⌚8am-10pm Mon-Wed, to midnight Thu & Fri, 9am-midnight Sat, to 10pm Sun; Ⓢ B/D to Grand St, F, J/M/Z to Delancey-Essex Sts) on Allen St makes a mean latte if you need a caffeine pick-me-up.

WARREN EISENBERG/SHUTTERSTOCK ©

TOP EXPERIENCE
ST MARKS PLACE

In New York every street tells a story, from the action unfurling before your eyes to the dense history hidden behind colorful facades. St Marks Place is one of the best strips of pavement for storytelling, as almost every building lining these blocks is rife with tales from a time when the East Village embodied a far more lawless spirit.

Third Ave to Ave A

Easily one of NYC's most famous streets, St Marks Place is also one of the city's smallest, occupying only three blocks between Astor Place and Tompkins Square Park. The road, however, is jam-packed with historical tidbits that would delight any trivia buff. The bar at 2 St Marks Place was once the famous Five-Spot, where jazz fiend Thelonious Monk got his start in the 1950s. Alexander Hamilton's widow Eliza lived in 4 St Marks Place in the 1830s; author James Fenimore Cooper *(Last of the Mohicans)* lived next door in number 6; and Yoko Ono's Fluxus artists descended upon the building in the 1960s. The buildings at 96 and 98 St Marks Place are immortalized on the cover of Led Zeppelin's *Physical Graffiti* album. Though it closed in the 1990s, 122 St Marks Place was the location of a popular cafe called Sin-é, where Jeff Buckley and David Gray often performed.

DON'T MISS

- Spying out the Mosaic Trail
- Tasty brunch at a cafe
- Tompkins Square Park
- Sake bombs at one of the basement Japanese bars
- Shopping for knickknacks and odd souvenirs

PRACTICALITIES

- Map p412, C2
- St Marks Pl, Ave A to Third Ave, East Village
- S 6 to Astor Pl, L to 3rd Ave or 1st Ave, F to 2nd Ave

The Mosaic Trail

As you walk, keep an eye out for the tile-encrusted street poles of the **Mosaic Trail** (Map p412; www.mosaicmannyc.com; St Marks Pl, btwn Astor Pl & Ave A, East Village; S 6 to Astor Pl). In the mid-1980s, a local Vietnam vet named Jim Power began decorating lampposts with bits of tile, mirror, ceramics, beads and coins as a way to deal with his PTSD and imbue the streets with colorful (and often political) art. Many of them portray local East Village landmarks or figures, such as 'CBGB,' (p130) 'Patti Smith' and 'PDT (Please Don't Tell)' (p123).

Astor Place

To the west of St Marks Place is Astor Place (p114), a crowded crisscrossing of streets anchored by a curious square sculpture that's affectionately (and appropriately) known to locals as 'The Cube.' A favorite meeting spot for neighborhood dwellers, this work of art – actually named *Alamo* – weighs over 1800lb and is made entirely of COR-TEN steel.

Originally Astor Place was the home of the Astor Opera House (now gone), which attracted the city's wealthy elite for regular performances in the mid-1800s. The square was also the site of the notorious Astor Place riots, a class struggle pitting immigrants against nativists that broke out between supporters of two rival Shakespearean actors, Edwin Forrest and William Macready. Police fired shots into the crowd, resulting in over two dozen deaths and more than 120 people injured.

Today the square is largely known as the former home of the *Village Voice* and the **Cooper Union** (Foundation Building, Great Hall; Map p412; www.cooper.edu; 7 E 7th St, btwn Third & Fourth Aves, East Village; S 6 to Astor Pl, N/R to 8th St-NYU) design-and-engineering institute.

Tompkins Square Park

St Marks Place terminates at a welcome clearing of green deep in the heart of the East Village. The 10.5-acre Tompkins Square Park (p114) honors Daniel Tompkins, who served as governor of New York from 1807 to 1817 (and as the nation's vice president after that, under James Monroe). Today the popular park is beloved by dog-walking locals, but it wasn't always a place for such clean fun. In the 1980s it was a dirty, needle-strewn, homeless encampment, unusable for folks wanting a place to stroll or picnic. A contentious turning point came when police razed the band shell and evicted more than 100 squatters living in a tent city in the park in 1988 (and again in 1991). That first eviction turned violent; the Tompkins Square Riot, as it came to be known, ushered in the first wave of yuppies in the dog run, fashionistas lolling on the grass and undercover narcotics agents trying to pass as druggie punk kids. These days there's not much drama, outside of the occasional music and arts festival that attempts to briefly reclaim the park's bohemian glory days – such as the **Charlie Parker Jazz Festival** held here every August.

TAKE A BREAK

In addition to all of its quirky and historical landmarks, St Marks has some wonderful places to stop for a bite. Weekend brunches in the East Village are a great bet, as the local restaurants are typically less expensive (and less scene-y) than the hot spots in nearby 'hoods. Try Cafe Mogador (p116), which fuses American favorites with an assortment of Middle Eastern plates.

Mamoun's (p115) falafel is a St Marks favorite and recently expanded to include ample seating.

If you've had enough of the busy streets, head up to 9th and have a beer or glass of wine at Immigrant (p126).

PUNK ROCK SHOPS

The East Village was once the home base for emerging punk-rock acts – many would frequent the clothing shops along St Marks. Although most joints have gone the way of the dodo in favor of more tourist-friendly wares, there are still a few spots that remain. Mainstay Trash & Vaudeville (p130) is still around, though it had to move from St Marks Pl to a few blocks over due to rising rents.

SIGHTS

You'll find a handful of key attractions in these twin neighborhoods, though many visitors come simply to explore the tree-lined blocks, particularly around Tompkins Square Park in the East Village. The Lower East Side has the lion's share of attractions, including the Tenement Museum, a great place to delve into NYC history. On nearby blocks, you'll find a high concentration of art galleries (particularly along Orchard St), as well as the cutting-edge New Museum of Contemporary Art. Other draws include a lavishly restored synagogue, a buzzing food market and the waterfront greenery of the East River Park.

East Village

ST MARKS PLACE — STREET

See p112.

TOMPKINS SQUARE PARK — PARK

Map p412 (www.nycgovparks.org; btwn E 7th & E 10th Sts & Aves A & B, East Village; 6am-midnight; ; S 6 to Astor Pl) This 10.5-acre park dating from 1879 is like a friendly town square for locals, who gather for chess at concrete tables, picnics on the lawn, and spontaneous guitar or drum jams on various grassy knolls. It's also the site of basketball courts, a fun-to-watch dog run (a fenced-in area where humans can unleash their canines), a mini-public swimming pool for kids, frequent summer concerts and an always-lively playground.

ASTOR PLACE — SQUARE

Map p412 (8th St, btwn Third & Fourth Aves, East Village; S N/R to 8th St-NYU, 6 to Astor Pl) Even with the Alamo, an iconic piece of public art more often referred to as 'The Cube,' restored after several years absence, this is not the Astor Place of old. No longer grungy, filled with gutter punks and squatters, this new iteration is also no longer a plaza. It's an orderly block that is situated between Broadway and Lafayette surrounded by sleek, glittery buildings and outfitted with well-designed benches and granite blocks good for people-watching.

Lower East Side

LOWER EAST SIDE TENEMENT MUSEUM — MUSEUM

See p109.

NEW MUSEUM OF CONTEMPORARY ART — MUSEUM

See p110.

MUSEUM AT ELDRIDGE STREET SYNAGOGUE — MUSEUM

Map p414 (212-219-0302; www.eldridgestreet.org; 12 Eldridge St, btwn Canal & Division Sts, Lower East Side; adult/child $14/8, Mon pay what you wish; 10am-5pm Sun-Thu, to 3pm Fri; S F to East Broadway, B/D to Grand St) This landmark house of worship, built in 1887, was a center of Jewish life before suffering a decline in the congregation in the late 1920s. After WWII, the main sanctuary was closed off and services relocated to the basement. The badly deteriorated synagogue was restored following a 20-year-long, $20-million restoration that was completed in 2007, and it now shines with its original splendor – it's a real stunner. Admission includes a **guided tour**, which departs hourly (last one is 4pm).

In addition to the restored portion of the synagogue, there's a hall of exhibits and artifacts about the history of Jewish life on the Lower East Side, as well as special events and seminars. Note that the museum is closed on all major Jewish and national holidays.

ANASTASIA PHOTO — GALLERY

Map p414 (212-677-9725; www.anastasia-photo.com; 143 Ludlow St, btwn Stanton & Rivington Sts, Lower East Side; 10am-6pm Tue-Sat; S F, J/M/Z to Delancey-Essex Sts) This small gallery specializes in documentary photography and photojournalism. Expect evocative, thought-provoking works covering subjects such as poverty in rural America, the ravages of war and disappearing cultures in Africa. Works are beautifully shot, and the staff member on hand can give a meaningful context to the images.

EAST RIVER PARK — PARK

Map p412 (www.nycgovparks.org/parks/east-river-park; FDR Dr & E Houston St, Lower East Side; sunrise-1am; S F to Delancey-Essex Sts)

ALPHABET CITY'S COMMUNITY GARDENS

After a stretch of arboreal abstinence in New York City, the community gardens of Alphabet City are breathtaking. A network of gardens was carved out of abandoned lots to provide the low-income and mainly Hispanic neighborhood (nicknamed 'Loisada,' for the local pronunciation of 'Lower East Side') with communal backyards. Trees and flowers were planted, sandboxes were built, found-art sculptures erected and domino games played – all within green spaces wedged between buildings or even claiming entire blocks. And while some were destroyed – in the face of much protest – to make way for the projects of developers, plenty of green spots have held their ground. You can visit most on weekends from April through October, when the gardens tend to be open to the public; many gardeners are activists within the community and are a good source of information about local politics.

Le Petit Versailles (Map p412; ☑212-529-8815; www.alliedproductions.org; 346 E Houston St, at Ave C, East Village; ☺2-7pm Wed-Sun Apr-Oct; ⑤F, J/M/Z to Delancey-Essex Sts) is a unique marriage of a verdant oasis and an electrifying arts organization, offering a range of quirky performances and screenings to the public. The 6th & B Garden (Map p412; www.6bgarden.org; E 6th St & Ave B, East Village; ☺1-6pm Sat & Sun Apr-Oct; ⑤6 to Astor Pl; L to 1st Ave) is a well-organized space that hosts free music events, workshops and yoga sessions; check the website for details. Three dramatic weeping willows and a koi pond grace the twin plots of La Plaza Cultural (Map p412; www.laplazacultural.com; 674 E 9th St, at Ave C, East Village; ☺10am-7pm Sat & Sun Apr-Oct; ⑤F to 2nd Ave; L to 1st Ave). Also check out the All People's Garden (Map p412; www.grownyc.org; 293 E 3rd St, btwn Aves C & D, East Village; ☺hours vary Apr-Oct; ⑤F to 2nd Ave) and Brisas del Caribe (Map p412; www.lungsnyc.org; 237 E 3rd St, btwn Aves B & C, East Village; ☺9am-3pm Tue-Thu Apr-Oct; ⑤F to 2nd Ave) – and feel free to pop into any open gardens you find while you're walking around the 'hood.

A map of all the area's gardens can be found on the website for Loisada United Neighborhood Gardens (www.lungsnyc.org).

In addition to the great ballparks, running and biking paths, 5000-seat amphitheater that hosts concerts, and expansive patches of green, this park has cool, natural breezes and fine views of the Williamsburg, Manhattan and Brooklyn Bridges.

✗ EATING

Here lies the epitome of what is beautiful in New York's dining scene: mind-blowing variety – which can cover the full spectrum of continents and budgets – in just a single city block. You'll find every type of taste-bud tantalizer from hole-in-the-wall Italian trattorias, Sichuan hot-pot dens, innovative sandwich joints, Ukrainian pierogi palaces, dozens of sushi and ramen spots, pizza parlors and falafel huts. And as gentrification deepens, the variety and quality (and cost) continue to rise.

✗ East Village

MAMOUN'S MIDDLE EASTERN $
Map p412 (☑646-870-5785; www.mamouns.com; 30 St Marks Pl, btwn Second & Third Aves, East Village; sandwiches $5-9, plates $9-13; ☺11am-1am Mon-Thu, to 4am Fri & Sat, to midnight Sun; ☑; ⑤6 to Astor Pl, L to 3rd Ave) This former grab-and-go outpost of the beloved NYC falafel chain has expanded its St Marks storefront with more seating inside and out. Late on weekends a line of inebriated bar-hoppers ends the night with a juicy shawarma covered in Mamoun's famous hot sauce. If you don't do lamb, perhaps a falafel wrap or a sustaining bowl of *fool mudammas* (stewed beans)?

DUN-WELL DOUGHNUTS PASTRIES $
Map p412 (☑646-998-5462; www.dunwelldoughnuts.com; 102 St Marks Pl, btwn First Ave & Ave A, East Village; doughnuts from $2.50; ☺8am-9pm Mon-Thu, to 10pm Fri, 9am-10pm Sat, 9am-9pm Sun; ☑; ⑤6 to Astor Pl) ✿ Brooklyn's finest

artisanal vegan doughnuts have made their way over the East River to this pocket-sized shop on St Marks Pl. Baked daily from organic ingredients, the luscious treats come in flavors both classic (glazed, cinnamon, chocolate) and bespoke (matcha pecan, French toast, peanut butter and strawberry). Wash them down with a fresh-pulled espresso.

CRIF DOGS — HOT DOGS $

Map p412 (☎212-614-2728; www.crifdogs.com; 113 St Marks Pl, btwn Ave A & First Ave, East Village; hot dogs $4.50-6.50; ⏰noon-2am Sun-Thu, to 4am Fri & Sat; Ⓢ L to 1st Ave) Although it often gets overshadowed by the secret bar it houses – PDT (p123), shhh – Crif Dogs is worth visiting in its own right if you're a hot-dog connoisseur. Its basic dog is solid, but it's really about the toppings: everything from onions and relish to jalapeños and bacon can be loaded into your bun.

MIKEY LIKES IT — ICE CREAM $

Map p412 (www.mikeylikesiticecream.com; 199 Ave A, btwn E 12th & E 13th Sts, East Village; scoop $4.50; ⏰noon-midnight Sun-Thu, to 2am Fri & Sat; Ⓢ L to 1st Ave) There's more than meets the eye at this tiny blue-and-white ice-cream shop. The homemade flavors are delicious and come in wild combinations: balsamic macerated strawberries with black pepper or banana ice cream with chocolate-covered peanuts. Founder and owner Mike Cole's inspirational story makes the hip-hop-inspired ice cream all the sweeter.

MUD SPOT — CAFE $

Map p412 (☎212-529-8766; www.onmud.com; 307 E 9th St, btwn Second & First Aves, East Village; mains $7-14; ⏰7:30am-midnight Mon-Fri, from 8am Sat & Sun; Ⓢ L to 3rd Ave; L to 1st Ave; 4/6 to Astor Pl) This 9th St nook is a favorite among East Villagers looking for a quick caffeine fix, a hearty breakfast after a long night out or a friendly place to chat with old friends (there's no wi-fi). The all-day brunch (coffee, craft beer or mimosa and any main course) is a deal at $21.50. Head out back for a surprisingly large garden.

RAI RAI KEN — RAMEN $

Map p412 (☎212-477-7030; www.rairaiken-ny.com; 218 E 10th St, btwn First & Second Aves, East Village; ramen $11-13; ⏰11:30am-10:30pm Sun-Thu, to 11:30pm Fri & Sat; Ⓢ L to 1st Ave; 6 to Astor Pl) Rai Rai Ken's storefront may only be the size of its door, but it's pretty hard to miss since there's usually a small congregation of hungry locals lurking out the front. Inside, low-slung wooden stools are arranged around the noodle bar, where the cooks busily churn out piping-hot portions of tasty pork-infused or chicken-broth ramen (or try the vegetarian option).

★MOMOFUKU NOODLE BAR — NOODLES $$

Map p412 (☎212-777-7773; https://momofukunoodlebar.com; 171 First Ave, btwn E 10th & E 11th Sts, East Village; mains $17-27; ⏰lunch noon-4:30pm Mon-Fri, to 4pm Sat & Sun, dinner 5:30-11pm Sun-Thu, to midnight Fri & Sat; 🌱; Ⓢ L to 1st Ave, 6 to Astor Pl) With just a handful of tables and a no-reservations policy, this bustling phenomenon may require you to wait. But you won't regret it: spicy short-rib ramen; ginger noodles with pickled shiitake; cold noodles with Sichuan sausage and Thai basil – it's all amazing. The ever-changing menu includes buns (perhaps brisket and horseradish), snacks (smoked chicken wings) and desserts. The open kitchen creates quite a bit of steam, but the devoted crowd remains unfazed.

Momofuku is part of David Chang's crazy-popular, now global, restaurant empire (www.momofuku.com). NYC outposts include two-Michelin-starred **Momofuku Ko** (8 Extra Pl, East Village), which serves up pricey tasting menus ($225) and has a prohibitive, we-dare-you-to-try reservations scheme; **Momofuku Ssäm Bar** (207 Second Ave, East Village), which features large and small meat-heavy dishes; chicken joint **Fuku** (four branches in Manhattan); and another Noodle Bar in the shopping center at Columbus Circle.

★VESELKA — UKRAINIAN $$

Map p412 (☎212-228-9682; www.veselka.com; 144 Second Ave, at E 9th St, East Village; mains $13-19; ⏰24hr; Ⓢ 6 to Astor Pl, L to 3rd Ave) This beloved vestige of the area's Ukrainian past has been serving up handmade pierogi (cheese, potato or meat dumplings), borscht and goulash since 1954. The cluttered spread of tables is available to loungers and carb-loaders all night long, though it's a great, warming pit stop any time of day, and a haunt for writers, actors and East Village characters.

CAFE MOGADOR — MOROCCAN $$

Map p412 (☎212-677-2226; www.cafemogador.com; 101 St Marks Pl, btwn First Ave & Ave A, East Village; mains $17-24; ⏰9am-11:30pm Sun-Thu, to

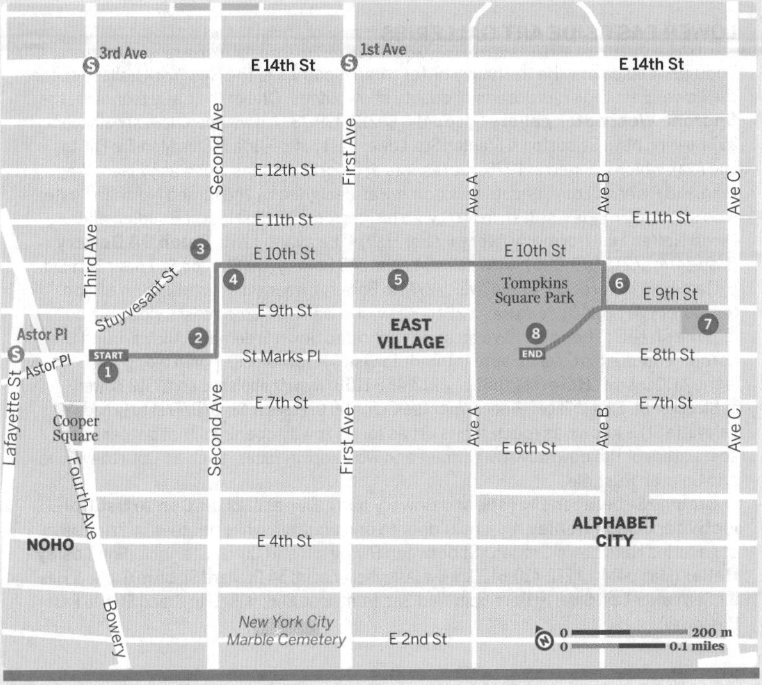

Neighborhood Walk
East Village Cultural Histories

START ST MARKS PL
END TOMPKINS SQUARE PARK
LENGTH 1 MILE; 1¼ HOURS

Historically the East Village has been home to successive waves of immigrant and cultural communities, remnants of which still haunt its streets. Walk down St Marks Pl to follow the 1 **Mosaic Trail** (p112), a series of tile artworks adorning utility poles started by Vietnam-vet Jim Power in the 1980s, when this was the main drag for NYC's vibrant, artistic counterculture.

Continue to Second Ave and turn left to find the terracotta facades of a 2 **public library and a former medical clinic** at Nos 135 and 137 Second Ave; built in 1884, they served the German immigrant community that once lived here. Another block north is 3 **St Mark's Church in-the-Bowery** (www.stmarksbowery.org ⏲10am-6pm Mon-Fri); in 1660 Dutch colonial governor Peter Stuyvesant built his family chapel here (he's buried in the crypt beneath), making this NYC's oldest religious site still in use.

Set into the southeast corner of E 10th St and Second Ave is the 4 **Yiddish Theater Memorial**, with names of actors and playwrights from the Jewish theaters that thrived here pre-WWII. Continue east along 10th St to the 5 **Russian & Turkish Baths** (p128), where locals have been *shvitzing* in the saunas since 1892.

Keep walking east to Ave B and turn right; No 151 was jazz saxophonist 6 **Charlie Parker's house** in the 1950s. Turn left onto E 9th St and continue to Ave C to explore 7 **La Plaza Cultural** (p115), one of the community gardens that dot 'Loisada,' the Hispanic eastern section of this neighborhood.

Finally, head back a block to end up at 8 **Tompkins Square Park** (p114), the green space that 's offered respite to the neighborhood's various demographics over the years: the German, Jewish and other European immigrants of the 1800s and early 1900s; Alphabet City's post-war Puerto Rican populace; the revolutionaries, and artists of the mid-20th century and today's young professionals and middle-class families.

LOWER EAST SIDE ART GALLERIES

Though Chelsea may be the heavy hitter when it comes to the New York gallery scene, the Lower East Side has dozens of quality showplaces. One of the early pioneers, the **Sperone Westwater gallery** (Map p414; ☑212-999-7337; www.speronewestwater.com; 257 Bowery, btwn E Houston & Stanton Sts, Lower East Side; ⊙10am-6pm Mon-Fri; ⑤F to 2nd Ave), which opened in 1975, represents art-world darlings, such as William Wegman and Richard Long, and its new home was designed by the famed Norman Foster, who's already made a splash in NYC with his designs for the Hearst Building and David Geffen Hall (formerly Avery Fisher Hall). The avant-garde **Salon 94 Bowery** (Map p414; ☑212-979-0001; www.salon94.com; 243 Bowery, cnr Stanton St, Lower East Side; ⊙11am-6pm Mon-Fri; ⑤F to 2nd Ave; J/Z/M to Bowery), near the New Museum of Contemporary Art (p110), features a 20ft LCD video wall that broadcasts video art out into the street. (They also have an annex secreted down Freemans Alley around the corner; enquire to make an appointment to visit.) A few blocks north along the Bowery is the 4000-sq-ft **Hole** (Map p412; ☑212-466-1100; www.theholenyc.com; 312 Bowery, at Bleecker St, East Village; ⊙noon-7pm Tue-Sun; ⑤6 to Bleeker St; B/D/F/M to Broadway-Lafayette St) – known as much for its art as for its rowdy openings that gather both scenesters of the downtown art circuit and well-known faces, such as Courtney Love and Salman Rushdie.

Broome St between Chrystie and Bowery has galleries such as **Con Artist Collective** and **Jack Hanley** right next door to one another, while another buzzing strip of galleries runs down Orchard St between Rivington and Canal Sts, including **Lesley Heller** (Map p414; ☑212-410-6120; www.lesleyheller.com; 54 Orchard St, btwn Grand & Hester Sts, Lower East Side; ⊙11am-6pm Wed-Sat, from noon Sun; ⑤B/D to Grand St; F to East Broadway).

midnight Fri & Sat; ⑤6 to Astor Pl) Mogador is a long-running East Village classic, serving fluffy piles of couscous, chargrilled lamb and *merguez* (a spicy lamb or beef sausage) with basmati rice and Arabic salad, as well as satisfying platters of hummus with chickpeas, tomato and parsley. The standouts, however, are the tagines – fragrantly spiced, claypot-simmered chicken or lamb dishes in four different sauces.

A garrulous young crowd packs the space, spilling out onto the small cafe tables on warm days. Brunch (served weekends from 9am to 4pm) is excellent. Family-owned since 1983, Mogador is now also in Williamsburg (133 Wythe Ave).

ESPERANTO LATIN AMERICAN **$$**

Map p412 (☑212-505-6559; www.esperantony. com; 145 Ave C, at E 9th St, East Village; mains $17-27; ⊙4-11pm Mon-Thu, to 2am Fri, 10am-2am Sat, 10am-11pm Sun; ⑤L to 1st Ave) A Brazilian-focused Latin fusion restaurant, Esperanto's vibrant green facade and large patio recall the gritty glory days of Alphabet City, before the trend toward gray-and-glass condos and sleek cocktail bars. Here you can sit outside all night sipping caipirinhas or enjoying a trio of ceviches (shrimp, salmon

and snapper) or strips of rare steak with chimichurri sauce.

UPSTATE SEAFOOD **$$**

Map p412 (☑646-791-5400; www.upstatenyc. com; 95 First Ave, at E 6th St, East Village; mains $16-20; ⊙5-10:30pm Sun-Wed, to 11pm Thu-Sat; ⑤F to 2nd Ave) Upstate keeps it simple: serving outstanding seafood dishes and craft beers. The small, always-changing menu features the likes of beer-steamed mussels, seafood stew, scallops over mushroom risotto, *uni* (urchin roe) and wondrous oyster selections. There's no freezer – seafood comes from the market daily, so you know you'll be getting only the freshest. Lines can be long, so go early.

LUZZO'S PIZZA **$$**

Map p412 (☑212-473-7447; www.luzzosgroup. com/luzzos-group-restaurants/luzzos; 211 First Ave, btwn E 12th & 13th Sts, East Village; pizzas $18-20; ⊙noon-11pm; ⑤L to 1st Ave) Fan-favorite Luzzo's occupies a thin, rustically designed sliver of real estate in the East Village, which is stuffed to the gills each evening as discerning diners feast on thin-crust pizzas, kissed with ripe tomatoes and cooked in a coal-fired stove. Cash only.

PRUNE AMERICAN $$

Map p412 (212-677-6221; www.prunerestaurant.com; 54 E 1st St, btwn First & Second Aves, East Village; dinner $19-28, brunch $15-19; noon-11pm Mon-Fri, 10am-3:30pm & 5:30-11pm Sat & Sun; S F to 2nd Ave) Expect lines around the block on the weekend, when the hungover show up to cure their ills with Prune's brunches and excellent Bloody Marys (in a dozen varieties). The small room is always busy as diners pour in for grilled trout with mint-and-almond salsa, seared duck breast and rich sweetbreads.

IPPUDO NY NOODLES $$

Map p412 (212-388-0088; www.ippudo.com/ny; 65 Fourth Ave, btwn 9th & 10th Sts, East Village; ramen $16-17; 11am-3:30pm & 5-11pm Mon-Thu, 11am-11pm Fri & Sat, to 10:30pm Sun; S R/W to 8th St-NYU; 4/5/6, N/Q/R/W, L to 14th St-Union Sq; 6 to Astor Pl) The good folks from Ippudo have kicked things up a notch here – they've taken their mouthwatering ramen recipe (truly, it's delicious) and spiced it up with sleek surrounds (hello shiny black surfaces and streamers of cherry red) and blasts of rock and roll on the overhead speakers.

WESTVILLE EAST AMERICAN $$

Map p412 (212-677-2033; http://westvillenyc.com; 173 Ave A, at E 11th St, East Village; mains $13-26; 10am-11pm Mon-Sat, to 10pm Sun; S L to 1st Ave; 6 to Astor Pl) Market-fresh veggies and mouthwatering mains are the name of the game at Westville, and it doesn't hurt that the cottage-chic surrounds are undeniably charming. It's a favorite among New Yorkers at lunchtime when they take a break from their jobs to scarf down kale salads or hot dogs.

KANOYAMA SUSHI $$

Map p412 (646-532-3083; www.kanoyama.com; 175 Second Ave, near E 11th St, East Village; rolls $4-20, mains $22-30; 5:30-11pm Sun-Thu, to midnight Fri & Sat; ; S L to 3rd Ave; L, N/Q/R/W, 4/5/6 to 14th St-Union Sq) Providing no-fuss sushi with fresh daily specials in the heart of the East Village, Kanoyama is a local favorite that has so far been overlooked by the city's big-name food critics (that might explain its unpretentious air). You can order sushi à la carte or in rolls, or choose from the many tempura plates.

LAVAGNA ITALIAN $$

Map p412 (212-979-1005; www.lavagnanyc.com; 545 E 5th St, btwn Aves A & B, East Village; mains $16-35; 6-11pm Mon-Thu, 5:30pm-midnight Fri, noon-3:30pm & 5pm-midnight Sat, noon-3:30pm & 5-11pm Sun; ; S F to 2nd Ave) Dark wood, flickering candles and a fiery glow from a somewhat-open kitchen help make homey Lavagna a late-night hideaway for lovers. But it's laid-back enough to make it appropriate for children, at least in the early hours before the smallish space fills up. Delicious pastas, thin-crust pizzas and hearty mains, such as baby rack of lamb, are standard fare.

HEARTH ITALIAN $$$

Map p412 (646-602-1300; www.restauranthearth.com; 403 E 12th St, at First Ave, East Village; dishes $16-26, tasting menu per person $74; 6-10pm Mon-Thu, to 11pm Fr & Sat, 10am-3pm & 6-10pm Sun; S L to 1st Ave; L, N/Q/R/W, 4/5/6 to 14th St-Union Sq) A staple for finicky, deep-pocketed diners, Hearth boasts a warm, brick-walled interior. The menu changes seasonally, but you can usually count on roasted meats and fish and well-seasoned sautéed veggies with a few standbys, such as liver pâté or sage-butter gnocchi.

Lower East Side

★**ESSEX MARKET** FOOD HALL $

Map p414 (www.essexmarket.nyc; 115 Delancey St, at Essex St, Lower East Side; 8am-8pm Mon-Sat, 10am-8pm Sun; ; S F, J/M/Z to Delancey-Essex Sts) Founded in 1940 in a cramped building across Delancey St, in 2019 this wide-ranging specialty food-and-dining market moved into expansive new digs. Browse fresh seafood, meats and artisanal cheeses before taking lunch upstairs to sunny, open-atrium seating. Vendors offer Scandinavian smoked fish, traditional Dominican food, Japanese bentos, Thai chicken, massive sandwiches, gourmet ice cream and much more.

KOSSAR'S BAGELS & BIALYS JEWISH $

Map p414 (212-473-4810; www.kossars.com; 367 Grand St, Lower East Side; baked goods from $1.15; 6am-6pm; S F/M, J/Z to Delancey-Essex Sts) Since 1936 Kossar's has been serving up Jewish baked goods like bagels, chocolate and cinnamon babka (a bread-like cake) and bialys. What's a bialy, you ask? Originating from Bialystok, Poland, it's a slightly flattened bread roll with a middle indent filled with roast onions or garlic – and it's

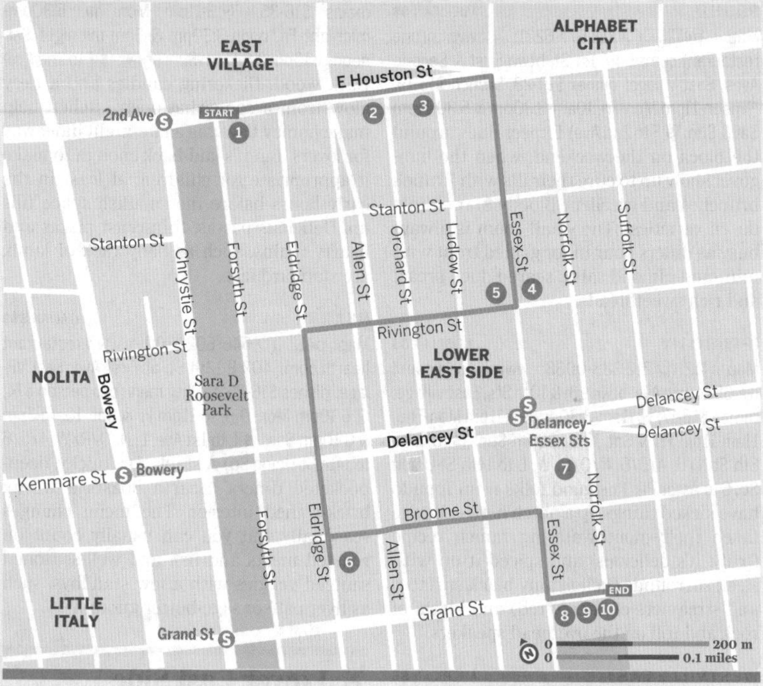

Neighborhood Walk
A Lower East Side Nosh

START YONAH SCHIMMEL KNISH BAKERY
END DOUGHNUT PLANT
LENGTH 1.1 MILES; 2½ HOURS

For generations the Lower East Side was home to successive waves of international immigrants. This walk will have you eating your way through some of NYC's most enduring culinary cultures.

Start on E Houston St with a fluffy potato knish from 1 **Yonah Schimmel** (founded 1910), and a classic NYC soda (an egg cream or a lime rickey). Farther east is delicatessen 2 **Russ & Daughters** (p130), where you can pick up some lox (smoked salmon) and cream cheese for tomorrow's breakfast. A block further is 3 **Katz's Delicatessen** (p122), where hot-pastrami sandwiches tower over the plate.

Head south on Essex, then turn left onto Rivington, where newcomer 4 **Supermoon Bakehouse** churns out flaky stuffed croissants with both sweet and savory fillings (get one of each!). Cross back over Essex to 5 **Economy Candy** (p131), stuffed with every sugary treat from your childhood (and many you've never heard of).

Continue west and turn left onto Eldridge St, walking another two blocks to devour fresh, handmade Chinese dumplings at 6 **Vanessa's Dumpling House**. Head to Broome St, turn right and continue four blocks to the brand-new home of local institution 7 **Essex Market** (p119), an expansive food hall with artisanal deli counters, gourmet grocers and an international array of kiosks serving everything from Dominican empanadas to Korean fried chicken.

Head to the corner of Essex and Grand to browse through barrels of pickled veg at local brinemeisters, the 8 **Pickle Guys** (p131). A few shops down, step into 9 **Kossar's** (p119) for some fresh bagels and bialys (and maybe a babka?) to take home for later. You gotta finish up with dessert, right? Three doors down, 10 **Doughnut Plant** has elevated the humble doughnut to high art with inventive ingredients like Valrhona chocolate and rosewater glaze.

delicious! Newer filling styles include olives and sun-dried tomatoes and pesto.

SUPERMOON BAKEHOUSE BAKERY $

Map p414 (www.supermoonbakehouse.com; 120 Rivington St, at Essex St, Lower East Side; pastries $4-9.5; ⏲8am-10pm Mon-Thu, to 11am Fri, 9am-11pm Sat, to 10pm Sun; Ⓢ F to Delancey St) This superfriendly Aussie-owned bakery, where the bakers can be seen doing their thing behind glass, produces perhaps Manhattan's most imaginative and remarkable baked croissants, both sweet and savory, from the hot apple pie or matcha-blueberry to the ham-and-cheese or the Reuben. Varying flavors of soft-serve ice cream and doughnuts round out the offerings.

YONAH SCHIMMEL KNISH BAKERY JEWISH $

Map p414 (☎212-477-2858; www.knishery.com; 137 E Houston St, at Forsyth St, Lower East Side; knishes $4-5; ⏲10am-7pm Mon-Sun; 🌱; Ⓢ F to Second Ave) Step back in time at this bakery-cafe that's been selling old-fashioned Jewish knishes – a pocket of baked dough filled with mashed potatoes, buckwheat, cabbage, spinach, blueberries and sweet cheese or other fillings – since 1910. Other classic dishes (potato pancakes, apple strudel) are available, as are egg cream and lime rickey sodas.

AN CHOI VIETNAMESE $

Map p414 (☎212-226-3700; http://anchoinyc.com; 85 Orchard St, btwn Broome & Grand Sts, Lower East Side; banh mi $11-15, mains $13-18; ⏲6pm-10:30pm Mon, from noon Tue-Thu, noon-11pm Fri & Sat, noon-10pm Sun; Ⓢ B/D to Grand St, F, J/M/Z to Delancey-Essex Sts) With faded communist party posters on the wall and a bar that looks like it was lifted out of the '70s, An Choi has cultivated a throwback style that denizens of the East Village love. It doesn't hurt that the food, simple Vietnamese dishes like pho (noodle soup) and banh mi (baguette) sandwiches, is tasty and not too expensive given the hipster credentials.

CHEEKY SANDWICHES SANDWICHES $

Map p414 (☎646-504-8132; www.cheekysandwiches.com; 35 Orchard St, btwn Hester & Canal Sts, Lower East Side; sandwiches $4.50-12; ⏲7am-10pm Sun-Thu, to midnight Fri & Sat; Ⓢ F to East Broadway) This ramshackle little eatery looks like it has been airlifted in from Cajun Country. The biscuit sandwiches are outstanding – try one topped with fried chicken, coleslaw and gravy. Add chicory coffee and bread pudding and you have a great, cheap meal.

DOUGHNUT PLANT PASTRIES $

Map p414 (☎212-505-3700; www.doughnutplant.com; 379 Grand St, at Norfolk St, Lower East Side; doughnuts $3-4; ⏲6:30am-8pm Sun-Thu, to 9pm Fri & Sat; Ⓢ F, J/M/Z to Delancey-Essex Sts) A New York legend, Doughnut Plant whips up sweet decadence in inventive flavors (pistachio, *tres leches,* cashew and orange blossom) made from all-natural ingredients. There are four other branches in town, including a handy location in Chelsea at 220 W 23rd St.

VANESSA'S DUMPLING HOUSE CHINESE $

Map p414 (☎212-625-8008; www.vanessas.com; 118a Eldridge St, btwn Grand & Broome Sts, Lower East Side; dumplings $2-8; ⏲9am-10:30pm; Ⓢ B/D to Grand St; J to Bowery; F to Delancey St) Tasty dumplings – filled with pork and chives, chicken and basil, shrimp, or just veggies – are whipped together in iron skillets at light speed and tossed into hungry mouths at unbeatable prices. Try them steamed, fried or in a bowl of steaming noodle soup.

★IVAN RAMEN RAMEN $$

Map p414 (☎646-678-3859; www.ivanramen.com; 25 Clinton St, btwn Stanton & E Houston Sts, Lower East Side; mains $15-21; ⏲12:30-10pm Sun-Thu, to 11pm Fri & Sat; Ⓢ F, J/M/Z to Delancey-Essex Sts, F to 2nd Ave) After creating two thriving ramen spots in Tokyo, Long Islander Ivan Orkin brought his talents back home. Few can agree about NYC's best ramen, but this intimate shop, where solo ramen heads sit at the bar watching their bowls take shape, is on every short list. The *tsukumen* (dipping-style) ramen with pickled collard greens and shoyu-glazed pork belly is unbeatable.

RUSS & DAUGHTERS CAFE JEWISH $$

Map p414 (☎212-475-4880; www.russanddaughterscafe.com; 127 Orchard St, btwn Delancey & Rivington Sts, Lower East Side; mains $18-23; ⏲9am-10pm Mon-Fri, from 8am Sat & Sun; Ⓢ F, J/M/Z to Delancey-Essex Sts) Sit down and feast on shiny boiled bagels and perhaps the best lox (smoked salmon) in the city in all the comfort of an old-school diner, in this extension of the storied Jewish delicatessen Russ & Daughters (p130), just up Orchard St. Aside from thick, smoky fish, there are potato latkes, borscht, eggs plenty of ways, and even chopped liver, if you must.

CASA MEZCAL MEXICAN $$

Map p414 (212-777-2600; www.casamezcalny.com; 86 Orchard St, btwn Broome & Grand Sts, Lower East Side; mains $17-34; 11:30am-11pm Sun-Thu, to midnight Fri & Sat; ; F, J/M/Z to Delancey-Essex Sts, B/D to Grand St) This festive space celebrates the rich culinary traditions of Mexico – and Oaxaca in particular. The high-ceilinged room is decorated with colorful paper streamers, masks, Day-of-the-Dead skulls, fetishes and even a stuffed turkey. Try regionally inflected dishes like the red snapper served with sweet potato puree and *xcatic* peppers and a tamarind margarita and you'll leave happy.

CLINTON STREET BAKING COMPANY AMERICAN $$

Map p414 (646-602-6263; www.clintonstreetbaking.com; 4 Clinton St, btwn Stanton & E Houston Sts, Lower East Side; mains $12-18; 8am-3:30pm & 5:30-10pm Mon-Fri, 9am-4:30pm Sat & Sun; F, J/M/Z to Delancey-Essex Sts, F to 2nd Ave) Mom-and-pop shop extraordinaire Clinton Street Baking Company takes the cake in so many categories – best pancakes, best muffins, best po'boys (Southern-style sandwiches), best biscuits etc – that you're pretty much guaranteed a stellar meal no matter what time you stop by. In the evening you can opt for 'breakfast for dinner' (pancakes, eggs Benedict), fish tacos or buttermilk fried chicken.

Weekend brunch can see hordes of locals lining up for an hour or more, so do your brunching during the week.

KUMA INN ASIAN $$

Map p414 (212-353-8866; www.kumainn.com; 113 Ludlow St, btwn Delancey & Rivington Sts, Lower East Side; small plates $9-20; 6-10pm Sun-Thu, to 11pm Fri & Sat; F, J/M/Z to Delancey-Essex Sts) Reservations are a must at this popular eating spot in a secretive 2nd-floor location (look for a small red door with 'Kuma Inn' painted on the concrete side). The Filipino- and Thai-inspired tapas runs the gamut from vegetarian summer rolls (with peanut plum sauce) to spicy drunken shrimp and deep-fried pork belly.

KATZ'S DELICATESSEN DELI $$

Map p414 (212-254-2246; www.katzsdelicatessen.com; 205 E Houston St, at Ludlow St, Lower East Side; sandwiches $12-23.50; 8am-10:45pm Mon-Wed, to 2:45am Thu, from 8am Fri, 24hr Sat, to 10:45pm Sun; F to 2nd Ave) Though visitors won't find many remnants of the classic, old-world Jewish Lower East Side dining scene, there are a few stellar holdouts, among them Katz's Delicatessen, where Meg Ryan faked her famous orgasm in the 1989 movie *When Harry Met Sally*. If you love classic deli grub like pastrami and salami on rye, it just might have the same effect on you.

These days the lines to get in are breathtakingly long, and the prices are high (Katz's signature hot pastrami sandwich costs a hefty $22.45). However, most sandwiches can very easily feed two people. Go very early or late to avoid the worst of the crowds.

FAT RADISH BRITISH $$$

Map p414 (212-300-4053; www.thefatradishnyc.com; 17 Orchard St, btwn Hester & Canal Sts, Lower East Side; mains $20-32; 5:30-10pm Sun-Tue, to 11pm Wed-Sat, also 11am-3:30pm Sat & Sun; F to East Broadway; B/D to Grand St) The young and fashionable pack into this dimly lit dining room with industrial touches. There's a loud buzz and people checking each other out, but the mains – typical of the local, seasonal, haute-pub-food fad – are worth your attention. Start with big briny oysters before moving on to heritage pork chops with glazed squash or crispy trout with cider-mustard wild greens.

FREEMANS AMERICAN $$$

Map p414 (212-420-0012; www.freemansrestaurant.com; Freeman Alley, off Rivington St, Lower East Side; mains lunch $16-34, dinner $27-38; 11am-11pm Mon-Thu, to 1am Fri, 10am-1am Sat, 10am-11pm Sun; F to 2nd Ave) Tucked at the end of Freeman Alley, this charmingly located and somewhat labyrinthine place draws a mostly hipster crowd who gather around the wooden tables to sip overflowing cocktails and nibble on dishes like roast chicken or slow-poached halibut. Potted plants and taxidermied antlers lend an endearing rustic-cabin vibe – a charming escape from the bustle (when it isn't crowded inside).

DRINKING & NIGHTLIFE

While not quite the '70s scene of CBGB and New York punk, the Lower East Side still clings to significant cachet as one of the coolest 'hoods in Manhattan. While some bars are favored by the 'bridge and tunnel' gang (partiers from the 'burbs), locals continue to establish and uncover new-minted clubs staging Manhattan's next indie-rock kings. In the East Village, the further east you go, the looser things get. You'll find dirty dive bars stuffed to the gills with students, and secret swanky lounges tucked behind the Japanese restaurant right next door. Things are positively packed come the weekend.

East Village

RUE B BAR

Map p412 (☎212-358-1700; www.rueb-nyc.com; 188 Ave B, btwn E 11th & E 12th Sts, East Village; ⏲6pm-4am; SL to 1st Ave) There's live jazz (and the odd rockabilly group) nightly from 9pm to midnight ($10 cover) at this tiny, amber-lit drinking den on a bar-dappled stretch of Ave B. A celebratory crowd packs the small space – so mind the tight corners, lest the trombonist end up in your lap.

BERLIN CLUB

Map p412 (☎reservations 347-586-7247; www.berlinundera.com; 25 Ave A, btwn E 1st & E 2nd Sts, East Village; occasional cover $5; ⏲8pm-2am Sun-Thu, to 4am Fri & Sat; SF to 2nd Ave) This brick-vaulted cavern beneath Ave A does its best to hide – access is through an unmarked door around the corner on the side of bar that seems to occupy Berlin's address, then steep stairs lead down into a dim, riotous indie lair. Once you're in, enjoy a night of rock, funk, disco, house and other party tunes in close proximity with your fellow revelers.

WAYLAND BAR

Map p412 (☎212-777-7022; www.thewaylandnyc.com; 700 E 9th St, cnr Ave C, East Village; ⏲4pm-4am Mon-Fri, 11am-4am Sat & Sun; SL to 1st Ave) Whitewashed walls, weathered floorboards and salvaged lamps give this urban outpost a Mississippi flair, which goes well with the live music (bluegrass, jazz, folk) featured Sunday to Wednesday nights. The drinks, though, are the real draw – try the 'I Hear Banjos-Encore,' made of apple-pie moonshine, rye whiskey and applewood smoke, which tastes like a campfire (but slightly less burning).

POURING RIBBONS COCKTAIL BAR

Map p412 (☎917-656-6788; www.pouringribbons.com; 225 Ave B, 2nd fl, btwn E 13th & 14th Sts, East Village; ⏲6pm-2am; SL to 1st Ave) Finding such a well-groomed and classy spot up a flight of stairs in Alphabet City is as refreshing as their drinks. Gimmicks and pretension are kept low; the flavors are exceptional. The encyclopedic cocktail menu could sate any appetite. Also, check out what could possibly be the largest collection of Chartreuse in NYC.

PDT BAR

Map p412 (☎212-614-0386; www.pdtnyc.com; 113 St Marks Pl, btwn Ave A & First Ave, East Village; ⏲6pm-2am Sun-Thu, to 4am Fri & Sat; S6 to Astor Pl, L to 1st Ave) PDT ('Please Don't Tell') scores high on novelty. Pick up the receiver in the phone booth at the hot-dog shop Crif Dogs (p116); once you're given the OK (reservations are recommended to avoid being turned away), the wall swings open and you step into an intimate, low-lit bar with the odd animal head on the wall and first-rate cocktails.

ANGEL'S SHARE BAR

Map p412 (☎212-777-5415; 6 Stuyvesant St, 2nd fl, near Third Ave & E 9th St, East Village; ⏲6pm-1:30am Sun-Wed, to 2am Thu, to 2:30am Fri & Sat; S6 to Astor Pl) Show up early and snag a seat at this hidden gem, behind a Japanese restaurant on the same floor. It's quiet and elegant, with seriously talented mixologists serving up creative cocktails, plus a top-flight collection of whiskeys. You can't stay if you don't have a table or a seat at the bar, and they tend to go fast.

OTTO'S SHRUNKEN HEAD BAR

Map p412 (☎212-228-2240; www.ottosshrunkenhead.com; 538 E 14th St, near Ave B, East Village; ⏲2pm-4am; SL to 1st Ave) Sling yourself into one of the curved vinyl booths at this rockabilly tiki bar with a Mai Tai or Zombie served up in a classic tiki mug (yours to keep for an extra $6). The back room hosts nightly live music, comedy, drag shows and the like, while DJs spin up front, and there's never a cover.

NIELSKLIIM/SHUTTERSTOCK ©

1. Tompkins Square Park (p114)
Dog-walking locals love this green space at the end of St Marks Place.

2. Eldridge Street Synagogue (p114)
A beautiful restoration allows the public to appreciate the splendour of this historic center of Jewish life.

3. Katz's Delicatessen (p122)
Loosen your belt after indulging in Katz's signature hot pastrami sandwich.

4. Lower East Side Tenement Museum (p109)
Learn about the hardships endured by immigrants living in 19th-century New York City.

3
KATZ'S
KATZ'S DELICATESSEN
Ludlow St

PHOENIX GAY & LESBIAN

Map p412 (☎212-477-9979; www.phoenixbarnyc.com; 447 E 13th St, btwn First Ave & Ave A, East Village; ⏲2pm-4am; ⓈL to 1st Ave) Literally risen from the ashes of its predecessor, The Bar (which burned down), The Phoenix is less 'divey' than it once was, but it's just as friendly. There's also happy hour from 2pm to 8pm, a pool table, karaoke and trivia nights.

PROLETARIAT BAR

Map p412 (www.proletariatny.com; 102 St Marks Pl, btwn Ave A & First Ave, East Village; ⏲5pm-2am Mon-Thu, from 2pm Fri & Sat, 2pm-midnight Sun; ⓈL to 1st Ave) The cognoscenti of NYC's beer world pack this tiny shop-front bar just west of Tompkins Square Park. Promising 'rare, new and unusual beers,' Proletariat delivers the goods with a changing lineup of brews you won't find elsewhere. Recent hits have included Brooklyn and New Jersey drafts from artisanal brewers.

IMMIGRANT BAR

Map p412 (☎646-308-1724; www.theimmigrantnyc.com; 341 E 9th St, btwn First & Second Aves, East Village; ⏲5pm-1am Mon-Fri, to 2am Sat & Sun; ⓈL to 1st Ave, 6 to Astor Pl) Combining wine bar and taproom within the intimate geometry of a 19th-century tenement building, this timber-floored little charmer has all the makings of a classic neighborhood local. The staff are knowledgeable and kind, mingling with faithful regulars while dishing out tangy olives and topping up glasses with imported snifters.

DEATH & CO COCKTAIL BAR

Map p412 (☎212-388-0882; www.deathandcompany.com; 433 E 6th St, btwn First Ave & Ave A, East Village; ⏲6pm-2am Sun-Thu, to 3am Fri & Sat; ⓈF to 2nd Ave, L to 1st Ave) Despite the morbid name, this award-winning cocktail bar is full of life. Relax in the dim, stylish interior and let the skilled bartenders shake, rattle and roll some of the most perfect cocktails in town (classics and new creations from $17) . It's usually packed – if there's no room they'll take your number and call once there is.

ABRAÇO CAFE

Map p412 (www.abraconyc.com; 81 E 7th St, btwn First & Second Aves, East Village; ⏲8am-10pm Tue-Sat, 9am-6pm Sun; ⓈF to 2nd Ave; L to 1st Ave; 6 to Astor Pl) Abraço is an East Village refuge in an open, ground-level space that serves up perfectly prepared espressos and lattes alongside housemade sweets. Find a table and sip your nicely balanced cappuccino while inhaling a slice of their dangerously addictive olive-oil cake.

AMOR Y AMARGO BAR

Map p412 (☎212-614-6818; www.amoryamargony.com; 443 E 6th St, btwn Ave A & First Ave, East Village; ⏲5pm-1am Sun-Thu, to 3am Fri & Sat; ⓈF to 2nd Ave; L to 1st Ave; 6 to Astor Pl) 'Love and Bitters' is a tiny but powerful specialist in crafty cocktails, showcasing its namesake selection of bitters. Ask the knowledgeable barkeeps for their advice on flavors. You won't be disappointed.

NOWHERE GAY

Map p412 (☎212-477-4744; www.nowherebarnyc.com; 322 E 14th St, btwn First & Second Aves, East Village; ⏲3pm-4am; ⓈL to 1st Ave) Dimly lit yet exuberantly welcoming, Nowhere is everything a local gay dive bar should be. There's a pool table, the drinks are strong and cheap, and a late-night **pizza joint** (Map p412; ☎212-228-2004; www.artichokepizza.com; 321 E 14th St; slices $5-6; ⏲11am-5am) across the street keeps crowds going till the wee hours. Themed events include bear-and-beard-focused night on Tuesdays and 'Fire in the Hole,' a monthly party for 'gingers and their admirers.'

COCK GAY

Map p412 (93 Second Ave, btwn E 5th & E 6th Sts, East Village; ⏲9pm-4am Mon & Tue, from 6pm Wed-Sun; ⓈF/M to 2nd Ave) A dark, dirty spot that's proud of its sleazy-chic reputation, this is the place to join lanky hipster boys and rage until you're kicked out at 4am. Varying theme nights present popular parties with live performers, DJs, drag-queen hostesses, nearly naked go-go boys and porn videos on constant loop. It's wild, friendly and cash only.

MCSORLEY'S OLD ALE HOUSE BAR

Map p412 (☎212-473-9148; www.mcsorleysoldalehouse.nyc; 15 E 7th St, btwn Second & Third Aves, East Village; ⏲11am-1am Mon-Sat, 1pm-1am Sun; Ⓢ6 to Astor Pl) Around since 1854 (it's thought to be New York's oldest continually operating bar), McSorley's feels far from the East Village veneer of cool. You're more likely to drink with frat boys, tourists and the odd fireman here. Still, it's hard to beat the cobwebs, sawdust floors and old-time New York bonhomie.

Lower East Side

FLOWER SHOP BAR

Map p414 (☎212-257-4072; www.theflowershopnyc.com; 107 Eldridge St, btwn Grand & Broome Sts, Lower East Side; ⏰5pm-midnight Sun & Mon, to 2am Tue-Sat; Ⓢ B/D to Grand St, J/Z to Bowery) Take the stairs under the humming restaurant of the same name to discover an eclectically furnished basement bar of such meticulously retro sensibility that you'll feel you've stumbled into a mash-up of your dad's pool room and your grandparents' 'best' room. The randomly assembled photos and posters often raise a smile, while flowery banquettes and good cocktails encourage lingering.

BAR GOTO COCKTAIL BAR

Map p414 (☎212-475-4411; www.bargoto.com; 245 Eldridge St, btwn E Houston & Stanton Sts, Lower East Side; ⏰5pm-midnight Tue-Thu & Sun, to 2am Fri & Sat; Ⓢ F to 2nd Ave) Maverick mixologist Kenta Goto has cocktail connoisseurs spellbound at his eponymous, intimate hot spot. Expect meticulous, elegant drinks that draw on Goto's Japanese heritage (the Umami Mary, with vodka, shiitake, dashi, miso, lemon, tomato and Clamato, is inspired), paired with authentic Japanese comfort bites, such as *okonomiyaki* (savory cabbage pancakes).

SEL RROSE COCKTAIL BAR

Map p414 (☎212-226-2510; www.selrrose.com; 1 Delancey St, btwn Bowery & Chrystie St, Lower East Side; ⏰4pm-3am Mon-Thu, to 4am Fri, 1pm-4am Sat, 1pm-2am Sun; Ⓢ B/D to Grand St, F to Delancey St) You're likely to see quite a few people on dates at this downtown spot, which serves up clever cocktails and a wide selection of oyster small plates and manages to exude quiet style despite its prominent corner location.

It also happens to be right across the street from the Bowery Ballroom (p129), making it perfect for a pre- or post-concert tipple.

TEN BELLS BAR

Map p414 (☎212-228-4450; www.tenbellsnyc.com; 247 Broome St, btwn Ludlow & Orchard Sts, Lower East Side; ⏰5pm-2am Mon-Fri, from 3pm Sat & Sun; Ⓢ F, J/M/Z to Delancey-Essex Sts) This charmingly tucked-away tapas bar has a grotto-like design, with flickering candles, dark tin ceilings, brick walls and a U-shaped bar that's an ideal setting for a conversation with a new friend.

The chalkboard menu hangs on both walls and features excellent wines by the glass, which go nicely with *boquerones* (marinated anchovies), *txipirones en su tinta* (squid in ink sauce) and regional cheeses. Come for happy hour when oysters are $1 each and a carafe of wine costs $15. The unsigned entrance is easy to miss; it's right next to the shop Top Hat.

ANOTHER SIDE OF GAY NYC

If Chelsea is a muscly, overachieving jock, then the Lower East Side is his wayward, punk, younger brother. Amid the frat dives and cocktail lounges you'll find many gay bars catering to guys who prefer flannels and scruff to tank tops and six-pack abs. Nowhere and Phoenix are great places to meet some new friendly faces, while the Cock caters to a friskier crowd. The drinks are also typically much cheaper.

ATTABOY COCKTAIL BAR

Map p414 (www.attaboy.us; 134 Eldridge St, btwn Delancey & Broome Sts, Lower East Side; ⏰6pm-4am; Ⓢ B/D to Grand St) One of those no-door-sign, speakeasy-vibe bars that are two-a-penny these days, this one is a notch above, serving knockout artisanal cocktails that will set you back $17 each. There is no menu, so let the expert bartenders guide you.

BEAUTY & ESSEX BAR

Map p414 (☎212-614-0146; www.beautyandessex.com; 146 Essex St, btwn Stanton & Rivington Sts, Lower East Side; ⏰5:30-11pm Mon & Tue, to midnight Wed & Thu, to 1am Fri, 11:30am-3pm & 5pm-1am Sat, 11:30am-11pm Sun; Ⓢ F, J/M/Z to Delancey-Essex Sts) Venture behind a tawdry pawn-shop front for a world of glamour. Beyond lies 10,000 sq ft of sleek restaurant-lounge space, complete with leather sofas and banquettes, dramatic amber-tinged lighting and a curved staircase that leads to yet another lounge-and-bar area. The exuberance, high prices and pretentious crowd give the place a Gatsby-esque vibe.

BARRIO CHINO COCKTAIL BAR

Map p414 (☎212-228-6710; www.barriochinony.com; 253 Broome St, btwn Ludlow & Orchard

LOCAL KNOWLEDGE

THE EAST VILLAGE'S RUSSIAN & TURKISH BATHS

Since 1892 this cramped, grungy downtown **spa** (Map p412; 212-674-9250; www.russianturkishbaths.com; 268 E 10th St, btwn First Ave & Ave A, East Village; full-day visit $52; noon-10pm Mon, Tue, Thu & Fri, from 10am Wed, from 9am Sat, from 8am Sun; S L to 1st Ave, 6 to Astor Pl) has been drawing a polyglot and eclectic mix: actors, students, frisky couples, singles on the make, Russian regulars and old-school locals, who strip down to their skivvies (or the roomy cotton shorts provided) and rotate between steam baths, an ice-cold plunge pool, a sauna and the sun deck.

Most hours are coed (clothing required), but there are several blocks of men-/women-only hours when clothing is optional (check the website). There are also massages, scrubs and Russian oak–leaf treatments (from $40). The cafe (mains $8 to $12) serves specials like Polish sausage and blinis; you can don one of the house-provided robes while eating.

A long-running and fairly operatic feud between co-owners David and Boris means days are split evenly between them. Passes and gift cards purchased from one manager can only be used during his hours. Check the website for more info on operating hours and the manager calendar.

Sts, Lower East Side; 10am-midnight Mon-Thu, 10am-1am Fri, 9am-1am Sat, 9am-midnight Sun; S F, J/M/Z to Delancey-Essex Sts) An eatery that spills easily into a party scene, with an airy Havana-meets-Beijing vibe and a focus on fine sipping tequilas. Or stick with fresh blood-orange or black-plum margaritas, guacamole and chicken tacos. Stop by on Tuesday night to hear DJs spinning Latin tunes.

ENTERTAINMENT

★METROGRAPH — CINEMA

Map p414 (212-660-0312; www.metrograph.com; 7 Ludlow St, btwn Canal & Hester Sts, Lower East Side; tickets $15; 11am-midnight Sun-Wed, to 2am Fri & Sat; ; S F to East Broadway, B/D to Grand St) The Lower East Side hasn't gentrified this far yet, giving the owners of this true movie mecca the chance to acquire a building adequate for their vision. It has two screens, both a state-of-the-art digital projector and an old 35mm reel-to-reel. The expertly curated films often form series on subjects such as Japanese Studio Ghibli or provocateur Gasper Noé.

ANYWAY CAFÉ — LIVE MUSIC

Map p412 (212-533-3412; www.anywaycafe.com; 34 E 2nd St, at Second Ave, East Village; noon-2am Sun-Thu, to 4am Fri & Sat; S F to 2nd Ave) This quirkily decorated, dimly lit basement bar has been hosting excellent live music every evening (no cover) for the past 25 years – a true NYC original. It's mainly jazz, everything from standards to gypsy or flamenco. There's a small menu of French-Russian cuisine as well as housemade vodka infusions in a dozen flavors. (Don't forget to tip the musicians.)

PERFORMANCE SPACE NEW YORK — THEATER

Map p412 (212-477-5829; www.performancespacenewyork.org; 150 First Ave, at E 9th St, East Village; S L to 1st Ave, 6 to Astor Pl) Founded in 1980 as Performance Space 122, this cutting-edge theater once housed in an abandoned public school now boasts state-of-the-art performance spaces, artist studios, a new lobby and a roof deck. The bones of the former schoolhouse remain, as does its experimental-theater bona fides: Eric Bogosian, Meredith Monk, the late Spalding Gray and Elevator Repair Service have all performed here.

ROCKWOOD MUSIC HALL — LIVE MUSIC

Map p414 (212-477-4155; www.rockwoodmusichall.com; 196 Allen St, btwn E Houston & Stanton Sts, Lower East Side; 5:30pm-2am Mon-Fri, from 2:30pm Sat & Sun; S F to 2nd Ave) Opened by indie rocker Ken Rockwood, this bread-box-size concert space has three stages and a rapid-fire flow of bands and singer-songwriters. If cash is tight, try stage 1, which has free shows, with a maximum of one hour per band (die-hards can see five or more performances a night). Music kicks off at 3pm on weekends and 6pm on weeknights.

ARLENE'S GROCERY LIVE MUSIC

Map p414 (www.arlenesgrocery.net; 95 Stanton St, btwn Orchard & Ludlow Sts, Lower East Side; cover $8-10; bar 5pm-4am Sun-Thu, 2pm-4am Fri & Sat; S F to 2nd Ave) This Lower East Side institution (found in a former bodega) has been hosting a wide swath of nightly live music – but especially local rock, punk and alternative bands – since 1995. Everyone from Arcade Fire to The Strokes to Lady Gaga has played here. Upstairs is a separate bar where you can keep the night going after the show.

SLIPPER ROOM LIVE PERFORMANCE

Map p414 (212-253-7246; www.slipperroom.com; 167 Orchard St, entrance on Stanton St, Lower East Side; from $10; doors open 1hr before performance; S F to 2nd Ave) This two-story club hosts offbeat shows, including some of the city's best burlesque performers, in each Friday's 'Slipper Room Show' (9:30pm; $20) and the outrageous romp 'Mr Choade's Upstairs Downstairs,' the city's longest-running variety show (9:30pm Saturday; $20). But whatever mix of acrobatics, sexiness, comedy and music you catch, you won't be disappointed. Event calendar and discounted tickets available online.

LA MAMA ETC THEATER

Map p412 (212-352-3101; www.lamama.org; 74a E 4th St, btwn Bowery & Second Ave, East Village; tickets from $20; S F to 2nd Ave) A longstanding home for onstage experimentation (the ETC stands for Experimental Theater Club), La MaMa is now a three-theater complex with a cafe, an art gallery, and a separate studio building that features cutting-edge dramas, sketch comedy and readings of all kinds. There are $10 tickets available for each show, available (until they run out) by booking online.

NUYORICAN POETS CAFÉ LIVE PERFORMANCE

Map p412 (212-780-9386; www.nuyorican.org; 236 E 3rd St, btwn Aves B & C, East Village; tickets $5-15; S F to 2nd Ave) Going strong since 1973, the legendary Nuyorican is home to poetry slams, hip-hop performances, plays, films, dance and music. It's living East Village history but also a vibrant, still-relevant nonprofit arts organization. Check the website for events and buy tickets online for the more-popular weekend shows. Or try out your lyrical skills at Monday's open-mic night (9pm; $8).

BOWERY BALLROOM LIVE MUSIC

Map p414 (800-745-3000, 212-533-2111; www.boweryballroom.com; 6 Delancey St, at Bowery, Lower East Side; S J/Z to Bowery, B/D to Grand St) This terrific, medium-size venue has the perfect sound and feel for well-known indie-rock acts such as The Shins, Jonathan Richman, Stephen Malkmus and Patti Smith.

SHOPPING

These neighborhoods cater to the strange, obscure and cutting edge. Secondhand stores trade in unique looks from worldwide names, while Obscura Antiques has you covered for skulls and Victorian-era medical equipment. The encroaching chain stores have zapped a little of the edginess, but many of the iconic old stores eg Trash & Vaudeville (p130) are still around. There's a particularly good stretch of clothing boutiques along 9th St between Second and First Aves.

East Village

OBSCURA ANTIQUES ANTIQUES

Map p412 (212-505-9251; www.obscuraantiques.com; 207 Ave A, btwn E 12th & E 13th Sts, East Village; 1-7:30pm; S L to 1st Ave) This eclectic trove pleases both curio-lovers and inveterate antique hunters. Here you'll find taxidermied animal heads, tiny rodent skulls and skeletons, butterfly displays in glass boxes, Victorian-era postmortem photography, disturbing little (dental?) instruments, German land-mine flags, old poison bottles and glass eyes. A Science Channel TV show, *Oddities* (2011–14), focuses on the shop, bizarre things, and those who seek them.

KIEHL'S COSMETICS

Map p412 (212-677-3171; 109 Third Ave, btwn 13th & 14th Sts, East Village; 10am-9pm Mon-Sat, 11am-7pm Sun; S L to 3rd Ave) Making and selling skincare products since it opened in NYC as an apothecary in 1851, this Kiehl's flagship store has doubled its shop size and expanded into an international chain, but its personal touch remains – as do the coveted, generous sample sizes.

TRASH & VAUDEVILLE CLOTHING

Map p412 (☎212-982-3590; www.trashandvaudeville.com; 96 E 7th St, btwn First Ave & Ave A, East Village; ⏰noon-8pm Mon-Thu, 11:30am-8:30pm Fri, to 9pm Sat, 1-7:30pm Sun; Ⓢ6 to Astor Pl) A vestige of the East Village heyday of the 1970s, Trash & Vaudeville is the go-to for punk, glam and rock clothing. It was once the boutique of choice for Debbie Harry and other Lower East Side luminaries, but now you'll find everyone from drag queens to themed partygoers scouting out the most ridiculous shoes, shirts and hair dye.

CONSIGLIERE COSMETICS

Map p412 (☎646-389-7482; www.shopconsigliere.com; 220 E 10th St, btwn First & Second Aves, East Village; ⏰noon-8pm Mon-Sat, to 7pm Sun; ⓈL to 1st Ave) Everything a well-groomed gentleman might need can be found in this small shop devoted to products for men's skin, hair, body and face – everything from moisturizers and skin masks to beard oil and preshave scrub. A small selection of accessories, such as leather toiletry travel bags, rounds out the offerings.

VERAMEAT JEWELRY

Map p412 (☎212-388-9045; www.verameat.com; 315 E 9th St, btwn First & Second Aves, East Village; ⏰noon-8pm; Ⓢ6 to Astor Pl; F/M to 2nd Ave) Designer Vera Balyura creates exquisite little pieces with a dark sense of humor in this delightful small shop on 9th St. Tiny, artfully wrought pendants, rings, earrings and bracelets appear almost too precious… until a closer inspection reveals zombies, Godzilla robots, animal heads, dinosaurs and encircling claws.

NO RELATION VINTAGE VINTAGE

Map p412 (L Train Vintage; ☎212-228-5201; www.ltrainvintagenyc.com; 204 First Ave, btwn E 12th & 13th Sts, East Village; ⏰noon-8pm Sun-Thu, to 9pm Fri & Sat; ⓈL to 1st Ave) Among the many vintage shops of the East Village, No Relation is a winner for its wide-ranging collections that run the gamut from designer denim and leather jackets to vintage flannels, funky sneakers, plaid shirts, irreverent branded T-shirts, varsity jackets, clutches and more. Sharpen your elbows: hipster crowds flock here on weekends.

DINOSAUR HILL TOYS

Map p412 (☎212-473-5850; www.dinosaurhill.com; 306 E 9th St, btwn First & Second Aves, East Village; ⏰11am-7pm; Ⓢ6 to Astor Pl) Through high windows glow the myriad colors of the handmade, unusual and stimulating items this small, old-fashioned and wholly wonderful toy store stocks. Czech marionettes, shadow puppets, micro building blocks, calligraphy sets, toy pianos, art and science kits, kids' music from around the globe, and wooden blocks in various languages, plus natural-fiber clothing for infants: there's so much to want.

JOHN VARVATOS FASHION & ACCESSORIES

Map p412 (☎212-358-0315; www.johnvarvatos.com; 315 Bowery, btwn E 1st & E 2nd Sts, East Village; ⏰noon-8pm Mon-Fri, from 11am Sat, noon-6pm Sun; ⓈF/M to 2nd Ave, 6 to Bleecker St) Occupying the former location of legendary punk club CBGB, this John Varvatos store goes to great lengths to acknowledge the site's rock-and-roll heritage, with records, high-end audio equipment and even electric guitars for sale alongside JV's denim, leather boots, belts and graphic tees. Sales associates dressed in Varvatos' downtown cool seem far removed from the Bowery's gritty past.

A-1 RECORDS MUSIC

Map p412 (☎212-473-2870; www.instagram.com/a1recordshop; 439 E 6th St, btwn First Ave & Ave A, East Village; ⏰1-9pm; ⓈF/M to 2nd Ave) One of the last of the many record stores that once graced the East Village, A-1 has been around for over two decades. The cramped aisles, filled with a large selection of jazz, funk and soul, draw vinyl fans and DJs from far and wide.

TOKIO 7 FASHION & ACCESSORIES

Map p412 (☎212-353-8443; www.tokio7.net; 83 E 7th St, near First Ave, East Village; ⏰noon-8pm; Ⓢ6 to Astor Pl) This revered, long-running consignment shop on a leafy stretch of E 7th St has good-condition designer labels for men and women at some fairly hefty prices. The owner's Japanese heritage is represented in pieces by Issey Miyake and Yohji Yamamoto, and you'll find a well-curated selection of Dolce & Gabbana, Prada, Chanel and other top labels.

Lower East Side

★RUSS & DAUGHTERS FOOD

Map p414 (☎212-475-4800; www.russanddaughters.com; 179 E Houston St, btwn Orchard & Allen Sts, Lower East Side; ⏰8am-6pm Fri-Wed, to 7pm Thu; ⓈF to 2nd Ave) Since 1914 this much-loved deli has served up Eastern European Jewish delicacies, such as caviar, herring, sturgeon and, of course, lox. Proudly owned by four generations of the Russ family, it's a great place to load up for a picnic or stock your fridge with breakfast goodies. Foodies, history buffs and interior designers will love it.

A Russ & Daughters Cafe (p121) with sit-down service is close by on Orchard St, but it's just as pleasant to order your 'Shtetl' (or other choice of bagel or bialy sandwich) and eat in nearby **Sara D Roosevelt Park** (Map p414; E Houston St, at Chrystie St, Lower East Side; ⑤F to Delancey-Essex Sts).

Polish immigrant Joel Russ started out selling herring from a barrel on the street, but with energy and determination built his way up to a storefront deli in 1914. In 1935 he made his daughters Hattie, Ida and Anne full partners, renaming the business and becoming the first-ever American company with 'and Daughters' in the name.

PICKLE GUYS FOOD

Map p414 (☑212-656-9739; www.pickleguys.com; 357 Grand St, at Essex St, Lower East Side; ⊙9am-6pm Sat-Thu, to 4pm Fri; ⑤F to East Broadway) Pucker up with pickled veg made the old-fashioned way at this kosher-certified shop that harks back to the classic Lower East Side. A few dozen barrels hold an array of briny goodness: sweet, sour and spicy varieties of pickled cucumbers, peppers, onions, olives, okra, mango and lots more, plus sauerkraut, horseradish and hot-dog relish. Ask for a free taste.

TOP HAT GIFTS & SOUVENIRS

Map p414 (☑212-677-4240; www.tophatnyc. com; 245 Broome St, btwn Ludlow & Orchard Sts, Lower East Side; ⊙noon-8pm Tue-Sat, 11am-7pm Sun; ⑤B/D to Grand St) Sporting curios from around the globe, this whimsical little shop is packed with intrigue: from vintage Italian pencils and handsomely miniaturized leather journals to beautifully carved wooden bird whistles. Looking for an endless rain album, a toy clarinet, Japanese fabrics, a crumpled map of the night sky or geometric Spanish cups and saucers? You'll find all these and more here.

REFORMATION CLOTHING

Map p414 (☑646-448-4925; www.thereformation.com; 156 Ludlow St, btwn Rivington & Stanton Sts, Lower East Side; ⊙noon-8pm Mon-Sat, to 7pm Sun; ⑤F to 2nd Ave, F, J/M/Z to Delancey-Essex Sts) 🌿 This stylish boutique sells beautifully designed garments with minimal environmental impact. Aside from its green credentials, it sells unique tops, blouses, sweaters and dresses, with fair prices in comparison to other Lower East Side boutiques.

MOO SHOES SHOES

Map p414 (☑212-254-6512; www.mooshoes.com; 78 Orchard St, btwn Broome & Grand Sts, Lower East Side; ⊙11:30am-8pm Mon-Sat, 11am-7pm Sun; ⑤F, J/M/Z to Delancey-Essex Sts) 🌿 This cruelty-free, earth-friendly boutique sells surprisingly stylish microfiber (faux leather) shoes, handbags and wallets. Look for fashionable pumps from Olsenhaus, rugged men's Oxfords by Novacos and sleek Matt & Nat wallets.

EDITH MACHINIST VINTAGE

Map p414 (☑212-979-9992; www.edithmachinist. com; 104 Rivington St, btwn Ludlow & Essex Sts, Lower East Side; ⊙noon-7pm Tue-Thu & Sat, to 6pm Sun, Mon & Fri; ⑤F, J/M/Z to Delancey-Essex Sts) To properly strut about the Lower East Side, you've got to dress the part. Edith Machinist can help you achieve that rumpled but stylish look in a hurry – a bit of vintage glam via knee-high soft suede boots, 1930s silk dresses and ballet-style flats.

ECONOMY CANDY FOOD

Map p414 (☑212-254-1531; www.economycandy. com; 108 Rivington St, at Essex St, Lower East Side; ⊙9am-6pm Tue-Fri, 10am-6pm Sat-Mon; ⑤F, J/M/Z to Delancey-Essex Sts) Bringing sweetness since 1937, this candy shop is stocked with goods in package and bulk, and is home to some beautiful antique gum machines. You'll find everything from childhood favorites like jelly beans, lollipops, gum balls, Cadbury imports, gummy worms and rock candy, to more grown-up delicacies such as halvah, green tea bonbons, hand-dipped chocolates, dried ginger and papaya.

BLUESTOCKINGS BOOKS

Map p414 (☑212-777-6028; www.bluestockings. com; 172 Allen St, btwn Stanton & Rivington Sts, Lower East Side; ⊙11am-11pm; ⑤F/M to Lower East Side-2nd Ave) This independent bookstore is the place to expand your horizons on feminism, queer and trans issues, globalism and African American studies, among other topics. It's also the site of an **organic, fair-trade cafe** with vegan treats, as well as myriad readings and speaking events.

West Village, Chelsea & the Meatpacking District

Neighborhood Top Five

❶ **High Line** (p134) Packing a picnic lunch from Chelsea Market and having a uniquely pastoral moment on the thin strand of green along the High Line as it soars above the gridiron.

❷ **Chelsea Galleries** Checking out the city's brightest art stars at top galleries, such as Pace Gallery (p141).

❸ **Washington Square Park** (p137) Walking through the park, pausing under the signature arch, then loitering at the fountain to eavesdrop on gossiping NYU kids.

❹ **Rubin Museum of Art** (p141) Exploring fascinating exhibitions from the Himalayas and beyond.

❺ **Stonewall National Monument** (p138) Taking a few moments to reflect on the night that sparked the LGBTIQ+ rights movement at this national park.

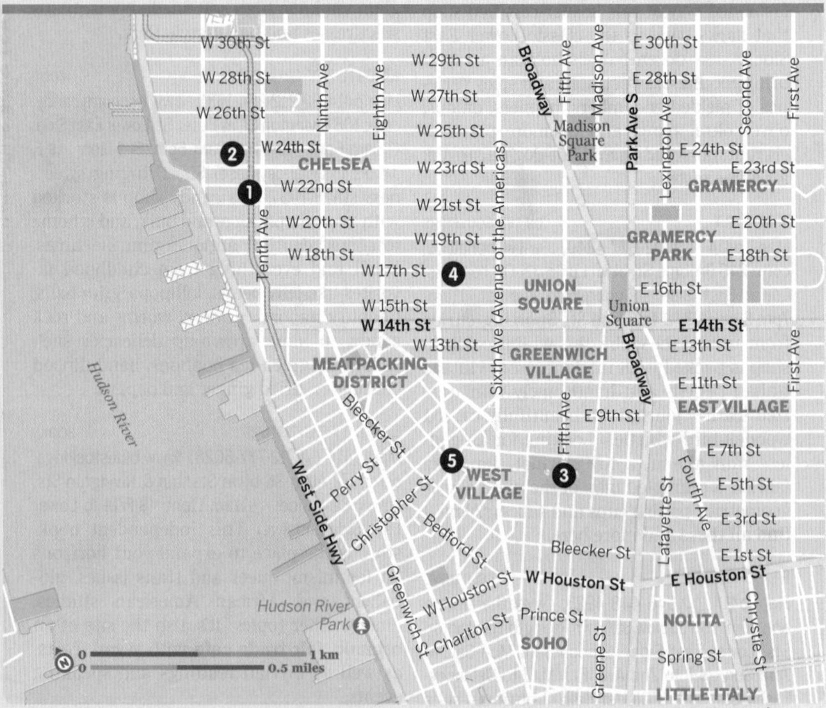

For more detail of this area see Map p416 and p420 ➡

Explore the West Village, Chelsea & the Meatpacking District

Quiet lanes carve their way between brown-brick town houses offering endless strolling for locals appreciating good weather or tourists coming to see what the fuss is about. The Village is indeed picturesque, and the best way to uncover its treasures is to simply have a wander. When you grow tired of walking the cobbled streets you'll find that you're never far from a cafe serving a frothy cappuccino or a glass of wine.

A stroll through the Meatpacking District, once filled with slaughterhouses, takes you past sleek boutiques and roaring nightclubs. Chelsea, just to the north, sits between the West Village and Midtown, and carries a bit of flavor from each. It's the de facto neighborhood for the city's gay community, and its broad avenues are lined with breezy cafes, themed bars and sweaty clubs. The neighborhood's gallery scene can be found in the West 20s.

The High Line, which travels from Gansevoort St at the southern end of the Meatpacking District to 30th St and the Hudson Yards project, is a way to cover a lot of ground with an elevated perspective – view street life and the Hudson River, and peek into the lives of New Yorkers living in apartments abutting the park.

Local Life

- **Eighth Avenue brunch** If you're a dude looking to meet (or at least look at) other dudes, but the cruisey bar scene isn't your style, try the weekend brunch scene along Eighth Ave for piles of friendly Chelsea boys drinking off their hangovers.
- **West Village cafes** The West Village is Manhattan's most desirable residential neighborhood, so do as the locals do and make the most of this quaint district filled with cute cafes. Grab a book and a latte and have a blissful afternoon of people-watching.
- **Imbibing art** Join the fashionable, art-minded crowds at the latest Chelsea gallery shows. Thursday night, when some galleries have openings (and free wine), is a good time to roam. In the Meatpacking District, the Whitney Museum of American Art is beloved by locals and tourists alike.

Getting There & Away

- **Subway** Sixth Ave, Seventh Ave and Eighth Ave have convenient subway stations, but public transportation slims further west. Take the A/C/E or 1/2/3 lines to reach this colorful clump of neighborhoods – disembark at 14th St or W 4th St-Washington Sq.
- **Bus** Try the M14, or the M8 if you're traveling across town and want to access the westernmost areas of Chelsea and the West Village by public transportation.

Lonely Planet's Top Tip

It's perfectly acceptable to arm yourself with a map (or rely on your smartphone) to get around the West Village's charming-but-challenging side streets. Even some locals have a tricky time finding their way! Just remember that 4th St makes a diagonal turn north – breaking away from usual east–west street grid – and you'll quickly become a Village pro.

Best Places to Eat

- Foragers Table (p152)
- Jeffrey's Grocery (p147)
- RedFarm (p147)
- Chelsea Market (p151)
- Blue Hill (p147)

For reviews, see p142

Best Places to Drink

- Employees Only (p152)
- Buvette (p153)
- Pier 66 Maritime (p157)
- Smalls (p158)
- Duplex (p159)

For reviews, see p152

Best Bookstores

- Printed Matter (p162)
- Strand Book Store (p161)
- Three Lives & Company (p160)
- 192 Books (p162)

For reviews, see p159

OLIVER FOERSTNER/SHUTTERSTOCK ©

TOP EXPERIENCE
HIGH LINE

Snaking through the Meatpacking District at 30ft above street level, this 1.5-mile urban park is a fabulous example of industrial reuse. Once a freight line linking slaughterhouses to the Hudson River, it fell into disuse by the 1980s, only to be resurrected as a green, art-strewn ribbon running between the high-rises, hotels and art galleries blossoming at its feet.

The Industrial Past

Long before the High Line was a beacon for eager tourists, happy-snapping families and New Yorkers seeking respite from the street-level grind, it was an unglamorous freight line running through neighborhoods of industry and slaughterhouses. In the early 1900s the western area around the Meatpacking District and Chelsea was the largest industrial section of Manhattan. With street-level freight lines causing disruption and even death (Tenth Ave was nicknamed 'Death Ave' for rail accidents that claimed over 500 lives), an elevated freight track was planned, and the 'West Side Elevated Line' moved its first train in 1933. The project drained over $150 million (equivalent to around $2 billion by today's dime) and took roughly five years to complete. After two decades of effective service, a rise in truck transportation led to an eventual decrease in use of the line; finally, in the 1980s, the rails became obsolete, quickly growing thick with wild foliage. Locals signed petitions to remove the eyesore the tracks had become, but in 1999 a committee called Friends of the High Line – founded by Joshua David and Robert Hammond – was formed to save the rusting iron and transform the tracks into a unique elevated green space.

DON'T MISS

- The amphitheater-style viewing platforms at 17th and 26th Sts
- Chelsea Market
- Mammoth sculptures at the Plinth

PRACTICALITIES

- Map p416, A2
- 212-500-6035
- www.thehighline.org
- Gansevoort St, Meatpacking District
- 7am-11pm Jun-Sep, to 10pm Apr, May, Oct & Nov, to 7pm Dec-Mar
- M14 crosstown along 14th St, M23 along 23rd St, S A/C/E, L to 8th Ave-14th St, 1, C/E to 23rd St, 7 to 34th St-Hudson Yards

A Green Future

On a warm spring day in 2009, the High Line – full of blooming flowers and broad-leaved trees – opened to the public, the first of three phases that today link the Meatpacking District and Midtown. Section 1 starts at Gansevoort St and runs parallel to Tenth Ave up to W 20th St. Full of sitting space in various forms – from giant chaises longues to bleacher-like benches – the first part quickly became the setting for various public works and activities, many geared toward the neighborhood's growing population of families. Two years later, Section 2 opened, adding another 10 blocks of greenified tracks. In 2014 the High Line's third section was completed, from 30th up to 34th St, going up to and around the West Side Rail Yards in a U-like fashion. As it veers west toward Twelfth Ave the path widens, and you have open views of the Hudson, with the rusting, weed-filled railroad tracks running alongside the walkway (the designers wanted to evoke the same sense of overgrown wilderness in the heart of the metropolis that greeted visitors who stumbled upon the tracks prior to the park's creation). This section also features a dedicated children's play area – a jungle gym made up of exposed beams covered in a soft play surface. Finally, in 2019, the last remaining section of the original rail structure was completed. Known as the Spur, this stretch extends east to 10th Ave, with a large-scale art space known as the Plinth as its focal point.

There are numerous access stairways along the park, including at Gansevoort, 14th, 16th, 17th, 20th, 23rd, 26th, 28th, 30th and 34th Sts. There are also elevators at Gansevoort, 14th, 16th, 23rd and 30th Sts.

A Unique Public Space

The High Line's civic influence extends far beyond being the trendsetter in Manhattan's regreening. As the West Village and Chelsea continue to embrace their newfound residential nature, the High Line is becoming less 'just' an unusual park and more an inspiring meeting point for families and friends. As you walk its length you'll find staffers wearing the signature double-H logo who can point you in the right direction or offer you additional information about the converted rails. There are also myriad staffers behind the scenes organizing public art exhibitions and activity sessions, especially in summer. Special tours and events explore a variety of topics: history, horticulture, design, art and food: check the schedule at www.thehighline.org for the latest.

GASTRONOMIC DELIGHTS

The High Line invites various gastronomic establishments from around the city to set up vending carts and stalls so that strollers can enjoy to-go items on the green. Expect a showing of the finest coffee and ice cream during the warmer months.

FRIENDS OF THE HIGH LINE

If you're interested in helping support the High Line through financial donations, you can become a member of the Friends of the High Line association through the park's website. 'Spike'-level members ($60) receive a discount at stores in the area, from Diane von Fürstenberg's boutique to **Amy's Bread** (Map p420; www.amysbread.com), a tasty food outlet in the Chelsea Market.

TAKE A BREAK

You'll find a wonderland of food vendors behind the brick walls of the Chelsea Market (p151), at the 14th St exit of the High Line.

If you feel like treating yourself after a long walk, head to the Top of the Standard (p156) for a pricey cocktail with a million-dollar view.

CHIE INOUE/SHUTTERSTOCK ©

TOP EXPERIENCE
WHITNEY MUSEUM OF AMERICAN ART

Even with Chelsea and the Meatpacking District's plenitude of galleries, the Whitney's collection of American art is exceptional. Its 63,000 sq ft of cleverly designed indoor- and outdoor-exhibition space is the perfect showcase for the world's foremost collection of 20th-century and contemporary American art.

The Building

Designed by Italian architect Renzo Piano, the Whitney's asymmetrical, glass-cloaked home quickly became a major landmark in the southern reaches of the Meatpacking District, housing myriad galleries, theaters, classrooms and outdoor spaces, and anchoring the first-opened section of the High Line. One gallery in particular is noteworthy – an 18,000-sq-ft space that is New York's largest column-free exhibition space. Once the decision was made to move from the Whitney's original, Marcel Breuer–designed home on Madison Ave, something on the scale of this nine-story cultural colossus was always likely. Commenced in 2010, it cost $422 million to build, and opened to great acclaim in 2015.

The Collection

The Whitney's collection of over 23,000 works by 3000+ different American artists assumes greater significance when you consider it's all 20th- and 21st-century work, much of it by still-practising artists. Works from the permanent collection you might expect to encounter include Sol LeWitt's *Five Towers* (1986), looking like the load-bearing frame of an abandoned building; several of Andy Warhol's 10 luridly colored *Mao Tse-Tung* prints (1972); Alice Neel's *Andy Warhol* (1970) for which the pop-art legend sat while recovering from a near-fatal shooting; Jasper Johns's *Three Flags* (1958); Marsden Hartley's early-modernist *Painting, Number 5* (1914–15); and plenty of comparable treasures.

DON'T MISS

- George Bellows, *Dempsey and Firpo*
- Joseph Stella, *The Brooklyn Bridge: Variation on an Old Theme*
- Alexander Calder, *Calder's Circus*

PRACTICALITIES

- Map p416, A2
- www.whitney.org
- 99 Gansevoort St, Meatpacking District
- adult/child $25/free, 7-10pm Fri pay-what-you-wish
- ⌚10:30am-6pm Mon, Wed, Thu & Sun, to 10pm Fri & Sat
- S A/C/E, L to 8th Ave-14th St

TOP EXPERIENCE WASHINGTON SQUARE PARK

What was once a potter's field and a square for public executions is now the unofficial town square of the Village. Encased in perfectly manicured brownstones and gorgeous twists of modern architecture, Washington Square Park is a striking garden space in the city – especially as you're welcomed by the iconic Stanford White Arch on the north side of the green.

A Storied History

Although now quite ravishing, Washington Square Park had a long and sordid history before finally blossoming into the paradigm of public space we see today (thanks largely to a $30 million renovation completed in 2014).

When the Dutch settled Manhattan to run the Dutch East India Company, they gave what is now the park to their freed Black slaves. The land was squarely between the Dutch and Native American settlements, so, in a way, the area acted as a buffer between enemies. Though somewhat marshy, it was arable land and farming took place for around 60 years.

At the turn of the 19th century, the municipality of New York purchased the land for use as a burial ground straddling the city's limit. At first the cemetery was mainly for indigent workers, but the space quickly reached capacity during an outbreak of yellow fever. Over 20,000 bodies remain buried under the park today.

By 1830 the grounds were used for military parades, and then quickly transformed into a park for the wealthy elite who were constructing lavish town houses along the surrounding streets.

DON'T MISS

- Stanford White Arch
- Central fountain
- Greek Revival houses surrounding the park
- The birdman, often found on a bench near the southwest entrance with dozens of pigeons roosting on him

PRACTICALITIES

- Map p416, G4
- www.nycgovparks.org
- Fifth Ave, at Washington Sq N, West Village
- closes midnight
-
- S A/C/E, B/D/F/M to W 4th St-Washington Sq, R/W to 8th St-NYU

A Political Stage

Washington Square Park has long provided a stage for political activity, from local protests against proposed changes to the shape and usage of the park, to issues of national importance such as the 1912 protests for better working conditions.

In 2007 Democratic Party candidate Barack Obama led a rally here to drum up support for his successful presidential bid. Turnout was, unsurprisingly, overwhelming.

Stanford White Arch

The iconic Stanford White Arch, colloquially known as the Washington Square Arch, dominates the park with its 72ft of beaming white Dover marble. Originally designed in wood to celebrate the centennial of George Washington's inauguration in 1889, the arch proved so popular that it was replaced with stone six years later and adorned with statues of the general in war and peace. In 1916 artist Marcel Duchamp famously climbed to the top of the arch by its internal stairway and declared the park the 'Free and Independent Republic of Washington Square.'

SIGHTS

If you're an art-lover, this trio of neighborhoods is simply not to be missed. The Whitney Museum of American Art (in the Meatpacking District) should feature prominently in any itinerary, followed by an exploration of Chelsea's galleries (in the West 20s) – the epicenter of NYC's art world. Other major sights include the High Line, a former rail line turned green space, the nearby Hudson River Park, which provides a tranquil setting for relaxing along the waterfront, as well as the historic Stonewall National Monument right in the center of the West Village and across the street from the eponymous bar.

West Village & the Meatpacking District

HIGH LINE — PARK

See p134.

WHITNEY MUSEUM OF AMERICAN ART — MUSEUM

See p136.

WASHINGTON SQUARE PARK — PARK

See p137.

STONEWALL NATIONAL MONUMENT — NATIONAL PARK

Map p416 (www.nps.gov/ston; W 4th St, btwn Christopher & Grove Sts, West Village; 9am-dusk; S 1 to Christopher St-Sheridan Sq, A/C/E, B/D/F/M to W 4th St-Washington Sq) In 2016 President Barack Obama declared Christopher Park, a small fenced-in triangle with benches and some greenery in the heart of the West Village, a national park and on it the first national monument dedicated to LGBTIQ+ history. It's well worth stopping here to reflect on the Stonewall uprising of 1969, when LGBTIQ+ citizens fought back against discriminatory policing of their communities – many consider the event the birth of the modern LGBTIQ+ rights movement in the US.

There's little ostentatious memorializing here, save a few plaques and two sets of slender white statues: a male couple and a female couple, holding hands and talking. Known as *Gay Liberation*, they are a tribute to the normalcy of gay life. Plenty of pilgrims give the monument the gravity it merits.

SALMAGUNDI CLUB — GALLERY

Map p416 (212-255-7740; www.salmagundi.org; 47 Fifth Ave, btwn W 11th & 12th Sts, West Village; 1-6pm Mon-Fri, to 5pm Sat & Sun; S 4/5/6, L, N/Q/R/W to 14th St-Union Sq) FREE Far removed from the flashy Chelsea gallery scene, the Salmagundi Club features several gallery spaces focusing on representational American art set in a stunning historic brownstone on Fifth Ave below Union Sq. The club is one of the oldest art clubs in the US (founded in 1871) and still offers classes and exhibitions for its members.

The gallery spaces are large with a wide-ranging collection of styles and mediums. The trip is worth it alone to linger a few minutes in the parlor decorated with period furniture and historic paintings.

WHITE COLUMNS — GALLERY

Map p416 (212-924-4212; www.whitecolumns.org; 91 Horatio St; 11am-6pm Tue-Sat; S A/C/E, L to 8th Ave-14th St) FREE Geographically, White Columns is part of the Meatpacking District, but aesthetically speaking, it's in Chelsea. The sedate, multiroom space hosts a wide range of installations and exhibits, some of which are by fairly well-known names, such as Andrew Serrano, Alice Aycock, Lorna Simpson and a White Columns founder, Gordon Matta-Clark.

GRACE CHURCH — CHURCH

Map p416 (212-254-2000; www.gracechurchnyc.org; 802 Broadway, at 10th St, West Village; noon-5pm, services daily; S R/W to 8th St-NYU; 6 to Astor Pl) This Gothic Revival Episcopal church, designed in 1843 by James Renwick Jr, was made of marble quarried by prisoners at 'Sing Sing,' the state penitentiary in the town of Ossining, 30 miles up the Hudson River (which, legend has it, is the origin of the expression 'being sent upriver'). After years of neglect, Grace Church has been beautifully restored.

It's now a National Landmark, whose elaborate carvings, towering spire and verdant, groomed yard are sure to stop you in your tracks as you make your way down this otherwise ordinary stretch of the Village. The stained-glass windows inside are stunning, and the soaring interior makes a perfect setting for the frequent musical programming (recently there was a series of 'Bach at Noon' organ concerts). Free guided tours are offered at 1pm on Sundays.

PIER 45 PARK

Map p416 (W 10th St, at Hudson River, West Village; S1 to Christopher St-Sheridan Sq) Still known to many as the Christopher St Pier, this is an 850ft-long finger of concrete, spiffily renovated with a grass lawn, flower beds, a comfort station, an outdoor cafe, tented shade shelters and a stop for the New York Water Taxi.

Now part of the Hudson River Park, it's a magnet for downtowners of all stripes, from local families with toddlers in daylight to mobs of young gay kids who flock here at night from all over the city (and beyond) thanks to the pier's long-established history as a gay cruising hangout. The spot offers sweeping views of the Hudson and cool, relieving breezes in the thick of summer.

ABINGDON SQUARE SQUARE

Map p416 (Hudson St, at 12th St, West Village; SA/C/E, L to 8th Ave-14th St) This historical dot on the landscape (just a quarter-acre) is a lovely little patch of green, home to grassy knolls, beds of perennial flowers and winding bluestone paths, as well as a popular Saturday Greenmarket. It's a great place to enjoy a midday picnic or rest after an afternoon of wandering the winding West Village streets.

NEW YORK UNIVERSITY UNIVERSITY

Map p416 (NYU; 212-998-4550; www.nyu.edu; Welcome Center, 50 W 4th St, West Village; SA/C/E, B/D/F/M to W 4th St-Washington Sq; N/R to 8th St-NYU) In 1831 Albert Gallatin, formerly Secretary of the Treasury under President Thomas Jefferson, founded an intimate center of higher learning open to all students, regardless of race or class background. He'd scarcely recognize the place today, as it's swelled to a student population of around 50,000, with more than 16,000 employees, and schools and colleges at six Manhattan locations.

It just keeps growing, too – to the dismay of landmark activists and business owners, who have seen buildings rapidly bought out by the academic giant (or destroyed through careless planning, such as with the historic Provincetown Playhouse)

TOP EXPERIENCE
HUDSON RIVER PARK

As its maritime industry dwindled, New York had to devise a future for the bristling ranks of piers left behind. The answer, stretching from Manhattan's southern tip to 59th St in Midtown, is the Hudson River Park.

The Hudson River Greenway, a long path running between the river and the busy West Side Hwy, invites strolling, blading, jogging and cycling. **Waterfront Bicycle Shop** (Map p416; 212-414-2453; www.bikeshopny.com; 391 West St, btwn W 10th & Christopher Sts, West Village; rental per hour/day $7.50/20; 10am-7pm; S1 to Christopher St-Sheridan Sq) is a convenient place to rent bikes. In summer, several boathouses offer kayak hire and longer excursions for the more experienced. There's also beach volleyball, basketball courts, a skate park and tennis courts. Families with kids have loads of options, including four playgrounds, a carousel (off W 22nd St) and mini-golf (Pier 25 off West St near N Moore St).

On warm summer evenings locals loll on the grass for people-watching and contemplation, while those seeking sunset revelry can join the sangria-loving crowds at the dockside *Frying Pan*, a historic ship serving food and drink from Pier 66 Maritime (p157).

DON'T MISS

- Kayaking on the river
- Sunset strolls
- Summertime drinks at *Frying Pan*

PRACTICALITIES

- Map p416, C7
- 9am-5pm Mon-Fri 212-627-2020
- www.hudsonriverpark.org
- West Village
- 6am-1am
-
- M23 crosstown bus, S1 to Christopher St, C/E to 23rd St

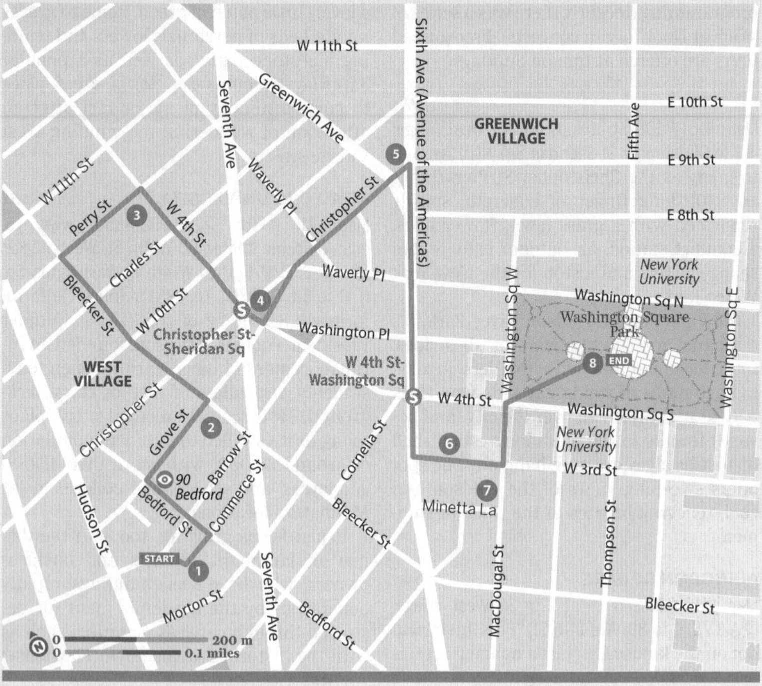

Neighborhood Walk
A Wander Through Greenwich Village

START COMMERCE ST
END WASHINGTON SQUARE PARK
LENGTH 1.2 MILES; ONE HOUR

Greenwich Village's brick-lined byways break Manhattan's signature grid pattern, striking off on tangents that beg to be explored on foot. Start at 1 **Cherry Lane Theatre** (p159), hidden in handsome Commerce St. Established in 1924, the Cherry is the city's longest continuously running off-Broadway establishment, and has hosted many famous playwrights and thespians.

Make a left on Bedford and turn right into Grove St (number 90, on the corner, may be familiar as the apartment building in *Friends*) to reach your first pit stop, 2 **Buvette** (p153). Literally 'snack bar,' this Francophile wine bar is ideal for people-watching.

Next, for another TV landmark, turn left up Bleecker St and make a right on Perry – 3 66 Perry Street is famous as Carrie Bradshaw's apartment in *Sex and the City*.

Turn right onto W 4th St and continue until you reach Christopher Park, home to the 4 **Stonewall National Monument** (p138). On the north side of the green is the legendary Stonewall Inn, where in 1969 LGBTIQ+ men and women rioted against routine police harassment, sparking what came to be known as the Gay Rights Movement.

Follow Christopher St to Sixth Ave to find the 5 **Jefferson Market Library** just north. Built as a courthouse in 1885, this gracious red-brick building rises from a tranquil garden of the same name.

Head south again through Sixth Ave's flurry of foot traffic, then turn left onto West 3rd St, looking for legendary jazz venue 6 **Blue Note** (p158) on your left. Sarah Vaughan, Lionel Hampton and other immortals have performed here; try to time your visit for jazz brunch on Sunday (11:30am or 1:30pm).

Turn right onto MacDougal St to reach the famous 7 **Comedy Cellar** (p157), where the likes of Jerry Seinfeld and Amy Schumer have performed, then double back, heading north on MacDougal to end your stroll in 8 **Washington Square Park** (p137), the village's unofficial town square.

and replaced with ugly dormitories or administrative offices. Still, some of its crevices are charming, such as the leafy courtyard at its School of Law, or impressively modern, like the Skirball Center for the Performing Arts, where top-notch dance, theater, music, spoken-word and other performances wow audiences at the 850-seat theater.

NYU's academic offerings are highly regarded and wide-ranging, especially its film, theater, writing, medical and law programs. For a unique experience that will put you on the fast track to meeting locals, sign up for a weekend or one-day class – from American history to photography – offered by the School of Professional Studies and Continuing Education, and open to all.

SHERIDAN SQUARE SQUARE

Map p416 (btwn Washington Pl & W 4th St, West Village; S1 to Christopher St-Sheridan Sq) The shape of a triangle, Sheridan Sq isn't much more than a few park benches and some trees surrounded by an old-fashioned wrought-iron gate. But its location (in the heart of gay Greenwich Village) has meant that it has witnessed every rally, demonstration and uprising that has contributed to New York's gay rights movement.

⊙ Chelsea

★PACE GALLERY GALLERY

Map p420 (☎212-421-3292; www.pacegallery.com; 540 W 25th St, btwn Tenth & Eleventh Aves, Chelsea; ⊙10am-6pm Tue-Sat; S1, C/E to 23rd St) With seven galleries across the world – including this eight-story Chelsea flagship – and decades of experience showing the work of such artists as Willem de Kooning, Barbara Hepworth and Julian Schnabel, gargantuan Pace is a landmark on any tour. With a glimmering exterior constructed from volcanic ash, the 75,000-sq-ft structure's spaces span an 18ft-ceiling gallery at street level, to more intimate confines like an appointment-only research library and a 6th-floor open-air terrace.

RUBIN MUSEUM OF ART GALLERY

Map p420 (☎212-620-5000; www./rubinmuseum.org; 150 W 17th St, btwn Sixth & Seventh Aves, Chelsea; adult/child $19/free, 6-10pm Fri free; ⊙11am-5pm Mon & Thu, to 9pm Wed, to 10pm Fri, to 6pm Sat & Sun; S1 to 18th St) The Rubin is the first museum in the Western world to dedicate itself to the art of the Himalayas and surrounding regions. Its impressive collection spans 1500 years to the present day, and includes Chinese embroidered textiles, Nepalese gilt-copper bodhisattvas, Pakistani stone sculptures and intricate Bhutanese paintings, as well as ritual objects and dance masks from various Tibetan regions. Fascinating rotating exhibitions have included *Victorious Ones*, comprising sculptures and paintings of the Jinas, the 24 founding teachers of Jainism.

GAGOSIAN GALLERY

Map p420 (☎212-741-1111; www.gagosian.com; 555 W 24th St, at Eleventh Ave, Chelsea; ⊙10am-6pm Mon-Sat; S1, C/E to 23rd St) International works dot the walls at the Gagosian. The ever-revolving exhibits feature the work of greats such as Jeff Koons, Andy Warhol and Jean-Michel Basquiat. Gagosian has five New York locations, and 12 more in San Francisco, London, Rome and other cities.

ARTECHOUSE GALLERY

Map p420 (www.artechouse.com/nyc; 439 W 15th St, Chelsea Market; adult/child $24/17; ⊙10am-10pm Sun-Thu, to 11pm Fri & Sat; SA/C/E, L to 8th Ave-14th St) The previously unused boiler room beneath historic Chelsea Market (p151) has finally found a tenant in Artechouse, a technology-forward creative space where digital projections deliver hallucinatory experiences through ambitiously large-scale installations. The innovative, 6000-sq-ft experimental art house is a departure from Chelsea's white-cube gallery circuit, with immersive and participatory elements that'll spark wonder in all manner of visitors.

ANDREA ROSEN GALLERY GALLERY

Map p420 (☎212-627-6000; www.andrearosengallery.com; 525 W 24th St, btwn Tenth & Eleventh Aves, Chelsea; ⊙10am-6pm Mon-Fri; S1, C/E to 23rd St) Oversized installations are the norm at this spacious gallery, where curators fill every inch of space (and the annex, Gallery 2, next door) in interesting ways. Rosen opened her gallery in 1990 and quickly made a name for herself. She has showcased John Currin's 'pale portraits,' Felix Gonzalez-Torres' 'Vultures' and

Tetsumi Kudo's oil paintings, to name just a few of her artists. Visits to the gallery are by appointment only.

CHELSEA HOTEL HISTORIC BUILDING

Map p420 (222 W 23rd St, btwn Seventh & Eighth Aves, Chelsea; S1, C/E to 23rd St) This red-brick hotel, built in the 1880s and featuring ornate iron balconies and no fewer than seven plaques declaring its literary landmark status, has played a major role in pop-culture history. It's where the likes of Mark Twain, Thomas Wolfe, Dylan Thomas and Arthur Miller hung out; Jack Kerouac allegedly crafted *On the Road* during one marathon session here; and it's where Arthur C Clarke wrote *2001: A Space Odyssey*.

Dylan Thomas died of alcohol poisoning while staying at the Chelsea Hotel in 1953, and Nancy Spungen died here after being stabbed by her Sex Pistols boyfriend Sid Vicious in 1978. Among the many celebs who have logged time living at the Chelsea are Joni Mitchell, Patti Smith, Robert Mapplethorpe, Stanley Kubrick, Dennis Hopper, Edith Piaf, Bob Dylan and Leonard Cohen, whose song 'Chelsea Hotel' recalls a romp with Janis Joplin (who spent time here, too).

Sadly, the hotel's days of artistry and intrigue are long gone. A decade-long saga of battles with permanent tenants plus revolving ownership sees its destiny in limbo; at the time of research, development for a luxury hotel with a restaurant and two bars was underway.

GENERAL THEOLOGICAL SEMINARY GARDENS

Map p420 (212-243-5150; www.gts.edu; 440 W 21st St, btwn Ninth & Tenth Aves, Chelsea; 10am-5pm Mon-Fri; S1, C/E to 23rd St) FREE Founded in 1817, this is the oldest seminary of the Episcopal Church in America. The school, which sits in the midst of the beautiful Chelsea historic district, has been working hard lately to make sure it can preserve its best asset – the garden-like campus snuggled in the middle of its full block of buildings – even as Chelsea development sprouts up all around it.

This peaceful haven is the perfect spot for finding respite, either before or after your neighborhood gallery crawl. To visit, ring the buzzer at the garden gate, located halfway down 21st St between Ninth and Tenth Aves.

EATING

With a bit of research and a little cash in your pocket, you can eat like royalty at every meal in these neighborhoods. The West Village is known for its classy, cozy and intimate spots, while the adjacent Meatpacking District's dining scene is generally more ostentatious, trend-driven and pricey. Chelsea strikes a balance between the two, with a brash assortment of *très*-gay eateries along ever-popular Eighth Ave (a must for see-and-be-seen brunch), and more cafes lining Ninth Ave further west.

West Village & the Meatpacking District

RED BAMBOO VEGAN $

Map p416 (212-260-7049; www.redbamboo-nyc.com; 140 W 4th St, btwn Sixth Ave & MacDougal St, West Village; mains $12-16; 12:30-11pm Mon-Thu, to 11:30pm Fri, from noon Sat, to 11pm Sun; ; SA/C/E, B/D/F/M to W 4th St-Washington Sq) Cajun soy 'shrimp', jerk-marinated soy 'chicken', 'cheesecake' so rich you can barely finish? The soul- and Asian-food temptations Red Bamboo concocts make it a must for vegans and vegetarians eager to try something different. Humble bare-wood furniture and a plain, tiled dining room relax the punters, while organic beers and wines complete the essentials for a night of culinary adventure.

MAMOUN'S MIDDLE EASTERN $

Map p416 (www.mamouns.com; 119 MacDougal St, btwn W 3rd St & Minetta Lane, West Village; sandwiches $4-7.50, plates $8-13; 11am-5am; SA/C/E, B/D/F/M to W 4th St-Washington Sq) This falafel and shawarma restaurant in lower Manhattan specializes in big, dripping platters and wraps that are served up quick and don't cost much. A NYC favorite, Mamoun's even has its own branded hot sauce. Be warned: it's not for anyone with a sensitive tongue. The West Village location is tiny, but there is some limited seating.

GANSEVOORT MARKET MARKET $

Map p416 (646-449-8400; www.gansevoortmarketnyc.com; 353 W 14th St, btwn Eighth & Ninth Aves, Meatpacking District; mains $10-15; 11am-9:30pm Mon-Thu, to 10:30pm Fri-Sun; ; SA/C/E, L to 8th Ave-14th St) Inside a brick building in the heart of the Meatpacking District is this buzzing food emporium. A raw, industrial space lit by skylights, it features a bar and over a dozen gourmet vendors slinging Korean bibimbap, poke bowls, ceviche, pizza, Japanese curry, ramen, Belgian waffles and more.

There's a communal seating area, and several food counters where you can sit around and watch the cooks in action while munching your meal.

MAH ZE DAHR BAKERY $

Map p416 (☎212-498-9810; www.mahzedahrbakery.com; 28 Greenwich Ave, btwn W 10th & Charles Sts, West Village; pastries from $3; ⏰7am-8pm Mon-Thu, to 9pm Fri, from 8am Sat, to 8pm Sun; Ⓢ A/C/E, L to 8th Ave-14th St) Tangy, creamy cheesecakes and spongy brioche doughnuts are on offer at this bakery opened by former financial advisor Umber Ahmad, who was discovered when she baked for one of her clients, celebrity chef Tom Colicchio. When you try one of the crumbly scones or rich brownies you'll understand why Colicchio suggested the change of career.

DOMINIQUE ANSEL KITCHEN BAKERY $

Map p416 (☎212-242-5111; www.dominiqueanselkitchen.com; 137 Seventh Ave, btwn Charles & W 10th Sts, West Village; pastries $6-9, sandwiches $14-16; ⏰9am-9pm; Ⓢ1 to Christopher St-Sheridan Sq) The much-garlanded creator of the cronut (croissant-doughnut hybrid) owns this small, sunlit bakery, where you can nibble on perfectly flaky croissants, brownies finished with smoked sage, lemon-yuzu butter tarts and many other heavenly treats (but no cronuts). There's also light savory fare, such as sausage, kale and lentil soup and an extra-large croque monsieur, served with salad.

COTENNA ITALIAN $

Map p416 (☎646-861-0175; www.cotenna.com; 21 Bedford St, btwn Downing & W Houston Sts, West Village; mains $14-16; ⏰11am-midnight Sun-Thu, to 1am Fri & Sat; Ⓢ1 to Houston St) Tucked away on a picturesque corner of the Village, this intimate, attractively designed eatery is a favorite on date night. It has a small menu of affordable pastas (from $16), bruschetta and grilled dishes, though you can also come for wine or cocktails and sharing plates, including *salumi* (cured meat) and cheese boards.

THELEWALA INDIAN $

Map p416 (☎212-614-9100; www.thelewalany.com; 112 MacDougal St, btwn Bleecker & W 3rd Sts, West Village; rolls $5-7; ⏰11:30am-2am Sun-Thu, to 5am Fri & Sat; Ⓢ A/C/E, B/D/F/M to W 4th St-Washington Sq) This small, rockin' place serves Calcutta-style street food: delicious rolls filled with minced lamb, paneer cheese, crispy okra and other ingredients. There are also *chaats* (savory snacks) and dishes like chickpea curry. Seating options – just a few counter stools – are limited, so get it to go and devour your rolls (you'll want more than one) in nearby Washington Square Park.

MOUSTACHE MIDDLE EASTERN $

Map p416 (☎212-229-2220; www.moustachepitzawest.com; 90 Bedford St, btwn Grove & Barrow Sts, West Village; pizzas $11-15; ⏰noon-11pm Sun-Thu, to 11:30pm Fri & Sat; Ⓢ1 to Christopher St-Sheridan Sq) In its warm, earthy space, small and delightful Moustache serves up rich, flavorful sandwiches (leg of lamb, *merguez* sausage, falafel), thin-crust pizzas, tangy salads and hearty specialties, such as *ouzi* (phyllo stuffed with chicken, rice and spices) and moussaka. The best start to a meal: a platter of hummus or baba ghanoush served with fluffy, piping-hot pita bread.

SAIGON SHACK VIETNAMESE $

Map p416 (☎212-228-0588; www.saigonshacknyc.com; 114 MacDougal St, btwn Bleecker & 3rd Sts, West Village; mains $7-10; ⏰11am-11pm Sun-Thu, to 1am Fri & Sat; Ⓢ A/CE, B/D/F/M to W 4th St-Washington Sq) Steaming bowls of pho (noodle soup), tangy *banh mi* (baguette) sandwiches and crunchy spring rolls await at this bustling wood-lined eatery just a few strides from Washington Square Park. The prices are fair and the food arrives in a hurry; the only downside: you might have to wait for a table as it's a popular draw for the NYU crowd.

CORNER BISTRO BISTRO $

Map p416 (☎212-242-9502; www.cornerbistrony.com; 331 W 4th St, btwn Jane & 12th Sts, West Village; burgers $10-13; ⏰11:30am-4am Mon-Sat, from noon Sun; Ⓢ A/C/E, L to 8th Ave-14th St) An old-school dive bar with cheap beers on tap – it all sounds pretty standard until you take a mouthwatering bite out of the bacon- and cheese-covered Corner Bistro burger. Nothing beats this juicy meat sandwich with a side scatter of fries.

OTTO ENOTECA PIZZERIA PIZZA $

Map p416 (212-995-9559; www.ottopizzeria.com; 1 Fifth Ave, entrance on E 8th St, West Village; pizzas $14-16; noon-11pm Mon-Thu, 11:30am-midnight Fri & Sat, to 11pm Sun; ; A/C/E, B/D/F/M to W 4th St-Washington Sq) Just north of Washington Square Park, this is a refreshingly affordable part of Mario Batali's empire, where thin pizzas are cooked on flat-iron griddles till they crackle. They come topped with items far beyond your standard pizza joint – asparagus, goat's cheese, egg, fresh chilies, capers, the best fresh mozzarella – and sauce that has the perfect balance of smoky and sweet.

TAÏM ISRAELI $

Map p416 (212-691-1287; www.taimfalafel.com; 222 Waverly Pl, btwn Perry & W 11th Sts, West Village; sandwiches $8.95-11.75; 11am-10pm; ; 1 to Christopher St-Sheridan Sq, 2/3 to 14th St, A/C/E, L to 8th Ave-14th St) This tiny joint whips up some of the best falafel in the city. You can order it Green (traditional style) or Harissa (with Tunisian spices) – whichever you choose, you'll get it stuffed into pita with tahini, salad and pickles, on a platter with sides such as Moroccan carrots and marinated beets, or over Israeli salad.

CAFFE REGGIO CAFE $

Map p416 (212-475-9557; www.caffereggio.com; 119 MacDougal St, near W 3rd St, West Village; sandwiches around $12; 9am-3am Sun-Thu, to 4am Fri & Sat; A/C/E, B/D/F/M to W 4th St-Washington Sq) This arty, ever-popular cafe is a visual treat with Renaissance paintings and marble-topped tables. Serving fresh pastries, panini, cakes, Italian milkshakes (try the 'delizioso') and delectable coffee since 1927, Reggio's claims to be the first American cafe to serve the cappuccino. You can question their claim, but it's hard to deny that they make a good one.

PEACEFOOD VEGAN $

Map p416 (212-979-2288; www.peacefoodcafe.com; 41 E 11th St, btwn University Pl & Broadway, West Village; mains $11-15; 10am-10pm; ; 4/5/6, L, N/Q/R to 14th St-Union Sq) Peacefood is a vegan and vegetarian diner's best friend with its tasty pizzas, roasted vegetable dishes, pan-seared dumplings and other delicacies. It gets crowded during the lunch and dinner rush, so prepare to eat in cramped quarters.

Local Life
Chelsea Galleries

Local knowledge comes in handy when navigating Chelsea's art spaces – the neighborhood's home to the densest concentration of galleries in NYC. Most lie in the 20s, between Tenth and Eleventh Aves, and open from Tuesday to Saturday (new openings are common on Thursday evening). Pick up Art Info's free Gallery Guide (with map) at most galleries, or visit www.chelseagalleries.nyc.

1 Paula Cooper Gallery

Exhibiting since 1968, **Paula** (www.paulacoopergallery.com; 524 West 26th St, btwn Tenth & Eleventh Aves; 10am-6pm Tue-Sat; 1, C/E to 23rd St) is a legend of the Chelsea scene. Conceptual and minimal art have long been a focus, although you're just as likely to stumble across photography by Sherrie Levine or an acoustic installation by Céleste Boursier-Mougenot.

2 Pace Gallery

Pace Gallery's (p141) eight-story flagship location showcases some of the leading artists of recent years, including Loie Hollowell, Sol LeWitt, David Hockney, Chuck Close and Robert Rauschenberg across 75,000 sq ft.

3 Gladstone Gallery

Barbara Gladstone made her name as a curator in the 1990s New York art world. Today her **gallery** (www.gladstonegallery.com; 515 W 24th St, btwn Tenth & Eleventh Aves; 10am-6pm Mon-Sat; 1, C/E to 23rd St) represents contemporary artists such as Brits Anish Kapoor and Sarah Lucas.

4 Gagosian

Gagosian (p141) offers a different vibe from Chelsea's stand-alone galleries, as it's part of a global network. You might also check out the 21st St location, which rivals some of the city's museums with its large-scale installations.

EDD WESTMACOTT/ALAMY STOCK PHOTO ©

Pace Gallery (p141)

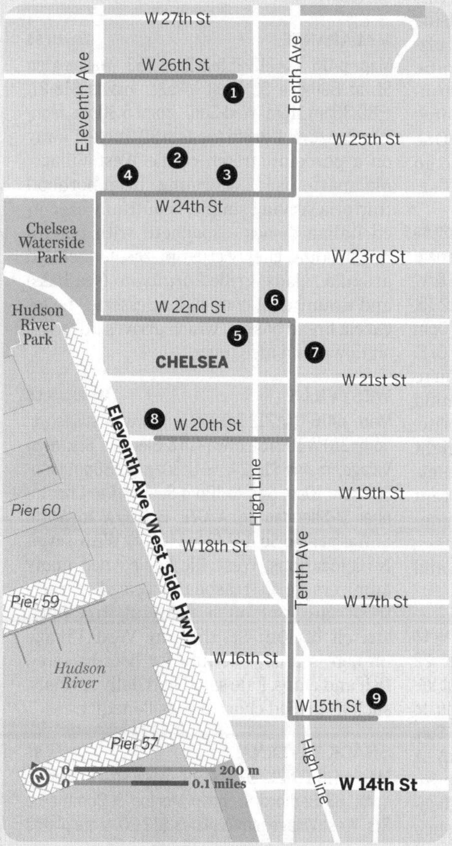

❺ Matthew Marks

Famous for exhibiting relationships with New York artists such as Nan Goldin and Terry Winters, **Matthew Marks** (www.matthewmarks.com; 522 W 22nd St, btwn Tenth & Eleventh Aves; ⌚10am-6pm Tue-Sat; Ⓢ1, C/E to 23rd St) is a true Chelsea pioneer. There are also other locations at 526 W 22nd St and 523 W 24th St.

❻ Tía Pol

Tía Pol (p152) is an intimate place for Basque and Spanish tapas, and is a great stop to refuel and reflect on the inspired works you've consumed in the area's galleries.

❼ 192 Books

It would be easy to walk right by the undemonstrative facade of this delightful little bookstore (p162), which makes a fine reprieve from the big gallery experience. Inside you'll find an edifying selection of literary works, plus artist monographs and children's books.

❽ David Zwirner

One of the major players in the art world, German curator **David Zwirner** (www.davidzwirner.com; 537 W 20th St, btwn Tenth & Eleventh Aves; ⌚10am-6pm Tue-Sat; Ⓢ1, C/E to 23rd St) opened this five-story, sustainability-certified gallery with 30,000 sq ft of exhibition space in 2013. Here he stages some of New York's most celebrated shows; *Infinity Mirrored Room* drew three-hour lines to see Yayoi Kusama's otherworldly light installations.

❾ Artechouse

For a change of pace amid the neighborhood's white-cube gallery scene, descend into the boiler room of Chelsea Market to Artechouse (p141), an immersive center where art and technology converge to conjure hallucinatory experiences through large-scale installations.

JEJU NOODLE BAR NOODLES $$

Map p416 (☎646-666-0947; www.jejunoodlebar.com; 679 Greenwich St, at Christopher St, West Village; noodles $18-19; ⊙5-10pm Sun-Wed, to 11pm Thu-Sat; 🚌M8 to Greenwich St-Christopher St, Ⓢ1 to Christopher St-Sheridan Sq) With classic ramen continuing to rampage across the world's tables, perhaps it's time to explore its variations – such as the Korean *ramyun* served at this welcoming restaurant on Christopher St's quieter western stretch. Start with *toro ssam bap* (fatty tuna, toasted seaweed, *tobiko* rice and scrambled egg) before slurping down a *so ramyun* – brisket and noodles in veal broth.

WILD PIZZA $$

Map p416 (☎212-929-2920; www.eatdrinkwild.com; 535 Hudson St, btwn Perry & Charles Sts, West Village; pizzas $14-17; ⊙11am-10pm Mon & Tue, to 11pm Wed-Sun; 🌶; Ⓢ1/2/3 to Christopher St-Sheridan Sq) Impress your gluten- or lactose-intolerant travel companions with this pizza spot where dietary-sensitive cuisine is the norm. In addition to gluten-free pizzas with toppings such as truffled ricotta, mushrooms and arugula, this relaxed farm-to-table restaurant also offers gluten-free pasta and vegan cheese upon request. One caveat: space is tight, so be prepared to go elbow-to-elbow with fellow diners.

MERMAID OYSTER BAR SEAFOOD $$

Map p416 (☎212-260-0100; www.themermaidnyc.com; 79 MacDougal St, btwn Bleecker & W Houston Sts, West Village; small plates $12-15, mains $25-29; ⊙5-10pm Mon-Thu, to 10:30pm Fri, from 4pm Sat, to 10pm Sun; ⓈA/C/E, B/D/F/M to W 4th St-Washington Sq) If you're craving a plate of oysters and don't mind a crowd, head to this West Village favorite. Happy hour is until 7pm daily (all night Monday) when you'll find young professionals crammed into the small restaurant unwinding over $8.50 glasses of champagne and $1.25 chef's-choice oysters. Squeeze yourself into a spot at the bar and enjoy.

BABU JI INDIAN $$

Map p416 (☎212-951-1082; www.babuji.nyc; 22 E 13th St, btwn University Pl & Fifth Ave, West Village; mains $16-28; ⊙dinner 5-11pm Sun-Thu, to midnight Fri & Sat, brunch 11am-3pm Sat & Sun; Ⓢ4/5/6, N/Q/R/W, L to 14th St-Union Sq) A playful spirit marks this Australian-run Indian restaurant near Union Sq. Many dishes play fast and loose with tradition, such as 'naan pizza' with sweet-pickled-chili butter, mushroom tikka with lemon-garlic sour cream and herbs, and tandoori-charred dorade with orange curry sauce, cucumber and daikon. A $62 tasting menu, obligatory for the entire party, can be matched with beers or wines.

MURRAY'S CHEESE BAR CHEESE $$

Map p416 (☎646-476-8882; www.murrayscheesebar.com; 264 Bleecker St, btwn Leroy & Morton Sts, West Village; mains $16-30; ⊙5-10pm Mon & Tue, to midnight Wed & Thu, from noon Fri, from 11am Sat, to 10pm Sun; ⓈA/C/E, B/D/F/M to W 4th St-Washington Sq) Lovers of fine cheeses no longer have to settle for takeout orders from Murray's famed West Village fromagerie (p162). Gourmet mac 'n' cheese, melted-cheese sandwiches, fondue, *raclette* and other cheese-centric dishes dominate the menu at this tile-lined eat and drinkery. You can also order a variety of cheeses à la carte.

MALAPARTE ITALIAN $$

Map p416 (☎212-255-2122; 753 Washington St, at Bethune St, West Village; mains $18-27; ⊙10:30am-11pm Wed-Sun, from 5:30pm Mon-Tue; ⓈA/C/E, L to 8th Ave-14th St) Tucked away on a peaceful stretch of the West Village, Malaparte is a charming neighborhood trattoria serving simple, beautifully executed Italian dishes – spaghetti with porcini mushrooms, chewy crust pizzas, fennel and arugula salads, grilled *branzino* (sea bass) and tiramisu (of course) for dessert. The focaccia bread basket, which arrives after you sit down, is a nice touch.

WESTVILLE AMERICAN $$

Map p416 (☎212-741-7971; www.westvillenyc.com; 210 W 10th St, btwn 4th & Bleecker Sts, West Village; mains $13-24; ⊙11:30am-10:30pm Mon-Fri, from 10am Sat, to 10pm Sun; Ⓢ1 to Christopher St-Sheridan Sq; A/C/E, B/D/F/M to W 4th St-Washington Sq; 1/2/3 to 14th St) With seven NYC locations, Westville has earned many admirers for its reasonably priced market-fresh fare. Set on a peaceful, tree-lined stretch of 10th St, the tiny West Village branch is a cozy setting for beer-battered fish and chips, kale salad and daily specials, such as grilled chorizo eggs Benedict.

SNACK TAVERNA GREEK $$

Map p416 (☎212-929-3499; www.snacktaverna.com; 63 Bedford St, btwn Morton & Commerce Sts, West Village; small plates $12-20, large plates

$26-30; ⏲11am-4:30pm & 5:30-11pm Mon-Sat, to 10pm Sun; Ⓢ A/C/E, B/D/F/M to W 4 St-Washington Sq; 1 to Christopher St-Sheridan Sq) So much more than your usual Greek restaurant, Snack Taverna eschews gyros for a seasonal selection of scrumptious small plates to accompany the flavorful selection of market mains. The regional wines are worth a miss, but the Med beers are surprisingly refreshing.

ALTA — TAPAS $$

Map p416 (☎212-505-7777; www.altarestaurant.com; 64 W 10th St, btwn Fifth & Sixth Aves, West Village; small plates $13-26; ⏲5:30-9:30pm Sun & Mon, to 10pm Tue-Thu, 5-10:45pm Fri & Sat; Ⓢ A/C/E, B/D/F/M to W 4th St-Washington Sq) This gorgeous town house highlights the neighborhood's quaintness, with plenty of exposed brick, wood beams, flickering candles, massive mirrors and romantic fireplace glows. A small-plates menu of encyclopedic proportions cures indecision with the likes of succulent lamb meatballs, seared scallops with pistachio, Japanese eggplant with époisses, fried goat's cheese and braised short rib. The wine list is outstanding, too.

URBAN VEGAN KITCHEN — VEGAN $$

Map p416 (☎646-438-9939; www.urbanvegankitchen.com; 41 Carmine St, btwn Bleecker & Bedford Sts, West Village; mains brunch $14-23, dinner $17-23; ⏲11am-11pm Mon-Thu, to midnight Fri, from 10am Sat, to 10:30pm Sun; 🖉; Ⓢ A/C/E, B/D/F/M to W 4th St-Washington Sq) This spot serves solid vegan cuisine in a moody, fun environment. Stop by for brunch and feast on chick-un and waffles with garlic kale and maple mustard aioli, or come for dinner and grab some double-decker seitan tacos.

★JEFFREY'S GROCERY — AMERICAN $$$

Map p416 (☎646-398-7630; www.jeffreysgrocery.com; 172 Waverly Pl, at Christopher St, West Village; mains $21-35; ⏲8am-11pm Mon-Wed, to 1am Thu-Fri, from 9:30am Sat, to 11pm Sun; Ⓢ 1 to Christopher St-Sheridan Sq) This West Village classic is a lively eating and drinking spot that hits all the right notes. Seafood is the focus: there's an oyster bar and beautifully executed mains such as mussels with green curry, coconut milk and herbs, a panko skate sandwch, and caviar toast. Meat dishes include hanger steak with fingerling potatoes and chimichurri sauce.

★REDFARM — FUSION $$$

Map p416 (☎212-792-9700; www.redfarmnyc.com; 529 Hudson St, btwn W 10th & Charles Sts, West Village; mains $20-58, dumplings $14-20; ⏲dinner 5-10:45pm Sun-Wed, to 11:30pm Thu-Sat, brunch 11am-2:30pm Sat & Sun; Ⓢ 1 to Christopher St-Sheridan Sq, A/C/E, B/D/F/M to W 4th St-Washington Sq) Experience Chinese cooking as unique, delectable artistry in this small, buzzing space. Diced tuna and eggplant bruschetta, crispy-skin smoked chicken with garlic and pastrami egg rolls are among the many stunning, genre-defying dishes. Other hits include lobster sautéed with egg and chopped pork, Kowloon filet-mignon tarts, and crispy duck and crab dumplings.

Waits can be long, and reservations are only made for parties of eight or more, so arrive early. The bar downstairs, **Decoy** (open 5pm to midnight Sunday to Wednesday, to 2am Thursday to Saturday), is part of RedFarm and specializes in Peking duck. It's usually less crowded, and takes smaller reservations, but only for parties willing to commit to the prix-fixe duck menu ($95 per person). Further RedFarm outlets have opened on the Upper West Side and in London.

★BLUE HILL — AMERICAN $$$

Map p416 (☎212-539-1776; www.bluehillfarm.com; 75 Washington Pl, btwn Sixth Ave & Washington Sq W, West Village; prix-fixe menu $95-108; ⏲5-11pm Mon-Sat, to 10pm Sun; Ⓢ A/C/E, B/D/F/M to W 4th St-Washington Sq) A place for Slow Food junkies with deep pockets, Blue Hill was an early crusader in the farm-to-table movement. Gifted chef-patron Dan Barber, who hails from a farm family in the Berkshires, MA, uses regional harvests to create his widely praised fare.

Expect judiciously seasoned, perfectly ripe vegetables that highlight proteins such as Montauk monkfish or Blue Hill Farm chicken. The space itself, set just below street level in a former speakeasy on a quaint village block, is sophisticated and serene. Reservations and 'elegant casual' dress are recommended, and cell phones and photography are forbidden in the dining room.

BAGATELLE — FRENCH $$$

Map p416 (☎212-488-2110; www.bagatellenyc.com; 1 Little W 12th St, btwn Ninth Ave & Hudson St, Meatpacking District; mains $29-54;

1

2

4

MILA PARH/SHUTTERSTOCK ©

1. Chelsea Market (p151)
Enjoy succulent lobster and other gastronomic delights at this popular food and craft market.

2. Washington Square Park (p137)
Hang out in heart of the Village.

3. The Stonewall Inn (p155)
This National Historic Monument is one of the birthplaces of the gay-rights movement.

4. Buvette (p153)
Settle in for drinks and dinner at this Francophile wine bar and restaurant.

GLYNNIS JONES/SHUTTERSTOCK ©

⏲11:30am-midnight Sun-Wed, to 1am Thu, to 2am Fri & Sat; S A/C/E, L to 8th Ave-14th St) At Bagatelle, elegant bentwood chairs, chandeliers, white linens and (ultimately) the bill conspire to give you the impression you're eating somewhere top-drawer in St-Tropez. Brunch, with a raw-seafood bar and plenty of refined egg dishes, is a favorite, but a dinner of French classics is also an occasion.

NIX VEGETARIAN **$$$**

Map p416 (☎212-498-9393; www.nixny.com; 72 University Pl, btwn E 10th & E 11th Sts, West Village; mains $26-28; ⏲5:30-10:30pm Mon-Thu, 5-11pm Fri, 10:30am-2:30pm & 5-11pm Sat, 10:30am-2:30pm & 5-10:30pm Sun; ✎; S 4/5/6, N/Q/R/W, L to 14th St-Union Sq) At this modest yet Michelin-starred restaurant, chefs John Fraser and Garrett Eagleton transform vegetables into beautifully executed dishes that delight the senses. Start with tandoor bread with dips such as red pepper and walnut, then move to more complex plates such as burrata with Granny Smith apples or cauliflower tempura with steamed buns and pickles.

CHUMLEY'S AMERICAN **$$$**

Map p416 (☎212-675-2081; www.chumleysnewyork.com; 86 Bedford St, btwn Grove & Barrow Sts, West Village; mains $29-36; ⏲5:30-10:15pm Mon-Thu, to 10:30pm Fri & Sat, 11:30am-3:30pm Sun; S 1 to Christopher St-Sheridan Sq, A/C/E, B/D/F/M to W 4th St-Washington Sq) Occupying the site of a legendary 1922 West Village speakeasy, Chumley's maintains its historic air while upgrading everything else. The ambitious seasonal menu includes arctic char cooked in parchment and a burger with two 4oz patties, bone marrow and shallots. Walls are lined with the portraits and book jackets of Prohibition-era writers, many of whom were once bar patrons.

ROSEMARY'S ITALIAN **$$$**

Map p416 (☎212-647-1818; www.rosemarysnyc.com; 18 Greenwich Ave, at W 10th St, West Village; mains $26-28, lunch/dinner prix fixe $24/34; ⏲8am-4pm & 5-11pm Mon-Thu, 8am-4pm & 5pm-midnight Fri, 10am-4pm & 5pm-midnight Sat, 10am-4pm & 5-11pm Sun; S 1 to Christopher St-Sheridan Sq) One of the West Village's hottest restaurants, Rosemary's serves high-end Italian fare that lives up to the hype. In a vaguely farmhouse-like setting, diners tuck into generous portions of house-made pastas, rich salads, and cheese and cured meat boards. Everything, from the beets with bitter greens and hazelnuts to the 'Meiller Farm' pork with orange mustard fruits, is incredible.

Some of the produce is grown in-house – or rather, *over* the house, with a state-of-the art rooftop garden producing crisp dandelion greens, plump zucchinis and mouthwatering tomatoes. Plan for crowds (reservations are only for groups of eight or more) or arrive early.

SUSHI NAKAZAWA SUSHI **$$$**

Map p416 (☎212-924-2212; www.sushinakazawa.com; 23 Commerce St, btwn Bedford St & Seventh Ave, West Village; prix-fixe menu $120 & $150; ⏲lunch 11:30am, 11:45am, 1:15pm & 1:30pm, dinner 5-10:15pm; S 1 to Christopher St-Sheridan Sq) The price is high, but the quality is phenomenal at this jewel-box-sized sushi spot that opened to much acclaim in 2013. There are no cooked dishes and little in the way of individual choice. Instead the meal is a 20-course fixed-price affair created by chef Daisuke Nakazawa, who served under Jiro Ono, probably the world's finest sushi chef.

MINETTA TAVERN BISTRO **$$$**

Map p416 (☎212-475-3850; www.minettatavernny.com; 113 MacDougal St, at Minetta Lane, West Village; mains $25-39; ⏲noon-3pm & 5:30pm-midnight Wed, to 1am Thu & Fri, 11am-3pm & 5:30pm-1am Sat, 11am-midnight Sun, 5:30pm-midnight Mon & Tue; S A/C/E, B/D/F/M to W 4th St-Washington Sq) Book in advance, or come early to snag a table on a weeknight, because Minetta Tavern is often packed to the rafters.

The snug red-leather banquettes, dark-paneled walls with B&W photos and glowing yellow bistro lamps will lure you in. The flavor-filled bistro fare – pan-seared marrow bones, roasted free-range chicken and briny mussels – will have you wishing you lived upstairs.

CAFÉ CLUNY BISTRO **$$$**

Map p416 (☎212-255-6900; www.cafecluny.com; 284 W 12th St, cnr W 12th & W 4th Sts, West Village; mains lunch $18-34, dinner $25-40; ⏲8am-10pm Mon, to 11pm Tue-Fri, from 9am Sat, to 10pm Sun; S A/C/E, L 8th Ave-14th St) Café Cluny brings the charm of Paris to the West Village, with woven bistro-style bar chairs, light wooden upholstery and a selection of *joie-de-vivre*-inducing platters. Service operates in three sections: brunch morning to afternoon, brasserie in the early evening and dinner at night. No matter the hour, the dishes are tasty and well prepared.

Chelsea

L'ARTE DEL GELATO ICE CREAM $

Map p420 (212-366-0570; www.lartedelgelato.com; Chelsea Market, 75 Ninth Ave, btwn W 15th & 16th Sts, Chelsea; ice cream $6-16; 11am-10pm; S A/C/E, L to 8th Ave-14th St) Sweet tooths will fawn over L'Arte Del Gelato, where gelato flavors are made fresh every day and come in over 20 varieties. It's the perfect snack to take up to the High Line – though L'Arte del Gelato also sells from a small cart along the greenway.

CHELSEA SQUARE DINER DINER $

Map p420 (212-691-5400; www.chelseasquareny.com; 368 W 23rd St, at Ninth Ave, Chelsea; mains breakfast $8-16, lunch & dinner $10-35; 24hr; S 1, C/E to 23rd St) This is one of the biggest and best of the old-school NYC diners. The food is tasty and its location in the heart of the Chelsea bar scene couldn't be better. During the day, you'll find old neighborhood regulars catching up over turkey clubs and Chelsea boys working on omelets after a long night out.

JUN-MEN RAMEN $$

Map p420 (646-852-6787; www.junmenramen.com; 249 Ninth Ave, btwn 25th & 26th Sts, Chelsea; ramen $16-19; 11:30am-3pm & 5-10pm Mon-Thu, to 11pm Fri & Sat; S 1, C/E to 23rd St) This tiny, ultramodern ramen joint whips up delectably flavored noodle bowls in variants of pork shoulder, spicy miso or uni mushroom (with sea urchin). Don't skip the appetizers: the yellowtail ceviche and barbecue pork buns are outstanding. Service is speedy, and it's fun to watch the adroit prep team in action in the tiny kitchen at center stage.

The wait can be long – go early to beat the crowds.

COOKSHOP AMERICAN $$

Map p420 (212-924-4440; www.cookshopny.com; 156 Tenth Ave, at W 20th St, Chelsea; mains brunch $14-18, lunch $16-25, dinner $23-34; 8am-11:30pm Mon-Fri, from 10am Sat, to 10pm Sun; ; S 1, C/E to 23rd St) A brilliant brunching pit stop before (or after) tackling the

TOP EXPERIENCE
CHELSEA MARKET

In a shining example of redevelopment and preservation, the Chelsea Market has transformed a former Nabisco factory – the Oreo cookie was invented here – into a shopping concourse catering to foodies and fashionistas. Take your pick of gastronomic delights from more than two dozen food vendors, including Mokbar (ramen with Korean accents), Bar Suzette (crepes), Num Pang (Cambodian sandwiches) and Doughnuttery (piping hot mini-doughnuts). For something more indulgent sample the first-rate seafood and raw bar at Cull & Pistol or stop by Friedman's Lunch for upscale American comfort food.

For nonfood offerings, browse Imports from Marrakesh, which specializes in Moroccan art and design; check out the latest literary hits at Posman Books; search for a new outfit at Anthropologie; or pick up a bottle at the expert-staffed Chelsea Wine Vault. At the Tenth Ave entrance is Artists and Fleas, a permanent market for local designers and craftspeople to sell their wares. It's the place to stop for a quirky new wallet, trendy pair of sunglasses or a piece of statement jewelry.

DON'T MISS

- Takumi Taco
- Doughnuttery
- Artists and Fleas

PRACTICALITIES

- Map p420, D5
- www.chelseamarket.com
- 75 Ninth Ave, btwn W 15th & W 16 Sts, Chelsea
- 7am-2am Mon-Sat, 8am-10pm Sun
- S A/C/E, L to 8th Ave-14th St

verdant High Line (p134) across the street, Cookshop is a lively place that knows its niche and nails it. Excellent service, eye-opening cocktails (good morning, Blushing Monk!), a perfectly baked bread basket, outdoor seating for warm days and inventive egg dishes make this a Chelsea favorite.

Beyond brunch you'll find great dinner dishes such as cornmeal-crusted skate with clam escabeche, chili and parsley potatoes, and a thoughtful vegetarian selection.

TÍA POL TAPAS **$$**

Map p420 (☎212-675-8805; www.tiapol.com; 205 Tenth Ave, btwn 22nd & 23rd Sts; small plates $7-16; ⏱5:30-11pm Mon, from noon Tue-Thu, to midnight Fri, from 11am Sat, to 10:30pm Sun; Ⓢ1, C/E to 23rd St) Churning out quality Spanish and Basque tapas in closet-size surrounds, Tía Pol is the real deal, as the hordes of locals swarming the entrance can attest. There's a great wine list and a tantalizing array of small plates: fried chickpeas, squid and ink with rice, cockles in white wine and garlic, and Navarran-style trout with serrano ham.

BLOSSOM VEGAN **$$**

Map p420 (☎212-627-1144; www.blossomnyc.com; 187 Ninth Ave, btwn 21st & 22nd Sts, Chelsea; mains lunch $14-24, dinner $22-25; ⏱noon-2:45pm & 5-9:30pm Mon-Thu, to 10pm Fri & Sat, to 9pm Sun; ✎; Ⓢ1, C/E to 23rd St) Cozily occupying a historic Chelsea town house, this beacon to hungry vegans is a peaceful, romantic dining spot that offers imaginative, all-kosher tofu, seitan and vegetable creations, some raw. Brunch dishes like tofu Benedict and Florentine impersonate animal proteins deliciously, while superb dinner mains such as the spaghetti squash cake and mushroom risotto with saffron-cashew cream need no affectations.

★FORAGERS TABLE AMERICAN **$$$**

Map p420 (☎212-243-8888; www.foragersmarket.com/restaurant; 300 W 22nd St, at Eighth Ave, Chelsea; mains $20-39; ⏱dinner 5:30-10pm Mon-Sat, to 9pm Sun, brunch 9am-3pm Sat & Sun; ✎; Ⓢ1, C/E to 23rd St) The owners of this outstanding restaurant run a 28-acre Hudson Valley farm, from which much of the seasonal menu is sourced. It changes frequently, but recent temptations included pan-roasted duck breast with poached pears, mushroom pappardelle with sherry and toasted almonds, and cauliflower with sweet-potato tahini and sumac onions.

Next door is the **gourmet market** (open 8am to 10pm Monday to Saturday, to 9pm Sunday), where you can browse goodies from organic produce to heavenly desserts. From 8am to 3:30pm Monday to Friday you're free to eat things bought here at the restaurant tables. There's also a **wine shop** with an excellent selection of natural wines from small producers.

DRINKING & NIGHTLIFE

Hedonism is de rigueur in these streets, which are perhaps more lavishly supplied with bars and clubs than anywhere else in NYC. In the West Village, keep heading west – the further you go toward the Hudson, the more likely you are to sidestep the NYU frat-party scene. Generally, the crooked lanes west of Sixth Ave are a good bet. The Meatpacking District is clubland, with sprawling, modern spaces boasting long cocktail lists, velvet-roped entrances and jaw-rattling sound systems. Chelsea is still a playground for gay men, but there are options for all tastes, from chic speakeasies to proper dive bars.

West Village & the Meatpacking District

★EMPLOYEES ONLY BAR

Map p416 (☎212-242-3021; www.employeesonlynyc.com; 510 Hudson St, btwn W 10th & Christopher Sts, West Village; ⏱6pm-4am; Ⓢ1 to Christopher St-Sheridan Sq) This divine cocktail bar, tucked behind a discreet green awning on Hudson St, is a world-beater. Ace mixologists shake up crazy libations like the Ginger Smash, and the wood-rich art deco space makes everyone feel glamorous. Open until 3:30am, the kitchen plays its part, too, producing delights such as bone-marrow poppers and spicy shrimp on polenta (mains $27 to $31).

HAPPIEST HOUR COCKTAIL BAR

Map p416 (☎212-243-2827; www.happiesthournyc.com; 121 W 10th St, btwn Greenwich St & Sixth Ave, West Village; ⏱5pm-late Mon-Fri, from 2pm Sat & Sun; ⓈA/C/E, B/D/F/M to W 4th St-Washington Sq; 1 to Christopher St-Sheridan Sq) A supercool, tiki-licious cocktail bar splashed with palm prints, '60s pop and playful mixed drinks that provide a chic take on the fruity beach cocktail. The crowd tends to be button-down after-work types and online daters. Beneath sits its serious sibling, **Slowly Shirley**, an art-deco-style subterranean temple to beautifully crafted, thoroughly researched libations.

BUVETTE WINE BAR

Map p416 (☎212-255-3590; www.ilovebuvette.com; 42 Grove St, btwn Bedford & Bleecker Sts, West Village; small plates $12-18; ⊙7am-2am; S1 to Christopher St-Sheridan Sq, A/C/E, B/D/F/M to W 4th St-Washington Sq) Buzzing with the animated conversation of locals, courting couples and theater types, this devotedly Francophile wine bar and restaurant makes a great rest stop amid a West Village backstreet wander. Enjoy a cocktail or a glass of wine, or settle in for a meal. Brunch dishes such as croque monsieurs are replaced by tartines and small plates at dinner.

MARIE'S CRISIS BAR

Map p416 (☎212-243-9323; 59 Grove St, btwn Seventh Ave & Bleecker St, West Village; ⊙4pm-3am Sun-Thu, to 4am Fri & Sat; S1 to Christopher St-Sheridan Sq, A/C/E, B/D/F/M to W 4th St-Washington Sq) Ageing Broadway queens, wide-eyed out-of-town youngsters, giggly tourists and various other fans of musical theater assemble around the piano here and take turns belting out campy show tunes, often joined by the entire crowd – and the occasional celebrity. It's old-school fun, no matter how jaded you might be when you go in. Non-flash photography is allowed, but video is not.

UNCOMMONS CAFE

Map p416 (☎646-543-9215; www.uncommonsnyc.com; 230 Thompson St, btwn W 3rd & Bleecker Sts, West Village; board games per hour/day $5/10; ⊙8:30am-midnight Mon-Thu, to 1am Fri & Sat, to 11pm Sun; 📶; SA/C/E, B/D/F/M to W 4th St-Washington Sq) If you can't get enough of board games, duck into this coffee shop, where a small fee gives you access to an enormous collection of new, popular and rare table-top games (also available for sale). The atmosphere is jovial and there's ample space to play, although it can get crowded during peak hours.

BELL BOOK & CANDLE BAR

Map p416 (☎212-414-2355; www.bbandcnyc.com; 141 W 10th St, btwn Waverly Pl & Greenwich Ave, West Village; ⊙5:30pm-2am Sun-Wed, to 4am Thu-Sat, also 11:30am-3:30pm Sat; SA/C/E, B/D/F/M to W 4th St-Washington Sq; 1 to Christopher St-Sheridan Sq) Step down into this candlelit gastropub for strong, inventive

COFFEE CULTURE

New York is no longer a second-string city when it comes to great coffee. Celebrated brewmasters, bringing technical wizardry and high-quality single-source coffee beans, have reinvented the simple cup of joe. For a mix of both classic and cutting-edge cafes, the West Village is a great place to start.

Stumptown Coffee Roasters (Map p416; ☎347-414-7802; www.stumptowncoffee.com; 30 W 8th St, at MacDougal St, West Village; ⊙7am-8pm; SA/C/E, B/D/F/M to W 4th St-Washington Sq) This renowned Portland roaster is helping to reinvent the NYC coffee scene with its exquisitely made brews. It has an elegant interior with coffered ceiling and walnut bar, though its few tables are often overtaken by the laptop-toting crowd.

Joe Coffee Company (Map p416; ☎212-924-6750; www.joecoffeecompany.com; 141 Waverly Pl, at Gay St, West Village; ⊙7am-8pm Mon-Fri, from 8am Sat & Sun; SA/C/E, B/D/F/M to W 4th St-Washington Sq) Superb coffee is served at this always-bustling joint sitting squarely on bucolic Waverly Pl in the heart of the Village. Some say this is the best cup of joe in town.

Blue Bottle (Map p420; www.bluebottlecoffee.com; 450 W 15th St, btwn 9th & 10th Aves, Chelsea; ⊙7am-6:30pm Mon-Fri, from 8am Sat & Sun; SA/C/E, L to 8th Ave-14th St) Blue Bottle may have originated in Oakland, but New Yorkers have happily embraced this high-quality third-wave roaster. Blue Bottle's small outpost across from the Chelsea Market uses scales and thermometers to make sure your pour-over or espresso is perfect. Grab one of the few window seats, or head to one of the mezzanine tables above the baristas.

libations with infused spirits and smoky mezcals and hearty late-night pub grub. A 20-something crowd gathers around the small, packed bar (for $1 oysters and happy-hour drink specials early in the night), though there's a lot more seating in the back, with big booths ideal for larger groups.

VIN SUR VINGT WINE BAR

Map p416 (☎212-924-4442; www.vsvwinebars.com; 201 W 11th St, btwn Seventh Ave & Waverly Pl, West Village; ⏲4pm-1am Mon-Fri, to 2am Sat & Sun; ⓈA/C/E, L to 8th Ave-14th St) A cozy spot just off Seventh Ave's bustle, Vin Sur Vingt is a slender wine bar with a strip of bar seating and a quaint row of two-seat tables, perfect for a first date. Warning: if you come for a pre-dinner drink, you'll inevitably be charmed into staying through dinner as you munch on the excellent selection of bar bites.

LE BAIN CLUB

Map p416 (☎212-645-7600; www.standardhotels.com; Standard, 848 Washington St, at 13th St, Meatpacking District; ⏲4pm-midnight Mon, to 4am Tue-Thu, from 2pm Fri & Sat, to 3am Sun; ⓈA/C/E, L to 8th Ave-14th St) This sweeping rooftop venue at the painfully hip Standard hotel (p339) sees a garish parade of party promoters who do their thing on any day of the week. Brace yourself for skyline views, a giant Jacuzzi on the dance floor, legendary DJs such as Tony Humphries and Danny Krivit and an eclectic crowd getting wasted on pricey snifters.

124 OLD RABBIT CLUB BAR

Map p416 (☎646-781-9646; www.rabbitclubnyc.com; 124 MacDougal St, at Minetta Lane, West Village; ⏲6pm-2am Sun-Thu, to 4am Fri & Sat; ⓈA/C/E, B/D/F/M to W 4th St-Washington Sq; 1 to Houston St) You'll wanna pat yourself on the back when you find this well-concealed bar (hint: look for the tiny word 'Rabbit' over the door). Once you're inside the narrow, cavern-like space with its low-key vibe, grab a seat at the dimly lit bar and reward yourself with a quenching stout or one of the dozens of imported brews.

LITTLE BRANCH COCKTAIL BAR

Map p416 (☎212-929-4360; 22 Seventh Ave, at Leroy St, West Village; ⏲7pm-2am Sun-Wed, to 3am Thu-Sat; Ⓢ1 to Houston St, A/C/E, B/D/F/M to W 4th St-Washington Sq) If it weren't for the lines later in the evening, you'd never guess that a charming bar lay beyond this plain metal door set into a brick wall on a triangular corner. Walking downstairs to the basement den feels like a throwback to Prohibition: patrons clink glasses and sip artfully prepared cocktails, and there are jazz performances Sunday through Thursday.

KETTLE OF FISH BAR

Map p416 (☎212-414-2278; www.kettleoffishnyc.com; 59 Christopher St, near Seventh Ave, West Village; ⏲3pm-4am Mon-Fri, from 2pm Sat & Sun; Ⓢ1 to Christopher St-Sheridan Sq; A/C/E, B/D/F/M to W 4th St-Washington Sq) Step into this former Jack Kerouac hangout, full of couches and plump chairs, and prepare to stay for a while because the crowd is simply beguiling. It's a dive bar, a sports bar and a gay bar in one, and everyone mixes happily.

ART BAR BAR

Map p416 (☎212-727-0244; www.artbar.com; 52 Eighth Ave, near Horatio St, Meatpacking District; ⏲4pm-4am; ⓈA/C/E, L to 8th Ave-14th St) A decidedly bohemian crowd favors Art Bar, which doesn't look like much up front (booths are crowded too close to the wooden bar), but it has more going on in the back. Grab your beer or a house special (usually martinis) and head for the couches, under a huge *Last Supper*-esque mural featuring Jimmy Dean and Marilyn Monroe, among others.

TROY LIQUOR BAR LOUNGE

Map p416 (☎212-699-2410; www.troyliquorbar.com; 675 Hudson St, at W 13th St (entrance on W 13th St), Meatpacking District; ⏲6pm-midnight Wed, to 2am Thu, to 4am Fri & Sat; ⓈA/C/E, L to 8th Ave-14th St) Tucked under Bill's Bar & Burger in the Meatpacking District is this indie-rock-loving, graffiti-scrawled hangout. Come for a game of foosball or hide away with your retro cocktail in one of the cave-like nooks.

FAT CAT BAR

Map p416 (☎212-675-6056; www.fatcatmusic.org; 75 Christopher St, btwn 7th Ave & Bleecker St, West Village; cover $3/5 on Sat & Sun; ⏲2pm-5am Mon-Thu, from noon Fri-Sun; Ⓢ1 to Christopher St-Sheridan Sq; A/C/E, B/D/F/M to W 4th St-Washington Sq) If $16 cocktails and fancy-schmancy Village boutiquery are getting you down, maybe it's time to pay a visit to this run-down little ping-pong hall. Fat Cat is a basement dive that draws a young, unpretentious crowd who want

DOWNTOWN GAY & LESBIAN BARS

Cubbyhole (Map p416; ☎212-243-9041; www.cubbyholebar.com; 281 W 12th St, at W 4th St, West Village; ⏰4pm-4am Mon-Fri, from 2pm Sat & Sun; Ⓢ A/C/E, L to 8th Ave-14th St) This West Village dive bills itself as 'lesbian, gay and straight friendly since 1994.' While the crowd's mostly ladies, it welcomes anyone looking for a drink in good company beneath a ceiling festooned with lanterns, toys and other ephemera. It's got a great jukebox, friendly bartenders and regulars who prefer to hang and chat rather than hook up and leave.

Eagle NYC (Map p420; ☎646-473-1866; www.eagle-ny.com; 554 W 28th St, btwn Tenth & Eleventh Aves, Chelsea; ⏰10pm-4am Mon-Sat, from 5pm Sun; Ⓢ 1, C/E to 23rd St) The Eagle is the choice for out-and-proud leather fetishists. Its two levels, roof deck and 'dark and sleazy' vibe are perfect for dancing, drinking and cruising, all done with abandon. There are frequent theme nights, so check the website lest you arrive without the appropriate attire (which may be nothing).

Gym Sportsbar (Map p420; ☎212-337-2439; www.gymsportsbar.com; 167 8th Ave; ⏰4pm-2am Mon-Thu, to 4am Fri, from 1pm Sat, to 2am Sun; Ⓢ A/C/E, L to 8th Ave-14th St) In the midst of Chelsea's famous gay nightlife scene, Gym Sportsbar offers a low-key vibe for LGBTIQ+ patrons. There are friendly bartenders, cheap drinks, a pool table in the back, a smoking patio out front and TVs throughout the bar playing whatever sport is in season. Weekday happy hour offers two-for-one drinks.

Henrietta Hudson (Map p416; ☎212-924-3347; www.henriettahudson.com; 438 Hudson St, at Morton St, West Village; ⏰4pm-2am Mon & Tue, to 4am Wed-Sun; Ⓢ 1 to Houston St) All sorts of young women, many from neighboring New Jersey and Long Island, storm this 'Bar & Girl,' where theme nights bring in spirited DJs spinning hip-hop, house, rock and other genres. Happy hour is 4pm to 7pm daily.

Julius' (Map p416; ☎877-746-0528; www.juliusbarny.com; 159 W 10th St, at Waverly Pl, West Village; ⏰1pm-4am Mon-Fri, from noon Sat & Sun; Ⓢ 1 to Christopher St-Sheridan Sq, A/C/E, B/D/F/M to W 4th St-Washington Sq) One of the oldest gay joints in NYC, Julius is a refreshingly unpretentious dive bar through and through. The clientele is a mix of the old queer vanguard and scruffy younger upstarts, and the food, cooked opposite the bar, is also without pretense (a burger or a grilled-cheese or chicken sandwich won't set you back more than $6).

Stonewall Inn (Map p416; ☎212-488-2705; www.thestonewallinnnyc.com; 53 Christopher St, at Christopher Park, West Village; ⏰2pm-4am Mon-Wed, from noon Thu-Sun; Ⓢ 1 to Christopher St-Sheridan Sq) Site of the 1969 Stonewall riots and a birthplace of the gay-rights movement, Stonewall is a National Historic Monument and a de facto place of pilgrimage. Despite its international fame, it's a friendly, unpretentious spot that welcomes everyone under the LGBTIQ+ rainbow (and their allies) to nightly events such as 'I Love the '90s' karaoke and drag bingo.

Monster (Map p416; ☎212-924-3558; www.monsterbarnyc.com; 80 Grove St, at Sheridan Sq, West Village; ⏰4pm-4am Mon-Fri, from 2pm Sat & Sun; Ⓢ 1 to Christopher St-Sheridan Sq; A/C/E, B/D/F/M W 4th St-Washington Sq) It's old-school gay-man heaven in here, with a small dance floor downstairs as well as a piano bar and cabaret space. Spirited theme nights range from Latino parties to drag-queen-hosted soirees.

Ty's (Map p416; ☎212-741-9641; www.tys.nyc; 114 Christopher St, btwn Bedford & Bleecker Sts, West Village; ⏰2am-2pm Mon-Wed, to 3am Thu, to 4am Fri & Sat, 1pm-3am Sun; Ⓢ 1 to Christopher St-Sheridan Sq; A/C/E, B/D/F/M to W 4th St-Washington Sq) New York's gay-bar scene has a reputation for catering to young, model types, but in the West Village you'll find many bars with a more welcoming atmosphere. Ty's has been an established presence in the neighborhood since the '70s. It caters to an older crowd and has a friendly, dive-bar vibe and dirt-cheap drinks.

to hang out, shoot some pool, play a little shuffleboard and maybe even get a ping-pong game going.

HIGHLANDS BAR

Map p416 (☎212-229-2670; www.highlands-nyc.com; 150 W 10th St, near Waverly Pl, West Village; ⏰5pm-1am Mon-Thu, to 3am Fri, from 11:30am Sat, to midnight Sun; Ⓢ1 to Christopher St-Sheridan Sq; A/C/E, B/D/F/M to W 4th St-Washington Sq) This handsome Scottish-inspired drinkery is a fine place to while away an evening. Exposed brick, a fireplace and a mix of animal heads, pheasant wallpaper, oil paintings and Edinburgh tartans on the walls bring more than a touch of the old country to the ambience. Scottish beers and spirits, plus haggis, Scotch eggs, shepherd's pie and other traditional bites round out the menu.

VOL DE NUIT PUB

Map p416 (☎212-982-3388; www.voldenuitbar.com; 148 W 4th St, btwn Sixth Ave & MacDougal St; ⏰4pm-1am Sun-Thu, to 3am Fri & Sat; ⓈA/C/E, B/D/F/M to W 4th St-Washington Sq) Even all the NYU students can't ruin this: a cozy Belgian beer bar with Delirium Tremens on tap and a few dozen bottle options, including Duvel and Lindemans Framboise (raspberry beer!). You can order *moules* (mussels) and *frites* (fries) to share at the front patio seats, the lounge, the communal wood tables or under the bar's dangling red lights.

TOP OF THE STANDARD BAR

Map p416 (☎212-645-7600; www.standardhotels.com; Standard, 848 Washington St, at W 13th St, Meatpacking District; ⏰4pm-midnight; ⓈA/C/E, L to 8th Ave-14th St) Afternoon tea and drinks morph into evening cocktails in this splendid perch atop the ever-so stylish Standard (p337) hotel.

Small plates ($12 to $20), such as English-pea ravioli or Moroccan shrimp with pickled raisins and Greek yogurt, are on hand to address any pangs of hunger, while live jazz and fabulous views complete the picture of sophistication.

WHITE HORSE TAVERN BAR

Map p416 (☎212-989-3956; www.whitehorsetavern1880.com; 567 Hudson St, at W 11th St, West Village; ⏰11am-2am; Ⓢ1 to Christopher St-Sheridan Sq) Run continuously since 1880 (it may be the second-oldest bar in NYC), this West Village institution is, understandably, on the tourist trail. Don't let that dampen your enjoyment of its pubby charms, including a pressed-tin ceiling and white-horse chandeliers: after all, Dylan Thomas and Jack Kerouac thought it was worth stopping here for a drink.

BRASS MONKEY BAR

Map p416 (☎212-675-6686; www.brassmonkeynyc.com; 55 Little W 12th St, at Washington St, Meatpacking District; ⏰11am-4am; ⓈA/C/E, L to 8th Ave-14th St) While most Meatpacking District bars tend toward the chic, the Monkey is more for beer lovers than those worrying about what shoes to wear. The multi-floor Monkey is at ease and down-to-earth, with squeaking wood floors and a nice long list of beers and whiskies.

The roof deck is a fine destination in warm weather.

ONE IF BY LAND, TWO IF BY SEA BAR

Map p416 (☎212-255-8649; www.oneifbyland.com; 17 Barrow St, btwn 7th Ave & W 4th St; ⏰5:30-9:30pm Sun-Thu, 5:15-10:30pm Fri & Sat; Ⓢ1 to Christopher St-Sheridan Sq; A/C/E, B/D/F/M to W 4th St-Washington Sq) Famous for its beef Wellington and graceful, aged location in Aaron Burr's old carriage house, this is quite possibly New York's favorite date restaurant. But it's even better as a quiet watering hole, perfect for an evening libation for those who need a break from the harried streets.

Chelsea

GALLOW GREEN BAR

Map p420 (☎212-564-1662; www.mckittrickhotel.com/gallow-green; 542 W 27th St, btwn Tenth & Eleventh Aves, Chelsea; ⏰5pm-midnight Mon-Wed, to 1am Thu & Fri, 11am-1am Sat, 11am-midnight Sun; Ⓢ1, C/E to 23rd St; 1 to 28th St) Run by the creative team behind Sleep No More (p157) theater, Gallow Green is a rooftop bar festooned with vines, potted plants and fairy lights. It's a great add-on before or after experiencing the show, with waitstaff in period costume, a live band most nights and tasty rum-filled cocktails. You'll want to make a reservation.

When the cold weather arrives, Gallow Green sets up 'the Lodge,' a cozy chalet, with various astonishingly filled rooms, complete with books, bunk beds, fur rugs, a rocking chair and a fireplace. For a woodsy escape without leaving Midtown, this is it.

PIER 66 MARITIME BAR

Map p420 (☎212-989-6363; www.pier66maritime.com; Pier 66, at W 26th St, Chelsea; ⏰noon-midnight May-Sep & warm days Apr & Oct; Ⓢ1, C/E to 23rd St) Salvaged from the bottom of the sea (or at least the Chesapeake Bay), the lightship *Frying Pan* and the two-tiered dockside bar where it's moored are fine go-to spots for a sundowner or two. On warm days the rustic open-air space brings in the crowds, who laze on deck chairs and drink ice-cold beers ($7/25 for a microbrew/pitcher).

You can also come for burgers ($13) cooked up on the sizzling grill or just sit back and admire the fine views across the water to Jersey City. In April and October the bar opens when the temperature rises above 65°F.

TIPPLER COCKTAIL BAR

Map p420 (☎917-261-7949; www.thetippler.com; 425 W 15th St, underneath Chelsea Market, Chelsea; ⏰4pm to 1am Sun-Thu, to 3am Fri & Sat; ⓈA/C/E, L to 8th Ave-14th St) Paying material homage to its once-industrial setting, this brick-and-wood cellar bar beneath Chelsea Market serves up properly blended cocktails ($15) and interesting craft beer. The decor makes use of materials from vintage sources – including an old NYC water tower and the nearby High Line – to create a warm and relaxing space.

BATHTUB GIN COCKTAIL BAR

Map p420 (☎646-559-1671; www.bathtubginnyc.com; 132 Ninth Ave, btwn W 18th & W 19th Sts, Chelsea; ⏰5pm-2am Mon-Wed, to 3am Thu, to 4am Fri, 4pm-4am Sat, 4pm-2am Sun; ⓈA/C/E, L to 8th Ave-14th St, 1, C/E to 23rd St, 1 to 18th St) Amid NYC's obsession with speakeasy-styled hangouts, Bathtub Gin manages to poke its head above the crowd with its super-secret front door hidden on the wall of the Stone Street Coffee Shop (look for the 'Stone Street Standard' sign).

Once inside, chill seating, soft background beats and kindly staff make it a great place to enjoy bespoke cocktails with friends.

PETER MCMANUS CAFE BAR

Map p420 (☎212-929-6196; www.petermcmanuscafe.com; 152 Seventh Ave, at 19th St, Chelsea; ⏰11am-4am Mon-Sat, from noon Sun; Ⓢ1 to 18th St; 1, C/E to 23rd St) Pouring drafts since the 1930s, this family-run dive is something of a museum to the world of the McManuses: photos of yesteryear, an old telephone booth and Tiffany glass. There's also greasy bar food to eat at the comfy green booths.

☆ ENTERTAINMENT

★SLEEP NO MORE THEATER

Map p420 (☎box office 212-904-1880; www.sleepnomorenyc.com; 530 W 27th St, btwn Tenth & Eleventh Aves, Chelsea; tickets from $100; ⏰sessions begin 4-7pm; Ⓢ1, C/E to 23rd St) One of the most immersive theater experiences ever conceived, *Sleep No More* is a loose, noir retelling of *Macbeth* set inside a series of Chelsea warehouses that have been redesigned to look like the 1930s-era 'McKittrick Hotel' (a nod to Hitchcock's *Vertigo*); the jazz bar, Manderley, is another Hitchcock reference, this time to his adaptation of Daphne du Maurier's *Rebecca*.

First staged in London, it's a choose-your-own-adventure kind of experience, where audience members are free to wander the elaborate rooms (ballroom, graveyard, taxidermy shop, lunatic asylum) and follow or interact with the actors, who perform a variety of scenes that can run from the bizarre to the risqué. Be prepared: you must check in *everything* when you arrive (jackets, bag, cell phone), and you must wear a mask, à la *Eyes Wide Shut*.

IFC CENTER CINEMA

Map p416 (☎212-924-7771; www.ifccenter.com; 323 Sixth Ave, at W 3rd St, West Village; adult/child tickets $16/13; 📶; ⓈA/C/E, B/D/F/M to W 4th St-Washington Sq) This art-house cinema in NYU land has a solidly curated lineup of new indies, cult classics and foreign films. Catch shorts, documentaries, mini festivals, '80s revivals, director-focused series, weekend classics and frequent special series, such as cult favorites *(The Shining, Taxi Driver, Aliens)* at midnight.

COMEDY CELLAR COMEDY

Map p416 (☎212-254-3480; www.comedycellar.com; 117 MacDougal St, btwn W 3rd St & Minetta Lane, West Village; cover $10-24; ⏰11am-3am; ⓈA/C/E, B/D/F/M to W 4th St-Washington Sq) This legendary, intimate comedy club beneath the Olive Tree cafe in the West Village features a cast of talented regulars (Colin Quinn, Judah Friedlander, Wanda Sykes), plus occasional high-profile drop-ins like Dave Chappelle, Jerry Seinfeld and Amy

Schumer. Its success has spawned offspring – locations in Las Vegas and at the **Village Underground**, around the corner at 130 W 3rd St.

ATLANTIC THEATER COMPANY THEATER

Map p420 (☎212-691-5919; www.atlantictheater.org; 336 W 20th St, btwn Eighth & Ninth Aves, Chelsea; S1, C/E to 23rd St; 1 to 18th St) Founded by David Mamet and William H Macy in 1985, the Atlantic Theater is a pivotal anchor for the off-Broadway community, hosting many Tony Award and Drama Desk winners over the last three decades.

NEW YORK LIVE ARTS DANCE

Map p420 (☎212-924-0077; www.newyorklivearts.org; 219 W 19th St, btwn Seventh & Eighth Aves, Chelsea; S1 to 18th St) You'll find a program of more than 100 experimental, contemporary performances annually at this sleek dance center, led by artistic director Bill T Jones. International troupes from Serbia, South Africa, Korea and beyond bring fresh works to the stage, with shows that will often include pre- or post-show discussions with choreographers or dancers.

GOTHAM COMEDY CLUB COMEDY

Map p420 (☎212-367-9000; www.gothamcomedyclub.com; 208 W 23rd St, btwn Seventh & Eighth Aves, Chelsea; S1, C/E to 23rd St) Fancying itself as a NYC comedy hall of fame, and backing it up with regular big names and Gotham All-Stars shows, this expanded club provides space for comedians who've cut their teeth on HBO, *The Tonight Show with Jimmy Fallon* and *The Late Show with Stephen Colbert*.

(LE) POISSON ROUGE LIVE MUSIC

Map p416 (☎212-505-3474; www.lpr.com; 158 Bleecker St, btwn Sullivan & Thompson Sts, West Village; SA/C/E, B/D/F/M to W 4th St-Washington Sq) This high-concept art space hosts a highly eclectic lineup of live music, with the likes of Deerhunter, Gary Bartz and Yo La Tengo performing in past years. There's a

ALL THAT JAZZ

The West Village remains the epicenter of NYC's jazz scene, with memorable performances at everything from divey basement clubs to polished music halls.

Blue Note (Map p416; ☎212-475-8592; www.bluenotejazz.com; 131 W 3rd St, btwn Sixth Ave & MacDougal St, West Village; ⊙box office 10am-6pm, doors open 6pm; SA/C/E, B/D/F/M to W 4th St-Washington Sq) With the likes of Sarah Vaughan, Lionel Hampton and Dizzy Gillespie gracing its stage since it opened in 1981, Blue Note is one of NYC's premier jazz clubs. Most shows are $20 to $45 at the bar or $35 to $55 at a table, but prices rise for the biggest stars. There's jazz brunch ($40) at 11:30am and 1:30pm Sunday.

Village Vanguard (Map p416; ☎212-255-4037; www.villagevanguard.com; 178 Seventh Ave S, btwn W 11th & Perry Sts, West Village; cover around $35; ⊙7:30pm-12:30am; S1/2/3 to 14th St, A/C/E, L to 8th Ave-14th St) Possibly NYC's most prestigious jazz club, the Vanguard has hosted literally every major star of the past 50 years. Starting in 1935 as a venue for beat poetry and folk music, it occasionally returns to its roots, but most of the time it's big, bold jazz all night long. The Vanguard Jazz Orchestra has been a Monday-night mainstay since 1966.

Smalls (Map p416; ☎646-476-4346; www.smallslive.com; 183 W 10th St, btwn W 4th St & Seventh Ave S, West Village; cover $20; ⊙7pm-3:30am Mon-Fri, from 4pm Sat & Sun; S1 to Christopher St-Sheridan Sq, A/C/E, B/D/F/M to W 4th St-Washington Sq) Living up to its name, this cramped but appealing basement jazz den offers a grab-bag collection of acts who take the stage nightly. Admission includes a come-and-go policy if you need to duck out for a bite, and there's an afternoon jam session on Saturday and Sunday that's not to be missed.

Mezzrow (Map p416; ☎646-476-4346; www.mezzrow.com; 163 W 10th St, at Seventh Ave, West Village; general admission $20; ⊙7:30pm-1:30am Sun-Thu, to 2am Fri & Sat; S1 to Christopher St-Sheridan Sq) This intimate basement jazz club opened its doors in 2014 and is run by the same folks behind nearby Smalls (p158), and admission (generally $20) gets you same-night entry to Smalls.

lot of experimentation and cross-genre pollination between classical, folk, opera and more.

KITCHEN THEATER

Map p420 (☎212-255-5793; www.thekitchen.org; 512 W 19th St, btwn Tenth & Eleventh Aves, Chelsea; Ⓢ A/C/E, L to 8th Ave-14th St) A loft-like experimental space in west Chelsea that also produces edgy theater, readings and music performances; Kitchen is where you'll find new, progressive pieces and works in progress from local movers and shakers.

DUPLEX CABARET

Map p416 (☎212-255-5438; www.theduplex.com; 61 Christopher St, at Seventh Ave S, West Village; cover $10-25; ⏲4pm-4am; Ⓢ1 to Christopher St-Sheridan Sq, A/C/E, B/D/F/M to W 4th St-Washington Sq) Cabaret, comedy and campy dance moves are par for the course at the legendary Duplex, on song since 1950. Pictures of Joan Rivers line the walls, and performers like to mimic her sassy form of self-deprecation while getting in a few jokes about audience members as well. It's a fun and unpretentious place, but certainly not for the bashful.

BAR NEXT DOOR LIVE MUSIC

Map p416 (☎212-529-5945; www.lalanternacaffe.com; 129 MacDougal St, btwn W 3rd & 4th Sts, West Village; cover $12-15; ⏲6pm-2am Sun-Thu, to 3am Fri & Sat; Ⓢ A/C/E, B/D/F/M to W 4th St-Washington Sq) One of the loveliest hangouts in the neighborhood, the basement of this restored town house is all low ceilings, exposed brick and romantic lighting. You'll find mellow, live jazz nightly, as well as the tasty Italian menu of the restaurant next door, La Lanterna di Vittorio.

CHERRY LANE THEATRE THEATER

Map p416 (☎212-989-2020; www.cherrylanetheater.org; 38 Commerce St, off Bedford St, West Village; Ⓢ1 to Christopher St-Sheridan Sq) A little backstreet theater of distinctive charm, Cherry Lane has a long and distinguished history. Started by poet Edna St Vincent Millay in 1924, it has given a voice to numerous playwrights and actors over the years, showcasing the early work of such dramaturgical heavyweights as Harold Pinter and Edward Albee. Readings, plays and spoken-word performances rotate frequently.

JOYCE THEATER DANCE

Map p420 (☎212-691-9740; www.joyce.org; 175 Eighth Ave, at W 19th St, Chelsea; Ⓢ1 to 18th St; 1, C/E to 23rd St; A/C/E, L to 8th Ave-14th St) A favorite among dance junkies thanks to its excellent sight lines and offbeat offerings, this is an intimate venue, seating 472 in a renovated cinema. Its focus is on traditional modern companies, such as Martha Graham, Stephen Petronio Company and Parsons Dance, as well as global stars, such as Dance Brazil, Ballet Hispanico and MalPaso Dance Company.

55 BAR LIVE MUSIC

Map p416 (☎212-929-9883; www.55bar.com; 55 Christopher St, at Seventh Ave, West Village; cover $15; ⏲1pm-4am; Ⓢ1 to Christopher St-Sheridan Sq) Dating back to the Prohibition era, this friendly basement dive is great for low-key shows without high covers or dressing up. There are regular performances twice nightly by quality artists-in-residence, some blues bands and Miles Davis' super '80s guitarist Mike Stern. There's a two-drink minimum.

ANGELIKA FILM CENTER CINEMA

Map p416 (☎212-995-2570; www.angelikafilmcenter.com; 18 W Houston St, at Mercer St, West Village; tickets $17; 👪; Ⓢ B/D/F/M to Broadway-Lafayette St) Angelika specializes in foreign and independent films and has some quirky charms (the rumble of the subway, long lines and occasionally bad sound). But its roomy cafe is a great place to meet and the beauty of its Stanford White–designed, beaux-arts building is undeniable.

SHOPPING

The West Village is home to lovely boutiques and other stores selling unique things with charm. High-end shoppers stick to top-label emporiums along Bleecker St between Bank and W 10th Sts. Chelsea offers antiques, art, discount fashion, chain stores and kitsch, along with the occasional bookstore and thrift shop. A highlight is the Chelsea Market, a huge concourse packed with top-shelf food, wine, fashion and home goods. The Meatpacking District is all about that sleek, high-ceilinged industrial-chic

vibe, selling the work of cutting-edge designers in expansive boutiques that cater to the serious shopper.

West Village & the Meatpacking District

★MURRAY'S CHEESE FOOD & DRINKS

Map p416 (212-243-3289; www.murrayscheese.com; 254 Bleecker St, btwn Morton & Leroy Sts, West Village; sandwiches $6-9; 8am-9pm Mon-Sat, 9am-8pm Sun; S A/C/E, B/D/F/M to W 4th St-Washington Sq, 1 to Christopher St-Sheridan Sq) Founded in 1940 by Spanish Civil War veteran Murray Greenberg, this is one of New York's best cheese shops. Former owner (now 'advisor') Rob Kaufelt is known for his talent for sniffing out the best curds from around the world: you'll find (and be able to taste) all manner of *fromage*, aged in cheese caves on site and in Queens.

MEADOW CHOCOLATE

Map p416 (212-645-4633; www.themeadow.com; 523 Hudson St, btwn W 10th & Charles Sts, West Village; 11am-9pm Mon-Thu, to 10pm Fri & Sat, to 8pm Sun; S 1 to Christopher St-Sheridan Sq) An import from Portland, this peaceful, pretty little shop is the place to go for single-origin chocolate, fine salt, honey and other pantry essentials. The owner selects exquisite chocolate from around the world (and has also written a 300-page book on salt). You may be offered hot, sticky chocolate (blended in-store), or popcorn generously sprinkled with truffle salt.

TRINA TURK CLOTHING

Map p416 (212-206-7383; www.trinaturk.com; 67 Gansevoort St, btwn Greenwich & Washington Sts, West Village; 11am-7pm Mon-Sat, noon-6pm Sun; S A/C/E, L to 8th Ave-14th St) Anyone with a yen for '70s-inspired prints should take themselves to the Trina Turk boutique. The wife and husband team behind the unisex brand have cultivated a range that harkens back to the vibrant heyday of California cool with shift dresses, floral blazers, statement pants, and swimsuits that range from board shorts to ultra-skimpy briefs.

PERSONNEL OF NEW YORK FASHION & ACCESSORIES

Map p416 (212-924-0604; www.personnelofnewyork.com; 9 Greenwich Ave, btwn Christopher & W 10th Sts, West Village; 11am-7:30pm Mon-Sat, noon to 6pm Sun; S A/C/E, B/D/F/M to W 4th St-Washington Sq; 1 to Christopher St-Sheridan Sq) This small, delightful indie shop sells women's designer clothing from unique labels from the East and West Coasts and beyond. Look for easy-to-wear Sunja Link dresses, jumpsuits by Ali Golden, statement-making jewelry by Marisa Mason and couture pieces by Rodebjer.

BEACON'S CLOSET VINTAGE

Map p416 (917-261-4863; www.beaconscloset.com; 10 W 13th St, btwn Fifth & Sixth Aves, West Village; 11am-8pm; S L, N/Q/R/W, 4/5/6 to 14th St-Union Sq) At Beacon's, which has three other locations in Brooklyn, you'll find a good selection of gently used clothing of a decidedly downtown/Brooklyn hipster aesthetic. Thrift shops are thin on the ground in this area, which makes this even more of a draw.

SATURDAYS FASHION & ACCESSORIES

Map p416 (347-246-5830; www.saturdaysnyc.com; 17 Perry St, at Waverly St, West Village; 10am-7pm; S A/C/E, L to 8th Ave-14th St; 1/2/3 to 14th St) For a strange sight in the West Village, stop by this eye-catching surf shop, complete with pricey boards by Tudor, Christenson and Haydenshapes. Of course, shopping here is more about buying into the surfing lifestyle – with stylish shades, board shorts, colorful tees and grooming products – for both you and your surfboard.

GREENWICH LETTERPRESS GIFTS & SOUVENIRS

Map p416 (212-989-7464; www.greenwichletterpress.com; 15 Christopher St, at Gay St, West Village; noon-6pm Sun & Mon, 11am-7pm Tue-Sat; S 1 to Christopher St-Sheridan Sq; A/C/E, B/D/F/M to W 4th St; 1/2/3 to 14th St) Founded by two sisters, this cute card shop specializes in wedding announcements and other specially made letterpress endeavors, so skip the stock postcards of the Empire State Building and send your loved ones a bespoke greeting card from this stalwart stationer.

THREE LIVES & COMPANY BOOKS

Map p416 (212-741-2069; www.threelives.com; 154 W 10th St, btwn Seventh Ave & Waverly Pl, West Village; 10am-8:30pm Mon-Sat, noon-7pm Sun; S 1 to Christopher St-Sheridan Sq; A/C/E, B/D/F/M to W 4th St-Washington Sq) Your neighborhood bookstore extraordinaire, Three Lives & Company is a wondrous spot that's tended by a coterie of exceptionally well-read individuals. A trip here is not just a pleasure, it's an adventure into the magical world of words.

IDLEWILD BOOKS BOOKS

Map p416 (☎212-414-8888; www.idlewildbooks.com; 170 Seventh Ave S, at Perry St, West Village; ⊙noon-8pm Mon-Thu, to 6pm Fri-Sun; S1 to Christopher St-Sheridan Sq, 2/3 to 14th St, A/C/E, L to 8th Ave-14th St) Named after JFK airport's original moniker, this indie travel bookstore gets feet seriously itchy. Books are divided by region and cover guidebooks as well as fiction, travelogues, history, cookbooks and other stimulating fare for delving into different corners of the world. The store also runs popular language classes in French, Italian, Spanish, Portuguese and German – see the website for details.

ODIN CLOTHING

Map p416 (☎212-243-4724; www.odinnewyork.com; 106 Greenwich Ave, btwn W 13th & W 12th Sts, West Village; ⊙noon-8pm Mon-Sat, to 7pm Sun; SA/C/E, L to 8th Ave-14th St, 1/2/3 to 14th St) Named after the mighty Norse god, Odin offers a bit of magic for men seeking a new look. The teeming boutique carries stylish labels such as Dickies Construct, Acne Studios and Second Layer, and gives rack space to up-and-coming designers. Stylin' extras include Albertus Swanepoel hats, Oliver Peoples sunglasses and Nikolai Rose jewelry.

FLIGHT 001 FASHION & ACCESSORIES

Map p416 (☎212-989-0001; www.flight001.com; 96 Greenwich Ave, btwn Jane St & W 12th St; ⊙11am-7pm Mon-Sat, noon-6pm Sun; SA/C/E, L to 8th Ave-14th St) Check out Flight 001's range of luggage and smaller bags by brands ranging from Bric's to Rimowa, kitschy 'shemergency' kits (breath freshener, lip balm, stain remover etc), brightly colored passport holders and leather luggage tags, travel guidebooks, toiletry cases, and a range of mini toothpastes, eye masks, pillboxes and the like.

MCNULTY'S TEA & COFFEE CO, INC FOOD & DRINKS

Map p416 (☎212-242-5351; www.mcnultys.com; 109 Christopher St, btwn Bleecker & Hudson Sts, West Village; ⊙10am-9pm Mon-Sat, 1-7pm Sun; S1 to Christopher St-Sheridan Sq) McNulty's is a sweet addition to the otherwise bawdy Christopher St. Its worn wooden floorboards, fragrant sacks of coffee beans and large glass jars of tea harken back to a different era of Greenwich Village. It's been selling gourmet teas and coffees here since 1895.

LOCAL KNOWLEDGE

FOR BOOK LOVERS

Beloved and legendary, the iconic **Strand Book Store** (Map p416; ☎212-473-1452; www.strandbooks.com; 828 Broadway, at E 12th St, West Village; ⊙9:30am-10:30pm; SL, N/Q/R/W, 4/5/6 to 14th St-Union Sq) embodies downtown NYC's intellectual bona fides – a bibliophile's Oz, where generations of book lovers carrying the store's trademark tote bags happily lose themselves for hours. In operation since 1927, the Strand sells new, used and rare titles, spreading an incredible 18 miles of books (over 2.5 million of them) among three labyrinthine floors.

Check out the extensive section on Americana on the 1st floor and browse eye-catching merchandise (iPhone covers, tote bags, paratrooper messenger bags). Or sell off your own tomes before you get back on the plane: the Strand buys or trades books at a side counter Monday through Saturday.

YOYA CHILDREN'S CLOTHING

Map p416 (☎646-336-6844; www.yoyanyc.com; 605 Hudson St, btwn Bethune & W 12th Sts, West Village; ⊙10am-6pm Mon-Sat, noon-5pm Sun, shorter hours winter; SA/C/E, L to 8th Ave-14th St) For well-made and stylishly curated kids' clothes and accessories, visit Yoya, which stocks such high-end brands as Bobo Choses, Bangbang Copenhagen and 1+ In The Family.

CO BIGELOW CHEMISTS COSMETICS

Map p416 (☎212-533-2700; www.bigelowchemists.com; 414 Sixth Ave, btwn 8th & 9th Sts, West Village; ⊙7:30am-9pm Mon-Fri, 8:30am-7pm Sat, 8:30am-5:30pm Sun; S1 to Christopher St-Sheridan Sq; A/C/E, B/D/F/M to W 4th St-Washington Sq) The 'oldest apothecary in America' is a favorite among New Yorkers and a convenient spot to grab upscale lotions and face masks, organic soaps and bath bombs, and basic toiletries. It's a fun place to test high-end products before you grab a tube of toothpaste.

FORBIDDEN PLANET — BOOKS

Map p416 (212-473-1576; www.fpnyc.com; 832 Broadway, btwn E 12th & 13th Sts, West Village; 10am-10pm Sun & Mon, from 9am Tue, 8am-midnight Wed, 9am-midnight Thu-Sat; S L, N/Q/R/W, 4/5/6 to 14th St-Union Sq) Indulge your inner sci-fi and fantasy nerd with heaps of comics, manga, graphic novels, posters and collectible toys.

The products represent everything from *Star Wars* and *Doctor Who* to the latest indie sensations. Check the website for upcoming book signings and other events.

EVOLUTION NATURE STORE — GIFTS & SOUVENIRS

Map p416 (212-343-1114; www.theevolutionstore.com; 687 Broadway, btwn W 3rd & W 4th Sts; 11am-8pm; S R/W to 8th Ave-NYU; 6 to Astor Pl) In the market for a shrunken head? Perhaps a dried scarab beetle? This SoHo favorite has display cases full of strange finds from all over the world. The store is cavernous and often busy, especially on weekends when people doing the SoHo boutique crawl wander in to ogle the oddities.

Chelsea

★ SCREAMING MIMIS — VINTAGE

Map p416 (212-677-6464; www.screamingmimis.com; 240 W 14th St, btwn Seventh & Eighth Aves, Chelsea; noon-8pm Mon-Sat, 1-7pm Sun; S A/C/E, L to 8th Ave-14th St) If you dig vintage, designer and rare threads, or flamboyant costumes, you may just scream, too. This funtastic shop carries an excellent selection of yesteryear pieces, organized by decade, from the '40s to the '90s. From prim beaded wool cardigans to suede minidresses, fluoro furs, white leather go-go boots, accessories and jewelry, the stock is in great condition.

192 BOOKS — BOOKS

Map p420 (212-255-4022; www.192books.com; 192 Tenth Ave, btwn W 21st & W 22nd Sts, Chelsea; 11am-7pm; S 1, C/E to 23rd St) This small indie bookstore in the thick of the gallery district shelves great selections of fiction, history, travel, art and criticism. Rotating art exhibits, during which the owners organize special displays of books related to the featured show or artist, are a treat. Frequent readings feature acclaimed authors and intellectuals.

PRINTED MATTER — BOOKS

Map p420 (212-925-0325; www.printedmatter.org; 231 Eleventh Ave, btwn 25th & 26th Sts, Chelsea; 11am-7pm Sat & Mon-Wed, to 8pm Thu & Fri, noon-6pm Sun; S 7 to 34th St-Hudson Yards; 1 to 28th St) Printed Matter is a wondrous little shop dedicated to limited-edition artist monographs and strange little zines.

Here you will find nothing carried by mainstream bookstores; instead, the trim shelves here are home to call-to-arms manifestos, critical essays about comic books, flip books that reveal Jesus' face through barcodes and how-to guides written by prisoners.

HOUSING WORKS THRIFT SHOP — VINTAGE

Map p420 (718-838-5050; www.housingworks.org; 143 W 17th St, btwn Sixth & Seventh Aves, Chelsea; 10am-7pm Mon-Sat, noon-6pm Sun; S 1 to 18th St) The flagship for 13 other branches around town, this shop with its swank window displays looks more boutique than thrift, but its selections of clothes, accessories, furniture, books and records are great value.

It's the place to go to find discarded designer clothes for a bargain, and all proceeds benefit the charity serving the city's HIV-positive and AIDS-affected homeless communities.

JEFFREY NEW YORK — FASHION & ACCESSORIES

Map p420 (212-206-1272; www.jeffreynewyork.com; 449 W 14th St, btwn Ninth & Tenth Aves, Chelsea; 10am-8pm Mon-Fri, to 7pm Sat, noon-6pm Sun; S A/C/E, L to 8th Ave-14th St) One of the pioneers in the Meatpacking District's makeover, Jeffrey sells several high-end designer clothing lines – Chanel, Gucci, Prada, Dior and company – as well as accessories and shoes.

DJs spinning pop and indie add to the very hip vibe.

INA — VINTAGE

Map p420 (212-334-6572; www.inanyc.com; 207 West 18th St, btwn Seventh & Eighth Aves, Chelsea; noon-8pm Mon-Sat, to 7pm Sun; S 1 to 18th St) This small but elegantly designed consignment store carries high-quality, gently used apparel and accessories. The prices are high and some of the staff have been known to be a tad sniffy, but you can occasionally unearth one-of-a-kind finds here.

SPORTS & ACTIVITIES

CHELSEA PIERS COMPLEX — HEALTH & FITNESS

Map p420 (☎212-336-6666; www.chelseapiers.com; Pier 62, at W 23rd St, Chelsea; ⏱5:30am-11pm Mon-Fri, 8am-9pm Sat & Sun; 👪; 🚌M23 to 12th Ave-W 23 St, Ⓢ1, C/E to 23rd St) This massive waterfront sports center caters to the athlete in everyone. You can hit endless golf balls at the four-level driving range, skate on an indoor ice rink or rack up strikes in a jazzy bowling alley. There's basketball at Hoop City, a sailing school for kids, batting cages, a huge gym and covered swimming pool, and indoor rock climbing.

A Multi-Sport Passport, which provides access to the gym, pool, golf club, skating rink and batting cage as well as free bowling-shoe rental, can be purchased from the desk at the golf club for $60. A few snack bars serve sandwiches and pizzas, so you can carb-load after your workout. Though the complex is somewhat cut off by the busy West Side Hwy (Eleventh Ave), the wide array of attractions here brings in the crowds; the M23 crosstown bus, which stops right at the main entrance, saves you the long, four-avenue trek from the subway. There's also a taxi stand outside, although during non-peak hours the line of cabs is fairly short.

NEW YORK GALLERY TOURS — TOURS

Map p420 (☎212-946-1548; www.nygallerytours.com; 526 W 26th St, at Tenth Ave, Chelsea; scheduled/private per person $29/300 minimum; ⏱scheduled tours Sat, private tours 10am-6pm Tue-Sun; Ⓢ1, C/E to 23rd St) You know you're supposed to check out the array of amazing modern-art galleries in Chelsea. But where to begin? This excellent guided tour takes you to a slew of galleries and provides helpful commentary along the way.

SCHOONER ADIRONDACK — CRUISE

Map p420 (☎212-627-1825; www.sail-nyc.com; Chelsea Piers Complex, Pier 62 at W 22nd St, Chelsea; tours $52-86; Ⓢ1, C/E to 23rd St) The two-masted *'Dack* hits the New York Harbor with four two-hour sails daily from May through November. The 1920s-style, 80ft *Manhattan* and 100ft *Manhattan II* yachts offer tours throughout the week.

Call or check the website for the latest times.

NEW YORK TRAPEZE SCHOOL — HEALTH & FITNESS

Map p416 (☎212-242-8769; www.newyork.trapezeschool.com; Pier 40, at West Side Hwy, West Village; per class $40-75; ⏱May-Oct; Ⓢ1 to Houston St) Fulfill your circus dreams on the flying trapeze in this tent by the river, located atop Pier 40. The school also has an indoor facility in South Williamsburg, Brooklyn, that's open year-round. Check the website for daily class times.

MNDFL — MEDITATION

Map p416 (☎212-477-0487; www.mndflmeditation.com; 10 E 8th St, btwn Fifth Ave & University Pl, West Village; 30/45/60min class $18/25/30; ⓈA/C/E, B/D, F/M to W 4th St-Washington Sq) The benefits of meditation are well-documented – and much needed by many of New York's harried residents. Take time out to clear your head with rejuvenating classes at this peaceful West Village outpost.

WEST 4TH STREET BASKETBALL COURTS — SPORTS

Map p416 (Sixth Ave, btwn 3rd & 4th Sts, West Village; ⓈA/C/E, B/D/F/M to W 4th St-Washington Sq) Also known as 'the Cage,' this small basketball court enclosed within chain-link fencing is home to some of the best streetball in the country. Though it's more touristy than its counterpart, Rucker Park in Harlem, that's also part of its charm, as the games held here in the center of the Village draw massive, excitable crowds, who often stand five-deep to hoot and holler for the skilled, competitive guys who play here.

Prime time is summer, when the W 4th St Summer Pro-Classic League, with daily high-energy games, hits the scene.

Union Square, Flatiron District & Gramercy

Neighborhood Top Five

❶ **Flatiron Building** (p167) Puzzling over the arresting triangularity and snapping photographs of one of New York's most iconic constructions.

❷ **Union Square** (p166) Watching the eclectic mix of New Yorkers pass by at this bustling town square, which transforms into a delightful Christmas market come late November.

❸ **Union Square Greenmarket** (p167) Inspecting fresh regional produce, meats and cheeses and sampling artisanal treats and baked goods at this frequent farmers market.

❹ **Raines Law Room** (p172) Sipping flawless cocktails in upholstered-leather luxury at this dimly lit bar that feels like it's from another era.

❺ **Eataly** (p169) Savoring a culinary trip through Italy at this gigantic, venerated food hall and market with a picturesque rooftop bar and restaurant.

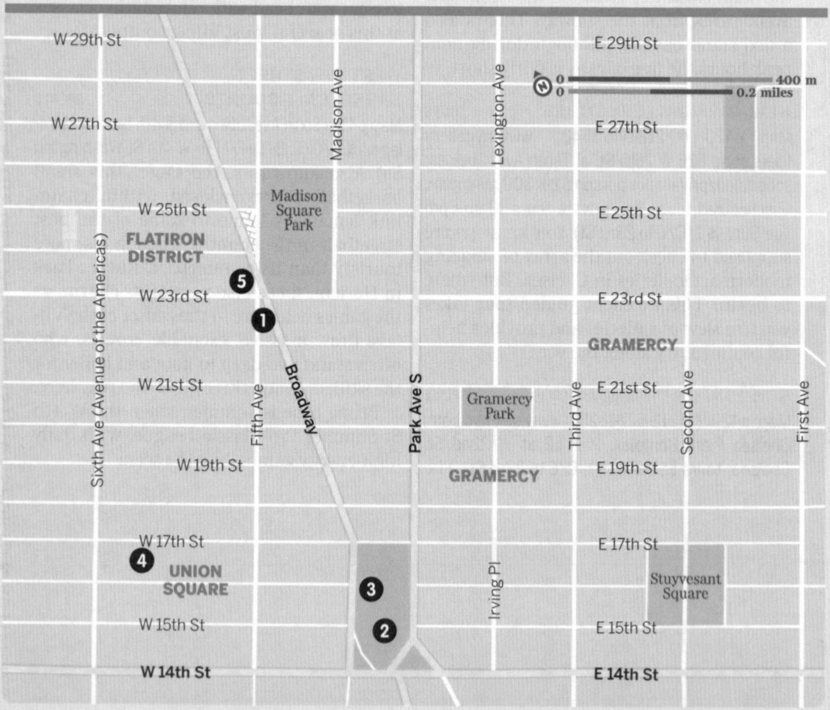

For more detail of this area see Map p422

Explore Union Square, Flatiron District & Gramercy

There's not a lot of ground to cover, so the best plan of attack is to use the two major public spaces – Union Square (p166) and Madison Square Park (p167) – as your anchors. From Union Square you'll feel the Village and university vibe (NYU is just south and the New School just to the west) spilling over with good cafes, sign-wielding protesters and buskers in the square itself. Walking east or west along 14th St takes you to the East or West Village respectively.

Up toward 23rd St you'll find the Flatiron Building (p167) looming over the commercial quarter that also bears its name, replete with crowded lunch spots and after-work watering holes. East of both public spaces is Gramercy, its distinctly residential vibe tempered with notable, buzzing restaurants.

In Madison Square Park you'll find young PR mavens chatting over lattes, harried lawyers getting away from the office for a moment of peace and, in the warmer months, foodies flocking to the Mad Sq Eats market.

Local Life

- **Mad Sq Eats** Each spring and fall, foodies flock to tiny General Worth Sq – wedged between Fifth Ave and Broadway, opposite Madison Square Park – for Mad Sq Eats (p169), a month-long culinary pop-up market. Its 30 or so vendors include some of the city's hottest eateries, cooking up anything from proper pizza to brisket tacos using top local produce.
- **Gourmet groceries** Eataly (p169) has made a name for itself as the place to go for Italophile food buffs, but locals do much more of their everyday shopping at health-conscious supermarket Whole Foods, at the southern end of Union Square.

Getting There & Away

- **Subway** A slew of subway lines converge below Union Square, running up Manhattan's East Side on the 4/5/6 lines, out to Williamsburg on the L, or to Queens on the N/Q/R lines. The L also travels to the West Side. The Q runs express to Herald Square and Times Square.
- **Bus** The M14A and M14D Select Bus Service (SBS) lines provide cross-town services along 14th St, while the M23 runs cross-town along 23rd St. The bus is better if you're traveling between two eastern points in Manhattan.

Lonely Planet's Top Tip

Human traffic can be overwhelming in Union Square, especially along 14th St. If you're in a rush, or trying to hoof it on foot, switch over to 13th St and you'll cover a lot more ground in much less time.

Best Places to Eat

- Eleven Madison Park (p171)
- Maialino (p171)
- Gramercy Tavern (p171)
- Clocktower (p171)
- Cosme (p171)

For reviews, see p169

Best Places to Drink

- Flatiron Room (p172)
- Raines Law Room (p172)
- Serra (p172)
- Old Town Bar & Restaurant (p172)
- Lillie's Victorian Establishment (p173)

For reviews, see p172

Best Places to Shop

- Union Square Greenmarket (p167)
- Fishs Eddy (p173
- ABC Carpet & Home (p174)
- Bedford Cheese Shop (p174)
- Books of Wonder (p174)

For reviews, see p173

TOP EXPERIENCE
UNION SQUARE

Union Square is like the Noah's Ark of New York, rescuing at least two of every kind from the curling seas of concrete. Amid the stone steps and fenced-in foliage you'll see denizens of every ilk: suited business types gulping fresh air during their lunch breaks, dreadlocked loiterers tapping beats on tablas and skateboarders flipping tricks on the southeastern stairs.

Riches & Rags

Opened in 1831, Union Square quickly became the central gathering place for those who lived in the mansions nearby. Concert halls and artist societies further enhanced the cultured atmosphere, and high-end shopping quickly proliferated along Broadway, which was dubbed 'Ladies' Mile.'

When the Civil War broke out, the vast public space (large by New York standards, of course) was center stage for protesters of all sorts, from union workers to political activists. By the height of WWI, the area had fallen largely into disuse, allowing politically and socially driven organizations like the American Civil Liberties Union, the Communist and Socialist Parties, and the Ladies' Garment Workers Union to move in. Many decades later, the square remains a popular site for political and social protests, as well as one of NYC's best regular farmers markets.

For an unforgettable, sweeping view of Union Square and the Empire State Building beyond, hit DSW, a 3rd-floor discount shoe store at the southern end of the square, or the cafe of the Whole Foods supermarket next door.

The Factory

After over a century of the continuous push-and-pull between dapper-dom and political protest, a third – artistic, if not thoroughly hippie-ish – ingredient was tossed into the mix when Andy Warhol moved his Factory to the 6th floor of the Decker Building at 33 Union Sq West. It was here, on June 3, 1968, that disgruntled writer Valerie Solanas shot Warhol three times, seriously wounding him. The ground floor of the building is now occupied by a brightly colored candy-store chain – very Warholian.

Metronome

A walk around Union Square will reveal a string of whimsical, temporary sculptures. Of the permanent offerings is an imposing equestrian statue of George Washington (one of the first public pieces of art in New York City) and a statue of peacemaker Mahatma Gandhi. Trumping both on the southeastern side of the square is a massive art installation that either earns confused stares or simply gets overlooked by passersby. A symbolic representation of the passage of time, *Metronome* has two parts: a digital clock with a puzzling display of numbers, and a wand-like apparatus with smoke puffing out of concentric rings. We'll let you ponder the latter while we give you the skinny on what exactly the winking orange digits denote: the 14 numbers must be split into two groups of seven: the seven from the left tell the current time (hour, minute, second, tenth-of-a-second) and the seven from the right are meant to be read in reverse order; they represent the remaining amount of time in the day.

DON'T MISS

- Union Square Greenmarket
- *Metronome* art installation
- The view from DSW shoe store
- Eclectics, sit-ins and buskers

PRACTICALITIES

- Map p422, D4
- www.unionsquarenyc.org
- 17th St, btwn Broadway & Park Ave S, Union Square
- S 4/5/6, N/Q/R, L to 14th St-Union Sq

SIGHTS

Though short on sights per se, there's lots happening on and around Union Square, which bustles with buskers, suits and appetite-piquing produce stalls. To the northwest are the dignified streets of Gramercy, while to the north is Madison Square Garden, where dogs and squirrels meet art installations, readings and a famous little burger shack.

UNION SQUARE
SQUARE

See p166.

UNION SQUARE GREENMARKET
MARKET

Map p422 (212-788-7476; www.grownyc.org/unionsquaregreenmarket; E 17th St, btwn Broadway & Park Ave S, Union Square; 8am-6pm Mon, Wed, Fri & Sat; S 4/5/6, N/Q/R/W, L to 14th St-Union Sq) Don't be surprised if you spot some of New York's top chefs prodding the produce here: Union Square's green market is arguably the city's most famous. Whet your appetite trawling the stalls, which peddle anything and everything from upstate fruit and vegetables to artisanal breads, cheeses and cider.

MADISON SQUARE PARK
PARK

Map p422 (212-520-7600; www.madisonsquarepark.org; E 23rd to 26th Sts, btwn Fifth & Madison Aves, Flatiron District; 6am-11pm; ; S R/W, F/M, 6 to 23rd St) This park defined the northern reaches of Manhattan until the island's population exploded after the Civil War. These days it's a much-welcome oasis from Manhattan's relentless pace, with a popular children's playground, dog-run area and the **Shake Shack** (Map p422; 646-889-6600; www.shakeshack.com; burgers $6-11; 9am-11pm) burger joint. It's also one of the city's most cultured parks, with specially commissioned art installations and (in the warmer months) activities ranging from literary discussions to live-music gigs. See the website for more information.

It's also the perfect spot from which to gaze up at the landmarks that surround it, including the Flatiron Building to the southwest, the Metropolitan Life Tower to the southeast and the New York Life Insurance Building, topped with a gilded spire, to the northeast.

Between 1876 and 1882 the torch-bearing arm of the Statue of Liberty was on display here, and in 1879 the first Madison Square Garden arena was constructed at

TOP EXPERIENCE
FLATIRON BUILDING

Designed by Daniel Burnham and built in 1902, the 20-story Flatiron Building has a narrow triangular footprint that resembles the prow of a massive ship. It also features a beaux-arts limestone and terracotta facade that gets more complex and beautiful the longer you stare at it. Until 1909 it was the world's tallest building.

Publisher Frank Munsey was one of the building's first tenants. From his 18th-floor offices he published *Munsey's Magazine*, which featured the work of short-story writer O Henry. His musings, the paintings of John Sloan and photographs of Alfred Stieglitz best immortalized the Flatiron back in the day. Actress Katharine Hepburn once quipped that she'd like to be admired as much as the grand old building.

While there are plans to transform the Flatiron into a luxurious five-star hotel, progress is on hold until the final business tenants willingly vacate the premises. In the meantime, the ground floor of the building's 'prow' has been transformed into a glassed-in art space. Past installations have included a life-size 3D-cutout replica of Edward Hopper's 1942 painting *Nighthawks*, its angular diner remarkably similar to the Flatiron's distinctive shape.

DON'T MISS

- The facade view from Madison Square Park
- Getting up close to the fine exterior detail
- Flatiron Prow art space

PRACTICALITIES

- Map p422, C2
- Broadway, cnr Fifth Ave & 23rd St, Flatiron District
- S N/R, F/M, 6 to 23rd St

TOP EXPERIENCE
GRAMERCY PARK

Manhattan's early Dutch settlers named the area now known as Gramercy 'Krom Moerasje' (Little Crooked Swamp). The swamp would meet its end in 1831, when lawyer and public official Samuel Ruggles purchased the land. He had the swamp drained and the land carved into 108 lots. Forty-two of these were set aside for an English-style private park, to be held in perpetuity by the residents of its surrounding 66 lots.

Almost two centuries later, **Gramercy Park** remains a private oasis. Only once has it been made accessible to nonresidents, when Union soldiers were permitted inside during the Draft Riots of 1863.

Many of the original town houses facing the park were replaced by high-rise apartment buildings through the 1920s. Along the park sits the **National Arts Club**; its elegance attests to the district's desirable pedigree. Indeed, Gramercy Park has had its fair share of illustrious residents. The town house at 4 Gramercy Park W was home to American publisher James Harper from 1847 to 1869. Mayor of New York City from 1844 to 1845, Harper's flouncy 'mayor's lights' still grace the front of the building. Another famous local was Stanford White, eponymous designer of the triumphal arch in Washington Square.

DON'T MISS

- A slow walk around the park to admire the stunning architecture of the surrounding buildings.
- Taking in a gallery show at the National Arts Club.

PRACTICALITIES

- Map p422, D3
- E 20th St, btwn Park & Third Aves, Gramercy
- SN/R, 6 to 23rd St

Madison Ave and 26th St. At the southeastern corner of the park, you'll find one of the city's few self-cleaning, coin-operated toilets (25¢).

NATIONAL ARTS CLUB ARTS CENTER

Map p422 (212-475-3424; www.nationalartsclub.org; 15 Gramercy Park S, Gramercy; galleries 10am-5pm Mon-Fri; SN/R, 6 to 23rd St) FREE Founded in 1898 to promote public interest in the arts, the National Arts Club holds art exhibitions, with free admission to the public during weekdays; check the website for upcoming shows as well as evening events. Calvert Vaux – one of the creators of Central Park – designed the building itself, with a picture-lined front parlor adorned with a beautiful, vaulted stained-glass panel. The mansion was once home to Samuel J Tilden, a former New York governor and the failed 1876 presidential candidate.

THEODORE ROOSEVELT BIRTHPLACE HISTORIC SITE

Map p422 (212-260-1616; www.nps.gov/thrb; 28 E 20th St, btwn Broadway & Park Ave S, Flatiron District; visitor center 9am-5pm, 40min guided tours 10am, 11am, 1pm, 2pm, 3pm & 4pm Tue-Sat; SR/W, 6 to 23rd St) FREE This National Historic Site is a bit of a cheat, since the physical house where the 26th president was actually born was demolished in his own lifetime. But this building is a worthy reconstruction by his relatives, who took painstaking steps to bring together original furniture from the residence with true-to-the-period restorations.

METROPOLITAN LIFE TOWER HISTORIC BUILDING

Map p422 (1 Madison Ave, btwn E 23rd & E 24th Sts, Flatiron District; SN/R, F/M, 6 to 23rd St) Completed in 1909, this 700ft-high clock tower soaring above Madison Square Park's southeastern corner is the work of Napoleon LeBrun, a Philadelphia-born architect of French stock. Italophiles may feel a certain déjà vu gazing at the tower as LeBrun's inspiration was Venice's world-famous *campanile* (bell tower) in Piazza San Marco. Ironically, this New World version is now older than its muse: the original Venetian tower collapsed in 1902, with its replacement not completed until 1912.

EATING

This trifecta of neighborhoods doesn't want for great food, and one of the city's best farmers markets operates year-round at Union Square. There are lots of highly regarded (and pricey) restaurants in the area, as well as a few good options for those dining on a budget.

BIG DADDY'S — DINER $

Map p422 (☎212-477-1500; www.bigdaddysnyc.com; 239 Park Ave S, btwn E 19th & E 20th Sts, Gramercy; mains $10-16; ⏰8am-midnight Mon-Thu, to 5am Fri & Sat, to 11pm Sun; ; Ⓢ6 to 23rd St; 4/5/6, L, N/Q/R/W to 14th St-Union Sq) Giant, fluffy omelettes, hearty burgers and heaps of tater tots (regular or sweet potato) have made Big Daddy's a top choice for both breakfast and late-night treats. The interior is all Americana kitsch, but unlike some theme restaurants the food doesn't break the bank and actually satisfies (and the kids' menu will please wee grumbling tums).

TACOMBI CAFÉ EL PRESIDENTE — MEXICAN $

Map p422 (☎212-242-3491; www.tacombi.com; 30 W 24th St, btwn Fifth & Sixth Aves, Flatiron District; tacos $4-9, quesadillas $7-8; ⏰11am-midnight Mon-Sat, to 10:30pm Sun; ; ⓈF/M, R/W to 23rd St) Channeling the cafes of Mexico City, pink-and-green Tacombi covers numerous bases, from juice and liquor bar to taco joint. Score a table, order a margarita and hop your way around a menu of Mexican street-food deliciousness. Top choices include *esquites* (grilled corn with *cotija* cheese and chipotle mayonnaise, served in a paper cup) and succulent carnitas tacos.

MAD SQ EATS — MARKET $

Map p422 (www.madisonsquarepark.org/mad-sq-food/mad-sq-eats; General Worth Sq, Flatiron District; ⏰spring & fall 11am-9pm; ⓈR/W, F/M, 6 to 23rd St) A biannual, pop-up culinary market with stalls run by some of the city's coolest eateries and hottest chefs. Bites span a range of street foods, from arancini and empanadas to lobster rolls and ice-cream sandwiches. See the website for dates and vendors.

EISENBERG'S SANDWICH SHOP — SANDWICHES $

Map p422 (☎212-675-5096; www.eisenbergsnyc.com; 174 Fifth Ave, btwn W 22nd & 23rd St, Flatiron District; sandwiches $4-14; ⏰7:30am-6pm Mon-Fri, 9am-5pm Sat, 10am-3pm Sun; ; ⓈR/W to 23rd St) This old-school diner – an anomaly on this mostly upscale stretch of real estate – is a comfy, quiet spot for traditional Jewish-diner fare like chopped liver, pastrami and whitefish salad. Grab a stool at the long bar and rub elbows with an eclectic mix of customers who know meatloaf isn't a joke dish.

BAR JAMÓN — TAPAS $$

Map p422 (☎212-253-2773; http://casamononyc.com; 125 E 17th St, btwn Irving Pl & Third Ave, Gramercy; tapas $6-24; ⏰5pm-2am Mon-Fri, noon-2am Sat & Sun; Ⓢ4/5/6, N/Q/R/W, L to 14th St-Union Sq) Around the corner from big brother Casa Mono (p172) lies Mario Batali's fun, communal Bar Jamón. Sniff, swill and sip your way across Spain's wine terroirs while grazing on superb, Catalan-inspired tapas like chorizo and pickled peppers or calamari with a perfectly salty olive tapenade.

EATALY — FOOD HALL $$

Map p422 (☎212-229-2560; www.eataly.com; 200 Fifth Ave, at W 23rd St, Flatiron District; ⏰7am-11pm; ; ⓈR/W, F/M, 6 to 23rd St) Mario Batali's sprawling temple to Italian gastronomy is a veritable wonderland. Feast on everything from vibrant *crudo* (raw fish) and *fritto misto* (tempura-style vegetables) to steamy pasta and pizza at the emporium's string of sit-down eateries. Alternatively, guzzle espresso at the bar and enjoy a custom-filled cannoli before scouring the shelves for a DIY picnic hamper that *nonna* would approve of.

Eataly's other assets include its rooftop beer garden, Serra (p172), and a busy schedule of on-site cooking and culinary appreciation classes. See the website for details.

MAX BRENNER — DESSERTS $$

Map p422 (☎646-467-8803; www.maxbrenner.com; 841 Broadway, btwn 13th & 14th Sts, Union Square; mains $17-24, desserts from $10; ⏰9am-1am Mon-Thu, to 2am Fri & Sat, to midnight Sun; Ⓢ4/5/6, N/Q/R/W, L to 14th St-Union Sq) Sweet-toothed Aussie Max Brenner is expanding waistlines in NYC with his cafe-cum-chocolate-bar. It's a Wonker-ful spot for a cocoa rush, whether it's sipping a chocolate martini, gobbling down peanut-butter-and-banana-chocolate crêpes, or nibbling nicely on an artisanal truffle. There is a full menu (great breakfast), but it's the chocolate that will leave you gaga.

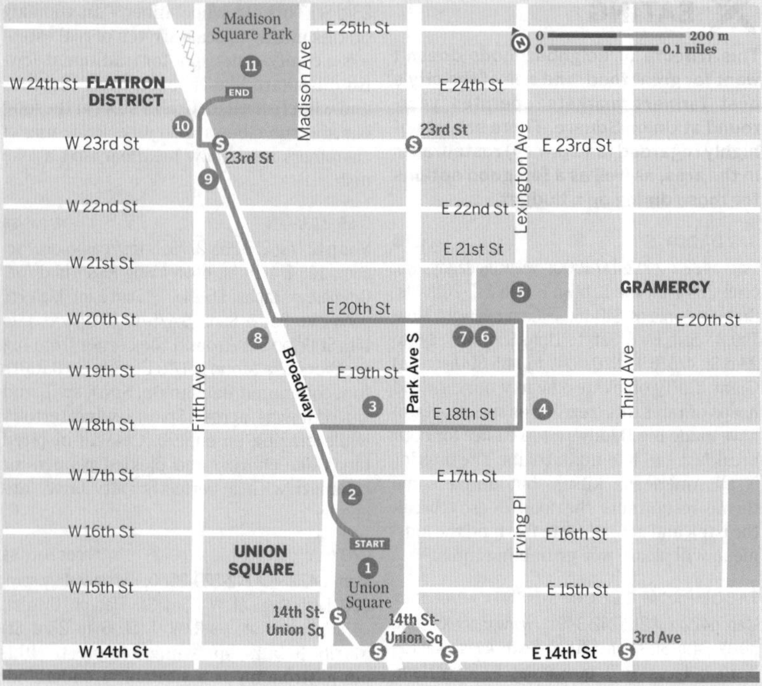

Neighborhood Walk
Be There, Be Square

START UNION SQUARE
END MADISON SQUARE PARK
LENGTH 1.2 MILES; ONE HOUR

Start at bustling park 1 **Union Square** (p166). Browse through crafts and fresh produce at the 2 **Greenmarket** (p167) and pause to people-watch the New Yorkers passing by (don't miss the chess masters at the southern end).

Two of New York's oldest drinking dens are nearby. On 18th St is 3 **Old Town Bar** (p172), whose ornate 1892 wood-and-mirror bar is a favorite for film shoots. Continue on to Irving Pl, where 4 **Pete's Tavern** (p173) has been pulling drafts since 1864. (According to legend, O Henry wrote his famous short story 'Gift of the Magi' here.)

Walk north on Irving Pl to see the Chrysler Building beyond the gates of 5 **Gramercy Park** (p168), the city's only private garden (local residents get a key). Turn left on 20th St to pass by two private social clubs in classic buildings. The 6 **Players Club** was founded in 1888 by Edwin Booth, a star actor of his day – his statue is in Gramercy Park – and brother of presidential assassin John Wilkes. The 7 **National Arts Club** (p168) was founded a decade later in the former mansion of New York governor Samuel Tilden, where you can browse free art galleries.

At Broadway and 20th St is the old 8 **Lord & Taylor Building** (cnr Broadway & E 20th St), former home of the famous Midtown department store (now a Brooks Brothers). This Second Empire–style construction (1870) stands in an area formerly nicknamed 'Ladies' Mile' for its once-abundant retail emporiums.

Head north on Broadway to where it meets Fifth Ave to the arrestingly triangular 9 **Flatiron Building** (p167), by Chicago architect Daniel Burnham. Admire its terracotta ornamentation from up close, then cross the street for wider views. Duck in to famed food hall 10 **Eataly** (p169) to grab some tasty Italian morsels to go, then head into leafy 11 **Madison Square Park** (p167) for a satisfying picnic lunch.

★MAIALINO ITALIAN $$$

Map p422 (212-777-2410; www.maialinonyc.com; Gramercy Park Hotel, 2 Lexington Ave, at 21st St, Gramercy; mains $24-58; 7:30-10am, noon-2pm & 5:30-10:30pm Mon-Thu, to 11pm Fri, 10am-2pm & 5:30-11pm Sat, to 10:30pm Sun; S 6, R/W to 23rd St) Fans reserve tables up to four weeks in advance at this Danny Meyer classic, but the best seats in the house are at the walk-in bar, with sociable, knowledgeable staffers. Wherever you're plonked, take your taste buds on a Roman holiday. Maialino's lip-smacking, rustic Italian fare is created using produce from the nearby Union Square Greenmarket (p167).

★ELEVEN MADISON PARK AMERICAN $$$

Map p422 (212-889-0905; www.elevenmadisonpark.com; 11 Madison Ave, btwn 24th & 25th Sts, Flatiron District; bar mains $35-50, tasting menu $175-335; 5:30-10pm Mon-Wed, to 10:30pm Thu, noon-1pm & 5:30-10:30pm Fri-Sun; S R/W, 6 to 23rd St) Eleven Madison Park consistently bags a spot on top restaurant lists. Frankly, we're not surprised: this revamped poster child of modern, sustainable American cooking is also one of only five NYC restaurants sporting three Michelin stars. Insane attention to detail, intense creativity and whimsy are all trademarks of chef Daniel Humm's approach.

After a revamp, it's now more accessible than ever thanks to the addition of dining tables in the bar. Here, an abbreviated tasting menu (five rather than 8 courses, for $175) can be had, or select mains ($35 to $50) from the core tasting menu. Reservations – for both the main dining room and bar tables – open on the first of the month for the following month. Dress to impress.

★CRAFT AMERICAN $$$

Map p422 (212-780-0880; www.craftrestaurant.com; 43 E 19th St, btwn Broadway & Park Ave S, Union Square; mains $33-69; 5:30-10pm Mon-Thu, to 11pm Fri, 5-11pm Sat, to 9pm Sun; ; S 4/5/6, N/Q/R/W, L to 14th St-Union Sq) Humming, high-end Craft flies the flag for small, family-owned farms and food producers, their bounty transformed into pure, polished dishes. Whether nibbling on flawlessly charred braised octopus, juicy roasted quail or pumpkin *mezzaluna* pasta with sage, brown butter and Parmesan, expect every ingredient to sing with flavor. Book ahead Wednesday to Saturday or head in by 6pm or after 9:30pm.

CLOCKTOWER BRITISH $$$

Map p422 (212-413-4300; www.theclocktowernyc.com; 5 Madison Ave, btwn 23rd & 24th Sts, Gramercy; dinner mains $27-47; 7-10:30am, 11:30am-2:30pm & 5:30-10pm daily, afternoon tea 3-5pm Fri-Sun; ; S F/M, R/W, 6 to 23rd St) Brits do it best at Jason Atherton's clubby, new A-lister, hidden away inside the landmark Metropolitan Life Tower (p168). This is the latest venture for the Michelin-starred British chef, its wood-and-stucco dining rooms setting a handsome scene for high-end comfort grub like beet-cured heritage pork chop with heirloom carrots and black pudding and a 'macaroni 'n' cheese' with slow-cooked ox cheek.

ABC KITCHEN AMERICAN $$$

Map p422 (212-475-5829; www.abckitchennyc.com; 35 E 18th St, at Broadway, Union Square; pizzas $18-23, dinner mains $25-37; noon-3pm & 5-10:30pm Mon-Wed, to 11pm Thu, to 11:30pm Fri, 11am-3pm & 5:30-11:30pm Sat, 11am-3pm & 5:30-10pm Sun; ; S 4/5/6, N/Q/R, L to 14th St-Union Sq) Looking part gallery, part rustic farmhouse, sustainable, produce-focused ABC Kitchen is the culinary avatar of the chichi home-goods department store ABC Carpet & Home (p174). Organic gets haute in dishes like wood-oven-roasted Maine lobster with lemon-chili vinaigrette, or crispy pork confit with smoked-bacon marmalade and braised turnips. For a more casual bite, try the scrumptious whole-wheat pizzas.

COSME MEXICAN $$$

Map p422 (212-913-9659; www.cosmenyc.com; 35 E 21st St, btwn Broadway & Park Ave S, Flatiron District; dinner dishes $19-29; noon-2:30pm & 5:30-11pm Mon-Thu, to midnight Fri, 11:30am-2:30pm & 5:30pm-midnight Sat, to 11pm Sun; ; S R/W, 6 to 23rd St) Mexican gets haute at this slinky, charcoal-hued restaurant, with innovative takes on south-of-the-border flavors from co-chefs Enrique Olvera and Daniela Soto-Innes. Subvert culinary stereotypes with the likes of delicate, invigorating scallops with avocado and jicama, a green mole with bok choy and purslane, herb guacamole or Cosme's cult-status duck carnitas. Book ahead or try your luck at the walk-in bar.

GRAMERCY TAVERN AMERICAN $$$

Map p422 (212-477-0777; www.gramercytavern.com; 42 E 20th St, btwn Broadway & Park Ave S, Flatiron District; tavern mains $34-36, dining room 3-course menu $134, tasting menus $164-184; ⏰tavern 11:30am-11pm Sun-Thu, to midnight Fri & Sat, lunch 11:30am-2pm, dinner 5-9:45pm Sun-Thu, to 10:30pm Fri & Sat; ; ⓈR/W, 6 to 23rd St) Seasonal, local ingredients drive this perennial favorite, a vibrant, country-chic institution aglow with copper sconces, murals and dramatic floral arrangements. Choose from two spaces: the walk-in-only tavern and its à la carte menu, or the swankier dining room and its fancier prix-fixe and degustation feasts. Regardless of where you sit, you'll find service is excellent. New Yorkers *love* this place: book ahead.

CASA MONO TAPAS $$$

Map p422 (☎212-253-2773; www.casamononyc.com; 52 Irving Pl, btwn 17th & 18th Sts, Gramercy; small plates $13-22; ⏰noon-11pm Sun-Tue, to midnight Wed-Sat; Ⓢ4/5/6, N/Q/R/W, L to 14th St-Union Sq) Another success story from restaurateur Mario Batali and chef Andy Nusser, Casa Mono features a long bar where you can sit and watch your Michelin-starred tapas being prepared, or dine at tables for more discreet conversation. Either way, get set for flavorful bites like creamy eggs with sea urchin, walnuts, lime and anchovy oil.

DRINKING & NIGHTLIFE

Perfectly made classic cocktails and robust wine lists are typical of the bars and lounges in Union Square, Flatiron District and Gramercy. Though these areas aren't packed with bars, what's here is generally classy and convivial: rooftop bars, Prohibition-style dens and one-of-a-kind hotel bars. If you need a regular-Joe kind of Irish drinking hole, try Third Ave north of 14th St.

RAINES LAW ROOM COCKTAIL BAR

Map p422 (www.raineslawroom.com; 48 W 17th St, btwn Fifth & Sixth Aves, Flatiron District; ⏰5pm-2am Mon-Thu, to 3am Fri & Sat, to 1am Sun; ⓈF/M to 14th St, L to 6th Ave, 1 to 18th St) A sea of velvet drapes and overstuffed leather lounge chairs, the perfect amount of exposed brick, expertly crafted cocktails using hard-to-find spirits – these folks are as serious as a mortgage payment when it comes to amplified atmosphere. There's no sign from the street; look for the '48' above the door and ring the bell to gain entry.

Reservations (recommended) are only accepted Sunday to Tuesday. Whatever the night, style up for a taste of a far more sumptuous era.

SERRA ROOFTOP BAR

Map p422 (☎212-937-8910; www.eataly.com; 200 Fifth Ave, at W 23rd St, Flatiron District; ⏰11:30am-10pm Sun-Thu, to 11pm Fri & Sat; ⓈF/M, R/W, 6 to 23rd St) The crown jewel of Italian food emporium Eataly (p169) is this covered rooftop garden tucked betwixt the Flatiron's corporate towers. The theme is refreshed each season, meaning you might find a Mediterranean beach escape one month and an alpine country retreat the next, but the setting is unfailingly impressive and food and drink always match up to the gourmet goodies below.

FLATIRON ROOM COCKTAIL BAR

Map p422 (☎212-725-3860; www.theflatironroom.com; 37 W 26th St, btwn Sixth Ave & Broadway, Flatiron District; ⏰5pm-2am Mon-Sat, to midnight Sun; ⓈR/W to 28th St, F/M to 23rd St) Vintage wallpaper, a glittering chandelier and hand-painted coffered ceilings make for a suitably elegant scene at this grown-up drinking den, its artfully lit cabinets graced with rare whiskeys. Fine cocktails pair nicely with high-end sharing plates, from deviled eggs with duck rillett to smoked oysters and charcuterie. Live music features most nights, including bluegrass and jazz. Reservations are highly recommended.

IRVING FARM ROASTERS CAFE

Map p422 (☎212-995-5252; www.irvingfarm.com; 71 Irving Pl, btwn 18th & 19th Sts, Gramercy; ⏰7am-8pm Mon-Fri, from 8am Sat & Sun; Ⓢ4/5/6, N/Q/R/W, L to 14th St-Union Sq) From keyboard-tapping scribes to gossiping friends and academics, this bustling downstairs cafe is never short of a crowd. Handpicked beans are lovingly roasted on a farm in the Hudson Valley (about 90 miles from NYC), and served alongside tasty edibles like Balthazar-baked croissants, granola, egg dishes, bagels and pressed sandwiches.

OLD TOWN BAR & RESTAURANT BAR

Map p422 (☎212-529-6732; www.oldtownbar.com; 45 E 18th St, btwn Broadway & Park Ave S, Union Square; ⏰11:30am-1am Mon-Fri, noon-1am Sat, 3pm-midnight Sun; ; Ⓢ4/5/6, N/Q/R/W, L to 14th St-Union Sq) It still looks like 1892 in here, with the mahogany bar, original tile floors and tin ceilings – the Old Town is an old-world drinking-man's classic. It's frequently used as an old-school shooting location for movies and TV (and even Madonna's 'Bad Girl' video). Most people settle into one of the snug wooden booths for beers and a burger (from $12.50).

BOXERS NYC GAY

Map p422 (☎212-255-5082; www.boxersnyc.com; 37 W 20th St, btwn Fifth & Sixth Aves, Flatiron District; ⏲4pm-2am Mon-Thu, to 3am Fri, 1pm-3am Sat, 1pm-3am Sun; SF/M, R/W, 6 to 23rd St) The beers and potential new buds are plentiful at this gay sports bar in the heart of the Flatiron District. There's football on TV, Buffalo wings at the bar, and shirtless waitstaff keeping the pool cues polished. To release your inner diva head there on a Monday for Karaoke Night.

LILLIE'S VICTORIAN ESTABLISHMENT BAR

Map p422 (☎212-337-1970; www.lilliesnyc.com; 13 E 17th St, btwn Broadway & Fifth Ave, Union Square; ⏲11:45am-4am Mon-Fri, from 11am Sat & Sun; S4/5/6, L, N/Q/R/W to 14th St-Union Sq) Step in and be taken to the era of petticoats and watch fobs with high, stamped-tin ceilings, red-velvet love seats and walls covered in vintage photographs in extravagant gilded frames – Lillie's feels every bit the traditional high-society Irish watering hole without falling into parody. Pub grub such as shepherd's pie helps fulfill the fantasy.

PETE'S TAVERN BAR

Map p422 (☎212-473-7676; www.petestavern.com; 129 E 18th St, at Irving Pl, Gramercy; ⏲11am-2:30am Sun-Wed, to 3am Thu, to 4am Fri & Sat; S4/5/6, N/Q/R/W, L to 14th St-Union Sq) With its original 19th-century mirrors, pressed-tin ceiling and rosewood bar, this dark, atmospheric watering hole serving up brews since 1864 has all the earmarks of a New York classic. You can get a respectable prime-rib burger here and choose from 17 draft beers, joined by everyone from post-theater couples to the odd celebrity (see photos by the restrooms).

ENTERTAINMENT

PEOPLES IMPROV THEATER COMEDY

Map p422 (PIT; ☎classes 212-563-7488; www.thepit-nyc.com; 123 E 24th St, btwn Lexington & Park Aves, Gramercy; 📶; SF/M, N/R, 6 to 23rd St) Aglow in red neon, this bustling comedy club serves up top-notch laughs at dirt-cheap prices. The string of nightly acts ranges from stand-up and improv to sketch and musical comedy. Come early to drink in the cheap and cheerful, lipstick-red bar. PIT also runs courses, including three-hour, drop-in improv workshops ($20) on weekend nights at its Midtown venue.

IRVING PLAZA LIVE MUSIC

Map p422 (☎212-777-6817; www.irvingplaza.com; 17 Irving Pl, at 15th St, Union Square; S4/5/6, N/Q/R, L to 14th St-Union Sq) Rocking since 1978, Irving Plaza has seen them all: the Ramones, Bob Dylan, U2, Pearl Jam, you name it. These days it's a great in-between stage for quirkier rock and pop acts, from riot grrrls Sleater-Kinney to hard rockers Disturbed. There's a cozy floor around the stage, and good views from the mezzanine.

SHOPPING

From rare children's books and artisanal cheeses, to one of New York's best-loved farmers markets, this block of neighborhoods harbors retail gems. However, today there are as many big chain stores as independent boutiques – particularly around the edges of Union Square and up Sixth Ave. Fourteenth St (more west than east) is a shopping adventure all of its own, hawking everything from guitars and furniture to sportswear, wigs and tattoos. For midrange to more upscale chains like Zara, Banana Republic, Club Monaco, J Crew, Anthropologie and Intermix, strut north up Fifth Ave.

FISHS EDDY HOMEWARES

Map p422 (☎212-420-9020; www.fishseddy.com; 889 Broadway, at E 19th St, Union Square; ⏲10am-9pm Mon-Fri, to 8pm Sat & Sun; SR/W, 6 to 23rd St) High-quality and irreverent design has made Fishs Eddy a staple in the homes of hip New Yorkers for years. Its store is a veritable landslide of mugs, plates, dish towels, carafes and anything else that belongs in a cupboard. Styles range from tasteful color blocking to delightfully outrageous patterns. The 'Brooklynese' line *(Cawfee, Shuguh, Sawlt* etc) makes for great souvenirs.

If you live in the US you don't have to worry about hauling your new flatware home: staff can arrange affordable shipping for you at the store.

ABC CARPET & HOME HOMEWARES

Map p422 (☎212-473-3000; www.abchome.com; 888 Broadway, at E 19th St, Flatiron District; ⊙10am-7pm Mon-Sat, noon-6pm Sun; S4/5/6, N/Q/R/W, L to 14th St-Union Sq) A mecca for home designers and decorators brainstorming ideas, this beautifully curated, seven-level temple to good taste heaves with all sorts of furnishings, small and large. Shop for easy-to-pack knickknacks, boho textiles and jewelry, as well as statement furniture, designer lighting, ceramics and antique carpets. Come Christmas the shop is a joy to behold and it's a great place to buy decorations.

RENT THE RUNWAY CLOTHING

Map p422 (www.renttherunway.com; 30 W 15th St, btwn Fifth & Sixth Aves, Union Square; ⊙8am-9pm Mon-Fri, 9am-8pm Sat, to 7pm Sun; SL, F/M to 14th St-6th Ave; 4/5/6, L, N/Q/R/W to 14th St-Union Sq) At the flagship store of this popular fashion-rental service anyone can pop in for an affordable fashion consultation ($30) for both planned and last-minute events. It's full of looks by high-end designers (Narciso Rodriguez, Badgley Mischka, Nicole Miller) available to rent. Perfect for those who pack light, but want to make a splash.

BEDFORD CHEESE SHOP FOOD

Map p422 (☎718-599-7588; www.bedfordcheeseshop.com; 67 Irving Pl, btwn E 18th & 19th Sts, Gramercy; ⊙8am-8pm Mon-Fri, 9am-8pm Sat, to 6pm Sun; S4/5/6, N/Q/R/W, L to 14th St-Union Sq) Whether you're after local, raw cow's-milk cheese washed in absinthe, or garlic-infused goat's-milk cheese from Australia, chances are you'll find it among the 200-strong selection at this outpost of Brooklyn's most-celebrated cheese vendor. Pair the cheesy goodness with artisanal charcuterie, deli treats and ready-to-eat sandwiches ($9 to $11.50), as well as a proud array of Made-in-Brooklyn edibles.

BOOKS OF WONDER BOOKS

Map p422 (☎212-989-3270; www.booksofwonder.com; 18 W 18th St, btwn Fifth & Sixth Aves, Flatiron District; ⊙10am-7pm Mon-Sat, 11am-6pm Sun; 👪; SF/M to 14th St, L to 6th Ave) Devoted to children's and young-adult titles, this wonderful bookstore is a great place to take little ones on a rainy day, especially when a kids' author is giving a reading or a storyteller is on hand. There's an impressive range of NYC-themed picture books, plus a section dedicated to rare and vintage children's books and limited-edition children's-book artwork.

PARAGON SPORTING GOODS SPORTS & OUTDOORS

Map p422 (☎212-255-8036; www.paragonsports.com; 867 Broadway, at E 18th St, Union Square; ⊙10am-8:30pm Mon-Fri, to 8pm Sat, 11am-7pm Sun; S4/5/6, L, N/Q/R/W to 14th St-Union Sq) Outfitting active New Yorkers since 1908, Paragon's goods sprawl across three floors of its giant corner store. With everything from team and solo sports equipment to beachwear, and travel and camping gear, you're sure to find what you need. Its shoe department has special machines to test your gait and help you find the perfect running shoe.

SPORTS & ACTIVITIES

NEW YORK CITY AUDUBON BIRDWATCHING

Map p422 (☎212-691-7483; www.nycaudubon.org; 71 W 23rd St, Suite 1523, at Sixth Ave, Flatiron District; tours & classes free-$170; SF/M to 23rd St) Throughout the year, the New York City Audubon Society runs bird-watching field trips (including seal- and waterbird-spotting on New York Harbor and eagle-watching in the Hudson Valley), plus lectures and beginners' birding classes. Its 'bird walks' in Central Park and Prospect Park are popular, so book ahead on the website.

Midtown

MIDTOWN EAST | FIFTH AVENUE | MIDTOWN WEST & TIMES SQUARE | MIDTOWN EAST & FIFTH AVENUE

Neighborhood Top Five

1 Rockefeller Center (p188) Playing Spot the Landmark at the jaw-dropping Top of the Rock observation deck, or taking a tour of NBC's historic TV studios.

2 Museum of Modern Art (p182) Hanging out with Picasso, Warhol and Rothko, or grabbing a spectacular bite to eat or a fine cocktail at this blockbuster museum.

3 Bryant Park (p191) Lunching alfresco, watching a movie under the stars or even just relaxing in this activity-filled Midtown oasis.

4 Jazz at Lincoln Center (p204) Gazing at the spectacular view while listening to world-class musicians hit their groove.

5 Broadway (p179) Adding a little sparkle to life with a toe-tapping, soul-lifting Broadway show.

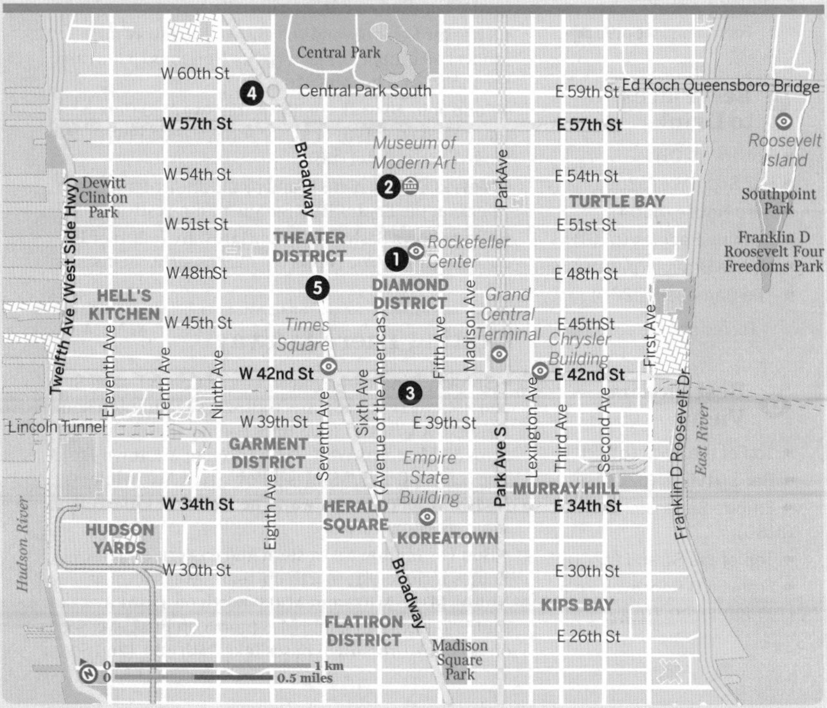

For more detail of this area see Map p424 and p428

Lonely Planet's Top Tip

Savoring Midtown's A-list restaurants without mortgaging the house is possible if you go for the prix-fixe lunch menu where available. Participants include Michelin-starred **Le Bernardin** (p198), which offers dishes featured in its evening menus. How far ahead you should book depends on the restaurant. It can sometimes be a one-month wait at Le Bernardin, which offers online reservations.

Best Places to Eat

- Le Bernardin (p198)
- O-ya (p196)
- Modern (p198)
- Totto Ramen (p196)
- Agern (p196)
- Hangawi (p195)

For reviews, see p195

Best Places to Drink

- Robert (p201)
- Bar SixtyFive (p200)
- Rum House (p204)
- Flaming Saddles (p201)
- Middle Branch (p200)
- The Campbell (p200)

For reviews, see p200

Best Skyline Views

- Top of the Rock (p193)
- Bar SixtyFive (p200)
- Empire State Building (p180)
- Top of the Strand (p200)
- Franklin D Roosevelt Four Freedoms Park (p190)

Explore Midtown

Midtown is big, brazen and best seen on foot, so slice it up and enjoy it bit by bit. The top end of Fifth Ave (around the 50s) makes for a fabled introduction, home to Tiffany & Co, the Plaza hotel (p340), the Museum of Modern Art (MoMA) (p182) and the Rockefeller Center's Top of the Rock (p193) observation decks. A day in Midtown East could easily incorporate rare manuscripts at the Morgan Library & Museum (p190), beaux-arts architecture at Grand Central Terminal (p184), the art deco lobby of the Chrysler Building (p186) and a tour of the United Nations (p190). If it's a rainy day, explore the gilded New York Public Library (p191).

In Midtown West, design and fashion buffs head to the Museum of Arts & Design (p194) and the Museum at FIT (p194). Between the two is blinding Times Square, most spectacular at night. Its residents include top-tier retail chains and a TKTS Booth (p179) selling cut-price Broadway tickets. Further west is Hell's Kitchen, packed with great eateries and gay venues.

Local Life

- **Dive bars** Stiff drinks, loosened ties and the whiff of nostalgia await at no-bull dive bars like Jimmy's Corner (p204) and Rudy's Bar & Grill (p204).
- **Theater** Look beyond the glitz of Broadway for innovative drama at Playwrights Horizons (p206) and Second Stage Theater (p208).
- **Food** Join all walks of life at time-warped Cuban diner Margon (p196) or go for some classic Jewish deli food at Ess-a-Bagel (p195).
- **Movies** Bring a blanket and picnic dinner for alfresco cinema at the Bryant Park Summer Film Festival (p191).
- **Drag shows** Sashay away to Hardware (p201) or Industry (p201) to see NYC's top queens strut their stuff.

Getting There & Away

- **Subway** Times Sq-42nd St, Grand Central-42nd St and 34th St-Herald Sq are Midtown's main interchange stations. A/C/E and 1/2/3 lines run north–south through Midtown West; 4/5/6 through Midtown East. The central B/D/F/M lines follow Sixth Ave, while N/Q/R/W follow Broadway. The 7, E and M lines offer some crosstown service.
- **Bus** For Midtown's western and eastern extremes. Routes include M11 (north on Tenth Ave; south on Ninth), M101, M102 and M103 (north on Third Ave; south on Lexington) and M15 (north on First Ave; south on Second). Crosstown buses take 34th and 42nd Sts.

INGUS KRUKLITIS/SHUTTERSTOCK ©

TOP EXPERIENCE
TIMES SQUARE

Love it or hate it, the intersection of Broadway and Seventh Ave – better known as Times Square – is New York City's heart. It's a restless, hypnotic torrent of glittering lights, giant billboards and raw urban energy that doesn't seem to have an off switch: it's nearly as busy in the wee hours as it is in the afternoon.

Hyperactive Heart

This is the New York of collective fantasies – the place where Al Jolson 'makes it' in the 1927 film *The Jazz Singer,* where photojournalist Alfred Eisenstaedt famously captured a lip-locked sailor and nurse on V-J Day in 1945, and where Alicia Keys and Jay-Z waxed lyrically about the concrete jungle.

But for several decades, the dream here was a sordid one. The economic crash of the early 1970s led to a mass exodus of corporations from Times Square. Billboard niches went dark, stores shut and once-grand hotels were converted into SRO (single-room occupancy) dives. While the adjoining Theater District survived, its respectable playhouses shared the streets with porn cinemas and strip clubs. That all changed with tough-talking former mayor Rudolph Giuliani who, in the 1990s, boosted police numbers and lured in a wave of 'respectable' retail chains, restaurants and attractions. By the new millennium, Times Square had gone from X-rated to G-rated, drawing almost 50 million visitors annually.

DON'T MISS

- Taking in Times Square from the TKTS Booth steps
- Seeing a Broadway show
- Sipping a drink at R Lounge (p204)
- Staring in awe at the sheer dazzle of it all

PRACTICALITIES

- Map p428, E5
- www.timessquarenyc.org
- Broadway, at Seventh Ave
- S N/Q/R/W, S, 1/2/3, 7 to Times Sq-42nd St

How the New York Times Made New Year's Eve

At the turn of the 20th century, Times Square was an unremarkable intersection known as Longacre Sq. This would change with a deal made between subway pioneer August Belmont and *New York Times* publisher Adolph Ochs. Heading construction of the city's

TOP TIP

In 2017, designated outdoor street-food areas launched in Times Square's pedestrian plazas (at the Broadway intersections with W 43rd and W 47th Sts), meaning it's now possible to bask in the warm glow of the neon lights sitting with a beer and taco in hand. There's also a **tourist information booth** (Map p428; ☎212-484-1222; www.timessquarenyc.org; Broadway Plaza, at W 45th St; ⏰8am-5pm; Ⓢ N/Q/R/W, S, 1/2/3, 7, A/C/E to Times Sq-42nd St).

TAKE A BREAK

For a panoramic overview, order a drink at the Renaissance Hotel's R Lounge (p204), which offers floor-to-ceiling glass windows over the neon-lit spectacle.

Times Square is so touristy and chaotic that if you want a proper meal, you're better off eating elsewhere. Fournos Theophilos (p196), a two-block walk east, is a quiet retreat for a delicious Greek lunch with baklava milkshakes.

first subway line (from Lower Manhattan to Harlem), Belmont astutely realized that a Midtown business hub would encourage use of the line (and maximize profit). Belmont approached Ochs, arguing that moving to Broadway and 42nd St would be a win-win for the broadsheet: an in-house subway station would mean faster distribution of the newspaper, but also more sales to the influx of commuters – and convinced mayor George B McClellan Jr to rename the square in honor of the broadsheet. In the winter of 1904–05, both the subway station and the *Times'* new headquarters at One Times Square made their debut.

In honor of the move, the *Times* hosted a New Year's Eve party in 1904, setting off fireworks from its skyscraper rooftop. By 1907, the square had become so built-up that fireworks were deemed a safety hazard, forcing the newspaper to come up with an alternative crowd-puller. It came in the form of a 700lb, wood-and-iron ball, lowered from the roof of One Times Square to herald the arrival of 1908.

Around one million people still gather in Times Square every New Year's Eve to watch a Waterford crystal ball descend from the building at midnight. Looking up, it's easy to forget that behind the current armor of billboards, the One Times Square building still exists. To see what it looked like in the days of Adolph Ochs, pay a visit to the beautiful DeWitt Wallace Periodical Room at the New York Public Library (p191), whose paintings by muralist Richard Haas include Times Square in the time of streetcars.

How Theater Came to Times Square

The neighborhood's first playhouse was the long-gone Empire, opened in 1893 and located on Broadway between 40th and 41st Sts. Two years later, cigar manufacturer and part-time comedy scribe Oscar Hammerstein opened the Olympia, also on Broadway, before opening the Republic – now children's theater **New Victory** (Map p428; ☎646-223-3010; www.newvictory.org; 209 W 42nd St, btwn Seventh & Eighth Aves; 👪; Ⓢ N/Q/R/W, S, 1/2/3, 7 to Times Sq-42nd St; A/C/E to 42nd St-Port Authority Bus Terminal) – in 1900. This led to a string of new venues, among them the still-beating **New Amsterdam Theatre** (Aladdin; Map p428; ☎866-870-2717; www.newamsterdamtheatre.com; 214 W 42nd St, btwn Seventh & Eighth Aves; ⏰box office 9am-8pm Mon-Fri, from 10am Sat, 10am-6:30pm Sun; 👪; Ⓢ N/Q/R/W, S, 1/2/3, 7 to Times Sq-42nd St; A/C/E to 42nd St-Port Authority Bus Terminal) and **Lyceum Theatre** (Map p428; www.shubert.nyc/theatres/lyceum; 149 W 45th St, btwn Sixth & Seventh Aves; Ⓢ N/R/W to 49th St).

The Broadway of the 1920s was well-known for its lighthearted musicals, commonly fusing vaudeville and music-hall traditions, and producing classic tunes like Cole Porter's 'Let's Misbehave.' But at the same time, Midtown's theater district was evolving as a platform for new American dramatists. One of the greatest was Eugene O'Neill (1888–1953). Born in Times Square at the long-gone Barrett Hotel (1500 Broadway), the playwright debuted many of his works here, including Pulitzer Prize winners *Beyond the Horizon* and *Anna Christie*. O'Neill's success on Broadway paved the way for other 20th-century American greats like Tennessee Williams, Arthur Miller and Edward Albee, who would come to be recognized for their serious talent by the establishment of the annual Tony Awards in 1947.

Brilliant Broadway

The dozens of Broadway and off-Broadway theaters near Times Square run everything from blockbuster musicals to new and classic drama. Unless there's a specific show you're after, the best – and cheapest – way to score tickets in the area is at the **TKTS Booth** (Map p428; www.tdf.org/tkts; Broadway, at W 47th St, Midtown; ⏲3-8pm Mon & Fri, 2-8pm Tue, 10am-2pm & 3-8pm Wed, Thu & Sat, 11am-7pm Sun; Ⓢ N/Q/R/W, S, 1/2/3, 7 to Times Sq-42nd St), where you can line up and get same-day discounted tickets for top Broadway and off-Broadway shows. Smartphone users can download the free TKTS app, which offers rundowns of both Broadway and off-Broadway shows, as well as real-time updates of what's available on that day. Always have a backup choice in case your first preference sells out, and never buy from scalpers on the street. Queues are usually shortest after 5:30pm – though the clever buy their tickets at the less-crowded South Street Seaport branch (p63).

The TKTS Booth is an attraction in its own right, with its illuminated roof of 27 ruby-red steps rising a panoramic 16ft 1in above Father Duffy Sq, named for a WWI army chaplain.

Today's Times Square

The iconic hourglass-shaped plaza is an unmissable homage to the hustle and bustle of big-city life. Almost as bright at 2am as it is at noon, and always jammed with people, Times Square proves that New York truly is the city that never sleeps. For some, it's hell on earth. Even so, if you can stroll along this short section of Broadway without feeling at least the tiniest twinge of awe, check your pulse. The massive billboards stretch half a skyscraper tall, and LED signs are lit for shows and performances. A mishmash of costumed characters on the square (from the cute, like Elmo, to the noble, like the Statue of Liberty, to the popular, like Marvel action heroes, to the just plain bizarre, like Naked Cowboy) mix with the jumble of humanity from every corner of the globe. Walk around and in minutes you'll hear more languages being spoken than you even knew existed. It's also an urban playground for public art and seasonal events, not forgetting the world's most famous spot to celebrate New Year's Eve.

Brill Building

At the northwest corner of Broadway and 49th, the humble-looking **Brill Building** (Map p428; 1619 Broadway, at W 49th St; Ⓢ N/R/W to 49th St; 1, C/E to 50th St) – its ground floor being redeveloped for retail – is widely considered the most important generator of popular songs in the Western world. In 1962, over 160 music businesses were based here, from songwriters and managers to record companies and promoters. It was a one-stop shop for artists, who could craft a song, hire musicians, cut a demo and convince a producer, all on-site. Among the legends who recorded here were Carole King, Bob Dylan, Joni Mitchell and Paul Simon.

TOP EXPERIENCE
EMPIRE STATE BUILDING

LOC WATIER/EYEEM/GETTY IMAGES ©

The Chrysler Building may be prettier, and One World Trade Center taller, but the queen bee of the New York skyline remains the Empire State Building. NYC's former tallest star has enjoyed close-ups in around a hundred films, from *King Kong* to *Independence Day.* Heading up to the top is as quintessentially New York as pastrami, rye and pickles.

By the Numbers

The statistics are astounding: 10 million bricks, 60,000 tons of steel, 6400 windows and 328,000 sq ft of marble. Built on the original site of the Waldorf-Astoria Hotel, construction took a record-setting 410 days, using seven million hours of labor and costing $41 million. It might sound like a lot, but it fell well below its $50 million budget. Coming in at 102 stories and 1454ft from top to bottom, the limestone tower opened for business on May 1, 1931. Generations later, Deborah Kerr's words to Cary Grant in *An Affair to Remember* still ring true: 'It's the nearest thing to heaven we have in New York.'

Observation Decks

Unless you're Ann Darrow (the unfortunate woman caught in King Kong's grip), heading to the top of the Empire State Building should leave you beaming. There are two observation decks. The open-air 86th-floor deck offers an alfresco experience, with telescopes (previously coin operated; now free) for close-up glimpses of the metropolis in action. Further up, at the top of the spire, the enclosed 102nd floor is New York's second-highest observation deck, trumped only by the observation deck at One World Trade Center. Needless to say, the views through the floor-to-ceiling windows over the city's five boroughs (and four neighboring states,

DON'T MISS

- Observation decks at sunset
- Live jazz Thursday to Saturday nights
- Art deco lobby with aluminum-relief mural

PRACTICALITIES

- Map p424, B7
- www.empirestatebuilding.com
- 20 W 34th St, btwn Fifth & Sixth Aves
- 86th-fl observation deck adult/child $38/32, incl 102nd-fl observation deck $58/52
- 8am-2am, last elevators up 1:15am
- S 6 to 33rd St, B/D/F/M, N/Q/R/W to 34th St-Herald Sq

weather permitting) are quite simply exquisite. The views from both decks are especially spectacular at sunset, when the city dons its nighttime cloak in dusk's afterglow.

An Ambitious Antenna

A locked, unmarked door on the 102nd-floor observation deck leads to one of New York's most outrageous pie-in-the-sky projects to date: a narrow terrace intended to dock zeppelins. Spearheading the dream was former New York governor Alfred E Smith, who went from failed presidential candidate in 1928 to head honcho of the Empire State Building project. When architect William Van Alen revealed the secret spire of his competing Chrysler Building, Smith went one better, declaring that the top of the Empire State Building would sport an even taller mooring mast for transatlantic airships. While the plan looked good on paper, there were two (major) oversights: dirigibles require anchoring at both ends (not just at the nose, as planned) and passengers (who travel in the zeppelin's gondola) cannot exit the craft through the giant helium-filled balloon. Regardless, it didn't stop them from trying. In September 1931, the *New York Evening Journal* threw sanity to the wind, managing to moor a zeppelin and deliver a pile of newspapers fresh out of Lower Manhattan. Though the ambitious plan for docking airships never got off the ground, years later an aircraft met up with the building with tragic consequences: a B-25 bomber crashed into the 79th floor on a foggy day in 1945, killing 14 people.

Language of Light

Since 1976, the building's top 30 floors have been floodlit in a spectrum of colors each night, reflecting seasonal and holiday hues, or even local sports teams, schools or charities. Famous combos include orange, white and green for St Patrick's Day; blue and white for Chanukah; white, red and green for Christmas; and the rainbow colors for Gay Pride weekend in June. For a full rundown of color schemes, check the website.

Sibling Comparisons

The Empire State Building was designed by the prolific architectural firm Shreve, Lamb and Harmon. According to legend, the skyscraper's conception began with a meeting between William Lamb and building co-financier John Jakob Raskob, during which Raskob propped up a No 2 pencil and asked, 'Bill, how high can you make it so that it won't fall down?' Shreve, Lamb and Harmon's other projects include the skyscraper at 500 Fifth Ave. To compare the soaring siblings, head to the northeast corner of Fifth Ave and 40th St.

TOP TIPS

Getting here very early (like 8am) or very late will help you avoid delays – as will buying tickets in advance online for an extra $2 convenience fee.

On the 86th floor between 10pm and 1am from Thursday to Saturday, the twinkling sea of lights below is accompanied by a live saxophone soundtrack (requests are welcome).

Download the Empire State Building tour app (free with your ticket) or stream the audio version live using the on-site free wi-fi.

TAKE A BREAK

You're just a short walk from Koreatown, with abundant eating options along 32nd St, including peaceful Hangawi (p195).

Or, stroll northward and lunch at the Bryant Park Grill (p193).

TOP EXPERIENCE

MUSEUM OF MODERN ART

MoMA boasts more A-listers than an Oscars after-party: Van Gogh, Matisse, Picasso, Warhol, Cassatt, Gaugin, Mondrian, Pollock and Bourgeois. Since its 1929 founding, the museum has amassed around 200,000 artworks, documenting the creativity of the late-19th century through to today. For art buffs, it's Valhalla. For the uninitiated, it's a crash course in all that is enthralling about art.

Collection Highlights

Works are rotated through the galleries every six months, so it's hard to say exactly what you'll find on display, but Van Gogh's phenomenally popular *The Starry Night* should be a sure bet – it's usually mobbed by a circle of star-struck fans wielding cameras. Other highlights of the collection include Picasso's *Les Demoiselles d'Avignon* and Henri Rousseau's *The Sleeping Gypsy,* not to mention iconic American works like Warhol's *Campbell's Soup Cans* and *Gold Marilyn Monroe,* Matisse's *Dance (I)* and Hopper's poignant *New York Movie.*

MoMA underwent a months-long redesign in 2019 by Diller Scofidio + Renfro, which added more than 40,000 sq ft of gallery space. The permanent collection has been curated as an overarching history of modern art, showcasing painting, sculpture, photography, film, architecture, industrial design and other disciplines, all set together in chronological segments on floors 5 (1880s–1940s), 4 (1940s–1970s) and 2 (1970s–present). Floor 3 features galleries for temporary exhibits, while the new 4th-floor

DON'T MISS

- Van Gogh's *Starry Night*
- The Abby Aldrich Rockefeller Sculpture Garden
- Dining at The Modern
- MoMA Book & Design Store

PRACTICALITIES

- MoMA
- Map p428, G2
- ☎212-708-9400
- www.moma.org
- 11 W 53rd St, btwn Fifth & Sixth Aves
- adult/child $25/free, 5:30-9pm Fri free
- ⌚10am-5:30pm Sat-Thu, to 9pm Fri & 1st Thu
- 👪
- Ⓢ E, M to 5th Ave-53rd St; F to 57th St

Kravis Studio will be a dedicated showcase for performance and other experimental art.

Generally speaking, Mondays and Tuesdays are the best (ie least-crowded) days to visit, except on public holidays. Friday evenings and weekends can be incredibly crowded and frustrating.

Abstract Expressionism

One of the greatest strengths of MoMA's collections is abstract expressionism, a radical movement that emerged in New York in the 1940s and boomed a decade later. Defined by its penchant for irreverent individualism and monumentally scaled works, this so-called New York School helped turn the metropolis into *the* epicenter of Western contemporary art. Among the stars on view are Mark Rothko's *No. 10* (1950), Jackson Pollock's *One: Number 31, 1950* and Lee Krasner's *Untitled* (1949).

Abby Aldrich Rockefeller Sculpture Garden

With architect Yoshio Taniguchi's reconstruction of the museum in 2004 came the restoration of the Sculpture Garden to the original, larger vision of Philip Johnson's 1953 design. Johnson described the space as a 'sort of outdoor room,' and on warm, sunny days, it's hard not to think of it as a soothing alfresco lounge. One resident that can't seem to get enough of it is Aristide Maillol's *The River,* a larger-than-life female sculpture that featured in Johnson's original garden. She's in fine company too, with fellow works from greats including Matisse, Giacometti, Calder and Picasso. Sitting sneakily above the garden's eastern end is *Water Tower,* a translucent resin installation by British artist Rachel Whiteread. The Sculpture Garden is open free of charge from 9:30am to 10:15am daily, except in inclement weather and during maintenance.

Film Screenings

Not only a palace of visual art, MoMA screens an incredibly well-rounded selection of celluloid gems from its collection of over 22,000 films, including the works of the Maysles Brothers and every Pixar animation film ever produced. Expect anything from Academy Award–nominated documentary shorts and Hollywood classics to experimental works and international retrospectives. Best of all, your museum ticket will get you in for free (though you'll still need to get a ticket for the film you want to see).

GALLERY CONVERSATIONS

To delve a little deeper into MoMA's collection, join one of the museum's talks and readings, which offer thought-provoking insight into specific works and exhibitions on view. The talks take place daily at 11:30am and 1:30pm. To check upcoming topics, visit the MoMA website and search for 'Gallery Sessions.'

TOP TIP

To maximize your time and create a plan of attack, download the museum's free smartphone app from the website beforehand. It's available in several different languages.

TAKE A BREAK

For communal tables and a casual vibe, nosh on Italian-inspired fare at **Cafe 2** (Map p428; ☎212-333-1299; www.momacafes.com; dishes $12-14; ⏲11am-5:30pm Sat-Thu, to 7:30pm Fri; 📶; Ⓢ E, M to 5th Ave-53rd St, F to 57th St).

For table service, opt for Terrace Café (p198), which features an outdoor terrace overlooking 53rd St.

JASON SPONSELLER/SHUTTERSTOCK ©

TOP EXPERIENCE
GRAND CENTRAL TERMINAL

Threatened by the opening of the original Penn Station, transport magnate Cornelius Vanderbilt transformed his 19th-century Grand Central Depot into a 20th-century showpiece. Grand Central Terminal is New York's most breathtaking beaux-arts building. Its chandeliers, marble and historic bars and restaurants are a porthole into an era when train travel and romance went hand in hand.

42nd St Facade

Clad in Connecticut Stony Creek granite at its base and Indiana limestone on top, Grand Central's showpiece facade is crowned by America's greatest monumental sculpture, *The Glory of Commerce* (also known as *Transportation*). Designed by the French sculptor Jules-Félix Coutan and rising 48ft, the piece was executed in Long Island City by local carvers Donnelly and Ricci. Once completed, it was hoisted up, piece by piece, in 1914. Its protagonist is a wing-capped Mercury, the Roman god of travel and commerce. To the left is Hercules in an unusually placid stance, while looking down on the mayhem of 42nd St is Minerva, the ancient guardian of cities. The clock beneath Mercury's foot contains the largest example of Tiffany glass in the world.

Main Concourse

Grand Central's centerpiece is more akin to a glorious ballroom than a thoroughfare. The marble floors are Tennessee pink, while the vintage ticket counters are Italian Bottocino marble. The vaulted ceiling is (quite literally) heavenly, its turquoise and

DON'T MISS

- Main beaux-arts facade
- Paul César Helleu's celestial mural
- Oysters under Rafael Guastavino's vaulted ceiling
- Cocktails at The Campbell
- Claus Meyer's Nordic-inspired gourmet bites

PRACTICALITIES

- Map p424, C5
- www.grandcentralterminal.com
- 89 E 42nd St, at Park Ave
- ⏲5:30am-2am
- S S, 4/5/6, 7 to Grand Central-42nd St, Metro North to Grand Central

gold-leaf mural depicting eight constellations... backwards. A mistake? Apparently not. Its French designer, painter Paul César Helleu, wished to depict the stars from God's point of view – from the out, looking in. The original, frescoed execution of Helleu's design was by New York–based artists J Monroe Hewlett and Charles Basing. Moisture damage saw it faithfully repainted (alas, not in fresco form) by Charles Gulbrandsen in 1944. By the 1990s, however, the mural was in ruins again. Enter renovation architects Beyer Blinder Belle, who restored the work, but left a small rectangular patch of soot (in the northwest corner, beneath the crab) as testament to just what a fine job they did.

Whispering Gallery, Oyster Bar & Restaurant, & Campbell Bar

The vaulted landing directly below the bridge linking the Main Concourse and Vanderbilt Hall is home to one of Grand Central's quirkier features, the so-called Whispering Gallery. If you're in company, stand facing the arched corners diagonally opposite each other and whisper something. If your partner proposes (it happens a lot), chilled champagne is just through the door at the Grand Central Oyster Bar & Restaurant (p196). It's hugely atmospheric (with a vaulted tiled ceiling by Catalan-born engineer Rafael Guastavino): the best spot is at the bar counter in front of the oyster shuckers. An elevator beside the restaurant leads up to another historic gem, the deliciously snooty bar The Campbell (p200).

Grand Central Goes Gourmet

Thronging Grand Central Market (p209) has long been a commuter foodie delight with its 240ft of fresh produce and artisan treats, but recently the terminal has taken things up a gear. A partnership with Claus Meyer, the Nordic chef who cofounded Noma in Denmark, has led to the launch of the Great Northern Food Hall (p195) in the airy, chandelier-lit Vanderbilt Hall. A major step up from the basement Dining Concourse, Meyer's handiwork offers Nordic-inspired gourmet bites using New York produce: flatbreads, hot sandwiches and *smørrebrød* (Danish open sandwiches) with fillings such as curried herring and egg yolk, alongside wine and artisan coffee. Next door, Meyer's stylish one-Michelin-starred restaurant, Agern (p196), serves fresh, zingy New Nordic cuisine and has an excellent lunch deal: two/three courses for $42/50.

GUIDED TOURS

The **Municipal Art Society** (Map p424; ☎212-464-8255; www.mas.org; tours adult/child from $30/20) runs 75-minute walking tours through Grand Central daily at 12:30pm. Tours start in front of Track 29 in the Main Concourse.

The **Grand Central Partnership** (Map p424; www.grandcentralpartnership.nyc) FREE also leads free, 90-minute tours of the terminal and the surrounding neighborhood on Fridays at 12:30pm, which commence on the southwest corner of E 42nd St and Park Ave.

THE PRESIDENT'S SECRET

Hidden away under the Waldorf-Astoria hotel is Grand Central's little-known Platform 61. One person who did know it well was President Franklin D Roosevelt. Determined to hide his wheelchair use from public view, Roosevelt made good use of the platform's freight elevator. Upon arrival at the station, the president would be driven straight out of his train carriage, along the platform and into the elevator...his public none the wiser.

TOP EXPERIENCE
CHRYSLER BUILDING

The 77-floor Chrysler Building makes most other skyscrapers look like uptight geeks. Designed by William Van Alen in 1930, it's the pinup for New York's most flamboyant art deco architecture. Constructed as the headquarters for Walter P Chrysler and his automobile empire, the ambitious $15 million building remains one of New York's most poignant symbols.

The Lobby

Although the Chrysler Building has no restaurant or observation deck, its lobby is a lavish consolation prize. Bathed in an amber glow, its Jazz Age vintage is echoed in its architecture – dark, exotic African wood and marble, contrasted against the brash steel of industrial America. The elaborately veneered elevators are especially beautiful, their Egyptian lotus motifs made of inlaid Japanese ash, Oriental walnut and Cuban plum-pudding wood. When the doors open, you almost expect Bette Davis to strut on out. Above you is painter Edward Trumbull's ceiling mural *Transport and Human Endeavor*. Purportedly the world's largest mural at 97ft by 100ft, its depiction of buildings, airplanes and industrious workers on Chrysler assembly lines shows the golden promise of industry and modernity.

The Spire

Composed of seven radiating steel arches reminiscent of the rising sun, the Chrysler Building's 185ft spire was as much a feat of vengeance as it was of modern engineering. Secretly constructed in the stairwell, the 200ft creation (dubbed 'the vertex') was raised through a false roof and anchored into place in an impressive 1½ hours. The novel reveal shocked and outraged architect H Craig Severance, who

DON'T MISS

- *Transport and Human Endeavor* lobby-ceiling mural
- William Van Alen's spire
- Building facade ornamentation
- Views from Third Ave and 44th St and the Empire State Building
- Chambellan and Delamarre's reliefs, Chanin Building

PRACTICALITIES

- Map p424, C5
- 405 Lexington Ave, at E 42nd St
- lobby 7am-6:30pm Mon-Fri
- S S, 4/5/6, 7 to Grand Central-42nd St

had hoped that his Manhattan Company skyscraper on Wall St would become the world's tallest building. The fait accompli was especially humiliating given that Severance had personally fallen out with architect William Van Alen, a former colleague. Karmic retribution may have been served with the 1931 debut of the even-taller Empire State Building, but Van Alen's crowning glory endures as a showstopping symbol of 20th-century daring.

The Gargoyles

If the spire is the building's diva, the gargoyles are its supporting cast. Pairs of gleaming steel American eagles look ready to leap from the corners of the 61st floor – they'd look Gothic, were it not for their distinctly art deco angular lines. Further down on the 31st floor, giant winged hubcaps echo the Chrysler radiator caps of the late 1920s. For a dramatic view of the gargoyles from street level, head to the corner of Lexington Ave and 43rd St and look up.

A Neighboring Gem

Across the street from the Chrysler Building, on the southwest corner of Lexington Ave and 42nd St, stands another art deco gem: the **Chanin Building** (Map p424; 122 E 42nd St, at Lexington Ave, Midtown East; Ⓢ S, 4/5/6, 7 to Grand Central-42nd St). Completed in 1929, the 56-story brick-and-terra-cotta tower is the work of unlicensed architect Irwin S Chanin, who teamed up with the legally recognized firm Sloan & Robertson to achieve his dream. Yet the star attraction here is the work of René Chambellan and Jacques Delamarre, creators of the exquisite bands of relief at the building's base. While birds and fish create a sense of whimsy in the lower band, the upper band of terra-cotta steals the show with its rich botanical carvings.

The Cloud Club

Balanced at the top of the Chrysler Building between 1930 and 1979 was the famed Cloud Club. Its regulars included tycoon John D Rockefeller, publishing magnate Condé Montrose and boxing legend Gene Tunney. The art deco–meets–Hunting Lodge hangout from floors 66 to 68 featured a lounge and dining rooms (including a private room for Walter Chrysler), as well as kitchens, a barber shop and a locker room with sneak cabinets for hiding booze during Prohibition. Chrysler merrily boasted about having the highest toilet in town.

CREMASTER 3

The Chrysler Building's lobby and crown feature in *Cremaster 3* (2002), an avant-garde film by award-winning visual artist and filmmaker Matthew Barney. The third installment of an epic five-part film project, it delivers a surreal take on the skyscraper's construction, fusing Irish mythology with genre elements from both zombie and gangster films. To read more about the project, check out www.cremaster.net.

TAKE A BREAK

If you just want a quickie snack, **99 Cent Pizza** (☎212-661-6221; 473 Lexington Ave, at 46th St; pizza slice $1; ⏲10am-midnight; Ⓢ S, 4/5/6, 7 to Grand Central-42nd St) is a few blocks away.

For something more relaxing, turn the corner and sit down to a fancier meal at **Sparks** (☎212-687-4855; www.sparkssteakhouse.com; 210 E 46th St, btwn Second & Third Aves, Midtown East; dinner mains $38-59; ⏲noon-11pm Mon-Thu, to 11:30pm Fri, 5-11:30pm Sat; 📶; Ⓢ S, 4/5/6, 7 to Grand Central-42nd St) – a steakhouse with gangster history.

TOP EXPERIENCE
ROCKEFELLER CENTER

This 22-acre 'city within a city' debuted at the height of the Great Depression. Taking nine years to build, it was America's first multiuse retail, entertainment and office space – a modernist sprawl of buildings (14 of which are the original art deco structures), outdoor plazas and big-name tenants.

DON'T MISS

- Sky-high views from Top of the Rock
- Sunset cocktails at Bar SixtyFive
- José Maria Sert's *American Progress*
- *Saturday Night Live* set (NBC Studio Tour)
- Skating at the Rockefeller Rink

PRACTICALITIES

- Map p424, B3
- www.rockefellercenter.com
- Fifth to Sixth Aves, btwn W 48th & 51st Sts
- S B/D/F/M to 47th-50th Sts-Rockefeller Center

Top of the Rock

There are views, and then there's *the* view from the Top of the Rock (p193). Crowning the central Comcast Building (aka 30 Rockefeller Plaza, formerly called the GE Building), 70 stories above Midtown, its blockbuster vista includes one icon that you won't see from atop the Empire State Building – *the* Empire State Building. If possible, head up just before sunset to see the city transform from day to night (if you're already in the area and the queues aren't long, purchase your tickets in advance to avoid the late-afternoon rush).

Public Artworks

Rockefeller Center features the work of 30 great artists, commissioned around the theme 'Man at the Crossroads Looks Uncertainly but Hopefully at the Future.' Paul Manship contributed the 18ft *Prometheus,* overlooking the sunken plaza, while Lee Lawrie made the 24ft-tall bronze *Atlas,* in front of the International Building (630 Fifth Ave). Isamu Noguchi's *News* sits above the entrance to the Associated Press Building (50 Rockefeller Plaza), and José Maria Sert's oil *American Progress* awaits in the lobby of the Comcast Building. The latter work replaced Mexican artist Diego Rivera's original painting, rejected by the Rockefellers for containing 'communist imagery' and destroyed (though a copy was made and is on display in Mexico City's Palacio de Bellas Artes).

NBC Studio Tour

TV comedy *30 Rock* gets its name from 30 Rockefeller Plaza, the real-life home of NBC TV. One-hour **NBC Studio Tours** (Map p424; ☎212-664-3700; www.thetouratnbcstudios.com; 30 Rockefeller Plaza, entrance at 1250 Sixth Ave; 1hr tours adult/child $33/29, children under 6yr not admitted; ⌚8:20am-2:20pm Mon-Thu, to 5pm Fri, to 6pm Sat & Sun, longer hours in summer; S B/D/F/M to 47th-50th Sts-Rockefeller Center) – enter from 1250 Sixth Ave – usually include a visit to Studio 8H, home of the iconic *Saturday Night Live* set. Tours have a strict 'no bathrooms policy' (empty your bladder beforehand!) and advance online reservations are strongly recommended. Across 49th St, opposite the plaza, is the glass-enclosed *NBC Today* show studio, broadcasting live from 7am to 11am on weekdays. If you fancy some screen time, head in by 6am to be at the front of the crowd.

Rockefeller Plaza

Come the festive season, Rockefeller Plaza is where you'll find New York's most famous **Christmas tree**. Ceremoniously lit just after Thanksgiving, it's a tradition that dates back to the 1930s, when construction workers set up a small tree on the site. In its shadow, Rink at Rockefeller Center (p210) is the city's most famous ice-skating rink. Although magical, it's also undeniably small and crowded. Opt for the first skating period (8:30am) to avoid a long wait. Come summer, the rink becomes a cafe.

TOP EXPERIENCE
ROOSEVELT ISLAND

Roosevelt Island, a 2-mile sliver of land in the East River between Manhattan and Queens, was long ignored by visitors and locals alike – except for quick trips on its aerial tram for the views. But since the long-awaited, stunning Franklin D Roosevelt Four Freedoms Park at the island's southern tip was completed in 2012, there's now an excellent reason to go.

Early Days

The Canarsee Native Americans called this tiny spit of land 'Minnahanonck' (Nice Island), which they sold as part of a larger parcel to the Dutch in 1633; from then it was used for livestock farming, and called 'Varckens Eylandt' (Hog Island). When the British took control of the area, the island was granted to the sheriff of New York, John Manning. After his death ownership transferred to his stepdaughter, Mrs Blackwell, and the island was called Blackwell's Island from the 1680s onward. In 1828 it was purchased by the city government, which used it to house various 'undesirables' by building a prison and medical facilities, including a mental-health hospital – the **Octagon** tower at its north end still stands as part of a residential complex – and the **Renwick Smallpox Hospital**, whose ruined, eerie-looking facade haunts the island's southern half. By the mid-20th century most of the institutions on 'Welfare Island' had been closed down or abandoned. In the 1970s, the city began redeveloping the island by renaming it in honor of President Franklin D Roosevelt and building a series of cookie-cutter brutalist apartment buildings along the island's main road. For years, the only thing Roosevelt Island really had to offer visitors were the views of Manhattan and the picturesque ruins of the old smallpox hospital.

Remembering a President

The island finally hit the architectural map in 2012, when a 4-acre memorial park (p190) to President Franklin D Roosevelt opened on its southern tip. Designed by architect Louis Kahn in 1972, its construction stalled later in the decade when Kahn died and New York City almost went into bankruptcy. William vanden Heuvel, former US ambassador and chairperson of the Four Freedoms Park Conservancy, kept the dream alive, and spent years raising funds and lobbying for the park's completion.

A High-Tech Future

In 2017, a fresh future for the island began with the opening of the first phase of a new advanced engineering school called Cornell Tech, a joint venture between Ivy League school Cornell University and the Technion – Israel Institute of Technology in Haifa. The $2-billion, high-tech campus, which is being built with some of the most energy-efficient technology in the world, is planned for completion via two further stages by 2037. It will eventually span 12 acres and is promised to create 28,000 new jobs and billions of dollars in economic benefits for the city.

DON'T MISS

- Franklin D Roosevelt Four Freedoms Park
- Viewing platform
- Aerial tram ride
- Renwick Smallpox Hospital ruins

PRACTICALITIES

- Map p424, G2
- www.rihs.us
- S F to Roosevelt Island, from Roosevelt Island Tramway Station, 2nd Ave at E 60th St

◉ SIGHTS

Midtown dazzles with several big-name sights, among them the megascreens and razzle of Times Square, modern-art temple MoMA, the observation decks of the Empire State Building and Rockefeller Center, and tours of the diplomatic United Nations. In their shadow lurk a number of lesser-known cultural options, from the marvelous manuscripts and interiors of the Morgan Library & Museum, to no-fee, fashion-focused Museum at FIT and neo-Gothic stunner St Patrick's Cathedral.

◉ Midtown East

GRAND CENTRAL TERMINAL
HISTORIC BUILDING

See p184.

CHRYSLER BUILDING
HISTORIC BUILDING

See p186.

ROOSEVELT ISLAND
AREA

See p189.

MORGAN LIBRARY & MUSEUM
MUSEUM

Map p424 (☑212-685-0008; www.themorgan. org; 225 Madison, at E 36th St, Midtown East; adult/child $22/free, 7-9pm Fri free; ⊙10:30am-5pm Tue-Thu, to 9pm Fri, 10am-6pm Sat, 11am-6pm Sun; ⑤6 to 33rd St) Incorporating the mansion once owned by steel magnate JP Morgan, this sumptuous cultural center houses a phenomenal array of manuscripts, tapestries and books (with no fewer than three Gutenberg Bibles). Adorned with Italian and Dutch Renaissance artworks, Morgan's personal study is only trumped by his personal library (East Room), an extraordinary, vaulted space with three stories of walnut bookcases, a 16th-century Dutch tapestry and zodiac-themed ceiling. The center's rotating exhibitions are often superb, as are its regular cultural events. Audioguides are free.

UNITED NATIONS
HISTORIC BUILDING

Map p424 (☑212-963-4475; http://visit.un.org; visitors gate First Ave at 46th St, Midtown East; guided tour adult/child $22/12, grounds access Sat & Sun Mar-Dec free; ⊙1hr tours 9am-4:45pm Mon-Fri, visitor center also open 10am-4:45pm Sat & Sun; ⑤S, 4/5/6, 7 to Grand Central-42nd St) New York is the home of the UN, a world-wide organization overseeing international law, security and human rights. The Le Corbusier–designed Secretariat building is off-limits, but guided tours cover the restored General Assembly Hall, Security Council Chamber, Trusteeship Council Chamber and Economic & Social Council (ECOSOC) Chamber, as well as exhibits about the UN's work and artworks donated by member states. Weekday tours must be booked on-line; kids under five not admitted. Photo ID is required.

Free walk-in access to the visitor center only is permitted on weekends (enter at 43rd Street). To the north of the UN complex, which technically stands on international territory, is a serene park featuring Henry Moore's *Reclining Figure*, as well as several other peace-themed sculptures.

FRANKLIN D ROOSEVELT FOUR FREEDOMS PARK
MEMORIAL

Map p424 (☑212-204-8831; www.fdrfourfreedomspark.org; Roosevelt Island; ⊙9am-7pm Wed-Mon Apr-Sep, to 5pm Wed-Mon Oct-Mar; ⑤F to Roosevelt Island, ⊞Roosevelt Island) FREE Dramatic design, presidential inspiration and a refreshing perspective on the NYC skyline make for an arresting trio at the Franklin D Roosevelt Four Freedoms Park. At the southern tip of Roosevelt Island (p189) on the East River, this remarkable monument honors America's 32nd president and his 1941 State of the Union speech. It's breathtakingly cinematic in its scale and effect: a luminous granite vision designed by renowned architect Louis Kahn in 1973, but only completed in 2012 – 38 years after Kahn's death.

A sweep of grand, stark steps lead up to a sloping triangular lawn. Fringed by linden trees, the lawn gently spills down to a bronze bust of Roosevelt by American sculptor Jo Davidson. Framing the sculpture is a granite wall, hand engraved with Roosevelt's rousing speech, in which he spoke of the four essential human freedoms he desired for the world: freedom of speech, freedom of worship, freedom from want and freedom from fear. The wall also serves to separate the bust from 'The Room,' a contemplative granite terrace clinging to the very tip of the island. The combination of lapping waves and hovering skyline are utterly mesmerizing. In front of the steps near the entrance to the park, the Gothic ruins of a 19th-century smallpox hospital only serves to accentuate the contemporary architecture beyond.

Although the F subway line will get you to Roosevelt Island, it's much more fun catching the aerial **tramway car** (☎212-832-4583; www.rioc.ny.gov/tramtransportation.htm; 60th St, at Second Ave; one-way $2.75; ⊙every 7-15 min 6am-2am Sun-Thu, to 3:30am Fri & Sat; Ⓢ N/Q/R, 4/5/6 to Lexington Ave-59th St), which glides above the East River, offering eagle-eye views of the Manhattan skyline. The monument is a 15-minute walk south of both the Roosevelt Island tramway car and subway stations.

JAPAN SOCIETY ARTS CENTER

Map p424 (www.japansociety.org; 333 E 47th St, btwn First & Second Aves, Midtown East; adult/child $12/10, 6-9pm Fri free; ⊙noon-7pm Tue-Thu, to 9pm Fri, 11am-5pm Sat & Sun; Ⓢ S, 4/5/6, 7 to Grand Central-42nd St) Elegant exhibitions of both traditional and contemporary Japanese art, textiles and design are the main draw at this calming cultural center, complete with indoor gardens and water features. Its theater hosts a range of films and dance and theatrical performances, while those wanting to dig deeper can browse through 14,000 volumes in the research library or attend one of its myriad lectures or workshops.

⊙ Fifth Avenue

EMPIRE STATE BUILDING OBSERVATORY, HISTORIC BUILDING

See p180.

ROCKEFELLER CENTER HISTORIC BUILDING

See p188.

NEW YORK PUBLIC LIBRARY HISTORIC BUILDING

Map p424 (Stephen A Schwarzman Building; ☎917-275-6975; www.nypl.org; 476 Fifth Ave, at W 42nd St; ⊙8am-8pm Mon & Thu, to 9pm Tue & Wed, to 6pm Fri, 10am-6pm Sat, 10am-5pm Sun, guided tours 11am & 2pm Mon-Sat, 2pm Sun; Ⓢ B/D/F/M to 42nd St-Bryant Park, 7 to 5th Ave) FREE Loyally guarded by 'Patience' and 'Fortitude' (the marble lions overlooking Fifth Ave), this beaux-arts show-off is one of NYC's best free attractions. When dedicated in 1911, New York's flagship library ranked as the largest marble structure ever built in the US, and to this day its recently restored **Rose Main Reading Room** steals the breath away with its lavish coffered ceiling. And it's not just for show: anybody who's working can use it, making it surely the most glamorous coworking space in the world.

That reading room only one of several glories inside, among them the **DeWitt Wallace Periodical Room** (1st floor). This extraordinary building is home to precious manuscripts by just about every author of note in the English language, as well as an original copy of the Declaration of Independence and a Gutenberg Bible. The **Map Division** is equally astounding, with a collection that holds some 431,000 maps, 16,000 atlases and books on cartography, dating from the 16th century to the present. To properly explore this mini-universe of books, art and architectural flourishes, join a **free guided tour** (departing from Astor Hall) or grab a **free audioguide** from the information desk (also in Astor Hall).

Across its branches, the NYPL keeps brains in gear with its string of lectures, seminars and workshops, with topics ranging from contemporary art to the writings of Jane Austen. You'll find some of the best at the main branch on 42nd St. You can search all happenings at the library's website.

BRYANT PARK PARK

Map p424 (☎212-768-4242; www.bryantpark.org; 42nd St, btwn Fifth & Sixth Aves, Midtown West; ⊙7am-midnight Mon-Fri, to 11pm Sat & Sun Jun-Sep, shorter hours Oct-May; Ⓢ B/D/F/M to 42nd St-Bryant Park, 7 to 5th Ave) European coffee kiosks, alfresco chess games, summer film screenings and winter ice skating: it's hard to believe that this leafy oasis was a crime-ridden hellscape known as 'Needle Park' in the '70s. Nestled behind the beaux-arts New York Public Library building, it's a whimsical spot for a little time-out from the Midtown madness. Fancy taking a beginner Italian language, yoga or juggling class, joining a painting workshop or signing up for a birding tour? There's a daily smorgasbord of quirky activities.

Among the park's attractions is the French-inspired, Brooklyn-made **Le Carrousel** (Map p424; www.bryantpark.org/amenities/le-carrousel; W 40th St, at Sixth Ave; ride $3; ⊙11am-8pm Jun-Oct, to 7pm Jan & Mar-May, reduced hours rest of year), offering rides. Frequent special events include the **Bryant Park Summer Film Festival** (⊙mid-Jun–Aug) FREE, popular with post-work crowds

SKYSCRAPERS IN MIDTOWN

Midtown's skyline is more than just the Empire State and Chrysler Buildings, with enough modernist and postmodernist beauties to satisfy the wildest of high-rise dreams. Here are six of Midtown's most notable.

Seagram Building (1956–58; 514ft) A textbook regular, the 38-floor **Seagram Building** (Map p424; 100 E 53rd St, at Park Ave, Midtown East; S 6 to 51st St; E, M to Fifth Ave-53rd St) is one of the world's finest examples of the international style. Its lead architect, Ludwig Mies van der Rohe, was recommended for the project by Arthur Drexler, then-curator of architecture at MoMA. With its low podium, colonnade-like pillars and bronze cladding, Mies cleverly references classical Greek influences.

Lever House (1950–52; 306ft) Upon its debut in 1952, 21-story **Lever House** (Map p424; 390 Park Ave, btwn E 53rd & E 54th Sts, Midtown East; S E, M to 5th Ave-53rd St) was at the height of the cutting-edge. The UN Secretariat Building was the only other skyscraper to feature a glass skin, an innovation that would redefine urban architecture. The building's form was equally bold: two counter-posed rectangular shapes consisting of a slender tower atop a low-rise base. The open courtyard features marble benches envisioned by Japanese American sculptor Isamu Noguchi, while the lobby exhibits contemporary art especially commissioned for the space.

Citigroup Center (1974–77; 915ft) With its striking triangular-cut roof and candy-like striped facade, Hugh Stubbins' 59-story **Citigroup Center** (Map p424; 601 Lexington Ave, at E 53rd St, Midtown East; S 6 to 51st St; E, M to Lexington Ave-53rd St) signaled a shift from the flat-roof sobriety of the international style. Even more dramatic is the building's base, which is cut away at the four corners, leaving the tower to perch dramatically on nine-story stilts. This unusual configuration allowed for the construction of St Peter's Lutheran Church on the site's northwest corner, which replaced the original neo-Gothic church demolished during the skyscraper's construction. The podcast *99% Invisible* has a fascinating episode about the building's dangerous structural flaws – found (and repaired) *after* its construction.

Hearst Tower (2003–06; 597ft) This 46-floor **tower** (Map p428; 949 Eighth Ave, btwn 56th & 57th Sts, Midtown West; S A/C, B/D, 1 to 59th St-Columbus Circle) is one of NYC's most creative works of contemporary architecture, not to mention one of its greenest; around 90% of its structural steel is from recycled sources. Designed by Foster & Partners, its diagonal grid of trusses evokes a jagged glass-and-steel honeycomb. The tower rises above the hollowed-out core of John Urban's 1928 cast-stone Hearst Magazine Building and the lobby is home to Richard Long's Riverlines, a 70ft mural made using mud from New York's Hudson River and England's River Avon.

Bank of America Tower (2004–09; 1200ft) Designed by Cook & Fox Architects, the 58-floor **Bank of America Tower** (One Bryant Park; Map p428; www.durst.org; Sixth Ave, at W 42nd St; S B/D/F/M to 42nd St-Bryant Park) is famed for its striking crystal shape, piercing 255ft spire and enviable green credentials. The stats are impressive: a clean-burning, on-site cogeneration plant providing around 65% of the tower's annual electricity requirements; CO_2-detecting air filters that channel oxygenated air where needed; and elevators designed to avoid empty-car trips. On the ground floor is the glass-walled public Urban Garden Room (8am to 8pm), used by locals in bad weather.

432 Park Avenue (2011–15; 1396ft) It's a case of 'thin is in' with the arrival of this 1396ft-tall, $1.3-billion **residential tower** (Map p424; www.432parkavenue.com; S N/Q/R to Lexington Ave-59th St) by Uruguayan architect Rafael Viñoly. The tower's clean, white, cubic facade, inspired by a 1905 trash can by Austrian designer Josef Hoffman, rises above the Midtown skyline like an impossibly slim square tube. It's currently the city's second-tallest building, upstaged only by One World Trade Center. (Measured to actual roof height, however, it's actually 28ft taller than its spire-crowned downtown rival.)

lugging cheese-and-wine picnics. Come Christmastime, the place becomes a winter wonderland, with holiday gift vendors lining the park's edge and a popular ice-skating rink sprouting in its middle. Lovely **Bryant Park Grill** (Map p424; ☎212-840-6500; www.arkrestaurants.com/bryant_park; mains $20-49, weekend brunch $28.50; ⌚11:30am-3:30pm & 5-11pm Apr-Dec, shorter hours Jan-Mar;) is the site of many a New York wedding come springtime, and when it's not closed for a private event, the patio bar is a perfect spot for a twilight cocktail. Next door you'll find its more casual alfresco sibling **Bryant Park Cafe** (Map p424; ☎212-840-6500; www.arkrestaurants.com/bryant_park; ⌚11:30am-10:30pm mid-Apr–Nov), a much-loved spot for after-five catch-ups that's open mid-April to November.

TOP OF THE ROCK — VIEWPOINT

Map p424 (☎212-698-2000, toll free 877-692-7625; www.topoftherocknyc.com; 30 Rockefeller Plaza, entrance on W 50th St, btwn Fifth & Sixth Aves; adult/child $38/32, sunrise/sunset combo $56/45; ⌚8am-midnight, last elevator at 11pm; SB/D/F/M to 47th-50th Sts-Rockefeller Center) Designed in homage to ocean liners and opened in 1933, this 70th-floor open-air observation deck sits atop 30 Rockefeller Plaza, the tallest skyscraper at the Rockefeller Center (p188). Top of the Rock beats the Empire State Building (p180) on several levels: it's less crowded, has wider observation decks (both outdoor and indoor) and offers a view of the Empire State Building itself. Before ascending, a fascinating 2nd-floor exhibition gives an insight into the legendary philanthropist behind the art deco complex.

If you don't have under-21s in tow, note that similar views can be had from the Rockefeller's 65th-floor Bar SixtyFive (p200)...and you don't need a ticket to Top of the Rock to get in.

ST PATRICK'S CATHEDRAL — CATHEDRAL

Map p424 (☎212-753-2261; www.saintpatrickscathedral.org; Fifth Ave, btwn E 50th & 51st Sts; ⌚6:30am-8:45pm; SB/D/F/M to 47th-50th Sts-Rockefeller Center, E/M to 5th Ave-53rd St) America's largest Catholic cathedral graces Fifth Ave with Gothic Revival splendor. Built at a cost of nearly $2 million during the Civil War (and spiffed up with a $200 million restoration in 2015), the building did not originally include the two front spires; those were added in 1888. Step inside to appreciate the Louis Tiffany-designed altar, gleaming below a 7000-pipe church organ, and Charles Connick's stunning Rose Window above the Fifth Ave entrance. Occasional walk-in guided tours are available; check the website for details.

PALEY CENTER FOR MEDIA — ARTS CENTER

Map p424 (☎212-621-6800; www.paleycenter.org; 25 W 52nd St, btwn Fifth & Sixth Aves; suggested donation adult/child $10/5; ⌚noon-6pm Wed & Fri-Sun, to 8pm Thu; SE, M to 5th Ave-53rd St) FREE This pop-culture repository offers more than 160,000 TV and radio programs from around the world on its computer catalog. Reliving your favorite TV shows on one of the center's consoles is a fun option on a rainy day, as are the excellent regular screenings, festivals, speakers and performers.

⊙ Midtown West & Times Square

TIMES SQUARE — AREA

See p177.

MUSEUM OF MODERN ART — MUSEUM

See p182.

★RADIO CITY MUSIC HALL — HISTORIC BUILDING

Map p428 (www.radiocity.com; 1260 Sixth Ave, at W 50th St; tours adult/child $31/27; ⌚tours 9:30am-5pm; ; SB/D/F/M to 47th-50th Sts-Rockefeller Center) This spectacular moderne movie palace was the brainchild of vaudeville producer Samuel Lionel 'Roxy' Rothafel. Never one for understatement, Roxy launched his venue on December 23, 1932, with an over-the-top extravaganza that included camp dance troupe the Roxyettes (mercifully renamed the Rockettes). Guided tours (75 minutes) of the sumptuous interiors include the glorious auditorium, Witold Gordon's classically inspired mural *History of Cosmetics* in the Women's Downstairs Lounge, and the VIP Roxy Suite, where luminaries such as Elton John and Alfred Hitchcock have been entertained.

As far as catching a show here goes, be warned: the vibe doesn't quite match the theater's glamour these days. That said, there are often some fabulous talents in the lineup, with past performers including

HUDSON YARDS

After six years and $25 billion, the first phase of Manhattan's new megadevelopment 'neighborhood' **Hudson Yards** (Map p428; ☎646-954-3100; www.hudsonyardsnewyork.com; W 30th to W 34th Sts, btwn Tenth & Twelfth Aves, Midtown West; S7 to 34th St-Hudson Yards) has finally opened. Five sheer glass skyscrapers of office space and luxury condos surround a manicured plaza, alongside a seven-story **mall** (Map p428; ☎646-954-3150; Tenth Ave at W 31st St, Midtown; ⊙shops 10am-9pm Mon-Sat, 11am-7pm Sun, restaurant hours vary; 📶) for upscale shopping and dining; promising interdisciplinary arts center The Shed (p207); and the Vessel, an Instagram-ready copper-clad basket of infinite staircases with river views. It might make you think more of gleaming Dubai than gritty New York, but then again, that's the point.

It's been decried by its critics as a soulless corporate playground for the wealthy and hyped by its boosters as a live-work-play 'city within a city' revitalizing the formerly industrialized far west of Midtown. As it's connected to the northern end of the High Line, crowds of visitors inevitably end up here, wandering through the Vessel and the shopping mall wondering what to do next. The Shed is worth a visit if there's a show on, as is bustling Spanish food hall Mercado Little Spain (p197). Beyond that Hudson Yards is more about style than substance – though you can also indulge in the thrill of its rarefied heights at **The Edge** (www.edgenyc.com), a large, prow-shaped balcony jutting out from the 101st floor that's New York's highest open-air observatory (adult/child from $36/31).

The second phase of the project, containing more office and residential high-rises, open plaza space and an elementary school on the site's western half, is due to be completed in 2024.

Lauryn Hill, Rufus Wainwright, Aretha Franklin and Dolly Parton. And while the word 'Rockettes' provokes eye rolling from most self-consciously cynical New Yorkers, fans of glitz and kitsch might just get a thrill from the troupe's annual **Christmas Spectacular**.

Same-day tickets are available at the box office inside the Sixth Ave entrance. Whether you book here or in advance online, expect horrendous queues to get into the show; it's hugely popular. Tour tickets are usually easy enough to book on the day, and tours depart from the entrance around the corner on W 50th St.

INTREPID SEA, AIR & SPACE MUSEUM — MUSEUM

Map p428 (☎877-957-7447; www.intrepidmuseum.org; Pier 86, Twelfth Ave at W 46th St; adult/child $33/24; ⊙10am-5pm Mon-Fri, to 6pm Sat & Sun Apr-Oct, 10am-5pm Mon-Sun Nov-Mar; 👪; 🚌westbound M42, M50 to 12th Ave, SA/C/E to 42nd St-Port Authority Bus Terminal) In WWII, the USS *Intrepid* survived both a bomb and kamikaze attacks. Thankfully, this hulking aircraft carrier is now a lot less stressed, playing host to a multimillion-dollar interactive military museum that tells its tale through videos, historical artifacts and frozen-in-time living quarters. The flight deck features fighter planes and military helicopters, which might inspire you to try the museum's high-tech flight simulators. Topical rotating exhibits add to the fun. Even if you're not into the subject matter, it's irresistibly absorbing and impressive.

MUSEUM AT FIT — MUSEUM

Map p428 (☎212-217-4558; www.fitnyc.edu/museum; 227 W 27th St, at Seventh Ave, Midtown West; ⊙noon-8pm Tue-Fri, 10am-5pm Sat; S1 to 28th St) FREE Fashionistas won't want to miss a visit to the fabulous sartorial exhibits at the Fashion Institute of Technology (FIT), which holds one of the world's richest collections of garments, textiles and accessories – more than 50,000 items spanning the 18th century to the present day. The school's museum features innovative, rotating exhibitions showcasing both permanent-collection items and on-loan curiosities. Exhibitions aside, the museum also hosts film screenings and talks, including with prolific fashion designers and critics.

MUSEUM OF ARTS & DESIGN — MUSEUM

Map p428 (MAD; ☎212-299-7777; www.madmuseum.org; 2 Columbus Circle, btwn Eighth

Ave & Broadway; adult/child $16/free, by donation 6-9pm Thu; ⏲10am-6pm Tue, Wed, Fri-Sun, to 9pm Thu; 👪; Ⓢ A/C, B/D, 1 to 59th St-Columbus Circle) MAD offers four floors of superlative design and handicrafts, from blown glass and carved wood to elaborate metal jewelry. Temporary exhibitions are innovative: one past show rendered fake news into art. The 6th floor houses resident artists' studios where you can interact with designers. During 'Studio Sundays,' professional artists lead family-friendly explorations of the galleries, followed by hands-on workshops inspired by the exhibitions. The gift shop sells fantastic contemporary jewelry, while 9th-floor restaurant/bar Robert (p201) is perfect for cocktails with a view.

VESSEL (TKA) ARCHITECTURE

Map p428 (☎646-954-3100; www.hudsonyardsnewyork.com; Hudson Yards, W 31st St off Tenth Ave, Midtown; ⏲10am-9pm; Ⓢ 7 to 34th St-Hudson Yards) FREE Sprouting 150ft high from the central plaza of Hudson Yards is the controversial construction called 'The Vessel.' Looking something like a giant, copper-colored, latticed beehive – it was allegedly inspired by step-wells in India – it features 154 flights of interlacing stairs across eight levels, offering novel views of the Hudson River (as well as a hell of a workout). Admission is free but timed tickets must be booked online or via smartphone using the digital kiosks at its base.

EATING

Midtown has no shortage of Michelin-starred restaurants but it's surprisingly hard to get a satisfying mid-priced meal. This is the heart of New York's touristville (not where most locals go out to eat), so you can expect plenty of mediocre chains and tourist-trap restaurants – especially around Times Square and the Theater District. But that's not to say it's a culinary desert: there's also the 'Curry Hill' district of Indian restaurants (Lexington Ave, roughly between 28th and 33rd Sts), cult-status ramen on W 52nd St, a speakeasy burger joint, vegetarian Korean and more.

Midtown East & Fifth Avenue

ESS-A-BAGEL DELI $

Map p424 (☎212-980-1010; www.ess-a-bagel.com; 831 Third Ave, at E 51st St, Midtown East; bagel sandwiches $3.50-5.50; ⏲6am-9pm Mon-Fri, to 5pm Sat & Sun; Ⓢ 6 to 51st St; E/M to Lexington Ave-53rd St) Fresh, toothsome bagels have made this kosher deli a veritable institution. Pick your style of bagel and choose from a sprawling display of cream cheeses and other fillings. For a classic, get scallion cream cheese with lox (smoked salmon), capers, tomato and red onion ($14.50). If the weather's fine, turn right into 51st St and lunch in pretty Greenacre Park.

GREAT NORTHERN FOOD HALL FOOD HALL $

Map p424 (www.greatnorthernfood.com; Grand Central Terminal, Vanderbilt Hall, 89 E 42nd St, at Park Ave; sandwiches $7-12; ⏲7am-11pm Mon-Fri, 6am-8pm Sat & Sun; 📶; Ⓢ S, 4/5/6, 7 to Grand Central-42nd St, 🚆Metro North to Grand Central-42nd St) Ensconced in the beautiful beaux-arts Vanderbilt Hall, this airy food hall has upped the ante for food in New York's grandest station terminal. Pull up a stool beneath the glamorous chandelier and enjoy a glass of wine, Danish beer or artisan coffee. Gourmet bites on offer mesh Nordic flair with New York produce. Hours differ for individual kiosks.

SMITH AMERICAN $$

Map p424 (☎212-644-2700; http://thesmithrestaurant.com; 956 Second Ave, at E 51st St, Midtown East; mains $22-33; ⏲7:30am-midnight Mon-Thu, to 1am Fri, 9am-1am Sat, 9am-midnight Sun; 📶; Ⓢ 6, E/M to 51st St) This bustling brasserie has an industrial-chic interior, sociable bar and well-executed grub. Much of the food is made from scratch, the seasonal menus a mix of nostalgic American and Italian inspiration (we're talking hot potato chips with blue-cheese fondue, spicy fried chicken with kale slaw, and Sicilian baked eggs with artichokes, spinach and spicy tomato sauce).

HANGAWI KOREAN $$

Map p424 (☎212-213-0077; www.hangawirestaurant.com; 12 E 32nd St, btwn Fifth & Madison Aves; mains lunch $13-29, dinner $19-30; ⏲5:30-10:15pm Mon, noon-2:30pm & 5:30-10:15pm Tue-Thu, to 10:30pm Fri, 1-10:30pm Sat, 5-9:30pm Sun; 🌱; Ⓢ B/D/F/M, N/Q/R/W to 34th St-Herald

Sq) Meat-free Korean is the draw at high-achieving Hangawi. Leave your shoes at the entrance and slip into a soothing, Zen-like space of meditative music, soft low seating and clean, complex dishes. Dishes include stuffed shiitake mushrooms, spicy kimchi-mushroom pancakes and a seductively smooth tofu claypot in ginger sauce. At lunchtime there's a four-course prix-fixe deal for $26.

★**O YA** SUSHI $$$

Map p424 (☎212-204-0200; www.o-ya.restaurant; 120 E 28th St; nigiri $6-25; ⏲5:30-10pm Mon-Sat; Ⓢ4/6 to 28th St) With the cheapest nigiri pairs at close to $15, this is not a spot you'll come to every day. But if you're looking for a special night out and sushi's in the game plan, come here for exquisite flavors, fish so tender it melts like butter on the tongue, and preparations so artful you almost apologize for eating them.

AGERN NEW NORDIC $$$

Map p424 (☎646-568-4018; www.agernrestaurant.com; Grand Central Terminal, 89 E 42nd St, at Park Ave; dinner mains $28-45, 2-/3-course prix-fixe lunch $42/50; ⏲11:30am-2:30pm & 5:30-10pm Mon-Fri, 5:30-10pm Sat; 📶✍; ⓈS, 4/5/6, 7 to Grand Central-42nd St, 🚆Metro North to Grand Central-42nd St) Showing off the sleek design principles and seasonal, creative flair you'd expect from an architect of Denmark's New Nordic food revolution, Claus Meyer's restaurant in Grand Central Station features deceptively simple dishes, such as endive with preserved blackberries and pork shoulder with sorrel. Agern is also relatively affordable – especially the $42 lunch menu.

GRAND CENTRAL OYSTER BAR & RESTAURANT SEAFOOD $$$

Map p424 (☎212-490-6650; www.oysterbarny.com; lower level, Grand Central Terminal, 89 E 42nd St, at Park Ave; oysters $2-4, mains $22-43; ⏲11:30am-9:30pm Mon-Sat; ⓈS, 4/5/6, 7 to Grand Central-42nd St) This buzzing bar and restaurant within Grand Central is hugely atmospheric, with a vaulted tiled ceiling by Catalan-born engineer Rafael Guastavino. Ignore the formal dining area on your left as you enter: the prize seats are at the sleek communal tables on your right, where diners happily slurp oysters as quick as staff can shuck them.

Most New Yorkers come for the two-dozen oyster varieties, handwritten onto a menu above the bar counter. But if you don't like oysters, you can feast from the extensive fish menu (the same menu is available in all dining areas). Dishes are clean and simple, and you can guarantee the star of the show will be the expertly cooked, generously sized seafood servings.

Midtown West & Times Square

★**TOTTO RAMEN** JAPANESE $

Map p428 (☎212-582-0052; www.tottoramen.com; 366 W 52nd St, btwn Eighth & Ninth Aves; ramen $14-18; ⏲noon-4:30pm & 5:30pm-midnight; ✍; ⓈC/E to 50th St) There might be two other Midtown branches but purists know that neither beats the tiny 20-seat original. Write your name and party size on the clipboard and wait your turn. Your reward: extraordinary ramen. Get the butter-soft *char siu* (pork), which sings in dishes like miso ramen (with fermented soybean paste, egg, scallion, bean sprouts, onion and homemade chili paste).

BURGER JOINT BURGERS $

Map p428 (☎212-708-7414; www.burgerjointny.com; Parker New York, 119 W 56th St, btwn Sixth & Seventh Aves; burgers $9-17; ⏲11am-11:30pm Sun-Thu, to midnight Fri & Sat; ✍; ⓈF to 57th St) With only a small neon burger as your clue, this speakeasy-style burger hut lurks behind the lobby curtain in the Parker New York hotel. Though it might not be as secret as it once was (you'll see the queues), it still delivers the same winning formula of graffiti-strewn walls, retro booths and attitude-loaded staff slapping up beef 'n' patty brilliance.

MARGON CUBAN $

Map p428 (☎212-354-5013; 136 W 46th St, btwn Sixth & Seventh Aves; sandwiches $9-10, mains $11-14; ⏲6am-5pm Mon-Fri, 7am-5pm Sat; ⓈB/D/F/M to 47th-50th Sts-Rockefeller Center) It's still 1973 at this ever-packed Cuban lunch counter, where orange Laminex and greasy goodness never went out of style. Go for gold with its legendary *cubano* sandwich (a pressed panino jammed with rich roast pork, salami, cheese, pickles, *mojo* sauce and mayo). It's obscenely good.

FOURNOS THEOPHILOS GREEK $

Map p428 (☎212-278-0015; www.fournos.com; 45 W 45th St, btwn Fifth & Sixth Aves; lunch

$12; 7am-10pm Mon-Sat, from 8am Sun, closed 4-5pm; ; S B/D/F/M to 47th-50th Sts-Rockefeller Center) Named in honor of a poor Greek painter who was paid for his art in food, Fournos Theophilos is a scrumptious archive of Greek food heritage in an area of Midtown that can feel like a culinary wasteland. Greek pies, pastries and even baklava milkshakes can be grabbed upfront in the bakery; head to the back for flavor-packed hot lunch boxes.

PENNSY FOOD HALL FOOD HALL $

Map p428 (www.thepennsy.nyc; 2 Pennsylvania Plaza, cnr 33rd St & Seventh Ave, Midtown West; mains from $9; 11am-9pm; ; S A/C/E, 1/2/3 to 34th St-Penn Station) A great addition to the much-maligned Penn Station is The Pennsy, an upmarket, streetside food hall offering slow-roasted pork-shoulder sandwiches from celebrity butcher Pat LaFrieda, ramen and rolls from Sabi Sushi, vegan comfort food from The Cinnamon Snail, Neapolitan-style pizza from Ribalta and more. There's also a full bar on the premises (open to 2am) and outdoor seating.

SOUVLAKI GR GREEK $

Map p428 (212-974-7482; www.souvlakigr.com; 162 W 56th St, at Seventh Ave; souvlaki $7-10, mains $13-29; 11am-11pm Sun-Thu, to midnight Fri & Sat; S N/Q/R/W to 57th St-7th Ave) Step out of Manhattan and into the Mediterranean – Souvlaki GR is a Greek restaurant in Midtown that offers a truly immersive dining experience. The interior is all cool blues and whites, with stone floors and trellis detailing over the bar. Of course, as the name suggests, you'll find impeccable souvlaki and other Greek specialties here.

MERCADO LITTLE SPAIN FOOD HALL $$

Map p428 (646-495-1242; www.littlespain.com; 501 W 30th St, at Tenth Ave, Hudson Yards, Midtown; mains from $12; 7am-10pm Sun-Thu, to 11pm Fri & Sat; ; S 7 to 34th St-Hudson Yards) Celebrity chef José Andrés has put his own spin on Euro food halls like Eataly (p1769) and Le District (p80) with Hudson Yards' buzzing new Mercado Little Spain. Explore the variety of Spanish cuisine via several sit-down restaurants and bars and a dozen kiosks serving Iberian specialties like *jamón*, paella, tapas, seafood, *pasteles* (pastries), Spanish wine and more.

DON ANTONIO PIZZA $$

Map p428 (646-719-1043; www.donantoniopizza.com; 309 W 50th St, btwn Eighth & Ninth Aves, Midtown West; pizzas $14-25; 11:30am-3:30pm & 4:30-11pm Mon-Thu, 11:30am-11pm Fri & Sat, to 10:30pm Sun; S C/E, 1 to 50th St) A top spot for authentic Neapolitan-style pizza, this hopping eatery is the offspring of Naples' historic pizzeria Starita. While New York concessions include a cocktail-shaking, solo-diner-friendly bar, the pies here are pure Napoli: chewy, thin-crust wonders with charred edges and sweet, ripe *sugo* (tomato sauce). All pizzas can be made using a wholewheat base, and they make gluten-free pizzas, too.

DHABA INDIAN $$

Map p424 (212-679-1284; www.dhabanyc.com; 108 Lexington Ave, btwn E 27th & E 28th Sts; mains $13-23; noon-midnight Mon-Thu, to 1am Fri & Sat, to 11pm Sun; ; S 6 to 28th St) Murray Hill (aka 'Curry Hill') has no shortage of subcontinental bites, but funky Dhaba packs one serious flavor punch. Mouthwatering standouts include the crunchy, tangy *lasoni gobi* (fried cauliflower with tomato and spices) and the insanely flavorful *murgh bharta* (minced chicken cooked with smoked eggplant).

DANJI KOREAN $$

Map p428 (212-586-2880; www.danjinyc.com; 346 W 52nd St, btwn Eighth & Ninth Aves, Midtown West; dishes $15-44; noon-2:30pm & 5pm-10:30pm Mon-Thu, to 11pm Fri, 11am-3pm & 5pm-11:30pm Sat, 11am-3pm & 4-9:30pm Sun; ; S C/E to 50th St) Young gun Hooni Kim woos palates with his Korean creations, served in a snug, whitewashed space. Lunch focuses on *bibimbap* (a traditional Korean rice dish), while the more

KOREATOWN (KOREA WAY)

Centered on W 32nd St between Fifth Ave and the intersection of Sixth Ave and Broadway, this Seoul-ful jumble of Korean-owned restaurants, shops, salons and spas will satiate any kimchi pangs. Businesses are dense on the ground and often occupy 2nd floors, some migrating east of Fifth Ave and to 31st and 33rd Sts. Bars and karaoke spots are plentiful and the block stays lively late into the night.

expansive dinner list offers small, medium and large plates. Thankfully, both offer Danji's cult-status *bulgogi* beef sliders, made with heavenly, butter-grilled buns. Head in early or prepare to queue. Vegetarian menu on request.

TERRACE CAFÉ CAFE $$

Map p428 (☎212-708-9400; www.momacafes.com; Museum of Modern Art, 11 W 53rd St, btwn Fifth & Sixth Aves, 6th fl; small plates $8-21; ⊙11am-5:30pm Sat-Thu, to 7:30pm Fri; 📶; Ⓢ E, M to 5th Ave-53rd St) Chic meets cafeteria at this full-service eatery at the Museum of Modern Art, which features seasonal American small plates and some cocktails, wine and beer. Sit inside under artworks by Kerstin Brätsch or on the terrace overlooking the skyscrapers of 53rd St.

VIRGIL'S REAL BARBECUE BARBECUE $$

Map p428 (☎212-921-9494; www.virgilsbbq.com; 152 W 44th St, btwn Broadway & Sixth Ave, Midtown West; mains $18-35; ⊙8am-11pm Sun-Thu, to midnight Fri & Sat; 📶; Ⓢ N/Q/R, S, 1/2/3, 7 to Times Sq-42nd St) Rather than specializing in one specific style of American BBQ, Virgil's celebrates them all. Indeed, the menu covers the entire BBQ map, from Memphis-style pork spare ribs, to Georgia chicken-fried steak and platters of sliced Texas beef brisket. Meats are smoked with a combo of hickory, oak and fruitwoods, keepin' fingers licked and clean.

★MODERN FRENCH $$$

Map p428 (☎212-333-1220; www.themodernnyc.com; 9 W 53rd St, btwn Fifth & Sixth Aves; 3-/6-course lunch $138/188, 6-course dinner $188; ⊙restaurant 11:30am-2pm & 5-9:30pm Mon-Thu, to 10:30pm Fri & Sat, closed Sun, bar room 11:30am-10pm Mon-Wed, to 10:30pm Thu-Sat, to 2:30pm Sun; 📶; Ⓢ E, M to 5th Ave-53rd St) Shining two (Michelin) stars bright, the Modern delivers rich, confident creations like foie-gras tart and 'ants on a log' peanut-butter cake. Service is friendly and meals presented in a light-filled space reminiscent of MoMA's galleries, with giant windows overlooking the sculpture garden.

★LE BERNARDIN SEAFOOD $$$

Map p428 (☎212-554-1515; www.le-bernardin.com; 155 W 51st St, btwn Sixth & Seventh Aves; prix-fixe lunch/dinner $93/165, tasting menus $170-198; ⊙11:45am-2:30pm & 4:45-10:30pm Mon-Thu, to 11pm Fri, 4:45-11pm Sat; Ⓢ 1 to 50th St; B/D, E to 7th Ave) The interiors may have been subtly sexed-up for a 'younger clientele' (the stunning storm-themed triptych is by Brooklyn artist Ran Ortner), but triple-Michelin-starred Le Bernardin remains a luxe, fine-dining holy grail. At the helm is French-born celebrity chef Eric Ripert, whose deceptively simple-looking seafood often borders on the transcendental. Life is short, and you only live (er, eat!) once.

The menu works simply: three lunch courses for $93 or four dinner courses for $165, with ample choices per course, and two tastings menus for those with more time and money. The dishes themselves are divided into three categories (Almost Raw, Barely Touched, Lightly Cooked), and most shine with delicious complexity. Book at least four weeks ahead for dinner and two weeks ahead for lunch.

NOMAD AMERICAN $$$

Map p428 (☎212-796-1500; www.thenomadhotel.com; NoMad Hotel, 1170 Broadway, at W 28th St; mains $28-46; ⊙noon-2pm & 5:30-10:30pm Mon-Thu, to 11pm Fri, 11am-2:30pm & 5:30-11pm Sat, to 10pm Sun; Ⓢ N/R, 6 to 28th St; F/M to 23rd St) Sharing the same name as the 'it kid' hotel (p340) it inhabits, and run by the perfectionist restaurateurs behind Michelin-starred Eleven Madison Park (p171), NoMad has become a local culinary highlight. With a series of distinctly different spaces – including an elegant 'parlor' and a snacks-only 'library' – it serves indulgent delicacies like seared venison and suckling pig with a chicory-and-dates confit. Book ahead.

TABOON MEDITERRANEAN $$$

Map p428 (☎212-713-0271; www.taboononline.com; 773 Tenth Ave, at 52nd St, Midtown West; meze dishes $12-24, mains $28-40; ⊙5-11pm Mon-Wed, to 11:30pm Thu & Fri, 11am-3:30pm & 5-11:30pm Sat, to 10pm Sun; Ⓢ C/E to 50th St) Taboon is Arabic for stone oven, and it's the first thing you'll see when stepping through the curtain into this warm, casually chic hot spot. Join urbane theater-goers and Hell's Kitchen muscle boys for Med-inspired dishes like sizzling shrimp with garlic and lemon or truffle-oil-drizzled egg *burek* (soft-poached egg in crispy phyllo dough). Reservations highly recommended…as are the oven-fresh breads.

Neighborhood Walk
Iconic Midtown Sights

START GRAND CENTRAL TERMINAL
FINISH ROCKEFELLER CENTER
LENGTH 1.8 MILES; 3½ HOURS

Start at beaux-arts marvel 1 **Grand Central Terminal** (p184). Stargaze at the Main Concourse ceiling, share sweet nothings at the Whispering Gallery and pick up a gourmet treat at the Grand Central Market.

Exit onto Lexington Ave and walk one block east along 44th St to Third Ave for a view of William Van Alen's 1930 masterpiece, the 2 **Chrysler Building** (p186). Slip into the Chrysler's sumptuous art deco lobby on 42nd St, lavished with exotic inlaid wood, marble and purportedly the world's largest ceiling mural.

Passing the ornately dressed 3 **Chanin Building** (p187), with its art deco gilt frieze above the door, head west to the stately 4 **New York Public Library** (p191). Step inside to peek at its spectacular Rose Reading Room, then have your market treat in neighboring 5 **Bryant Park** (p191). On the northwest corner of 42nd St and Sixth Ave soars the 6 **Bank of America Tower** (p192), NYC's fifth-tallest building and one of its most ecofriendly.

Head north along Sixth Ave to 47th St: the 7 **Diamond District**, home to more than 2600 independent jewelry businesses; whimsical diamond-shaped street lamps guard either end of the street. Walk toward Fifth Ave, taking in its swirl of busy traders. Turn left into Fifth Ave and admire the splendor of 8 **St Patrick's Cathedral** (p193), its impressive rose window the work of American artist Charles Connick.

Your last stop is 9 **Rockefeller Center** (p188), a magnificent complex of art deco skyscrapers and sculptures. Visit the main plaza and its golden statue of Prometheus. Then either head to the 70th floor of 30 Rockefeller Plaza for an unforgettable vista at the 10 **Top of the Rock** (p193) observation deck – or, if it's after 5pm, head straight up for a cocktail at 11 **Bar SixtyFive** (p200), where you can toast the Empire State Building at eye level.

DRINKING & NIGHTLIFE

The massive belly of Manhattan covers about everyone – cheesy tourists, partying suburbanites, martini princesses, you name it. The drinking holes east of Times Square may be a little more old-school than to the west, but they're among the most atmospheric in town, from historic pubs to baronial hideaways. Head to Midtown West and quench your thirst anywhere from lofty cocktail bars to sleazy dive joints and even a country-and-western gay bar. Those around Seventh Ave, Times Square and Hell's Kitchen are within easy striking distance of Broadway theaters.

Midtown East & Fifth Avenue

★THE CAMPBELL — COCKTAIL BAR

Map p424 (☎212-297-1781; www.thecampbellnyc.com; Grand Central Terminal, D Hall, 89 E 42nd St; ⏲noon-2am; Ⓢ S, 4/5/6, 7 to Grand Central-42nd St) In 1923 this hidden-away hall was the office of American financier John W Campbell. It later became a signalman's office, a jail and a gun storage before falling into obscurity. In 2017 it was restored to its original grandeur, complete with the stunning hand-painted ceiling and Campbell's original safe in the fireplace. Come for cocktails and you'll feel like you're waiting for Rockefeller or Carnegie to join you.

Try to book ahead Thursday to Sunday. It's a little tricky to find: take the elevator in the corridor next to the oyster bar (p196).

MIDDLE BRANCH — COCKTAIL BAR

Map p424 (☎212-213-1350; 154 E 33rd St, btwn Lexington & Third Aves, Midtown East; ⏲4pm-2am; Ⓢ 6 to 33rd St) Brainchild of the late cocktail deity Sasha Petraske, bi-level Middle Branch injects some much-needed drinking cred in beer-and-margarita-centric Murray Hill. Eye-candy bartenders whip up some of Midtown's sharpest libations, from faithful classics to playful reinterpretations like the Island Old Fashioned (made with Bacardi Reserva Ocho).

LITTLE COLLINS — COFFEE

Map p424 (☎212-308-1969; www.littlecollinsnyc.com; 667 Lexington Ave, btwn E 55th & E 56th Sts, Midtown East; ⏲7am-5pm Mon-Fri, 8am-4pm Sat & Sun; Ⓢ E, M to 53rd St; 4/5/6 to 59th St) Co-owned by Aussie expat Leon Unglik, Little Collins emulates the celebrated cafes of his hometown Melbourne: understatedly cool, welcoming spaces serving superlative coffee and equally tasty grub. The cafe is home to NYC's very first Modbar: high-tech, under-the-counter brewers that look like sleek chrome taps. Don't miss the avocado 'Smash' ($10.25). Milk and cream come served in Lilliputian milk bottles.

Midtown West & Times Square

BAR SIXTYFIVE — COCKTAIL BAR

Map p424 (☎212-632-5000; www.rainbowroom.com/bar-sixty-five; 30 Rockefeller Plaza, entrance on W 49th St; ⏲4:30pm-midnight Mon-Fri, 4-9pm Sun, closed Sat; Ⓢ B/D/F/M to 47th-50th Sts-Rockefeller Center) Sophisticated SixtyFive sits on level 65 of the central building of Rockefeller Center (p188), making it the highest vantage point in Midtown that doesn't require a ticket. Views are undeniably breathtaking, but at peak times it can feel like a cattle market: walk-ins are herded into a central standing area. If you want to sit down by a window, you'll need to reserve a table.

BAR CENTRALE — BAR

Map p428 (☎212-581-3130; www.barcentralenyc.com; 324 W 46th St, btwn Eighth & Ninth Aves, Midtown West; ⏲5-11:30pm; Ⓢ A/C/E to 42nd St-Port Authority) Set in an old brownstone, this unmarked bar is a favorite of Broadway actors, often seen here post-curtain debriefing and unwinding to sultry jazz. It's an intimate spot with a no-standing policy, so consider calling ahead (reservations are taken up to a week in advance). It's just up the stairs to the left of Joe Allen's.

TOP OF THE STRAND — COCKTAIL BAR

Map p424 (☎646-368-6426; www.topofthestrand.com; Marriott Vacation Club Pulse, 33 W 37th St, btwn Fifth & Sixth Aves, Midtown East; ⏲5pm-midnight Sun & Mon, to 1am Tue-Sat; 📶; Ⓢ B/D/F/M, N/Q/R to 34th St) For that 'Oh my God, I'm in New York' feeling, head to the Marriott Vacation Club Pulse (formerly the Strand) hotel's rooftop bar, order a martini (extra dirty) and drop your jaw. Sporting comfy cabana-style seating, a refreshingly mixed-age crowd and a

GAY BARS IN HELL'S KITCHEN

Industry (Map p428; ☎646-476-2747; www.industry-bar.com; 355 W 52nd St, btwn Eighth & Ninth Aves; ⏰5pm-4am; Ⓢ C/E, 1 to 50th St) What was once a parking garage is now one of the hottest gay bars in Hell's Kitchen – a slick, 4000-sq-ft watering hole with handsome lounge areas, a pool table and a stage for top-notch drag divas. Head in between 5pm and 9pm for the two-for-one drinks special or squeeze in later to party with the eye-candy party hordes. Cash only.

Therapy (Map p428; ☎212-397-1700; www.therapy-nyc.com; 348 W 52nd St, btwn Eighth & Ninth Aves, Midtown West; ⏰5pm-2am Sun-Thu, to 4am Fri & Sat; Ⓢ C/E, 1 to 50th St) Multilevel Therapy was the first gay men's lounge/club to draw throngs to Hell's Kitchen, and it still pulls a crowd with its nightly shows (from live music to interviews with Broadway stars) and decent grub served Sunday to Friday (the quesadillas are especially popular). Drink monikers match the theme: 'Oral Fixation' and 'Freudian Sip,' to name a few.

Hardware (Map p428; ☎212-924-9885; www.hardware-bar.com; 697 Tenth Ave, btwn 47th & 48th Sts, Midtown West; ⏰noon-4am; Ⓢ C/E to 50th St) This unassuming gay bar on the western fringes of Hell's Kitchen is home to some of the best drag shows in town, with top queens from NYC and beyond strutting their stuff nightly, as well as weekend afternoons for 'Skinny Brunch' (no food but there are $5 mimosas and Bloody Marys).

Flaming Saddles (Map p428; ☎212-713-0481; www.flamingsaddles.com/nyc; 793 Ninth Ave, btwn W 52nd & W 53rd Sts, Midtown West; ⏰3pm-4am Mon-Fri, 2pm-4am Sat & Sun; Ⓢ C/E to 50th St) A country-and-western gay bar in Midtown! *Coyote Ugly* meets *Calamity Jane* at this Hell's Kitchen hangout, complete with studly bar-dancing barmen in skintight jeans, aspiring urban cowboys and a rough 'n' ready vibe. Slip on them Wranglers or chaps and hit the Saddle: you're in for a fun and boozy ride.

Boxers NYC (Map p428; ☎212-951-1518; www.boxersnyc.com; 742 Ninth Ave, at W 50th St, Midtown West; ⏰4pm-2am Mon-Thu, to 4am Fri, noon-4am Sat, noon-2am Sun; Ⓢ C/E, 1 to 50th St) A gay sports bar offering football on TV, spicy buffalo wings, buff topless waitstaff and a rooftop deck. The original branch (p173) is in the Flatiron District.

retractable glass roof, its view of the Empire State Building is simply unforgettable.

ROBERT — COCKTAIL BAR

Map p428 (☎212-299-7730; www.robertnyc.com; Museum of Arts & Design, 2 Columbus Circle, btwn Eighth Ave & Broadway; ⏰11:30am-10pm Mon & Tue, to 11pm Wed-Fri, 10:30am-11pm Sat, to 10pm Sun; Ⓢ A/C, B/D, 1 to 59th St-Columbus Circle) Perched on the 9th floor of the Museum of Arts & Design (p194), '60s-inspired Robert is technically a high-end, Modern American restaurant. While the food is satisfactory, we say visit late afternoon or post-dinner, find a sofa and gaze out over Central Park with a MAD Manhattan (bourbon, blood-orange vermouth and liqueured cherries). Check the website for live jazz sessions.

WAYLON — BAR

Map p428 (☎212-265-0010; www.thewaylon.com; 736 Tenth Ave, at W 50th St; ⏰4pm-4am Mon-Thu, noon-4am Fri-Sun; Ⓢ C/E to 50th St) Slip on your spurs, partner, there's a honky-tonk in Hell's Kitchen! Kick back at this saloon-style watering hole, where the jukebox keeps good folks dancing to Tim McGraw's broken heart, the barkeeps pour American whiskeys and tequila, and the grub includes Texan-style Frito pie and pulled-pork sandwiches. For live country-and-western sounds, stop by Thursdays between 8pm and 11pm.

STUMPTOWN COFFEE ROASTERS — COFFEE

Map p424 (☎855-711-3385; www.stumptowncoffee.com; 18 W 29th St, btwn Broadway & Fifth Ave; ⏰6am-8pm Mon-Fri, from 7am Sat & Sun; Ⓢ R/W to 28th St) Stylin' baristas in fedora hats brewing killer coffee? No, you're not in Williamsburg, you're at the Manhattan outpost of Portland's cult-status coffee roaster. The queue is a small price to pay for proper espresso, so count your blessings. It's standing-room only, though weary punters might find a seat in the adjacent Ace Hotel (p339) lobby.

1

JEFF WHYTE/SHUTTERSTOCK ©

EQROY/SHUTTERSTOCK ©

1. Vessel (TKA; p195)
For a great cardio workout, explore 'The Vessel', a network of 154 flights of stairs at Hudson Yards.

2. Top of the Rock (p193)
Head up to the Rockefeller Center's 70th-floor open-air observation deck for stunning views across Manhattan.

3. Intrepid Sea, Air & Space Museum (p194)
Hop into a flight simulator at this interactive military museum.

4. Bryant Park (p191)
Play chess, learn a language or join a yoga class at this leafy oasis beneath Midtown's skyscrapers.

LET GO MEDIA/SHUTTERSTOCKW ©

RUM HOUSE COCKTAIL BAR

Map p428 (☎646-490-6924; www.therumhousenyc.com; 228 W 47th St, btwn Broadway & Eighth Ave; ⊙noon-4am; SN/R/W to 49th St) This slice of old New York is revered for its rums and whiskeys. Savor them straight up or mixed in impeccable cocktails like 'The Escape,' a potent piña-colada take. Adding to the magic is nightly live music, spanning solo piano tunes to jaunty jazz trios and sentimental divas. Bartenders here are careful with their craft; don't expect them to rush.

R LOUNGE BAR

Map p428 (Renaissance Hotel; ☎212-261-5200; www.rloungetimessquare.com; Two Times Sq, 714 Seventh Ave, at W 48th St; ⊙5-11pm Sun & Mon, to 11:30pm Tue-Thu, to midnight Fri & Sat; SN/R/W to 49th St) It might not be the most-fashionable spot for a drink in town, but this hotel bar delivers a spectacular, floor-to-ceiling view of Times Square that's hard to beat.

JIMMY'S CORNER BAR

Map p428 (☎212-221-9510; 140 W 44th St, btwn Sixth & Seventh Aves; ⊙noon-4am Mon-Sat, from 3pm Sun; SN/Q/R/W, 1/2/3, 7 to 42nd St-Times Sq; B/D/F/M to 42nd St-Bryant Park) This welcoming, unpretentious dive is run by an old boxing trainer – as if you wouldn't guess by all the framed photos of boxing greats (and lesser-known fighters, too). The jukebox, which covers Stax to Miles Davis, is kept low enough for postwork gangs to chat away. Long and narrow, the place looks like it would fit in a train car.

RUDY'S BAR & GRILL BAR

Map p428 (☎646-707-0890; www.rudysbarnyc.com; 627 Ninth Ave, at W 44th St, Midtown West; ⊙8am-4am Mon-Sat, noon-4am Sun; 📶; SA/C/E to 42nd St-Port Authority Bus Terminal) The big pantless pig in a red jacket out front marks Hell's Kitchen's best divey hangout, with cheap pitchers of Rudy's draft beers, half-circle vinyl booths covered in red duct tape, and free hot dogs. A mix of folks come to flirt or watch muted Knicks games as classic rock plays.

☆ ENTERTAINMENT

★RICHARD RODGERS THEATRE THEATER

Map p428 (Hamilton; ☎tickets 877-250-2929; www.hamiltonmusical.com; 226 W 46th St, btwn Seventh & Eighth Aves; ⊙box office 10am-8pm Mon-Sat, noon-6pm Sun; SN/R/W to 49th St) This theater opened in 1926 and is unique for several reasons. It was the first to allow all patrons to enter through one set of doors (generally there were separate entrances for low-price ticket holders, aka riff-raff, to come through). It also has the honor of being the venue for the highest number of Best Play and Best Musical Tony Awards.

Broadway's hottest ticket, Lin-Manuel Miranda's acclaimed musical *Hamilton,* uses contemporary hip-hop beats to recount the story of America's first secretary of the treasury, Alexander Hamilton. Inspired by Ron Chernow's best-selling biography, the show has won a flock of awards, with 11 Tony Awards (including Best Musical), a Grammy for its triple-platinum cast album and the Pulitzer Prize for Drama.

Book tickets at least six months in advance or be prepared to pay high resale rates on the ticket sites. Alternatively, head to the online ticket lottery, which can be accessed at www.luckyseat.com or via the dedicated Hamilton app (yes, this show is *that* popular). Winners can purchase one or two $10 front-row tickets (in honor of the man himself, who graces the 10-dollar bill).

★JAZZ AT LINCOLN CENTER JAZZ

Map p428 (☎Dizzy's Club Coca-Cola reservations 212-258-9595, Rose Theater & Appel Room tickets 212-721-6500; www.jazz.org; Time Warner Center, 10 Columbus Circle, Broadway at W 59th St; SA/C, B/D, 1 to 59th St-Columbus Circle) Perched atop the Time Warner Center, Jazz at Lincoln Center comprises three state-of-the-art venues: midsized **Rose Theater**; panoramic, glass-backed **Appel Room**; and intimate, atmospheric **Dizzy's Club Coca-Cola**. It's the last of these that you're most likely to visit, given its nightly shows (cover charge $5 to $45). The talent here is often exceptional, as are the dazzling Central Park views.

★CARNEGIE HALL LIVE MUSIC

Map p428 (☎212-247-7800; www.carnegiehall.org; 881 Seventh Ave, at W 57th St; tours adult/child $17/12; ⊙1hr tours 11:30am, 12:30pm, 2pm & 3pm Mon-Fri, 11:30am & 12:30pm Sat Sep-Jun; SN/R/W to 57th St-7th Ave) The legendary Carnegie Hall may not be the world's biggest concert hall, nor its grandest, but it's definitely one of the most acoustically blessed. Opera, jazz and folk greats feature in the **Isaac Stern Auditorium**, with edgier jazz, pop, classical and world music in the

TV TAPINGS

Wanna be part of a live studio audience for the taping of one of your favorite shows? NYC is the place to do it. Follow the instructions here to gain access to some of TV's big-ticket tapings.

Saturday Night Live (www.nbc.com/saturday-night-live) One of the most popular NYC-based shows, and known for being difficult to get into. That said, you can try your luck by getting your name into the mix in the fall, when seats are assigned by lottery. Simply send an email to snltickets@nbcuni.com in August, or line up on the 48th St side of Rockefeller Plaza on the day of the show for the 7am distribution of standby tickets. You can choose a stand-by ticket for either the 8pm dress rehearsal or the 11:30pm live broadcast. The tickets are limited to one per person and are issued on a first-come, first-served basis. You will need to bring valid photo ID when the ticket is issued, as well as to the show later that day. Audience members must be 16 or over.

The Late Show with Stephen Colbert Tickets for this hugely popular late-night show are available online, but they commonly sell out on the day of their release. Check *The Late Show*'s official Twitter account (@colbertlateshow) and Facebook page for release date announcements, usually made one to two months in advance. If you do manage to reserve tickets, you will need to line up outside the **Ed Sullivan Theater** (Map p428; www.showclix.com/event/thelateshowwithstephencolbert; 1697 Broadway, btwn W 53rd & W 54th Sts) no later than 2pm on the day of taping. Given that the show is intentionally overbooked to ensure capacity, arrive early to increase your chance of getting in. *The Late Show* tapes Monday through Friday at 5pm. Audience members must be 18 or over.

The Daily Show with Trevor Noah (Map p428; www.showclix.com/event/thedailyshowwithtrevornoah; 733 Eleventh Ave, btwn W 51st & W 52nd Sts) Sign up online to catch this popular news parody show. Reservations for shows are released on a gradual basis a few weeks before, so it pays to keep visiting the website. Tapings take place at 6pm and end by 8:30pm Monday through Thursday. Check-in begins at 4pm, but consider arriving early as there is no guarantee of entry. Audience members must be aged 18 or over.

Last Week Tonight with John Oliver Tickets to this biting British comedian's news recap show are available at www.lastweektickets.com up to a month in advance of taping dates. The show is taped at 6:30pm on Sunday at the **CBS Broadcast Center** (Map p428; www.lastweektickets.com; 528 W 57th St, btwn Tenth & Eleventh Aves) and audience members are requested to arrive at least 40 minutes in advance. Minimum age of admission is 18.

Full Frontal with Samantha Bee (www.samanthabee.com) Samantha Bee offers incisive and utterly hilarious commentary on the politicos and scandal makers hogging the current news headlines. Her late-night shows are taped at 5:45pm on Wednesday. Go online to get tickets.

For more show ticket details, visit the websites of individual TV stations, or check out www.nycgo.com/articles/tv-show-tapings.

popular **Zankel Hall**. Intimate **Weill Recital Hall** hosts chamber music, debut performances and panel discussions.

From September to June, Carnegie Hall runs **guided tours** (adult/child $17/12) of the building, shedding light on the venue's storied history (these are walk-in, but subject to performance and rehearsal schedules, so check the website before heading in). There's also the **Rose Museum**, which explores the venue's illustrious history through archival treasures (open 11am to 4:30pm; closed late July to mid-September).

★BIRDLAND — JAZZ

Map p428 (☎212-581-3080; www.birdlandjazz.com; 315 W 44th St, btwn Eighth & Ninth Aves; cover $30-50; ⏲5pm-1am; 📶; Ⓢ A/C/E to 42nd St-Port Authority Bus Terminal) This bird's got a slick look, not to mention the legend – its name comes from bebop legend Charlie Parker (aka 'Bird'), who headlined at

LOCAL KNOWLEDGE

BROADWAY BARGAINS

Unless booked many months in advance, must-see Broadway musicals can be prohibitively expensive. Discount ticket agent TKTS (p179) offers great deals daily, though rarely to the most in-demand shows. For these, your best bet for last-minute discounts is at the theater box office itself.

Many of the hottest shows – including Hamilton (p204) and Book of Mormon – run ticket lotteries, usually online via their website or www.luckyseat.com, but sometimes at the theater itself. If your name is drawn, the show is yours for a steal. The bad news: tickets are limited and in such high demand that you do need to be lucky to get them.

Other shows offer a limited number of general rush tickets, available each morning when the box office opens. Again, tickets are limited and in high demand, translating into early-morning queues and long waits.

Several shows also offer Standing Room Only (SRO) tickets, allowing patrons to stand through the performance in numbered spaces the width of a standard seat, usually at the back of the orchestra. Commonly between $27 and $40, SRO tickets can be especially tricky to land, as they are generally only available if the show is sold out. While there's no foolproof way to predict a sold-out show in advance, shows that sell out often include *Hamilton* and *Book of Mormon.* Policies can change, so always check the specific show's website before hitting the theater, toes and fingers crossed.

Birdland's former 52nd St location, along with Miles, Monk and just about everyone else (their photos are up on the walls). The 44th St club is intimate; come for the electrifying Big Band session on Fridays at 5:30pm.

SIGNATURE THEATRE THEATER

Map p428 (☎tickets 212-244-7529; www.signaturetheatre.org; 480 W 42nd St, btwn Ninth & Tenth Aves, Midtown West; ⓢA/C/E to 42nd St-Port Authority Bus Terminal) Looking good in its Frank Gehry–designed home – complete with three theaters, bookstore and cafe – Signature Theatre is devoted to the work of playwrights-in-residence, past and present. Featured dramatists have included Tony Kushner, Edward Albee, Anna Deavere Smith and Kenneth Lonergan. The theater also runs talks with playwrights, directors, designers and actors. Aim to book performances one month in advance.

EUGENE O'NEILL THEATRE THEATER

Map p428 (Book of Mormon; ☎tickets 877-250-2929; www.bookofmormonbroadway.com; 230 W 49th St, btwn Broadway & Eighth Ave; ⊙box office 10am-8pm Mon-Sat, noon-6pm Sun; ⓢN/R/W to 49th St, 1 to 50th St, C/E to 50th St) The Eugene O'Neill Theatre's shows have ranged from family-friendly *Annie* all the way to uproarious *The Best Little Whorehouse in Texas,* with nearly as wild a commercial ride as well – it's been bought and sold and renamed numerous times over its nearly a century lifetime. Playwright Neil Simon once owned it, before selling in 1982 to its current owners.

Subversive, obscene and ridiculously hilarious, *The Book of Mormon,* a cutting musical satire, is the work of *South Park* creators Trey Parker and Matt Stone and *Avenue Q* composer Robert Lopez. Winner of nine Tony Awards, it tells the story of two naive Mormons on a mission to 'save' a Ugandan village. Book at least three months ahead for the best choice of prices and seats, or pay a premium at shorter notice. Alternatively, try your luck at the online lottery (www.luckyseat.com). Winners – announced two hours before curtain – get in for a bargain $32. Once the winners are called, a limited number of standing-room tickets go on sale at the box office for $27 (subject to availability; expect queues to form).

PLAYWRIGHTS HORIZONS THEATER

Map p428 (☎212-564-1235; www.playwrightshorizons.org; 416 W 42nd St, btwn Ninth & Tenth Aves, Midtown West; ⓢA/C/E to 42nd St-Port Authority Bus Terminal) An excellent place to catch what could be the next big thing, this veteran 'writers' theater' is dedicated to fostering contemporary American works. Notable past productions include Annie Baker's Pulitzer Prize–winning *The Flick,* Kenneth Lonergan's *Lobby Hero,* Bruce

Norris' Tony Award–winning *Clybourne Park,* and Doug Wright's *I Am My Own Wife* and *Grey Gardens.*

LYRIC THEATRE
THEATER
Map p428 (☑Ticketmaster 877-250-2929; www.lyricbroadway.com; 214 W 43rd St, btwn Seventh & Eight Aves, Midtown West; ⊙box office 10am-8pm Mon-Sun; ⑤N/Q/R, S, 1/2/3, 7 to 42nd St-Times Sq) Set behind the facades of two century-old Broadway houses is this state-of-the-art theater opened in 1997 as part of the New 42nd St revitalization project. Its current production is the popular two-part play *Harry Potter and the Cursed Child,* beloved of Potterheads of all ages and winner of six Tony Awards.

GERSHWIN THEATRE
THEATER
Map p428 (Wicked; ☑212-586-6510, tickets 877-250-2929; www.wickedthemusical.com; 222 W 51st St, btwn Broadway & Eighth Ave, Midtown West; ⑤C/E, 1 to 50th St) The former Uris Theatre is one of the largest theaters on Broadway, seating nearly 2000. One of NYC's biggest flops played here: *Via Galactica* (a musical by *Hair* composer Galt MacDermot), which closed after only seven performances and lost more than a million dollars. Its many successes include *Singin' in the Rain,* the original production of *Oklahoma!* and, currently, *Wicked.*

MINSKOFF THEATRE
THEATER
Map p428 (The Lion King; ☑212-869-0550, tickets 866-870-2717; www.lionking.com; 200 W 45th St, at Seventh Ave, Midtown West; ♿; ⑤N/Q/R, S, 1/2/3, 7 to Times Sq-42nd St) The expansive Minskoff Theatre has been hosting shows, pageants and events since 1973. It currently is the home to Disney's *The Lion King.*

ROUNDABOUT THEATRE COMPANY
THEATER
Map p428 (☑212-719-1300; www.roundabouttheatre.org; 111 W 46th St, btwn Sixth & Seventh Aves, Midtown West; ⑤N/Q/R to 49th St; B/D/F/M to 47th-50th Sts) The Harold and Miriam Steinberg Center for Theatre is a state-of-the-art, dual-theater venue where the Roundabout Theatre Company stages works by emerging and established playwrights, as well as revivals of classic plays and musicals. They also mount productions at their flagship **American Airlines Theatre** on W 42nd St, the **Stephen Sondheim Theatre** on W 43rd St and **Studio 54** on W 54th St.

UPRIGHT CITIZENS BRIGADE THEATRE
COMEDY
Map p428 (UCB; ☑212-366-9176; www.ucbtheatre.com; 555 W 42nd St, btwn Tenth & Eleventh Aves, Hell's Kitchen; free-$14; ⊙7:30pm-midnight; ⑤A/C/E to 42nd St-Port Authority) Comedy sketch shows, improv and variety reign at the new location of the legendary venue, which receives drop-ins from casting directors and often features well-known figures from TV. Entry is cheap, and so is the beer and wine. You'll find quality shows happening nightly, from either 6pm or 7:30pm, though the Sunday-night Asssscat 3000 improv session is always a riot.

MADISON SQUARE GARDEN
LIVE PERFORMANCE
Map p428 (MSG, 'the Garden'; www.thegarden.com; 4 Pennsylvania Plaza, Seventh Ave, btwn 31st & 33rd Sts; ⑤A/C/E, 1/2/3 to 34th St-Penn Station) NYC's major performance venue – part of the massive complex housing Penn Station (p380) – hosts big-arena performers, from Kanye West to Madonna. It's also a sports arena, with **New York Knicks** (www.nba.com/knicks) and **New York Liberty** (https://liberty.wnba.com) basketball games and **New York Rangers** (www.nhl.com/rangers) hockey games, as well as boxing and events like the **Annual Westminster Kennel Club Dog Show** (www.westminsterkennelclub.org).

THE SHED
ARTS CENTER
Map p428 (☑646-455-3494; www.theshed.org; 545 W 30th St, at Tenth Ave, Hudson Yards, Midtown; ⊙exhibits 11am-6pm Tue, Wed & Sun, to 8pm Thu-Sat; ⑤7 to 34th St-Hudson Yards) Hudson Yards' most interesting building is this puffy-looking, Diller Scofidio + Renfro–designed multimedia arts center. It commissions original works across a range of disciplines, with two performance spaces, two art galleries, an arts-focused bookshop and large lobby bar-lounge. The inaugural season included artists as diverse as Björk, Renee Fleming, Boots Riley, Trisha Donnelly, Arvo Pärt and Sia.

AUGUST WILSON THEATER
THEATER
Map p428 (☑Ticketmaster 877-250-2929; www.jujamcyn.com; 245 W 52nd St, btwn Broadway & Eighth Ave, Midtown West; ⊙box office 10am-8pm Mon-Sat, noon-6pm Sun) This 1200-seat venue, which dates from 1925, was named for Pulitzer Prize–winning playwright August Wilson just weeks after his death

in 2005. It's the home of *Mean Girls,* Tina Fey's musical adaptation of her classic film about the perils of navigating social cliques in high school.

AMBASSADOR THEATRE THEATER

Map p428 (Chicago; ☎tickets 212-239-6200; www.chicagothemusical.com; 219 W 49th St, btwn Broadway & Eighth Ave; ⊙box office 10am-8pm Mon-Sat, noon-6pm Sun; ⓈN/R/W to 49th St; 1, C/E to 50th St) The landmark 1920s Ambassador Theatre is curiously built kitty-corner on the lot, enabling the small space to have more seating. It's currently the venue for the classic musical *Chicago,* one of Broadway's longest-running and most-popular shows.

DON'T TELL MAMA CABARET

Map p428 (☎212-757-0788; www.donttellmamanyc.com; 343 W 46th St, btwn Eighth & Ninth Aves, Midtown West; ⊙4pm-2:30am Sun-Thu, to 3:30am Fri & Sat; ⓈN/Q/R, S, 1/2/3, 7 to Times Sq-42nd St) Piano bar and cabaret venue extraordinaire, Don't Tell Mama is an unpretentious little spot that's been around for more than 30 years and has the talent to prove it. Its regular roster of performers aren't big names, but true lovers of cabaret who give each show their all. Singing waitstaff add to the fun.

SECOND STAGE THEATER THEATER

Map p428 (Tony Kiser Theater; ☎tickets 212-246-4422; www.2st.com; 305 W 43rd St, at Eighth Ave, Midtown West; ⊙box office noon-6pm Sun-Fri, to 7pm Sat; ⓈA/C/E to 42nd St-Port Authority Bus Terminal) This nonprofit theater company is famed for debuting the work of talented emerging writers as well as that of the country's more-established names. If you're after well-crafted contemporary American theater, this is a good place to find it.

CAROLINE'S ON BROADWAY COMEDY

Map p428 (☎212-757-4100; www.carolines.com; 1626 Broadway, at 50th St, Midtown West; ⓈN/R/W to 49th St; 1, C/E to 50th St) You may recognize this big, bright, mainstream classic from comedy specials filmed here on location. It's a top spot to catch US comedy big guns and sitcom stars. Tickets for most shows are around $20.

NEW YORK CITY CENTER DANCE

Map p428 (☎212-581-1212; www.nycitycenter.org; 131 W 55th St, btwn Sixth & Seventh Aves, Midtown West; ⓈN/Q/R to 57th St-7th Ave) This Moorish, red-domed landmark hosts dance troupes (including the Alvin Ailey American Dance Theater), theater productions, the New York Flamenco Festival in February or March and the popular Fall for Dance Festival in September or October.

SHOPPING

Midtown is home to the fabled, department-store-studded shopping strips of Madison and Fifth Aves, the diamond-trading hub of W 47th St, and a collection of eclectic, independent stores selling everything from rare books and autographed Hollywood shots to designer rainwear. If you're a self-made style maven, hit the Garment District (around Seventh Ave in the 30s) for massive shops peddling DIY fashion props. Not much, other than gift shops and corporate behemoths like Disney or the M&M store, can survive Times Square's astronomic rents. Down in Herald Square lies Macy's, the largest store in the Western Hemisphere.

Midtown East & Fifth Avenue

★ARGOSY BOOKS

Map p424 (☎212-753-4455; www.argosybooks.com; 116 E 59th St, btwn Park & Lexington Aves, Midtown East; ⊙10am-6pm Mon-Fri, to 5pm Sat; Ⓢ4/5/6 to 59th St; N/Q/R to Lexington Ave-59th St) Bookstores like this are becoming as rare as the books they contain, but since 1925 this six-story landmark has stocked fine antiquarian items such as books, old maps, art monographs and more. There's also an interesting booty of Hollywood, historical and literary memorabilia, from personal letters and signed books to autographed publicity stills. Prices range from costly to clearance.

SAKS FIFTH AVENUE DEPARTMENT STORE

Map p424 (☎212-753-4000; www.saksfifthavenue.com; 611 Fifth Ave, at E 50th St; ⊙10am-8:30pm Mon-Sat, 11am-7pm Sun; ⓈB/D/F/M to 47th-50th Sts-Rockefeller Center, E, M to 5th Ave-53rd St) Comprising a whopping 650,000 sq ft of retail space, Saks' 10-floor flagship store is home to the 'Shoe Salon,' NYC's biggest women's-shoe department. Other strengths include the revamped beauty floor and men's departments, the latter home to a coloring salon by Joel Warren and a sharply edited offering of fashion-forward labels. The store's January sale is legendary.

BLOOMINGDALE'S DEPARTMENT STORE

Map p424 (212-705-2000; www.bloomingdales.com; 1000 Third Ave, at E 59th St; 10am-8:30pm Mon-Sat, 11am-7pm Sun; ; S4/5/6 to 59th St; N/R/W to Lexington Ave-59th St) Blockbuster Bloomie's is something like the Metropolitan Museum of Art of the shopping world – historic, sprawling, overwhelming and packed with bodies, but you'd be sorry to miss it. Raid the racks for clothes and shoes from a who's who of US and global designers, including many 'new-blood' collections. Refueling pit stops include a branch of cupcake heaven Magnolia Bakery.

GRAND CENTRAL MARKET MARKET

Map p424 (www.grandcentralterminal.com/market; Grand Central Terminal, Lexington Ave, at 42nd St, Midtown East; 7am-9pm Mon-Fri, 10am-7pm Sat, 11am-6pm Sun; SS, 4/5/6, 7 to Grand Central-42nd St) It's not all trains at Grand Central Station. The station also holds a 240ft corridor lined with perfectly coiffed fresh produce and artisanal treats. Stock up on anything from fresh crusty bread and fruit tarts to sushi, chicken pot pies, Spanish quince paste, loose-leaf tea, antipasti and roasted coffee beans. There's even a Murray's Cheese stall, peddling milky wonders such as cave-aged Gruyère.

NEW YORK TRANSIT MUSEUM STORE GIFTS & SOUVENIRS

Map p424 (212-878-0106; www.nytransitmuseumstore.com; Grand Central Terminal, 89 E 42nd St, at Park Ave, Midtown East; 8am-8pm Mon-Fri, 10am-6pm Sat & Sun; SS, 4/5/6, 7 to Grand Central-42nd St) For NYC souvenirs with a twist, stop by this shop next to the stationmaster's office in Grand Central Terminal, which carries a comprehensive supply of swag themed to NYC public transit: mugs, T-shirts and hats for your favorite subway line, jewelry made from old tokens, bags and pencil cases, toy trains and much more.

Midtown West & Times Square

★MOMA MUSEUM & DESIGN STORES GIFTS & SOUVENIRS

Map p428 (212-708-9700; www.momastore.org; 11 W 53rd St, btwn Fifth & Sixth Aves; 9:30am-6:30pm Sat-Thu, to 9pm Fri; SE, M to 5th Ave-53rd St) The newly redesigned flagship design store at the Museum of Modern Art (p182) is a fabulous spot for souvenir shopping. Besides gorgeous books (from art and architecture to culture critiques and kids' picture books), you'll find art posters and one-of-a-kind knickknacks. For furniture, homewares, jewelry, bags and artsy gifts, head to the **MoMA Design Store** (10am to 6:30pm daily) across the street.

BERGDORF GOODMAN DEPARTMENT STORE

Map p424 (212-753-7300; www.bergdorfgoodman.com; 754 Fifth Ave, btwn W 57th & 58th Sts; 10am-8pm Mon-Sat, 11am-7pm Sun; SN/R/W to 5th Ave-59th St, F to 57th St) Not merely loved for its Christmas windows (New York City's best), plush BG, at this location since 1928, leads the fashion race, led by its industry-leading fashion director Linda Fargo. A mainstay of ladies who lunch, its draws include exclusive collections and a coveted women's-shoe department. The men's store is situated across the street.

FINE & DANDY FASHION & ACCESSORIES

Map p428 (212-247-4847; www.fineanddandyshop.com; 445 W 49th St, btwn Ninth & Tenth Aves, Midtown West; 11:30am-7:30pm Mon-Sat, from 12:30pm Sun; SC/E to 50th St) This pocket-square-sized haberdashery specializes in retro fashion accessories for the dapper folk among us, with everything from proper bow ties, ascots, embroidered suspenders and cuff links to tie pins, straw boaters and newsboy caps, cigarette cases and watch fobs. (They even sell spats.) You've never seen so much tweed, tartan, paisley and argyle in one spot before.

FAO SCHWARZ TOYS

Map p424 (800-326-8638; www.faoschwarz.com; 30 Rockefeller Plaza; 10am-8pm Mon-Thu, to 9pm Fri & Sat, to 7pm Sun; ; SB/D/F/M 47-50 Sts-Rockefeller Center) New Yorkers mourned the loss of this landmark toy store (c 1862) when it closed its famed flagship on Fifth Ave in 2015 (you might remember Tom Hanks playing a giant floor keyboard there in the movie *Big*). It was resurrected in this new Rockefeller location in 2018, looking jazzier than ever. Even the keyboard has made a comeback upstairs.

NEPENTHES NEW YORK FASHION & ACCESSORIES

Map p428 (☎212-643-9540; www.nepenthesny.com; 307 W 38th St, btwn Eighth & Ninth Aves; ⊙noon-7pm Mon-Sat, to 5pm Sun; **S** A/C/E to 42nd St-Port Authority Bus Terminal) Occupying an old sewing machine shop in the Garment District, this cult Japanese collective stocks edgy menswear from the likes of Engineered Garments and Needles, known for their quirky detailing and artisanal production value, with a vintage-inspired Americana workwear feel. Accessories include bags and satchels, hats, gloves, eyewear and footwear.

B&H PHOTO VIDEO ELECTRONICS

Map p428 (☎212-444-6600; www.bhphotovideo.com; 420 Ninth Ave, btwn W 33rd & 34th Sts; ⊙9am-7pm Mon-Thu, to 2pm Fri, 10am-6pm Sun, closed Sat; **S** A/C/E to 34th St-Penn Station) Visiting NYC's most-popular camera and electronics shop is an experience in itself – it's massive and crowded, and bustling with tech-savvy Hasidic Jewish salesmen. Your chosen item is dropped into a plastic tub, which then moves up and across the ceiling-high conveyor belts to the purchase area (which requires waiting in another line).

MACY'S DEPARTMENT STORE

Map p428 (☎212-695-4400; www.macys.com; 151 W 34th St, at Broadway, Midtown West; ⊙10am-10pm Mon-Sat, to 9pm Sun; **S** B/D/F/M, N/Q/R/W to 34th St-Herald Sq; A/C/E to Penn Station) Occupying most of an entire city block, the country's largest department store covers most bases, with fashion, furnishings, kitchenware, sheets, cafes and hair salons. It's more 'midpriced' than 'exclusive,' stocking mainstream labels and big-name cosmetics. The store also houses an NYC Information Center (p390) with information desk, free city maps and 10% store-discount vouchers for tourists (bring valid ID).

SPORTS & ACTIVITIES

CENTRAL PARK BIKE TOURS CYCLING

(☎212-541-8759; www.centralparkbiketours.com; 203 W 58th St, at Seventh Ave; adult rentals per 2hr/day $25/45, 2hr tours adult/child $49/35; ⊙rentals 8am-8pm Mon-Sat, to 6pm Sun Apr-Oct, 9am-5pm daily Nov-Mar, tours 9am, 10am, 1pm & 4pm; **S** A/C, B/D, 1 to 59th St-Columbus Circle) This place rents out a variety of good bikes, including e-bikes, and leads two-hour guided tours of Central Park and the Brooklyn Bridge area. If you book through its website, tours are discounted by 30%.

MANHATTAN COMMUNITY BOATHOUSE KAYAKING

Map p428 (www.manhattancommunityboathouse.org; Pier 96, at W 56th St, Hudson River Park; ⊙10am-6pm Sat & Sun Jun–mid-Oct, plus 5:30-7:30pm Mon-Wed Jun-Aug; M12 to 12th Ave/56th St, **S** A/C, B/D, 1 to 59th St-Columbus Circle) FREE Fancy a quick glide on the mighty Hudson? This volunteer-run boathouse offers free kayaking on summer weekends. It also offers free classes in kayaking technique and safety.

RINK AT ROCKEFELLER CENTER ICE SKATING

Map p424 (☎212-332-7654; www.therinkatrockcenter.com; Rockefeller Center, Fifth Ave, btwn W 49th & 50th Sts; adult $25-33, child $15, skate rental $13; ⊙8:30am-midnight mid-Oct–Apr; **S** B/D/F/M to 47th-50th Sts-Rockefeller Center) From mid-October to April, Rockefeller Plaza is home to New York's most famous ice-skating rink. Carved out of a recessed oval with the 70-story art deco Rockefeller Center (p188) towering above, plus a massive Christmas tree during the holiday season, it's incomparably magical.

LUCKY STRIKE BOWLING

Map p428 (☎646-829-0170; www.luckystrikesocial.com; 624-660 W 42nd St, btwn Eleventh & Twelfth Aves, Midtown West; individual games $9-12, shoe rental $6.50; ⊙noon-midnight Sun-Wed, to 1am Thu, to 2am Fri & Sat; **S** A/C/E to 42nd St-Port Authority Bus Terminal) One of the world's few bowling alleys with a dress code, Lucky Strike has pricey drinks, plush lounge fittings and a fashion-conscious crowd – which makes the whole experience more akin to a nightclub than a bowling alley. Book ahead. After 7pm it's ages 21 and over only.

Upper East Side

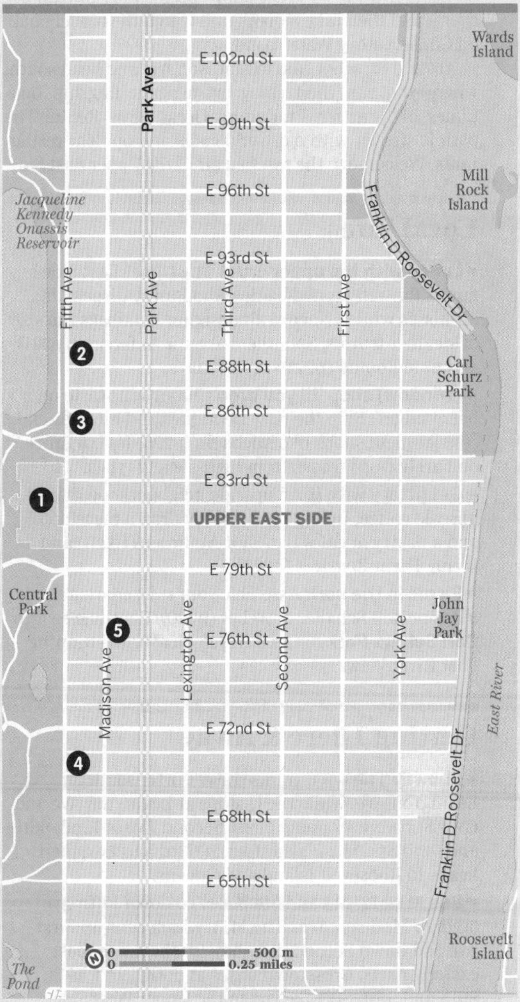

For more detail of this area see Map p430

Neighborhood Top Five

❶ **Metropolitan Museum of Art** (p214) Spending a few hours (or weeks) wandering amid the priceless cultural treasures.

❷ **Guggenheim Museum** (p213) Walking the spiral ramp of Frank Lloyd Wright's iconic architectural design on the trail of its latest installations of modern art.

❸ **Neue Galerie** (p218) Gazing at the lush, gilded paintings of Gustav Klimt, followed up by a leisurely lunch of Viennese specialties at the museum's elegant cafe.

❹ **Frick Collection Concerts** (p224) Listening to classical music on a Sunday evening, in a beaux-arts mansion surrounded by priceless paintings and sculptures.

❺ **Bemelmans Bar** (p222) Sipping an early evening cocktail at this elegant, mural-lined bar that hearkens back to the city's glorious Jazz Age.

Lonely Planet's Top Tip

The Upper East Side is the epitome of old-school opulence, especially the area that covers the blocks from 60th to 86th Sts between Park and Fifth Aves. If you're looking for eating and drinking spots that are easier on the wallet, head east of Lexington Ave. First, Second and Third Aves are lined with less pricey neighborhood venues.

Best Places to Eat

- Tanoshi (p221)
- Café Boulud (p221)
- Levain Bakery (p220)
- Papaya King (p220)
- Café Sabarsky (p221)
- Sfoglia (p220)

For reviews, see p219

Best Places to Drink

- Bemelmans Bar (p222)
- UES NYC (p222)
- Pony Bar (p224)
- Jeffrey (p222)
- Caledonia (p224)
- Auction House (p224)

For reviews, see p222

Best Places to Shop

- Blue Tree (p225)
- Tiny Doll House (p225)
- Michael's (p225)
- Mary Arnold Toys (p225)
- Albertine (p225)

For reviews, see p225

Explore the Upper East Side

There are infinite ways to tackle this large, well-heeled neighborhood. Begin with a walk south down Fifth Ave from 96th St, down historic Museum Mile, which is studded with vintage mansions and prestigious cultural institutions. Start early if you can – visiting the Metropolitan Museum of Art (p214) alone can easily take up an entire morning (or more). Enter Central Park just south of the 79th St Tranverse and join the hordes picnicking or lying about Cedar Hill; in wintertime you'll see local children sledding. Stroll south to the sculpture of *Alice in Wonderland* – a great photo op for kids to clamber over – and then take a break and watch the model boats on Conservatory Water pond.

At 72nd St, scoot east to Madison Ave and head south, where you can then enjoy extravagant flagship boutiques like Cartier, Prada and Oscar de la Renta. The path is strewn with old-world cafes and opulent restaurants. Welcome to the rarefied air of the Upper East Side.

Local Life

- **Lunch with the upper crust** The Upper East Side is famed for well-coiffed 'ladies who lunch,' dispensing air kisses while armed with designer handbags the size of steamer trunks. Spot them at Sant Ambroeus (p221) and Café Boulud (p221) on weekdays.
- **(Window) shop 'til you drop** Champagne taste on a beer budget? Skip the ritzy boutiques and hit high-end consignment shops like Michael's (p225) for bargains on barely worn frocks from high-society types.
- **Get jittery with it** An upscale neighborhood drinks upscale coffee. Indulge in a freshly drawn macchiato and a pastry at cafes like Sant Ambroeus (p221) and Irving Farm Roasters (p222).
- **Picnic in the park** Assemble your own charcuterie at old-time deli Schaller & Weber (p220). Continue east to **Carl Schurz Park** for an alfresco meal with stunning East River views.

Getting There & Away

- **Subway** The 4/5/6 trains travel north–south on Lexington Ave, while the Q stops at Lexington Ave and 63rd St before stopping along Second Ave at 72nd, 86th and 96th Sts. The F also stops at 63rd and Lex, then heads to Roosevelt Island and Queens.
- **Bus** M1, M2, M3 and M4 buses go down Fifth Ave (and up Madison Ave). The M15, which runs up First Ave and down Second, is handy for the area's most easterly parts. Crosstown buses at 66th, 72nd, 79th, 86th and 96th Sts take you to the Upper West Side.

TOP EXPERIENCE
GUGGENHEIM MUSEUM

A sculpture in its own right, this building by architect Frank Lloyd Wright almost overshadows the collection of 20th-century art inside. Even before it opened, the inverted ziggurat structure was derided by some critics but hailed by others, who welcomed it as a beloved architectural icon. Since its opening, this unusual structure has appeared in countless postcards, TV programs and films.

Abstract Roots

The Guggenheim came out of the collection of Solomon R Guggenheim, a New York mining magnate who began acquiring abstract art in his 60s at the behest of his art adviser, an eccentric German baroness named Hilla Rebay. In 1939, with Rebay serving as director, Guggenheim opened a temporary museum on 54th St titled the Museum of Non-Objective Painting. (Incredibly, it had grey velour walls, piped-in classical music and burning incense.) Four years later, the pair commissioned Wright to construct a permanent home for the collection.

Like most developments in New York City, the project took forever to come to fruition. Construction was delayed for almost 13 years due to budget constraints, the outbreak of WWII and outraged neighbors who weren't all that excited to see a giant concrete spaceship land in their midst. Construction was finally completed in 1959 – after both Wright and Guggenheim had passed away.

DON'T MISS

- Temporary Rotunda exhibitions (with unusual viewpoints)
- Brunch at the Wright restaurant
- Museum shop

PRACTICALITIES

- Map p430, A3
- ☎212-423-3500
- www.guggenheim.org
- 1071 Fifth Ave, at E 89th St
- adult/child $25/free, cash-only pay-what-you-wish 5-8pm Sat
- ⏲10am-5:30pm Wed-Fri, Sun & Mon, to 8pm Sat, to 9pm Tue
- [family-friendly]
- [S]4/5/6, Q to 86th St

Bring on the Critics

When the Guggenheim opened its doors in October 1959, the ticket price was 50¢ and the works on view included pieces by Wassily Kandinsky, Alexander Calder and abstract expressionists Franz Kline and Willem de Kooning.

The structure was savaged by the *New York Times*, but others quickly celebrated it as one of the country's most beautiful buildings. Whether Wright intended to or not, he had given the city one of its most recognizable landmarks.

To the Present

A renovation in the early 1990s added an eight-story tower to the east, which seamlessly provided an extra 50,000 sq ft of exhibition space. These galleries feature rotating exhibitions from the permanent collection, while the ramps of the Rotunda are occupied by temporary exhibits.

The museum's holdings include works by Kandinsky, Picasso and Jackson Pollock. Over time, other key additions have included paintings by Monet, Van Gogh and Degas, sculpture by Constantin Brancusi, photographs by Robert Mapplethorpe, and key surrealist works donated by Guggenheim's niece Peggy.

Visiting the Museum

The museum's ascending ramp displays rotating exhibitions of modern and contemporary art. Though Wright intended visitors to go to the top and wind their way down, the cramped single elevator makes this difficult. Exhibitions, therefore, are installed from bottom to top.

TOP EXPERIENCE
METROPOLITAN MUSEUM OF ART

This sprawling, encyclopedic museum, founded in 1870, houses one of the world's largest and most important art collections, with more than two million individual objects, from Egyptian temples to American paintings. 'The Met' attracts over six million visitors a year to its 17 acres of galleries, making it the largest single-site attraction in NYC. In other words: plan on spending some time here.

Egyptian Art

The museum has an unrivaled collection of ancient Egyptian art, some of which dates back to the Paleolithic era. Located to the north of the Great Hall, the 39 Egyptian galleries open dramatically with one of the Met's prized pieces: the **Tomb of Perneb** (c 2300 BCE), an Old Kingdom burial chamber crafted from limestone. From here, a web of rooms is cluttered with funerary stelae, carved reliefs and fragments of pyramids. Don't miss the intriguing models from the **Tomb of Meketre**, clay figurines meant to help in the afterlife, in Gallery 105. These eventually lead to the **Temple of Dendur** (Gallery 131), a sandstone temple to the goddess Isis given to the US by Egypt in 1965. It resides in a sunny atrium gallery with a reflecting pool – a must-see for the first-time visitor.

European Paintings

Want Renaissance? The Met's got it. On the museum's 2nd floor, the European Paintings galleries display a stunning collection of masterworks. This includes more than 1700 canvases from the roughly 500-year period starting in the

DON'T MISS

- Temple of Dendur
- Paintings by Caravaggio, El Greco, Vermeer and other old masters
- Damascus Room in the Islamic Art galleries

PRACTICALITIES

- Map p430, A5
- ☎212-535-7710
- www.metmuseum.org
- 1000 Fifth Ave, at E 82nd St
- 3-day pass adult/senior/child $25/$17/free, pay-what-you-wish for NY State residents
- ⌚10am-5:30pm Sun-Thu, to 9pm Fri & Sat
- [family-friendly]
- S 4/5/6, Q to 86th St, 6 to 77th St

13th century, with works by every important painter from Duccio to Rembrandt. In fact, everything here is, literally, a masterpiece. At the time of writing, the skylights in these galleries were being replaced to improve the quality of light within. Once completed, hours spent viewing these many powerful works will be even more enjoyable.

Art of the Arab Lands

In the southeastern corner of the 2nd floor you'll find the Islamic galleries, with 15 incredible rooms showcasing the museum's extensive collection of art from the Middle East, and Central and South Asia. In addition to garments, secular decorative objects and manuscripts, you'll find a magnificent 14th-century mihrab (prayer niche) from Iran, lined with elaborately patterned blue, white and yellow tile work (Gallery 455). There's also a superb array of Ottoman textiles (Gallery 459), a medieval-style **Moroccan court** (Gallery 456) and the 18th-century **Damascus Room** (Gallery 461).

American Wing

In the northwestern corner, the two-floor American Wing showcases a wide variety of decorative and fine art from throughout US history. These include everything from colonial portraiture to Hudson River School art – not to mention Emanuel Leutze's massive canvas of *Washington Crossing the Delaware* (Gallery 760). What the permanent collection lacks, though, is a serious body of Native American art. In 2018–19 a landmark exhibition showcased 116 works of sculpture, painting, textiles and regalia from more than 50 indigenous North American cultures. The works were gifts, donations and loans from the Diker Collection, considered to be the most significant private collection of Native American art in the US.

Greek & Roman Art

The 27 galleries devoted to classical antiquity are another Met doozy. From the Great Hall, a passageway takes you through a barrel-vaulted room flanked by the chiseled torsos of Greek figures. This spills right into one of the Met's loveliest spaces: the airy **Greek and Roman sculpture court** (Gallery 162), full of marble carvings of gods and historical figures. The statue of a bearded Hercules from CE 68–98, with a lion's skin draped about him, is particularly awe-inspiring.

FOR KIDS

The most popular galleries with children are generally the Egyptian, African and Oceania galleries (check out the Asmat body masks), and the collection of medieval arms and armor. The Met hosts plenty of youth-centric events (see the website) and distributes a museum brochure and map made specially for kids.

THE MET'S MASCOT

In Gallery 111 you'll find a small, blue-glazed faience hippopotamus that was sealed into an Egyptian tomb 3900 years ago to guard its owner in the afterlife. Nicknamed 'William,' he's the Met's unofficial mascot. If you'd like your own guardian hippo, head to the **museum shop** on the 1st floor, where you can buy bright-blue William figurines, plush toys, ties, T-shirts, magnets and children's books.

TAKE A BREAK

The museum's casual **Petrie Court Café** (11am to 4:30pm) sells tasty salads, soups, pastas and hot sandwiches, plus wine and a good selection of tea – all served in an airy setting with floor-to-ceiling views of Central Park.

For more views with a cocktail in hand, head to the Met's Cantor Roof Garden Bar (p222).

Metropolitan Museum of Art

PLAN OF ATTACK

From the Great Hall, just inside the main entrance, walk through the Egyptian galleries to the ❶ **Temple of Dendur**, dramatically set in a glass-walled gallery.

Stroll through the Charles Engelhard Court, a soaring sunlit atrium packed with American sculptures, to the Arms and Armor galleries. Examine the meticulous craftsmanship of the 16th-century ❷ **Armor of Henry II of France**. The next room (Gallery 371) has four fully armored, mounted horsemen.

Head back into the American Wing and up to the 2nd floor to see the massive ❸ **Washington Crossing the Delaware**. Continue on to the jaw-dropping collection of European masters. Don't miss the Caravaggios in Gallery 621, especially ❹ **The Denial of Saint Peter**.

Cut through the Photography section to 19th- and Early 20th-Century European Paintings and Sculpture for works by Monet, Renoir, Van Gogh and Gauguin. In Gallery 822 is Van Gogh's ❺ **Wheat Field with Cypresses**, which he painted shortly after his famous *Starry Night* (on display at the Museum of Modern Art).

Nearby are the Islamic Art galleries, where you'll find an elaborate ❻ **Mihrab** (prayer niche) next to a medieval-style Moroccan court with gurgling fountain (Gallery 456).

Walk downstairs to the Met's trove of ancient Greek and Roman works. In the largest gallery is the intricate marble sarcophagus ❼ **Triumph of Dionysos and the Seasons**. In the Oceania halls next door is vivid tribal art from New Guinea, including the three ❽ **Asmat Body Masks**; overhead is a painted ceiling from a Kwoma ceremonial house.

Continue to the Modern and Contemporary Art galleries for paintings by O'Keeffe, Dalí, Miró, Hopper and more; Picasso's high cubist ❾ **Still Life with a Bottle of Rum** is in Gallery 905. For a well-earned break, take the nearby elevators to the summertime Cantor Roof Garden Bar or try the stylish Petrie Court Café around the corner.

The Denial of Saint Peter Gallery 621
Painted in the final months of Caravaggio's short, tempestuous life, this magnificent work is a masterpiece of storytelling.

Wheat Field with Cypresses Gallery 822
Van Gogh painted this during a fevered period of production in the summer of 1889, while staying voluntarily at a mental asylum near Arles, France.

Mihrab Gallery 455
One of the world's finest religious architectural decorations, this 8th-century prayer niche from Iran was created by joining cut glazed tiles into a richly ornate mosaic.

Still Life with a Bottle of Rum Gallery 905
Picasso painted this in 1911, during the period when he and Georges Braque developed their new style of cubism together.

Asmat Body Masks Gallery 354
A New Guinea costume like this was worn to represent the spirit of someone who recently died, and featured in ritual dances of the Asmat people.

Triumph of Dionysos and the Seasons Gallery 162
On this marble sarcophagus, you'll see the god Dionysos seated on a panther, joined by four figures representing (from left to right) winter, spring, summer and fall.

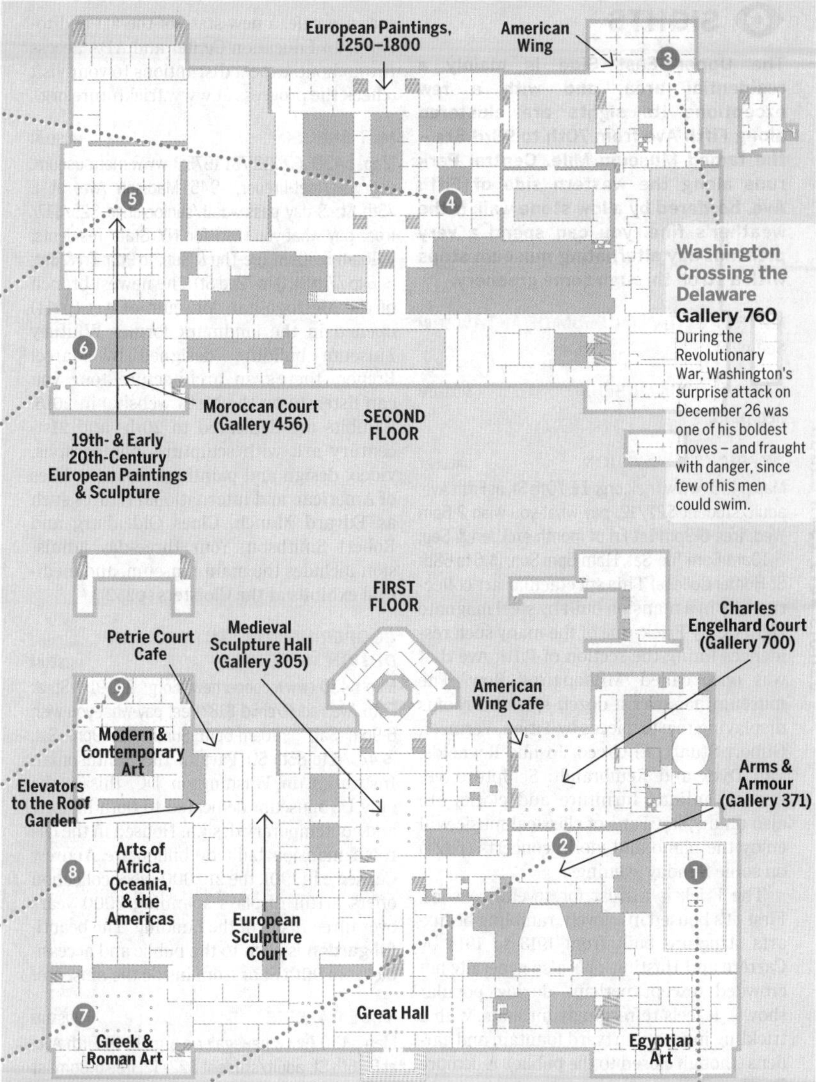

Washington Crossing the Delaware Gallery 760

During the Revolutionary War, Washington's surprise attack on December 26 was one of his boldest moves – and fraught with danger, since few of his men could swim.

Armor of Henry II of France Gallery 374

Look closely to see creatures, gods and warriors among the dense foliate scrolls, including Apollo chasing the nymph Daphne on the shoulders.

Temple of Dendur Gallery 131

One of the Met's must-see sights, this temple was built by order of Caesar Augustus. The Roman emperor and ruler of Egypt had many temples built in honor of Egyptian deities.

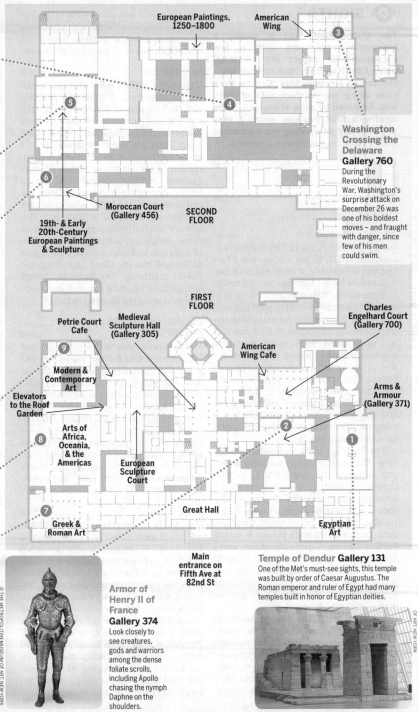

SIGHTS

The Upper East Side is mainly a residential area, and with a few exceptions its sights are clustered along Fifth Ave from 70th to 93rd Sts – the famed Museum Mile. Central Park runs along the western side of Fifth Ave, bordered by a low stone wall. If the weather's fine, you can spend a very pleasant day alternating museum stops with a stroll through some greenery.

METROPOLITAN MUSEUM OF ART MUSEUM

See p214.

GUGGENHEIM MUSEUM MUSEUM

See p213.

★FRICK COLLECTION GALLERY

Map p430 (www.frick.org; 1 E 70th St, at Fifth Ave; adult/student $22/12, pay-what-you-wish 2-6pm Wed, free 6-9pm 1st Fri of month excl Jan & Sep; ⏲10am-6pm Tue-Sat, 11am-5pm Sun; Ⓢ6 to 68th St-Hunter College) This spectacular art collection sits in a mansion built by steel magnate Henry Clay Frick, one of the many such residences lining the section of Fifth Ave that was once called 'Millionaires' Row.' The museum has over a dozen splendid rooms displaying masterpieces by Titian, Vermeer, Gilbert Stuart, El Greco, Joshua Reynolds, Van Dyck and Rembrandt. Sculpture, ceramics, antique furniture and clocks are also on display. Fans of classical music will enjoy the piano and violin concerts (p224) on some Sunday evenings.

The Frick is a treat for several reasons. First, it's housed in a lovely, rambling beaux-arts structure built from 1913 to 1914 by Carrère and Hastings; it's also generally not crowded (except perhaps during popular shows). It feels refreshingly intimate, with a trickling indoor courtyard fountain and gardens (though closed to the public). A demure **Portico Gallery** displays decorative works and sculpture. (Note that children under 10 years are not admitted to the museum.) And, finally, free lectures from curators or experts in the field are usually offered in conjunction with special exhibitions.

A worthwhile audio tour (available in several languages) is included in the admission price. Beginning in 2020, the museum is undertaking a restoration and expansion project, eventually opening up new galleries on the 2nd floor of the house and adding private state-of-the-art conservation laboratories, a cafe, a new state-of-the-art auditorium, an Education Center and ADA access throughout: expect disruptions to your visit (check the progress at www.frickfuture.org).

MET BREUER MUSEUM

Map p430 (☎212-731-1675; www.metmuseum.org/visit/met-breuer; 945 Madison Ave, at E 75th St; 3-day pass adult/senior/child $25/$17/free, pay-what-you-wish for NY State residents; ⏲10am-5:30pm Tue-Thu & Sun, to 9pm Fri & Sat; Ⓢ6 to 77th St, Q to 72nd St) The newest branch of the Metropolitan Museum of Art (p214) opened in the landmark former Whitney Museum building (designed by Marcel Breuer; there's an architecture tour you can listen to on the Met's website) in 2016. Exhibits are dedicated to 20th- and 21st-century art, with sculpture, photographs, video, design and paintings from the likes of American and international figures such as Edvard Munch, Claes Oldenburg and Robert Smithson. Your three-day admission includes the main museum, and medieval exhibits at the Cloisters (p252).

COOPER-HEWITT SMITHSONIAN DESIGN MUSEUM MUSEUM

Map p430 (www.cooperhewitt.org; 2 E 91st St, at Fifth Ave; adult/child $18/free, pay-what-you-wish 6-9pm Sat; ⏲10am-6pm Sun-Fri, to 9pm Sat; Ⓢ4/5/6 to 86th St) Part of the Smithsonian Institution in Washington DC, this is the only US museum dedicated to both historic and contemporary design. Housed in the 64-room mansion built by billionaire Andrew Carnegie in 1901, the 210,000-piece collection offers artful displays spanning 3000 years over three floors of the building. The beautiful **garden** is open to the public and accessible from 90th St or from inside the museum.

NEUE GALERIE MUSEUM

Map p430 (www.neuegalerie.org; 1048 Fifth Ave, at E 86th St; adult/student $22/12, free 5-8pm 1st Fri of month; ⏲11am-6pm Thu-Mon; Ⓢ4/5/6, Q to 86th St) This restored Carrère and Hastings mansion from 1914 is a resplendent showcase for Austrian and German art, featuring works by Paul Klee and Ernst Ludwig Kirchner, and incredible collections of Gustav Klimt and Egon Schiele. In pride of place on the 2nd floor is Klimt's golden 1907 *Portrait of Adele Bloch-Bauer I* – acquired for the museum by cosmetics magnate Ronald Lauder for a whopping $135 million. The fascinating story of the painting's history is told in the 2015 film *Woman in Gold*.

This is a small but beautiful place, with winding staircases and wrought-iron banisters. It also has a lovely, street-level eatery, Café Sabarsky (p221); downstairs, **Café Fledermaus** serves the same menu and absorbs the overflow. Avoid weekends (and the free-admission first Friday of the month) if you don't want to deal with gallery-clogging crowds. Note that children aged under 12 are not admitted to the museum, though Family Mornings are offered on select Sundays.

GRACIE MANSION HISTORIC BUILDING

Map p430 (www.nyc.gov/gracie; East End Ave, at E 88th St; ⌚tours 10am, 11am & 5pm Mon; Ⓢ Q to 86th St) FREE This Federal-style home served as the country residence of merchant Archibald Gracie in 1799. Since 1942, it's been the residence of New York's mayors and their families (with the exception of Michael Bloomberg, who preferred his own plush Upper East Side apartment). The house has been added to and renovated over the years. To visit, you'll have to reserve a spot online for one of the hour-long house tours held one day a week (less frequently during the holiday season).

The estate's 11 acres of grounds were turned into the pleasant, riverside **Carl Schurz Park**. It's popular with local joggers and dog owners, and its lovely promenade – which offers panoramic views of the East River, several islands and the Triborough Bridge – is one of the Upper East Side's hidden gems.

ASIA SOCIETY & MUSEUM MUSEUM

Map p430 (☎212-288-6400; www.asiasociety.org; 725 Park Ave, cnr E 70th St; adult/child $12/free, free 6-9pm Fri Sep-Jun; ⌚11am-6pm Tue-Sun, to 9pm Fri Sep-Jun; Ⓢ 6 to 68th St-Hunter College; Q to 72nd St) Founded in 1956 by John D Rockefeller III (an avid collector of Asian art), this cultural center hosts fascinating exhibits (Buddhist art of Myanmar, retrospectives of leading Chinese artists, contemporary Southeast Asian art), as well as Jain sculptures and Nepalese Buddhist paintings. Daily **tours** (free with admission) are offered at 2pm Tuesday through Sunday year-round and at 6:30pm Friday (excluding summer months). Note the museum is generally closed for three weeks or so in August and June for turning over exhibitors.

JEWISH MUSEUM MUSEUM

Map p430 (☎212-423-3200; www.thejewishmuseum.org; 1109 Fifth Ave, btwn E 92nd & 93rd Sts; adult/child $18/free, Sat free, pay-what-you-wish 5-8pm Thu; ⌚11am-5:45pm Mon-Tue & Fri, 11am-8pm Thu, 10am-5:45pm Sat & Sun; 👪; Ⓢ Q, 6 to 96th St) This gem occupies a French-Gothic mansion from 1908, housing 30,000 items of Judaica including torah shields and hanukah lamps, as well as sculpture, painting and decorative arts. It does not, however, include any historical exhibitions relating to the Jewish community in New York. Temporary exhibits are often excellent, featuring retrospectives on influential figures such as Art Spiegelman or Leonard Cohen, as well as world-class shows on luminaries like Marc Chagall and Modigliani.

TEMPLE EMANU-EL SYNAGOGUE

Map p430 (www.emanuelnyc.org; 1 E 65th St, at Fifth Ave; ⌚10am-4pm Sun-Thu, to 2pm Fri; Ⓢ 6 to 68th St-Hunter College) FREE Founded in 1845 as the first Reform synagogue in New York, this temple, completed in 1929, is now one of the largest Jewish houses of worship in the world. An imposing Romanesque structure, it is more than 175ft long and 100ft tall, with a brilliant, hand-painted ceiling featuring gold details. It is best to call ahead before visiting because the synagogue regularly closes for funerals and other events. Services (6pm Fridays and 10:30am Saturdays) are open to all.

MUSEUM OF THE CITY OF NEW YORK MUSEUM

Map p430 (www.mcny.org; 1220 Fifth Ave, btwn E 103rd & 104th Sts; suggested admission adult/child $20/free; ⌚10am-6pm; Ⓢ 6 to 103rd St) Situated in a Georgian Colonial Revival-style building at the top end of Museum Mile, this local museum focuses solely on New York City's past, present and future. Don't miss the 28-minute film *Timescapes* (on the ground floor), which charts NYC's growth from a tiny trading post for Native Americans to burgeoning metropolis.

EATING

High-end diners should dress the part for a meal at upmarket restaurants, where conversation is often hushed and service extremely white-tablecloth-formal. But go a little lower on the foodie totem pole here and you'll be pleasantly surprised not only by the sheer number of options, but by the fun and breezy vibe in the dining rooms.

★**LEVAIN BAKERY** BAKERY $

Map p430 (www.levainbakery.com; 1484 Third Ave, btwn E 83rd & E 84th Sts; cookies $4; ⏲6am-9pm; S 4/5/6 to 86th St) Levain's world-famous cookies are unlike anything you have ever tasted. Tempting you in four flavors – chocolate chip walnut, dark chocolate chip, dark chocolate peanut butter chip and oatmeal raisin – these heavyweight clumps of confection clock in at a whopping 6oz and are damn near as thick as a brick. Clear your schedule.

★**PAPAYA KING** HOT DOGS $

Map p430 (www.papayaking.com; 179 E 86th St, at Third Ave; hot dogs $3-4.50; ⏲8am-midnight Sun-Thu, to 1am Fri & Sat; S 4/5/6, Q to 86th St) The *original* hot-dog-and-papaya-juice shop, from 1932, over 40 years before crosstown rival Gray's Papaya (p235) opened, Papaya King has lured many a New Yorker to its neon-lit corner for a cheap and tasty snack of hot dogs and fresh-squeezed papaya juice. (Why papaya? The informative wall signs will explain all.) Try the Homerun, with sauerkraut and New York onion relish.

JG MELON PUB FOOD $

Map p430 (☎212-744-0585; www.jgmelon-nyc.com; 1291 Third Ave, at E 74th St; mains $8.50-33; ⏲11:30am-3am Mon-Wed, to 4am Thu-Sat, to 1am Sun; S Q to 72nd St) JG's is a loud neighborhood pub that has been serving reasonably priced drinks and coveted, old-school juicy burgers ($11.75) on tea plates since 1972. It's a local favorite for both eating and drinking (the Bloody Marys are excellent) and it gets crowded in the after-work hours. Cash only.

EJ'S LUNCHEONETTE DINER $

Map p430 (☎212-472-0600; www.ejsluncheonette.com; 1271 Third Ave, at 73rd St; breakfast $7.50-19.50, mains $11.50-22; ⏲8am-10pm; 👪; S Q to 72nd St) When comfort food is what Upper East Siders need, EJ's is where they come. Always full of chatter, this lovely retro diner has kept its head up over the years, with well-polished 1940s chrome and turquoise booths and Formica tables. Fluffy egg dishes, burgers, steak sandwiches and meatloaf with mushroom gravy are all equally satisfying.

SCHALLER & WEBER MARKET $

Map p430 (www.schallerweber.com; 1654 Second Ave, cnr E 86th St; sausages from $8 per 12oz; ⏲10am-8pm Mon-Sat, noon-6pm Sun; S Q, 4/5/6 to 86th St) This award-winning charcuterie and delicatessen is a holdover from when the Yorkville neighborhood was a largely German enclave. It sells over 15 varieties of sausage made at its factory in Pennsylvania – such German classics as *bauernwurst* and *weisswurst,* chicken bratwurst, cheddar-stuffed brat', Irish bangers, Polish kielbasa and more – alongside imported European goodies: cheese, pickles, condiments, chocolate, wine and beer.

LA ESQUINA TAQUERÍA MEXICAN $

Map p430 (The Corner; www.esquinanyc.com; 1420 Second Ave, cnr E 73rd St; tacos $4.50; ⏲11am-10pm Sun-Thu, to 11pm Fri & Sat; 🌶; S Q to 72nd St) This chain of hip new taquerías has acutely designed retro decor – its locations all look like 1950s diners that got stuck in time – but the Mexican menu is full of modern, yet authentic, takes on chicken quesadillas, *barbacoa* lamb-shoulder tacos, *elote callejero* (grilled corn with mayo, cheese and chili powder) and tortilla soup. Crowd- *and* wallet-pleasing.

WILLIAM GREENBERG DESSERTS BAKERY $

Map p430 (☎212-861-1340; www.wmgreenbergdesserts.com; 1100 Madison Ave, btwn E 82nd & 83rd Sts; baked goods from $1.75; ⏲8am-6:30pm Mon-Fri, to 6pm Sat, 9:30am-4:30pm Sun; 👪; S 4/5/6 to 86th St) Stop in at this Manhattan institution for its signature New York–style black-and-white cookies – soft, cakey discs dipped in vanilla and chocolate glazes (grab a box of minis for the trip home). Classic egg-cream sodas come in three flavors; its brownies are divine, too. Take-out only.

HEIDI'S HOUSE BY THE SIDE OF THE ROAD AMERICAN $$

Map p430 (☎212-249-0069; www.heidishouse.net; 308 E 78th St, btwn 1st & 2nd Aves; mains $17-35; ⏲5-10pm Mon, to 11pm Tue-Thu, to midnight Fri, 4pm-midnight Sat, 4-10pm Sun; S 4/6 to 77th St) Wildly out of place on the UES (it's a compliment), this downhome restaurant-bar is a local favorite, dishing out gussied up comfort food like numerous cast-iron mac 'n' cheeses (with bacon from 'properly fed piggies,' chorizo, lobster, mushrooms and white truffle oil and more), an excellent burger, and daily-changing specials like ribeyes with jalapeño tomato relish or chicken ragù.

SFOGLIA ITALIAN $$

Map p430 (☎212-831-1402; www.sfogliarestaurant.com; 1402 Lexington Ave, btwn E 92nd &

93rd Sts; mains $19-39; ⏲5:30-10pm Sun-Mon, to 10:30pm Tue-Sat; Ⓢ4/6 to 96th St) This upscale, trendy Italian (originally a Nantucket transplant) makes for a pretty idyllic date night out for the culinarily enlightened. The pappardelle *alla bolognese* is a step removed from Bologna and bucks tradition (it should be tagliatelle) but that's not to say this menu mainstay isn't divine, while the lemony chicken *al mattone* (pressed with a brick) is rustic fowl perfection.

DRUNKEN MUNKEY INDIAN $$

Map p430 (☎646-998-4600; www.drunkenmunkeynyc.com; 338 E 92nd St, btwn First & Second Aves; mains $18-34; ⏲4:30pm-2am Mon-Tue & Fri, to 3am Wed-Thu, 11:30am-3am Sat, 11am-2am Sun; 📶; ⓈQ, 6 to 96th St) This lively lounge channels colonial-era Bombay with vintage wallpaper, cricket-ball door handles and jauntily attired waitstaff. The monkey chandeliers may be pure whimsy, but the craft cocktails (favoring gin, not surprisingly) and tasty curries are serious business. Expect a good level of spice in Anglo-Indian dishes like masala Bombay lamb chops and Goan pork vindaloo. Book ahead.

SANT AMBROEUS ITALIAN $$

Map p430 (☎212-570-2211; www.santambroeus.com; 1000 Madison Ave, btwn E 77th & 78th Sts; panini $7-9, mains $21-69; ⏲7am-11pm Mon-Fri, from 8am Sat & Sun; ✎; Ⓢ6 to 77th St) Behind a demure facade lies this dressy Milanese bistro and cafe that oozes old-world charm. The long granite counter up front dispenses rich cappuccinos, pastries and mini panini (grilled with the likes of cotto ham and San Daniele prosciutto DOP); the elegant dining room behind dishes up northern Italian specialties, such as breaded veal chop, risotto and tagliatelle al ragù.

Don't miss its famed gelato. You can also find the same delicious espresso, pastries and panini at its **coffee bar** (Map p430; ☎212-339-4051; www.santambroeus.com; entrance on E 61st St, 540 Park Ave; ⏲7am-8pm Mon-Fri, from 8am Sat & Sun; ⓈF, Q to Lexington Ave-63rd St, 4/5/6 to 59th St), located further south in the Loews Regency Hotel.

WRIGHT AMERICAN $$

Map p430 (☎212-423-3665; www.guggenheim.org; Guggenheim Museum, 1071 Fifth Ave, at E 89th St; mains $20-27; ⏲11:30am-3:30pm Mon-Fri, from 11am Sat & Sun; 📶; Ⓢ4/5/6, Q to 86th St) The Wright restaurant at the Guggenheim (p215), serving such dishes as kohlrabi fritters, house-made pasta and seared salmon (the menu changes regularly), is somewhat overshadowed by its gleaming-white, modernist design aesthetic. Four intricately woven canvas collages by Sarah Crowner were installed in early 2017. On weekends it serves brunch.

CAFÉ SABARSKY AUSTRIAN $$

Map p430 (www.neuegalerie.org/cafes/sabarsky; 1048 Fifth Ave, at E 86th St; mains $19-32; ⏲9am-6pm Mon & Wed, to 9pm Thu-Sun; Ⓢ4/5/6 to 86th St) The lines can get long at this popular cafe evoking an opulent, turn-of-the-century Vienna coffeehouse. The Austrian specialties, courtesy of *Michelin*-starred chef Kurt Gutenbrunner, include crepes with smoked trout, goulash soup and roasted bratwurst – all beautifully presented. There's also a mouthwatering list of specialty sweets, including a divine Sacher torte (dark chocolate cake with apricot confiture).

CANDLE CAFE VEGAN $$

Map p430 (☎212-472-0970; www.candlecafe.com; 1307 Third Ave, btwn E 74th & 75th Sts; mains $16-22; ⏲11:30am-10pm Mon-Fri, from 11am Sat, 11am-9:30pm Sun; ✎; ⓈQ to 72nd St) The moneyed yoga set piles into this minimalist vegan cafe serving a long list of sandwiches, salads, comfort food and market-driven specials. The specialty here is the house-made seitan. There is a juice bar, a gluten-free menu and organic cocktails.

★TANOSHI SUSHI $$$

Map p430 (www.tanoshisushinyc.com; 1372 York Ave, btwn E 73rd & 74th Sts; chef's sushi selection $95-100; ⏲seatings 6pm, 7:30pm & 9pm Tue-Sat; ⓈQ to 72nd St) It's not easy to snag one of the 22 stools at Tanoshi, a wildly popular, pocket-sized sushi spot. The setting may be humble, but the flavors are simply magnificent. Only sushi is on offer and only *omakase* (chef's selection) – which might include Hokkaido scallops, kelp-cured flake or mouthwatering *uni* (sea urchin). BYO beer, sake or whatnot. Reserve well in advance via website only.

★CAFÉ BOULUD FRENCH $$$

Map p430 (☎212-772-2600; www.cafeboulud.com/nyc; 20 E 76th St, btwn Fifth & Madison Aves; breakfast $13-29, mains $39-52; ⏲7-10:30am, noon-2:30pm & 5:30-10:30pm Mon-Fri, 8-10:30am, 11:30am-2:30pm & 5:30-10:30pm Sat, 8-10:30am, 11:30am-3pm & 5-10pm Sun; ✎; Ⓢ6 to 77th St) This *Michelin*-starred bistro by Daniel

Boulud attracts a rather staid crowd with its globe-trotting French-Vietnamese cuisine. Seasonal menus include classics like bass 'en paupiette,' as well as fare such as duck with sour cherry and baby fennel.

The inventive farmers-market section will appeal to vegetarians, and foodies on a budget will be interested in the two-/three-course prix-fixe lunch ($39/45); locals come for breakfast. The restaurant is a long-standing Upper East Side fixture and, as such, easier to get reservations at than many other *Michelin*-starred New York restaurants (book two weeks ahead for Saturday nights). The adjacent 40-seat **Bar Pleiades** (www.barpleiades.com; ⊙noon-midnight Sun-Thu, to 1am Fri & Sat) serves seasonal cocktails.

DRINKING & NIGHTLIFE

Drinking options on the Upper East Side have traditionally been either pricey, luxe lounges or frat-house sports bars ('Beer pong, anyone?'). Times are changing, however, with downtown-cool cocktail lounges and classy gastropubs opening up in recent years, especially alongside the transformative Second Ave subway line.

★UES NYC — COCKTAIL BAR

Map p430 (☎646-559-5889; www.theuesnyc.com; 1707 Second Ave, btwn E 88th & 89th Sts; ⊙5pm-late Mon-Sat; SQ to 86th St) Scooping delicious ice cream by day, this candy-colored parlor lets rip as a speakeasy by night. Cocktails ($15 to $25) are named after Upper East Side landmarks, such as 'Meet me at the Met' and '2nd Avenue Subway.' Beware: there's a dress code, so no sneakers, flip-flops, ripped jeans or T-shirts.

Entrance to the dimly lit 'Storage Room' is through the wall of ice-cream tubs at the back of the shop (you have to find the switch). On Sundays it becomes a cinema from 8pm and the dress code is forgiven.

★BEMELMANS BAR — LOUNGE

Map p430 (☎212-744-1600; www.thecarlyle.com; Carlyle Hotel, 35 E 76th St, at Madison Ave; ⊙noon-1:30am; 📶; S6 to 77th St) Sink into a chocolate-leather banquette and take in the glorious, old-school elegance at this atmospheric bar – the sort of place where the waiters wear white jackets and serve martinis, a pianist tinkles on a baby grand and the ceiling is 24-carat gold leaf. The walls are covered in charming murals by the bar's namesake Ludwig Bemelmans, famed creator of the *Madeline* books.

FLORA BAR — BAR

Map p430 (☎646-558-5383; www.florabarnyc.com; Met Breuer, 945 Madison Ave, lower fl, at E 75th St; ⊙bar 11:30am-3:30pm & 5:30-10pm, cafe 10am-5:30pm Tue-Sun; 📶; S6 to 77th St, Q to 72nd St) Forget that this is essentially a museum bar in the Met Breuer (p218); Flora is a sophisticated drinking lounge that shows off the building's architectural extravagance. Park yourself at the marble bar or curl into a deep modernist armchair to marvel at the double-story concrete cathedral and gigantic glass wall that leads to a sunken garden: an oasis beneath Madison Ave.

IRVING FARM ROASTERS — COFFEE

Map p430 (☎646-861-2949; www.irvingfarm.com; 1424 Third Ave, at E 81st St; ⊙7am-7pm Mon-Fri, from 8am Sat & Sun; S6 to 77th St, 4/5/6 to 86th St) This pioneering New York artisanal coffeehouse serves full-bodied espressos and single-origin pour-overs, along with a small yet tasty cafe menu. This is the largest of its 10 Manhattan locations, with a roomy seating area at the back. Its policy is 'no wi-fi' – bring a book.

CANTOR ROOF GARDEN BAR — ROOFTOP BAR

Map p430 (www.metmuseum.org/visit/dining; Metropolitan Museum of Art, 1000 Fifth Ave, 5th fl, at E 82nd St; ⊙11am-4:30pm Sun-Thu, to 8:15pm Fri & Sat mid-Apr–Oct; 📶; S4/5/6 to 86th St) The sort of setting you can't get enough of (even if you are a jaded local). Located atop the Met, this rooftop bar sits right above Central Park's tree canopy, allowing for splendid views of the park and the city skyline all around. Sunset is when you'll find fools in love...then again, it could all be those martinis.

JEFFREY — CRAFT BEER

Map p430 (www.thejeffreynyc.com; 311 E 60th St, btwn First & Second Aves; ⊙11am-2am; SN/R/W to Lexington Ave-59th St) In the shadow of the Queensboro Bridge right under the Roosevelt Island Tramway, this unpretentious craft-beer and cocktail bar packs in gaggles of post-work pursuers of hops but with hardly a hipster beard in sight (the Bearded Alchemist notwithstanding!). The

Neighborhood Walk **Memorable Manhattan Movies**

START BLOOMINGDALE'S
END METROPOLITAN MUSEUM OF ART
LENGTH 1.5 MILES; TWO HOURS

An exploration of Manhattan's most storied film sites takes you past movie locations big and small. Start at **1 Bloomingdale's** (p209), where Darryl Hannah and Tom Hanks shattered televisions in *Splash* (1984) and Dustin Hoffman hailed a cab in *Tootsie* (1982). West of here, 10 E 60th St is the site of the now-defunct **2 Copacabana**, a nightclub (now an upscale restaurant) that hosted Ray Liotta and Lorraine Bracco in *Goodfellas* (1990) and a coked-up lawyer played by Sean Penn in *Carlito's Way* (1993).

Continue west to **3 Central Park** (p228), which has appeared in *The Royal Tenenbaums* (2001), *Ghostbusters* (1983), *The Muppets Take Manhattan* (1983), *Barefoot in the Park* (1967) and the cult classic *The Warriors* (1979). From here, head east to Park Ave. At 620 Park Ave (at 65th St) is the building that housed **4 John Malkovich's apartment** in Charlie Kaufman's *Being John Malkovich* (1999). Six blocks north and one and a half blocks east is 171 E 71st St, a town house featured in one of the most famous movies ever filmed in New York: this was **5 Holly Golightly's apartment** in *Breakfast at Tiffany's* (1961). Continuing east to Third Ave, you'll find **6 JG Melon** (p220) at the corner of 74th St; grab a beer and burger at the site of a meeting between Dustin Hoffman and Meryl Streep in *Kramer vs Kramer* (1979).

Head west to Madison Ave; the posh **7 Carlyle Hotel**, at the corner of 76th St, is where Woody Allen and Dianne Wiest had a date from hell in *Hannah and Her Sisters* (1986). From the Carlyle, it's a short walk north and west to **8 1030 Fifth Ave** where Carrie Bradshaw (Sarah Jessica Parker) and Mr Big (Chris Noth) lived it up together in *Sex and the City 2* (2010). Across the street, the **9 Metropolitan Museum of Art** (p214) at 82nd St and Fifth Ave, is where Angie Dickinson had a fatal encounter in *Dressed to Kill* (1980) and Billy Crystal chatted up Meg Ryan in *When Harry Met Sally* (1989).

custom-built draft system spits suds from 29 rotating taps – which are best enjoyed in the wonderful beer garden.

PONY BAR CRAFT BEER

Map p430 (www.theponybar.com; 1444 First Ave, btwn E 75th & 76th Sts; 3pm-4am Mon-Tue & Thu-Fri, to 1:30am Wed, noon-4am Sat & Sun; SQ/R to 72nd St) The best craft-beer destination in Upper Manhattan, Pony Bar pours exclusively American craft (including cask-conditioned ales) with a near total devotion to New York State breweries. You'll find 20 rotating taps and a whole lot of rustic hardwoods (the bar, the seating, the barrels, the canoe...). If you're in pursuit of a locally devout hoptopia in UES, look no further.

CALEDONIA BAR

Map p430 (www.caledoniabar.com; 1609 Second Ave, btwn E 83rd & 84th Sts; 5pm-2am Mon-Thu, 4pm-4am Fri & Sat, 4pm-1am Sun, happy hour to 7pm Mon-Fri; SQ, 4/5/6 to 86th St) The name of this unpretentious, dimly lit bar is a dead giveaway: it's devoted to Scotch whisky, with over a hundred single malts to choose from (be they Highlands, Islands, Islay, Lowlands or Speyside), as well as some blends and even a few from the US, Ireland and Japan.

The bartenders know their stuff and will be happy to make recommendations.

ETHYL'S ALCOHOL & FOOD BAR

Map p430 (www.ethylsnyc.com; 1629 2nd Ave, btwn E 84th & 85th Sts; 5pm-2am Mon-Wed, to 4am Thu, 4pm-4am Fri & Sat, 4pm-2am Sun; SQ/R to 86th St) This funky, divey 1970s-themed bar harks back to the gritty, artsy NYC of yore, before famed punk club CBGB became a fashion boutique. (The $14 cocktails make it decidedly modern.) There's '60s/'70s music nightly from bands or DJs, plus go-go dancers and occasional burlesque shows, and a famed *Fi-Dolla* ($5) burger.

DAISY BAR

Map p430 (646-964-5756; www.thedaisynyc.com; 1641 Second Ave, cnr E 85th St; 4pm-1am Mon-Wed, to 4am Thu & Fri, 11am-4am Sat, 11am-1am Sun; SQ, 4/5/6 to 86th St) Swish gastropub Daisy serves craft cocktails and creative, seasonal bar plates like pork belly with poached egg and mustard-cumin vinaigrette and oxtail ragù fusilli. Unlike most other Upper East Side bars, there are no TVs or packs of loud partygoers here – it's a laid-back, low-lit spot, with art deco touches, good grooves, skilled bartenders and a friendly crowd.

AUCTION HOUSE BAR

Map p430 (www.theauctionhousenyc.com; 300 E 89th St, at Second Ave; 6:30pm-1am Sun-Thu, to 4am Fri & Sat; SQ to 86th St) Dark maroon doors lead into a candlelit hangout that's perfect for a relaxing drink. Victorian-style couches and fat, overstuffed easy chairs are strewn about the wood-floored rooms. Take your well-mixed cocktail to a seat by the fireplace and admire the scene reflected in the gilt-edged mirrors propped up on the walls.

☆ ENTERTAINMENT

FRICK COLLECTION CONCERTS CLASSICAL MUSIC

Map p430 (212-547-0715; www.frick.org/programs/concerts; 1 E 70th St, at Fifth Ave; $45; S6 to 68th St-Hunter College) Every two to four weeks, the opulent Frick Collection (p218) hosts a Sunday 5pm concert that brings in world-renowned performers, such as cellist Yehuda Hanani and violinist Thomas Zehetmair: check the website for the schedule.

92ND STREET Y ARTS CENTER

Map p430 (212-415-5500; www.92y.org; 1395 Lexington Ave, at E 92nd St; box office 30min prior to ticketed events; ; SQ, 6 to 96th St) In addition to its wide spectrum of concerts, dance performances, literary readings and family-friendly events, this nonprofit cultural center hosts an excellent lecture and conversation series. Playwright Edward Albee, cellist Yo-Yo Ma, comedian Steve Martin and novelist Salman Rushdie have all taken the stage here.

CAFÉ CARLYLE JAZZ

Map p430 (212-744-1600; www.thecarlyle.com; Carlyle Hotel, 35 E 76th St, at Madison Ave; cover $75-225, 2-course food minimum $80; shows 8:45pm & 10:45pm Mon-Sat, close early Jan, Jul, Aug & early Sep; S6 to 77th St) This swanky spot at the Carlyle Hotel draws top-shelf talent. Bring mucho bucks: the cover charge doesn't include food or drinks, and there's a minimum spend. The dress code is 'chic' – gentlemen, wear a jacket.

SHOPPING

Madison Ave isn't for amateurs. Some of the globe's glitziest shops line the stretch from 60th St to 72nd St, with flagship boutiques from the world's top designers, including Gucci, Prada and Cartier. A handful of consignment stores offer preloved designer deals. Further east, a range of more general – though still upmarket – stores line Lexington, Third and Second Aves, with everything from cosmetics and fashion to books and quirky gifts.

★TINY DOLL HOUSE — ARTS & CRAFTS

Map p430 (www.tinydollhousenewyorkcity.com; 314 E 78th St; ⊙11am-5pm Mon-Fri, to 4pm Sat; Ⓢ4/6 to 77th St) If the Carrie Stettheimer dollhouse at the Museum of the City of New York turned you on or you're otherwise in the market for a dream dollhouse, this fascinating shop is NYC's only store dedicated to dollhouses and miniature accessories. The tiny worlds offered here come in a variety of styles (Victorian, Chippendale, contemporary) and are rendered in stunning detail.

The shop, started by owner Leslie Edelman over 25 years ago, is worth a look-see even if it's not exactly the sort of souvenir you can lug home.

★BLUE TREE — FASHION & ACCESSORIES

Map p430 (☎212-369-2583; www.bluetreeny.bigcartel.com; 1283 Madison Ave, btwn E 91st & 92nd Sts; ⊙10am-6pm Mon-Fri, from 11am Sat & Sun, closed Sun Jan-Apr; Ⓢ4/5/6 to 86th St) This charming (and expensive) little boutique, owned by actress Phoebe Cates Kline (of *Fast Times at Ridgemont High* fame), sells a dainty array of women's clothing, jewelry, cashmere scarves, Lucite objects, whimsical accessories and unconventional home design.

ALBERTINE — BOOKS

Map p430 (☎212-650-0070; www.albertine.com; 972 Fifth Ave, btwn E 78th & 79th Sts; ⊙11am-7pm Mon-Sat, to 6pm Sun; Ⓢ4/5/6 at 86th St) This wonderful two-story bookstore, which opened in 2014 as part of the French embassy's cultural programming, caters to enthusiasts of French literature. It stocks fiction, nonfiction and children's books in French, as well as English translations of French classics – along with rare offerings such as 18th-century editions from Diderot and Rousseu.

MARY ARNOLD TOYS — TOYS

Map p430 (☎212-744-8510; www.maryarnoldtoys.com; 1178 Lexington Ave, btwn E 80th & 81st Sts; ⊙9am-6pm Mon-Fri, from 10am Sat, 10am-5pm Sun; 👪; Ⓢ4/5/6 to 86th St) Several generations of Upper East Siders have spent large chunks of their childhood browsing the stuffed shelves of this personable local toy store, opened in 1931. Its range is extensive – stuffed animals, action figures, science kits, board games, arts and crafts, educational toys – even Lomo cameras for budding retro photographers.

Check the website for free monthly events, such as scavenger hunts or Lego-making sessions.

DIPTYQUE — PERFUME

Map p430 (☎212-879-3330; www.diptyqueparis.com; 971 Madison Ave, cnr E 76th St; ⊙10am-7pm Mon-Sat, noon-6pm Sun; Ⓢ6 to 77th St) Come out smelling like a rose – or wisteria, jasmine, cypress or sandalwood – at this olfactory oasis. Parisian company Diptyque has been creating signature scents since 1961, using innovative combinations of plants, woods and flowers.

MICHAEL'S — CLOTHING

Map p430 (☎212-737-7273; www.michaelsconsignment.com; 1125 Madison Ave, btwn E 84th & 85th Sts; ⊙10am-6:30pm Mon-Sat, to 8pm Thu, noon-6pm Sun, closed Sun Jul & Aug; Ⓢ6 to 77th St) In operation since the 1950s and as of 2018 in a new street-facing location, this vaunted Upper East Side resale store features high-end labels, including Chanel, Gucci, Prada and Jimmy Choo. Almost everything on display is less than two years old. It's pricey but cheaper than shopping the flagship boutiques on Madison Ave.

SHAKESPEARE & CO — BOOKS

Map p430 (☎212-772-3400; www.shakeandco.com; 939 Lexington Ave, at E 69th St; ⊙7:30am-8pm Mon-Fri, 8am-7pm Sat, 9am-6pm Sun; 📶; Ⓢ6 to 68th St-Hunter College) No relation to the Paris seller, this popular bookstore is one of NYC's great indie options. There's a wide array of contemporary fiction and nonfiction, and art and local history books, plus a small but unique collection of periodicals, while an Espresso book machine churns out print-on-demand titles. A small cafe serves coffee, tea and light meals.

Upper West Side & Central Park

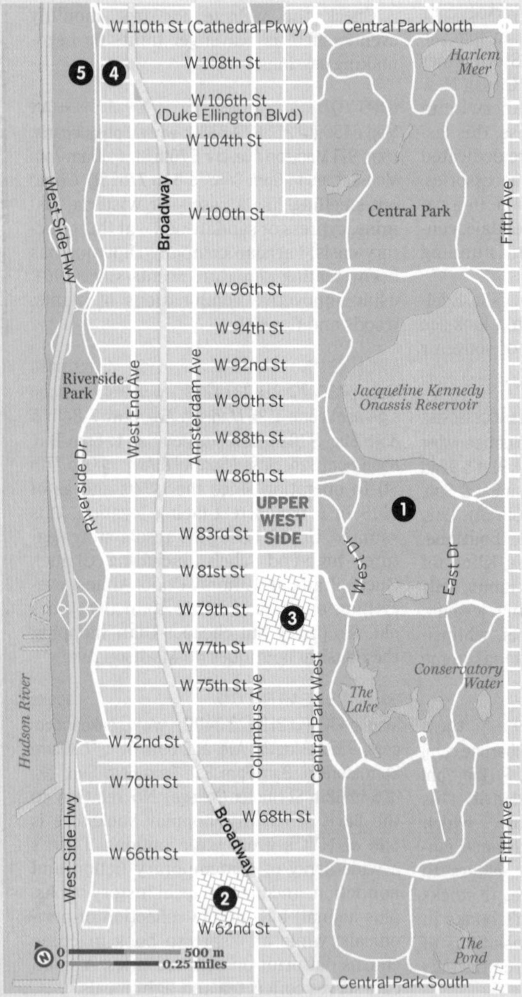

Neighborhood Top Five

❶ **Central Park** (p228) Escaping the urban madness with a day of picnicking on Sheep Meadow, row-boating on the lake and strolling the grand Literary Walk.

❷ **Lincoln Center** (p232) Plunging into the sheer depth of artistic choices with some of the world's best opera, ballet, classical music, film and theater.

❸ **American Museum of Natural History** (p234) Walking among some of the world's largest dinosaurs and running your hand along the pitted surface of the biggest meteorite in the US.

❹ **Nicholas Roerich Museum** (p233) Taking a pilgrimage to Tibet through the mind of a remarkable man, all inside a beautiful 19th-century town house.

❺ **Riverside Park** (p233) Jogging, cycling or even just strolling along the Hudson waterfront as the sun goes down over the river's far shore.

For more detail of this area see Map p432

Explore the Upper West Side & Central Park

The central western section of Manhattan offers a lot of ground to cover, so the best plan of attack will depend on what you want to see. Traveling with tykes? Dazzle their budding brains with a visit to the American Museum of Natural History (p234), followed by a journey through the sprawling wonderland that is Central Park (p228). (The street running parallel to the park, Central Park West, is lined with stately apartment buildings that are lovely to admire if you can deal with the real-estate envy.) If the arts are high on your list, head to Lincoln Center (p232), where the Metropolitan Opera, the New York Philharmonic and the New York City Ballet offer vibrant doses of culture. But if your idea of a good time is just ambling around a neighborhood, then take in the sights on and around Broadway in the 70s, an area packed with bustling shops and fine architecture. To experience a quieter green space, head to Riverside Park (p233), along the far western edge of Manhattan, for a nice long stroll with views of the Hudson River – particularly lovely at sunset.

Local Life

- **Go fishing** Wood-smoked lox. Briny pickled herring. Meaty sturgeon. It doesn't get more Upper West Side than examining the seafood treats at Zabar's (p243) and Barney Greengrass (p238).
- **Central chill** Tourists in Central Park (p228) rush between sights. Make like a local by picking out a patch of green with good views and letting the world pass by.
- **Catch a flick** Manhattan's die-hard film buffs get their quality cinema courtesy of the Film at Lincoln Center (p241).
- **Late-night munchies** Nothing is more New York than soaking up the evening's liquor damage with a 2am hot dog from Gray's Papaya (p235).

Getting There & Away

- **Subway** The 1, 2 and 3 lines are good for destinations between Broadway and the river; take the B or C train for museums and Central Park (which can be accessed from every side). The A/C, B/D and 1 stop at 59th St-Columbus Circle, at Central Park's southwestern corner, and go north from there; the N/R/W line goes to the southeast. The 2 or 3 stops at the northern gate in Harlem.
- **Bus** The M104 runs along Broadway; the M10 along the park's scenic western edge. Crosstown routes at 66th, 72nd, 79th, 86th and 96th Sts go through the park to the Upper East Side, stopping at Central Park West and Fifth Ave – not inside the park.

Lonely Planet's Top Tip

The best way to cover all 840 acres of Central Park is by bicycle; Central Park Bike Tours (p244) and Toga Bike Shop (p244) offer rentals. A full ride of the Central Park loop is 6.2 miles long, and takes in hilly and flat terrain (the northern half being hillier than the south). Get more information and a park map at the Central Park Conservancy website (www.centralparknyc.org).

Best Places to Eat

- Absolute Bagels (p235)
- Cafe Luxembourg (p236)
- Awadh (p236)
- Jin Ramen (p235)
- Jacob's Pickles (p236)

For reviews, see p234 ➡

Best Places to Drink

- Dead Poet (p239)
- Empire Rooftop (p239)
- Prohibition (p241)
- Irving Farm Roasters (p239)

For reviews, see p239 ➡

Best Live Music Spots

- Metropolitan Opera House (p241)
- SummerStage (p242)
- Smoke (p242)
- Beacon Theatre (p242)

For reviews, see p241 ➡

T PHOTOGRAPHY/SHUTTERSTOCK ©

TOP EXPERIENCE
CENTRAL PARK

With more than 800 acres of picturesque meadows, ponds and woods, Central Park might seem to be Manhattan in its raw state. But the park, designed by Frederick Law Olmsted and Calvert Vaux, is the result of serious engineering: thousands of workers shifted 10 million cartloads of soil to transform swamp and rocky outcroppings into the 'people's park' of today.

Birth of a Park

In the 1850s, this area of Manhattan was occupied by pig farms, a garbage dump, a bone-boiling operation and an African American village. It took 20,000 laborers two decades to transform this terrain into a park. Today, Central Park has more than 24,000 trees, 136 acres of woodland, 21 playgrounds and seven bodies of water – and more than 38 million visitors a year.

Bethesda Terrace & the Mall

The arched walkways of **Bethesda Terrace** (66th to 72nd St; SB, C to 72nd St), crowned by the **Bethesda Fountain** (SB, C to 72nd St), at 72nd St, have long been a gathering area for New Yorkers. To the south is **the Mall** (Literary Walk; btwn 67th & 72nd Sts; 6am-1am; SN/R/W to 5th Ave-59th St), featured in countless movies, a promenade shrouded in mature North American elms. The southern stretch, known as **Literary Walk**, is flanked by statues of famous authors.

Central Park Zoo

This small **zoo** (Map p432; 212-439-6500; www.centralparkzoo.com; 64th St, at Fifth Ave; adult/child $20/15, without 4D Theater $14/9; 10am-5pm Mon-Fri, to 5:30 Sat & Sun Apr-Oct, 10am-4:30pm

DON'T MISS

- The Mall
- Jackie O Reservoir
- Bethesda Fountain
- Conservatory Garden

PRACTICALITIES

- Map p432, D5
- www.centralparknyc.org
- 59th to 110th Sts, btwn Central Park West & Fifth Ave
- 6am-1am
- SA/C, B/D to any stop btwn 59th St-Columbus Circle & Cathedral Pkwy (110th St)

Nov-Mar; ; S N/R to 5th Ave-59th St), which gained fame for its part in the DreamWorks animated movie *Madagascar,* is home to penguins, snow leopards and lemurs. Feeding times in the sea lion and penguin tanks make for a rowdy spectacle. The attached petting zoo, **Tisch Children's Zoo**, has alpacas and mini-Nubian goats and is perfect for small children.

Conservatory Water & Alice in Wonderland

North of the zoo (at 74th St) is Conservatory Water, where model sailboats drift and kids scramble about on a toadstool-studded *Alice in Wonderland* statue. There are Saturday story hours (www.hcastorycenter.org) at 11am from June to September at the Hans Christian Andersen statue, to the west of the water.

Great Lawn & the Ramble

The **Great Lawn** (Map p432; btwn 79th & 85th Sts; Apr-mid-Nov; S B, C to 86th St) is a massive emerald carpet at the center of the park, surrounded by ball fields and London plane trees. (It's where Simon & Garfunkel played their famous 1981 concert.) Immediately to the southeast is Delacorte Theater (p242), home to an annual Shakespeare in the Park festival, as well as Belvedere Castle (p244), a bird-watching lookout. Further south is the leafy **Ramble** (Map p432; btwn 73rd & 78th Sts; S B,C to 81st St-Museum of Natural History), a popular birding destination. On the southeastern end is the Loeb Boathouse (p244), home to a waterside restaurant that offers rowboat rentals and gondola rides.

Jacqueline Kennedy Onassis Reservoir

The reservoir (at 90th St) takes up almost the entire width of the park and serves as a gorgeous reflecting pool for the city skyline. It is surrounded by a 1.58-mile track that draws legions of joggers in the warmer months. Nearby, at Fifth Ave and 90th St, is a statue of New York City Marathon founder Fred Lebow, peering at his watch.

Strawberry Fields

This tear-shaped **garden** (Map p432; at W 72nd St; S C, B to 72nd St) serves as a memorial to former Beatle John Lennon, who lived directly across the street in the **Dakota Building** (Map p432; 1 W 72nd St, at Central Park West; S B, C to 72nd St) and was fatally shot there. The garden, which was partially funded by his widow Yoko Ono, is composed of a grove of stately elms and a tiled mosaic that reads, simply, 'Imagine.' Visitors can listen to an audioguide to Strawberry Fields, narrated by Yoko, at www.centralparknyc.org/imagine.

CONSERVATORY GARDEN

If you want a little peace and quiet (as in, no runners, cyclists or buskers), the 6-acre **Conservatory Garden** (Fifth Ave at E 105th St; S 6 to 103rd St) serves as one of the park's official quiet zones. And it's beautiful, to boot: bursting with crabapple trees, meandering boxwood and, in the spring, lots of flowers. Otherwise, you can catch maximum calm (and max birdlife) in all areas of the park just after dawn.

TAKE A BREAK

Consider packing a picnic from the assortment of gourmet goodies at Zabar's (p243) or **Eli's Essentials** (646-755-3999; www.elizabar.com/elis-essentials-.aspx; 1270 Madison Ave, at E 91st St; buffet per lb $16.95, sandwiches from $7.50; 7am-11pm; ; S 6 to 96th St), both a short hop from the park.

Inside the park you can dine alfresco at casual **Le Pain Quotidien** (www.lepainquotidien.com; Mineral Springs Pavilion, Central Park, off West Dr; mains $7.50-17; 7am-7pm, closes earlier winter; ; S B, C to 72nd St), or class things up a bit with a meal in the elegant Loeb Boathouse (p239).

Central Park

THE LUNGS OF NEW YORK

The rectangular patch of green that occupies Manhattan's heart began life in the mid-19th century as a swampy piece of land that was carefully bulldozed into the idyllic nature-scape you see today. Since officially becoming Central Park, it has brought New Yorkers of all stripes together in interesting and unexpected ways. The park has served as a place for the rich to show off their fancy carriages (1860s), for the poor to enjoy free Sunday concerts (1880s) and for activists to hold be-ins against the Vietnam War (1960s).

Since then, legions of locals – not to mention travelers from all kinds of faraway places – have poured in to stroll, picnic, sunbathe, play ball and catch free concerts and performances of works by Shakespeare.

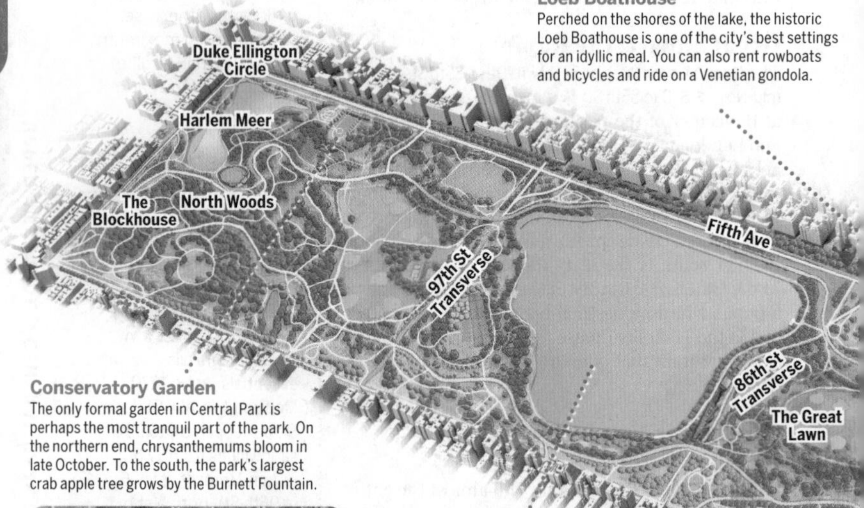

Loeb Boathouse
Perched on the shores of the lake, the historic Loeb Boathouse is one of the city's best settings for an idyllic meal. You can also rent rowboats and bicycles and ride on a Venetian gondola.

Conservatory Garden
The only formal garden in Central Park is perhaps the most tranquil part of the park. On the northern end, chrysanthemums bloom in late October. To the south, the park's largest crab apple tree grows by the Burnett Fountain.

STUDIOLASKA/SHUTTERSTOCK © FOUNTAIN SCULPTOR: BESSIE POTTER VONNOH

Jacqueline Kennedy Onassis Reservoir
This 106-acre body of water covers roughly an eighth of the park's territory. Its original purpose was to provide clean water for the city. Now it's a good spot to catch a glimpse of water birds.

LULU AND ISABELLE/SHUTTERSTOCK ©

Belvedere Castle
A so-called 'Victorian folly,' this Gothic-Romanesque castle serves no other purpose than to be a very dramatic lookout point. It was built by Central Park co-designer Calvert Vaux in 1869.

The park's varied terrain offers a wonderland of experiences. There are quiet, woodsy knolls in the north. To the south is the reservoir, crowded with joggers. There are European gardens, a zoo and various bodies of water. For maximum flamboyance, hit the Sheep Meadow on a sunny day, when all of New York shows up to lounge.

Central Park is more than just a green space. It is New York City's backyard.

FAST FACTS

- ➡ The landscape architects were Frederick Law Olmsted and Calvert Vaux.
- ➡ Construction commenced in 1858.
- ➡ The park covers 843 acres.
- ➡ Hundreds of movies have been shot on location, from Depression-era blockbuster *Gold Diggers* (1933) to monster-attack flick *Cloverfield* (2008).

Conservatory Water
This pond is popular in the warmer months, when children sail their model boats across its surface. Conservatory Water was inspired by 19th-century Parisian model-boat ponds and figured prominently in EB White's classic book, *Stuart Little*.

CHRISTOPHER PENLER/SHUTTERSTOCK ©

KRIDSADA KAMSOMBAT/SHUTTERSTOCK ©

Bethesda Fountain
This neoclassical fountain is one of New York's largest. It's capped by the *Angel of the Waters*, which is supported by four cherubim. The fountain was created by bohemian-feminist sculptor Emma Stebbins in 1868.

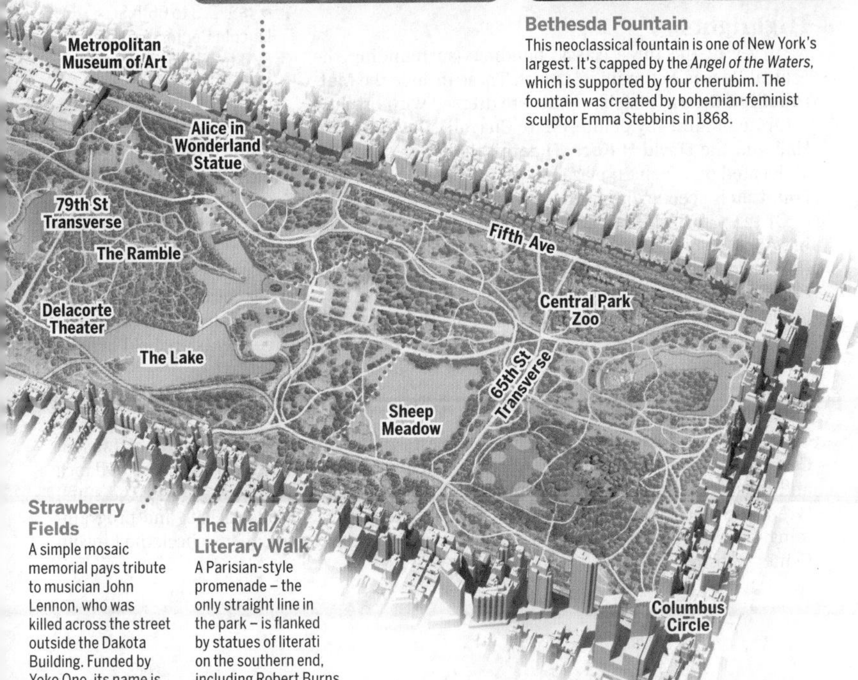

Strawberry Fields
A simple mosaic memorial pays tribute to musician John Lennon, who was killed across the street outside the Dakota Building. Funded by Yoko Ono, its name is inspired by the Beatles song 'Strawberry Fields Forever.'

The Mall/Literary Walk
A Parisian-style promenade – the only straight line in the park – is flanked by statues of literati on the southern end, including Robert Burns and Shakespeare. It is lined with rare North American elms.

TOP EXPERIENCE
LINCOLN CENTER

This stark arrangement of gleaming modernist temples contains some of Manhattan's most important performance spaces, home to the finest opera, ballet and symphony orchestra in New York City. Various other venues are tucked in and around the 16-acre campus, including two theaters, two film-screening centers and the world-renowned Juilliard School for performing arts.

A History of Building & Rebuilding

Built in the 1960s, this imposing arts campus replaced a neighborhood of tenements called San Juan Hill (gleefully bulldozed by urban planner Robert Moses), a predominantly African American neighborhood where the exterior shots for the movie *West Side Story* were filmed. In addition to being a controversial urban-planning move, Lincoln Center wasn't exactly well received at an architectural level – it was relentlessly criticized for its conservative design, fortresslike aspect and poor acoustics. For the center's 50th anniversary (2009–10), Diller Scofidio + Renfro and other architects gave the complex a much-needed and critically acclaimed freshening up.

Highlights

A survey of the three classic buildings surrounding the central Revson Fountain is a must. These include the **Metropolitan Opera** (its lobby walls are dressed with brightly saturated murals by painter Marc Chagall), **David Geffen Hall** and the **David H Koch Theater**, the latter designed by Philip Johnson. (These are all located on the main plaza at Columbus Ave, between 62nd and 65th Sts.) The **Revson Fountain** is spectacular in the evenings when it puts on Las Vegas–like water shows.

Of the refurbished structures, there are a number that are worth examining, including **Alice Tully Hall**, now displaying a very contemporary translucent, angled facade, and the **David Rubenstein Atrium** (Map p432; ☎212-721-6500; http://atrium.lincolncenter.org; 61 W 62nd St, at Broadway; ⏰atrium 8am-10pm Mon-Fri, from 9am Sat & Sun, box office noon-7pm Mon-Sat, to 5pm Sun; Ⓢ1 to 66th St-Lincoln Center), a public space behind the Empire Hotel offering a lounge area (with free wi-fi), a cafe and an information desk. Free events are held here on Thursday evenings, and this is also where Lincoln Center tours depart.

Performances & Screenings

On any given night, there are numerous performances happening throughout Lincoln Center – and even more in summer, when **Lincoln Center Out of Doors** (a series of dance and music concerts) and **Midsummer Night Swing** (ballroom dancing under the stars) lure those who love their culture alfresco. For details on seasons, tickets and programming – which runs the gamut from opera to dance to theater to ballet – check the Lincoln Center website.

DON'T MISS

- Revson Fountain
- Marc Chagall murals
- Attending a performance

PRACTICALITIES

- Map p432, B7
- ☎212-875-5456, tours 212-875-5350
- www.lincolncenter.org
- Columbus Ave, btwn W 62nd & 66th Sts
- tours adult/student $25/20
- ⏰tours 11:30am & 1:30pm Mon-Sat, 3pm Sun
- ♿
- Ⓢ1, 2, 3 to 66th St-Lincoln Center, A/C or B/D to 59th St-Columbus Circle

SIGHTS

The stretch of Manhattan west of Central Park was once a lively mix of African American, Latino and German Jewish immigrant communities. (This is where you'll find some of the best smoked fish in town.) In more recent decades, it has become a base for well-to-do artsy types, young professionals and the stroller set. While long stretches of Broadway are lined with charmless chain stores, the rest of the neighborhood is an architectural bonanza featuring beaux arts, baroque, neo-Gothic and postwar styles. Some of the poshest pads line Central Park West, among them the Dakota, where John Lennon once lived.

CENTRAL PARK — PARK

See p228.

LINCOLN CENTER — ARTS CENTER

See p232.

★NICHOLAS ROERICH MUSEUM — MUSEUM

Map p432 (☎212-864-7752; www.roerich.org; 319 W 107th St, btwn Riverside Dr & Broadway; ⊙noon-5pm Tue-Fri, from 2pm Sat & Sun; S1 to Cathedral Pkwy 110th St) FREE This compelling little museum, housed in a three-story town house from 1898, is one of Manhattan's best-kept secrets. It displays 150 paintings by the prolific Nicholas Konstantinovich Roerich (1874–1947), a Russian-born poet, philosopher and painter. His most remarkable works are his stunning depictions of the Himalayas, where he and his family settled in 1928. Indeed, his mountainscapes are truly a wonder to behold: icy Tibetan peaks in shades of blue, white, green and purple, channeling a Georgia O'Keeffe/Rockwell Kent vibe.

NEW-YORK HISTORICAL SOCIETY — MUSEUM

Map p432 (☎212-873-3400; www.nyhistory.org; 170 Central Park West, at W 77th St; adult/child $22/6, by donation 6-8pm Fri, library free; ⊙10am-6pm Tue-Thu & Sat, to 8pm Fri, 11am-5pm Sun; 👪; SB, C to 81st St-Museum of Natural History) As the antiquated hyphenated name implies, the Historical Society is the city's oldest museum, founded in 1804 to preserve historical and cultural artifacts. Its collection of more than 60,000 objects is quirky and fascinating and includes everything from George Washington's inauguration chair to a 19th-century Tiffany ice-cream dish (gilded, of course). However, it's far from stodgy, having moved into the 21st century with renewed vigor and purpose.

Redesigned with a sleek and modern aesthetic and an emphasis on interactive technology, the building houses several museums in one. The 4th floor is now occupied by the immersive Center for Women's History, the only one of its kind in a major American museum, part of the revamped Henry Luce III Center. Plus, there's a children's museum, lectures and other educational activities. An Oval Office replica is also on the cards, along with a new permanent exhibition dedicated to American presidents.

A few other notable treasures of the permanent collection include a leg brace worn by President Franklin D Roosevelt and photographer Jack Stewart's graffiti-covered door from the 1970s (featuring tags by known graffiti writers such as Tracy 168). In the lobby, be sure to look up: the ceiling mural from Keith Haring's 1986 'Pop Shop' hangs above the admissions desk.

RIVERSIDE PARK — PARK

Map p432 (www.riversideparknyc.org; Riverside Dr, btwn W 59th & 155th Sts; ⊙6am-1am; 👪; S1/2/3 to any stop btwn 72nd & 125th Sts) A classic beauty designed by Central Park creators Frederick Law Olmsted and Calvert Vaux, this waterside spot, running north on the Upper West Side and banked by the Hudson River from W 59th to 155th Sts, is lusciously leafy. Plenty of bike paths, playgrounds and dog runs make it a family favorite. Views from the park make the Jersey side of the Hudson look quite pretty.

From late March through October (weather permitting), lively waterside restaurant **West 79th Street Boat Basin Café** (Map p432; ☎212-496-5542; www.boatbasincafe.com; W 79th St, at Henry Hudson Parkway; mains $8-22; ⊙noon-11pm Apr-Oct, weather permitting; S1 to 79th St) serves a light menu at the level of 79th St. **Pier i Café** (Map p432; ☎212-362-4450; www.piericafe.com; at W 70th St & Riverside Blvd; mains $13-24; ⊙8am-midnight May-Oct; S1/2/3 to 72nd St), an outdoor cafe nine blocks south on the waterfront, is another option.

AMERICAN FOLK ART MUSEUM — MUSEUM

Map p432 (☎212-595-9533; www.folkartmuseum.org; 2 Lincoln Sq, Columbus Ave, btwn W 65th & 66th Sts; ⊙11:30am-7pm Tue-Thu & Sat, noon-7:30pm Fri, noon-6pm Sun; S1 to 66th St-Lincoln

TOP EXPERIENCE
AMERICAN MUSEUM OF NATURAL HISTORY

Founded in 1869, this classic museum contains a veritable wonderland of some 34 million artifacts, plus a cutting-edge planetarium. From October through May, it's home to the Butterfly Conservatory, featuring 500-plus butterflies from around the globe. Perhaps best known are its Fossil Halls containing nearly 600 specimens, including the skeletons of a massive mammoth and a fearsome *Tyrannosaurus rex*.

There are plentiful animal exhibits, galleries devoted to gems and an IMAX theater. The Hall of Ocean Life contains dioramas devoted to ecology and conservation, as well as a beloved 94ft replica of a blue whale suspended from the ceiling. At one entrance you're greeted by a 63ft, 19th-century canoe, carved by the Haida people of British Columbia.

For the space set, the Rose Center for Earth & Space is the star of the show. Its mesmerizing glass-box facade – home to space-show theaters and the planetarium – is an otherworldly setting. *Dark Universe*, narrated by Neil deGrasse Tyson and screening frequently, explores the mysteries and wonders of the cosmos.

The museum gets swamped on weekends. Aim to go early on a weekday.

DON'T MISS

- *Tyrannosaurus rex* (4th floor)
- Hall of Ocean Life (1st floor)
- Hayden Big Bang Theater (2nd floor)

PRACTICALITIES

- Map p432, C5
- ☎212-769-5100
- www.amnh.org
- Central Park West, at W 79th St
- suggested admission adult/child $23/13
- ⏱10am-5:45pm
- Ⓢ C to 81st St-Museum of Natural History; 1 to 79th St

Center) FREE This small institution offers rotating exhibitions in three small galleries. Past exhibits have included quilts made by 19th-century soldiers and sculptures by a celebrated Ghanaian coffin-maker of forts through which slaves were trafficked. The gift shop is a trove of unique, artsy items: books, jewelry, accessories, scarves, home decor etc. There's free music on Wednesdays (2pm) and Fridays (5:30pm).

STRAUS PARK PARK

Map p432 (www.nycgovparks.org; Broadway, btwn W 106th & 107th Sts; Ⓢ1 to 103rd or 110th Sts) This leafy little triangle is dedicated to the memory of Ida and Isidor Straus, a wealthy couple (Isidor owned Macy's) who died together in 1912 on the *Titanic*, when Ida insisted on staying with her husband instead of boarding a lifeboat. A curving granite exedra bears a fitting biblical quote: 'Lovely and pleasant were they in their lives and in their death they were not divided.'

CHILDREN'S MUSEUM OF MANHATTAN MUSEUM

Map p432 (☎212-721-1223; www.cmom.org; 212 W 83rd St, btwn Amsterdam Ave & Broadway; $15; ⏱10am-5pm Tue-Fri & Sun, to 7pm Sat; 👪; ⓈB, C to 81st St-Museum of Natural History, 1 to 86th St) This small museum features interactive exhibits scaled down for the 0 to 10-year-old set, including toddler discovery programs and exhibits that stimulate play, such as perennial favorites like the Talking Dragon, *Dora the Explorer*–themed rooms and an 8ft mural wall for fingerpainting. The outdoor seasonal *Dynamic H_2O* water exhibits shed light on NYC's aqueduct and watershed system.

EATING

Though not particularly a dining destination, this huge swath of Manhattan nonetheless manages to serve everything from old-style bagels to fancy French cassoulet to the latest in New American cooking. Broadway, Amsterdam Ave and Columbus Ave all have interesting indie neighborhood cafes and restaurants once you get a little north of Lincoln Center.

★ABSOLUTE BAGELS BAGELS $

Map p432 (2788 Broadway, btwn W 107th & 108th Sts; bagels from $1.25; ⏲6am-9pm; S1 to Cathedral Parkway 110th St) A bagel shop run by Thai immigrants might be puzzling to connoisseurs, but one thing's for sure: many folks – most of whom wait in a line down the block – agree this is the city's best. With a degree in look-away decor and appalling coffee, it's all about the bagels: heft and crunch on point, perfectly boiled and wonderfully satisfying.

★ÉPICERIE BOULUD DELI $

Map p432 (☎212-595-9606; www.epicerieboulud.com; 1900 Broadway, at W 64th St; sandwiches $8-14.50; ⏲7am-10pm Mon, to 11pm Tue-Sat, 8am-10pm Sun; 📶🥗; S1 to 66th St-Lincoln Center) A deli from star chef Daniel Boulud is no ordinary deli. Forget ham on rye – here you can order suckling pig confit, *jambon de Paris* and Gruyère on pressed ciabatta, or paprika-spiced flank steak with caramelized onions and three-grain mustard.

CAFE LALO DESSERTS $

Map p432 (☎212-496-6031; www.cafelalo.com; 201 W 83rd St, btwn Amsterdam & Columbus Aves; desserts $5-10; ⏲8am-1am Mon-Thu, to 4am Fri, 9am-4am Sat, to 2am Sun; S1 to 79th St, B, C to 81st St-Museum of Natural History) The vintage French posters and marble-topped tables make this longtime Upper West Side date spot feel like a Parisian cafe. But really – you're here for the mind-blowing array of desserts: choose (if you can) from over 30 different cakes, 23 flavors of cheesecake, 10 types of pie, a dozen kinds of fruit tart, cookies, pastries, zabaglione, chocolate mousse and more.

JIN RAMEN JAPANESE $

Map p432 (☎646-657-0755; www.jinramen.com; 462 Amsterdam Ave, btwn W 82nd & 83rd Sts; mains $13-19; ⏲lunch 11:30am-3:30pm, dinner 5-11pm Mon-Thu, to midnight Fri & Sat, to 10pm Sun; 🥗; S1 to 79th St) This buzzing little joint off Amsterdam Ave serves delectable bowls of piping hot ramen. *Tonkotsu* (pork broth) ramen is a favorite, though vegetarians also have tantalizing options. Don't neglect the appetizers: *shishito* peppers, pork buns and *hijiki* salad.

The mix of rustic wood elements, exposed bulbs and red industrial fixtures gives the place a cozy vibe.

SILVER MOON BAKERY BAKERY $

Map p432 (www.silvermoonbakery.com; 2740 Broadway, at W 105th St; pastries $4-6.50; ⏲7:30am-8pm Mon-Fri, 8am-7pm Sat & Sun; S1 to 103rd St) A small patisserie and boulangerie that brings a bit of Left Bank love to Morningside Heights. Folks line up in droves for the baked good and sweet treats of Judith Norell, who decided to hang up her harpsichord and flee to baking school in Paris before opening Silver Moon.

Some say her challah is New York's best (try the challah croissant) but her brioche, baguettes and muffins are famed far and wide as well (go for the Morning Glory muffin, made with apples, carrots, raisins, coconut, sunflower seeds and spices, among other tidbits). Sidewalk seating in suitable weather makes for a lazy morning.

HUMMUS PLACE MIDDLE EASTERN $

Map p432 (☎212-799-3335; www.hummusplace.com; 305 Amsterdam Ave, btwn W 74th & 75th Sts; mains $12.50-17; ⏲11am-10pm Mon-Fri, 10:30am-10:30pm Sat, 10:30am-10pm Sun; 🥗; S1/2/3 to 72nd St) Israeli-owned Hummus Place is cuter than its no-frills facade suggests; its eight tables tucked below street level front a cramped, open kitchen and pack in the crowds for sublime hummus platters, served warm and with various toppings – mushrooms, whole chickpeas, fava-bean stew with chopped egg.

You'll also find tasty salads, *shakshuka* and stuffed grape leaves.

PEACEFOOD CAFE VEGAN $

Map p432 (☎212-362-2266; www.peacefoodcafe.com; 460 Amsterdam Ave, at W 82nd St; mains $11-18; ⏲10am-10pm; 📶🥗; S1 to 79th St) This bright and airy vegan haven dishes up a popular fried seitan panini (served on homemade focaccia and topped with cashew cheese, arugula, tomatoes and pesto), as well as pizzas, roasted-vegetable plates and an excellent quinoa salad. There are daily raw specials, energy-fueling juices and rich desserts, plus a more substantial dinner menu served 5pm to 10pm.

GRAY'S PAPAYA HOT DOGS $

Map p432 (☎212-799-0243; www.grayspapayanyc.com; 2090 Broadway, at W 72nd St, entrance on Amsterdam Ave; hot dogs $2.95; ⏲24hr; S1/2/3, B, C to 72nd St) It doesn't get more New York than bellying up to this classic stand-up joint – founded by a former partner

1

RMBARRICARTE/GETTY IMAGES ©

2

4

EILEEN_10/SHUTTERSTOCK ©

1. Loeb Boathouse (p239)
Rent a rowboat after enjoying a fine meal at this lakeside restaurant in Central Park.

2. Lincoln Center (p232)
Home to some of New York's finest performing arts.

3. American Folk Art Museum (p233)
Fascinating exhibits showcasing the nation's folk-art journey through time.

4. American Museum of Natural History (p234)
Gape in awe at prehistoric beasts, a blue whale and even the mysterious cosmos at this wonderland for young and old.

PIO3/SHUTTERSTOCK ©

of crosstown rival Papaya King (p220) – in the wake of a beer bender. The lights are bright, the color palette is 1970s and the hot dogs are unpretentiously good.

JACOB'S PICKLES AMERICAN $$

Map p432 (212-470-5566; www.jacobspickles.com; 509 Amsterdam Ave, btwn W 84th & 85th Sts; mains $14-26; 10am-12:30am Mon & Tue, to 1:30am Wed, to 2am Thu & Fri, 9am-2am Sat, to 12:30am Sun; S1 to 86th St) Jacob's elevates the humble pickle to exalted status at this dark, loud and boisterous good-time eatery. Aside from briny cukes and other preserves, you'll find heaping portions of upscale comfort food, such as catfish tacos, buttermilk chicken and pancakes, and cheeseburger mac 'n' cheese.

The biscuits are top-notch. Two dozen or so draft craft beers showcase brews from coast to coast.

AWADH NORTH INDIAN $$

Map p432 (646-861-3241; www.awadhnyc.com; 2588 Broadway, btwn W 97th & 98th Sts; mains $13-26; 5-11pm Mon-Fri, noon-3pm & 5-11pm Sat & Sun; S1/2/3 to 96th St) This dark-toned, upscale North Indian gem harkens back to the culinary heritage of Lucknow and the cuisine of aristocratic Nawabs. Chef Gaurav Anand will transport you to the subcontinent with his transcendent *galouti* kebabs (melt-in-your-mouth minced lamb patties with spices, a Lucknow street-food legend) and anything cooked *dum phukt* style: meat and/or rice slow cooked inside a dough-sealed clay pot.

The results are stunning. Look no further than *Awadh gosht biryani,* a tender lamb and rice dish that is as good as anything this writer has ever had in Lucknow; and they are not afraid to light you up if you ask for 'Indian spicy.' Be sure to book in advance.

BLOSSOM ON COLUMBUS VEGAN $$

Map p432 (212-875-2600; www.blossomnyc.com; 507 Columbus Ave, btwn W 84th & 85th Sts; mains lunch $16-25, dinner $19-25; 11:30am-3:30pm & 5-9:45pm Mon-Sat, from 10:30am Sun; ; SB, C, 1 to 86th St) The elegantly modern surrounds at this vegan restaurant elevate the plant-based menu to a higher realm. Opt for something veggie-forward like the roasted red and yellow beet, chickpea and cranberry kale salad, or else go for something a bit, um, meatier – pan-seared seitan cutlets with white wine, lemon and capers.

BARNEY GREENGRASS DELI $$

Map p432 (212-724-4707; www.barneygreengrass.com; 541 Amsterdam Ave, at W 86th St; mains $5.25-28, fish platters $37-67; deli 8am-6pm Tue-Sun, cafe 8:30am-4pm Tue-Fri, to 5pm Sat & Sun; S1 to 86th St) The self-proclaimed 'King of Sturgeon,' Barney Greengrass serves the same heaping dishes of eggs and salty lox, luxuriant caviar and melt-in-your-mouth chocolate babkas that first made it famous when it opened over a century ago. Fuel up in the morning at casual tables amid the crowded produce counters, or take lunch at the serviced cafe in an adjoining room.

★CAFE LUXEMBOURG BRASSERIE $$$

Map p432 (212-873-7411; www.cafeluxembourg.com; 200 W 70th St, btwn Amsterdam & West End Aves; mains lunch $19-35, dinner $26-40; 8am-10pm Mon & Tue, to 11pm Wed-Fri, 9am-11pm Sat, to 10pm Sun; S1/2/3 to 72nd St) This quintessential French bistro is generally crowded with locals – and it's no mystery why: the setting is understatedly elegant, the staff genuinely friendly, and there's an outstanding menu to boot. The classics – steak tartare, *moules frites* (mussels and fries), seasonal roast chicken – are all deftly executed, and its proximity to Lincoln Center makes it a perfect pre-show destination.

BOULUD SUD MEDITERRANEAN $$$

Map p432 (212-595-1313; www.bouludsud.com; 20 W 64th St, btwn Broadway & Central Park West; 3-course prix fixe 5-7pm Mon-Sat $65, mains lunch $25-35, dinner $31-63; 11:30am-2:30pm & 5-11pm Mon-Fri, 11am-3pm & 5-11pm Sat, to 10pm Sun; ; S1 to 66th St-Lincoln Center) Pearwood paneling and a yellow-grey palette lend a 1960s *Mad Men* feel to Daniel Boulud's restaurant championing cuisines from the Mediterranean and North Africa. Dishes such as Moroccan tagines, spicy green shakshouka and Sardinian lemon saffron linguini emphasize seafood, vegetables and regional spices. Look out for specials, like the express lunch ($26), pretheater menu ($65) and happy pasta hour (50% off).

SMITH AMERICAN $$$

Map p432 (212-496-5700; https://thesmithrestaurant.com; 1900 Broadway, at W 63rd St; mains $18-47; 7:30am-midnight Mon-Thu, to 1am Fri, 9am-1am Sat, 9am-midnight Sun; ; S1 to 66th St-Lincoln Center, A/C, B/D to 59th St-Columbus Circle) On a restaurant-lined strip across from Lincoln Center, this always-buzzing bistro serves high-end comfort food with seasonal accents: grilled shrimp with quinoa tabbouleh, burgers with raclette and green peppercorn sauce, and short rib ragù are a few recent selections. There's also a raw bar and myriad drink selections. On warm days, there's open-air seating in front.

LAKESIDE RESTAURANT AT LOEB BOATHOUSE — AMERICAN $$$

Map p432 (212-517-2233; www.thecentralparkboathouse.com; Central Park Lake, Central Park, near E 74th St; mains lunch $26-38, dinner $30-46; restaurant noon-3:45pm Mon-Fri, from 9:30am Sat & Sun year-round, 5:30-9:30pm Mon-Fri, from 6pm Sat & Sun Apr-Nov; S B, C to 72nd St, 6 to 77th St) Perched on the northeastern tip of the Central Park Lake with views of the midtown skyline in the distance, the Loeb Boathouse provides one of New York's most idyllic spots for a meal. That said, you're paying for the setting. While the food is generally good (crab cakes are the standout; $21), the service can be indifferent.

If you want to experience the location without having to lay out the bucks, a better bet is to hit the adjacent open-air bar, where you can enjoy cocktails on the lake. In winter, the indoor bar area (to the left as you enter) is also a decent option for a drink with a view. The dour express cafe is set back from the lakeside windows but still has partial views.

DRINKING & NIGHTLIFE

As a historic family neighborhood, the Upper West Side isn't exactly the number-one destination for hard-core drinkers. Restaurants and cafes that morph into bars by night is more the style around here, though there's also a standout cocktail lounge and one of Manhattan's largest rooftop bars.

PLOWSHARES COFFEE — COFFEE

Map p432 (www.plowsharescoffee.com; 2730 Broadway, btwn W 104th & 105th Sts; 7am-7pm Mon-Fri, from 8am Sat & Sun; S 1 to 103rd St) Plowshares got in the specialty coffee game way back in 2008, when this small but exquisite espresso haven opened in the Bloomingdale district of the UWS. Your coffee is pulled from the Pagani of espresso machines: an $18,000 hand-built Slayer, of which just about as many exist as do the aforementioned made-to-order Italian car. A connoisseur's delight.

EMPIRE ROOFTOP — ROOFTOP BAR

Map p432 (www.empirehotelnyc.com; 44 W 63 St, at Broadway; 3pm-1am Mon-Wed, to 2am Thu & Fri, 11am-2am Sat, to 1am Sun; ; S 1 to 66th St-Lincoln Center) Sprawled across the top of the Empire Hotel, this stylish rooftop bar is one of New York's most expansive drinking spaces in the sky at 8000 sq ft. A bright, glass-roofed wing strewn with palms and sofas is perfect for winter and has a retractable roof for summer, and there's a handful of outdoor terraces.

IRVING FARM ROASTERS — COFFEE

Map p432 (www.irvingfarm.com; 224 W 79th St, btwn Broadway & Amsterdam Ave; 7am-9pm Mon-Fri, from 8am Sat & Sun; S 1 to 79th St) Tucked into a little ground-floor shop, the Upper West Side branch of this popular local coffee chain is bigger on the inside – beyond the coffee counter the space opens up into a backroom with a sunny skylight. Enjoy a menu of light meals along with your freshly pulled espresso or on-tap cold brew. No wi-fi.

OWL'S TAIL — COCKTAIL BAR

Map p432 (www.owlstail.com; 215 W 75th St, btwn Broadway & Amsterdam Ave; 4:30pm-1am Mon-Thu, 4pm-2am Fri, 11:30am-2am Sat, 11:30am-1am Sun; ; S 1/2/3 to 72nd St) A snazzy neighborhood cocktail bar that feels more downtown than UWS with its cozy banquet sofa seating, tiled flooring and industrially bent lighting. Owl art, from Northwest Coast style to wooden carvings to a stupendous mural, pepper the place. The highly social L-shaped bar is your perfect perch for popular beat-the-heat cocktails like Bicycle Thief (Campari, gin, grapefruit, lemon, simple syrup and seltzer).

DEAD POET — BAR

Map p432 (www.thedeadpoet.com; 450 Amsterdam Ave, btwn W 81st & 82nd Sts; noon-4am; ; S 1 to 79th St) This narrow, mahogany-paneled pub is a neighborhood favorite. It takes its Guinness pours seriously, and features cocktails named after deceased masters of verse, including a Walt Whitman Long Island Iced Tea ($14) and a Pablo

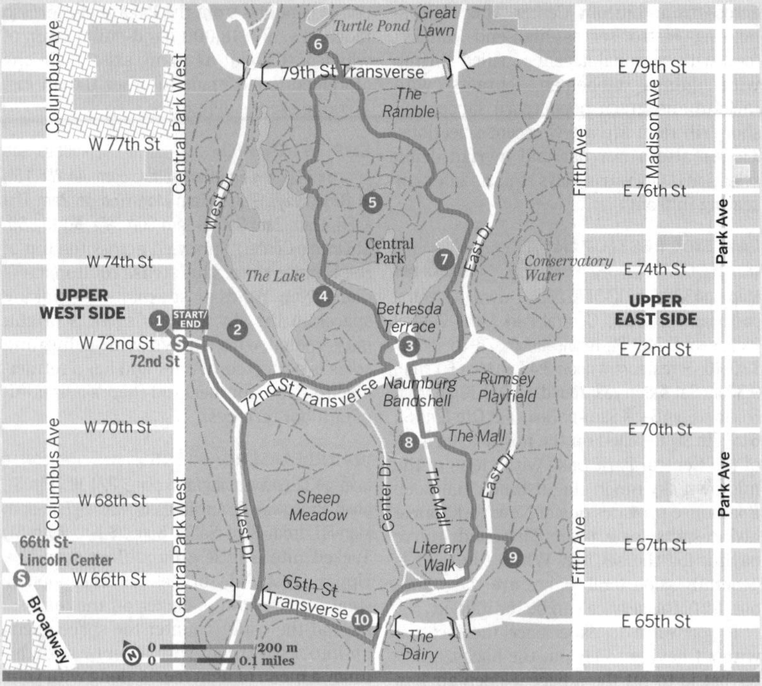

Neighborhood Walk
A Walk in the Park

START DAKOTA BUILDING
END DAKOTA BUILDING
LENGTH 2.5 MILES; TWO HOURS

Central Park is arguably the world's most famous green space, a storied work of urban beauty that clocks in at 843 acres spanning 51 NYC blocks. In a word, it's huge. Consider this stroll through the park as a brief, family-friendly intro – numerous museums and attractions warrant detours.

Enter the park at W 72st St in front of the 1 **Dakota Building** (p229) – it was here that Beatles frontman John Lennon both lived and died (he was assassinated out front in 1980). His iconic memorial sits across the street just beyond the park entrance at 2 **Strawberry Fields** (p229), a rite of pilgrimage for all who appreciate Lennon's cultural and musical impact. Continue about 0.4 miles into the park's center to the neoclassical 3 **Bethesda Fountain** (p228); dating to 1868, it's one of the park's most photographed destinations and a popular meeting point. Head north following the lakeshore – crossing the park's longest bridge, the cast-iron 4 **Bow Bridge** along the way – to reach the 5 **Ramble** (p229), Central Park's leafy 38-acre wooded thicket.

North of the Ramble is 6 **Belvedere Castle** (p244), a 19th-century castle with a bird-watching deck. Feeling peckish? Turn back for 0.3 miles south toward the lake, where the 7 **Loeb Boathouse** (p239) awaits for refueling. Continuing south for another 0.3 miles brings you to 8 **the Mall** (p228), a promenade flanked by a Literary Walk on the southern end. Continue south yet again, this time for around 0.2 miles to the 9 **Balto Statue**. A favorite with kids, this bronze statue immortalizes a heroic dog that woofed it 674 miles to deliver medicine during a 1925 diphtheria outbreak in Alaska. Continuing south still to the 10 **Central Park Carousel**, which has been twirling adults and kids alike since 1871 (though not the same model) – you'll hear its Wurlitzer rolls from a distance. Head back north toward the Dakota the same way you came in – with music on your mind.

Neruda spiced-rum sangria ($13). Feeling adventurous? Order the signature cocktail ($15), a secret recipe of seven alcohols – you even get to keep the glass.

GEBHARD'S BEER CULTURE
CRAFT BEER

Map p432 (www.beerculture.nyc/gebhards; 228 W 72nd St, btwn West End Ave & Broadway; ⏲4pm-2am Mon, from 11:30am Tue-Sun; Ⓢ1/2/3 to 72nd St) One of two locations in the city (the other is Hell's Kitchen), cozy Gebhard's is one of the most serious hophead havens on the Upper West Side. You'll find 16 taps of New York–heavy craft, but brews can flow from anywhere from California to Canada. Wash it all down with burgers, tacos, hot dogs and other alcohol-absorbing pub grub.

PROHIBITION
BAR

Map p432 (www.prohibition.net; 503 Columbus Ave, btwn W 84th & 85th Sts; ⏲4:30pm-2am Sun-Thu, to 3:30am Fri & Sat; 📶; ⓈB, C to 86th St) This buzzing drinking den features a live band every night on the front-room stage, though decibel levels are low enough that your ears won't bleed. The back room is band-free (though it's piped in via CCTV); for those who prefer a little action, there's a billiard table.

☆ ENTERTAINMENT

★METROPOLITAN OPERA HOUSE
OPERA

Map p432 (☎tickets 212-362-6000, tours 212-769-7028; www.metopera.org; Lincoln Center, Columbus Ave at W 64th St; tickets $25-480; ⏲box office 10am-10pm Mon-Sat, noon-6pm Sun; Ⓢ1 to 66th St-Lincoln Center) New York's premier opera company is the place to see classics such as *La Boheme, Madame Butterfly* and *Macbeth*. It also hosts premieres and revivals of more contemporary works, such as John Adams' *The Death of Klinghoffer*. The season runs from September to May. Tickets start at $25 and can get close to $500.

Note that the box seats can be a bargain, but unless you're in boxes right over the stage, the views are dreadful: seeing the stage requires sitting with your head cocked over a handrail – a literal pain in the neck.

For last-minute ticket buyers there are other deals. You can get bargain-priced standing-room tickets (from $20 to $30) from 10am on the day of the performance. (You won't see much, but you'll hear everything.) Monday through Friday at noon and Saturdays at 2pm, a number of rush tickets are put on sale for starving-artist types – just $25 for a seat; these are available online only. Matinee tickets go on sale four hours before curtain.

Don't miss the gift shop, which is full of operatic knickknacks (like binoculars), and an extensive collection of classical music – many from past Met performances.

For a behind-the-scenes look, the **Met Opera Guild** (www.metguild.org) runs guided tours ($30) weekdays at 3pm and Sundays at 10:30am and 1:30pm during the performance season.

The 2016–17 season marked the 50th anniversary of the Met's home in Lincoln Center.

★NEW YORK CITY BALLET
DANCE

Map p432 (☎212-496-0600; www.nycballet.com; Lincoln Center, Columbus Ave at W 63rd St; tickets $39 to $204; ⏲box office 10am-7:30pm Mon, to 8:30pm Tue-Sat, 4:30am-7:30pm Sun; 👪; Ⓢ1 to 66th St-Lincoln Center) This prestigious company was first directed by renowned Russian-born choreographer George Balanchine in the 1940s. Today, it's the largest ballet organization in the US, performing 23 weeks a year at Lincoln Center's David H Koch Theater. Rush tickets for those under age 30 are $30. During the holidays the troupe is best known for its annual production of *The Nutcracker* (tickets go on sale in September: book early).

FILM AT LINCOLN CENTER
CINEMA

Map p432 (☎212-875-5610; www.filmlinc.com; W 65th St, Lincoln Center, btwn Broadway & Amsterdam Ave; Ⓢ1 to 66th St-Lincoln Center) Film at Lincoln Center is one of New York's cinematic gems, providing an invaluable platform for a wide gamut of documentary, feature, independent, foreign and avant-garde art pictures. Films screen in one of two facilities at Lincoln Center: the **Elinor Bunin Munroe Film Center** (☎box office 212-875-5232; adult/student $15/12), a more intimate, experimental venue, or the **Walter Reade Theater** (☎212-875-5601), with wonderfully wide, screening-room-style seats.

AMERICAN BALLET THEATRE
DANCE

Map p432 (☎212-477-3030; www.abt.org; Lincoln Center, David H Koch Theater, W 64th St, at Columbus Ave; Ⓢ1 to 66th St-Lincoln Center) Founded

SUMMER HAPPENINGS IN CENTRAL PARK

During the warm months, Central Park is home to countless cultural events, many of which are free. The two most popular are **Shakespeare in the Park** (www.publictheater.org/free-shakespeare-in-the-park; Jun-Aug; S A/B/C to 81st St-Museum of Natural History), which is managed by the Public Theater, and **SummerStage** (www.cityparksfoundation.org/summerstage; Rumsey Playfield, Central Park, access via Fifth Ave & 69th St; May-Oct; ; S 6 to 68th St-Hunter College), a series of free concerts.

Tickets for Shakespeare in the Park are given out at noon on the day of the performance, but if you want to be sure of getting a seat, line up by 8am and make sure you have something to sit on, and your entire group with you. Tickets are free and there's only two per person; no latecomers are allowed in line. Note that you also need to register for a free Public Theater Patron ID and show it to qualify for the free tickets; apply online at www.publictheater.org.

SummerStage concert venues are generally opened to the public 1½ hours prior to the start of the show. But if it's a popular act, start queuing up early or you won't get in.

in 1937, this traveling company presents a classic selection of ballets at the Metropolitan Opera House every spring (generally in May), with a shorter season at the David H Koch Theater in the fall.

NEW YORK PHILHARMONIC CLASSICAL MUSIC

Map p432 (212-875-5656; www.nyphil.org; Lincoln Center, Columbus Ave at W 65th St; tickets $29-125; ; S 1 to 66 St-Lincoln Center) The oldest professional orchestra in the US (dating to 1842) holds its season every year at David Geffen Hall; music director Jaap van Zweden took over from Alan Gilbert in 2017. The orchestra plays a mix of classics (Tchaikovsky, Mahler, Haydn) and contemporary works, as well as concerts for children.

If you're on a budget, check out the open rehearsals held several times a month (starting at 9:45am) on the day of the concert for only $22. In addition, students with a valid school ID can pick up rush tickets for $21.50 to $23.50 online before some events; check the website for options.

DELACORTE THEATER THEATER

Map p432 (www.publictheater.org; Central Park, enter at W 81st St; S B, C to 81st St-Museum of Natural History) Every summer the Public Theater (p102) heads here to present its fabulous free productions of Shakespeare in the Park, which founder Joseph Papp began back in 1954, before the lovely, leafy, open-air theater was even built. Productions are usually superb and it's a magical experience: waiting in line for tickets is a rite of passage for newcomers to the city.

BEACON THEATRE LIVE MUSIC

Map p432 (212-465-6500; www.beacontheatre.com; 2124 Broadway, btwn W 74th & 75th Sts; box office 11am-7pm Mon-Sat; S 1/2/3 to 72nd St) This historic 1928 theater is a perfect medium-size venue with 2829 seats (not a terrible one in the house) and a constant flow of popular acts from ZZ Top to Bob Dylan (plus comedians like Jerry Seinfeld and Patton Oswalt). A 2009 restoration left the gilded interiors – a mix of Greek, Roman, Renaissance and rococo design elements – totally sparkling.

SMOKE JAZZ

Map p432 (212-864-6662; www.smokejazz.com; 2751 Broadway, btwn W 105th & 106th Sts; 5:30pm-3am Mon-Sat, from 11am Sun; S 1 to 103rd St) This swank but laid-back lounge – with good stage views from plush sofas – brings out old-timers and local faves, such as George Coleman and Wynton Marsalis. Covers cost $15 to $40 plus dinner (the bar seats run at a $20 minimum spend). Purchase tickets online for weekend shows.

Late nights Wednesday to Sunday you can stop by for free shows (no cover but $20 minimum applies) that kick off at midnight.

SHOPPING

The lower stretch of Broadway that runs through the Upper West Side has been colonized by chain stores; instead, head further north for more interestiunique shopping stops, especially on and around Columbus Ave.

★ **ZABAR'S** FOOD

Map p432 (☎212-787-2000; www.zabars.com; 2245 Broadway, at W 80th St; ⏰8am-7:30pm Mon-Fri, to 8pm Sat, 9am-6pm Sun; S1 to 79th St) A bastion of gourmet kosher foodie-ism, this sprawling local market has been a neighborhood fixture since the 1930s. And what a fixture it is! It features a heavenly array of cheeses, meats, olives, caviar, smoked fish, pickles, dried fruits, nuts and baked goods, including pillowy, fresh-out-of-the-oven *knishes* (Eastern European–style potato dumplings wrapped in dough; $3).

With cramped and crowded aisles, the shopping experience can feel like a bit of a scrum. Grab a number at the specialty counters upon entering – the wait can be long. Upstairs is an entire floor of oft-overlooked houseware products and next door is a sit-down cafe.

T2 TEA

Map p432 (☎646-998-5010; www.t2tea.com; 188 Columbus Ave, btwn W 68th & 69th Sts; ⏰11am-7pm; S1 to 66th St-Lincoln Center, B, C to 72nd St) Aficionados of the brewed leaf will find more than 150 varieties at this outpost of an Australian tea company: oolong, green, black, yellow, herbals, you name it. But you don't just have to go by smell – the staff will brew samples of anything you care to try on the spot. It also carries a selection of tea-related gifts.

ICON STYLE VINTAGE

Map p432 (☎212-799-0029; www.iconstyle.net; 104 W 70th St, near Columbus Ave; ⏰11am-8pm Tue-Fri, to 7pm Sat, noon-6pm Sun; S1/2/3 to 72nd St) This tiny gem of a vintage shop specializes in antique fine and costume jewelry dating from the 1700s to 1970s, but also stocks carefully curated dresses, gloves, bags and hats. Half of the shop is covered in strikingly restored apothecary units, with the goods displayed in open drawers. Stop by and indulge your inner Grace Kelly.

BOOK CULTURE BOOKS

Map p432 (☎212-595-1962; www.bookculture.com; 450 Columbus Ave, btwn W 81st & 82nd Sts; ⏰9am-10pm Mon-Sat, to 8pm Sun; 👪; SB, C to 81st St-Museum of Natural History) The warm aesthetic and friendliness of this neighborhood bookstore belies its size and selection. It caters not just to literary types but to gift hunters looking for mod backpacks, design-oriented homewares, NYC-themed items and fancy stationery. Parents flock to the large downstairs kids' space, which hosts regular story-time sessions in several languages (check the website for times).

MAGPIE ARTS & CRAFTS

Map p432 (www.magpienewyork.com; 488 Amsterdam Ave, btwn W 83rd & 84th Sts; ⏰11am-7pm Mon-Sat, to 6pm Sun; S1 to 86th St) 🍃 This charming little shop carries a wide range of ecofriendly objects: elegant stationery, beeswax candles, hand-painted mugs, organic-cotton scarves, recycled-resin necklaces, hand-dyed felt journals and wooden earth puzzles are a few things that may catch your eye. Most products are fair-trade, made of sustainable materials or locally designed and made.

WEST SIDE KIDS TOYS

Map p432 (www.westsidekidsnyc.com; 498 Amsterdam Ave, at W 84th St; ⏰11am-7pm Mon-Thu, from 10am Fri & Sat, 11am-6pm Sun; S1 to 86th St) A great place to pick up a gift for that little someone special, no matter their age. In stock are lots of hands-on activities and fun educational games, as well as puzzles, mini musical instruments, science kits, magic sets, old-fashioned wooden trains and New York–themed kids' books.

GRAND BAZAAR NYC MARKET

Map p432 (☎212-239-3025; www.grandbazaarnyc.org; 100 W 77th St, near Columbus Ave; ⏰10am-5:30pm Sun; SB, C to 81st St-Museum of Natural History, 1 to 79th St) One of the oldest open-air shopping spots in the city, browsing this friendly, well-stocked flea market is a perfect activity for a lazy Upper West Side Sunday morning. You'll find a bit of everything here, including vintage and contemporary furnishings, antique maps, custom eyewear, hand-woven scarves and more.

WESTSIDER RECORDS MUSIC

Map p432 (☎212-874-1588; www.westsiderbooks.com; 233 W 72nd St, btwn Broadway & West End Ave; ⏰11am-7pm Mon-Thu, to 9pm Fri & Sat, noon-6pm Sun; S1/2/3 to 72nd St) Featuring more than 30,000 LPs, this shop has got you covered when it comes to everything from funk to jazz to classical, plus opera, musical theater, spoken word, film soundtracks and other curiosities. (Don't miss the $1 bins up front.) It's a good place to lose all track of time – as is its **bookstore** (Map p432; ☎212-362-0706; 2246 Broadway, btwn W 80th & 81st Sts; ⏰10am-9pm; S1 to 79th St) further uptown.

🏃 SPORTS & ACTIVITIES

CENTRAL PARK BIKE TOURS
CYCLING

Map p432 (☑212-541-8759; www.centralpark biketours.com; 203 W 58th St, btwn Broadway & 7th Ave; bike rentals per hour/day adult from \$10.50/28, child \$9/23; ⊙8am-8pm; 🖪; ⑤1/2/3 to 59th St-Columbus Circle) The official bike-rental outfitter of NYC Parks has over 3000 bikes in 12 locations around the city (you can't miss their green-shirted touts around the edges of the park). This outlet is one of two along 58th St just south of the park. Two-hour guided tours of the park (\$30) are also offered. Helmet and bike locks are included in the rates.

WOLLMAN SKATING RINK
SKATING

Map p432 (☑212-439-6900; www.wollmanskating rink.com; Central Park, btwn E 62nd & 63rd Sts; adult Mon-Thu \$12, Fri-Sun \$19, child \$6, skate rentals \$10; ⊙10am-2:30pm Mon & Tue, to 10pm Wed & Thu, to 11pm Fri & Sat, to 9pm Sun late Oct-early Apr; 🖪; ⑤F to 57 St, N/R/W to 5th Ave-59th St) This rink is much larger than the Rockefeller Center skating rink (p210), and not only does it allow all-day skating but its position at the southeastern edge of Central Park also offers magical views. There's locker rental for \$5 and a spectator fee of \$5. Cash only.

BELVEDERE CASTLE
BIRDWATCHING

Map p432 (☑646-790-4833; www.central parknyc.org; Central Park, at W 79th St; ⊙9am-7pm mid-Jun–mid-Aug, 10am-5pm mid-Aug–mid-Jun; 🖪; ⑤1/2/3, B, C to 72nd St) For a DIY birding expedition with kids, borrow a 'Discovery Kit' at Belvedere Castle in Central Park, which comes with binoculars, a bird book, colored pencils and paper – a perfect way to get the kids excited about birds. Picture ID is required.

LOEB BOATHOUSE
BOATING

Map p432 (☑212-517-2233; www.thecentralpark boathouse.com; Central Park, btwn 74th & 75th Sts; boating per hour \$15, each additional 15min \$3; ⊙10am-7pm; 🖪; ⑤B, C to 72nd St, 6 to 77th St) Central Park's boathouse has a fleet of 100 rowboats, as well as a Venetian-style gondola that you can reserve for up to six people if you'd rather someone else do the paddling (\$45 for 30 minutes, reserved with the restaurant itself). Rentals include life jackets and require ID and a \$20 deposit. Cash only.

Rentals are weather permitting and available virtually all year as long as the temperature is above about 50°F (10°C).

TOGA BIKE SHOP
CYCLING

Map p432 (☑212-799-9625; www.togabikes.com; 110 West End Ave, btwn W 64th & 65th Sts; rentals per 24hr hybrid/road bike \$35/150; ⊙11am-7pm Mon-Wed & Fri, to 8pm Thu, 10am-6pm Sat, 11am-6pm Sun; ⑤1 to 66th St-Lincoln Center) This friendly, long-standing bike shop is conveniently located right next to the Hudson River bike path (and only a few blocks from Central Park) and rents out both hybrid and road models (but no children's bikes). Rental prices include a helmet.

Harlem & Upper Manhattan

MORNINGSIDE HEIGHTS | HARLEM | EAST HARLEM | HAMILTON HEIGHTS & SUGAR HILL | WASHINGTON HEIGHTS & INWOOD | HAMILTON HEIGHTS | INWOOD

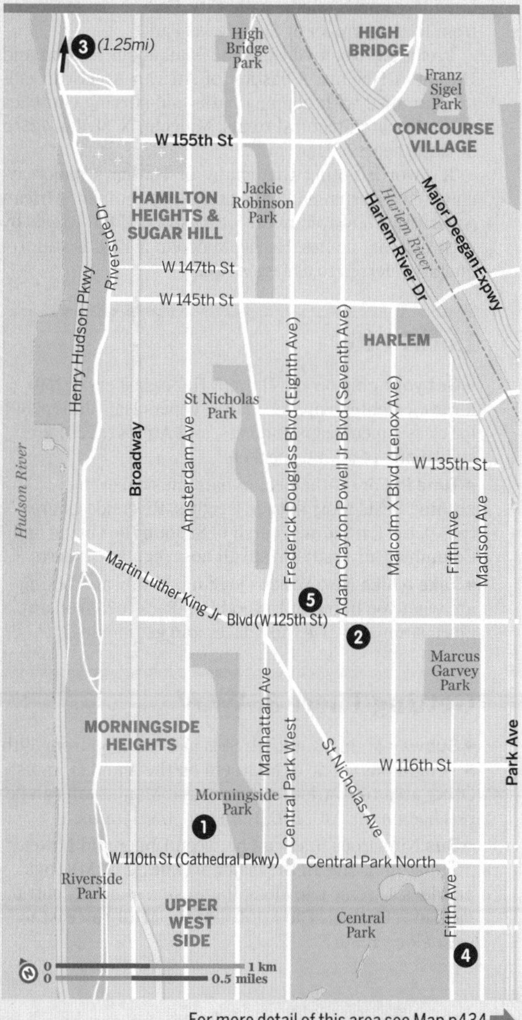

For more detail of this area see Map p434

Neighborhood Top Five

1 Cathedral Church of St John the Divine (p247) Exploring the fine artistry and hidden treasures inside the gloriously epic yet still-unfinished St John the Divine, the largest house of worship in the US.

2 Studio Museum in Harlem (p249) Seeing the world through African American eyes at this small but thoughtfully curated museum.

3 Met Cloisters (p252) Taking a fantastical journey into the Middle Ages at this monastic reconstruction, replete with Flemish tapestries and other medieval masterpieces.

4 El Museo del Barrio (p251) Catching cutting-edge exhibitions from the Latin American diaspora in East Harlem.

5 Apollo Theater (p250) Joining the celebratory crowds at this venerable concert hall in the heart of Harlem.

Lonely Planet's Top Tip

Manhattan's uptown communities tend to be locally minded, with bars, restaurants and shops catering to a neighborhood crowd. These establishments tend to be sleepiest on weekday mornings and liveliest in the evenings and on weekends.

To make the most of your visit, hit one of the museums or historic sights in the afternoon, then stick around for dinner when these areas come to life.

Best Places to Eat

- Red Rooster (p256)
- Seasoned Vegan (p255)
- Dinosaur Bar-B-Que (p255)
- Sylvia's (p255)
- BLVD Bistro (p255)

For reviews, see p253

Best Places to Drink

- Silvana (p258)
- Shrine (p258)
- 67 Orange St (p258)
- Ginny's Supper Club (p258)

For reviews, see p258

Best Live Jazz

- Marjorie Eliot's Parlor Jazz (p258)
- Apollo Theater (p250)
- Ginny's Supper Club (p258)

For reviews, see p258

Explore Harlem & Upper Manhattan

The top half of Manhattan is a lot of territory to cover, with many points of interest a distance away from one another and no subways to take you across town (the bus is an option). So pick a neighborhood (or, better yet, a couple of contiguous neighborhoods) and stick to it. If you like your cities to feel a little bit country, then head to Inwood, which has parks with Hudson River views and a spectacular museum (p252). Work your way down the West Side to the gargantuan Cathedral Church of St John the Divine and the environs of Columbia University (p250), where academics roam. The university's massive new Manhattanville campus, along with City College, is separated from Harlem proper by St Nicholas Park.

Prefer an urban vibe? Then it's all about Harlem and Hamilton Heights, a bastion of African American culture jammed with hopping bars, soul-stirring churches and a few architectural treats. Malcolm X Blvd at 125th St is the heart of Harlem.

It's worth noting that many of Harlem's major avenues have been renamed in honor of prominent African Americans; however, many locals still call the streets by their original names. Hence, Malcolm X Blvd is still frequently referred to as Lenox Ave.

Local Life

- **Get your chic on** Hit Harlem Haberdashery (p259) for eye-catching apparel, Flamekeepers Hat Club (p259) for classic men's caps and hats, and Atmos (p259) for stylish one-of-a-kind sneakers.
- **Tune in** For off-the-beaten-path musical events, nothing beats Morningside Heights. Riverside Church (p251), the Cathedral Church of St John the Divine and Columbia University (p250) all host regular concerts.
- **Take a hike** New Yorkers jogging, hiking and biking are what you'll find at Inwood Hill Park (p253) on any given sunny day. Tie those laces and get moving.

Getting There & Away

- **Subway** Main drag 125th St is just one stop from 59th St–Columbus Circle in Midtown on the A and D trains. Other areas of Harlem and northern Manhattan can be reached on the A/C, B/D, 1/2/3 and 4/5/6 trains.
- **Bus** Numerous lines run between Upper and Lower Manhattan along all the major avenues. The M10 bus provides a scenic trip along the western side of Central Park into Harlem. The M100 and the M101 run east to west along 125th St.

FELIX LIPOV/SHUTTERSTOCK ©

TOP EXPERIENCE

CATHEDRAL CHURCH OF ST JOHN THE DIVINE

The largest place of worship in America has yet to be completed – and probably won't be anytime soon. But this glorious Episcopal cathedral nonetheless commands attention with its ornate Gothic-style facade, booming vintage organ and extravagantly scaled nave – twice as wide as London's Westminster Abbey.

Visiting the Cathedral

Hour-long Highlight Tours are offered at 11am and 1pm Monday through Friday, and 11am Saturday. One-hour Vertical Tours take you on a steep climb to the top of the cathedral (bring a flashlight) at 10am Monday, noon on Wednesday and Friday, and noon and 2pm on Saturday. Two services worth experiencing are the Blessing of the Animals, a pet-owner pilgrimage held on the first Sunday of October; and the Blessing of the Bikes, which takes place on a Saturday in mid- to late April – local roll in on everything from slick road bikes to chill beach cruisers.

Keith Haring Triptych

Behind the choir is the white-gold and bronze triptych *Life of Christ*, carved by '80s pop artist Keith Haring (1958–90). It's one of the last works of art he produced prior to succumbing to an AIDS-related illness aged 31.

DON'T MISS

- Portal sculptures
- Great Rose Window
- Great Organ
- Keith Haring Triptych

PRACTICALITIES

- Map p434, B6
- ☎tours 212-316-7540
- www.stjohndivine.org
- 1047 Amsterdam Ave, at W 112th St, Morningside Heights
- adult/student $10/8, highlights tour $15, vertical tour $20/18
- ⏲9am-5pm Mon-Sat, 12:30-2:30pm Sun
- Ⓢ B/C, 1 to 110th St-Cathedral Pkwy

Great Organ

The cathedral's Great Organ – one of the world's most powerful – was originally installed in 1911. It was expanded in 1952 and now contains 8500 pipes arranged in 141 ranks. A

2001 fire damaged the instrument, but a five-year restoration resurrected it.

The Nave

Illuminated by the Great Rose Window (America's largest stained-glass window), the nave is lined with two magisterial sets of 17th-century tapestries. The Barberini Tapestries depict scenes from Christ's life, while the Mortlake Tapestries, based on cartoons by Raphael, show the Acts of the Apostles.

The Portal Sculptures

Two rows of sculptures carved in the 1980s and '90s by British artist Simon Verity frame the cathedral's western entrance. Its central pillar features St John the Divine himself, who penned the Book of Revelation; you'll see the Four Horsemen of the Apocalypse beneath his feet. Depictions of devastation abound – among the most frightful is a statue of Jeremiah, third on the right, on a base that portrays the New York City skyline – Twin Towers included – being destroyed.

An Unfinished History

The first cornerstone for the cathedral was laid on St John's Day in 1892, but construction was hardly smooth. Engineers had to dig 70ft in order to find bedrock to which they could anchor the building. Architects died or were fired, and in 1911, the initial Romanesque design was exchanged for a bigger, Gothic-inspired plan.

Depleted funds have seen construction regularly halted. The north tower remains unbuilt, and a 'temporary' domed roof, constructed out of terracotta tile in 1909, still rises above the epicenter of the church. A raging fire in 2001 caused significant damage, including to the north transept, which is yet to be rebuilt.

If it is ever completed, the 601ft-long cathedral will rank as the world's third-largest church, behind Rome's St Peter's Basilica and Côte d'Ivoire's Basilica of Our Lady of Peace at Yamoussoukro.

CIVIL RIGHTS

The cathedral was involved in the Civil Rights movement as far back as the early 1950s and has regularly worked with members of the community on issues of inequity. It is also a long-running cultural outpost, hosting holiday concerts, lectures and exhibits, and it has been the site of memorial services for many famous New Yorkers, including trumpeter Louis Armstrong, poet and activist Audre Lorde, and artist Keith Haring.

TAKE A BREAK

Join the Columbia University student crowd for delicious American fare at Community Food & Juice (p253).

Hit the well-loved **Tom's Restaurant** (Map p434; ☎212-864-6137; www.tomsrestaurant.net; 2880 Broadway, at 112th St; mains $10-15, sandwiches $6-9.50; ⏰7am-1am Tue-Thu, 24hr Fri-Mon; 📶; Ⓢ1 to 110th St) for diner food.

STUDIO MUSEUM HARLEM
MISSION
The Studio Museum in Harlem is the nexus for artists of African descent locally, nationally and internationally and for work that has been inspired and influenced by black culture. It is a site for the dynamic exchange of ideas about art and society.

JEFFREY ISAAC GREENBERG 3/ALAMY STOCK PHOTO ©

TOP EXPERIENCE
STUDIO MUSEUM IN HARLEM

For more than 40 years, this treasured museum has showcased influential African American artists. Yet it's not just another art display center – it is a significant point of connection for a breadth of Harlem cultural figures, who enjoy a rotating selection of exhibitions, film screenings, gallery talks and more.

Collecting African American Artists

The permanent collection is small (just under 2000 objects), but it is rich. The Studio Museum has been an important patron to African American artists, and the collection features work by more than 400 of them. This includes important pieces by painter Jacob Lawrence, photographer Gordon Parks and collagist Romare Bearden – all of whom are represented in major museum collections in the US. Additional works include those by a new generation of artists, such as Nigeria-born Njideka Akunyili Crosby, who was awarded a MacArthur Genius Award in 2017 for her large-scale collage and photo transfer-based paintings that navigate the cultural complexities of the transnational experience.

A New Beginning

The current museum is being dismantled to make way for a new building, which is scheduled to emerge on the present location in 2021. The museum's temporary programming space, Studio Museum 127, is located at 429 W 127th St between Amsterdam and Convent Aves. Hours are Thursday through Sunday from noon to 6pm.

DON'T MISS

- Rotating art exhibitions
- Photography by James VanDerZee
- The well-stocked gift shop

PRACTICALITIES

- Map p434, C5
- ☎212-864-4500
- www.studiomuseum.org
- 144 W 125th St, at Adam Clayton Powell Jr Blvd, Harlem
- suggested donation $7, Sun free
- ⏲noon-9pm Thu & Fri, 10am-6pm Sat, noon-6pm Sun
- S 2/3 to 125th St

SIGHTS

Latino culture is the focus of East Harlem's El Museo del Barrio, while Harlem's Studio Museum and Schomburg Center for Research in Black Culture fly the flag for African American expression. During the Harlem Renaissance, the northern edge of the neighborhood was dubbed 'Sugar Hill' as it was here that the Harlem elite lived the 'sweet life.' Columbia University and America's largest cathedral dominate Morningside Heights, while Washington Heights takes its name from America's first president, who set up a fort here during the Revolutionary War. Topping the lot is Inwood, home to the Metropolitan Museum of Art's medieval booty.

Morningside Heights

CATHEDRAL CHURCH OF ST JOHN THE DIVINE — CATHEDRAL

See p247.

COLUMBIA UNIVERSITY — UNIVERSITY

Map p434 (www.columbia.edu; Broadway, at W 116th St, Morningside Heights; S1 to 116th St-Columbia University) Founded in Lower Manhattan in 1754 as King's College, the oldest university in New York is now one of the world's premier research institutions. In 1897 the Ivy League school moved to its current location (the site of a former asylum), where its stately, gated campus offers plenty of cultural happenings.

The principal point of interest is the **main courtyard** (located on either side of College Walk, at 116th St), which is surrounded by various Italian Renaissance-style buildings. In the northern half, you'll find the statue of the open-armed *Alma Mater* seated before the Low Memorial Library. On the eastern end of College Walk, at the corner of Amsterdam Ave, is Hamilton Hall, a key site during the famous student uprising of 1968.

Your best bet for navigating the grounds is to download architectural historian Andrew Dolkart's self-guided audio tour (www.columbia.edu/content/self-guided-walking-tour.html) from the Columbia University website.

TOP EXPERIENCE
APOLLO THEATER

More than simply historic, Harlem's Apollo Theater is a swinging testament to Harlem's astounding musical legacy. Originally a whites-only burlesque joint, the neoclassical venue reinvented itself in 1934 with 'Jazz à la Carte.' Soon after, virtually every major Black artist was performing here, from Duke Ellington and Louis Armstrong to Count Basie and Billie Holiday.

The Apollo introduced the legendary Amateur Night in 1934. Its long list of then-unknown competitors includes Ella Fitzgerald, Gladys Knight, Jimi Hendrix, the Jackson 5 and Lauryn Hill. The event still kicks off every Wednesday night and its wild and ruthless crowd is as fun to watch as tomorrow's next big things. Beyond Amateur Night is a thriving year-round program of music, dance, master classes and special events, with shows spanning Cuban salsa tributes to Afro-Latin jazz suites.

While guided tours of the interior are available only for groups of 20 or more with advance reservations, individuals are welcome to join group tours based on availability. Take the tour and expect to see a fragment of the Tree of Hope, a long-gone elm performers would rub for good luck before taking to the stage.

DON'T MISS

- Amateur Night
- Guided tours
- Tree of Hope

PRACTICALITIES

- Map p434, C5
- tickets 800-745-3000, tours 212-531-5337
- www.apollotheater.org
- 253 W 125th St, btwn Frederick Douglass & Adam Clayton Powell Jr Blvds, Harlem
- tickets from $24
- S A/B/C/D, 2/3 to 125th St

GENERAL ULYSSES S GRANT NATIONAL MEMORIAL

MEMORIAL

Map p434 (☎212-666-1640; www.nps.gov/gegr; Riverside Dr, at 122nd St, Morningside Heights; ⊙10am-5pm Wed-Sun; S1 to 125th St) FREE Popularly known as Grant's Tomb ('Who's buried in Grant's Tomb?' 'Who?' 'Grant, stupid!' goes a classic joke), this landmark holds the remains of Civil War hero and 18th president Ulysses S Grant and his wife, Julia. Completed in 1897 – 12 years after his death – the imposing granite structure is the largest mausoleum in America. A gallery covers key events in Grant's life. Rangers lead guided tours at various times throughout the day and answer questions about the general and statesman.

Seventeen Gaudí-inspired mosaic benches, designed by Chilean artist Pedro Silva in the 1970s, surround the mausoleum. It's a downright hallucinatory installation – and a good spot to contemplate the musings of the late, great comedian George Carlin, who was known to light up here back in the day.

RIVERSIDE CHURCH

CHURCH

Map p434 (☎212-870-6700; www.trcnyc.org; 490 Riverside Dr, at 120th St, Morningside Heights; ⊙9am-5pm; S1 to 116th St) This imposing neo-Gothic beauty was built by the Rockefeller family in 1930. While the sparseness of the interior evokes an Italian Gothic style, the stained-glass windows in the narthex are actually Flemish, dating back to the 16th century. The church rings its 74 carillon bells with an extraordinary 20-ton bass bell (the world's largest) at 10:30am and 3pm on Sunday. Interdenominational services are held at 10:45am on Sunday, with free tours offered immediately after (at 12:30pm).

Harlem

STUDIO MUSEUM IN HARLEM

MUSEUM

See p249.

SCHOMBURG CENTER FOR RESEARCH IN BLACK CULTURE

MUSEUM

Map p434 (☎917-275-6975; www.nypl.org/locations/schomburg; 515 Malcolm X Blvd, at 135th St, Harlem; ⊙10am-6pm Mon & Thu-Sat, to 8pm Tue & Wed; S2/3 to 135th St) FREE The nation's largest collection of documents, rare books and photographs relating to the African American experience resides at this scholarly center run by the New York Public Library. It's named after Arthur Schomburg, a Black Puerto Rican activist who amassed a singular collection of manuscripts, slave narratives and other important artifacts. Regular exhibitions, lectures and film screenings are held on-site.

LOCAL KNOWLEDGE

555 EDGECOMBE AVE

When completed in 1916, this brick **beaux-arts giant** (Map p434; 555 Edgecombe Ave, at 160th St, Washington Heights; SA/C to 163rd St-Amsterdam Ave; 1 to 157th St) was Washington Heights' first luxury apartment complex, with a concierge, a separate workers' entrance and no fewer than three elevators. It was initially available only to whites, but the neighborhood's transformation from predominantly Irish and Jewish to African American saw the building's residents become mostly Black by the 1940s.

Its tenants would include some of New York's most prominent African Americans, among them boxer Joe Louis and music heavyweights Lena Horne, Count Basie, Duke Ellington and Billy Strayhorn. Today the building's cultural legacy lives on every Sunday afternoon, when veteran musician Marjorie Eliot (p258) throws open the doors to her apartment, inviting anyone and everyone into her living room for one of the city's most enchanting jazz jams.

East Harlem

EL MUSEO DEL BARRIO

MUSEUM

Map p434 (☎212-831-7272; www.elmuseo.org; 1230 Fifth Ave, btwn 104th & 105th Sts, East Harlem; suggested donation adult/student/child $9/5/free; ⊙11am-6pm Wed-Sat, noon-5pm Sun; S6 to 103rd St) *Bienvenido* to one of New York's premier Latino cultural institutions, with thoughtful rotating exhibitions that span all media, from painting and photography to video and site-specific installations. The shows often highlight El Museo's strong permanent collection, which includes pre-Columbian artifacts, traditional folk works and a stellar array of postwar art made by a wide range of Latino artists.

The museum includes pieces by well-known historical figures such as Chilean surrealist Roberto Matta and established contemporary artists such as Félix González-Torres and Pepón Osorio.

Hamilton Heights & Sugar Hill

HAMILTON GRANGE HISTORIC BUILDING

Map p434 (646-548-2310; www.nps.gov/hagr; St Nicholas Park, at 141st St; 9am-5pm Wed-Sun, guided tours 10am, 11am & 2pm; S A/C, B/D to 145th St) FREE This Federal-style retreat belonged to Founding Father Alexander Hamilton, who owned a 32-acre country estate here in the early 1800s. Unfortunately, Hamilton was able to enjoy his abode for only two years before his life was cut short in a fatal duel with political rival Aaron Burr. Moved from Convent Ave to its present location in 2008, the building is one of several Hamilton-related sights seeing an increase in visitors – by some 75% – thanks to Lin-Manuel Miranda's musical, *Hamilton*.

HAMILTON HEIGHTS HISTORIC DISTRICT AREA

Map p434 (Convent Ave & Hamilton Tce, btwn 141st & 145th Sts, Hamilton Heights; S A/C, B/D to 145th St) Two parallel streets in Hamilton Heights – Convent Ave and Hamilton Tce – contain a landmark stretch of historic limestone and brownstone town houses from the period between 1866 and 1931. Wes Anderson fans may recognize the turreted building on the southeastern corner of Convent Ave and 144th St from the film *The Royal Tenenbaums*.

Washington Heights & Inwood

★**MET CLOISTERS** MUSEUM

(212-923-3700; www.metmuseum.org/cloisters; 99 Margaret Corbin Dr, Fort Tryon Park; 3-day pass adult/senior/child $25/17/12, pay-as-you-wish for residents of NY State & students from CT, NY and NJ; 10am-5:15pm Mar-Oct, to 4:45pm Nov-Feb;

FULL PEWS: HARLEM GOSPEL CHURCH SERVICES

What started as an occasional pilgrimage has turned into a tourist-industry spectacle: entire busloads of travelers now make their way to Harlem every Sunday to attend a gospel service. The volume of visitors is so high that some churches turn away people due to space constraints. In some cases, tourists have been known to outnumber congregants.

Naturally, this has led to friction. Many locals are upset by visitors who chat during sermons, leave in the middle of services or show up in skimpy attire. Plus, for some, there's the uncomfortable sense that African American spirituality is something to be consumed like a Broadway show.

The churches, to their credit, remain welcoming spaces. But if you do decide to attend, be respectful: dress modestly (Sunday best!), don't take pictures and remain present for the duration of the service. Also, keep in mind that most churches will not allow large backpacks.

Sunday services generally start at 10am or 11am and can last for two or more hours. There are roughly five dozen participating churches. The soulful Sunday gospel services at **Abyssinian Baptist Church** (Map p434; 212-862-7474; www.abyssinian.org; 132 Odell Clark Pl, btwn Adam Clayton Powell Jr & Malcolm X Blvds, Harlem; tourist gospel service 11:30am Sun mid-Sep–Jul; S 2/3 to 135th St) are the city's most famous. Arrive at least an hour before the service to queue up, and abide by the strict entry rules: no tank tops, flip-flops, shorts, leggings or backpacks. Others include **Canaan Baptist Church** (Map p434; 212-866-0301; www.cbccnyc.org; 132 W 116th St, btwn Adam Clayton Powell Jr & Malcolm X Blvds, Harlem; service 10am Sun; ; S 2/3 to 116th St), a neighborhood church founded in 1932, and **Convent Avenue Baptist Church** (Map p434; 212-234-6767; www.conventchurch.org; 420 W 145th St, at Convent Ave, Hamilton Heights; services 8am & 11am Sun; S A/C, B/D or 1 to 145th St), which has been conducting traditional baptist services since the 1940s.

If you're less interested in the preaching and more interested in the feel-good singing and celebration, a number of Harlem spots offer Sunday gospel brunches, including Sylvia's (p255) and Ginny's Supper Club (p258).

S A to 190th St) On a hilltop overlooking the Hudson River, the Cloisters is a curious architectural jigsaw, its many parts made up of various European monasteries and other historic buildings. Built in the 1930s to house the Metropolitan Museum's medieval treasures, its frescoes, tapestries and paintings are set in galleries that sit around a romantic courtyard, connected by grand archways and topped with Moorish terracotta roofs. Among its many rare treasures is the beguiling tapestry series *The Hunt of the Unicorn* (1495–1505).

Also worth seeking out is the remarkably well-preserved 15th-century Annunciation Triptych (Merode Altarpiece). Then there's the stunning French 12th-century Saint-Guilhem and Bonnefant cloisters, the latter featuring plants used in medieval medicine, magic, ceremony and the arts, and with views over the Hudson River.

Your ticket gives you three-day admission to the Cloisters as well as the Metropolitan Museum of Art (p214) and the Met Breuer (p218). Note that although the Dyckman St subway station looks closest to the museum, there are steep slippery steps between the station and the entrance; use 190th St station instead and walk through the park.

INWOOD HILL PARK — PARK

(www.nycgovparks.org/parks/inwoodhillpark; Dyckman St, at the Hudson River, Inwood; ⏰6am-1am; S A to Inwood-207th St) This 196-acre oasis contains the last natural forest and salt marsh in Manhattan and evidence suggests the land was used by Native Americans in the 17th century. It's a cool escape in summer and a great place to explore anytime, as you'll find hilly paths for hiking and mellow, grassy patches and benches for quiet contemplation. It's so bucolic that the treetops serve as frequent nesting sites for bald eagles. On summer weekends, join locals who barbecue at designated grills.

MORRIS-JUMEL MANSION MUSEUM — HISTORIC BUILDING

Map p434 (☎212-923-8008; www.morrisjumel.org; 65 Jumel Tce, at 160th St, Washington Heights; adult/child $10/free; ⏰10am-4pm Tue-Fri, to 5pm Sat & Sun; S C to 163rd St-Amsterdam Ave) Built in 1765 as a country retreat for Roger and Mary Morris, this columned mansion is the oldest house in Manhattan. It is also famous for having briefly served as George Washington's headquarters after it was seized by the Continental Army in 1776. The mansion's beautifully appointed rooms contain many original furnishings, including a bed that reputedly belonged to Napoleon. Hour-long guided tours run on weekends (Saturday at noon, Sunday at 2pm; $12).

SYLVAN TERRACE — HISTORIC SITE

Map p434 (Sylvan Tce, Washington Heights; S C to 163rd St-Amsterdam Ave) The wooden houses on storybook Sylvan Terrace – resplendent with their high narrow stoops, dentiled canopies and boldly paneled wooden doors – constitute NYC's first attempt at building affordable abodes for workers. The street itself is graced by its original late-19th-century gas lamps, while its cobblestones are Belgian, not Dutch, as is the case in Lower Manhattan and Brooklyn.

EATING

Harlem remains justifiably famous for its soul food, both classic and reinvented, with a growing number of international options. Catering to the students and teachers of Columbia University, Morningside Heights offers cheap late-night diners and convivial bistro-style hangouts. Frederick Douglass Blvd, Adam Clayton Powell Jr Blvd and Malcolm X Blvd (Lenox Ave) are becoming prime stomping ground for gourmands, with interesting independent cafes and restaurants popping up all the time.

Morningside Heights

PISTICCI — ITALIAN $$

Map p434 (☎212-932-3500; www.pisticcinyc.com; 125 La Salle St, Morningside Heights; mains $15-24; ⏰noon-11pm Mon-Fri, from 11am Sat & Sun; 🍷; S 1 to 125th St) 🌿 When the weather is lousy, Pisticci makes a fine retreat, with its cozy two-room interior graced by low-lit chandeliers, vintage paintings and globe lights over the bar. Creative cocktails make a fine prelude to the excellent Italian fare and daily specials like baked tilapia. Many vegetables are grown at Pisticci's upstate farm (don't miss the grilled eggplant).

COMMUNITY FOOD & JUICE — AMERICAN $$

Map p434 (☎212-665-2800; www.community restaurant.com; 2893 Broadway, btwn 112th & 113th Sts, Morningside Heights; sandwiches $12-15,

WORTH A DETOUR

THE BRONX

The Bronx is a big borough, with numerous points of interest spread all about. Your best bet is to focus on one specific area or a couple of contiguous neighborhoods. You could easily combine a visit to Bronx Zoo or the New York Botanical Garden with an exploration of Arthur Ave in neighboring Belmont. Similarly, an early-afternoon tour of Yankee Stadium is easily followed by a snoop around Bronx Museum. The B/D subway line makes travel a breeze between Bronx Museum and Edgar Allan Poe Cottage. From the latter, it's an easy 0.2-mile walk west to Kingsbridge Rd subway station, from where the 6 line heads north to nearby Woodlawn Cemetery. Some highlights include the following:

➡ Seventh-inning-stretching at a baseball game in one of America's most famous sports venues, **Yankee Stadium** (Map p434; ☑212-926-5337; www.mlb.com/yankees; 1 E 161st St, at River Ave; tours $20; ⑤B/D, 4 to 161st St-Yankee Stadium).

➡ Exploring the 50 acres of the beautifully landscaped **New York Botanical Garden** (☑718-817-8716; www.nybg.org; 2900 Southern Blvd; all-garden pass Mon-Fri adult/child $23/10, Sat & Sun $28/12, grounds only NYC residents $15/4, Wed & 9-10am Sat grounds admission free; ◷10am-6pm Tue-Sun; ☖; ☗Metro-North to Botanical Garden) – particularly stunning in springtime.

➡ Dabbling in a different kind of wild life at New York's historic **Bronx Zoo** (☑718-220-5100; www.bronxzoo.com; 2300 Southern Blvd; full-experience adult/child Apr-Oct $37/27, Nov-Mar $29/21, pay-as-you-wish general admission Wed; ◷10am-5pm Mon-Fri, to 5:30pm Sat & Sun Apr-Oct, 10:30am-4:30pm Nov-Mar; ⑤2, 5 to West Farms Sq-E Tremont Ave).

➡ Pushing your cultural boundaries at the **Bronx Museum** (Map p434; ☑718-681-6000; www.bronxmuseum.org; 1040 Grand Concourse, at 165th St; ◷11am-6pm Wed, Thu, Sat & Sun, to 8pm Fri; ⑤B/D to 167th St) **FREE**, an unexpectedly brilliant museum.

➡ Paying your respects to Duke Ellington and Herman Melville at beautiful **Woodlawn Cemetery** (☑718-920-0500, 877-496-6352; www.thewoodlawncemetery.org; Webster Ave, at E 233rd St; ◷8:30am-4:30pm; ⑤4 to Woodlawn).

➡ Contemplating the haunting words of a great American writer at **Edgar Allan Poe Cottage** (☑718-881-8900; www.bronxhistoricalsociety.org/poe-cottage; 2640 Grand Concourse, at Kingsbridge Rd; adult/child $5/3; ◷10am-3pm Thu & Fri, to 4pm Sat, 1-5pm Sun; ⑤B/D to Kingsbridge Rd).

➡ Browsing food stalls to live music on a warm summer night at the **Bronx Night Market** (www.thebronxnightmarket.com; Fordham Plaza at E Fordham Rd; street food from $5; ◷4-10pm Sat May-Oct; ⑤B/D to Fordham Rd, ☗Metro-North to Fordham).

When hunger strikes, head over to Arthur Ave in Belmont, a much-loved strip lined with nostalgic Italian eateries serving up delicacies from the Old World. Get mozzarella and prosciutto sandwiches at **Casa della Mozzarella** (☑718-364-3867; www.facebook.com/casadellamozzarella; 604 E 187th St, at Arthur Ave; sandwiches $6-13; ◷7:30am-6pm Mon-Sat, to 1pm Sun; ⑤B/D to Fordham Rd, ☗Metro-North to Fordham), pizza at **Zero Otto Nove** (☑718-220-1027; www.zeroottonove.com/locations/bronx; 2357 Arthur Ave, at 186th St; pizzas $12-18, dinner mains $19-31; ◷noon-2:30pm & 4:30-10pm Tue-Thu, to 11pm Fri & Sat, 1-9pm Sun; ☖; ⑤B/D to Fordham Rd, ☗Metro-North to Fordham) or pretty much anything at **Tra Di Noi** (☑718-295-1784; www.tradinoi.com; 622 E 187th St; mains $15-22; ◷noon-9pm Tue-Sun; ⑤B/D to Fordham Rd, ☗Metro North to Fordham).

Afterwards, head south to Mott Haven to expand your literary horizons at **Lit. Bar** (Map p434; ☑347-955-3610; www.thelitbar.com; 131 Alexander Ave; ◷noon-8pm Sun & Mon, to 10pm Tue-Sat; ⑤6 to 3rd Avenue-138th St), a cool new indie bookstore/wine bar. Finish up at nearby **Bronx Brewery** (☑718-402-1000; www.thebronxbrewery.com; 856 E 136th St, btwn Willow & Walnut Aves; ◷3-7pm Mon-Wed, to 8pm Thu, to 10pm Fri, noon-10pm Sat, noon-7pm Sun; ⑤6 to Cypress Ave) with wood-fired pizzas and locally brewed craft beer.

mains $14-24; ⌚8am-9:30pm Mon-Thu, to 10pm Fri, 9am-10pm Sat, to 9:30pm Sun; ; S1 to 110th St) The convivial, spacious Community is a brunch staple for frenzied families and hungover Columbia University students. Get here before 10:30am or be prepared to wait for your veggie scramble or sausage-and-egg biscuit sandwich. Better yet, skip the weekend brunch rush and stop in for a candlelit dinner. Both the fluffy blueberry pancakes and the veggie burger deserve an A.

Harlem

SEASONED VEGAN VEGAN $

Map p434 (212-222-0092; www.seasonedvegan.com; 55 St Nicholas Ave, at 113th St, Harlem; mains $10-21; ⌚5-10pm Tue-Fri, from 11am Sat, 11am-9pm Sun; ; S2/3 to 110th St or 116th St) Run by a mother-and-son team, the Seasoned Vegan has earned a loyal following for its delicious twist on soul food. Everything here is organic, kosher and made entirely without animal products. You'll find creative takes on barbecued ribs (made with lotus root and fermented soy), po'boys (with yams) and mac 'n' cheese (made with cashew milk).

CHARLES' PAN-FRIED CHICKEN AMERICAN $

Map p434 (212-281-1800; 2461 Frederick Douglass Blvd, btwn 151st & 152nd Sts, Harlem; fried chicken from $12; ⌚11am-10:30pm Mon-Sat, noon-9:30pm Sun; SB/D to 155th St) It's a hole-in-the-wall, but charismatic Charles Gabriel makes some of the best fried chicken in the city. Crisp and beautifully seasoned, it's served with sides including collard greens, yams, mac 'n' cheese and corn bread. Don't expect designer touches: just unadorned tables, food on trays, and proof that a book (or chicken joint) mustn't be judged by its cover.

SYLVIA'S SOUTHERN US $$

Map p434 (212-996-0660; www.sylviasrestaurant.com; 328 Malcolm X Blvd, btwn 126th & 127th Sts, Harlem; mains $15-28; ⌚8am-10:30pm Mon-Sat, 11am-8pm Sun; S2/3 to 125th St) Founded by Sylvia Woods in 1962, this Harlem icon has been dazzling Harlemites and visitors (including a few presidents) with its lip-smackingly good down-home Southern cooking – succulent fried chicken, baked mac 'n' cheese and cornmeal-dusted catfish, plus requisite sides like collard greens. Come on Sundays for the gospel brunch, and book ahead to avoid the overwhelming scrum for a table.

MAISON HARLEM FRENCH $$

Map p434 (212-222-9224; www.maisonharlem.com; 341 St Nicholas Ave, at 127th St, Harlem; mains $18-34; ⌚11am-midnight Mon-Thu, to 1am Fri, 10am-1am Sat, to midnight Sun; ; SA/C, B/D to 125th St) Run by two French *amis,* this swinging little bar-bistro is like a second home for locals, who drop in at all hours to nibble on French toast, slurp onion soup, or loosen their belts over slow-cooked duck-leg confit. For the full effervescent effect, head here on weekends when DJs and wine-fueled merriment may just lead to dancing.

BLVD BISTRO AMERICAN $$

Map p434 (212-678-6200; www.boulevardbistrony.com; 2149 Frederick Douglass Blvd, at 116th St, Harlem; mains $16-28; ⌚11am-3:30pm & 5-11pm Tue-Fri, 9am-4pm & 6-11pm Sat, 10am-6pm Sun; SB/C to 116 St) Bustling BLVD Bistro takes quality seasonal produce and turns it into subtly tweaked Southern soul food. Heading the kitchen is Mississippi-born Carlos Swepson, whose roots shine bright in dishes like blueberry-packed buttermilk pancakes, seven-cheese macaroni with apple-wood-smoked bacon, and oh-so-fine biscuits and sausage gravy.

DINOSAUR BAR-B-QUE BARBECUE $$

Map p434 (212-694-1777; www.dinosaurbarbque.com; 700 W 125th St, at Twelfth Ave, Harlem; mains $12-26; ⌚11:30am-11pm Mon-Thu, to midnight Fri & Sat, noon-10pm Sun; S1 to 125th St) Jocks, hipsters, moms and pops: everyone dives into this honky-tonk rib bar for a rockin' feed. Get messy with dry-rubbed, slow-pit-smoked ribs, slabs of juicy steak and succulent burgers, or watch your waistline with the lightly seasoned grilled-chicken options. The few vegetarian choices include a fantastic version of Creole-spiced deviled eggs.

REVERENCE FUSION $$$

Map p434 (www.reverence.nyc; 2592 Frederick Douglass Blvd; 5-course tasting menu $98; ⌚6-10:30pm Tue-Sat; SA/B/C to 135 St) After pioneering San Francisco's underground supper clubs, noted chef Russell Jackson made his NYC debut in 2019 with a five-course tasting menu of Asian, French and Latin American influences. Dishes like Peruvian *uni* cooked in shiso butter or *gougères* stuffed with tofu and fermented berries are enjoyed only in the moment – Jackson put the kibosh on photography of any sort.

★RED ROOSTER AMERICAN $$$

Map p434 (☎212-792-9001; www.redroosterharlem.com; 310 Malcolm X Blvd, btwn W 125th & 126th Sts, Harlem; mains lunch $21-29, dinner $23-40; ⊙11:30am-3pm & 4:30-10:30pm Mon-Thu, to 11:30pm Fri, 10am-3pm & 4:30-11:30pm Sat, to 10pm Sun; S 2/3 to 125th St) Transatlantic superchef Marcus Samuelsson laces upscale comfort food with a world of flavors at his cool brasserie. Mac 'n' cheese joins forces with lobster, blackened catfish pairs with pickled mango, and Swedish meatballs salute Samuelsson's home country. The DJ-led bar atmosphere is as good, if not better, than the food: roll in after midnight on weekends and it's still buzzing.

Hamilton Heights

HARLEM PUBLIC AMERICAN $

Map p434 (☎212-939-9404; www.harlempublic.com; 3612 Broadway, at 149th St, Hamilton Heights; mains $13-16; ⊙11am-1am Sun-Thu, to 2am Fri & Sat; S 1, A/C, B/D to 145th St) Amiable hipsters at the bar, old-school funk on the speakers and finger-licking bar grub: Harlem Public sets the scene for a night out. Celebrate neighborhood discoveries with mouthwatering feel-good food, whether it's a soft-shell crab sando or a plate of breakfast poutine. The drinks menu showcases all things local, from Brooklyn craft beers to small-batch upstate New York liquors.

Inwood

NEW LEAF AMERICAN $$

(☎212-568-5323; www.newleafrestaurant.com; 1 Margaret Corbin Dr, Inwood; mains $16-38; ⊙noon-8pm Mon-Thu, to 9pm Fri & Sat, 11am-8pm Sun; S A to 190th St) Nestled in Fort Tryon Park, a short walk from the Cloisters (p254), this 1930s stone building feels like a country tavern. Settle in for market-fresh ingredients in bistro-style dishes such as salmon with seasonal vegetables or watermelon salad with feta cheese, kalamata olives and mint. If possible, grab a table on the all-weather patio for that garden-party vibe.

Local Life
Harlem Soul

Harlem: the neighborhood where Billie Holiday crooned; where Ralph Ellison penned *Invisible Man,* his epic novel on truth and intolerance; where acclaimed artist Romare Bearden pieced together his first collages. Simultaneously vibrant and effusive, brooding and melancholy, Harlem is the deepest recess of New York's soul.

❶ Malcolm Shabazz Harlem Market

Trawl the low-key, semi-enclosed **Malcolm Shabazz Harlem Market** (Map p434; 52 W 116th St, btwn Malcolm X Blvd & Fifth Ave, Harlem; ⊙10am-8pm; 🚹; S 2/3 to 116th St) FREE, run by the Malcolm Shabazz Mosque, where slain Muslim orator Malcolm X once preached. Pick up African jewelry, textiles, drums, leather goods and oils, or get your hair braided.

❷ Sylvia's

An institution for down-home Southern delights, Sylvia's (p255) has drawn locals, visitors, celebrities and even a few presidents with authentic soul food since the 1960s. Dishes conjure a '*hallelujah*', and the popular gospel brunch is a spirited Sunday affair.

❸ Strivers' Row

On the blocks of 138th and 139th Sts, **Strivers' Row** (Map p434; W 138th & 139th Sts, btwn Frederick Douglass & Adam Clayton Powell Jr Blvds, Harlem; S B, C to 135th St) is graced with 1890s town houses. Ever since ambitious African Americans first moved here in the 1920s and gave the area its nickname, these buildings have housed some of Harlem's greatest luminaries, like blues veteran WC Handy and singer-dancer Bill 'Bojangles' Robinson.

❹ Shrine

A mainstay on Harlem's nightlife circuit, Shrine (p258) may look like a dive from the outside, but inside its small stage hosts an incredible lineup of music every night of the week. Beats range from calypso, Afropunk and French electro to Latin jazz and straight-up soul. Several

CHIE INOUE/SHUTTERSTOCK ©

Apollo Theater (p250)

bands play each night, the beer is cheap and the crowd's as eclectic as the music.

5 Apollo Theater

One of the best places to catch a concert in Harlem is the Apollo Theater (p252). Ella Fitzgerald debuted here in 1934, at one of the theater's earliest Amateur Nights. Eight decades on, Amateur Night takes place every Wednesday (February to November), notorious crowds and all.

6 Flamekeepers Hat Club

Harlem's Gilded Age lives on at Flamekeepers Hat Club (p261), a friendly corner boutique lined with elegant hats and caps. If you can't decide, seek Marc Williamson's keen eye.

7 Minton's

Bebop was incubated at this formal jazz-and-dinner club (p260), where greats like Thelonious Monk, Dizzy Gillespie and Charlie Parker were all regulars. Listed on the National and New York State Registers of Historic Places, it's a place to dress, impress and savor sweet grooves over decadent Southern fare.

DRINKING & NIGHTLIFE

The swath of Manhattan above 125th St is not especially known for its bar scene. That said, you will find some stellar options up here, including good craft beer and several live-music joints that have redefined the nightlife scene in Harlem.

★SHRINE BAR

Map p434 (www.shrinenyc.com; 2271 Adam Clayton Powell Jr Blvd, btwn 133rd & 134th Sts, Harlem; 4pm-4am; S 2/3 to 135th St) It may look like a dive from outside, but friendly, unpretentious Shrine is one of the best places in Harlem (if not New York) to hear live bands without a cover charge. Musicians take to its small stage every day with blues, reggae, Afro-beat, funk and indie rock. Beer is cheap and the crowd is as eclectic as the music.

SILVANA BAR

Map p434 (646-692-4935; www.silvana-nyc.com; 300 W 116th St, Harlem; 8am-4am; S 2/3 to 116th St) This appealing Middle Eastern cafe and shop whips up tasty hummus and falafel plates; the real draw, though, is the hidden downstairs club, which draws a friendly, easygoing local crowd with good cocktails and live bands (kicking off around 6pm) followed by DJs. The lineup is anything-goes, with jazz, Cuban *son*, reggae and Balkan gypsy punk all in the rotation.

GINNY'S SUPPER CLUB COCKTAIL BAR

Map p434 (212-421-3821; www.ginnyssupperclub.com; 310 Malcolm X Blvd, btwn W 125th & 126th Sts, Harlem; cover charge $25; 6pm-midnight Thu, to 3am Fri & Sat, brunch 10:30am-12:30pm Sun; S 2/3 to 125th St) Looking straight out of the TV series *Boardwalk Empire*, this roaring basement supper club is rarely short of styled-up regulars sipping cocktails, nibbling on soul and global bites – from the Red Rooster (p256) kitchen upstairs – and grooving to live jazz from 7:30pm Wednesday to Saturday. Don't miss the weekly Sunday gospel brunch.

HARLEM HOPS CRAFT BEER

Map p434 (646-998-3444; www.harlemhops.com; 2268 Adam Clayton Powell Jr Blvd, btwn 133th & 134th Sts, Harlem; 4pm-midnight Sun-Thu, to 2am Fri & Sat; ; S 2/3 to 135th St) Harlem's only 100% African American–owned beer bar has its home 'hood emblazoned on the ceiling in neon lights, and bratwurst and meat pies on the menu. Pair with a habanero beef pie with African spices, and settle in. The beers are mostly small batch, niche offerings; ask the staff for recommendations.

67 ORANGE STREET COCKTAIL BAR

Map p434 (212-662-2030; www.67orangestreet.com; 2082 Frederick Douglass Blvd, btwn 112th & 113th Sts; 5pm-midnight Mon & Tue, to 2am Wed & Thu, to 4am Fri, 6pm-4am Sat, to midnight Sun; S B,C to 116th St) Named after the address where NYC's first Black-owned bar stood (back in the 1840s!), 67 Orange Street serves up beautifully crafted cocktails in a cozy, speakeasy-like setting. Exposed brick, flickering candles and original artwork on the walls make a fine backdrop for sipping creative elixirs like the red rosemary gin, with its rooibos-infused gin and refreshing rosemary.

THE CHIPPED CUP CAFE

Map p434 (212-368-8881; www.chippedcupcoffee.com; 3610 Broadway, btwn 148th & 149th Sts, Hamilton Heights; 7am-8pm Mon-Fri, 8am-8pm Sat & Sun; ; S 1, A/C, B/D to 145th St) Hipsterdom gets all cozy at the Chipped Cup, where coffee-slurping scribes and students work away among dainty teacups, worn novels and quirky artwork. If the weather is behaving, order a latte and *pain au chocolat*, grab a copy of the *New York Times* and rediscover life's simpler pleasures in the garden.

ENTERTAINMENT

★MARJORIE ELIOT'S PARLOR JAZZ JAZZ

Map p434 (212-781-6595; 555 Edgecombe Ave, Apartment 3F, at 160th St, Washington Heights; donations appreciated; 3:30pm Sun; S A/C to 163rd St-Amsterdam Ave; 1 to 157th St) Each Sunday the charming Ms Eliot provides one of New York's most magical experiences: free, intimate jazz jams in her own apartment. Dedicated to her two deceased sons, the informal concerts feature a revolving lineup of talented musicians, enchanting guests from all over the globe. Go early, as this event is popular (there's usually a line by 2:45pm).

MINTON'S JAZZ

Map p434 (212-243-2222; www.mintonsharlem.com; 206 W 118th St, btwn St Nicholas Ave & Adam Clayton Powell Jr Blvd; $20-25 or $30 food purchase minimum; 6-11pm Wed-Sat, noon-3pm & 6-10pm Sun; S B/C, 2/3 to 116th St) Birthplace of bebop, this Harlem jazz-and-dinner club is a formal spot for catching live music. Everyone from Dizzy Gillespie to Louis Armstrong has jammed here, and dinner (mains $22 to $46) in its tinted-mirror-lined dining room is an experience to behold. Book ahead, dress to impress and savor Southern flavors while catching live, honey-sweet jazz.

MAYSLES DOCUMENTARY CENTER CINEMA

Map p434 (☎212-537-6843; www.maysles.org; 343 Malcolm X Blvd, btwn 127th & 128th Sts, Harlem; films from $12; S2/3 to 125th St) This small, not-for-profit cinema founded by the late director Albert Maysles (of *Grey Gardens* fame) shows documentary and other independent films – particularly some excellent works coming out of Africa. Check the website for details of screenings and events, which also include Q&A sessions with filmmakers, lectures and live performances.

AMORE OPERA OPERA

Map p434 (☎347-948-4588; www.amoreopera.org; Riverside Theatre, 91 Claremont St, btwn 120th & 122nd Sts; tickets from $40; S1 to 116th St, 1 to 125th St) This company, formed by members of the now-defunct Amato Opera, presents well-known works such as *The Magic Flute, La Bohème* and *The Mikado* at the Riverside theater. The appeal? Much cheaper tickets and a more intimate setting than most opera venues. They offered Zoom performances throughout 2020 and 2021. See their website for news on live shows.

SHOPPING

HARLEM HABERDASHERY FASHION

Map p434 (☎646-707-0070; www.harlemhaberdashery.com; 245 Malcolm X Blvd, btwn 122nd & 123rd Sts, Harlem; ⊙noon-8pm Mon-Sat; S2/3 to 125th St) Keep your wardrobe fresh at this uberhip uptown boutique, which has covetable apparel in all shapes and sizes. Lovely T-shirts, high-end sneakers, dapper woven hats, bespoke leather jackets and jazzy sunglasses are among the ever-changing collections on display, plus chic homewares and their own line of craft spirits.

FLAMEKEEPERS HAT CLUB FASHION

Map p434 (☎212-531-3542; www.flamekeepershatclub.com; 273 W 121st St, at St Nicholas Ave, Harlem; ⊙noon-7pm Tue & Wed, to 8pm Thu-Sat, to 6pm Sun; SA/C, B/D to 125th St) Polish your look at this dapper hat boutique owned by affable Harlem designer Marc Williamson. Constructed from the likes of fur, wool felt and straw, his one-of-a-kind fedoras, pork pies, news boys and berets are hand-stitched, distressed, and adorned with patches and ribbons before hitting the shelves of the shop. Prices range from $110 to $1000.

REVOLUTION BOOKS BOOKS

Map p434 (☎212-691-3345; www.revolutionbooksnyc.org; 437 Malcolm X Blvd at 132nd St, Harlem; ⊙noon-9pm Tue-Sun; S2/3 to 135th St) This fiercely independent bookstore stocks a range of titles related to social issues, politics, gender studies and human rights. There are author readings once a week or so. Check the website for upcoming events.

ATMOS SHOES

Map p434 (☎212-666-2242; www.atmosny.com; 203 W 125th St, at Adam Clayton Powell Jr Blvd; ⊙10am-8pm Mon-Sat, noon-7pm Sun; SA/C, B/D, 2/3 to 125th St) Sneaker fetishists both high and low sprint to Atmos to pimp their feet (Method Man from the Wu-Tang Clan has been seen here). A top spot for high-end kicks, limited-edition releases and rereleases, the Harlem store is well-known for its collaborations with partners including Nike, Puma and K-Swiss.

SPORTS & ACTIVITIES

RIVERBANK STATE PARK HEALTH & FITNESS

Map p434 (☎212-694-3600; www.parks.ny.gov/parks/93; entrance via 145th St at Riverside Dr, Hamilton Heights; pool adult/child $2/1, fitness room $5, ice skating adult/child $5/3, roller skating $1.50, skate rental $6; ⊙6am-11pm; 👪; S1 to 145th St) This 28-acre, five-building facility, perched atop a wastewater-treatment plant (not as crazy as it sounds), has an Olympic-size indoor pool, an outdoor lap pool, a fitness room, basketball and tennis courts, a running track around a soccer field, a playground and a roller-skating rink (with ice skating from November to March).

TREAD CYCLING

(☎212-544-7055; www.treadbikeshop.com; 250 Dyckman St; per hr/day $8/30; ⊙10am-7pm Mon-Sat, to 6pm Sun; 👪; SA to Dyckman St) Located in Inwood Hill Park, right off the New York Greenway Bike Trail, is this family-friendly rental shop – perfect for when you want to navigate the long and winding paths of Upper Manhattan on wheels.

Brooklyn

BROOKLYN HEIGHTS, DOWNTOWN BROOKLYN & DUMBO | BOERUM HILL, COBBLE HILL, CARROLL GARDENS & RED HOOK | FORT GREENE, CLINTON HILL & BED-STUY | PARK SLOPE, GOWANUS & SUNSET PARK | PROSPECT HEIGHTS, CROWN HEIGHTS & FLATBUSH | WILLIAMSBURG, GREENPOINT & BUSHWICK | CONEY ISLAND & BRIGHTON BEACH

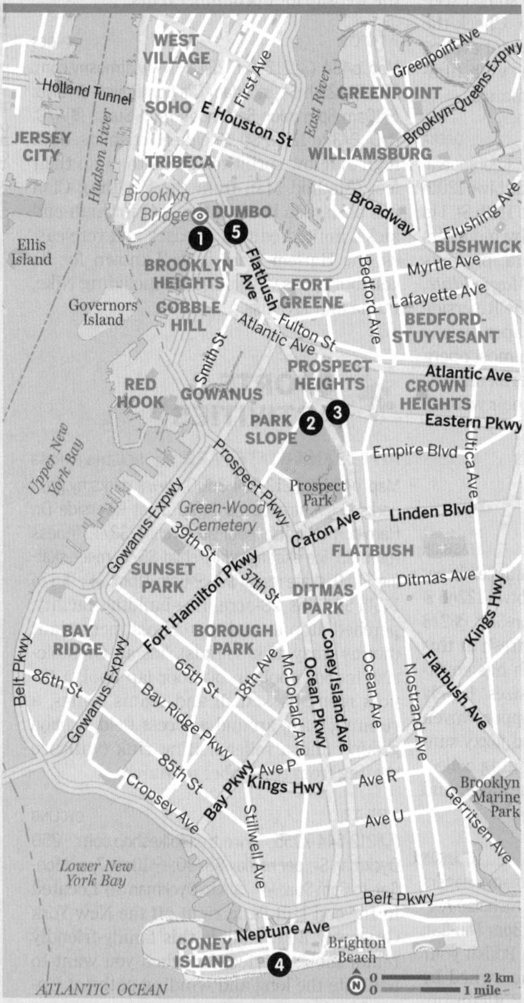

For more detail of this area see Map p436, p438, p440, p443 and p444

Neighborhood Top Five

❶ **Brooklyn Bridge Park** (p263) Running, cycling, lounging, skating, bouldering – and more – at these 85 acres of multifarious parkland perfectly situated along the East River.

❷ **Prospect Park** (p264) Wandering through the 600 acres of woodlands, meadows, lakes and more in the park that Central Park designers Vaux and Olmsted considered their crowning achievement.

❸ **Brooklyn Museum** (p265) Discovering the collections of Brooklyn's largest museum, from one of the nation's finest exhibits of ancient Egyptian art to groundbreaking feminist art from the 1970s.

❹ **Coney Island** (p275) Riding a wooden roller coaster, strolling the boardwalk and taking in colorful street art in murals in this fun-time, seaside district.

❺ **Brooklyn Flea** (p299) Browsing through dozens of tables of vintage clothes, old LPs, antiques, housewares and other interesting bric-a-brac at Brooklyn's favorite weekend arts/flea market.

Explore Brooklyn

Home to more than 2.6 million people spread across 71 sq miles, Brooklyn is a universe unto its own. There's much to see here, from charming brownstone-lined neighborhoods and beautifully landscaped parks to cutting-edge art galleries and seaside amusement parks.

For day-trips, it is best to pick a neighborhood and stick to it. South Brooklyn, especially Brooklyn Heights and neighboring Dumbo, offers lots of history and great Manhattan views. Prospect Park is just as magnificent a green space as Central Park (and only slightly smaller), and many of the neighborhoods surrounding it are great for architectural walks, window shopping and cafe-hopping. In the same area are two other big draws: the sprawling Brooklyn Museum and the Brooklyn Botanic Gardens.

Fans of vintage amusement parks and beachside strolls should head to Coney Island. For nightlife, north Brooklyn is the place to be. The trendy enclave of Williamsburg lies just a single subway stop from Manhattan and is loaded with bars and restaurants. Greenpoint and Bushwick have more indie cred, with atmospheric drinking dens and live-music spots.

Local Life

➡ **Rock and roll** Hit the hot music spots in Williamsburg and Bushwick to hear the latest indie sounds.

➡ **Park sloping** Join the stroller brigade for a lap or two around Prospect Park (p264). Or go window-shopping and cafe-hopping on Fifth Ave.

➡ **Farmers markets** Shop at the Saturday produce markets – Grand Army Plaza (p299), Fort Greene Park (p269), Borough Hall and McCarren Park (p274).

➡ **Recreation** Brooklyn Bridge Park (p263) has ample amusement: pickup basketball, idle strolls or bike rides, or just lying on the grass,taking in the skyline views.

Getting There & Away

➡ **Subway** Seventeen lines travel to/from Brooklyn; all run through downtown. Key routes from Manhattan include the A/C, 2/3, 4/5, B/D/F, N/R/Q and L trains. The G runs only between Queens and Brooklyn, from Long Island City to south of Prospect Park.

➡ **Bus** Take the B61 or B57 for Red Hook. The B62 runs from downtown Brooklyn to Williamsburg/Greenpoint.

➡ **Boat** The **NYC Ferry** (Map p436; www.ferry.nyc; S 10th St, off Kent Ave, Williamsburg; one-way trip $2.75; 🚌B32, Q59 to Kent Ave, Ⓢ J/M/Z to Marcy Ave) runs services to Brooklyn from Manhattan's Wall St and E 34th St, with stops including Dumbo, Williamsburg, Greenpoint, Sunset Park and Brooklyn Navy Yard.

➡ **Taxi** Apple-green Boro Taxis can pick up passengers only in Upper Manhattan and the four outer boroughs (but can drop off anywhere in NYC). Hail them on the street or request one through the Curb smartphone app.

Lonely Planet's Top Tip

For a sense of the city as it was, wander around Brighton Beach. Under the elevated tracks on Brighton Beach Ave, the bustling Russian district known as 'Little Odessa' is packed with greengrocers and emporiums dispensing smoked fish and pierogi. On the street, you'll find a cross section of humanity – from grandmas to sulky teens – chattering in dozens of different languages as the trains rumble overhead. It's unmistakably New York.

Best Places to Eat

➡ Olmsted (p284)
➡ Modern Love (p286)
➡ Miss Ada (p281)
➡ Smorgasburg (p281)
➡ Juliana's (p278)
➡ Zenkichi (p286)

For reviews, see p278 ➡

Best Places to Drink

➡ House of Yes (p291)
➡ Brooklyn Barge (p292)
➡ Radegast Hall & Biergarten (p292)
➡ Union Hall (p290)
➡ Maison Premiere (p291)

For reviews, see p287 ➡

Best Green Spaces

➡ Prospect Park (p264)
➡ Brooklyn Bridge Park (p263)
➡ Brooklyn Botanic Garden (p270)
➡ Fort Greene Park (p269)
➡ East River State Park (p274)

TOP EXPERIENCE
BROOKLYN BRIDGE

One of NYC's most-photographed sights, and an engineering masterpiece, Brooklyn Bridge opened in 1883. With a then-unequalled span of 1596ft, it became the first land connection between Brooklyn and Manhattan, as well as the world's first steel suspension bridge. This timeless example of urban design has inspired poets, writers and painters – even today, it never fails to dazzle.

The Bridge's Heavy Toll

German-born engineer John Roebling designed the bridge, but after contracting tetanus when his foot was crushed by a ferry at Fulton Landing, he died before construction even began. His son, Washington Roebling, assumed responsibility for the project, which lasted 14 years. However, Roebling junior also became a victim, contracting 'the bends' from working underwater in a pressurized *caisson*. Bedridden within sight of the bridge for many years, he relied on his wife, Emily Warren Roebling, herself a mathematician and engineer, to oversee construction in his stead. She also had to deal with budget overruns and unhappy politicians. Aside from the Roeblings, at least 27 workers died during the bridge's construction. And there was one final tragedy to come: in 1883, six days after the official opening, a massive crowd of pedestrians was bottlenecked at a stairway when rumours of a collapse, possibly started in jest, set off a stampede in which dozens were injured and 12 were crushed to death.

Crossing the Bridge

A stroll across the Brooklyn Bridge usually figures quite high on the 'must-do' list for NYC visitors. The pedestrian walkway affords wonderful views of Lower Manhattan, while observation points under the support towers offer brass 'panorama' histories of the waterfront. It's about a mile across the bridge, which can take 20 to 40 minutes to walk, depending on how often you stop to admire the view.

DID YOU KNOW?

➡ In May 1884, circus impresario PT Barnum marched 21 elephants over the bridge to prove to skeptics that the structure was safe.

PRACTICALITIES

➡ Map p443, B1

➡ S 4/5/6 to Brooklyn Bridge-City Hall, J/Z to Chambers St, R/W to City Hall, S 2/3 to Clark St, A/F to High St-Brooklyn Bridge Station

TOP EXPERIENCE
BROOKLYN BRIDGE PARK

A stunning example of industrial regeneration, this 85-acre, multi-use waterfront park skirts the East River for 1.3 miles from Jay St in Dumbo to the west end of Atlantic Ave in Cobble Hill. It has revitalized a barren shore and its once-decaying piers into a scenic playground for all-comers: local amblers, camera-toting tourists and families with kids in tow.

Empire Fulton Ferry

This section of the park, between the Brooklyn and Manhattan Bridges in the northern section of Dumbo, contains a sweeping grassy lawn with stunning views of the East River. As well as the lovingly restored 1922 Jane's Carousel (p266), there are shrubby landscaped gardens and walking tracks to find the best vantage point for that essential Brooklyn Bridge photograph. The park is bordered on one side by the Empire Stores (p267), a cluster of Civil War-era warehouses that now house restaurants, shops and acclaimed avant-garde theater St Ann's Warehouse (p294).

Pier 1

Picnicking, playgrounds and photography are all invited by the three lawns on Pier 1, just south of the Brooklyn Bridge. The largest of the park's piers, this is the stage for free events from May through August, including free films, screened against the stunning backdrop of Manhattan; plus dance parties, group yoga classes, and kid-friendly activities; check the park's website for the event calendar. At the north end of the pier, you can catch the **NYC Ferry** (Map p443; www.ferry.nyc; Pier 1; adult one-way $2.75) South Brooklyn and East River services to Manhattan.

DON'T MISS

- A stroll across the Brooklyn Bridge
- Taking photographs of NYC's two most charismatic bridges
- Empire Fulton Ferry at sunset

PRACTICALITIES

- Map p443, A1
- www.brooklynbridgepark.org
- East River Waterfront, btwn Atlantic Ave & John St, Brooklyn Heights/Dumbo
- 6am-1am, some sections to 11pm
- B63 to Pier 6/Brooklyn Bridge Park, B25 to Old Fulton St/Elizabeth Pl, East River or South Brooklyn routes to Dumbo/Pier 1, A/C to High St-Brooklyn Bridge, 2/3 to Clark St, F to York St

Pier 6

At the southern end of the park, off Atlantic Ave, Pier 6 is kid central. Between the flower beds and lawns are fantastic playgrounds: a sandbox, water jets, water slides, swings and more!) Jog with Fido at the dog run, use the beach-volleyball courts and relax at seasonal concessions (May to October) like pizza place Fornino (p278), which has a rooftop deck that's perfect for sundowners.

Other Areas

Main Street Park, just south of the Manhattan Bridge, has a bouldering wall, a dog run, a nautical-themed playground, a pebble beach and the Park Authority's Environmental Education Center.

A direct pedestrian link to Brooklyn Heights, **Squibb Park Bridge** leads from Columbia Heights between Middagh and Cranberry Sts directly down to Pier 1. At the time of research, there were plans in motion to replace it by a steel version.

Pier 2 is all about sweat, with a roller rink, an outdoor gym with free fitness equipment, courts for bocce, handball, basketball and shuffleboard, and free kayaking (thrice weekly, June through August). **Pier 3** has more lawns and granite steps for sitting and contemplating, while **Pier 4** has a small beach where you can launch a paddle boat or dip your toes in the East River. **Pier 5** has sports fields and cycling paths, a 'picnic peninsula' with shade umbrellas and barbecues, and an **Ample Hills** ice-cream kiosk.

TOP EXPERIENCE
PROSPECT PARK

Though Central Park is New York's most storied green space, its 19th-century architects, Frederick Olmsted and Calvert Vaux, considered Prospect Park their true *chef d'œuvre.* Between its looping bridges, scenic lake, broad meadow and the only swath of forest in Brooklyn, you might agree. Opened in 1867, 585-acre Prospect Park today receives roughly 10 million visitors a year.

Grand Army Plaza

Carrying a distinctly Parisian feel, this monumental plaza with its dominant ceremonial arch sits at the intersection of Flatbush Ave and Prospect Park West, marking the beginning of Eastern Pkwy and the entrance to Prospect Park. The arch was built in the 1890s as a memorial to Union soldiers who fought in the Civil War; there's also a bust of John F Kennedy nearby. The Greenmarket (p299) is held here Saturdays from 8am to 4pm year-round.

Long Meadow

Reaching for an unbroken mile, the longest meadow in any urban park in the USA, this 90-acre expanse lies to the south of the park's formal entrance at Grand Army Plaza. Long Meadow is a super area for strolling and lounging, filled with pickup ball games, frolicking dogs and families flying kites. On the south end is the **Picnic House**, with a snack stand and public bathrooms.

Children's Corner

Near Flatbush Ave, the Children's Corner contains a terrific 1912 **carousel** (per ride $2.50, open noon to 6pm from Thursdays to Sundays and public holidays), originally from Coney Island. The **Prospect Park Zoo** (Map p440; www.prospectparkzoo.com; adult/child $10/7; ⏲10am-5pm Mon-Fri, to 5:30pm Sat & Sun Apr-Oct, to 4:30pm Nov-Mar) is also here, home to sea lions, red pandas, wallabies and a small petting zoo. To the northeast of the carousel is the 18th-century **Lefferts Historic House** (Map p440; www.prospectpark.org/lefferts; adult/child $3/free; ⏲noon-5pm Thu-Sun Apr-Jun, Sep & Oct, to 6pm Jul & Aug, to 4pm Sat & Sun Nov & Dec), where kids can imagine themselves on an 18th-century Brooklyn Dutch farm.

LeFrak Center at Lakeside

A 26-acre, all-season activity **complex** (Map p440; www.lakesideprospectpark.com; 171 East Dr, near Ocean & Parkside Aves; skating $7.25-10, skate rental $7, boat rental per hr $16-36, bike rental per hr $13-38; ⏲hours vary) provides a focus for locals burning off energy in Prospect Park. From late March to mid-October there are kayaks and pedal boats to cast out on the lake, plus there are walking trails, rental bikes, roller-skating and on sunny summer days sprinklers flick on at the cooling kids' play area. In winter the center offers indoor and outdoor ice-skating. The partly alfresco cafe is a shaded place for refreshments.

Audubon Center Boathouse

Sitting on a northern finger of Prospect Park Lake, the photogenic boathouse (aka Prospect Park Audubon Center) hosts a range of pop-up events throughout the year: guided bird-watching, free yoga, nature-themed art exhibitions, hands-on craft activities for kids and more. From the boathouse, there's a trailhead for more than 2.5 miles of woodsy **nature trails**. The mile-long route along Lullwater Creek is very scenic; a slightly shorter trail plunges into the Midwood, offering views of the park's oldest trees. Check the website for directions or ask at the boathouse.

DON'T MISS

- Audubon Center Boathouse
- Long Meadow
- Lullwater Creek

PRACTICALITIES

- Map p440, E3
- www.prospectpark.org
- Grand Army Plaza
- ⏲5am-1am
- S 2/3 to Grand Army Plaza, F, G to 15th St-Prospect Park, B, Q to Prospect Park, Q to Parkside Ave

TOP EXPERIENCE
BROOKLYN MUSEUM

This five-story, 560,000-sq-ft beaux-arts building was designed in the early 1890s by McKim, Mead & White, a leading architectural powerhouse. It was conceived as the largest single-site museum in the world – though it was significantly scaled back when Brooklyn was incorporated into NYC (it's now New York's third-largest museum). There is ancient art, lavish 19th-century interiors and cutting-edge contemporary work.

Egyptian Art

A particular highlight is the excellent collection of Egyptian art, which spans a period of 5000 years. Housed in the 3rd-floor galleries, it includes bas-reliefs and Roman-era portraits, some of which are drawn from the museum's ongoing excavations in Egypt. A mummy chamber holds sarcophagi and ritual objects. Seek out the Wilbour Plaque, a limestone fragment showing the vivid profile of Queen Nefertiti facing a male figure, likely Akhenaten (father of Tutankhamun) dating to 1352–1336 BCE.

American Art

Don't miss a trip to the 5th floor to see the museum's colossal collection of American art, including an iconic full-length portrait of George Washington by Gilbert Stuart; Childe Hassam's celebrated 1900 urban landscape, *Late Afternoon, New York, Winter;* and watercolors by late-19th-century portraitist John Singer Sargent.

DON'T MISS

- Egyptian funerary gallery
- *The Dinner Party*
- American art
- Visible Storage Center

PRACTICALITIES

- Map p440, F3
- ☎718-638-5000
- www.brooklynmuseum.org
- 200 Eastern Pkwy, Prospect Park
- adult/child $16/free
- ⏱11am-6pm Wed & Fri-Sun, to 10pm Thu year-round, to 11pm 1st Sat of month Oct-Dec & Feb-Au
- Ⓢ2/3 to Eastern Pkwy-Brooklyn Museum

A Room of Their Own

This is one of the few mainstream arts institutions to devote permanent space to showcasing the works of women artists. The 8300-sq-ft Elizabeth Sackler Center for Feminist Art on the 4th floor exhibits an engaging mix of one-person and historical shows ranging from radical Black women artists to video installations and photography. At the gallery's core, you'll find Judy Chicago's absorbing 1979 installation, *The Dinner Party,* with place settings for 39 mythical and historical women; it somehow succeeds in being imposing and intimate.

Other Highlights

Housing more than 1.5 million objects, the museum has worthwhile galleries devoted to African sculpture, Islamic design, Latin American textiles and contemporary art. For a peek behind the scenes, head to the Visible Storage and Study Center on the 5th floor to see glass cases stuffed with everything from Tiffany lamps and Brooklyn-fashioned ceramics to vintage bicycles and Spanish colonial artifacts.

On the first Saturday of every month except September, the museum stays open until 11pm and hosts a free evening of art, performances and live music (sometimes there's even a dance floor set up). It's a big draw for families.

SIGHTS

Brooklyn Heights, Downtown Brooklyn & Dumbo

Brooklyn's engines of industry are today a collection of waterside neighborhoods. Former warehouses and piers have found new uses, but the 19th-century atmosphere is attractively preserved.

When Brooklyn ferry services started in the early 1800s, well-to-do Manhattanites began building beautiful houses in **Brooklyn Heights**. The piers are now recreational areas with lawns gazing towards Manhattan's skyscrapers. East lies cobblestone **Dumbo** ('Down under the Manhattan Bridge overpass'), beyond which Vinegar Hill hoards a few special restaurants. South is the **downtown** area, where high-rise condos are the backdrop to Brooklyn's present-day money-making enterprises.

BROOKLYN BRIDGE — BRIDGE

See p262.

BROOKLYN BRIDGE PARK — PARK

See p263.

JANE'S CAROUSEL — HISTORIC SITE

Map p443 (718-222-2502; www.janescarousel.com; Old Dock St, Brooklyn Bridge Park, Dumbo; tickets $2; 11am-7pm Wed-Mon mid-May–mid-Sep, to 6pm Thu-Sun mid-Sep–mid-May; ; F to York St, A/C to High St-Brooklyn Bridge) Behold the star attraction of the north end of Brooklyn Bridge Park (p263): a vintage carousel built by the Philadelphia Toboggan Company back in 1922. In 1984 it was purchased by Dumbo artist Jane Walentas, who spent the next two decades faithfully restoring the vintage paint scheme on the ornate, carved-wood elements before the carousel took up its current plum spot beneath New York's two most photographed bridges.

The carousel has 48 horses, two chariots and 1200 lights, and is the first of its kind to be placed on the National Register of Historic Places. The working treasure is housed in a clear acrylic pavilion designed by Pritzker Prize–winning architect Jean Nouvel.

BROOKLYN HISTORICAL SOCIETY — MUSEUM

Map p443 (718-222-4111; www.brooklynhistory.org; 128 Pierrepont St, Brooklyn Heights; suggested admission adult/child $10/free; noon-5pm Wed-Sun; R to Court St, 2/3, 4/5 to Borough Hall) Housed in a majestic, landmarked 1881 building with striking terracotta details, this museum is devoted to all things Brooklyn. Its priceless collection contains a rare 1770 map of NYC and a signed copy of the Emancipation Proclamation. Exhibits on Brooklyn life and history rotate regularly. Peek into the stunning 33,000-book **Othmer Library**, with its original 19th-century balcony of black ash.

The lobby **gift shop** (open noon to 5pm daily) is a fantastic resource for Brooklyn-themed books and upscale gifts.

The society also organizes regular exhibitions and neighborhood walks; check the website for details.

BROOKLYN HEIGHTS PROMENADE — VIEWPOINT

Map p443 (www.nycgovparks.org; btwn Orange & Remsen Sts, Brooklyn Heights; 24hr; N/R/W to Court St, 2/3 to Clark St, A/C to High St-Brooklyn Bridge) Six of the east–west streets of well-to-do Brooklyn Heights (such as Montague and Clark Sts) lead to the neighborhood's number-one attraction: a narrow, paved walking strip with breathtaking views of Lower Manhattan and New York Harbor that is blissfully removed from the busy Brooklyn–Queens Expwy (BQE) over which it sits. This little slice of urban beauty, over 1800ft in length, is fiercely defended by locals against development proposals. A great spot for a sunset walk.

An innovatively designed footbridge called the **Squibb Park Bridge**, just past the northern end of the promenade, links it with the shoreside Pier 1 in Brooklyn Bridge Park (p263).

NEW YORK TRANSIT MUSEUM — MUSEUM

Map p443 (718-694-1600; www.mta.info/mta/museum; 99 Schermerhorn St, at Boerum Pl, Downtown Brooklyn; adult/child $10/5; 10am-4pm Tue-Fri, 11am-5pm Sat & Sun; ; 2/3, 4/5 to Borough Hall; R to Jay St-MetroTech) Occupying an old subway station built in 1936 (and out of service since 1946), this kid-friendly museum takes on 100-plus years of getting around town. The best part is the downstairs area, on the platform, where you can climb aboard 20 original subway and elevated train cars dating to 1907. Temporary exhibitions highlight the subway's fascinating history, from its grueling construction to the art of map design.

EMPIRE STORES HISTORIC BUILDING

Map p443 (www.empirestoresdumbo.com; 53-83 Water St, Dumbo; ⌚8am-7:30pm; 🚌B25 to Water/Main Sts, ⓈF to York St, A/C to High St-Brooklyn Bridge) Built just after the Civil War, the Empire Stores are a vestige of Brooklyn's historic waterfront, which once supported 3 miles of brick warehouses stacked with coffee, sugar and tobacco. Retaining its original structure and features, it's been rehabilitated as an upscale hub of commerce and culture across 360,000 sq ft. **Time Out**'s chic food market, complete with avocado toast, Mexican fusion and Michelin-star ramen, is the highlight; head to the 5th floor for remarkable views and alfresco tables.

Boerum Hill, Cobble Hill, Carroll Gardens & Red Hook

Cobble Hill and **Boerum Hill** (respectively, west and east of Court St) are light on sightseeing but brimming with home-style restaurants, disarmingly friendly bars and attractive 19th-century houses. Genteel **Carroll Gardens** (south of here) is also a trove of brownstones, restaurants and tree-lined streets.

Further south, comparatively isolated **Red Hook** was one of the first parts of Brooklyn settled by Europeans (the Dutch dubbed it 'Roode Hoek' because of its tapered shape and ruddy soil). Galleries occupy old warehouses, while seafood and barbecue restaurants are a sticky-fingered highlight.

RED HOOK WINERY WINERY

Map p438 (☎347-689-2432; www.redhookwinery.com; 175 Van Dyke St, Pier 41, Suite 325a, Red Hook; ⌚noon-6pm; ⓈF to Smith-9th Sts then 🚌B61 to Van Brunt/Beard Sts) Sip wines from across New York in this stripped-bare tasting room, lined with barrels and crowded with chardonnay-sipping locals every weekend. Though the grapes are plucked from Finger Lakes and Long Island vineyards, every drop is produced right here. At this waterside winery, the cabernet sauvignon and riesling tastes even better looking out over the water.

COFFEY PARK PARK

Map p438 (www.nycgovparks.org/parks/coffey-park; Verona St, btwn Richards & Dwight Sts, Red Hook; ⌚6am-1am; 👪; ⓈF to Smith-9th Sts then then 🚌B61 to Van Brunt/King Sts) FREE This neighborhood park in the heart of Red Hook is flanked by hedges and trees, with lawns where families picnic, adjacent basketball courts and a kids' playground with swings.

Named for an Irish-American former district leader, Coffey Park also hosts NYC Summer Stage concerts and other free events.

> LOCAL KNOWLEDGE
>
> **MANHATTAN BRIDGE VIEW**
>
> Crowds gather where Front St meets Washington St to point their cameras at Manhattan Bridge, which frames the Empire State Building between its mighty girders. The view is appealing, but the elbow-to-elbow photo shoots aren't – go early if you're set on snapping this specific view, or better yet seek out other angles from the parks between Brooklyn and Manhattan Bridges.

INVISIBLE DOG GALLERY

Map p438 (☎347-560-3641; www.theinvisibledog.org; 51 Bergen St, btwn Smith & Court Sts, Boerum Hill; ⌚1-7pm Thu-Sat, to 5pm Sun; ⓈF, G to Bergen St) FREE In a converted factory dating to 1863, the Invisible Dog is an interdisciplinary arts center that embodies the spirit of Brooklyn's creativity. Check the calendar on their website to be sure something is showing in this airy, three-story space; there are frequent free exhibitions on the ground floor, where the unadorned warehouse backdrop makes art shows pop.

Fort Greene, Clinton Hill & Bed-Stuy

Stately brownstone buildings, cultural attractions and an enviable food scene give these neighborhoods their charm, though their industrial histories are soaked in sweat and blood.

Spreading eastward from Downtown Brooklyn beyond Flatbush Ave, leafy **Fort Greene** is home to a cultural lightning-rod, the Brooklyn Academy of Music (p294). North lies the Brooklyn Navy Yard, a historic shipbuilding site brought to new lustre. Moving east is neighborly drinking and dining in **Clinton Hill**, poet Walt Whitman's old stomping ground, while **Bedford-Stuyvesant** (aka Bed-Stuy) is the heart of African-American culture in Brooklyn.

Neighborhood Walk
Brownstones & Bridges

START ST GEORGE HOTEL
END JANE'S CAROUSEL
LENGTH 2 MILES; TWO HOURS

Studded with historic structures, Brooklyn Heights also has sublime views of Manhattan. Start at Clark and Henry Sts, at the base of the 30-story 1 **St George Hotel**. Built between 1885 and 1930, it was once the city's largest hotel. Scenes from *The Godfather* were filmed here.

Two blocks north on Orange St is 2 **Plymouth Church**. In the mid-19th century, Henry Ward Beecher gave abolitionist sermons here. Abraham Lincoln worshiped here during his 1860 presidential campaign.

Continue west on Orange, then south on Willow St. The yellow mansion at 70 Willow served as 3 **Truman Capote's house** while he was writing *Breakfast at Tiffany's*. Continue south, turning right on Pierrepont St. The street turns into 4 **Montague Tce**, lined with old brownstones. Thomas Wolfe penned *Of Time and the River* at No 5.

From here, turn left along Remsen St and right along Hicks St. Turning right along Joralemon St, lined with terraced houses in shades of brick, green and powder blue. Continue beneath the expressway and emerge facing 5 **Pier 5**, part of Brooklyn Bridge Park. These restored riverbank spaces have mixed-use walking and cycling paths that meander close to the water. Turning right, walk north past Pier 5's barbecue and picnic zones, and the small sandy beach at 6 **Pier 4**. Detour slightly to enjoy the flush of lawns and trees at 7 **Pier 3**. Continue past Piers 2 and 1 for increasingly spectacular views of the Manhattan skyline across the water. At the southern edge of 8 **Pier 1** is a salt marsh sheltered by salvaged granite.

Nearby is 9 **Fulton Ferry Landing**. George Washington made an important hasty retreat here during the Battle of Long Island in 1776. From here, follow Water St under the 10 **Brooklyn Bridge** (p262) (opened 1883), and past the Civil War–era brick warehouses of the 11 **Empire Stores** (p267); grab a snack on the 5th floor. The walk ends at Empire Fulton Ferry, home to the gleaming 1922 12 **Jane's Carousel** (p266).

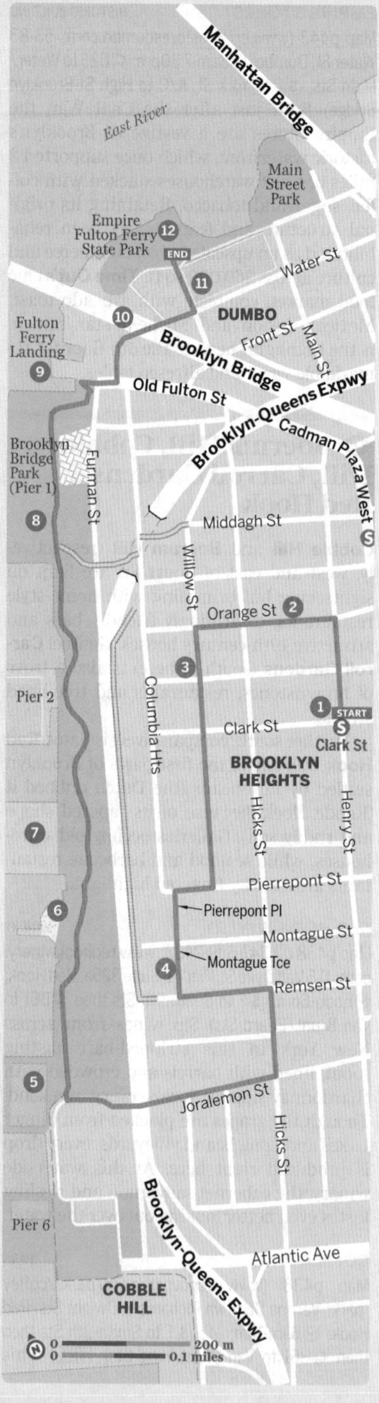

MUSEUM OF CONTEMPORARY AFRICAN DIASPORAN ARTS MUSEUM

Map p438 (MoCADA; ☎718-230-0492; www.mocada.org; 80 Hanson Pl, at S Portland Ave, Fort Greene; adult/student/child $8/4/free; ⊙central galleries noon-7pm Wed, Fri & Sat, to 8pm Thu, to 6pm Sun, exterior galleries 10am-7pm Mon-Fri; Ⓢ C to Lafayette Ave, B/D, N/Q/R, 2/3, 4/5 to Atlantic Ave-Barclays Center) This small museum in a brownstone building hosts thought-provoking, multidisciplinary installations exploring social and political issues facing people of the African Diaspora. Through rotating exhibitions, from contemporary art and photography to multimedia deep dives into history, the museum attempts to rediscover cultural traditions lost during colonization and the transatlantic slave trade. The museum also hosts performance pieces, music nights, artist talks and discussions.

Don't miss the on-site shop, with its range of one-of-a-kind art, jewelry, apparel and home decor by contemporary designers.

BRIC HOUSE ARTS CENTER

Map p438 (☎718-683-5600; www.bricartsmedia.org; 647 Fulton St, cnr Rockwell Pl, Fort Greene; ⊙gallery 11am-7pm Tue-Fri, to 5pm Sat & Sun; Ⓢ B, Q/R to DeKalb Ave, 2/3, 4/5 to Nevins St) This long-running Brooklyn arts organization (responsible for the free, summer **Celebrate Brooklyn! Festival** (Prospect Park Bandshell, near Prospect Park W & 11th St, Park Slope; ⊙Jun–mid-Aug) in Prospect Park, among other things) is housed in an impressive 40,000-sq-ft space. The multidisciplinary arts complex stages art exhibitions, media events and a wide range of cultural fare – poetry slams, plays, concerts, dance performances – inside its 400-seat theater. There's also a glassworking facility (which also has exhibitions) next door.

FORT GREENE PARK PARK

Map p438 (www.fortgreenepark.org; btwn Myrtle & DeKalb Aves & Washington Park & St Edwards St, Fort Greene; ⊙6am-1am; 👪; Ⓢ B, Q/R to DeKalb Ave, C to Lafayette St, G to Fulton St) War history and a hilly aspect make 30-acre Fort Greene Park a rewarding space to ramble. Forts from the Revolutionary War and War of 1812 were retired by 1847 when this tract of land became Brooklyn's first park (a measure championed by Walt Whitman, then editor of the *Brooklyn Daily Eagle*). By 1896, Calvert Vaux and Frederick Olmsted – designers of Central Park and Prospect Park – were resculpting its rugged expanse. It's popular for its tennis courts, ball fields and playground.

At the center of the park stands the **Prison Ship Martyrs' Monument**, at the time of its construction the world's tallest Doric column at 149ft. Designed by Stanford White (of prominent architectural firm McKim, Mead & White), it was built in 1905 to memorialize the 11,500 American prisoners of war who died in wretched conditions in British prison ships during the American Revolution. Some of their remains are interred in a crypt beneath its base.

Particularly in summer, it's worth checking the website for kid-friendly events, historical walking tours, yoga sessions and more. If you're there on a Saturday don't miss the year-round Greenmarket (p299) featuring all kinds of fresh regional produce, held at the southeastern corner of the park. In autumn months (from September to mid-November) it's joined by an **artisan market** featuring locally made artwork and crafts from independent artists.

KINGS COUNTY DISTILLERY DISTILLERY

Map p443 (☎347-689-4211; www.kingscountydistillery.com; 299 Sands St, at Navy St, Brooklyn Navy Yard; tours $16; ⊙tours 3pm & 5pm Tue-Thu, 3pm, 5pm & 7pm Fri, hourly 1-6pm Sat, 1pm, 3pm & 5pm Sun, tasting room noon-10pm Mon-Sat, to 8pm Sun; 🚌B62, B67 to Sands/Navy Sts, Ⓢ F to York St) Set in an 1899 brick building in the Brooklyn Navy Yard, this distillery uses New York grain to create some mighty smooth craft spirits. Come on a 45-minute **guided tour** (advance booking recommended) for a look at the distilling process and a tasting, with a bit of a history thrown in – the 19th-century Whiskey Wars, which erupted in nearby Vinegar Hill, devastated Brooklyn. Whether or not you join the tour, the atmospheric **bar-tasting room** pours flights and shakes cocktails.

BLDG 92 MUSEUM

(☎718-907-5932; www.bldg92.org; 63 Flushing Ave, at Carlton Ave, Brooklyn Navy Yard; ⊙noon-6pm Wed-Sun; 🚌B57, B69 to Cumberland St/Flushing Ave, Ⓢ G to Fulton St, F to York St) FREE A museum and gallery built in to the Brooklyn Navy Yard, BLDG 92 tells Brooklyn's living history, from the navy yards to its present-day innovators and designers. Three floors of exhibition rooms showcase the shipbuilding history that made Brooklyn, with some gripping testimony from characters of the time...women welders working 10-hour days while fighting for equal pay with the men, we salute you.

Check ahead on the website for regular tours of the Brooklyn Navy Yard.

Park Slope, Gowanus & Sunset Park

Known for tree-lined streets and graceful brownstone houses, **Park Slope** is Brooklyn's answer to Manhattan's Upper West Side. This former working-class area is today filled with couples with toddlers and designer dogs, who stroll between brunch places, boutiques and 585-acre Prospect Park (p266), Brooklyn's most beautiful green space. West lies quirky **Gowanus**, whose pungent canal has spawned its own monster mythology. Stretching south along Third Ave, adjoining the historical and picturesque Green-Wood Cemetery, are **Greenwood Heights** and **Sunset Park**. Neither has major sights, but bargain-hunters take note: each has great-value hotels.

PROSPECT PARK PARK

See p264.

SUNSET PARK PARK

Map p440 (www.nycgovparks.org/parks/sunset-park; btwn 41st & 44th Sts & Fifth & Seventh Aves, Sunset Park; ; B63 to 42nd or 44th St, S R to 45th St, D, N to 36th St) Sunset Park is a lovely hangout spot: on summer evenings, families keep cool in its Olympic-size outdoor swimming pool, and kids love its large, modern playground. It's small enough to walk around easily, large enough to spread out for picnics and relaxation, and features incredible views of New York Harbor and the Statue of Liberty from its highest point. You'll also find basketball, volleyball and handball courts, and some ever-elusive public restrooms.

Prospect Heights, Crown Heights & Flatbush

Endowed with multifarious dining scenes and tree-lined streets, the neighborhoods that are located east and south of Prospect Park (p264) are a springboard to big-hitters like the Brooklyn Museum (p265) and botanic garden.

Prospect Heights is filled with families, young professionals and scattered restaurants. Eastern Pkwy runs through **Crown Heights**, a largely Caribbean and African American neighborhood with a significant Hasidic Jewish community. East and south are sedate **Prospect Lefferts Gardens** and **Ditmas Park**, home to beautiful 19th-century brownstones. Below is **Flatbush**, founded by the Dutch in the mid-1600s, with Caribbean and Haitian flavors but fewer attractions.

BROOKLYN MUSEUM MUSEUM

See p265.

★BROOKLYN BOTANIC GARDEN GARDENS

Map p440 (☎718-623-7200; www.bbg.org; 150 Eastern Pkwy, Prospect Park; adult/student/child $15/8/free, 8am-noon Fri free, Tue-Fri Dec-Feb free; 8am-6pm Tue-Fri, from 10am Sat & Sun Mar-Oct, shorter hours Nov-Feb; ; S 2/3 to Eastern Pkwy-Brooklyn Museum, B, Q to Prospect Park) Opened in 1911 and now one of Brooklyn's most picturesque sights, this 52-acre garden is home to thousands of plants and trees and a **Japanese garden** where river turtles swim alongside a Shinto shrine. The best times to visit are late April or early May, when the blooming cherry trees (a gift from Japan) are celebrated in Sakura Matsuri – the **Cherry-Blossom Festival** (late Apr/early May), or fall, when the deciduous trees blaze their colours.

A network of trails runs throughout the gardens, connecting popular sections devoted to native flora, bonsai trees, a wood covered in bluebells and a rose garden. The **Discovery Garden** is a hands-on, immersive space for kids, with regular family activities. There's also a good cafe (with outdoor seating, of course).

There are three entrances; the most convenient one is immediately west of the Brooklyn Museum (p265). The Washington Ave entrance around the corner (at President St) leads to a striking eco-designed **visitor center** with a 'living roof' covered in a thriving diversity of plants. It's also possible to enter just north of Prospect Park subway station (corner of Empire Blvd and Flatbush Ave).

WEEKSVILLE HERITAGE CENTER HISTORIC SITE

(☎718-756-5250; www.weeksvillesociety.org; 158 Buffalo Ave, btwn St Marks Ave & Bergen

WORTH A DETOUR

GREEN-WOOD CEMETERY

If you want to enjoy a slice of scenic Brooklyn in total peace and quiet, make for **Green-Wood Cemetery** (Map p440; ☎718-768-7300; www.green-wood.com; 500 25th St, at Fifth Ave, Greenwood Heights; ⊙8am-5pm Oct-Mar, 7am-7pm Apr-Sep; P; S R to 25th St) FREE. This historic burial ground set on the borough's highest point covers 478 hilly acres with more than 7000 trees (many of which are over 150 years old); its myriad tombs, mausoleums, lakes and patches of forest are connected by a looping network of roads and footpaths, making this a perfect spot for some aimless rambling.

Founded in 1838 as a rural cemetery with Manhattan views, Green-Wood has over 560,000 'permanent residents,' including notable and historic personalities such as inventors Samuel Morse and Elias Howe, abolitionist Henry Ward Beecher, designer Louis Comfort Tiffany, artist Jean-Michel Basquiat and Susan Smith McKinney-Steward, the first African-American woman in New York state to gain a medical degree.

Don't miss **Battle Hill**, the cemetery's highest point, where Washington's Continental Army lost to British and Hessian troops during the 1776 Battle of Long Island (aka the Battle of Brooklyn). The event is commemorated by the 7ft statue of Minerva, the Roman goddess of wisdom, whose upright arm waves to the Statue of Liberty, facing back from a few miles across the harbor. The hill is located in the northeast sector of the cemetery, off Battle Ave. Musical legend Leonard Bernstein and Brooklyn Dodgers owner Charles Ebbets are both buried in the vicinity.

Admission is free, as are the maps available at the entrance. On Wednesdays at 1pm you can take a two-hour trolley-bus tour ($20 per person; advance online booking recommended). Note the squawking green-monk parakeets nesting within the nooks of the glorious Gothic entry gate – some allegedly broke free from an airport crate in the 1960s and started a colony that's lived here ever since.

Tip: pack mosquito repellent in the summer.

St, Crown Heights; tours adult/student $8/6; ⊙9:30am-6pm Tue-Fri, tours 3pm Tue-Thu; S A/C to Ralph Ave, 2/3 Utica Ave) In 1838 a former enslaved man by the name of James Weeks purchased a tract of land on the fringes of Brooklyn's settled areas to build a free African American community of entrepreneurs, doctors, laborers and craftspeople. The village was absorbed into Brooklyn, but three historic wooden houses (known as the Hunterfly Road Houses) have been preserved.

Small exhibitions of photography and local history are free to visit during opening hours, but tours of the houses are greatly more rewarding.

BROOKLYN CHILDREN'S MUSEUM — MUSEUM

(☎718-735-4400; www.brooklynkids.org; 145 Brooklyn Ave, at St Marks Ave, Crown Heights; $11; ⊙10am-5pm Tue, Wed & Fri, to 6pm Thu, to 7pm Sat & Sun; 👪; S A/C to Kingston-Throop Aves, 2/3 to Kingston Ave) A bright-yellow, L-shaped structure houses this hands-on kids' favorite, founded in 1899 as the first children's museum in the US. The collection contains almost 30,000 cultural objects (musical instruments, masks and dolls) and natural-history specimens (rocks, minerals and a complete Asian-elephant skeleton). But Brooklyn is very much in the house, with a re-created bodega, a pizza joint, and a Caribbean market that kids can play-act in. The canopied rooftop area, with greenery and play areas, is a highlight.

WYCKOFF HOUSE MUSEUM — HISTORIC BUILDING

(☎718-629-5400; www.wyckoffmuseum.org; 5816 Clarendon Rd, at E 59th St, East Flatbush; suggested donation adult/child $5/3; ⊙tours 1-4pm Fri & Sat, by arrangement Tue-Thu; S 2, 5 to Newkirk Ave then 🚌B8 to Kings Hwy St) Built in 1652, Pieter Claesen Wyckoff House is New York City's oldest building and one of the oldest in the US. A working farm until 1901, this Dutch Colonial H-frame house has shingled walls and split doors; outside is a community vegetable garden. Guided tours (usually half-hourly) explain the family's history and successive additions made to the house in the 18th and 19th centuries. Located in East Flatbush, a solid hour by public transportation from Downtown Brooklyn – for history fanatics only.

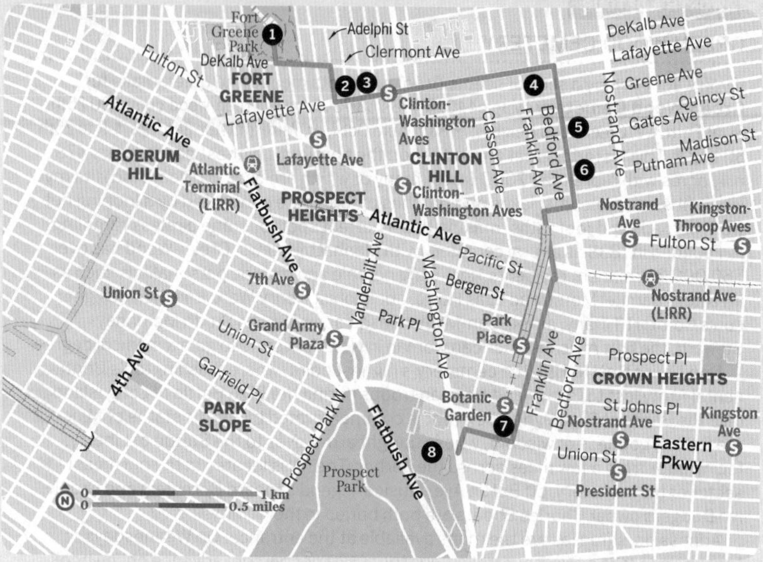

Local Life
Fort Greene to Prospect Park

Linking Brooklyn's two most attractive green spaces, this 3.5-mile walk starts at historic Fort Greene Park, tours cafes and cultural landmarks in Clinton Hill and Bed-Stuy, and finishes at the fringe of expansive Prospect Park.

1 Fort Greene Park
A stroll across pleasant 30-acre Fort Greene Park (p269) is a bracing way to kick off the day. Climb the hill to the Prison Ship Martyrs' Monument for military history and views of Manhattan. On Saturday morning there's a Greenmarket at the southeast corner of the park, where you can peruse locally sourced cheeses, baked goods and seasonal produce.

2 Brownstones & Local Flavors
The pleasant neighborhood surrounding the park is also called Fort Greene. Restaurant-lined DeKalb Ave, on the park's southern flank, is one of its main commercial strips, while the side streets have some of Brooklyn's loveliest residential architecture. From the park's southwestern corner, dip one block beyond DeKalb to Lafayette Ave for tapas at convivial Olea (p281).

3 Clinton Hill
Continuing east along Lafayette Ave, you'll pass intriguing buildings like the stately 1906-built **Masonic Temple** (on the corner with Clermont Ave) as you cut through the neighborhood of Clinton Hill.

4 Bed-Stuy Pitstop
After less than 10 minutes' walk, you'll cross into the neighborhood of Bed-Stuy, rich in African American cultures and boasting numerous noteworthy places to eat. Make sure you stop for a passion-fruit or dulce de leche doughnut at Dough (p281).

5 Biggie Mural
Turning south along Bedford Ave, after a few blocks you'll come face to face with one of Bed-Stuy's most beloved sons. Christopher Wallace, better known as hip-hop legend the Notorious B.I.G., stares regally from a **mural** on the corner with Quincy St.

6 Museum of African Art
Almost four blocks south is a repository of traditional and contemporary African art. If you're here on a weekday step inside the **museum** (www.bedstuymuseum.org; 1157 Bedford Ave, Ste 1, Bed-Stuy; by donation;

JUMIS/SHUTTERSTOCK ©

Clinton Hill

10am-3pm, tours by appointment) to see ceremonial masks, headdresses, fertility figures and more from diverse African countries.

7 Franklin Avenue

It's a very pleasant 25-minute walk, past bustling cafes and hang-worthy bars, to reach your next destination. Break up the journey by stopping for cookies and cocktails at sweet-toothed bar Butter & Scotch (p293).

8 Prospect Park

Just one block west is the enormous green escape of Prospect Park. Consider touring the many-splendored Botanic Garden (p270), if you arrive early enough; otherwise take your time through the park's meandering paths (or call it a day at a bar or restaurant on Classon and Washington Aves).

Williamsburg, Greenpoint & Bushwick

An international byword for beards, body art, bustling bars and fixed-wheel bikes, **Williamsburg** is now well and truly gentrified. Artists and students piled in to the postindustrial neighborhood, then since the late 1990s its revitalized streets received a stampede of property developers sowing eye-watering rents. Street art, coffee joints and avant-garde nightspots remain, making this an exciting neighborhood to explore. But the seamy up-and-comer is now **Bushwick**, to the east. North lies **Greenpoint**, Brooklyn's now-gentrifying 'Little Poland,' with enough casual restaurants and bars to recall its working-class immigrant roots.

CITY RELIQUARY MUSEUM

Map p436 (718-782-4842; www.cityreliquary.org; 370 Metropolitan Ave, near Havemeyer St, Williamsburg; adult/child $7/free; noon-6pm Thu-Sun; S G to Metropolitan Ave, L to Lorimer St) You knew Brooklyn was bizarro, but this repository for New York–related ephemera is something else. Tenderly curated displays exhibit objects from the recent past, like seltzer bottles, postcards of Lady Liberty and decaying confetti. Push through the antique subway turnstile to learn about local character 'Little Egypt' in a peep-show-style booth, admire mosaic shrines out the back, and stick around for a drink maybe (check out the website for occasional events).

BROOKLYN ART LIBRARY GALLERY

Map p436 (718-388-7941; www.sketchbookproject.com; 28 Frost St, btwn Union Ave & Lorimer St, Williamsburg; 10am-6pm Wed-Sun; S L to Lorimer St) FREE Enjoy an intimate glimpse into the creative minds of artists, both professional and amateur, at Brooklyn Art Library, which has assembled the world's largest collection of artist sketchbooks. More than 41,000 sketchbooks line the walls, containing a wild mix of graphic design, collage, fine art, poetry, irreverent comics and personal essays. Notebooks in baskets on the tables are free for visitors to browse (don't grab from the shelves).

If you feel inspired after paging through a few books, join in on the creative, cathartic fun. You can buy a sketch book ($30 for the 5"x7" book that each artist must use) and fill it with whatever you like; let your imagination run wild or use one of the suggested yearly themes. Once received by the library (you can mail it back from home) it will be added to the collection. Contributors from over 130 countries have added their sketchbooks. For a snappier way to leave your mark, take a picture in the photo booth to add to their collection.

MCCARREN PARK PARK

Map p436 (☎718-965-6580; www.nycgovparks.org/parks/mccarren-park; N 12th St, at Bedford Ave, Williamsburg; ⏰pool 11am-3pm & 4-7pm late May-early Sep; 👪; Ⓢ G to Nassau Ave, L to Bedford Ave) The grassy 35-acre McCarren Park makes a good picnic spot, and barbecues and bikinis define the action on warm summer weekends. On sweltering days you might want to head to the free **swimming pool** – a huge, historic community spot that reopened in 2012 after being closed for almost three decades. Go early to avoid the worst of the crowds. Free movies and live-music nights are held on Wednesdays in July and August (see www.summerscreen.org for details).

EAST RIVER STATE PARK PARK

Map p436 (☎718-782-2731; www.parks.ny.gov/parks/155; Kent Ave, btwn N 7th & N 9th Sts, Williamsburg; ⏰9am-9pm May-Sep, to 7pm Oct-Apr; 🚌B32 to Kent Ave/N 6th St, Ⓢ L to Bedford Ave) This 7-acre waterfront park is a slice of greenery with sublime views of Manhattan and cobbled vestiges of its cargo-handling past. It's home to plenty of events and activities in summer, with picnic tables, playgrounds and the odd concert. There's also summer-only ferry service to Governors Island (p74) and year-round service on the **NYC Ferry** (Map p436; www.ferry.nyc; N 6th St, N 5th St Pier & Park, off Kent Ave, Williamsburg; one-way trip $2.75; 🚌B32 to N 6th St, Ⓢ L to Bedford Ave). No pets allowed. Saturdays in the warmer months see the park given over to Smorgasburg (p281), the country's largest outdoor food market.

BROOKLYN BREWERY BREWERY

Map p436 (☎718-486-7422; www.brooklynbrewery.com; 79 N 11th St, btwn Berry St & Wythe Ave, Williamsburg; tours Mon-Thu $18, Sat & Sun free; ⏰tasting room 5-11pm Mon-Thu, 5pm-midnight Fri, noon-midnight Sat, noon-8pm Sun, tours 1-6pm Sat & Sun, reserve ahead Mon-Fri; Ⓢ L to Bedford Ave) Harking back to a time when this area of New York was a beer-brewing center, the Brooklyn Brewery not only brews and serves tasty local suds but also offers 45-minute tours of its facilities. Tours offered from Monday to Thursday include tastings of four beers, plus history and insight into the brewery; reserve a tour spot online. Note that sandals and high-heeled shoes are not allowed on tours.

On weekends, tours are free (just show up) but don't include tastings; buy refreshing brews at the bar. Or you can skip the tour altogether and just while away a weekend afternoon in the bare-bones tasting room.

Interesting fact: the brewery's cursive logo was designed by none other than Milton Glaser, of 'I Heart New York' fame, who did the job in exchange for a share of the profits and free beer for life.

LOCAL KNOWLEDGE

BUSHWICK STREET ART

Further cementing Bushwick's status as Brooklyn's coolest neighborhood is **Bushwick Collective** (www.instagram.com/thebushwickcollective; Bushwick; Ⓢ L to Jefferson St) FREE, an outdoor gallery of murals by some of the most talented street artists in NYC and beyond. The works change regularly, and can be found mainly along Jefferson and Troutman Sts between Cypress and Knickerbocker Aves, with others along Gardner Ave (north of Flushing Ave). Other street art can be found around the Morgan Ave L stop, particularly on Seigel and Grattan Sts.

The latter two streets are conveniently near Roberta's and Pine Box Rock Shop – great places to stop for a pizza or some drinks.

Though overall safe to visit, Bushwick still has occasional incidents of crime, so pay attention to your surroundings in this area, especially late at night and on weekends.

TOP EXPERIENCE
CONEY ISLAND AMUSEMENT PARKS

Coney Island – a name synonymous in American culture with antique seaside fun and frolicking – achieved worldwide fame as a working-class amusement park and beach-resort area at the turn of the 20th century. After decades of decline, its kitschy charms have experienced a 21st-century revival. Though it's no longer the booming attraction it once was, it still draws crowds of tourists and locals alike for legendary roller-coaster rides, hot dogs and beer on the beachside boardwalk.

Luna Park (Map p444; ☎718-373-5862; www.lunaparknyc.com; 1000 Surf Ave, at W 10th St; ⏲Apr-Oct; ⓈD/F, N/Q to Coney Island-Stillwell Ave) is one of Coney Island's most popular amusement parks and contains one of its most legendary rides: the Cyclone ($10), a wooden roller-coaster that reaches speeds of 60mph and makes near-vertical drops. In a neighboring park is the 150ft-tall pink-and-mint-green **Deno's Wonder Wheel** (Map p444; ☎718-372-2592; www.denoswonderwheel.com; 1025 Riegelmann Boardwalk, at W 12th St; rides $10; ⏲from noon Jul & Aug, Sat & Sun Apr-Jun, Sep & Oct; 👪; ⓈD/F, N/Q to Coney Island-Stillwell Ave), which has been delighting New Yorkers since 1920 as the best place to survey Coney Island from up high.

DON'T MISS

- Cyclone roller-coaster ride
- Cold beer at Ruby's
- Nathan's Famous hot dogs

PRACTICALITIES

- Map p444, C2
- Surf Ave & Boardwalk, btwn W 15th & W 8th Sts
- ⓈD/F, N/Q to Coney Island-Stillwell Ave

WILLIAMSBURG BRIDGE BRIDGE

Map p436 (www.nyc.gov/html/dot/html/infrastructure/williamsburg-bridge.shtml; S 5th St, Williamsburg; ⓈJ/M/Z to Marcy Ave) Built in 1903 to link Williamsburg and the Lower East Side (at Delancey St), this steel-frame suspension bridge helped transform the area into a teeming industrial center. At the time it was the longest suspension bridge on earth, a behemoth with its 1600ft span and all-steel towers. While the Brooklyn Bridge is the more attractive bridge, the Williamsburg Bridge's foot and bike paths offer excellent views of Manhattan and the East River, plus it connects two neighborhoods with numerous bars and restaurants.

Coney Island & Brighton Beach

Located an hour by subway from midtown Manhattan, Coney Island was once New York City's most popular beachside amusement area. After decades in the doldrums, revitalization has brought the summertime crowds back for hot dogs, roller coasters, minor-league baseball games and strolls down the boardwalk.

Situated directly to the east along the boardwalk is Brighton Beach, dubbed 'Little Odessa' for its large population of Ukrainian and Russian families. Running under the elevated subway tracks, its bustling main street, Brighton Beach Ave, is lined with Slavic shops, restaurants and cafes.

CONEY ART WALLS PUBLIC ART

Map p444 (www.coneyartwalls.com; 3050 Stillwell Ave, off Surf Ave, Coney Island; ⏲noon-8pm Jun-Sep; ⓈD/F, N/Q to Coney Island-Stillwell Ave) **FREE** This open-air public museum of street art features 35 freestanding walls transformed each season into colorful murals by emerging and renowned graffiti artists from around the world (including pioneers such as Daze and Lee Quiñones). On summer weekends, food trucks and live music make it one big Instagram-worthy street party.

1

MATT MUNRO/LONELY PLANET ©

2

1. Radegast Hall & Biergarten (p292)
This popular Williamsburg drinking spot has re-created an early-20th-century Germanic beer hall.

2. Brooklyn Museum (p265)
Houses a comprehensive collection of artefacts, including Egyptian art and Latin American textiles.

3. Manhattan Bridge view (p267)
Capture this classic shot of the Manhattan Bridge perfectly framed by buildings along Washington St.

4. Coney Island (p275)
Ride the wooden rollercoaster then stroll the boardwalk at this old-school amusement park.

4

PHOTRAVEL_RU/SHUTTERSTOCK ©

JUANA NUNEZ/SHUTTERSTOCK ©

3

TTSTUDIO/SHUTTERSTOCK ©

EATING

Brooklyn's culinary identity, hard to pin down and argued over with the passion of Talmudic scholars, is nevertheless assured. Why else would Manhattanites trek out to the far reaches of Kings County for a meal these days? Credentialed, ambitious chefs have created their own subspecies of restaurant here – small, retro, bespoke and locavore. Williamsburg and Greenpoint have perhaps the greatest variety, followed by the nexus of Carroll Gardens, Cobble Hill and Park Slope; honorable mention goes to a few gems in the Fort Greene, Clinton Hill and Bed-Stuy areas. Concentrated world-food wonderlands extend from Sunset Park to Brighton Beach.

Brooklyn Heights, Downtown Brooklyn & Dumbo

DEKALB MARKET HALL FOOD HALL $

Map p443 (☎929-359-6555; www.dekalbmarkethall.com; City Point, 445 Albee Sq W, at DeKalb Ave, Downtown Brooklyn; snacks from $6, mains from $12; ⏰7am-10pm; 📶; Ⓢ B, Q/R to DeKalb Ave, 2/3 to Hoyt St, A/C, G to Hoyt-Schermerhorn) Brooklyn's largest food hall arrays more than 40 street-food vendors and gourmet grab-and-go options within the City Point retail center's basement. Choose from hand-made pierogi and beer, churros, crepes, arepas (cornmeal bread sandwiches), French patisserie, tacos, brimming bagels and plenty more. One of Downtown Brooklyn's best options for a quick feed.

Hours for individual vendors vary but there's always someone dishing up something tasty.

GOVINDA'S VEGETARIAN LUNCH INDIAN $

Map p443 (☎718-855-6714; http://iskconnyc.com/govindas-vegetarian-lunch; 305 Schermerhorn St, btwn Bond & Nevins Sts, Downtown Brooklyn; mains $7-12; ⏰noon-3:30pm Mon-Fri; 🥬; Ⓢ 2/3, 4/5 to Nevins St, A/C, G to Hoyt-Schermerhorn) A simple, wholesome all-vegetarian buffet is served in the basement of a Hare Krishna temple, nourishing devoted vegheads and downtown workers who seek an oasis of calm on their lunch hour. Daily specials might be anything from veggie kofta or eggplant parmigiana to spicy broccoli and squash, and there are always vegan options.

★JULIANA'S PIZZA $$

Map p443 (☎718-596-6700; www.julianaspizza.com; 19 Old Fulton St, btwn Water & Front Sts, Brooklyn Heights; pizzas $20-32; ⏰11:30am-10pm, closed 3:15-4pm; 🥬; Ⓢ A/C to High St-Brooklyn Bridge) Legendary pizza maestro Patsy Grimaldi offers delicious, thin-crust perfection in both classic and creative combos – like the No 1, with mozzarella, *scamorza affumicata* (an Italian smoked cow's cheese), pancetta, scallions and white truffles in olive oil. Note that Juliana's closes for 45 minutes every afternoon to stoke the coal-fired pizza oven.

ALMAR ITALIAN $$

Map p443 (☎718-855-5288; www.almardumbo.com; 111 Front St, btwn Adams & Washington Sts, Dumbo; mains lunch $13-16, dinner $17-45; ⏰8am-10:30pm Mon-Thu, to 11pm Fri, 9am-11pm Sat, 10am-5pm Sun; Ⓢ F to York St, A/C to High St-Brooklyn Bridge) This welcoming restaurant serves breakfast, lunch and dinner in a homey, wood-lined space. The roasted fish and eggplant parmigiana are exemplary but if you're into pasta, don't miss the rich, delicious lamb and olive ragu or *cavatelli* (pasta shells) with mussels, clams, shrimp and cherry tomatoes. The hands-down brunch highlight is fluffy 'egg in a cloud' on brioche.

SUPERFINE AMERICAN $$

Map p443 (☎718-243-9005; www.superfine.nyc; 126 Front St, at Pearl St, Dumbo; mains lunch $12-18, dinner $21-38; ⏰11:30am-3pm & 6-11pm Tue-Sat, 10am-3pm & 6-10pm Sun; Ⓢ F to York St) 🌿 This casual hangout with an understated, bare-brick aesthetic is known for Sunday brunches, where locals sip Bloody Marys while DJs spin lazy tunes. The menu features breakfast burritos and buttermilk pancakes for brunch, and fish tacos and sandwiches for lunch. Dinners sprinkle in European bistro staples (grass-fed steak au poivre, spaghetti carbonara) and the ingredients are seasonal and locally sourced.

FORNINO AT PIER 6 ITALIAN $$

Map p443 (☎718-422-1107; www.fornino.com; Pier 6, Brooklyn Bridge Park; pizzas $15-16; ⏰10am-midnight Memorial Day–mid-Sep, weather permitting Apr, May & Oct; 🚌B63 to Brooklyn Bridge Park/Pier 6, Ⓢ 2/3, 4/5 to Borough Hall,

R to Court St) From the end of May through mid-September, Fornino dishes out excellent wood-fired pizza, sandwiches, beer and Italian treats right on Pier 6. The rooftop deck with picnic tables and spectacular views of Lower Manhattan is a great spot for groups.

The restaurant also opens in April, May and October when the weather's fine (check their Instagram account), but it closes completely in winter. Gluten-free bases are available.

RIVER CAFE AMERICAN **$$$**

Map p443 (☎718-522-5200; www.rivercafe.com; 1 Water St, near Old Fulton St, Brooklyn Heights; fixed-price menus dinner 3/6 courses $145/175, lunch $54, brunch $67; ⊙dinner 5:30-11pm, lunch 11:30am-2pm Sat, brunch 11:30am-2:30pm Sun; SA/C to High St-Brooklyn Bridge) Situated at the foot of the Brooklyn Bridge, this floating wonder offers unrivaled views of downtown Manhattan – not to mention solidly rendered modern American cooking. Standouts include Wagyu steak tartare, chicken with truffle stuffing, huckleberry-glazed duck breast and poached Nova Scotia lobster. The atmosphere is sophisticated (jackets required at dinner) but incurably romantic.

VINEGAR HILL HOUSE AMERICAN **$$$**

Map p443 (☎718-522-1018; www.vinegarhillhouse.com; 72 Hudson Ave, btwn Water & Front Sts, Vinegar Hill; mains dinner $25-34, brunch $15-18; ⊙dinner 6-10:30pm Mon-Thu, to 11pm Fri & Sat, 5:30-10pm Sun, brunch 10:30am-3:30pm Sat & Sun; B62 to York Ave/Navy St, SF to York St) Tucked into out-of-the-way Vinegar Hill (east of Dumbo), this homey spot is decked out with thrift-store bric-a-brac. Don't let the low-key decor fool you: the menu is bracingly fresh and unfussy, featuring cast-iron chicken with shallots and sherry-vinegar jus and rigatoni with rich lamb ragù and pecorino. Original craft cocktails use rhubarb amaro and sparkling cider to refreshing effect.

THE BEST OF BROOKLYN PIZZA

New York is known for a lot of things: screeching subways, towering skyscrapers, bright lights. It is also known for its pizza, which comes in gooey, chewy, sauce-soaked varieties. These are some of the top places in Brooklyn to grab a slice or a whole pie:

Di Fara Pizza (☎718-258-1367; www.difarapizzany.com; 1424 Ave J, cnr E 15th St, Midwood; pizza slices $5-6, toppings $1-2; ⊙noon-9pm; SQ to Ave J) In operation since 1965 in the Midwood section of Brooklyn, this slice joint is truly old-school, overseen by long-time proprietor Dom DeMarco.

Totonno's (Map p444; ☎718-372-8606; www.totonnosconeyisland.com; 1524 Neptune Ave, at W 16th St, Coney Island; pizzas $20-23, extra toppings $2.50; ⊙noon-8pm Thu-Sun; ✎; SD/F, N/Q to Coney Island-Stillwell Ave) A classic, family-owned Coney Island pizzeria that makes pies till the dough runs out.

Grimaldi's (Map p443; ☎718-858-4300; www.grimaldis-pizza.com; 1 Front St, cnr of Old Fulton St, Brooklyn Heights; pizzas $20-22; ⊙11:30am-10:45pm Mon-Thu, to 11:45pm Fri, noon-11:45pm Sat, to 10:45pm Sun; SA/C to High St-Brooklyn Bridge) Legendary pizzas (and legendary lines) abound at this tourist magnet in Brooklyn Heights.

Juliana's (p278) The home of pizza legend Patsy Grimaldi's celebrated return to the Brooklyn dining scene in 2013.

Lucali (p280) Neapolitan-style pies started as a hobby for this noted Carroll Gardens *pizzaiolo* (pizza maker).

Roberta's (p287) Divine pies with inventive topping combos are whisked out of brick ovens at the confluence of Bushwick and East Williamsburg.

If you want to try several pizzas in one go, sign up for an outing with **Scott's Pizza Tours** (☎212-913-9903; www.scottspizzatours.com; tours incl pizza from $55), which will take you to the most vaunted (and heavily mozzarella-topped) slices around the city by foot or by bus.

Boerum Hill, Cobble Hill, Carroll Gardens & Red Hook

★FOB
FILIPINO $$

Map p438 (☎718-852-8994; www.fobbrooklyn.com; 271 Smith St, Carroll Gardens; mains $16-24; ⏲5:30-10:30pm daily, plus 11am-3pm Sat & Sun; SF, G to Bergen St or Carroll St) Homestyle Filipino barbecue is lovingly prepared at FOB (meaning 'fresh off the boat'). Hospitable waitstaff conjure up beer-braised spare ribs, flounder grilled in banana leaf and sauce-drowned skewers of barbecued pork, while boba slushies add a sugar rush to the proceedings. It's casual, but FOB also makes a trim date spot – particularly if you land an outdoor table.

FOB also serves one of Brooklyn's standout brunches, with choices like seared spam with mustard, or smoked milkfish, always with savorous garlic rice and fried eggs.

MILE END
DELI $

Map p438 (☎718-852-7510; www.mileenddeli.com; 97a Hoyt St, Boerum Hill; sandwiches $11-21; ⏲8am-4pm Mon, 8am-10pm Tue-Thu, 8am-11pm Fri, 10am-11pm Sat, 10am-10pm Sun; SA/C, G to Hoyt-Schermerhorn) You can almost taste the smoked meats as you enter this small Boerum Hill eatery, which has exposed-brick walls and a couple of communal tables. Try potato latkes smothered in apple sauce and sour cream for breakfast, or a smoked beef brisket on rye with mustard ($16) – the bread is sticky soft and the meat will melt in your mouth.

HOMETOWN BAR-B-QUE
BARBECUE $$

Map p438 (☎347-294-4644; www.hometownbarbque.com; 454 Van Brunt St, Red Hook; meat per 0.5lb $12-14, sides $4-9; ⏲noon-11pm Tue-Thu, to midnight Fri & Sat, to 10pm Sun; SF, G to Smith-9th Sts then 🚌B61 to Van Brunt/Van Dyke Sts) Devotees of lamb belly, brisket and sweet pulled pork queue reverently for juicy BBQ at this casual home-style restaurant in Red Hook. Haul your tray, heavy with ribs, Italian sausage, cornbread and all the trimmings, to a convivial wooden table. There's also a bar stirring up craft cocktails; rock up on Friday or Saturday evening for live music.

RED HOOK LOBSTER POUND
SEAFOOD $$

Map p438 (☎718-858-7650; www.redhooklobster.com; 284 Van Brunt St, Red Hook; lobster rolls $24-28, mains $18-28; ⏲11:30am-9pm Mon-Thu, 11am-10pm Fri & Sat, 11am-9pm Sun; 🚌B61 to Van Brunt & Verona Sts) You may have seen its food truck vending lobster rolls across New York, so why not stop by the flagship restaurant? Nautical decor, with roughly whitewashed planks and lobster wallpaper, set the tone. The menu bursts with northeast seafood favorites and twists on the theme, like lobster mac 'n' cheese. Maine lobsters await their fate in tanks at the entrance.

★BUTTERMILK CHANNEL
AMERICAN $$

Map p438 (☎718-852-8490; www.buttermilkchannelnyc.com; 524 Court St, at Huntington St, Carroll Gardens; mains brunch $13-18, lunch $14-22, dinner $24-30; ⏲11:30am-3pm & 5-10pm Mon-Thu, 11:30am-3pm & 5-11:30pm Fri, 10am-3pm & 5-11:30pm Sat, 10am-3pm & 5-10pm Sun; SF, G to Smith-9th Sts) Taking comfort food to rare heights, Buttermilk Channel is a bustling, friendly place beloved of locals. Brunch is dominated by French toast and syrup-drowned pancakes, while buttermilk-fried chicken and duck meatloaf feature on the dinner menu, always complemented by a head-lightening array of cocktails. Named for the tidal strait between Brooklyn and Governors Island, its weekend brunch draws large crowds.

LUCALI
PIZZA $$

Map p438 (☎718-858-4086; www.lucalibrooklyn.com; 575 Henry St, at Carroll St, Carroll Gardens; pizzas $24, toppings $3; ⏲5:45-11pm Wed-Mon; 👪; 🚌B57 to Court & President Sts, SF, G to Carroll St) One of New York's tastiest pizzas comes from this unlikely little spot run by dough virtuoso Mark Iacono. Pizzas are all one size, with crisp but pliant crusts, fresh tomato sauce and superfresh mozzarella. Toppings are limited, but the Brooklyn accent is for real. Cash only; beer or wine are BYOB. Worth the long wait.

FRANKIES 457 SPUNTINO
ITALIAN $$

Map p438 (☎718-403-0033; www.frankies457.com; 457 Court St, btwn 4th Pl & Luquer St, Carroll Gardens; snacks from $4.50, sandwiches $12-17, mains $14-23; ⏲11am-11pm Sun-Thu, to midnight Fri & Sat; 👪; SF, G to Smith-9th Sts) Frankies is a neighborhood magnet, attracting local couples, families and plenty of Manhattanites with hearty pasta dishes like cavatelli with hot sausage and gnocchi with fresh ricotta. But as a *spuntino* (snack joint), this place is more about the small plates, with a seasonal menu that boasts salads flecked with pecorino and walnuts, local and Italian cheeses, cured meats and heavenly crostini.

Fort Greene, Clinton Hill & Bed-Stuy

★DOUGH BAKERY $

(☎347-533-7544; www.doughdoughnuts.com; 448 Lafayette Ave, cnr Franklin Ave, Bed-Stuy; doughnuts around $3; ⊙6am-9pm; 📶; Ⓢ G to Classon Ave) Situated on the border of Clinton Hill and Bed-Stuy, this tiny, out-of-the-way bakery takes the business of doughnuts seriously – making light, chewy 'nuts in frequent small batches to ensure peak freshness. The brioche-style dough is twice-proved, fried, then rolled in a changing array of glazes and toppings, including salted chocolate caramel, passion fruit, dulche de leche and hibiscus.

GREEN GRAPE ANNEX CAFE $

Map p438 (☎718-858-4791; www.greenegrape.com/annex; 753 Fulton St, at S Portland Ave, Fort Greene; breakfasts & sandwiches $7-11; ⊙7am-9pm Mon-Thu, 7am-10pm Fri, 8am-10pm Sat, 8am-9pm Sun; 🖉; Ⓢ G to Fulton St, C to Lafayette Ave) Weathered sofas and creeper plants draped across whitewashed walls...Green Grape Annex follows an understated hipster aesthetic to the letter, and the result is a relaxed, airy cafe. The coffee's superb and there are soups, veg bowls and sandwiches (from avocado to 'fig and pig toast') to ease the hunger pangs of punters distractedly tapping the keys of their laptops.

★MISS ADA MEDITERRANEAN $$$

Map p438 (☎917-909-1023; www.missadanyc.com; 184 DeKalb Ave, at Carlton Ave, Fort Greene; mains $18-27; ⊙5:30-10:30pm Tue-Thu, to 11:30pm Fri & Sat, 11am-2:30pm & 5:30-10:30pm Sun; 🖉; Ⓢ G to Fulton St, G to Clinton-Washington Aves, B, Q/R to DeKalb Ave) Chef-owner Tomer Blechman presents dishes inspired by Mediterranean flavors and recipes from his native Israel: octopus with eggplant, za'atar-seasoned salmon and *shakshuka* (eggs baked in spicy tomato with goat's cheese). Many are flavored with herbs grown in the backyard, which features canopied dining in warmer months. And Miss Ada? A misdirection: *misada* is Hebrew for restaurant. Reserve far in advance.

LOCAL KNOWLEDGE

SMORGASBURG!

The largest **foodie event** (www.smorgasburg.com; mains from $10; ⊙Williamsburg 11am-6pm Sat, Prospect Park 11am-6pm Sun; 👪) in Brooklyn (perhaps the US) brings together more than 100 vendors selling an incredible array of goodness. Seize stuffed calamari or Afghan comfort food; queue for fusion inventions like ramen burgers and pizza cupcakes; or wash down Colombian arepas (cornbread sandwiches) with lavender lemonade. Most vendors accept cards.

Locations can change each season, so check the website. Most recently the Smorg has been held in Williamsburg in East River State Park (p274) on Saturday, and Prospect Park near Lakeside (p264) on Sunday.

PEACHES SOUTHERN US $$

(☎718-942-4162; www.peachesbrooklyn.com; 393 Lewis Ave, at MacDonough St, Bed-Stuy; mains $14-23; ⊙11am-10pm Mon-Thu, to 11pm Fri & Sat, 10am-10pm Sun, closed 4-5pm; Ⓢ A/C to Utica Ave) A homey atmosphere and beloved Southern staples – like cornmeal-crusted catfish and shrimp po' boys – have won Peaches a loyal following. Shrimp and grits with a creamy mushroom sauce is popular at all hours, while the granola-crusted French toast and turkey sausage omelette are in demand at brunch. Vegetarian options are limited to plant-based burgers and various side dishes.

OLEA MEDITERRANEAN $$$

Map p438 (☎718-643-7003; www.oleabrooklyn.com; 171 Lafayette Ave, at Adelphi St, Fort Greene; mains brunch $11-18, dinner $18-32; ⊙10am-11pm Sun-Thu, to midnight Fri & Sat; 🖉; Ⓢ C to Lafayette Ave; G to Clinton-Washington Aves) Though it looks humble, the crowds arriving at this Mediterranean restaurant promise greatness and the exceptional tapas-style dishes deliver. Olea's day starts with Greek-inflected breakfasts (try the 'Green Eggs and Lamb') and continues with Spanish-style dainties like goat's cheese croquettes and *patatas bravas* (fried potatoes with aioli). Come evening, the kitchen sizzles with hanger steak, garlic prawns and wine-drenched meatballs.

ROMAN'S ITALIAN $$$

Map p438 (☎718-622-5300; www.romansnyc.com; 243 DeKalb Ave, btwn Clermont & Vanderbilt Aves, Fort Greene; mains $20-38; ⏰5-11pm Sun-Thu, to midnight Fri & Sat, brunch 11am-3pm Sat & Sun; 🚌B38, B69 to Vanderbilt/DeKalb Aves, ⓈG to Clinton-Washington Aves) Solo diners nursing the daily 'sour' or 'bitter' cocktail at the bar are just as welcome at Roman's as larger parties of blow-ins or tables full of regulars. All are soon happily hunched over seasonally changing Italian food: perhaps yellowfin tuna with black rice and eggplant, or fusilli with pesto that zings with olive oil and freshly crushed basil.

Park Slope, Gowanus & Sunset Park

AMPLE HILLS CREAMERY ICE CREAM $

Map p440 (☎347-725-4061; www.amplehills.com; 305 Nevins St, at Union St, Gowanus; ice cream from $4.75; ⏰noon-11pm Sun-Thu, to midnight Fri & Sat; 📶🖊; ⓈR to Union St, F, G to Carroll St) Though Ample Hills' Red Hook location now churns the ice cream, this scoop shop serves the small chain's magnificently creative flavors – honeycomb, butter cake, vegan-friendly mango and cherry-lime, plus 'It Came From Gowanus,' a chocolatey swirl of cookies and brownies, inspired by the dark depths of the Gowanus canal. Grab a cone and head up to the roof deck.

★**FOUR & TWENTY BLACKBIRDS** BAKERY $

Map p440 (☎718-499-2917; www.birdsblack.com; 439 Third Ave, cnr 8th St, Gowanus; slices $6, whole pies $42; ⏰8am-8pm Mon-Fri, from 9am Sat, 10am-7pm Sun; 📶; ⓈR to 9th St) Inspired by their grandma, sisters Emily and Melissa Elsen use local fruit and organic ingredients to create NYC's best pies, hands down. Any time is just right to drop in for a slice – salted-caramel apple, lavender-honey custard or other seasonally changing flavors – and a cup of Stumptown coffee.

KORZO EASTERN EUROPEAN $$

Map p440 (☎718-499-1199; www.korzorestaurant.com; 667 Fifth Ave, btwn 19th & 20th Sts, Greenwood Heights; mains $17-21; ⏰11:30am-11:30pm Mon-Fri, from 11am Sat & Sun; ⓈR to Prospect Ave) The story of Korzo begins with love forged in the ski resorts of former Czechoslovakia, and finds its happy ending in the husband-and-wife owners' mutual affection for *halusky,* Central European–style gnocchi. The restaurant effortlessly mingles old-country classics, like dumplings and wurst, with some of Brooklyn's best burgers and beer-battered fish. Cocktails like the vegetal, ginger-spiced 'Beet'Tini' add extra warmth.

BABA'S PIEROGIES POLISH $

Map p440 (☎718-222-0777; www.babasbk.com; 295 Third Ave, at Carroll St, Gowanus; 5/9 dumplings from $9/11; ⏰11:30am-10pm Tue-Sat, to 9pm Sun & Mon; 🖊; ⓈR to Union St) Granny's recipes have been passed down to these Brooklyn purveyors of plump *pierogi* (Polish dumplings), whose soft dough is stuffed with cheese and potato, feta and spinach, or even mac 'n' cheese, before being boiled to perfection. There are vegan options, too, like dumplings crammed with sauerkraut or potato.

KING DAVID TACOS TACOS $

Map p440 (☎929-367-8226; www.kingdavidtacos.com; Grand Army Plaza, Prospect Park; tacos $4; ⏰7-11am Mon-Fri, to 2pm Sat, 8am-1pm Sun; 🖊; Ⓢ2/3 to Grand Army Plaza) Texan native Liz Solomon found NYC missing one thing: Austin-style breakfast tacos. So in 2017 she started to make her own, shipping flour tortillas in from Texas and filling them with smoked bacon, chorizo, eggs and other satisfying breakfast combos. Her outdoor stand at Grand Army Plaza offers four varieties, made that morning and ready to go, plus cold-brew coffee.

BAKED IN BROOKLYN BAKERY $

Map p440 (☎718-499-1818; www.bakedinbrooklynny.com; 755 Fifth Ave, btwn 25th & 26th Sts, Greenwood Heights; pastries from $2.50; ⏰7am-7pm Mon-Sat, 8am-4pm Sun; ⓈR to 25th St) The flagship bakery for a popular local brand of baked goods is small, but filled to the brim with treats: flaky Danish pastries, buttery croissants, brownies, crisp and savory pita chips, gooey cookies and more.

Coffee is served as well, which makes it a perfect morning or afternoon treat, especially after a visit to Green-Wood Cemetery (p271) across the street.

LUKE'S LOBSTER SEAFOOD $

Map p440 (☎347-457-6855; www.lukeslobster.com; 237 Fifth Ave, btwn Carroll & President Sts, Park Slope; lobster roll from $17, chowder $7-12; ⏰noon-10pm Mon-Thu, from 11am Fri-Sun; 👪; ⓈR to Union Ave) Spreading across NYC

BROOKLYN COOKBOOKS

Locally sourced products, ecological sustainability and large doses of culinary creativity are all hallmarks of Brooklyn's celebrated dining scene. To learn more about the magic behind the cuisine – and more importantly how to make the dishes at home – check out the following titles:

➡ *The New Brooklyn Cookbook* (2010) Recipes, stories and culinary insights from 31 of Brooklyn's top restaurants.

➡ *Roberta's Cookbook* (2013) Diver scallops in plum juice, orecchiette with oxtail ragu and glorious pizza perfection.

➡ *Four & Twenty Blackbirds Pie Book* (2013) Take your pastry skills up a notch with these tantalizing recipes by the Elsen sisters.

➡ *Franny's: Simple, Seasonal, Italian* (2013) An essential reference for making memorable pizzas, pastas and gelato at home.

➡ *The Frankies Spuntino Kitchen Companion & Cooking Manual* (2010) Beautifully designed cookbook packed with recipes of reimagined Italian American comfort fare.

➡ *Brooklyn Brew Shop's Beer Making Book* (2011) Easy-to-follow guide for making refreshing brews at home.

➡ *One Girl Cookie* (2012) Moist, tender whoopie pies and other sweet indulgences.

➡ *The Mile End Cookbook* (2012) Reinventing Jewish comfort food.

➡ *The Macaroni's in the Basement* (2014) Italian-American home cooking in post-WWII Brooklyn.

➡ *Butter & Scotch: Recipes from Brooklyn's Favorite Bar & Bakery* (2016) Sweet-toothed recipes for cake and cocktail connoisseurs.

➡ *Veganomicon: 10th Anniversary Edition* (2017) Celebrated Brooklyn chef Isa Chandra Moskowitz teaches you how to whip up delicious vegan fare like you'll find at her East Williamsburg restaurant.

For the latest on the borough's dining scene, seek out *Edible Brooklyn* magazine (www.ediblebrooklyn.com).

(and far beyond) from the East Village, this chain of seafood 'shacks' works directly with fishers to ensure the provenance of its crustacea. Favorites include the lobster bisque, the clam and lobster chowders, and the staple lobster roll (a quarter crustacean on bread with mayonnaise and lemon butter).

SIDECAR AMERICAN **$$**

Map p440 (☎718-369-0077; www.sidecarbrooklyn.com; 560 Fifth Ave, btwn 15th & 16th Sts, Park Slope; mains $14-27; ⊙6pm-1am Mon, 11am-1am Tue-Thu & Sun, 11am-3am Fri & Sat; Ⓢ R to Prospect Ave) Upscale American cuisine is beautifully conceived at Sidecar, an atmospheric spot with stamped-tin ceiling and leather boot seating. Classic dishes are given a modern touch, such as buttermilk fried chicken served with a savory root mash, and a club salad that muddles gruyère and tart apple into its medley of turkey and sun-dried tomato.

LOT 2 AMERICAN **$$**

Map p440 (☎718-499-5623; www.lot2restaurant.com; 687 Sixth Ave, btwn 19th & 20th Sts, Greenwood Heights; mains $18-32; ⊙6-10pm Wed & Thu, 6-10:30pm Fri & Sat, 5-9:30pm Sun; 🚌B63, B67, B69 to 18th St, Ⓢ R to Prospect Ave) This rustic, intimate spot serves high-end comfort food in Greenwood Heights, south of Park Slope. The menu is small but big on flavors. Try the grilled-cheese sandwich (with cheddar, provolone and Parmesan), brick chicken with nettle pesto, or an outstanding burger with thick-cut, duck-fat fries. The Sunday three-course special is a deal at $35 ($17 for kids).

Prospect Heights, Crown Heights & Flatbush

★AMPLE HILLS CREAMERY ICE CREAM **$**

Map p440 (☎347-240-3926; www.amplehills.com; 623 Vanderbilt Ave, at St Marks Ave, Prospect Heights; ice cream from $4.50; ⊙noon-10pm Sun-Thu, to 11pm Fri & Sat; ⓈB, Q to 7th Ave, 2/3 to Grand Army Plaza) Taking its name from Walt Whitman's 'Crossing Brooklyn Ferry,' Ample Hills makes superb ice cream from organic ingredients. Each Ample Hills outlet has one location-specific flavor; in Prospect Heights it's the salty-sweet 'Commodore', studded with homemade honeycomb and potato chips coated in chocolate. Everything is made from scratch with fresh, hormone-free milk and cream at their factory in Red Hook.

CATFISH CAJUN **$$**

Map p440 (☎347-305-3233; www.catfishnyc.com; 1433 Bedford Ave, btwn Prospect & Park Pl, Crown Heights; mains $14-22; ⊙kitchen 11am-3:30pm & 5pm-2am, bar 11am-2am; Ⓢ2/3, 4/5 to Franklin Ave, A/C to Nostrand Ave) Catfish serves Cajun cuisine with flair, in an atmosphere that is sheer fun. Rich, garlicky shrimp 'n' grits join jambalaya (veg, spicy rice and andouille sausage) and beer-braised pulled pork on the menu. Portions are generous enough to threaten your appetite for bourbon-drenched bread pudding (push through the pain barrier, it's worth it). Free bingo on Monday nights.

High-quality cocktails employing retro libations like absinthe, sweet vermouth and rye encourage boozy dinners. Aim for the 5pm to 7pm weekday happy hour for reduced-price drinks and $1 oysters.

CHUKO JAPANESE **$**

Map p440 (☎347-425-9570; www.chukobk.com; 565 Vanderbilt Ave, cnr Pacific St, Prospect Heights; ramen $15; ⊙noon-3pm & 5:30-10pm Sun-Thu, to 11pm Fri & Sat; ⓥ; ⓈB/Q to 7th Ave, 2/3 to Bergen St) This contemporary, minimalist ramen shop brings a top-notch noodle game to Prospect Heights. Steaming bowls of al dente ramen are paired with one of several spectacularly silky broths, including an excellent roasted pork and a full-bodied vegetarian. The appetizers are *very* worthwhile, like the crispy brussels sprouts and fragrant salt-and-pepper chicken wings.

LINCOLN STATION CAFE **$**

Map p440 (☎718-399-2211; www.stationfoods.com; 409 Lincoln Pl, near Washington Ave, Prospect Heights; sandwiches $10-12, dinner mains $8-17; ⊙7am-9pm Mon-Fri, from 8am Sat & Sun; Ⓢ2/3 to Eastern Pkwy-Brooklyn Museum) Somewhere between old-school bistro and upmarket espresso joint is brick-lined Lincoln Station, where folks amass around the long center table, fresh cold brew in hand, awaiting their order of sandwiches stuffed with avocado and cheddar or brisket with blue cheese. By night the kitchen opens up, offering juicy rotisserie chicken, lamb chili and a veggie lasagna.

Proximity to the Brooklyn Museum (p265), Brooklyn Botanic Garden (p270) and Prospect Park (p264) makes this a fine halt on a whistle-stop tour of some of the borough's best sights. Bonus points for the designated laptop-free zones, to fend off the office space atmosphere that befalls many Brooklyn cafes.

BERG'N FOOD HALL **$**

Map p440 (www.bergn.com; 899 Bergen St, btwn Classon & Franklin Aves, Crown Heights; mains $13-16; ⊙approximately 9am-11pm, bar 11am-late Tue-Sun; ; ⓈC, 2/3, 4/5 to Franklin Ave) From the team behind Smorgasburg (p281) and Brooklyn Flea (p299), Berg'n is a large factory-feeling food hall with long wooden tables where you can feast on smoky brisket (Mighty Quinn's), gourmet grilled cheese and burgers (LandHaus), Shanghai-inspired street food (Jianbing) and blistered, hand-stretched pizzas (Pizza by Charlie). There's also a coffee stand and a bar serving a dozen local and regional microbrews.

TOM'S RESTAURANT DINER **$**

Map p440 (☎718-636-9738; www.tomsbrooklyn.com; 782 Washington Ave, at Sterling Pl, Prospect Heights; mains $8-14; ⊙7am-5pm Mon-Fri, to 9pm Sat, 8am-8pm Sun; Ⓢ2/3 to Eastern Pkwy-Brooklyn Museum) Open since 1936, Tom's traffics in Brooklyn nostalgia and delivers good, greasy-spoon cooking three blocks from the Brooklyn Museum (p267). Breakfast is served all day and it's a deal: huge spinach-stuffed omelettes with home fries, crab cakes and unrivaled blueberry-ricotta pancakes with lemon zest. For a classic, order an egg cream (milk, soda and chocolate syrup, topped with cream). Cash only.

★OLMSTED AMERICAN **$$$**

Map p440 (☎718-552-2610; www.olmstednyc.com; 659 Vanderbilt Ave, btwn Prospect Pl & Park Pl, Prospect Heights; small plates $14-17, large plates $23-24; ⊙dinner 5:30-10pm Mon-Thu, 5-10:30pm Fri & Sat, 5-9:30pm Sun, brunch 11:30am-2:30pm Fri, 11am-3pm Sat & Sun; ⓈB, Q to 7th Ave) Chef-owner Greg Baxtrom, alumnus of a string of hot kitchens, cooks such outstanding, seasonally inspired food that even Manhattanites cross the river to eat here. Much of the menu comes from the restaurant's backyard garden – which doubles as a lovely spot for cocktails or dessert. Whether pork belly with dandelion, carrot crepe, or scallops with chanterelles, sensational flavors are almost guaranteed.

CHERYL'S GLOBAL SOUL FUSION $$

Map p440 (☎347-529-2855; www.cherylsglobalsoul.com; 236 Underhill Ave, btwn Eastern Pkwy & St Johns Pl, Prospect Heights; sandwiches $8-17, dinner mains $16-25; ⊙8am-4pm Mon, to 10pm Tue-Thu & Sun, to 11pm Fri & Sat; ; S2/3 to Eastern Pkwy-Brooklyn Museum) Around the corner from the Brooklyn Museum (p265) and botanic garden (p270), this homey brick-and-wood favorite serves unpretentious cooking that draws on a world of influences: Moroccan tagine, Korean-style rib-eye, jerk chicken, mussels in Thai curry, homemade quiche and a long list of satisfying sandwiches. There are a couple of veggie options plus a separate kids' menu. Expect long waits for weekend brunch.

SCREAMER'S PIZZA VEGAN $

Map p440 (☎718-623-6000; www.screamerspizzeria.com; 685 Franklin Ave, at Prospect Pl, Crown Heights; slices from $3.25; ⊙noon-midnight; ; S2/3, 4/5 Franklin Ave) In a city of pizza lovers, it's hard to break the mold. But this buzzy, candy-colored joint has won a loyal following for its all-vegan slices, adorned with almond-based ricotta, vegan chorizo, seitan pepperoni and other plant-based toppings.

Williamsburg, Greenpoint & Bushwick

KARCZMA POLISH $

(☎718-349-1744; www.karczmabrooklyn.com; 136 Greenpoint Ave, Greenpoint; mains $11-16; ⊙noon-10:30pm Sun-Thu, to 11:30pm Fri & Sat; SG to Greenpoint Ave) There's no better way to soak up Greenpoint's Polish flavors than at this tavern-style restaurant. Slip into a booth, admire the rustic decor, and order sour soup in a puffy bread bowl, pork knuckle in beer, grilled *kielbasa* (sausage) or *pierogi*, ear-shaped dumplings stuffed with potato. Weekday lunch specials are mighty filling ($12.50), but allow space for Polish draft beer.

CRIF DOGS HOT DOGS $

Map p436 (☎718-302-3200; www.crifdogs.com; 555 Driggs Ave, at N 7th St, Williamsburg; hot dogs $4.50-6.50; ⊙noon-2am Sun-Thu, to 4am Fri & Sat; ; SL to Bedford Ave) Many a late-night Billyburg excursion ends up at this laid-back hot-dog joint, with no-nonsense beef-and-pork and veggie weiners done how you like, with two dozen toppings to choose from. Get a draft beer and a side of tater tots, order your dog with pineapple, sauerkraut or Swiss cheese, and keep the party going.

DUN-WELL DOUGHNUTS VEGAN $

Map p436 (☎347-294-0871; www.dunwelldoughnuts.com; 222 Montrose Ave, at Bushwick Ave, East Williamsburg; doughnuts $2.50-2.75; ⊙7am-7pm Mon-Fri, from 8am Sat & Sun; ; SL to Montrose Ave) 'Brooklyn's finest artisanal vegan doughnuts' might sound like peak hipster, but here reality exceeds the hype. Light, almost croissant-like doughnuts are made daily with organic ingredients in myriad flavors, including blueberry French toast, eggnog, lemon poppyseed, pumpkin crunch, cinnamon sugar, vanilla chip and chocolate peanut.

PETER PAN DONUT & PASTRY SHOP BAKERY $

Map p436 (☎718-389-3676; www.peterpandonuts.com; 727 Manhattan Ave, btwn Norman & Meserole Aves, Greenpoint; doughnuts from $1.25; ⊙4:30am-8pm Mon-Sat, to 7pm Sun; SG to Nassau Ave) On the main drag in Greenpoint, Peter Pan doesn't go in for gimmicks or fancy presentation, just soft doughnuts made from long-perfected recipes, and other gone-in-two-bites baked goods. More substantial eats are also baked and filled on site, like breakfast sandwiches on house-baked rolls or bagels (try the bacon-egg-and-cheese on a toasted poppy-seed roll), all at rock-bottom prices.

BUTCHER'S DAUGHTER VEGETARIAN $

Map p436 (☎347-763-1421; www.thebutchersdaughter.com; 271 Metropolitan Ave, btwn Driggs Ave & Roebling St, Williamsburg; mains $13-18; ⊙8am-10pm; ; SL to Bedford Ave) This wryly named vegetarian restaurant is supremely relaxing, with a light-flooded dining room and rejuvenating (often vegan-friendly) meals. Brunch fans clamor for the French toast, gluten-free vegan waffles and curried avocado toast, always with a vitamin-packed juice or kick-ass espresso. Efficient service and primo people-watching make this a must-eat at weekends.

CHAMPS DINER VEGAN $

Map p436 (☎718-599-2743; www.champsdiner.com; 197 Meserole St, btwn Humboldt St & Bushwick Ave, East Williamsburg; breakfast $11-16, sandwiches & burgers $12-20; ⊙9am-midnight; ☑; ⓈL to Montrose Ave) The classic diner experience receives a plant-based makeover at Champs. The menu is packed with all-American classics like Philly cheese steaks, Nashville hot 'chicken' and burritos, the only difference being they're all vegan variants. Tuck into a tofu scramble or French toast, slurp on a cookie-dough shake, and take your coffee with nut, soy or oat milks.

The setting is a quintessential American diner, with tiled floor, booths and counter-side stools for casual and solo diners...only through a hip East Williamsburg filter.

Weekend brunch sees lines out the door – if you don't want to wait, head around the corner and try the brunch at local bar **Tradesman** (Map p436; ☎718-386-5300; www.tradesmanbar.com; 222 Bushwick Ave, at Meserole St, East Williamsburg; ⊙5pm-2am Mon-Thu, noon-4am Fri & Sat, noon-2am Sun; ; ⓈL to Montrose Ave).

LITTLE SKIPS CAFE $

(☎718-484-0980; www.littleskips.nyc; 941 Willoughby Ave, at Charles Pl, Bushwick; snacks & sandwiches $8-11; ⊙7am-8pm Mon-Fri, from 8am Sat & Sun; ☑; ⓈJ/M to Myrtle Ave) It's requires attention to detail to create a cafe this artfully haphazard. Little Skips is decked in art, all creaky wooden floors and mismatched seating, and pours astoundingly good coffee. There's a community focus, with weekly open-mics, live music and art shows, plus an earth-conscious menu featuring vegan BLT sandwiches, chilled artichoke soup and (the classic) avocado toast.

★MODERN LOVE VEGAN $$

Map p436 (☎929-298-0626; www.modernlovebrooklyn.com; 317 Union Ave, at S 1st St, East Williamsburg; mains brunch $16-18, dinner $18-24; ⊙5:30-10pm Tue-Thu, 5:30-11pm Fri, 10am-2:30pm & 5-11pm Sat, 10am-2:30pm & 5-10pm Sun; ☑; ⓈG to Metropolitan Ave, L to Lorimer St) Celebrated chef Isa Chandra Moskowitz's 'swanky vegan comfort food' has been received with open, watering mouths in Williamsburg. The restaurant is a lovely date spot with sultry lighting and immaculate service, while dishes include 'mac 'n' shews' (with creamy cashew cheese), truffled poutine and a lip-smacking Korean BBQ bowl with glazed tofu and kimchi. It's always buzzing, so consider booking.

★ZENKICHI JAPANESE $$$

Map p436 (☎718-388-8985; www.zenkichi.com; 77 N 6th St, at Wythe Ave, Williamsburg; tasting menus veg/regular $65/75; ⊙5:30-11:30pm Sun-Thu, to midnight Fri & Sat; ☑; ⓈL to Bedford Ave) Created by a homesick Tokyo chef, this hushed restaurant promises peace and pleasure in equal proportions. Sink into one of the secluded booths, order the *omakase* (regularly changing tasting menu, for a minimum of two guests) and abandon yourself to a precise succession of delights: silky tofu, miso-marinated cod, and seasonal sashimi.

★FETTE SAU BARBECUE $$

Map p436 (☎718-963-3404; www.fettesaubbq.com; 354 Metropolitan Ave, btwn Havemeyer & Roebling Sts, Williamsburg; meats per 0.5lb $12-15, sides $4-8; ⊙5-11pm Mon, from noon Tue-Sun; ⓈL to Bedford Ave) The atmosphere is unfussy, but the reverence for smoky meat is indubitable at the 'Fat Pig,' Brooklyn's best house of barbecue. The cement floor and inside-outside feel echo the garage that once operated from this space, while shared trestles and an 'order by the pound' system put lovers of brisket, pulled pork, smoked chicken and ancho-chili-spiced sausage further at ease.

FIVE LEAVES AMERICAN $$

Map p436 (☎718-383-5345; www.fiveleavesny.com; 18 Bedford Ave, at Lorimer St, Greenpoint; mains breakfast or lunch $10-19, dinner $15-27; ⊙8am-1am; B48, B62 to Lorimer St, ⓈG to Nassau Ave) An anchor of the Greenpoint scene, Five Leaves draws a mix of neighborhood regulars to outdoor tables and the vintage-filled interior. Stop by in the morning for ricotta pancakes, brûléed grapefruit and great espresso, or at lunch for a bacon-avocado or fish sandwich with truffle fries. Cocktails seem designed for day drinking (like their Bloody Mary and coffee-coconut Tiger's Milk).

RABBITHOLE BISTRO $$

Map p436 (☎718-782-0910; www.rabbitholerestaurant.com; 352 Bedford Ave, btwn S 3rd & S 4th Sts, Williamsburg; mains breakfast & lunch $15-17, dinner $19-25; ⊙9am-11pm; ☑; B62 to S 4th St, ⓈJ/Z, M to Marcy Ave) The rustic warmth of Rabbithole's dining room (rough-hewn tables, brick walls, a tailor's dummy and other eclectica) is matched by its kitchen (they cook their own pastries) and by relaxed, attentive staff. The breakfast menu (offered until 5pm) features New York favorites like eggs Benedict and French toast with mascarpone. Come evening, the quaint tin-ceilinged eatery transforms into a gastropub.

PAULIE GEE'S PIZZA $$
(☎347-987-3747; www.pauliegee.com; 60 Greenpoint Ave, btwn West & Franklin Sts, Greenpoint; pizzas $15-20; ⏱6-11pm Mon-Fri, 5-11pm Sat, 5-10pm Sun; ; ; Ⓢ G to Greenpoint Ave) Greenpoint's best pizza place has a cozy cabin-in-the-woods vibe, with flickering candles and old-school soundtrack. Diners huddle over creatively topped thin-crust pizzas. Vegan pizzas and desserts go above and beyond the cheese-less standards you'll find elsewhere, with ingredients like cashew ricotta, vegan fennel sausage and kale pesto. Oh and vegan dessert pizza, cheesecake and pie? Yes to all three!

OKONOMI & YUJI RAMEN JAPANESE $$
Map p436 (www.okonomibk.com; 150 Ainslie St, btwn Lorimer & Leonard Sts, Williamsburg; set menus $21-35, ramen $17-24; ⏱9am-3pm & 6-11pm Mon-Sat, to 10pm Sun; Ⓢ L to Lorimer St, G to Metropolitan Ave) For breakfast without the eggy mainstays or a refreshing lunch, make a pilgrimage to this exquisite wood-lined eatery. By day it's Okonomi, serving only set menus: a small vegetable dish, baked egg, seven-grain rice and fish (choose from four preparations, like salt-roasted or kelp-cured), accompanied by green tea. By evening, it serves noodles as Yuji Ramen. Walk-ins only.

★ROBERTA'S PIZZA $$
Map p436 (☎718-417-1118; www.robertaspizza.com; 261 Moore St, near Bogart St, East Williamsburg; pizzas $17-21; ⏱11am-midnight Mon-Fri, from 10am Sat & Sun; ; Ⓢ L to Morgan Ave) This hiply renovated warehouse restaurant in one of Brooklyn's booming food enclaves makes some of the best pizza in NYC. Service is relaxed, but the brick-oven pies are serious: chewy, fresh and topped with knowing combinations of outstanding ingredients. The classic margherita is sublime; more adventurous palates can opt for near-legendary options like 'Beastmaster' (gorgonzola, pork sausage and jalapeño).

MARLOW & SONS AMERICAN $$$
Map p436 (☎718-384-1441; www.marlowandsons.com; 81 Broadway, btwn Berry St & Wythe Ave, Williamsburg; mains lunch $15-18, dinner $34-36; ⏱8am-10pm Sun-Thu, to 11pm Fri & Sat, closed 4-5:30pm Sat & Sun; Ⓢ J/Z, M to Marcy Ave) The dimly lit, wood-lined space feels like an old farmhouse cafe, and hosts a buzzing nighttime scene as diners and drinkers crowd in for oysters, tip-top cocktails and a changing daily menu of locavore specialties, such as grilled bluefish, sour cabbage pancakes and tuna melt on brioche. Brunch is a big draw, so prepare for lines (or book ahead by phone or online).

Coney Island & Brighton Beach

NATHAN'S FAMOUS HOT DOGS $
Map p444 (☎718-333-2202; www.nathansfamous.com; 1310 Surf Ave, at Stillwell Ave, Coney Island; hot dogs from $5; ⏱10am-11pm Mon-Thu, to midnight Fri, 9am-midnight Sat, to 11pm Sun; ; Ⓢ D/F to Coney Island-Stillwell Ave) The hot dog was invented in Coney Island in 1867, which means that eating a frankfurter is practically obligatory here. The top choice: Nathan's Famous, founded by Polish immigrant Nathan Handwerker in 1916. The hot dogs are the real deal, but the menu runs the gamut from fried clams to fried chicken fingers.

DRINKING & NIGHTLIFE

Brewpubs. Dives. Cocktail lounges. Unassuming neighborhood joints. When it comes to booze, Brooklyn's got a bit of everything – including oodles of retro 1920s and '30s style. Williamsburg has the most vibrant nightlife scene concentrated in one spot, but other neighborhoods have the advantage of less crowded and more relaxed options. Hit Bushwick for under-the-radar bars, Boerum Hill and Cobble Hill for buzzy bars with a local feel, and Gowanus for neighborhood flavor in distinctive venues.

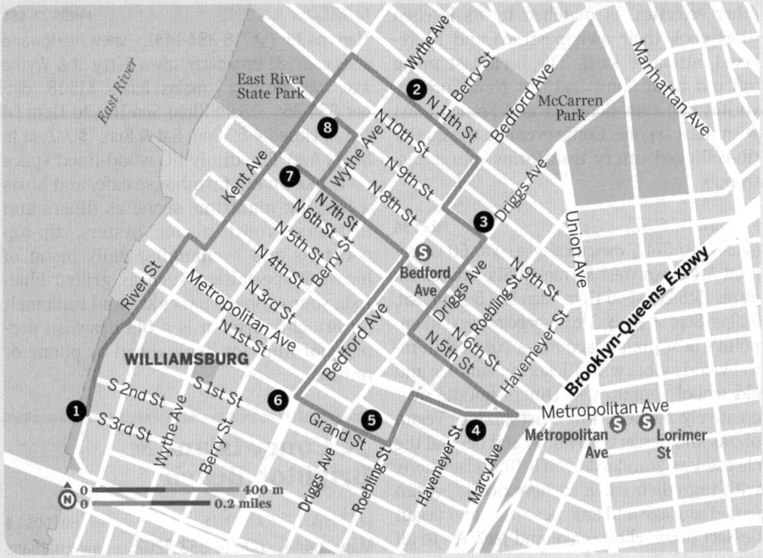

Local Life
Exploring Williamsburg

Now the nightlife epicenter of Brooklyn (and, dare we say it, NYC), Williamsburg owes its growth to working-class communities of Latino, Italian and Polish migrants. This erstwhile bohemian magnet has seen the starving artists move to Bushwick for cheaper rents, leaving gleaming condos and refurbished brownstones to professionals and hip young families. There's lots to explore, from vintage-cocktail dens to shops selling one-of-a-kind creations from local craftspeople.

1 Seeing Green
Industrial-styled **Domino Park** (Map p436; www.dominopark.com; River St, btwn S 2nd & S 3rd Sts; 6am-1am; ; B32, Q59 to Kent Ave/S 1st St) has active distractions like bocce, a kids' playground and an elevated walkway with marvelous views of Manhattan.

2 Homegrown Hops
Once upon a time Williamsburg was the center of beer-brewing in New York. Continuing the tradition, the Brooklyn Brewery (p276) serves rich ales and hoppy IPAs in an on-site tasting room and offers 45-minute tours into beer history and its own brewing techniques.

3 Hipster Threads
Intrigued or envious of Brooklynites' eclectic fashion sense? Create your own mix of retro finds, repurposed vintage and art-print T-shirts at much-loved resale shop **Buffalo Exchange** (Map p436; 718-384-6901; www.buffaloexchange.com; 504 Driggs Ave, at N 9th St; 11am-8pm Mon-Sat, noon-7pm Sun; S L to Bedford Ave).

4 Bodega Ephemera
For a glimpse of curious old objects from the city's days of yore, visit City Reliquary (p275), a full-to-bursting museum of NYC relics, from vintage postcards to exhibits on the 1939 World's Fair.

5 Latin American Detour
A visual delight, **Fuego 718** (Map p436; 718-302-2913; https://fuego718.business.site; 249 Grand St, btwn Roebling St & Driggs Ave; noon-7pm Sun-Fri, to 8pm Sat; S L to Bedford Ave) transports you south of the border with Day of the Dead boxes, colorful frames and mirrors, and kitsch and crafts from Mexico, Peru and beyond. We defy you to leave without a skull-adorned hand mirror or metal ornament from Haiti.

Domino Park

❻ More Brooklyn Booze
Crank that time machine back one more notch at retro Maison Premiere (p291), which features bespoke cocktails, oysters and other treats with a smart Southern vibe.

❼ Maker Multiverse
If it's a weekend, browse the aisles of Artists & Fleas (p299), a shopping warren of more than 75 booths featuring locally crafted jewelry, accessories, artworks, cosmetics, housewares and vintage records and clothes.

❽ Vinyl Valhalla
Williamsburg is home to the lone American outpost of legendary UK record store Rough Trade (p299), a warehouse-sized dream for music lovers and LP collectors that also hosts frequent in-store concerts of upcoming talents, with tickets usually not more than $15. You can finish up your neighborhood stroll with a latte from the in-store cafe.

Brooklyn Heights, Downtown Brooklyn & Dumbo

MONTERO BAR & GRILL BAR

Map p443 (646-729-4129; 73 Atlantic Ave, at Hicks St, Brooklyn Heights; noon-4am; 2/3, 4/5 to Borough Hall) Montero's is the real deal: an anachronistic, neon-fronted, Pabst-peddling longshoreman's bar that's weathered every change thrown at this corner of Brooklyn since WWII. Its eclectic decor (ship's wheels, nautical miscellany) recalls the maritime types who once drank here, though these days the soundtrack is regular karaoke rather than sailors' yarns.

FLOYD BAR

Map p443 (718-858-5810; www.floydny.com; 131 Atlantic Ave, btwn Henry & Clinton Sts, Brooklyn Heights; 5pm-4am Mon-Thu, from 4pm Fri, from 1pm Sat & Sun; ; B61, B63 to Atlantic Ave/Henry St, 2/3, 4/5 to Borough Hall; R to Court St) This glass-front bar is home to young flirters who cuddle on tattered antique sofas while beer-swillers congregate around a 40ft indoor bocce court (games are free, first-come, first-served, outside of league nights). A good local hang that rouses nostalgia for small-town drinking from the vintage signs to the noisy clientele.

Boerum Hill, Cobble Hill, Carroll Gardens & Red Hook

ROBERT BAR BAR

Map p438 (347-853-8687; www.robertbarbrooklyn.com; 104 Bond St, btwn Atlantic Ave & Pacific St, Boerum Hill; 5pm-2am Mon-Thu, to 4am Fri & Sat, to 1am Sun; A/C, G to Hoyt-Schermerhorn) With a side-room dartboard and jukebox full of 1970s and '80s hits, this place looks kinda like a dive bar, but the young, cool Brooklyn crowd listening to live DJs under a domino-tiled ceiling gives it away as something hipper. There are craft beers and a custom cocktail menu with drinks named after the jukebox songs.

CLOVER CLUB COCKTAIL BAR

Map p438 (718-855-7939; www.cloverclubny.com; 210 Smith St, near Baltic St, Cobble Hill; 4pm-2am Mon-Thu, to 4am Fri, 10:30am-4am Sat, 10:30am-1am Sun; B57 to Smith & Douglass

Sts, S F, G to Bergen St) Cocktails are certainly shaken with aplomb at this retro-elegant bar, but there's no pretension at Clover Club. Converse over fabulous tiki drinks, libations infused with lavender and bell peppers, and happy-hour specials like $8 Aperol Spritz (4pm to 7pm Monday to Friday). Mocktails, too, are given loving attention, with headache-free concoctions of elderflower, agave and sugar snap peas.

61 LOCAL BAR

Map p438 (☎718-875-1150; www.61local.com; 61 Bergen St, btwn Smith St & Boerum Pl, Boerum Hill; ⊙7am-midnight Mon-Thu, to 1am Fri, 9am-1am Sat, 9am-midnight Sun; ☏; S F, G to Bergen St) Employing a classic Brooklyn bar aesthetic with its brick interior, 61 Locals pulls a laid-back crowd thanks to mellow-mannered bar staff and a great selection of NYC-brewed and other craft beers. Coffee-sipping creatives on laptops and new-mother groups hold down the fort during the day.

★ SUNNY'S BAR

Map p438 (☎718-625-8211; www.sunnysredhook. com; 253 Conover St, btwn Beard & Reed Sts, Red Hook; ⊙5pm-midnight Mon, 4pm-2am Tue, 4pm-4am Wed, 3pm-4am Thu & Fri, 11am-4am Sat, 11am-midnight Sun; S F, G to Carroll St then ☒B61 to Van Dyke/Van Brunt Sts) Surviving since the late 1800s, Sunny's cultivates a charming, throwback atmosphere: nautical miscellany, model ships, everything but the barnacles. The longshoremen are long gone, but loyal regulars and newcomers alike arrive to play drunken sailor at the long bar and out in the yard. Foot-stomping bluegrass and other banjo-pickin' events liven the place up, usually on Thursdays and Sundays.

Hurricane Sandy dealt the bar a tough blow and it struggled to rebound from the damage. The bar's legendary owner Sunny Balzano passed away in 2016 and real-estate-related threats have loomed for years. *Sunny's Nights: Lost and Found at a Bar on the Edge of the World* by Tim Sultan (2016) is a loving portrait of the bar and its owner.

🍷 Fort Greene, Clinton Hill & Bed-Stuy

BLACK FOREST BROOKLYN BEER HALL

Map p438 (☎718-935-0300; www.blackforest brooklyn.com; 733 Fulton St, btwn S Elliot Pl & S Portland Ave, Fort Greene; ⊙noon-midnight Mon-Fri, 10am-midnight Sat, 10am-10pm Sun; S G to Fulton St, A, C to Lafayette Ave) Two German Brooklynites opened this hip take on a traditional beer hall, with dark ceiling timbers, exposed brick and waiters in red-checked shirts serving up draft liters of local and German lagers, pilsners, wheat beers and more. Have it all by ordering a flight of 13 different beer tasters, and delay decision-making further with a platter of different wursts.

The Teutonic menu also offers schnitzels, *spätzle* (noodles) with goulash, and a few vegetarian options such as beer-battered mushrooms and *flammkuchen* (Alsatian 'pizza').

A second location opened on Boerum Hill's Smith St in 2017.

🍷 Park Slope, Gowanus & Sunset Park

UNION HALL BAR

Map p440 (☎718-638-4400; www.unionhallny. com; 702 Union St, near Fifth Ave, Park Slope; ⊙4pm-4am Mon-Fri, 1pm-4am Sat & Sun; S R to Union St) Anyone seeking an authentically Brooklyn night out should look no further than Union Hall. This bar and event space is located in a converted warehouse and boasts a double-sided fireplace, towering bookshelves, leather couches and two full-size indoor bocce courts (a ball game similar to boules). Head to the basement for live music and comedy.

SEA WITCH BAR

Map p440 (☎347-227-7166; www.seawitchnyc. com; 703 Fifth Ave, btwn 21st & 22nd Sts, Greenwood Heights; ⊙5pm-2am Mon-Thu, 4pm-4am Fri, noon-4am Sat, noon-2am Sun, kitchen to midnight Sun-Thu, to 1am Fri & Sat; ☒B63 to 5th Ave/21st St, S R to 25th St) Better-looking than the average maritime-themed bar, Sea Witch snares an easygoing crowd in among its nautical miscellany, mermaid mural and backlit bottles. The tank of clownfish and anemones at the bar means you can find Nemo in between Brooklyn-brewed ales (there are 20 beers on tap) and smoky mezcal cocktails. Unspool your sailors' yarns in the patio out back.

ROYAL PALMS BAR

Map p440 (☎347-223-4410; www.royalpalms shuffle.com; 514 Union St, btwn Third Ave & Nevins St, Gowanus; ⊙6pm-midnight Mon-Thu, 6pm-2am Fri, noon-2am Sat, to 10pm Sun; S R to Union St)

If you're hankering for some sports but prefer your activity close to your bar stool, the faux-Floridian Royal Palms is for you. Inside this 17,000-sq-ft space are 10 full-size shuffleboard courts ($40 per hour), plus board games (massive Jenga, oversize Connect Four), draft brews, cocktails and snacks provided by a different food truck each week. Over-21s only.

GREENWOOD PARK BEER GARDEN

Map p440 (☎718-499-7999; www.greenwoodparkbk.com; 555 Seventh Ave, btwn 19th & 20th Sts, Greenwood Heights; ⊙noon-1am Sun-Thu, to 3am Fri & Sat, shorter hours in winter; 📶👪; 🚌B67, B69 to 18th St, ⓈF, G to 15th St-Prospect Park) Only in Brooklyn is a beer garden easily mistaken for an auto scrap yard…and all the better for it. Around the corner from Green-Wood Cemetery (p271), this 13,000-sq-ft indoor/outdoor beer hall in an open, industrial setting is a clever reconfiguration of a former gas station and mechanic's shop, with a rockin' soundtrack. Family-friendly by day, strictly 21-and-over after 7pm. Cash only.

GINGER'S BAR LESBIAN

Map p440 (☎718-788-0924; 363 Fifth Ave, at 5th St, Park Slope; ⊙5pm-4am Mon-Fri, from 2pm Sat & Sun; ⓈF, G, R to 4th Ave-9th St) This bright blue-and-yellow watering hole is a hub for the local lesbian community and comes complete with a friendly bartender, a jukebox, a pool table, a small courtyard out back for the warmer months and lots of regulars. Happy hour runs from 5pm to 8pm nightly.

Prospect Heights, Crown Heights & Flatbush

★BUTTER & SCOTCH BAR

Map p440 (☎347-405-6266; www.butterandscotch.com; 818 Franklin Ave, btwn Eastern Pkwy & Union St, Crown Heights; ⊙5pm-midnight Mon-Thu, 3pm-2am Fri, noon-2am Sat, noon-midnight Sun; Ⓢ2/3, 4/5 to Franklin Ave) With cocktail names like 'Smash the Patriarchy,' it's clear that this emporium of indulgence has a feminist ethos. The ingenious women who own it also have a fondness for birthday cake and they blend a lip-smacking vegan pina colada. Delicious combinations at this bar-bakery include cookies with White Russians (vodka and milk) and cocktails that pair beautifully with s'mores and key-lime pie.

WEATHER UP COCKTAIL BAR

Map p440 (www.weatherupnyc.com; 589 Vanderbilt Ave, at Dean St, Prospect Heights; ⊙5:30pm-2am) Walk through the barely-marked entrance into a dimly lit den of dark wood and tile, joining an elegant throng of cocktail aficionados. Sit at the bar to watch the bartenders expertly mix your drink from the seasonal menu, or take refuge in the booth at the back. A back patio offers candlelit seclusion within leafy trellised walls. Cash only.

FRIENDS AND LOVERS BAR

Map p440 (☎917-979-3060; www.fnlbk.com; 641 Classon St, btwn Pacific & Dean Sts, Crown Heights; ⊙5pm-2am Sun-Thu, to 4am Fri & Sat; ⓈA/C to Franklin Ave) A youngish crowd piles into this spirited, unpretentious bar and it's even better when the back room hosts comedy (usually every Wednesday, plus occasional Thursdays, Fridays and Saturdays – check their calendar online). There's a very happy hour (or should that be 'messy hour'?) between 5pm and 9pm from Wednesdays to Saturdays, when cut-price beer-and-shot deals reign supreme. Cash only.

Williamsburg, Greenpoint & Bushwick

★HOUSE OF YES CLUB

(www.houseofyes.org; 2 Wyckoff Ave, at Jefferson St, Bushwick; tickets free-$60; ⊙usually 7pm-4am Wed-Sat; ⓈL to Jefferson St) 🍃 Anything goes at this hedonistic warehouse venue, with two stages, three bars and a covered outdoor area that offers some of the most creative themed performance and dance nights in Brooklyn. You might see aerial-silk acrobats, punk bands, burlesque shows, drag shows, performance artists, or DJs as revered as Jellybean Benítez spinning disco, soul, house and other delights.

★MAISON PREMIERE COCKTAIL BAR

Map p436 (☎347-335-0446; www.maisonpremiere.com; 298 Bedford Ave, btwn S 1st & Grand Sts, Williamsburg; ⊙2pm-2am Sun-Wed, to 4am Thu-Sat; ⓈL to Bedford Ave) Perched on a stool in Maison Premiere, it's hard not to be seduced by this New Orleans–style oyster and cocktail bar, from antique pictures and soft lighting to suspender-wearing staff. Contemplate a small plate ($13 to $19) – perhaps shrimp cocktail or littleneck clams – and enjoy the maracas sound of cocktail shakers preparing another round of Spring Pimm's and gimlets.

BROOKLYN BARGE BEER GARDEN

(929-337-7212; www.thebrooklynbarge.com; 79 West St, btwn West St & East River, Greenpoint; 4pm-midnight Mon & Tue, noon-1am Wed-Fri, 11am-1am Sat, 11am-midnight Sun; ; S G to Greenpoint Ave) Bracing breezes and expansive views of Manhattan's skyline make this floating barge Greenpoint's most invigorating drinking hole. Moored to land via a wooden bridge, the alfresco bar serves local draft beers, good cocktails plus some wines and cider. Reducing any impetus to leave is a menu of sharer plates like Thai-chili wings, tacos and lobster rolls from the repurposed-shipping-container kitchen.

PARTNERS COFFEE

Map p436 (347-586-0063; www.partnerscoffee.com; 125 N 6th St, btwn Bedford Ave & Berry St, Williamsburg; 6:30am-7pm; ; S L to Bedford Ave) The flagship of a small chain roaster bringing aromatic pour-overs, smooth flat whites and punchy *cortados* (espresso with a dash of milk) to the streets of Billyburg. Even if it does follow all the unspoken rules of Williamsburg cafe design (bare brick and wood, retro miscellany on display…) it's an enjoyable place to hang.

RADEGAST HALL & BIERGARTEN BEER HALL

Map p436 (718-963-3973; www.radegasthall.com; 113 N 3rd St, at Berry St, Williamsburg; noon-late Mon-Fri, 11am-late Sat & Sun; S L to Bedford Ave) This reimagining of an early-20th-century Germanic beer hall is not all gimmick: the huge selection of European and local brews, kitchen slinging schnitzel and goulash (mains $21 to $29), roistering ranks of tables and free live music nightly make it a bona fide Williamsburg house of assembly. The framed posters of Prussian nobility and Gothic fonts add to the atmosphere.

SPUYTEN DUYVIL BAR

Map p436 (718-963-4140; www.spuytenduyvilnyc.com; 359 Metropolitan Ave, btwn Havemeyer & Roebling Sts, Williamsburg; 5pm-2am Mon-Fri, noon-3am Sat, noon-2am Sun; S L to Lorimer St, G to Metropolitan Ave) This low-key, beer-centric Williamsburg bar looks as though it was pieced together from a rummage sale, with crimson-painted pressed-tin ceilings, book shelves and a vintage bike mounted on the walls, and mismatched thrift-store furniture. The selection of beer (Belgian especially) is staggering, with knowledgeable bar staff primed to steer you to Danish beers or Normandy ciders.

If you get peckish working through the blackboard of 'rare and obscure' beers, plates of imported cheese and charcuterie (from $8) can provide ballast. There's a large, leafy backyard that's open in good weather.

ROCKA ROLLA BAR

Map p436 (486 Metropolitan Ave, at Rodney St, Williamsburg; noon-4am; S G to Metropolitan Ave, L to Lorimer St) Named for Judas Priest's first album, this bar reels in rockers with its Misfits logos, taxidermied buffalo heads and, of course, neon Judas Priest sign. It keeps them around with cheap drinks and a guitar-heavy, old-school soundtrack. It's the best kind of dive bar: grungy and loud but friendly enough to be accessible to timid first-timers.

MOONLIGHT MILE COCKTAIL BAR

(718-389-3904; www.themoonlightmilegpt.com; 200 Franklin St, at India St, Greenpoint; 4pm-1am Mon-Thu, 1pm-2am Fri & Sat, 1pm-midnight Sun; S G to Greenpoint Ave) A library of whiskies lines the bar at this rocking cocktail bar in Greenpoint, finding their way into classic and reinvented cocktails via the dextrous manipulations of the friendly mixologists (we like the smoky 'Foggy Mountain Manhattan'). Non-aficionados of whisky also have plenty to enjoy, with oatmeal stouts, blood-orange ciders and wines by the glass.

THE ROOKERY BAR

(718-483-8048; www.therookerybar.com; 425 Troutman St, btwn St Nicholas & Wyckoff Aves, Bushwick; noon-4am Mon-Fri, from 11am Sat & Sun; S L to Jefferson St) Dominated by an imposing-yet-welcoming horseshoe bar that claims the center of the room, the Rookery acknowledges its industrial past (as many places do in this art- and bar-rich corner of Bushwick) but keeps things cosy, contemporary and crucially, friendly. There's a beer garden out front for warm weather, plus pints of draft beer, whiskeys and a playful (occasionally spicy) set of cocktails.

SPRITZENHAUS33 BEER HALL

Map p436 (347-987-4632; www.spritzenhaus33.com; 33 Nassau Ave, at Guernsey St, Greenpoint; 4pm-4am Mon-Wed, noon-4am Thu-Sun; S G to Nassau Ave) Beer lovers shouldn't miss this place on the edge of McCarren Park, an open, somewhat industrial 6000-sq-ft beer hall with 20 or so beers on tap and dozens more by the bottle. German, Belgian and North American microbrews dominate, and there's lots of meaty pub grub (sausages mostly, but the Belgian fries with truffle oil are also a hit).

LEMON'S BAR

Map p436 (☎718-460-8006; www.lemonsbk.com; 80 Wythe Ave, 6th fl, Wythe Hotel, at N 11th St, Williamsburg; ⏲5pm-1am Mon-Thu, 2pm-2am Fri, noon-2am Sat, noon-midnight Sun; Ⓢ L to Bedford Ave, G to Nassau Ave) This bar atop the Wythe Hotel (p344) has a sunny color scheme, vacation vibes and magnificent picture-window views of Manhattan. There's a respectable cocktail list and an OK wine and beer list, along with small plates and snacks to sustain energy levels when DJs rock the house. The outdoor area closes an hour or two before the bar, keeping neighbors happy.

HOTEL DELMANO COCKTAIL BAR

Map p436 (☎718-387-1945; www.hoteldelmano.com; 82 Berry St, at N 9th St, Williamsburg; ⏲5pm-2am Mon-Thu, 5pm-3am Fri, 2pm-3am Sat, 2pm-2am Sun; Ⓢ L to Bedford Ave) Drink in a taste of the old New York at this effortlessly stylish cocktail bar with old, smoky mirrors, unpolished floorboards and vintage chandeliers. Nestle into a booth or sit at the curving, marble-topped bar, peruse the 100-bottle wine list and watch keen-eyed, burly-armed barkeeps shake smoky bourbon cocktails, concoctions of gin and rosewater, and other seasonally changing intoxicants.

BOSSA NOVA CIVIC CLUB CLUB

(☎718-443-1271; www.facebook.com/bossanovacivicclub; 1271 Myrtle Ave, at Hart St, Bushwick; ⏲7pm-4am; Ⓢ M to Central Ave) Yet another reason you never need to leave Brooklyn, this smallish hole-in-the-wall club is a great place to get your groove on, with DJs spinning house, EDM and techno in a (somewhat) tropical-themed interior. There's a great sound system, fairly priced drinks and a celebratory crowd that's there to dance. A $10 cover applies after midnight on Friday and Saturday.

SEY COFFEE COFFEE

Map p436 (www.seycoffee.com; 18 Grattan St, East Williamsburg; ⏲7am-7pm Mon-Fri, 8am-7pm Sat & Sun; 📶; Ⓢ L to Morgan Ave) We don't say 'best coffee in East Williamsburg' lightly, with so many talented bean-crafters hereabouts. But SEY's mad-scientist attention to detail ensures impeccable brews, plus the presentation is artful and the atrium-style setting awash in natural light.

PINE BOX ROCK SHOP BAR

Map p436 (☎718-366-6311; www.pineboxrockshop.com; 12 Grattan St, btwn Morgan Ave & Bogart St, East Williamsburg; ⏲4pm-2am Mon & Tue, 4pm-4am Wed-Fri, 2pm-4am Sat, noon-2am Sun; Ⓢ L to Morgan Ave) This entertainment upstart in a rickety former casket factory is run by a friendly vegan musician couple. There are more than a dozen draft beers to choose from, as well as widely lauded, spicy Bloody Marys – like everything else, none of its ingredients contain animal products. Local artwork graces the walls, and a back room hosts regular gigs and comedy.

BLUE BOTTLE COFFEE COFFEE

Map p436 (☎510-653-3394; www.bluebottlecoffee.com; 76 N 4th St, Williamsburg; coffees $4-5; ⏲6:30am-7pm Mon-Fri, 7am-7:30pm Sat & Sun; 📶; Ⓢ L to Bedford Ave) While many argue in favor of Brooklyn's home-grown coffee spots, there's a reason this West Coast roaster-brewer also has many fans. Blue Bottle prepares its beans in a vintage Probat roaster, and all drinks are carefully brewed to order (be prepared to wait a bit).

CLEM'S PUB

Map p436 (☎718-387-9617; www.clemsbrooklyn.com; 264 Grand St, at Roebling St, Williamsburg; ⏲2pm-4am Mon-Fri, from noon Sat & Sun; Ⓢ L to Lorimer St, G to Metropolitan Ave) A retro rock soundtrack and vintage fittings ease punters in to this easygoing Williamsburg watering hole. It has a long bar, overseen by friendly bartenders (and dust-gathering taxidermied boar heads). There are a few outdoor tables perfect for summer people-watching.

BERRY PARK ROOFTOP BAR

Map p436 (☎718-782-2829; www.berryparkbk.com; 4 Berry St, at N 14th St, Williamsburg; ⏲noon-late Mon-Fri, from 11am Sat & Sun, shorter hours winter; Ⓢ G to Nassau Ave, L to Bedford Ave) This sports-loving bar with a 2nd-floor rooftop space is a real crowd-pleaser. There are several huge screens for watching premier-league-soccer matches and NFL games, with 14 beers on tap to sip as the action unfolds. A nightclub atmosphere takes hold on Friday and Saturday nights, with DJs spinning tunes and twinkly views of Manhattan's skyline from the rooftop deck.

Coney Island & Brighton Beach

RUBY'S BAR & GRILL BAR

Map p444 (718-975-7829; www.rubysbar.com; 1213 Riegelmann Boardwalk, btwn Stillwell Ave & W 12th St, Coney Island; 10:30am-10pm Mon-Thu, to 1am Fri, to midnight Sat & Sun Apr-Sep, weekends only Oct; S D/F, N/Q to Coney Island-Stillwell Ave) The oldest and only dive bar on the Coney Island boardwalk, Ruby's has been around since 1934, and in the family of the eponymous Ruby since 1972. It's a little sanitised these days, but still a great place to grab a stool, order a pint of Ruby's Ale and watch the waves (and salty locals) roll in.

ENTERTAINMENT

★BROOKLYN ACADEMY OF MUSIC PERFORMING ARTS

Map p438 (BAM; 718-636-4100; www.bam.org; 30 Lafayette Ave, at Ashland Pl, Fort Greene; ; S B/D, N/Q/R, 2/3, 4/5 to Atlantic Ave-Barclays Center) Founded in 1861 (the year the Civil War erupted), BAM is the country's oldest performing-arts center. Spanning several venues in the Fort Greene area, the complex hosts innovative works of opera, modern dance, music, cinema and theater – everything from 'retro-modern' Mark Morris Group ballets and Laurie Anderson multimedia shows to avant-garde Shakespeare productions, comedy and kids' shows.

The 1908 Italian Renaissance–style Peter J Sharp Building houses the **Howard Gilman Opera House** (showing opera, dance, music and more) and the four-screen **Rose Cinemas** (tickets $16-18), showing first-run, indie and foreign films in gorgeously vintage-feel theaters; the on-site bar and restaurant, **BAM Café**, stages free jazz, R&B and pop performances on Friday and Saturday. A block away on Fulton St is the **Harvey Lichtenstein Theater** (Harvey Lichtenstein Theater; 651 Fulton St, at Rockwell Pl; S B, Q/R to DeKalb Ave, 2/3, 4/5 to Nevins St), aka 'the Harvey,' which stages cutting-edge, contemporary plays and sometimes radical interpretations of classics. Around the corner from the Sharp building is the **Fisher Building** (www.bam.org/fisher; 321 Ashland Pl, at Lafayette Ave), with its more intimate 250-seat theater.

From October through December, BAM hosts its acclaimed **Next Wave Festival** (tickets from $32), which presents an array of international avant-garde theater and dance, and artist talks. Buy tickets early.

★ST ANN'S WAREHOUSE THEATER

Map p443 (718-254-8779; www.stannswarehouse.org; 45 Water St, at Old Dock St, Dumbo; B25 to Water/Main Sts, S A/C to High St-Brooklyn Bridge, F to York St) This handsome red-brick building, a Civil War–era tobacco warehouse, is the first permanent home of avant-garde performance company St Ann's. The 'warehouse' – a high-tech, flexible 320-seat theater – is ideal for staging genre-bending theater, music, dance and puppet performances.

★BARBÈS LIVE MUSIC

Map p440 (347-422-0248; www.barbesbrooklyn.com; 376 9th St, at Sixth Ave, Park Slope; requested donation for live music $10; 5pm-2am Mon-Thu, 2pm-4am Fri & Sat, 2pm-2am Sun; S F, G to 7th Ave, R to 4th Ave-9th St) This compact bar and performance space, named after a neighborhood in Paris with a strong North African flavor, is owned by French musicians (and longtime Brooklyn residents). There's live music all night, every night: an impressively eclectic lineup including Balkan brass, contemporary opera, Afro-Peruvian grooves, West African funk and other diverse sounds.

★NATIONAL SAWDUST LIVE PERFORMANCE

Map p436 (646-779-8455; www.nationalsawdust.org; 80 N 6th St, at Wythe Ave, Williamsburg; 10am-1am Mon-Fri, noon-11pm Sat & Sun; ; B32 to Wythe Ave-N 6th St, S L to Bedford Ave) Covered in wildly hued murals, this cutting-edge space for classical and new music has come a long way since its days as a sawdust factory, with artists as diverse as Pussy Riot and Yo La Tengo performing within. The angular, high-tech interior stages contemporary opera with multimedia projections, electro-acoustic big-band jazz and concerts by experimental composers, alongside less common genres.

BELL HOUSE LIVE PERFORMANCE

Map p440 (718-643-6510; www.thebellhouseny.com; 149 7th St, btwn Second & Third Aves, Gowanus; 5pm-late; ; S F, G, R to 4th Ave-9th St) This 1920s warehouse in the light-industrial grid of Gowanus showcases high-profile live music and variety, spanning indie rockers, DJ nights, comedy shows, burlesque parties and more. The handsomely converted performance area holds up to 500 beneath its timber rafters, and the little Front Lounge has flickering candles, leather armchairs and plenty of beers behind the long oak bar.

JALOPY LIVE MUSIC

Map p438 (☎718-395-3214; www.jalopytheatre.org; 315 Columbia St, btwn Hamilton Ave & Woodhull St, Columbia St Waterfront District; ⏰4-9pm Mon, noon-midnight Tue-Sun; 👪; Ⓢ F, G to Carroll St then 🚌B61 to Columbia/Carroll Sts) This tavern, and music and teaching space, at the fringes of Carroll Gardens and Red Hook is a fun, DIY kind of affair, where the beer's cold and you can usually catch a bluegrass, country, klezmer or ukulele show. There are freebies like open-mic nights (Tuesdays) and old-school blues and folk at Roots 'n' Ruckus (Wednesdays); consult the website.

NITEHAWK CINEMA CINEMA

Map p436 (☎718-782-8370; www.nitehawkcinema.com; 136 Metropolitan Ave, btwn Berry & Wythe Sts, Williamsburg; adult/child $13/10; Ⓢ L to Bedford Ave) This indie triplex has a fine lineup of first-run and repertory films, a good sound system and comfy seats. Amplifying the experience is the fact that you can dine and drink throughout the movie, thanks to stealthy wait staff who slink to and fro armed with hot popcorn chicken, vegan 'pulled-pork' sandwiches, soft-serve ice cream and cocktails themed by whatever movies are showing.

ALAMO DRAFTHOUSE CINEMA

Map p443 (☎718-513-2547; www.drafthouse.com; 445 Albee Sq W, at DeKalb Ave, City Point, Downtown Brooklyn; tickets $17.50; ⏰box office opens 45min before first screening; Ⓢ B, Q/R to DeKalb Ave, 2/3 to Hoyt St, A/C, G to Hoyt-Schermerhorn) The NYC branch of this Texas-based moviehouse phenomenon shows both first-run movies and special presentations in big-screen cinemas with wide, cushy seats and small tables. Throughout the show, waiters slink through the aisles to bring draft beers, daiquiris, vegan burgers and pulled-pork sandwiches right to your seat.

LITTLEFIELD LIVE PERFORMANCE

Map p440 (www.littlefieldnyc.com; 635 Sackett St, btwn Third & Fourth Aves, Gowanus; tickets from $8; Ⓢ R to Union St) This performance and art space occupying a 6200-sq-ft former textile warehouse showcases a wide range of live music and other shows, including comedy, storytelling, theater, dance, film screenings and trivia nights. Mondays bring a riotous comedy lineup; other regular events include the groan-inducing game show *Punderdome 3000,* oddball variety shows and trivia competition *Nerd Nite*. No under-21s.

> **WHAT'S ON**
>
> Visit the websites of Free Williamsburg (www.freewilliamsburg.com), Brooklyn Based (www.brooklynbased.com), Greenpointers (www.greenpointers.com) and Bushwick Daily (www.bushwickdaily.com) to keep tabs on the latest music gigs, art openings and more.

★KINGS THEATRE THEATER

Map p440 (☎box office 718-856-5464; www.kingstheatre.com; 1027 Flatbush Ave, at Tilden Ave, Flatbush; ⏰box office noon-5:30pm Mon-Sat; Ⓢ 2, 5 to Beverly Rd) This dream palace from the twilight of cinema's pre-Depression heyday is a nostalgic landmark and a top-notch concert venue to boot. Allowed to fall derelict in the 1970s, it was sensitively restored in 2015. Today, the gold-and-red lobby, elaborately painted ceiling and plush chairs are gloriously reborn, while events are as diverse as Russian ballet, classic rock and horror screenings.

MCU PARK BASEBALL

Map p444 (☎718-372-5596; www.brooklyncyclones.com; 1904 Surf Ave, at W 17th St, Coney Island; tickets $10-19, all tickets Wed $10; Ⓢ D/F, N/Q to Coney Island-Stillwell Ave) The minor-league baseball team **Brooklyn Cyclones**, part of the New York–Penn League and interborough rivals of the **Staten Island Yankees**, plays at this beachside park just off Coney Island boardwalk.

THEATER FOR A NEW AUDIENCE PERFORMING ARTS

Map p438 (Polonsky Shakespeare Center; ☎tickets 866-811-4111; www.tfana.org; 262 Ashland Pl, cnr Fulton St, Fort Greene; ⏰box office 9am-9pm Mon-Fri, 10am-6pm Sat & Sun; Ⓢ 2/3, 4/5 to Nevins St, B, Q/R to Dekalb Ave) Part of the emerging cultural district surrounding BAM, the Theater for a New Audience opened in late 2013 in an ultramodern, ecofriendly building inspired by London's Cottesloe Theatre. The calendar features avant-garde productions of works by Shakespeare, Ibsen and Strindberg, as well as more recent works by playwrights like Richard Maxwell and his theater company the New York City Players.

PUPPETWORKS PUPPET THEATRE

Map p440 (718-965-3391; www.puppetworks.org; 338 Sixth Ave, at 4th St, Park Slope; adult/child $11/10; office 10am-2:30pm; ; S F, G to 7th Ave) In a tiny theater in Park Slope, this nonprofit outfit stages delightful marionette shows that earn rave reviews from pint-size critics. Catch puppet adaptations of classics like *Beauty and the Beast, The Frog Prince* and (of course) *Pinocchio*. Most shows happen on Saturday and Sunday at 12:30pm and 2:30pm. Cash only.

MUSIC HALL OF WILLIAMSBURG LIVE MUSIC

Map p436 (718-486-5400; www.musichallofwilliamsburg.com; 66 N 6th St, btwn Wythe & Kent Aves, Williamsburg; tickets $10-65; S L to Bedford Ave) This popular venue is *the* place to see indie bands in Brooklyn – everyone from They Might Be Giants to Teenage Fanclub and Kendrick Lamar has played here. For many groups playing New York, this is their one and only spot. It has an intimate feel (capacity is 550) and typically programs several shows of various genres per week.

EASTVILLE COMEDY CLUB COMEDY

Map p438 (347-889-5226; https://eastvillecomedy.com; 487 Atlantic Ave, btwn Nevins St & Third Ave, Boerum Hill; S 2, 3, 4, 5 to Nevins St or, S Atlantic Terminal) A welcoming bar and diverse program combine for big laughs and community vibes at this comedy club. Shows take place in a tiled back room where local comedians take to the stage (including occasional big names). There's table service during shows; complementing the beers and wines are guilty pleasures like chocolate popcorn and various candies. Bonus: no drink minimum.

WARSAW LIVE MUSIC

Map p436 (718-387-5252; www.warsawconcerts.com; 261 Driggs Ave, Polish National Home, at Eckford St, Greenpoint; B43 to Graham/Driggs Aves, S G to Nassau Ave, L to Bedford Ave) What do *pierogi* (Polish dumplings) have in common with punk rock? Why, this rockin' stage inside the no-frills and friendly Polish National Home! There are good views in the old ballroom for shows ranging from death metal to Mongolian folk rock and sultry funk. Polish ladies serve *bigos* (cabbage stew), kielbasa sandwiches and beers under the disco balls. Cash only.

KNITTING FACTORY LIVE MUSIC

Map p436 (347-529-6696; http://bk.knittingfactory.com; 361 Metropolitan Ave, at Havemeyer St, Williamsburg; tickets from $5; S L to Lorimer St, G to Metropolitan Ave) A longtime outpost for folk, indie and experimental music in New York, Williamsburg's Knitting Factory is where to go to see everything from '90s rock to afropunk, comedy and emo karaoke. The stage is small and intimate. A separate barroom has a soundproof window with stage views.

BARGEMUSIC CLASSICAL MUSIC

Map p443 (718-624-4924; www.bargemusic.org; Fulton Ferry Landing, Brooklyn Heights; tickets adult/student from $35/20; S A/C to High St-Brooklyn Bridge) The chamber-music concerts held on this 125-seat converted coffee barge (built c 1899) are a unique, intimate affair. For more than 40 years, it has been a beloved venue, with beautiful views of the East River and Manhattan. Concerts run between one hour and 90 minutes long. No restrooms on board (go at public conveniences in Brooklyn Bridge Park before the show starts).

BARCLAYS CENTER STADIUM

Map p440 (917-618-6100; www.barclayscenter.com; cnr Flatbush & Atlantic Aves, Prospect Heights; S B/D, N/Q/R, 2/3, 4/5 to Atlantic Ave-Barclays Center) The Brooklyn Nets in the NBA (formerly the New Jersey Nets) hold court at this high-tech stadium. Basketball aside, Barclays also stages boxing, professional wrestling, major concerts and shows by big names; Ariana Grande, Justin Bieber, KISS and Cirque de Soleil have all rocked the stadium.

SHOPPING

Whatever your preferred flavor of retail therapy, Brooklyn's got it. Dumbo, Williamsburg and Greenpoint are full of home-design shops, vintage furniture and clothing stores, and indie boutiques, bookstores and record shops. In southern Brooklyn, you'll find some satisfying browsing (and good consignment) in the vicinity of Boerum and Cobble Hills. Atlantic Ave, running east to west near Brooklyn Heights, is sprinkled with antique stores, while Park Slope features a good selection of laid-back clothing shops.

Brooklyn Heights, Downtown Brooklyn & Dumbo

POWERHOUSE ARENA BOOKS

Map p443 (☎718-666-3049; www.powerhousearena.com; 28 Adams St, cnr Water St, Dumbo; ⏰11am-7pm Mon-Fri, 10am-7pm Sat, 11am-6pm Sun; 📶; Ⓢ A/C to High St-Brooklyn Bridge, F to York St) Snarky greetings cards, souvenirs and books (from tattoo flash to children's reads) are carefully curated inside Powerhouse Arena, which stands snug beneath the Manhattan Bridge. It's a pleasure to browse, and a nexus of Brooklyn's cultural scene, hosting changing art exhibitions, book-launch parties and creative events.

SAHADI'S FOOD

Map p443 (☎718-624-4550; www.sahadis.com; 187 Atlantic Ave, btwn Court & Clinton Sts, Brooklyn Heights; ⏰9am-7pm Mon-Sat; Ⓢ 2/3, 4/5 to Borough Hall) The smell of freshly roasted coffee and spices envelops shoppers who enter this beloved Middle Eastern delicacies shop. The olive bar boasts two dozen kinds and there are mountains of breads, cheeses, nuts and hummus. Its varied shelves are ideal for assembling a picnic before heading to Brooklyn Bridge Park (p263).

FULTON MALL SHOPPING CENTER

Map p443 (Fulton St, from Boerum Pl to Flatbush Ave, Downtown Brooklyn; 👪; Ⓢ A/C, F, R to Jay St-MetroTech, B, Q/R to DeKalb Ave, 2/3, 4/5 to Nevins St) This outdoor shopping experience has been around for a long time, and features everything from big-name department stores such as Macy's to local favorites like Dr Jays. Stores such as H&M, Gap, Banana Republic and Nordstrom Rack make it a magnet for Brooklynites looking to give their credit card a workout. Toy stores and fast-food places add family appeal.

Boerum Hill, Cobble Hill, Carroll Gardens & Red Hook

BOOKS ARE MAGIC BOOKS

Map p438 (☎718-246-2665; www.booksaremagic.net; 225 Smith St, at Butler St, Carroll Gardens; ⏰10am-9pm Mon-Fri, 9am-9pm Sat, to 7pm Sun; 👪; Ⓢ F, G to Bergen St) Opened in 2017 by novelist Emma Straub and her designer husband, this independent bookstore has won over Brooklyn's resident bookworms, not only with its well-curated selection of established and new authors but also with regular free literary events, including author talks and discussion panels. After perusing the shelves, you can also stock up on cute stationery, tote bags and other accessories.

TWISTED LILY PERFUME

Map p438 (☎347-529-4681; www.twistedlily.com; 360 Atlantic Ave, btwn Bond & Hoyt Sts, Boerum Hill; ⏰noon-7pm Tue-Sun; Ⓢ F, G to Hoyt-Schermerhorn)

READING BROOKLYN

Brooklyn's literary roots run deep, with a range of local talents who have shaped American literature, not to mention the countless authors living here today. Here are a few quintessential reads from celebrated Brooklyn authors present and past:

- *Leaves of Grass* (1855) Walt Whitman's love letter to New York; 'Crossing Brooklyn Ferry,' is a particularly poignant part of his poetic celebration of life.
- *A Tree Grows in Brooklyn* (1943) Betty Smith's affecting coming-of-age story set in the squalid tenements of Williamsburg.
- *Sophie's Choice* (1979) William Styron's blockbuster centers on a trio battling their postwar neuroses from a boarding house in Flatbush.
- *Motherless Brooklyn* (1999) Jonathan Lethem's brilliant and darkly comic tale of small-time hoods is set in Carroll Gardens and other parts of Brooklyn.
- *Literary Brooklyn* (2011) Evan Hughes provides an overview of great Brooklyn writers and their neighborhoods, from Henry Miller's Williamsburg to Truman Capote's Brooklyn Heights.
- *Manhattan Beach* (2017) Pulitzer Prize–winning author Jennifer Egan's novel follows a young woman working in the Brooklyn Navy Yard during WWII.

Come out smelling like a rose (or, if you'd prefer, almond, clary sage or orange blossom) from this 'fragrance boutique and apothecary' specializing in unusual scents from around the world. The attentive staff will help you shop by fragrance for personalized perfumes, scented candles, and skincare and grooming products.

BLACK GOLD RECORDS MUSIC

Map p438 (☎347-227-8227; www.blackgoldbrooklyn.com; 461 Court St, btwn 4th Pl & Luquer St, Carroll Gardens; ⏲7am-7pm Sun-Thu, 7am-8pm Fri, 8am-8pm Sat, 8am-7pm Sun; **S**F, G to Smith-9th Sts) Records, coffee, antiques and taxidermy await you in this darkly delightful Court St gem. Sample vintage vinyl – from disco and funk to heavy metal – on the turntable and enjoy a damn good cup of coffee, ground and brewed individually. Want to peruse creepy vintage board games or stuffed beavers? Find them here.

BROOKLYN STRATEGIST GAMES

Map p438 (☎718-576-3035; www.thebrooklynstrategist.com; 333 Court St, btwn Sackett & Union Sts, Carroll Gardens; ⏲11am-11pm Mon-Fri, 10am-11pm Sat, 10am-8pm Sun; 👪; **S**F, G to Carroll St) Whether you're into *Settlers of Catan* or checkers, this community games store has something for you. Besides the large selection of games for sale, $10 (per person) gets you four hours to play any of the several hundred games in its huge library. Tuesday nights there's open-play chess and board games; a small cafe keeps you fueled. Great rainy-day option.

Fort Greene, Clinton Hill & Bed-Stuy

GREENLIGHT BOOKSTORE BOOKS

Map p438 (☎718-246-0200; www.greenlightbookstore.com; 686 Fulton St, at S Portland Ave, Fort Greene; ⏲10am-10pm; **S**C to Lafayette Ave, B/D, N/Q/R, 2/3, 4/5 to Atlantic Ave-Barclays Center) This independent bookstore has been a neighborhood mainstay for more than a decade. How does it stick around in the age of Amazon? Friendly, book-loving staff, a great selection of kids' books and works by local authors, a calendar of readings and talks, plus loyal, literary Brooklynites who prefer to shop local. Great selection of Brooklyn- and NYC-themed books.

Park Slope, Gowanus & Sunset Park

BEACON'S CLOSET VINTAGE

Map p440 (☎718-230-1630; www.beaconscloset.com; 92 Fifth Ave, at Warren St, Park Slope; ⏲noon-9pm Mon-Fri, 11am-8pm Sat & Sun; **S**2/3 to Bergen St, B, Q to 7th Ave) Rifle through the racks for bright vintage clothing, zany accessories and footwear at the Park Slope branch of this NYC thrift-store stalwart.

There's a much bigger branch in Greenpoint (p300) and another one in Bushwick (p300).

BROOKLYN SUPERHERO SUPPLY CO GIFTS & SOUVENIRS

Map p440 (☎718-499-9884; www.superherosupplies.com; 372 Fifth Ave, btwn 5th & 6th Sts, Park Slope; ⏲noon-6pm Tue-Sun; 👪; **S**F, G, R to 4th Ave-9th St) This curious shop sells capes, masks, utility belts, invisibility goggles, buckets of antimatter and other essentials for budding superheroes…but the on-sale items are a mere distraction from the behind-the-scenes heroism. All sales provide support for 826NYC, a nonprofit organisation that helps students improve their writing and literacy skills (the classroom area is concealed behind one of the shelves).

LEROY'S PLACE ARTS & CRAFTS

Map p440 (☎718-369-4200; www.leroysplace.com; 353 Seventh Ave, btwn 10th & 11th Sts, Park Slope; ⏲noon-7pm Wed-Sun; 👪; **S**F, G to 7th Ave) Is it a gallery, boutique or event space? No matter: inside whimsical Leroy's Place, you'll pose inside art installations, browse gifts from fine jewelry to zany T-shirts, and keep the kids amused with oversized monster puppets.

Williamsburg, Greenpoint & Bushwick

QUIMBY'S BOOKSTORE NYC BOOKS

Map p436 (☎718-384-1215; www.quimbysnyc.com; 536 Metropolitan Ave, btwn Union Ave & Lorimer St, Williamsburg; ⏲11am-10pm Mon-Sat, to 7pm Sun; **S**G to Metropolitan Ave, L to Lorimer St) A bookstore with renegade spirit, this offshoot of the renowned indie outlet in Chicago spotlights Brooklyn authors and assembles counter-culture writing on travel, the occult, LGBTIQ+ culture, music and more. In between are archly humorous greetings cards, poetry pamphlets, postcards, phrenology prints, mounted beetles, small-press productions...everything an anarchist shopper could desire. Weekly events include readings and photography exhibitions.

ROUGH TRADE MUSIC

Map p436 (☎718-388-4111; www.roughtradenyc.com; 64 N 9th St, btwn Kent & Wythe Aves, Williamsburg; ⊙11am-11pm Mon-Sat, to 9pm Sun; 📶; Ⓢ L to Bedford Ave) This 10,000-sq-ft record store – a London import – has a cult following as a shopping experience and hangout for music-lovers. Deep racks of vinyl and CDs fill the warehouse-like space, with listening stations to tempt fans from their usual genres. There are also books, magazines and merchandise to browse. In-store DJs spin discs, and coffee is available from on-site Brompton Bike Cafe, encourage lingering.

A small stage hosts acts as diverse as Gang of Four and the Get Up Kids (tickets start at $10 bought in advance or $12 on the door). Upstairs there are free table-tennis tables.

CATBIRD JEWELRY

Map p436 (☎718-599-3457; www.catbirdnyc.com; 219 Bedford Ave, btwn N 4th & N 5th Sts, Williamsburg; ⊙noon-8pm Mon-Fri, 11am-7pm Sat, noon-6pm Sun; Ⓢ L to Bedford Ave) Specializing in dainty jewelry, such as moonstone rings, exquisite necklaces and minimalist anklets, Catbird is a fixture of

LOCAL KNOWLEDGE

BROOKLYN MARKETS

When the weekend arrives, Brooklynites are out and about, strolling the stoop sales and hitting the markets. Here are a few good places to unearth something unusual:

Brooklyn Flea (Map p443; www.brooklynflea.com; 80 Pearl St, Manhattan Bridge Archway, Anchorage Pl, at Water St, Dumbo; ⊙10am-5pm Sun Apr-Oct; 🚌B67 to York/Jay Sts, Ⓢ F to York St) Every Sunday from spring through to early fall, 80-odd vendors sell their wares inside a giant archway under the Manhattan Bridge. There is everything from antique goods to records, vintage clothes, bouquets of flowers, quirky handicrafts and housewares, even wormwood liqueur. Snack on flavored doughnuts or a slice while contemplating if a kimono or Brooklyn print T-shirt will fit into your rucksack.

Artists & Fleas (Map p436; ☎917-488-4203; www.artistsandfleas.com; 70 N 7th St, btwn Wythe & Kent Aves, Williamsburg; ⊙10am-7pm Sat & Sun; Ⓢ L to Bedford Ave) Over 75 purveyors of rough-stone jewelry, scented candles, extra-strength CBD oil and art-print T-shirts assemble at this indoor market, where smooth tunes waft from the DJ deck and drip coffee fuels shoppers. This uber-hip shopping experience also has two smaller locations in Manhattan which are open daily, one in SoHo, the other inside the Chelsea Market (p151).

Fort Greene Greenmarket (Map p438; ☎212-788-7476; www.grownyc.org; Fort Greene Park, cnr Cumberland St & DeKalb Ave, Fort Greene; ⊙8am-3pm Sat; 🖉; 🚌B38 to DeKalb Ave/Carlton St, Ⓢ G to Fulton St, C to Lafayette Ave) This beloved neighborhood farmers market is held at the southeastern corner of Fort Greene Park (p269) every Saturday, year-round. Purveyors of local and regional produce are reliably in attendance, offering everything from Hudson Valley ducks, charcuterie and wild-caught fish to organic fruits, aged cheeses and small-batch baked goods – other produce follows the seasons, such as maple syrup (winter) and cut flowers (spring).

Grand Army Plaza Greenmarket (Map p440; www.grownyc.org; Grand Army Plaza, cnr Prospect Park W & Flatbush Ave, Prospect Park; ⊙8am-4pm Sat; Ⓢ 2, 3 to Grand Army Plaza) Held at the southern edge of Grand Army Plaza every Saturday, this long-standing farmers market boasts stalls laden with local and regional produce – from pastries, dairy and vodka to merino wool and candles – and a few fun food trucks. It's a good spot to grab a picnic before heading into Prospect Park (p264).

Williamsburg's artisanal scene. The compact shop stocks its own work – produced in a studio located just a few blocks away – as well as pieces from independent jewelers from around the world. Everything is made from either sterling silver or gold (recycled or fair-trade), and features conflict-free gems.

DESERT ISLAND COMICS COMICS

Map p436 (718-388-5087; www.desertislandbrooklyn.com; 540 Metropolitan Ave, btwn Union Ave & Lorimer St, Williamsburg; 2-7pm Mon, noon-8pm Tue-Sun; ; S L to Lorimer St, G to Metropolitan Ave) A comic store lives or dies by the encyclopedic knowledge of its staff, and Desert Island sure knows its stuff.

A breezy welcome and good advice make it all the easier to navigate through hundreds of comics, graphic novels, local zines, prints, games and handmade artists' books, while good tunes spin on the turntable out the back.

BEACON'S CLOSET VINTAGE

Map p436 (718-486-0816; www.beaconscloset.com; 74 Guernsey St, btwn Nassau & Norman Aves, Greenpoint; 11am-8pm; S G to Nassau Ave) This 5500-sq-ft warehouse of vintage clothing is both a gold mine and a gauntlet. Arranged by color themes, its circular racks of coats, dresses, polyester tops and '90s-era T-shirts take time and determination to conquer. The committed will also find sequin-studded shoes, flannel shirts, hats, handbags, costume jewelry and retro sunglasses.

There are other store branches that are located in **Bushwick** (Map p436; 718-417-5683; www.beaconscloset.com; 23 Bogart St, btwn Varet & Cook Sts, Bushwick; 11am-8pm; S L to Morgan Ave), Park Slope (p298) and Manhattan.

SPOONBILL & SUGARTOWN BOOKS

Map p436 (718-387-7322; www.spoonbillbooks.com; 218 Bedford Ave, btwn N 5th & N 4th Sts, Williamsburg; 10am-10pm; S L to Bedford Ave) Williamsburg's favorite bookstore has community at its heart. The shelves brim with social justice tomes, rad art and intriguing coffee-table books, along with used and rare titles, and locally made works not found elsewhere. Check the website for upcoming readings and book-launch parties.

SPORTS & ACTIVITIES

BROOKLYN BOWL BOWLING

Map p436 (718-963-3369; www.brooklynbowl.com; 61 Wythe Ave, btwn N 11th & N 12th Sts, Williamsburg; lane rental per 30min $25, shoe rental $5; 6pm-late Mon-Fri, from noon Sat & Sun; ; S L to Bedford Ave, G to Nassau Ave) This impressive bowling alley has 16 lanes surrounded by sofas and brick walls. Brooklyn Bowl also hosts concerts throughout the week, and there's good food available (like French bread pizzas, wings and veg bowls). Saturdays from noon to 5pm and Sundays to 6pm are all-ages Family Bowl hours. Night bowling is for ages 21 and over only.

BROOKLYN BOULDERS CLIMBING

Map p440 (347-834-9066; www.brooklynboulders.com; 575 Degraw St, at Third Ave, Gowanus; day pass $36, shoe & harness rental $14; 7am-midnight Mon-Fri, to 10pm Sat & Sun; S R to Union St) Brooklyn's biggest indoor climbing arena is housed in an airy and vibrant space on an industrial block in the Gowanus neighborhood. Ceilings top out at 30ft inside this 18,000-sq-ft facility, and its caves and freestanding 17ft boulder and climbing walls offer routes for both beginners and experts. There are overhangs of 15, 30 and 45 degrees.

BROOKLYN BRAINERY WALKING

Map p440 (347-292-7246; www.brooklynbrainery.com; 190 Underhill Ave, btwn Sterling & St Johns Pls, Prospect Heights; S 2/3 to Grand Army Plaza) This community educational resource hosts one-off evening talks and hands-on courses – on everything from shorthand to vegan Chinese food to coding – and also offers guided walking tours with themes such as native plants and Dutch history.

RED HOOK BOATERS KAYAKING

Map p438 (www.redhookboaters.org; Louis Valentino Jr Park, cnr Coffey & Ferris Sts, Red Hook; 1-4pm Sun Jun-Sep & 6-8pm Thu mid-Jun–mid-Aug; ; S F, G to Smith-9th Sts then B61 to Van Brunt/Coffey Sts) FREE This volunteer-run boathouse, located in Red Hook, offers free kayaking in the small embayment off Louis Valentino Jr Park. Once in the water, you'll have beautiful views of Lower Manhattan and the Statue of Liberty. Check the website for the latest times before making the trip out. There are life jackets for kids; under-14s must be accompanied by an adult.

Queens

LONG ISLAND CITY | ASTORIA | JACKSON HEIGHTS | FLUSHING & CORONA | WOODSIDE | ELMHURST | FLUSHING

Neighborhood Top Five

❶ **MoMA PS1** (p303) Feeling inspired at the Museum of Modern Art's cross-river cultural hub, with paintings, sculpture and site-specific installations.

❷ **Museum of the Moving Image** (p306) Reliving your favorite film and TV moments at Astoria's contemporary tribute to the small and silver screens.

❸ **Rockaways** (p307) Heading out to the seaside by subway (or better yet ferry) for surfing, rock-loving waterfront eateries and miles of shimmering beaches.

❹ **Roosevelt Avenue** (p313) Taking a snack crawl through Latin America, via food trucks along this melting-pot avenue.

❺ **Flushing** (p310) Immersing yourself in bustling Asian street life and feasting on chewy Chinese noodles, plump dumplings and plenty more.

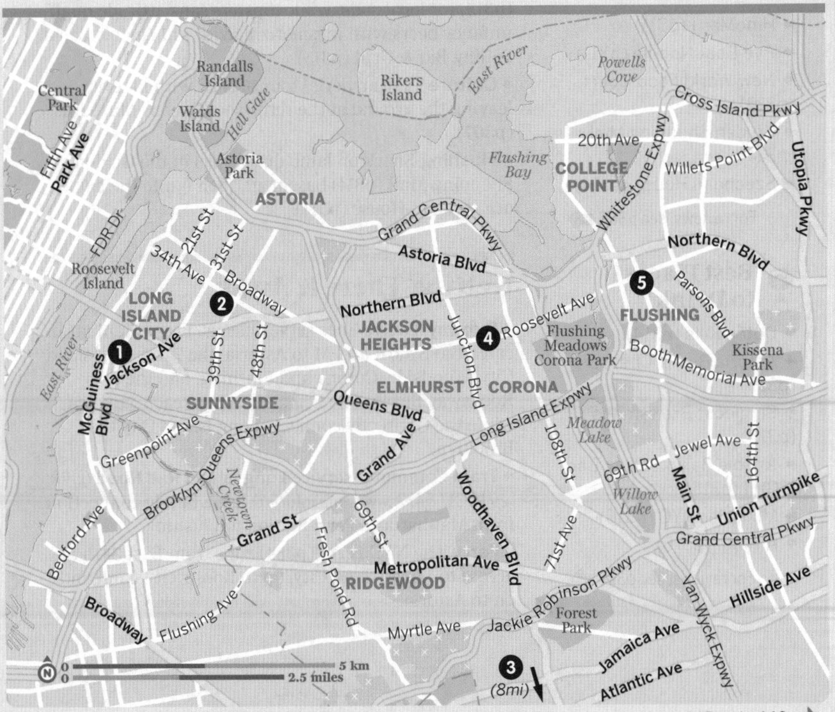

For more detail of this area see Map p445 and p446

Lonely Planet's Top Tip

Beat Manhattan hotel prices while sleeping with a view of that famous skyline in a sleek designer bedroom. Queens' growing list of swanky hotels, many cleverly repurposing industrial real estate, makes it the ideal place to rest your head at reasonable rates, yet remain close to the action.

Best Places to Eat

- Casa Enrique (p309)
- Bahari Estiatorio (p312)
- Mombar (p312)
- Addā (p308)
- Taverna Kyclades (p312)

For reviews, see p308

Best Asian Cuisine

- HinoMaru (p311)
- Pye Boat Noodle (p311)
- New World Food Court (p313)
- Golden Shopping Mall (p314)
- Szechuan House (p314)

For reviews, see p308

Best Places to Drink

- Dutch Kills (p314)
- Astoria Bier & Cheese (p315)
- Singlecut Brewsmiths (p315)
- Anable Basin Sailing Bar & Grill (p315)
- Mikkeller NYC (p316)
- Alewife (p315)

For reviews, see p314

Explore Queens

Queens is NYC's biggest and most-populated borough – anywhere else, it would be a major city in its own right. So where to begin?

Start with a day in Long Island City, home to contemporary art hubs MoMA PS1 and SculptureCenter (p306). Watch the sun set from Gantry Plaza State Park (p305), and sip-and-sup on neighborly Vernon Blvd. Spend a day or two exploring Astoria, taste-testing a variety of eateries, sipping local brews, and checking out the Museum of the Moving Image (p307). If it's summer, catch an alfresco film at Socrates Sculpture Park (p305).

With its jumble of street foods, Asian groceries and kitschy malls, Flushing (home to NYC's biggest Chinatown) also merits a full-day adventure. Or you can spend the morning on Main St and Roosevelt Ave, then hit neighboring Corona for the Queens Museum (p307), Louis Armstrong House (p306) or New York Hall of Science (p308) for the kids. If it's hot, tackle the surf at Rockaway Beach (p307), home to NYC's coolest beach scene.

Local Life

- **Hangouts** Brew fans head to Astoria Bier & Cheese (p315) for local suds, while hipsters sans attitude quaff unfancy beers with mesmerizing views at Anable Basin Sailing Bar & Grill (p315).
- **Culture** Take an aerial tour of NYC without ever leaving the ground at the retro-cool Queens Museum (p307).
- **Flushing** Snack on lamb dumplings in the Golden Shopping Mall (p314) basement, then ignite the palate at Szechuan House (p314).

Getting There & Away

- **Subway** Twelve lines serve Queens. From Manhattan, catch the N/Q/R and M to Astoria, the 7 to Long Island City, Woodside, Corona and Flushing, and the A to Rockaway Beach. The E, J and Z lines reach Jamaica, while the G directly connects Long Island City to Brooklyn.
- **Train** Commuter service **Long Island Rail Road** (LIRR; ☎718-217-5477; www.mta.info/lirr) has a handy connection from Manhattan's Penn Station to Flushing.
- **Ferry** The NYC Ferry (p384) runs from East 34th St across to Long Island City, up to Roosevelt Island and on to Astoria.

TOP EXPERIENCE
MOMA PS1

The smaller, hipper sibling of Manhattan's Museum of Modern Art, MoMA PS1 hunts down razor-sharp art and serves it in an ex-school locale. Here you'll be peering at videos through floorboards and debating the meaning of nonstatic structures while staring through a hole in the wall. Nothing is predictable. Best of all, admission is free with your MoMA ticket within 14 days of your visit.

Roots, Radicals & PS1 Classics

PS1 first hit the scene in the 1970s. This was the age of Dia, Artists' Space and the New Museum – new-gen projects showcasing the city's thriving experimental, multimedia art scene. In 1976, Alanna Heiss – a supporter of art in alternative spaces – took possession of an abandoned school building in Queens and invited artists like Richard Serra, James Turrell and Keith Sonnier to create site-specific works. The end result was PS1's inaugural exhibition, *Rooms*. Surviving remnants include Richard Artschwager's oval-shaped wall 'blps' and Alan Saret's light-channeling *The Hole at P.S.1, Fifth Solar Chthonic Wall Temple,* on the north wing's 3rd floor. These works are part of the museum's long-term installations, which also include Pipilotti Rist's video *Selbstlos im Lavabad* (Selfless in the Bath of Lava) – viewable through the lobby floorboards – and Turrell's awe-inspiring *Meeting,* where the sky is the masterpiece.

Summer 'Warm Up' Parties

On Saturday afternoons from July 4 through Labor Day, rock on at one of New York's coolest weekly music/culture events, Warm Up. It's a hit

DON'T MISS

- Temporary and long-term exhibitions
- Summer 'Warm Up' parties
- Sunday Sessions

PRACTICALITIES

- Map p446, B5
- 718-784-2084
- www.momaps1.org
- 22-25 Jackson Ave, Long Island City
- suggested donation adult/child $10/free, NYC residents or with MoMA ticket free, Warm Up party online/at venue $18/22
- noon-6pm Thu-Mon, Warm Up parties noon-9pm Sat Jul-early Sep
- S G, 7 to Court Sq, E/M to Court Sq-23rd St

BOOKSTORE

Seek further enlightenment at **Artbook** (Map p446; ☎718-433-1088; www.artbook.com/artbookps1.html; 22-25 Jackson Ave, Long Island City; ⏰noon-6pm Thu-Mon; Ⓢ E/M to Court Sq-23rd St, G, 7 to Court Sq), the MoMA PS1 bookstore. Stock up on MoMA exhibition catalogs, coffee-table tomes, art-theory titles and out-of-print fodder. You'll also find contemporary culture, film and performance titles; art, architecture and design journals; magazines; and new media. Scan the Artbook website for occasional readings and exhibition-based events.

TAKE A BREAK

Greek chef Mina Stone offers Greek comfort food in the museum's restaurant, appropriately named Mina's (p309).

A few blocks from the museum, the LIC Market (p309) serves creative American dishes.

with everyone from verified hipsters to plugged-in music geeks, who spill into the MoMA PS1 courtyard to eat, drink and catch a stellar lineup of top bands, experimental music and DJs. Featured artists have included acid-house deity DJ Pierre and techno pioneer Juan Atkins. It's like one big block party, albeit with better music and art than your usual neighborhood slap-up. Linked to it is the annual YAP (Young Architects Program) competition, in which one design team is selected to transform the museum courtyard with a large-scale structure that provides shade and creative party space.

Sunday Sessions

Another cultural treat is the Sunday Sessions, on Sundays November to April (for the 2019–20 season but timeframes vary yearly). Spanning lectures, film screenings, live music and performance art and beyond, the lineup has included experimental comedy, postindustrial noise jams and Latin art-house dance. One week you might catch a symphony debut, the next an architectural performance from Madrid. Upcoming events are listed on the MoMA PS1 website.

Architecture

Built in the Renaissance Revival style and dating back to the early 1890s, the MoMA PS1 building housed the first school in Long Island City. Low attendance forced its closure in 1963. A three-year, award-winning restoration by LA-based architect Frederick Fisher in the mid-1990s saw the addition of the building's outdoor galleries and main entrance.

SIGHTS

The Queens Tourism Council (www.itsinqueens.com) website offers information on attractions and events, while the Queens Council on the Arts (www.queenscouncilarts.org) promotes art in the borough. For a more personalized introduction, Hunter College urban-geography professor Jack Eichenbaum leads many unusual Walking Tours (p318) of Queens' ethnic neighborhoods, including a full-day walk/subway ride along the 7 train line.

Long Island City

Despite being only a 10-minute ride on the 7 train to Midtown, Long Island City remained undeveloped and undiscovered for decades. Now many years into its mini-boom, it remains on the edge of cool. Several cutting-edge art museums and repurposed industrial buildings lend it the prototypical vibe of a hip New York City neighborhood just past pioneering stage. There are great views to be had, particularly from Gantry Plaza State Park along the river.

To get there, take the G to 21st St or the NYC Ferry.

MOMA PS1 GALLERY

See p303.

★NOGUCHI MUSEUM MUSEUM

Map p446 (☎718-204-7088; www.noguchi.org; 9-01 33rd Rd, at Vernon Blvd, Long Island City; adult/child $10/free, 1st Fri of month free; ⌚10am-5pm Wed-Fri, 11am-6pm Sat & Sun; 🚌Q103, Q104 to Vernon Blvd-33 Rd, Ⓢ N/W to Broadway) Both the art and the context in which it's displayed here are the work of LA-born sculptor, designer and landscape architect Isamu Noguchi, famous for iconic lamps and coffee tables, as well as elegant, abstract stone sculptures. Artifacts are displayed in serene indoor galleries and a minimalist sculpture garden, forming a complete aesthetic vision and an oasis of calm. The 1st floor holds the permanent collection, while the upstairs gallery shows temporary exhibitions.

GANTRY PLAZA STATE PARK STATE PARK

Map p446 (www.nysparks.com/parks/149; 4-09 47th Rd, Long Island City; ⌚8am-10pm; Ⓢ 7 to Vernon Blvd-Jackson Ave) This 12-acre riverside park directly across the water from the United Nations has gorgeous uninterrupted views of the Manhattan skyline. It's nicely designed, with public lounges for panoramic chilling, and attracts a good mix of Queens families. The restored gantries – in service until 1967 – are testament to the area's past as a loading dock for rail-car floats and barges.

Dating back to 1936, the giant Pepsi-Cola sign at the park's northern end is an icon of Long Island City. It once topped a nearby Pepsi bottling plant, which has been since demolished. This is also a handy spot for catching ferries across to E 34th St, or up to Roosevelt Island and Astoria.

SOCRATES SCULPTURE PARK PARK

Map p446 (www.socratessculpturepark.org; 32-01 Vernon Blvd, Astoria; ⌚9am-dusk; Ⓢ N/W to Broadway) FREE First carved out of an abandoned dump by sculptor Mark di Suvero, Socrates is now a city park on the river's edge with beautiful views and a rotating series of installations. Try to time a visit with free events – such as yoga on weekends from mid-May to late September, and Wednesday-night movies in July and August.

KAUFMAN ARTS DISTRICT ARTS CENTER

Map p446 (www.kaufmanartsdistrict.com; 34-12 36th St, Astoria; Ⓢ M/R to Steinway St, N/Q to 36th Ave) Anchored by the legendary **Kaufman Astoria Studios** at 34-12 36th St, this up-and-coming district comprises more than 24 blocks of Queens' cultural heart – you can say you knew it before it became the new Chelsea. In addition to key institutions like the Museum of the Moving

WORTH A DETOUR

FARM LIFE

Frolic with cows, sheep and goats at **Queens County Farm Museum** (☎718-347-3276; www.queensfarm.org; 73-50 Little Neck Pkwy, Floral Park; ⌚10am-5pm; 👪; 🚌Q46 to Little Neck Pkwy) FREE, the last patch of farmland within the city limits. It's a long way from Manhattan, but for anyone with an interest in urban agriculture – or kids who need a break from city energy – this is a tranquil destination. It hosts an annual powwow for tribes from all over America, plus many seasonal events (including a haunted house in late October).

Image, the KAD puts on events, workshops and public art pieces around the area (see the website for a calendar), and there are plenty of restaurants and bars to pop into between gallery visits.

SCULPTURECENTER GALLERY

Map p446 (☎718-361-1750; www.sculpture-center.org; 44-19 Purves St, Long Island City; suggested donation $10; ⏲11am-6pm Thu-Mon; Ⓢ7 to 45th Rd-Court House Sq, E, M to 23rd St-Ely Ave, G to Long Island City-Court Sq) Down a dead-end street, in a former trolley repair shop, SculptureCenter pages Berlin with its edgy art and industrial backdrop. Its hangar-like main gallery and cavernous underground space show both emerging and established artists. It's always a worthwhile add-on to a visit to nearby MoMA PS1 (p303).

Astoria

Home to the largest Greek community in the world outside Greece, this is obviously the place to find amazing Greek bakeries, restaurants and gourmet shops, mainly along Broadway. An influx of Eastern European, Middle Eastern and Latino immigrants, not to mention young artsy types (especially aspiring actors), have created a rich and diverse mix. A reminder that movie-making started in Astoria in the 1920s; the Museum of the Moving Image exposes some of the mysteries of the craft with amazing exhibits and screenings in its ornate and renovated theater.

★MUSEUM OF THE MOVING IMAGE MUSEUM

Map p446 (www.movingimage.us; 36-01 35th Ave, btwn 36th & 37th Sts, Astoria; adult/child $15/9, 4-8pm Fri free; ⏲10:30am-5pm Wed & Thu, to 8pm Fri, to 6pm Sat & Sun; 👪; ⓈM/R to Steinway St) This supercool complex is one of the world's top film, TV and video museums. Galleries show the best of a collection of 130,000-plus artifacts, including Elizabeth Taylor's wig from *Cleopatra*, an epic bounty of vintage TVs and cameras, 19th-century optical toys and a room of vintage arcade games. Interactive displays – such as a DIY flip-book station – show the science behind the art. The museum also has fantastic temporary exhibitions and regular film screenings; check the website for details.

Jackson Heights

Spread out in a 50-block area from 70th to 90th Sts between Roosevelt and 34th is one of the nicest NYC neighborhoods that few New Yorkers know about. Roosevelt Ave is not to be missed. It's a veritable United Nations, best appreciated by chowing down at a restaurant or several. South Asians and Latinos from every community south of the border to the tip of Patagonia have significant presences. To get here, take the 7 to 74th St-Broadway or E/F/M/R to Jackson Heights-Roosevelt Ave.

Flushing & Corona

The intersection of Main St and Roosevelt Ave, downtown Flushing, can feel like the Times Square of a city a world away from NYC. Immigrants from all over Asia, primarily China and Korea, populate this exuberant neighborhood, and its markets and restaurants burst with the delicious and exotic.

To the southeast is Corona, most notable for Flushing Meadows Corona Park, Queens' massive green heart. Besides several worthwhile museums, the park (created to host the 1939 World's Fair) also contains the USTA Billie Jean King National Tennis Center, where the US Open is held every August.

★LOUIS ARMSTRONG HOUSE NOTABLE BUILDING

Map p445 (☎718-478-8274; www.louisarmstronghouse.org; 34-56 107th St, Corona; adult/child $12/8; ⏲10am-5pm Wed-Fri, from noon Sat & Sun, last tour 4pm; Ⓢ7 to 103rd St Corona Plaza) At the peak of his career and with worldwide fame at hand, legendary trumpeter Armstrong settled in this modest Queens home, and lived there until his death in 1971. The place has been immaculately preserved in groovy style, down to the dazzling retro-turquoise kitchen. Guided tours (40 minutes) tell Armstrong's story through audio clips and insightful commentary on some of the objects connected to the great jazz man.

FLUSHING MEADOWS CORONA PARK PARK

Map p445 (www.nycgovparks.org/parks/fmcp; Grand Central Pkwy, Corona; ⏲24hr; Ⓢ7 to Mets Willets Point) FREE Central Queens' biggest attraction is this 1225-acre park, built for the

WORTH A DETOUR

ROCKAWAY BEACH

Immortalized by the Ramones' 1977 song 'Rockaway Beach,' America's largest urban **beach** (beach 6am-9pm, boardwalk to 10pm; Q52-SBS to Rockaway Beach Blvd-Beach 92 St, NYC Ferry from Wall St-Pier 11, S A to Beach-90 St) – and one of the city's best – is just a $2.75 trip on the A train from Manhattan (or the same price on the ferry). Less crowded than Coney Island and with a wilder feel, Rockaway Beach is a long stretch with two social hubs.

On the west end, **Jacob Riis Park** (718-318-4300; www.nyharborparks.org/visit/jari.html; Gateway National Recreation Area, Rockaway Beach Blvd, Queens; 9am-5pm Memorial Day-Labor Day; P; Q35 & Q22 to Jacob Riis Park, Sat, Sun & holidays from Pier 11, Wall St, to Riis Landing, Rockaway), part of the 26,000-acre Gateway National Recreation Area, mostly draws families. This area is also home to the cool green ruins of Fort Tilden, a decommissioned coastal artillery installation from WWI.

On the east end, starting around Beach 108th St, is a burgeoning scene of hipsters, artists and locavore food options, fronting the city's only designated surfing beaches (at Beach 92nd St and going east). On the boardwalk here, concrete concession booths peddle treats such as lobster rolls, ceviche and hipster pizza.

Extending from near JFK International Airport, the salty, marshy **Jamaica Bay Wildlife Refuge** covers the water north of the Rockaways' barrier island. As one of the most important migratory bird and wetland habitats along the eastern seaboard, it attracts more than 325 bird species in spring and fall, as they snap up all sorts of briny sea creatures like clams, turtles, shrimp and oysters. Each season brings different visitors. Spring features warblers and songbirds, and American woodcocks in late March. In mid-August shorebirds start to move south, landing here from Canada and fueling up for the trip to Mexico. Fall is when migrating hawks and raptors get mobile, along with ducks, geese, monarch butterflies and thousands and thousands of dragonflies. Birders and naturalists get the most action around the east pond, though casual visitors will enjoy the more scenic and better maintained west pond trail, which has a loop path of 2 miles. Just make sure to wear mud-resistant shoes, insect repellent and sunscreen, carry some water and watch out for poison ivy.

To get to the **visitor center** (718-318-4340; www.nyharborparks.org; Cross Bay Blvd, Broad Channel; trails sunrise-sunset, visitor center 9am-5pm; Q53 to Cross Bay Blvd/Wildlife Refuge, S A/S to Broad Channel) FREE, exit at Broad Channel station, walk west along Noel Rd to Cross Bay Blvd, turn right (north) and walk for 0.7 miles, and the center will be visible on the left side of the road.

1939 World's Fair and dominated by Queens' most famous landmark, the stainless-steel **Unisphere** (24hr; S 7 to 111th St or Mets Willets Point) – it's the world's biggest globe: 120ft high and weighing 380 tons. Facing it is the former New York City Building, now home to the fantastic Queens Museum.

Just south are three weather-worn, Cold War–era New York State Pavilion Towers, part of the New York State Pavilion for the 1964 World's Fair. (You may recognize them as alien spaceships from the film *Men in Black*.) If entering the park from the north, via the 7 train, look for the 1964 World's Fair mosaics by Salvador Dalí and Andy Warhol. Also nearby is Citi Field (p317), and the **USTA Billie Jean King National Tennis Center** (Map p445; 718-760-6200; https://ustanew2.gotennissource.com; S 7 to Mets Willets Point). Head west over the Grand Central Pkwy to find a few more attractions, including the New York Hall of Science (p308). The park has sports grounds, too, on its eastern and southern edges. The top-notch Astroturf soccer fields are popular for soccer, and there's a pitch-and-putt golf course that's lit up for golfers at night.

QUEENS MUSEUM MUSEUM

Map p445 (QMA; 718-592-9700; www.queensmuseum.org; suggested donation adult/child $8/free; 11am-5pm Wed-Sun; S 7 to 111th St or Mets Willets Point) The Queens Museum is one of the city's most unexpected pleasures. Its most famous installation is the *Panorama of New York City,* a gob-smacking

WHY ARE QUEENS ADDRESSES HYPHENATED?

If you've spent more than a day or two in Manhattan, you'll know that getting the hang of navigation is pretty simple: Generally speaking, avenues run north–south, streets run east–west increasing in number from north to south. Queens? Not so much. But there is a bit of rhyme and reason to the borough's funky hyphenated addresses and overuse of avenues, lanes, drives, roads, streets and terraces (one amazing example in Forest Hills sees a consecutive five-block run of 68th St, 68th Rd, 68th Dr, 69th Ave and 69th Rd!).

Before Queens was incorporated into New York City in 1898, it was a series of unrelated towns and villages each with their own street nomenclature (there were 40 Washington Streets alone!). Something had to be done but it didn't happen until 1911 – 100 years after Manhattan's grid system began.

Today, the Queens grid system has 167 avenues that go east–west (Long Island City to Queens Village) and 271 streets that go north–south (Whitestone to Rockaway) – Manhattan's total opposite. But here's the most confusing bit: Addresses have two sets of double-digit numbers separated by a dash. The two pre-dash numbers indicate the closest cross street/avenue while the two post-dash numbers designate the building or house number (the lowest number starts nearest to that cross street). Exceptions, of course, are rampant.

So the Museum of the Moving Image in Astoria is at 36-01 35th Ave, so that means it's on 35th Ave between 36th St and 37th St and is the first building from 36th St. Got it?

Ah, *fuhgeddaboudit!*

9335-sq-ft miniature NYC, with all buildings accounted for and a 15-minute dusk-to-dawn light simulation. The museum also hosts top exhibitions of global contemporary art, reflecting the diversity of Queens. A fascinating exhibit explores some of the most interesting and avant-garde NYC designs that never came to fruition, realized through drawings and 3-D models.

The museum is housed in a historic building constructed for the 1939 World's Fair (and once home to the UN), and you'll find a retro-fabulous collection of memorabilia from both the '39 and '64 fairs on display (with reproductions in the gift shop).

NEW YORK HALL OF SCIENCE MUSEUM

Map p445 (☎718-699-0005; www.nysci.org; 47-01 111th St; adult/child $16/13, admission free 2-5pm Fri & 10-11am Sun; ⌚9:30am-5pm Mon-Fri, 10am-6pm Sat & Sun; Ⓢ7 to 111th St) Occupying a weird 1965 building, rippling with stained glass, this science museum is unapologetically nerdy. An outdoor mini-golf course and North America's largest science playground don't require as much brain power, but inside highlights include operating a Mars Rover, a Charles and Ray Eames (of Eames chairs fame)–designed *Mathematica* exhibit and *Connected Worlds*, an animated, interactive showcase allowing kids to manage water and plant growth in six environments (jungle, desert, wetlands, mountain valley, reservoir and plains).

EATING

Spanakopita? *Khao man gai? Encebol de mariscos?* If it exists, you can devour it in Queens. Head to Long Island City for locavore eateries, and to Astoria for anything from Greek to bagels – here hot spots include 30th Ave, Broadway (lying between 31st and 35th Sts) and 31st Ave. Steinway Ave between Astoria Blvd and 30th Ave is Astoria's 'Little Cairo.' Further east, Elmhurst is home to a cluster of straight-outta-Bangkok Thai options, while Roosevelt Ave is perfect for a Latin food-truck crawl. At the end of the 7 subway line lies Flushing, New York's 'Chinatown without the tourists.'

Long Island City

ADDÃ INDIAN $

Map p446 (☎718-433-3888; www.addanyc.com; 31-31 Thomson Ave, Long Island City; mains $9-25; ⌚noon-3pm & 5-9pm Mon-Thu, noon-3pm & 5-9:30pm Fri & Sat; 📶; Ⓢ7 to 33 St-Rawson St) Sandwiched between a National Guard recruiting office and a 7-Eleven, you might not look twice at Addã, which is Indian slang for 'place to hang out.' But inside, a Mumbaiker-Delhiite-Bengali trio do foodie-embraced Northern Indian among walls plastered with subcontinent periodicals and corrugated galvanized steel. The succulent and fragrant chicken biryani is perfection, slow-cooked inside a dough-sealed clay pot.

Chef Chintan Pandya brings *Michelin*-starred experience to the kitchen and you'll finds nods to his Maharashtrian heritage as well (Malvani prawn curry, for example). Lunch specials ($9 to $15) cannot be beat. And don't concern yourself with the spice level – you get it the way it's supposed to be, no more, no less.

CANNELLE PATISSERIE
BAKERY $

Map p446 (☑718-937-8500; www.cannelle patisserie.com; 5-11 47th Ave, Long Island City; pastries from $3; ⌚6:30am-8pm Mon-Fri, from 7am Sat, 7am-6pm Sun; 🚇; ⑤7 to Vernon Blvd-Jackson Ave) A surprising source of flawless French pastry, this cafe sits on a slick block in new-build LIC – but one bite of a flaky croissant, a gemlike fruit tart or a gooey macaroon will take you straight to Paris. This is a branch of the original business, set in an even more unlikely location: a dreary strip mall in Jackson Heights.

MINA'S
GREEK $

Map p446 (www.minas.nyc; 22-25 Jackson Ave, Long Island City; mains $8-20; ⌚noon-6pm Wed-Thu & Sat & Sun, to 8pm Fri; ⑤E/M to Court Sq-23rd St, G, 7 Court Sq) Chef-fashionista Mina Stone took over this coveted spot inside the school-turned-museum MoMA PS1 in late 2019 (no need to pay museum admission) and calls on her Greek grandmother for the inspiration behind her slow-cooked, home-style cuisine – the kind typically found only on family dinner tables throughout Greece.

JOHN BROWN SMOKEHOUSE
BARBECUE $

Map p446 (☑347-617-1120; www.johnbrown seriousbbq.com; 10-43 44th Dr, Long Island City; mains $9-17; ⌚11:30am-10pm Mon-Thu. to 11pm Fri, noon-11pm Sat, Sun noon-9pm; ⑤E/M to Court Sq-23rd St) Red-checked tablecloths, local craft beers on tap and the heavenly scent of beef brisket and burnt ends set the stage for a carnivorous feast at this Kansas City–style barbecue joint. It's an unfussy affair – order at the counter, then grab a seat – there are also tables on a back terrace where bands play most nights (7pm to 9pm).

CYCLO
VIETNAMESE $

Map p446 (www.cyclolic.com; 5-51 47th Ave, btwn Vernon Blvd & 5th St, Long Island City; mains $11-16; ⌚noon-3:30pm & 5-10pm Mon-Thu, to 10:30pm Fri, noon-3:30pm Sat, noon-10pm Sun; 🚇; ⑤7 to Vernon Blvd-Jackson Ave) Set in a humdrum brick building just off Vernon Blvd, Cyclo has a cozy interior of wood-paneled walls and rustic tables – just right for noshing on warm, perfectly crusted banh mi (Vietnamese baguettes with pickled daikon and carrot, cucumber, cilantro, sriracha, Vietnamese ham, roasted ground pork and pâté). More substantial options include claypots, pho, vermicelli salads and stir-fries.

★CASA ENRIQUE
MEXICAN $$

Map p446 (☑347-448-6040; www.henrinyc.com/casa-enrique.html; 5-48 49th Ave, btwn Vernon Blvd & 5th St, Long Island City; mains $13-24; ⌚5-11pm Mon-Fri, 11am-3:30pm & 5-11pm Sat & Sun; ⑤7 to Vernon Blvd-Jackson Ave, G to 21st St) Don't let the unassuming facade fool you: Cosme Aguilar, Enrique's Chiapas-born chef-patron, is classically trained, winning a *Michelin* star – Queens only – every year from 2015 to 2019 for his high-end renditions of Mexican favorites.

Expect such delights as tequila-marinated carne asada (grilled skirt steak), *mole de piaxtla* (Pueblan-style chicken and rice with a spicy chocolate sauce) and tacos stuffed with slow-cooked cow's tongue. Seating is limited, so make a reservation.

TOURNESOL
FRENCH $$

Map p446 (☑718-472-4355; www.tournesolnyc.com; 50-12 Vernon Blvd, btwn 50th & 51st Aves, Long Island City; mains $9-23; ⌚5:30-10:30pm Mon, 11:30am-3pm & 5:30-10:30pm Tue-Thu, 11:30am-3pm & 5:30-11:30pm Fri & Sat, 11am-3:30pm & 5-10pm Sun; ⑤7 to Vernon Blvd-Jackson Ave) The kitchen rarely strays beyond the familiar ground of French bistro cooking, but that's just what devoted regulars come here for. Brunch dishes such as croque monsieur and eggs Florentine give way to more involved lunch and dinner plates such as the highly regarded steak-*frites* or duck with celery purée and honey sauce.

LIC MARKET
CAFE $$

Map p446 (☑718-361-0013; www.licmarket.com; 21-52 44th Dr, Long Island City; mains lunch $12-16, dinner $21-48; ⌚10am-3:30pm Sun-Mon, 10am-3:30pm & 6-10pm Tue-Sat; 🚇; ⑤E, M to 23rd St-Ely Ave, 7 to 45th Rd-Court House Sq) 🌿 Local creatives and office workers mix at this cool

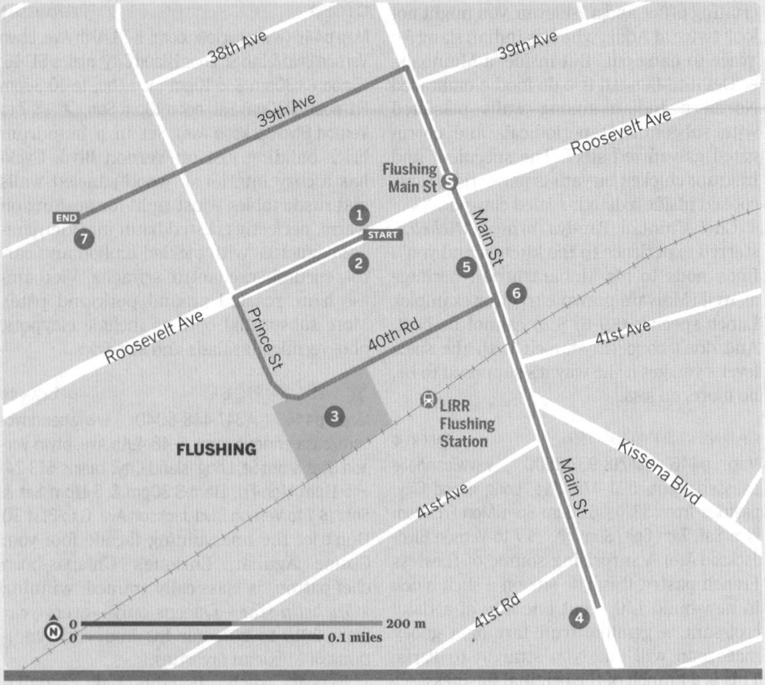

Neighborhood Walk
Chinatown in Flushing

START ROOSEVELT AVE
END 39TH AVE
LENGTH 1 MILE; 2½ HOURS

Bring an appetite before you start this food-loving stroll through Flushing, home to New York's biggest and most authentic Chinatown. Start off with a beautifully prepared oolong at 1 **Fang Gourmet Tea** (p316). It's hidden in the back of a mini-mall and is a Zen-like retreat from the frenzy outside. Cross busy Roosevelt Ave to find 2 **Soy Bean Chen Flower Shop** (p314) – aside from pretty roses and fragrant peonies, this shop has a counter in front that serves silky portions of superfresh tofu, with a side of ginger syrup for drizzling on top. Take your warm treat around the corner to 3 **Bland Playground**, which has benches that provide a fine setting for relaxation.

Continue along 40th Rd and turn right onto people-packed Main St, Flushing's most vibrant thoroughfare. Just past 41st Rd, take the stairs leading down to the 4 **Golden Shopping Mall** (p314). Here you'll find a chaotic jumble of food stalls serving a variety of delicacies.

Once sated, walk back up Main St just past 40th Rd. You'll see the line first – that's 5 **Tiger Sugar** (p316), one of the best bubble-tea purveyors in the world and its only North American location. You'll want to order the Black Sugar Boba + Pearl with Cream Mousse. Drink in hand, head back to Main St and walk across the street to the 6 **New World Food Court** (p313). This bustling shopping mall has a magnificent food court on the lower level. Aside from culinary curiosities from China, you'll also find Korean, Thai and Vietnamese fare. Don't miss the hand-pulled noodles served at Lan Zhou Noodles. Exiting the mall, continue north on Main to 39th Ave and turn left. Two blocks on you'll reach the Hyatt Place Hotel. Head inside and take the elevator to the 10th floor, where you'll find 7 **Leaf Bar & Lounge** (p316). High above the din below, you can nurse a cocktail while reflecting on the day's culinary adventures.

little cafe, trimmed in local artwork and cooking pots. Brunchy winners include the 'sausage and onions' sandwich (fried eggs, breakfast sausage, cheddar and caramelized onion), while ever-changing lunch and dinner options can include pork tenderloins, soulful risottos and slow-cooked duck hash, all washed down with natural wines.

M WELLS STEAKHOUSE STEAK $$$

Map p446 (☎718-786-9060; www.magasinwells.com; 43-15 Crescent St, Long Island City; mains $27-65; ⊙5-10pm Sun-Tue, to 11pm Wed-Sun; 📶; Ⓢ E/M to Court Sq-23rd St, G, 7 to Court Sq) Carnivores with a taste for decadence will appreciate Quebecois chef Hugue Dufour's satisfying take on steak. Try the showstopping New York strip, with its Korean-style maple rub, or opt for the perfectly tender Wagyu flank steak. There's always a homemade pasta, plus a side of poutine for homesick Canadians. Loud, exuberant ambience. Reserve on weekends.

Astoria

★AMPLE HILLS CREAMERY ICE CREAM $

Map p446 (www.amplehills.com; 34-02 30th Ave, btwn 34 & 35th Sts, Astoria; small/medium/large $4.50/5.50/7; ⊙noon-midnight; Ⓢ W to 30th Ave) There is only one Queens location of this storied Brooklyn-born creamery, which has been voted the best ice cream in the US by the *Food Network*. They weren't joking! Folks line up to get down with wildly imaginative flavors churned from organic ingredients and hormone-free milk and cream at their Gowanus factory-shop (p282).

★HINOMARU JAPANESE $

Map p446 (☎718-777-0228; www.hinomaruramen.com; 33-18 Ditmars Blvd, Astoria; ramen $14-16; ⊙noon-10:30pm; Ⓢ N/Q to Astoria Ditmars Blvd) You won't stumble across too many *Michelin*-listed ramen houses but this casual Astoria noodle bar helmed by chef Koji Miyamoto deserves all the attention it gets. The signature New York-style *tonkatsu* ramen swims in a rich and creamy, perfectly spiced pork bone broth cooked for 17 hours to suck out all of that marrowy goodness.

★PYE BOAT NOODLE THAI $

Map p446 (☎718-685-2329; www.facebook.com/pyeboatnoodle; 35-13 Broadway, btwn 35th & 36th Sts, Astoria; mains $10-13.50; ⊙11:30am-3:30pm & 4-10:30pm Mon-Thu, 11:30am-11pm Fri & Sat, 11:30am-10:30pm Sun; 🖉; Ⓢ N/W to Broadway, M/R to Steinway St) Young Thai waitresses in matching fedoras greet you at this cute place decked out like an old-fashioned country house. The specialty is rich, star-anise-scented boat noodles, topped with crispy pork crackling. There's also *yen ta fo* (delicate seafood soup, tinted with red-bean paste) – a rarity in NYC and good with a side of papaya salad (off-menu request: add funky fermented crab).

ARTOPOLIS BAKERY $

Map p446 (www.artopolis.us; 23-18 31st St, btwn 23rd Rd & 23rd Ave, Astoria; pastries & cookies per lb $12-17; ⊙7am-8pm Mon-Fri, 8am-9pm Sat, 8am-7pm Sun; Ⓢ N/W to Astoria Blvd) Considered among Greeks in the know to be NYC's best Hellenic bakery, Artopolis – the City of Breads – drops the Aegean sweetness on Astoria. Greek specialties abound, but we're partial to the *melomakarona* (honey-drenched, orange-flavored cookies) and the traditional baklava (though it comes in a nontraditional Nutella version, too!). It's located discreetly in a strip mall and easy to miss.

KING SOUVLAKI FOOD TRUCK $

Map p446 (☎917-416-1189; www.kingsouvlakiofastoria.com; 31st St, at 31st Ave, Astoria; sandwiches $7-10; ⊙9am-11pm Mon, to midnight Tue-Wed, to 5am Thu-Sat, 11am-11pm Sun; Ⓢ N/W to Broadway) Follow the scent of chargrilled decadence (not to mention the plumes of smoke wafting along 31st St) to this celebrated food truck, one of the best in Astoria and going strong since 1979. Come for the pita sandwiches stuffed with mouthwatering morsels of pork, chicken, lamb or *loukaniko* sausage, along with a side of feta-topped Greek fries.

STRAND SMOKEHOUSE BARBECUE $

Map p446 (☎718-440-3231; www.thestrandsmokehouse.com; 25-27 Broadway, Astoria; mains $11-16; ⊙4pm-midnight Tue-Thu, to 1am Fri, noon-2am Sat, noon-midnight Sun; 📶; Ⓢ N/W to Broadway) This good old-fashioned southern-style BBQ restaurant is usually one large party. There is live music on weekends (Friday and Saturday at 8am, Sunday at 2pm) and a full bar with local craft brews (16 taps) and moonshine cocktails. Of course, there are also hearty plates of ribs, brisket and pastrami, plus delectable sides like homemade cornbread and spicy mac 'n' cheese.

ROSARIO'S PIZZA $

Map p446 (www.rosariospizzaastoria.com; 22-55 31st St, Astoria; slice $2.50, sandwiches $7-9; ⏲8:30am-7:30pm Mon-Sat; ✎; Ⓢ N/Q to Astoria Ditmars Blvd) Rosario's is a fully stocked Italian deli, its meats and cheeses dazzling in their own right. But its brilliant secret is its flawless, crisp-crust pizza, sold by the slice, cheese only (don't even bother asking for toppings). It's hidden at the back – ask if you don't see any in the display case.

BROOKLYN BAGEL & COFFEE COMPANY BAKERY $

Map p446 (www.brooklynbagelandcoffeecompany.com; 35-05 Broadway, Astoria; bagels $1.40; ⏲6am-3:30pm Mon-Fri, to 4:30pm Sat & Sun; Ⓢ N/Q to Broadway; M/R to Steinway St) It may be in Queens, not Brooklyn, but there's little confusion about the caliber of the bagels here. With a good crust and a chewy interior, they come in a number of fine variations, including sesame, onion, garlic and whole-wheat everything (even occasionally French toast!). Mix and match with a dazzling repertoire of flavored cream cheese, including chipotle and cinnamon walnut raisin.

★BAHARI ESTIATORIO GREEK $$

Map p446 (☎718-204-8968; www.bahariestiatorio.com; 31-14 Broadway, btwn 31st & 32nd Sts, Astoria; mains $10-29; ⏲noon-midnight; ✎; Ⓢ N/W to Broadway) Locally loved Bahari is a cut above most Astoria Greek restaurants, offering a broad range of charcoal-grilled fish and meat and traditional casseroles alongside creamy béchamel-topped moussaka and ready-made sides like velvety slow-cooked beans and spinach-flecked rice. The welcoming, switched-on staff can be seen posing with Al Pacino in photos on the wall.

KABAB CAFE EGYPTIAN $$

Map p446 (☎718-728-9858; 25-12 Steinway St, Astoria; mains $7-18; ⏲1-5pm & 6-10pm Tue-Sun; ✎; Ⓢ N/Q to Astoria Blvd) Chef Ali is a big personality and an anchor on the Steinway strip known as Little Egypt – though his creative, earthy food, often served straight from the frying pan to your plate, ranges much further than his Alexandrian roots. Start with mixed apps, for fluffy green Egyptian-style falafel, then pick any lamb dish.

MOMBAR EGYPTIAN $$

Map p446 (☎718-726-2356; 25-22 Steinway St, Astoria; mains $14-26; ⏲5-11pm Tue-Sun; ✎; Ⓢ N/Q to Astoria Blvd) A legendary restaurant located in the Steinway strip of Arab businesses, Mombar is worth a visit for the decor alone – its collage style of found objects was assembled over years as chef Mustafa saved money to open the place. It's a jewel-box setting for his refined Egyptian food; definitely order the signature *mombar* – a light, rice-stuffed sausage.

TAVERNA KYCLADES GREEK $$

Map p446 (☎718-545-8666; www.tavernakyclades.com; 33-07 Ditmars Blvd, Astoria; mains $15-46; ⏲noon-11pm Mon-Sat, to 10pm Sun; 📶; Ⓢ N/Q to Astoria Ditmars Blvd) Kyclades is tops when it comes to Greek seafood – and repeat diner Bill Murray agrees. Simple classics include succulent grilled octopus and whole fish, backed up with *saganaki* (pan-fried cheese) and a hearty salad. Skip the overpriced Kyclades Specialty, and go early to beat the daunting line. (Ironically, the Manhattan location, in the East Village, is less crowded.)

VESTA TRATTORIA & WINE BAR ITALIAN $$

Map p446 (☎718-545-5550; www.vestavino.com; 21-02 30th Ave, Astoria; pizzas $17-20, mains $18-25; ⏲noon-4pm & 5-10pm Mon-Thu, to 11pm Fri, 11:30am-3pm & 4:30-11pm Sat, 11am-3pm & 4:30-10pm Sun; Ⓢ N/Q to 30th Ave) Vesta is one of those neighborhood secrets, with chatty regulars at the bar, local art on the walls and organic produce from a Brooklyn rooftop farm.

The menu is simple and seasonal, with satisfying steamed mussels with garlic crostini, bubbling thin-crust pizzas and wide-ranging mains along the likes of orecchiette with summer squash and toasted pine nuts and wild-boar lasagna.

Woodside

SRIPRAPHAI THAI $$

Map p446 (☎718-899-9599; www.sripraphai.com; 64-13 39th Ave, Woodside; mains $10-26; ⏲11:30am-9:30pm Thu-Tue; Ⓢ 7 to 69th St) Sripraphai was the first restaurant in New York City to serve Thai food for Thai people, with no punches pulled. In some ways it has been outpaced by newer, more single-minded restaurants (the menu here is epic, drawn from all over the country), but it is still a legend and a satisfying place for a big dinner of everything from curries to heavenly fried soft-shell crab. They accept cash only.

LOCAL KNOWLEDGE

ROOSEVELT AVENUE FOOD CRAWL

When it comes to sidewalk grazing, it's hard to beat Roosevelt Ave and its army of late-night Latino food trucks, carts and secret delis. Just one stroll from 90th St to 103rd St will have you sipping on *champurrados* (a warm, thick corn-based chocolate drink), nibbling on a *cemita* (Mexican sandwich) and making a little more room for some Ecuadoran fish stew. It's cheap, authentic and quintessentially Queens. Hungry? Then set off on a taste-testing mission of Roosevelt Ave's best.

On the south side of Roosevelt head for the intersection with Forley St. Here you'll find the celebrated food stall **Taco Veloz** (Map p446; 86-10 Roosevelt Ave, Jackson Heights; tacos from $3; ⏲noon-2am; S7 to 90th St-Elmhurst), which whips up delicious tacos as well as first-rate *cemitas* ($7).

A short stroll further east along Roosevelt Ave lies the corner deli **La Esquina del Camarón** (Map p446; ☎347-885-2946; 80-02 Roosevelt Ave, Jackson Heights; shrimp cocktail $9-25; ⏲11am-9pm Mon-Fri, to 7:30pm Sat & Sun; S7 to 82nd St-Jackson Heights). Never mind the nondescript entrance; head to the back where you'll find a food counter where skilled staffers whip up some of the best shrimp cocktails on the planet. They come loaded with shrimp (and/or octopus) and are topped with sliced avocado – zingy, refreshing and mouthwateringly good.

Keep rolling along Roosevelt Ave to Warren St. A major Warren St star is **El Guayaquileño** (www.elguayaquileno.com; 9551 Roosevelt Ave, btwn Junction Blvd & Warren St, Jackson Heights; mains $13-25; ⏲8am-10pm; S7 to Junction Blvd), famous for its Ecuadoran *encebollado* – a stew made of tuna, yuca, cilantro, onion, lemon, cumin and toasted corn kernels. It's flavorsome, wonderfully textured and a meal in itself. If you're more in the mood for something meaty, the food truck a few feet away serves roast pig with crackling and all the fixings.

Elmhurst

HK FOOD COURT — FOOD HALL $

Map p446 (8202 45th Ave, btwn 82nd St & Broadway, Elmhurst; prices vary; ⏲9:30am-10pm Sun-Thu, 10am-10:30pm Sat & Sun; SM/R to Elmhurst Ave) This new Asian food hall – moved over from Flushing – is a cornucopia of 26 vendors that will transport you across Asia.

Choices include Japanese, Thai, Vietnamese; and regional Chinese including Fuzhou, Henan, northwest halal and Sichuan.

KHAO KANG — THAI $

Map p446 (www.khaokangnyc.com; 76-20 Woodside Ave, Elmhurst; meals $9-9.50; ⏲11am-9pm Tue-Sun; SE/F/M/R to Jackson Heights-Roosevelt Ave; 7 to 74 St-Broadway) This place offers new-era Thai food at its best, where you can eat like a business-luncher in Bangkok, pointing at two or three hot, ready-made dishes – creamy-hot pumpkin with eggs and basil, caramelized pork and more – to eat over rice. It's fast and inexpensive, but doesn't skimp on style. Desserts are a treat too.

Flushing & Corona

★NEW WORLD FOOD COURT — FOOD HALL $

Map p445 (www.newworldmallny.com; 136-20 Roosevelt Ave, btwn Main & Union Sts, Flushing; mains $7-12; ⏲10:30am-10pm; ✎; S7 to Flushing Main St) Head to the basement to choose from 30 some-odd purveyors of Eastern culinary wonders, from hand-pulled Lanzhou noodles to Korean-style barbecue, deftly pleated dumplings, sushi, bubble tea and Vietnamese pho.

Come with an appetite and perhaps the willingness to try such dishes as fish-stomach soup and rice noodles with Liuzhou snails (we're partial to the spicy vegetable noodles at Chong Qing Xiao Mian). A second entrance leads off Main St. There's also a sprawling Asian supermarket in the mall.

★NAN XIANG XIAO LONG BAO — DUMPLINGS $

Map p445 (☎718-321-3838; www.nan-xiang.com; 39-16 Prince St, One Fulton Sq, Flushing; dumplings $5-6.60; ⏲8am-midnight, to 1am Fri & Sat; S7 to Flushing Main St) Juicy, savory soup dumplings; thick, sticky noodles; spicy wontons – everything you'd want from a dumpling house you'll find at cash-only Nan Xiang Xiao Long Bao. Expect a line, but tables tend to open up quickly and the dishes come out fast. Bring some friends and order in excess.

After closing its far more modest Flushing address nearby in 2019, this NYC legend was moving into much larger, more contemporary digs at One Fulton Sq – check ahead if it has reopened by the time you read this.

GOLDEN SHOPPING MALL CHINESE $

Map p445 (41-28 Main St, Flushing; meals from $7; ⏲10am-9:30pm; Ⓢ7 to Flushing Main St) A chaotic jumble of hanging ducks, airborne noodles and greasy Laminex tables, Golden Mall's basement food court dishes up fantastic hawker-style grub. Don't be intimidated by the lack of English menus: most stalls have at least one English speaker, and the regulars are usually happy to point out their personal favorites, whether it's Lanzhou hand-pulled noodles or spicy pig ears.

SOY BEAN CHEN FLOWER SHOP TOFU $

Map p445 (☎718-321-3982; 135-26 Roosevelt Ave, btwn Prince & Main Sts, Flushing; small/large tofu $2/3.50; ⏲7am-9pm; Ⓢ7 to Flushing Main St) To find this easy-to-miss place on busy Roosevelt Ave look for the flower displays – the main order of business here. For foodies, though, the tiny tofu counter at the front is the real draw. Silky, heavenly dollops of creamy tofu – known as *dou fu hua* – are spooned up steaming hot in to-go containers, then drizzled with ginger-honey syrup. If you think tofu is bland and uninspiring, this place is a game changer.

HUNAN KITCHEN OF GRAND SICHUAN CHINESE $$

Map p445 (☎718-888-0553; www.hunankitchenofgrandsichuanny.com; 42-47 Main St, Flushing; mains $5.50-33; ⏲11am-9:30pm; Ⓢ7 to Flushing Main St) Work up a sweat at this respectable Flushing restaurant, best known for its specialties from Hunan province. Standout dishes include a deliciously salty white-pepper smoked beef, tender chicken with hot red pepper, and lovely warming fish soup. If you're in a large group, order the house specialty: BBQ duck, Hunan-style.

LIUYISHOU HOTPOT CHINESE $$

Map p445 (☎778-732-0201; www.liuyishouna.com; 136-76 39th Ave, Flushing; items $2.99-27.99; ⏲11:30am-11:30pm; 📶; Ⓢ7 to Flushing Main St) This Chinese export – one of three US locations – has become Flushing's...ahem... hottest pot since its late 2018 opening. Pick your soup base (the animated servers tried to steer us from the 'special spicy,' warning us it was too much, but it was perfect!), then pile in your chosen ingredients.

Lotus root, Chinese cabbage, head-on shrimp, sole, bamboo shoots and an epic, often-Instragramed wheel of thinly sliced lamb and beef that serves about 75 ($16; we're kidding, obviously) are great choices, but there's way more where that came from. It's especially fun for groups.

SZECHUAN HOUSE SICHUAN $$

Map p445 (☎718-762-2664; www.szechuanhouseflushing.com; 133-47 Roosevelt Ave, Flushing; mains $14-27; ⏲11am-11pm; Ⓢ7 to Flushing Main St) Purported to be the oldest continuously operated Sichuan restaurant in Flushing, Szechuan House often finds itself at the top of NYC best-of lists for China's fiery regional cuisine.

Like it hot? The dan-dan noodles, laced with minced pork and chili oil, are not for the faint of heart; nor the sliced fish with peppercorn, either.

DRINKING & NIGHTLIFE

Queens' mighty sprawl has pockets of nightlife action catering mostly to its diverse local base – with themes ranging from Greek and Croatian to Irish and Jamaican. River-hugging neighborhoods Astoria and Long Island City tend to bring the most Manhattanites over for a curious night out.

Long Island City

★DUTCH KILLS COCKTAIL BAR

Map p446 (www.dutchkillsbar.com; 27-24 Jackson Ave, btwn Queens & Dutch Kills Sts, Long Island City; ⏲5pm-2am Sun-Thu, to 3am Fri & Sat; ⓈE/M/R to Queens Plaza, G to Court Sq) Named for the area where Dutch settlers first established themselves around Newtown Creek, this moodily lit bar is all about atmosphere and amazing craft cocktails.

Enter through the nondescript door beneath a blinking neon 'bar' sign on an old industrial building, and whistle up an expertly mixed Headless Horseman, or select another from the list of classic house cocktails ($15).

ALEWIFE CRAFT BEER

Map p446 (www.alewife.beer; 5-14 51st Ave, Long Island City; 4-11pm Mon, 4pm-1am Tue-Thu, to 3am Fri, 11am-3pm Sat, 11am-11pm Sun; S 7 to Vernon Blvd-Jackson Ave) Considered LIC's top craft-beer destination by beer geeks in the know, Alewife's cozy 28-draft brewpub and cosmic/alien-themed brews often push boundaries (go for its one-barrel experimental Scullery series or any number of imperial IPA, stouts and other heavy-hitting styles). There's elevated pub grub like pork-belly pho and chicken-confit tacos as well.

ANABLE BASIN SAILING BAR & GRILL BAR

Map p446 (www.anablebasin.com; 44th Dr & East River, Long Island City; 3:30pm-midnight Mon-Fri, from noon Sat, noon-2am Sun Mar-Oct; S E/M to Court Sq-23rd St) Navigating past slumbering factories and industrial grit to this waterside warehouse on the East River feels like a bit of an adventure. Once you've arrived, however, you'll be rewarded with a mesmerizing view of Manhattan. Stake out a picnic table around sunset and watch the spires of Midtown light up while you sip bottles of Kona Longboard.

BIEROCRACY BEER HALL

Map p446 (www.bierocracy.com; 12-23 Jackson Ave, Long Island City; 4pm-midnight Mon-Wed, to 1am Thu, to 2am Fri, 11am-2am Sat, 11am-11pm Sun; S 7 to Vernon Blvd-Jackson Ave, G to 21st St) Anyone looking to grab a beer and watch the game will feel right at home at this large, Eastern European–inspired beer hall, which is perfect for big groups and families. It comes with large projector screens all around the seating areas. There's an extensive beer list, as well as fish and chips, dark beer goulash and big, doughy pretzels.

SWEETLEAF COFFEE

Map p446 (www.sweetleafcoffee.com; 10-93 Jackson Ave, Long Island City; 7am-7pm Mon-Fri, from 8am Sat & Sun; ; S G to 21st St, 7 to Vernon Blvd-Jackson Ave) Looking for a place to curl up with a warm drink and a good book? Sweetleaf has a study-like atmosphere, with plush couches and chairs, making an enticing spot for a relaxing, low-key coffee-shop experience.

Astoria

★ ASTORIA BIER & CHEESE BEER HALL

Map p446 (www.milkandhops.com; 34-14 Broadway, Astoria; noon-11pm Mon-Thu, to midnight Fri & Sat, to 10pm Sun; S N/Q to Broadway, M/R to Steinway St) At this funky bar-shop hybrid in Astoria, you can foam that upper lip with 10 seasonal, mostly local drafts, or pick from hundreds of canned and bottled options to take home or swill on-site. There's an impressive cheese and charcuterie selection, with creative grilled cheeses ($8 to $14) and mouthwatering sandwich combos (like Iberian *jamón serrano* with cave-aged Gruyère).

SINGLECUT BEERSMITHS MICROBREWERY

Map p446 (www.singlecut.com; 19-33 37th St, btwn 19th & 20th Aves, Astoria; 5-10pm Wed, 4-11pm Thu, 1pm-midnight Fri, 11am midnight Sat, 11am-1pm Sun; ; Q101 from 20th Ave/Steinway) The wonderful waft of juice and hops smacks you upside the head when you enter Astoria's best craft brewery, a haven for hopheads where at least half of the 16 taps are often devoted to potent IPAs and DIPAs.

BOHEMIAN HALL & BEER GARDEN BEER GARDEN

Map p446 (718-274-4925; www.bohemianhall.com; 29-19 24th Ave, btwn 29th & 31st Sts, Astoria; 5pm-1am Mon-Thu, to 3am Fri, noon-3am Sat, to midnight Sun; S N/W to Astoria Blvd) This Czech community center kicked off NYC's beer-garden craze, and nothing quite matches it for space and heaving drinking crowds, which pack every picnic table under the towering trees in summer. There's Czech food such as schnitzels and goulash (mains $10 to $20), but the focus is on cold and foamy Czech beers, augmented by local craft brews.

ALBATROSS GAY

Map p446 (www.albatrossastoria.com; 3619 24th Ave, btwn 23rd & 24th Aves, Astoria; 5pm-4am Mon-Sat, from 1pm Sun; S N/W to Astoria Blvd) Queens' oldest LBGTQ bar, Albatross remains the preferred seat of action for the resident hot and bothered. Saturday-night drag with resident queen Sutton Lee Seymour is legendary, but there are karaoke nights, drag bingo, RuPaul's Drag Race viewing parties and other outlandish events. But it's also just the best gay bar in Queens to catch a cocktail and a chat.

KINSHIP COFFEE COFFEE

Map p446 (www.www.facebook.com/kinshipcoffee; 32-14 Steinway St, btwn Broadway & 34th Ave, Astoria; ⌚6:30am-9pm Mon-Fri, from 8am Sat & Sun; 📶; **S**M/R/E to Steinway St) Astoria's top caffeine haunt, Kinship brews Heart (Portland, OR) and Tandem (Portland, ME) beans, doing the usual Third Wave things with espresso ($3.25), including a cold concoction with tonic. There's avocado toast, sandwiches and pastries to munch on and a studious back area for tucking away.

VITE VINOSTERIA WINE BAR

Map p446 (☎718-278-8483; www.facebook.com/vitebar; 31-05 34th St, Astoria; ⌚4-11pm Mon-Thu, noon-3pm & 4-11:30pm Fri-Sun; **S**N/W to Broadway) First-rate wines by the glass (from $11), delectable Italian fare and a welcoming vibe are a few reasons to fall for this easygoing, wine-forward restaurant just a short stroll from the subway. Their nearby wine bar closed, but this original location soldiers on, offering well-balanced Nebbiolas and braised lamb shanks in a more upscale environment.

Flushing

★TIGER SUGAR TEAHOUSE

Map p445 (www.tigersugar.com; 40-10 Main St, Flushing; medium tea $4-5.50; ⌚11am-9:30pm; **S**7 to Flushing Main St) Get in line for bubble tea? You're damn right. The first North American outlet of the wildly popular Tiger Sugar, which has swept across Asia like a tsunami since its opening in 2017, arrived in Flushing in 2019 and the lines are real. Its secret recipe brown-sugar syrup, cooked with the boba in large pots, and mixed with Horizon organic milk, creates a tiger-stripe-like effect down the sides of the cup (hence the name). If you can't sweat the line, Yi Fang is nearby and also outstanding.

MIKKELLER NYC CRAFT BEER

Map p445 (www.mikkellernyc.com; 126th St at 38th Ave, Citi Field btwn Bullpen & Right Field Gates, Flushing; ⌚4-10pm Wed-Thu, noon-midnight Fri & Sat, noon-10pm Sun; 📶; **S**7 to Mets Willets Point) Few American baseball stadiums can boast a craft-beer selection like Mikkeler NYC's 60 taps but you don't need to be attending a Mets game to imbibe in their sought-after liquid. Danes Mikkel Borg Bjergsø and Kristian Klarup Keller's Mikkeller are bonafide brew whisperers who have taken their craft worldwide, including – since 2018 – right into this hallowed sport ground.

LEAF BAR & LOUNGE BAR

Map p445 (☎718-865-8158; www.leafbarandlounge.com; 133-42 39th Ave, Hyatt Place, 10th fl, btwn College Point Blvd & Prince St, Flushing; ⌚5pm-1am Mon-Thu, to 2am Fri & Sat, to midnight Sun; **S**7 to Flushing Main St) This handsomely designed drinking spot draws the neighborhood's cool crowd. Come for happy-hour specials from 5pm to 8pm, well-made cocktails and creative Asian small plates like 'molten cheeseburger' spring rolls or chicken wings with General Tso's sauce ($7 to $9). The rooftop perch atop the Hyatt Place hotel offers decent views above the chaos of Flushing below.

FANG GOURMET TEA TEAHOUSE

Map p445 (www.fangtea.com; 135-25 Roosevelt Ave, btwn Prince & Main Sts, Flushing; tea $5-15; ⌚10:30am-7:30pm; **S**7 to Flushing Main St) This tranquil little tea parlor offers a welcome retreat from the bustle of Flushing's Chinatown. Tucked in the back of a mini-mall, Fang Gourmet Tea has an astonishing selection of high-end teas, from subtle roasted oolongs to herbaceous greens and exotic varieties like silver-needle white tea and Yunnan-style Pu'er tea. Tastings start at $5.

COOP BAR

Map p445 (☎718-358-9333; www.thecoopnyc.com; 133-42 39th Ave #103, Flushing; ⌚noon-2am Sun-Wed, to 3am Thu-Sat; **S**7 to Flushing Main St) Crisp cocktail culture meets Korean fusion food at the COOP, located in the middle of Flushing's bustling main drag. Enjoy a full meal of Korean delicacies, or just order a round of small plates such as pork-belly sliders or kimchi egg rolls (mains $13 to $30). The chic vibe makes it a perfect place to start a night out.

ENTERTAINMENT

★TERRAZA 7 LIVE MUSIC

Map p446 (☎347-808-0518; www.terraza7.com; 40-19 Gleane St, at Roosevelt Ave, Elmhurst; tickets from $7; ⌚4pm-4am; **S**7 to 82nd St-Jackson Heights) Come to Queens for multicultural eats, then stay for equally diverse sounds at this cool bi-level performance space. It makes creative use of the tiny room, with live bands playing from a loft above the bar from 8pm most nights. Latin jazz is the mainstay, but performers can hail from as far away as Morocco.

CREEK & THE CAVE COMEDY

Map p446 (☎box office 917-806-6692; www.creeklic.com; 10-93 Jackson Ave, btwn 11th St & 49th Ave, Long Island City; ⊙11am-2am Sun-Thu, to 4am Fri & Sat; Ⓢ7 to Vernon Blvd-Jackson Ave) The biggest and best known of a handful of fringy comedy clubs in the neighborhood, Creek and the Cave has two stages, a Mexican restaurant (mains $12 to $17), a chilled-out backyard and a bar with eight well-maintained pinball machines. With so much fun in one place, it's no surprise it's a kind of clubhouse for young comedy scenesters.

CITI FIELD STADIUM

Map p445 (www.mlb.com/mets; 120-01 Roosevelt Ave, Flushing; Ⓢ7 to Mets Willets Point) The home of the New York Mets, the city's underdog baseball team, Citi Field opened in 2009, replacing the earlier Mets HQ, Shea Stadium. In contrast to the very contemporary interior features, the facade has a somewhat old-fashioned pattern of arches; the food offerings, far removed from hot dogs and peanuts, range from barbecued brisket to thin-crust pizza.

SHOPPING

Shops in Queens reflect its diverse population, with international grocery stores and niche retailers such as vendors of Mexican rodeo gear or Indian wedding outfits. Roosevelt Ave is a lively walk for retail opportunities.

★LOCKWOOD GIFTS & SOUVENIRS

Map p446 (http://lockwoodshop.com; 32-15 33rd St, Astoria; ⊙11am-8pm; ⓈN/W to Broadway) A whimsical shop that's packed with great gift ideas, including plenty of intriguing Queens-related objects. You'll find vintage wall hangings, hip baby gear, scented candles, flasks disguised as sunscreen and essential accessories for the kitchen, including provocative oven mitts and kitchen towels: 'Fuck, I Love Cheese,' 'Bitch, I am the Secret Ingredient' and so on. Lockwood also has both a stationery and a clothing store a few doors up and around the corner.

ASTORIA BOOKSHOP BOOKS

Map p446 (☎718-278-2665; www.astoriabookshop.com; 31-29 31st St, btwn 31st Ave & Broadway, Astoria; ⊙11am-7pm; ⓈN/W to Broadway) A much-loved indie bookshop with ample shelf space dedicated to local authors, Astoria is a good spot to pick up a title about the Queens dining scene or the borough's wide-ranging ethnic diversity. A stalwart of the community, Astoria also hosts author readings, discussion groups, writing workshops and kids' storytelling (every Thursday at 11am).

ALL THE RIGHT CLOTHING

(www.alltheright.com; 9130 Corona Ave, btwn 91st Pl & 92nd St, Elmhurst; ⊙11am-9pm Mon-Sat, noon-7pm Sun; Ⓢ7 to 90th St) This bastion of hip-hop couture, Queens-themed gear and street-art materials in Elmhurst has attracted the likes of rappers Nikki Minaj and French Montana, among others. Limited-edition Nike sneakers climb the walls, which are tagged by storied graffiti artists from New York (Tats Cru's Seen and BG183), Japan (Shiro) and beyond, so it's a bit of a museum as well.

LOVEDAY 31 VINTAGE

Map p446 (www.facebook.com/loveday31nyc; 3306 31st Ave, Astoria; ⊙1-8pm Tue-Fri, from noon Sat, noon-7pm Sun; ⓈN/W to 30th Ave) Fashion-conscious Astorians have a certain fondness for this sweet little boutique, with its well-curated selection of dresses, blouses, tops, scarves, shoes, jewelry and sunglasses. Bonus points for the helpful staff. The prices are quite reasonable, and there's usually a discount rack out the front.

MIMI & MO FASHION & ACCESSORIES

Map p446 (www.mimiandmonyc.com; 4545 Center Blvd, Long Island City; ⊙11am-7pm Mon-Sat, 10am-5pm Sun; Ⓢ7 to Vernon Blvd-Jackson Ave) Located near the waterfront, this sunny boutique stocks a fine assortment of wares, including soft cotton graphic T-shirts, Herschel hats, Happy Socks, Nest candles and one-of-a-kind gift cards. There's gear for kids too: colored pencils, crafty games and clothing, among other things.

SPORTS & ACTIVITIES

WORLD'S FARE TOURS TOURS
(www.chopsticksandmarrow.com; 3hr tours incl food $95) Dedicated Queens eater Joe DiStefano leads three culinary tours around the borough's fantastic ethnic eateries. Focus on Flushing's vibrant Chinatown, the Himalayan dumpling eateries clustered in Jackson Heights or the Southeast Asian goodness of Elmhurst.

GEOGRAPHY OF NEW YORK CITY WITH JACK EICHENBAUM WALKING
(☎718-961-8406; www.geognyc.com; 2hr/full-day tour $20/49) Urban geographer Jack Eichenbaum leads insightful walking (and sometimes subway) tours around Queens, focusing on the strange collisions between planning and reality, history and diverse modern use. See the website for the current status of his tours.

NEW YORK SPA CASTLE SPA
(☎718-888-9893; http://ny.spacastleusa.com; 131-10 11th Ave, at 131st St, College Point; weekday/weekend $50/60; ⏲8am-midnight; Ⓢ7 to Flushing Main St, then shuttle bus) A slice of cutting-edge Korean bathhouse culture in an industrial corner of Queens, this 100,000-sq-ft spa complex is a bubbling dream of mineral and massage pools, saunas of dazzling variety, steam rooms and waterfalls. It also has a food court, beauty treatments and massages (50 minutes from $95).

A free shuttle bus runs to/from the One Hotel on the corner of Northern Blvd and Union St, a few blocks north of the Flushing–Main St subway station. Shuttles generally depart every 10 and 40 minutes past the hour – but check the schedule online before making the trip out.

CLIFFS CLIMBING
Map p446 (☎718-729-7625; www.thecliffsclimbing.com; 11-11 44th Dr, Long Island City; day pass $32, with shoes/harness rental $44; ⏲6am-midnight Mon-Thu, 9am-10pm Sat & Sun; ⓈE/M to Court Sq-23rd St, 7 to Court Sq) New York's largest indoor climbing facility has more than 30,000 sq ft of climbing surface, with some 125 top-rope stations, 16ft top-out bouldering, a rappel tower and auto-belays for climbers without a partner.

There's also a gym with exercise equipment, plus group classes (yoga and core workouts).

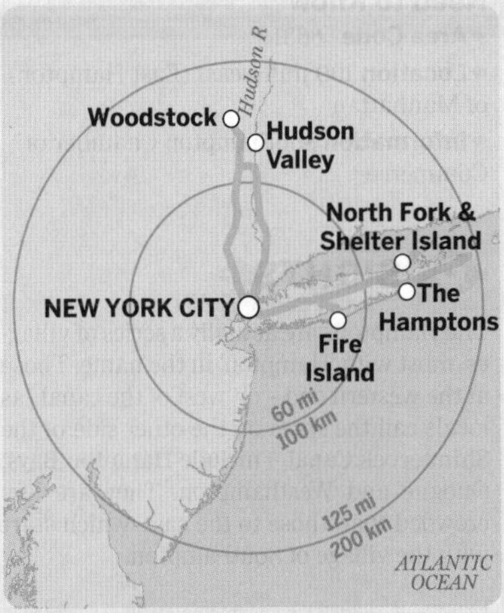

Day Trips from New York City

The Hamptons p320

The summertime capital of New York's moneyed set is a sweeping coastline studded with opulent mansions that host see-and-be-seen summer parties. Surprises include Native American sites, charming village main streets and wild state parks.

Fire Island p322

This car-free getaway ramps up in summer with tiny rental bungalows, chill beach bars and, at one end, a famous gay scene, roaring with drag queens and carefree clubs. The wild setting, with sand streets and miles of beaches, restores calm.

North Fork & Shelter Island p323

Wine tasting at Long Island's vineyards is a fun day's ramble, capped by main-street strolling and alfresco dining at waterside Greenport.

Hudson Valley p325

You could spend weeks exploring this region, with great hiking, open-air sculpture, charming towns and historic homes of American greats (Irving, Roosevelt and Vanderbilt included).

Woodstock p328

Supplement your pilgrimage to hippiedom with a round of antiquing and quiet walks in protected parks.

The Hamptons

Explore

This string of villages is a summer escape for Manhattan's wealthiest, who zip to their mansions by helicopter. Mere mortals take the Hampton Jitney bus and chip in on rowdy rental houses. Behind the glitz is a long cultural history, as noted artists and writers have lived here. Beneath the glamour, the gritty and life-risking tradition of fishing continues. The area is small and connected by often traffic-clogged Montauk Hwy.

The Best...

➡ **Sight** Parrish Art Museum

➡ **Place to Eat** Clam Bar at Napeague

➡ **Place for a Beach Stroll** Montauk Point State Park

Top Tip

In search of summer solitude? Plan to visit this area on a weekday – weekends are stuffed to the gills with refugees from the urban jungle.

Getting There & Away

➡ **Car** Take the Midtown Tunnel out of Manhattan onto I-495/Long Island Expwy.

➡ **Bus** The Hampton Jitney (www.hamptonjitney.com; one way from $30) is a 'luxury' express bus. Its Montauk line departs from Manhattan's East Side, with stops on Lexington Ave between 77th and 76th Sts, then 69th St, 59th St and 40th St. It makes stops at villages along Rte 27 in the Hamptons.

➡ **Train** The Long Island Rail Road (LIRR; www.mta.info/lirr; furthest zone one way off-peak/peak $22.25/30.50) leaves from Penn Station in Manhattan, making stops in West Hampton, Southampton, Bridgehampton, East Hampton and Montauk.

Getting Around

The app-driven, cool turquoise converted school buses offered by Hampton Hopper (www.hamptonhopper.com) are an economical, hassle-free way around the towns; they run into the bar hours.

Need to Know

➡ **Area Code** ☎631

➡ **Location** 100 miles east (East Hampton) of Manhattan

➡ **Information** Southampton Chamber of Commerce

SIGHTS

The Hamptons are actually a series of villages, most with 'Hampton' in the name. Those at the western end – or 'west of the canal,' as locals call the spots on the other side of the Shinnecock Canal – include Hampton Bays, Quogue and Westhampton. They are less crowded than those to the east, which start with the village of Southampton.

Southampton

Compared with some of its neighbors, Southampton is a rather conservative, old-money spot. It's home to sprawling old mansions, awe-inspiring churches, a main street with no 'beachwear' allowed, and some lovely beaches.

★ PARRISH ART MUSEUM MUSEUM

(☎631-283-2118; www.parrishart.org; 279 Montauk Hwy, Water Mill; adult/child $12/free; ⏲10am-5pm Wed-Mon, to 8pm Fri) In a sleek, long barn designed by Herzog & de Meuron, this institution spotlights local artists such as Jackson Pollock, Willem de Kooning, Chuck Close and William Merritt Chase.

Temporary exhibitions change over five times throughout the year; seven of the galleries are dedicated to permanent works that are curated from a 3000-strong collection. For more Pollock, make reservations to see his nearby paint-drizzled studio and home.

SOUTHAMPTON HISTORY MUSEUM MUSEUM

(☎631-283-2494; www.southamptonhistory.org; 17 Meeting House Lane; adult/child $5/free; ⏲11am-4pm Wed-Sat Mar-Dec) Before the Hamptons were the Hamptons, there was this clutch of buildings, now nicely maintained and spread around Southampton. The main museum is Rogers Mansion, once owned by a whaling captain. You can also visit a former dry-goods store, now occupied by a local jeweler, around the corner at 80 Main St; and a 17th-century homestead, the Halsey House (adult/child $5/free, Saturday only, July to September).

Bridgehampton & Sag Harbor

To the east of Southampton, Bridgehampton is tiny but packed with trendy boutiques and restaurants. Head 7 miles north from here to reach the old whaling town of Sag Harbor, on Peconic Bay, edged with historic homes. You can pick up a walking-tour map at Sag Harbor Historical Society.

SAG HARBOR WHALING & HISTORICAL MUSEUM MUSEUM
(☎631-725-0770; www.sagharborwhalingmuseum.org; 200 Main St; adult/child $8/3; ⏲10am-5pm May-Oct) The cool collection here includes actual artifacts from 19th-century whaling ships: sharp flensing knives, battered pots for rendering blubber, delicate scrimshaw and more. It's a bit surreal to see photos of the giant mammals in a village that's now a cute resort town.

East Hampton

Don't be fooled by the oh-so-casual-looking summer attire, heavy on pastels and sweaters tied around the neck – the sunglasses alone are probably equal to a month's rent. Some of the highest-profile celebrities have homes here.

POLLOCK-KRASNER HOUSE ARTS CENTER
(☎631-324-4929; www.pkhouse.org; 830 Springs Fireplace Rd; Sat $10, guided tours Thu & Fri $15; ⏲noon-5pm Sat, guided tours noon, 2pm & 4pm Thu & Fri May-Oct) Tour the home of husband-and-wife art stars Jackson Pollock and Lee Krasner. While lacking in actual Pollock works (there's only one, 1938's *Composition with Red Arc and Horses*), it's worth it just to see the paint-spattered floor of Pollock's studio (the wall splatter belongs to Krasner). Although you could simply show up on a Saturday at the time of writing, due to parking problems, plans were in the works to change to a reservations/guided tour-only plan Thursday through Saturday.

EAST HAMPTON MARINE MUSEUM MUSEUM
(www.easthamptonhistory.org; 301 Bluff Rd, Amagansett; adult/child $8/5; ⏲10am-4pm Fri & Sat Jul & Aug) One of your last outposts before you drive on to Montauk, this small museum dedicated to the fishing and whaling industries is more interesting than its counterpart in Sag Harbor, full of old harpoons, boats half the size of their prey, shipwrecked cannons and beautiful exhibitions, including a B&W photographic tribute to the local fishers and their families and watercolors by Claus Hoie.

Montauk

Toward the east-pointing tip of Long Island's South Fork, you'll find the mellow town of Montauk, aka 'The End,' and the famous surfing beach **Ditch Plains**. With the surfers have come affluent hipsters and boho-chic hotels (often vintage roadside motels revamped for the modern age), but the area is still far less of a scene than the Hamptons, with proudly blue-collar residents and casual seafood restaurants.

MONTAUK POINT STATE PARK STATE PARK
(☎631-668-3781; www.parks.ny.gov; 2000 Montauk Hwy/Rte 27; per car $8; ⏲dawn-dusk) Covering the eastern tip of the South Fork is Montauk Point State Park, with its impressive lighthouse. A good place for windswept walks, surfing, surf fishing (with permit) and seal-spotting – call the park for the schedule; rangers will set up spotting scopes to better view the frisky pinnipeds. The vehicle entrance fee is enforced from 8am to 4pm.

MONTAUK POINT LIGHTHOUSE LIGHTHOUSE
(www.montauklighthouse.com; 2000 Montauk Hwy; adult/child $12/5; ⏲10:30am-5:30pm Sun-Fri, to 7pm Sat mid-Jun–Aug, shorter hours mid-Apr–mid-Jun & Sep-Nov) This is the fourth-oldest active lighthouse in the US, commissioned by George Washington and built in 1796. It's a nice climb, but the 15-person limit may involve a wait and a test of one's claustrophobia limits. The payoff is the view, which stretches to the eastern horizon. Suffolk County bus 10C heads here from East Hampton and Montauk.

SLEEPING

★MARRAM BOUTIQUE HOTEL $$$
(☎631-668-2050; www.www.marrammontauk.com; 21 Oceanview Tce; d $300-600; P❄📶🏊) New in 2019, this revamped golden age

motel now sits strikingly dressed in a cedar and mahogany exterior opposite the Terrace beach surf break. Marram (dune grass) leaps from the minidunes that pepper the property, leading to minimalist rooms awash in extraordinary design: white oak ceilings and furniture, Waterworks bathroom fixtures, poured concrete flooring and Morocco-evoking Tadelakt plaster walls.

EATING

★AMBER WAVES FARM AMERICAN $
(www.amberwavesfarm.org; 367 Main St, Amagansett; mains $10-17; kitchen 8am-3pm Wed-Mon, market 7am-7pm Jun-Aug, shorter hours rest of year;) In a fairy-tale setting under maple trees flanked by blooming hydrangeas, this organic farm-to-table food stand is the reason you come to the Hamptons (besides the beaches and P. Diddy parties). Breakfast brings incredibly fresh and innovative dishes, such as tostadas with crispy mushrooms, potatoes, slaw and picked veggies, and delectable baked goods (herb/cheddar/kale scones, heirloom tomato focaccia).

★CLAM BAR AT NAPEAGUE SEAFOOD $$
(631-267-6348; www.clambarhamptons.com; 2025 Montauk Hwy, Amagansett; mains $10-29; 11:30am-8pm Apr-Oct, to 6pm Nov & Dec) You won't get fresher seafood or saltier waitstaff, and holy mackerel, those lobster rolls are good, even if you choke a bit on the price ($24 to $28). Three decades in business – the public has spoken – with cash only, of course. Locals favor this one. Find it on the road between Amagansett and Montauk. Winter hours are weather permitting.

SHOPPING

★WYETH HOMEWARES
(https://wyeth.nyc; 3654 Montauk Hwy, Sagaponack; 10am-6pm) Wyeth is the sort of place where you can't tell exactly what is going on inside as you pass by on the road but you are compelled to stop and check it out. And you're so glad you did. Inside is a treasure trove of mid-century modern design worthy of an afternoon of browsing.

Fire Island

Explore

Fire Island is a skinny, 50-mile-long barrier island most notable for the absence of cars. Sand streets, concrete paths and boardwalks connect the dozen or so tiny residential communities, and the only traffic is fat-tire bikes and the little wagons regulars haul their belongings in. Several enclaves are famed getaways for the gay community, but there's something for everyone here, including families, couples and single travelers – gay and straight alike. The island is federally protected as the Fire Island National Seashore, and much of it is wild dunes and windswept forest. In summer, expect hamlets jam-packed with nightclubs next to neighboring stretches of sand where you'll find nothing but pitched tents and deer. Don't forget bug repellent: the mosquitoes are both fierce and abundant on Fire Island. While day trips are easy here, staying for a night or two is a real treat (even if hotel offerings aren't great), especially in the quieter spring and fall.

The Best...

➡ **Sight** Sunken Forest
➡ **Place to Eat** Sand Castle
➡ **Place to Drink** CJ's

Top Tip

On summer weekends, skip out before 3pm on Sunday or (better) spend the night and leave Monday – the line for the ferry on Sunday evenings is impossible.

Getting There & Away

➡ **Car** Take the Long Island Expwy to Exit 53 (Bayshore), 59 (Sayville) or 63 (Patchogue).

➡ **Train** Take the LIRR to one of three stations with connections to the ferries: Patchogue, Bayshore or Sayville.

➡ **Fire Island Ferries** (631-665-3600; www.fireislandferries.com; 99 Maple Ave, Bay Shore; one-way adult/child $11/6) run from near the Bay Shore LIRR station to Kismet, Ocean Beach and other western communities. Sayville Ferries go from Sayville to Cherry Grove and Fire Island Pines. Davis Park Ferry goes to Davis Park and Watch Hill.

Need to Know

- **Area Code** 631
- **Location** 60 miles east of Manhattan
- **Information** www.fireisland.com

SIGHTS

The gem-like parts of Fire Island are the car-free zones in the center (rather than the ends, reached by causeways). Davis Park, Fair Harbor, Kismet, Ocean Bay Park and Ocean Beach combine small summer homes with tiny clusters of basic grocery stores and restaurants. Of these communities, Ocean Beach ('OB' to locals) is the liveliest, with a miniature downtown by the ferry port and a little strip of bars. Perhaps the most infamous villages are those that have evolved into gay destinations: Cherry Grove and The Pines, in the center of Fire Island. Biking between towns isn't feasible, as streets turn into deep sand. For exploring further than you can walk, Fire Island Water Taxi runs a lateral ferry service along the bay side – but this shuts down in October, along with most other tourist-oriented businesses.

SUNKEN FOREST FOREST

(631-597-6183; www.nps.gov/fiis; Fire Island; visitor center mid-May–mid-Oct) FREE This 300-year-old forest, a surprisingly dense stretch of trees behind the dunes, is easily accessible via a 1.5-mile boardwalk trail looping through it. It's pleasantly shady in summer, and vividly colored when the leaves change in fall. It's accessible by its own **ferry** (631-589-0810; www.sayvilleferry.com; 41 River Rd, Sayville) stop (Sailors Haven, where there's also a visitor center), or a long walk in the winter season, after the ferry shuts down. Ranger-guided tours available.

The beach straight south of here is also an impressively wild, yet reasonably accessible, stretch of the island. A Sunken Forest Trail Guide is available via email from the National Park Service.

EATING & DRINKING

CJ'S AMERICAN $$

(631-583-9890; www.cjsfireisland.com; 479 Bay Ave, Ocean Beach, Fire Island; mains $15-34; 11am-midnight Sun-Thu, to 4am Fri & Sat) Open year-round, CJ's is raucous and fun and a great place to wait for your ferry. It's packed on summer weekend nights, so get here early. Renowned for its 'rocket fuel' frozen drink, it's owned by the nearby Palms Hotel.

SAND CASTLE SEAFOOD $$$

(631-597-4174; www.fireislandsandcastle.com; 106 Lewis Walk, Cherry Grove, Fire Island; mains $24-33; 11am-11pm Mon, Tue & Thu-Sat, from 9:30am Sun May-Sep;) One of Fire Island's only oceanfront (rather than bayfront) options, Sand Castle serves satisfying appetizers (fried calamari, seafood chowder) and lots of seafood temptations (mussels, octopus carpaccio, grilled King Salmon).

> **WORTH A DETOUR**
>
> **LONG BEACH**
>
> Beautiful **Long Beach** (www.www.longbeachny.gov), one of the best stretches of sand in the area, is only a few miles outside New York City's limits. It's easily accessible by train and has clean beaches, a hoppin' main strip with ice-cream shops, cafes and restaurants within walking distance of the ocean, a thriving surf scene and many city hipsters. The downside: a $15 day-use fee, purchasable at designated beach entrances (Minnesota Ave, Neptune Blvd, Long Beach Blvd and Lafayette Blvd). Long Island Rail Road runs 'beach getaways,' which include discounted admission and round-trip train fare during summer, with departures from both New York's Penn Station and Atlantic Terminal in Brooklyn.

North Fork & Shelter Island

Explore

The North Fork is known for its bucolic farmland and vineyards (though weekends can draw rowdy limo-loads on winery crawls). Rte 25, the main road through **Jamesport**, **Cutchogue** and **Southold**, is pretty and edged with farm stands; the less-traveled Rte 48 also has many wineries.

The largest town on the North Fork is laid-back **Greenport**, with working fishing boats, a history in whaling and a **vintage carousel** (www.villageofgreenport.org; Mitchell Park; $2; ⏲10am-9pm Jun-Aug, shorter hours rest of year) in Mitchell Park. It's compact and easily walkable from the LIRR station.

Like a pearl in Long Island's claw, Shelter Island rests between the North and South Forks. The island is a smaller, more low-key version of the Hamptons, with a touch of maritime New England. Parking is limited; long **Crescent Beach**, for instance, has spots only by permit. If you don't mind a few hills, it's a nice place to visit by bike, and Mashomack Nature Preserve is a wildlife lover's dream.

The Best...

- **Sight** Mashomack Nature Preserve
- **Place to Eat** North Fork Table & Inn
- **Place to Drink** Shinn Estate

Top Tip

The North Folk wineries are an easy DIY adventure. Consider taking the train out to Long Island and renting a car there (Riverhead is a good place to look). Prices are cheaper than in Manhattan and you'll save time, gas and frustration.

Getting There & Away

- **Bus** The Hampton Jitney bus picks up passengers on Manhattan's East Side on 96th, 83rd, 77th, 69th, 59th and 40th Sts, and makes stops in 10 North Fork villages.
- **Car** Take the Midtown Tunnel out of Manhattan, which will take you onto I-495/Long Island Expwy. Take this until it ends at Riverhead and follow signs onto Rte 25 for all points east.
- **Train** Take the LIRR Ronkonkoma Branch line, with trips leaving from New York Penn Station and Brooklyn and running all the way out to Greenport.

Need to Know

- **Area Code** ☎631
- **Location** ☎100 miles east of Manhattan
- **Information** ☎Long Island Wine Council (631-722-2220; www.liwines.com)

SIGHTS & ACTIVITIES

MASHOMACK NATURE PRESERVE — NATURE RESERVE

(☎631-749-1001; www.nature.org/Mashomack; Rte 114, Shelter Island; suggested donation adult/child $3/2; ⏲9am-5pm Jul & Aug, closed Tue Apr-Jun & Sep-Oct, shorter hours rest of year) The 2000 acres of this Shelter Island reserve, shot through with creeks and marshes, are great for kayaking, birding and hiking (no cycling allowed). Take precautions against ticks, an ever-present problem on the island.

ORIENT BEACH STATE PARK — BEACH

(☎631-323-2440; www.parks.ny.gov/parks/106; 40000 Main Rd, Orient; per car $10, kayaks per hour $25; ⏲8am-4pm) A sandy slip of land at the end of the North Fork, where you can swim in the calm ocean water (July and August only; 10:30am to 6pm) or rent kayaks to paddle in the small bay. True believers can view four different lighthouses, including the Orient Point Lighthouse, known as 'the coffee pot' for its stout bearing. To best see the lighthouse, go up the road to Orient Point County Park, which has a half-mile trail to a white-rock beach.

★SHINN ESTATE — WINERY

(☎631-804-0367; www.shinnestatevineyards.com; 2000 Oregon Rd, Mattituck; tastings $16-28; ⏲10:30am-5pm Mon-Thu, to 7pm Fri-Sat, to 6pm Sun) This restored 1880s farmhouse and winery lures oenophiles in the know not only for its excellent, age-worthy wines often touted as Long Island's best (biodynamic and organic to boot, though not certified), but its luxury, four-bedroom B&B as well (doubles from $260). If you're in for a tasting, the alluring picnic tables and couches are perfect for lazing away with its Coalescence white blend or Malbec overlooking 25 acres of bucolic perfection.

KONTOKOSTA WINERY — WINERY

(☎631-477-6977; www.kontokostawinery.com; 825 North Rd, Greenport; tastings $16; ⏲11am-5pm Sun-Thu, to 6pm Fri & Sat) One of the newer kids on the North Fork wine block, yet already producing award-winning vintages. You'll be as wowed by the scenery – it's the only local tasting room with a Sound view –

as by what's in your glass. No limos, buses or vans means a more serene scene.

VINTAGE TOURS WINE

(☎631-765-4689; www.vintagetour1.com; tours incl lunch $99-112) Drink all you like – a driver takes care of the rest on this five- to six-hour tour of four wineries in the North Fork, with a behind-the-scenes peek at one of the operations. Pick-up is from your lodgings.

EATING & DRINKING

★NORTH FORK TABLE & INN AMERICAN $$$

(☎631-765-0177; www.nofoti.com; 57225 Main Rd, Southold; mains $33-45, 5-course tasting menu $125; ⏱5:30-8pm Mon-Thu, to 9:30pm Fri, 5-9.30pm Sat, 5-8pm Sun, plus 11:30am-2pm & Sat & Sun; 📶) A favorite foodies' escape, this four-room inn (rooms from $250) has an excellent farm-to-table restaurant, run by alums of the esteemed Manhattan restaurant Gramercy Tavern. Dinner is served nightly (along with weekend brunch), but if you're hankering for a gourmand-to-go lunch ($5.50 to $21), the inn's food truck is parked outside Friday to Monday from 11:30am to 3:30pm (daily July and August).

CLAUDIO'S SEAFOOD $$$

(☎631-477-0627; www.claudios.com; 111 Main St, Greenport; mains $19-52; ⏱11:30am-9pm Sun-Thu, to 10pm Fri & Sat May-Oct; 📶) This Greenport legend was the nation's oldest restaurant continuously owned by the same family (the Portuguese Claudio clan; since 1870) until 2018 when it was sold to three Greenport loyalist families who have carried on its mostly seafood-heavy traditions with a modern upgrade. Dishes include swordfish ragù, spaghetti with clams, fresh oysters and dry-aged steaks (from Kansas).

For a more casual meal and an epic outdoor bar, hit Claudio's Waterfront on the nearby pier (mains $17 to $26).

MOUSTACHE BREWING BREWERY

(www.moustachebrewing.com; 400 Hallett Ave, Riverhead; ⏱3-8pm Mon, Thu & Fri, noon-7pm Sat, noon-6pm Sun; 📶) In true craft fashion, this hop-lovers' haven occupies a warehouse space in Riverhead; 25 taps and few bells and whistles await connoisseurs, with an emphasis on double IPAs and European-style brews. Food trucks on occasion.

Hudson Valley

Explore

Winding roads along either side of the Hudson River take you by picturesque farms, Victorian cottages, apple orchards and old-money mansions built by New York's elite. Painters of the Hudson River School romanticized these landscapes, especially the region's famous fall foliage – you can see their work at art museums in the area as well as in NYC. Autumn is a particularly beautiful time for a trip up this way. The eastern side of the river feels more populated – less so the further north you go – while the western side has a rural feel, with hills leading into the Catskills mountain region.

The Best...

➡ **Sight** Dia:Beacon

➡ **Place to Eat** Roundhouse Restaurant & Lounge

➡ **Place to Hike** Harriman State Park

Top Tip

Food lovers should set their sights on Rhinebeck and Beacon, which have some of the best restaurants in the area.

Getting There & Away

➡ **Car** From Manhattan, take the Henry Hudson Pkwy across the George Washington Bridge to Palisades Pkwy. Head for the New York State Thruway to Rte 9W or Rte 9, the scenic river routes. You can also take the Taconic State Pkwy north from Ossining, a pretty road in autumn.

➡ **Bus** Short Line (www.coachusa.com) runs regular trips to Bear Mountain, Harriman, Hyde Park, Rhinebeck and other destinations.

➡ **Train** The Metro-North (www.mta.info/mnr) train makes several stops on the Lower and Middle Hudson Valleys (take the Hudson Line). Amtrak runs to Hudson.

Need to Know

➡ **Area Code** ☎845

➡ **Location** 95 miles north of Manhattan

➡ **Information** Dutchess Tourism, Beacon Tourist Information

SIGHTS & ACTIVITIES

Lower Hudson Valley

Several magnificent homes can be found near Tarrytown and Sleepy Hollow. The formerly industrial town of Beacon has become an outpost of contemporary art, while the galleries and antique shops of historic Hudson attract a wealthier set of weekenders. If you have a car, cross to the west bank of the Hudson River to explore Harriman State Park and adjacent Bear Mountain State Park, with views down to Manhattan from its 1303ft peak.

★STORM KING ART CENTER GALLERY

(☎845-534-3115; www.stormking.org; 1 Museum Rd, off Old Pleasant Hill Rd, New Windsor; adult/child $18/8; ⏲10am-5:30pm Wed-Sun Apr-Oct, to 4:30pm Nov & Dec) This 500-acre sculpture park, established in 1960, has works by the likes of Barbara Hepworth, Mark di Suvero, Andy Goldsworthy and Isamu Noguchi. All have been carefully sited across the grassy estate's natural breaks and curves.

There's also a visitor center, a cafe and some indoor galleries. A free tram shuttle loops throughout the park; you can also rent bicycles by the hour (weekday/weekend $10/12) or for the day ($34/44). From late May through September the center is open to 8pm Friday and Saturday, and in September and October they're also open on Mondays. Check the website for details of package bus tours from NYC.

BEAR MOUNTAIN STATE PARK STATE PARK

(☎845-786-2701; www.parks.ny.gov; Palisades Pkwy/Rte 6, Bear Mountain; per car $10; ⏲8am-dusk) The main draw here are the views of the Manhattan skyline from the 1303ft peak (accessible by car), but there's also ice skating in winter and boating and swimming in summer. There are several scenic roads snaking their way past secluded lakes with gorgeous vistas. Entrance fee collected daily late June to early September, and Saturdays and Sundays only from mid-September to mid-June; some amenities have individual costs as well.

KYKUIT HISTORIC BUILDING

(☎914-366-6900; www.hudsonvalley.org; 200 Lake Rd, Pocantico Hills; tour adult/child from $27/25; ⏲tours Thu-Sun May-Sep & early Nov, Wed-Mon Oct) Built by oil tycoon John D Rockefeller as his summer home and completed in 1913, this 40-room mansion is listed on the National Register and has lovely grounds landscaped by Frederick Law Olmsted. On display as sculptures around the estate and in an underground art gallery is a remarkable collection of modern art including works by Picasso, Chagall and Warhol.

Admission is only by tour, which depart from **Philipsburg Manor** (☎914-366-6900; www.hudsonvalley.org; 381 N Broadway, Sleepy Hollow; adult/child $14/8; ⏲tours 10:30am-3:30pm Wed-Sun May–mid-Nov); hours vary. A shuttle bus will take you out to the estate from here. Tickets are $2 cheaper if bought online.

HARRIMAN STATE PARK STATE PARK

(☎845-947-2444; www.parks.ny.gov; Seven Lakes Dr, Bear Mountain Circle, Ramapo; per car late May-Sep $10; ⏲dawn-dusk) This park on the west side of the Hudson covers 72 sq miles and provides swimming, hiking, camping, 200 miles of walking trails, and a visitor center.

A seven-plus mile section of the **Appalachian Trail** (www.appalachiantrail.org) runs through here and it's not uncommon to see grizzled hikers with walking sticks, loaded down with packs, alongside the highway or peeking out from the forest like creatures from a secret world.

WASHINGTON IRVING'S SUNNYSIDE HISTORIC BUILDING

(☎914-591-8763, Mon-Fri 914-631-8200; www.hudsonvalley.org; 3 W Sunnyside Lane, Tarrytown; adult/child $14/8; ⏲tours 10:30am-4pm Wed-Sun May–mid-Nov) Washington Irving, famous for tales such as *The Legend of Sleepy Hollow*, built this imaginative home, which he said had more nooks and crannies than a cocked hat. Tour guides in 19th-century costume tell good stories, and the wisteria Irving planted a century ago still climbs the walls. Tickets are $2 cheaper if bought online.

The closest train station to Sunnyside is Irvington, one stop before Tarrytown.

Beacon

★DIA:BEACON GALLERY
(☎845-440-0100; www.diaart.org; 3 Beekman St, Beacon; adult/child $15/free; ⏱11am-6pm Thu-Mon Apr-Oct, to 4pm Thu-Mon Nov & Dec, to 4pm Fri-Mon Jan-Mar) The 300,000-sq-ft former Nabisco box-printing factory beside the Hudson River is now a storehouse for a series of stunning monumental works by the likes of Richard Serra, Dan Flavin, Louise Bourgeois and Gerhard Richter. The permanent collection is complemented by temporary shows of large-scale sculptures and installations, making this a must-see for contemporary art fans. Guided tours (free with admission) are offered on weekends at 12:30pm and 2pm.

Poughkeepsie & Hyde Park

HOME OF FRANKLIN D ROOSEVELT HISTORIC BUILDING
(☎845-229-5320; www.nps.gov/hofr; 4097 Albany Post Rd; adult/child $20/free, museum/house only adult/child $10/free; ⏱tours every 30min 9am-4pm) Rangers lead interesting hour-long tours around Springwood, the home of Franklin D Roosevelt (FDR) who won a record four presidential elections and led America from the Great Depression through WWII. Considering his family wealth, it's a modest abode, but can be unpleasantly crowded in summer. Intimate details have been preserved, including his desk – left as it was the day before he died – and the hand-pulled elevator he used to hoist his polio-stricken body to the 2nd floor.

The home is part of a 1520-acre estate, formerly a working farm, which also includes the simple marble tomb where FDR and Eleanor (and their dog Fala) were interred, various walking trails and the **FDR Presidential Library and Museum** (☎845-486-7770; www.fdrlibrary.org; 4079 Albany Post Rd; adult/child $20/free, museum/house only adult/child $10/free; ⏱9am-6pm Apr-Oct, to 5pm Nov-Mar), which details important achievements in FDR's presidency. Admission tickets last two days and include the Springwood tour and the presidential library.

Note that Springwood has a series of repair projects planned. Check on their status before visiting.

WALKWAY OVER THE HUDSON VIEWPOINT
(☎845-834-2867; www.walkway.org; 61 Parker Ave, Poughkeepsie; ⏱7am-sunset) This is the main eastern entrance (with parking) to what was once a railroad bridge (built in 1889) crossing the Hudson. Today it's the world's longest pedestrian bridge – 1.28 miles – and a state park. The 212ft-high span provides breathtaking views along the river.

If you have time, there's a 3.6-mile loop walking trail you can follow across this bridge and back along the Mid-Hudson Bridge to Poughkeepsie.

There's also a free elevator that takes you straight up to the walkway at the river's edge, located in Upper Landing Park (83 N Water St). Note that the elevator opens at 9am and closes 90 minutes before the bridge does.

Hudson

★OLANA HISTORIC SITE
(☎518-828-0135; www.olana.org; 5720 Rte 9G; house tours adult/child $15/free; ⏱grounds 8:30am-sunset daily, house tours 10am-5pm Tue-Sun mid-May–Oct, 10am-4pm Fri-Sun Nov-May) This is one of the finest of the Hudson Valley mansions, as its owner, celebrated landscape painter Frederic Church, designed every detail, inspired by his travels in the Middle East and his appreciation of the beautiful views across the Hudson to the Catskills. The 'Persian fantasy' house is extraordinary and it's well worth booking ahead for a tour of the interior, where you can also see many of Church's paintings.

There are also guided walking and driving tours of the grounds (which you're free to explore in your own car as well). Olana underwent a major rejuvenation which was completed in 2018.

EATING

★ROUNDHOUSE RESTAURANT & LOUNGE AMERICAN **$$**
(☎845-765-8369; www.rhbeacon.com; 2 E Main St, Beacon; mains $20-34; ⏱lounge 3-9pm Mon-Thu, 11:30am-10pm Fri & Sat, 11am-8pm Sun, restaurant 5-10pm Fri & Sat, 11am-3pm Sun) Situated with stunning waterfall views, the Roundhouse restaurant pulls out all the culinary stops, with dishes celebrating

the cream of Hudson Valley produce. The seasonal menu offers American favorites, as well as the occasional curveball such as rice bowls, or (in winter) filling bowls of ramen. During the week, the lounge offers a more subdued, but no less delicious, menu.

GRAZIN' DINER BURGERS **$$**
(☎518-822-9323; www.grazinburger.com; 717 Warren St, Hudson; burgers $11.50-19.50; ⊙noon-8pm Mon-Thu, to 9:30pm Fri, 9am-9:30pm Sat, 9am-6pm Sun) If retro cred from the converted 1940 diner weren't enough, Grazin' goes above and beyond with their burgers, made with grass-fed, organic beef sourced from their own 500-acre farm a few miles up the road (which is also approved for its humane conditions by the Animal Welfare Institute). This may be the freshest burger you've ever had.

★**BLUE HILL AT STONE BARNS** AMERICAN **$$$**
(☎914-366-9600; www.bluehillfarm.com; 630 Bedford Rd, Pocantico Hills; set menu $278; ⊙5-10pm Wed-Sat, 1-7:30pm Sun) Go maximum locavore at chef Dan Barber's farm (which also supplies his Manhattan restaurant). Settle in for an eye-popping multicourse feast based on the day's harvest (allow three hours), where the service is as theatrical as the presentation. Be sure to book at least a month in advance. The dress code prefers jackets and ties for gentlemen; shorts are not permitted.

By day, visitors are welcome to tour **Stone Barn Center for Food & Agriculture** (☎914-366-6200; www.stonebarnscenter.org; 630 Bedford Rd, Pocantico Hills; ⊙10am-4pm Wed-Sun) , which has a basic takeout cafe.

Woodstock

Explore

A minor technicality: the 1969 music festival was actually held in Bethel, an hour's drive west. Nonetheless, the town of Woodstock still attracts an arty, music-loving crowd and cultivates the free spirit of that era, with rainbow-tie-dye style and local grassroots everything, from radio to a respected indie film festival and a farmers market (fittingly billed as a farm festival).

The Best...

➡ **Sight** Woodstock Artists Association & Museum

➡ **Place to Eat** Garden Cafe

➡ **Place to Drink** Station Bar & Curio

Top Tip

Bring an empty bag – you never know what you'll unearth in the many antique shops and markets (plus weekend yard sales!) found in the area.

Getting There & Away

➡ **Car** Take the New York State Thruway (via the Henry Hudson Pkwy north from Manhattan) or I-87 to Rte 375 for Woodstock, Rte 32 for Saugerties or Rte 28 for other points.

➡ **Bus** Frequent buses from NYC to Saugerties and Woodstock (from $30, three hours) are operated by Trailways (www.trailwaysny.com).

Need to Know

➡ **Area Code** ☎845

➡ **Location** 110 miles north (Saugerties) of Manhattan

SIGHTS & ACTIVITIES

CENTER FOR PHOTOGRAPHY AT WOODSTOCK ARTS CENTER
(☎845-679-9957; www.cpw.org; 59 Tinker St; ⊙noon-5pm) FREE Founded in 1977, this creative space gives classes, hosts lectures and mounts exhibitions that expand the strict definition of the art form, thanks to a lively artist-in-residence program.

This was formerly the Café Espresso, and Bob Dylan once had a writing studio above it – that's where he typed up the liner notes for *Another Side of Bob Dylan* in 1964. Janis Joplin was a regular performer.

WOODSTOCK ARTISTS ASSOCIATION & MUSEUM MUSEUM
(WAAM; ☎845-679-2940; www.woodstockart.org; 28 Tinker St; ⊙noon-5pm Wed, Thu & Sun, to 6pm Fri & Sat) FREE WAAM has been supporting artists working in the Catskills since 1919. Exhibitions in its several galleries

WORTH A DETOUR

SAUGERTIES

Around 10 miles northeast of Woodstock, the town of Saugerties (www.discover saugerties.com) dates back to the Dutch settling here in the mid-17th century. Today it's well worth making a day trip to a couple of local attractions. **Opus 40 Sculpture Park & Museum** (☎845-246-3400; www.opus40.org; 50 Fite Rd, Saugerties; adult/child $10/3; ⏰10:30am-5:30pm Thu-Sun late May-Nov) is where artist Harvey Fite worked for nearly four decades to coax an abandoned quarry into an immense work of land art, all sinuous walls, canyons and pools. The picturesque 1869 **Saugerties Lighthouse** (☎845-247-0656; www.saugertieslighthouse.com; 168 Lighthouse Dr, Saugerties; tour suggested donation adult/child $5/3; ⏰trail dawn-dusk), on the point where Esopus Creek joins the Hudson, can be reached by a half-mile nature trail. Classic rock lovers may also want to search out **Big Pink** (www.bigpinkbasement.com; Parnassus Lane, West Saugerties; house $625; ❄📶), the house made famous by Bob Dylan and the Band, although note it's on a private road. It's possible to stay at both the lighthouse and Big Pink, but you'll need to book well ahead.

include historic pieces as well as current creative output from members of this venerable arts association. The attached shops sells glassware, ceramics, textiles and jewelry made by local artisans.

OVERLOOK MOUNTAIN HIKING

(Meads Mountain Rd; ⏰dawn-dusk) Several strenuous hikes branch out from this trailhead part of the way up Overlook Mountain and a five-minute drive from downtown Woodstock. The forest up here has a few fun finds, including a fire tower and the ruins of an abandoned hotel.

EATING

★GARDEN CAFE VEGAN $

(☎845-679-3600; www.thegardencafewoodstock.com; 6 Old Forge Rd; mains $9-22; ⏰11:30am-9pm Mon & Wed-Fri, 10am-9pm Sat & Sun; 📶🖉) 🍃 All the ingredients used at this relaxed, charming cafe are organic. The food served is appealing, tasty and fresh, and includes salads, sandwiches, rice bowls and veggie lasagna. It also serves freshly made juices, smoothies, organic wines, craft beers and coffee made with a variety of nondairy milks. In nice weather you can sit outside in the large garden.

SHINDIG AMERICAN $

(☎845-684-7091; www.woodstockshindig.com; 1 Tinker St; mains $11-15; ⏰10am-9pm Tue & Wed, 9am-10pm Thu-Sat, 9am-9pm Sun; 📶) What's not to love about this cheery little cafe-bar? It serves breakfast until 3pm, there's a great range of craft beers and inventive cocktails, and the trout BLT puts a tasty new twist on the classic sandwich.

DRINKING & NIGHTLIFE

STATION BAR & CURIO BAR

(☎845-810-0203; www.stationbarandcurio.com; 101 Tinker St; ⏰4pm-2am Mon-Thu, noon-2am Fri-Sun) The 1900 Ulster & Delaware Railroad Company station that this bar occupies was once located 10 miles south in Brown's Station, a village now lying beneath the Ashokan Reservoir. It offers eight local craft beers on tap, many more by the bottle, cocktails and wine. Live jazz and blues is played here most weekends.

Sleeping

With over 60 million visitors descending upon the city every year, you can expect that hotel rooms fill up quickly. Accommodations options range from boxy cookie-cutter rooms in Midtown high-rises to stylish boutique options downtown. You'll also find a few B&Bs set in residential neighborhoods as well as budget-conscious hostels sprinkled about the metropolis.

The Basics

Expect high prices and small spaces. Rates waver by availability, not by high-season or low-season rules. You'll pay dearly during holidays. Accommodations fill quickly, especially in summer and December, and range from cookie-cutter chains to stylish boutiques.

Brooklyn and Queens offer better value; Long Island City has a few bargain designer hotels, and Staten Island has affordable B&Bs if you don't mind a ferry ride. A few hostels are scattered throughout NYC.

Reservations are essential – walk-ins are practically impossible and rack rates are almost always unfavorable relative to online deals. Reserve your room as early as possible and make sure you understand your hotel's cancellation policy. Expect check-in to be in the middle of the afternoon and check-out to be late morning.

Room Rates

New York City doesn't have a high or low season. Room rates fluctuate based on availability; most hotels use a booking algorithm. If you're looking to find the best room rates, flexibility is useful and stays for three or more days can reduce rates. On weekends, try business hotels in the Financial District.

How to Book

In New York City, the average room rate is well over $300. But don't let that scare you as there are great deals to be had – almost all of which can be found through savvy online scouring. Above all, book early: it's common to see lower rates for stays booked three days or more in advance. In B&B and boutique properties, where there's a range of room styles, the smaller (read: cheaper) accommodations are snapped up weeks in advance. If you don't have your heart set on a particular property, check generic booking websites – but scrutinize whether rates include taxes, resort fees and other add-ons. If you do know where you want to stay, booking directly through the hotel's website will probably get you the best deals and package rates.

Sleeping in Brooklyn

Just a short train ride across the East River and you'll find more bang for your buck. Downtown Brooklyn and Williamsburg have ever-increasing numbers of chic hotels, while small B&Bs in classic houses can be found in residential areas such as Prospect Lefferts Gardens and Ditmas Park. Sunset Park has several affordable chain hotels, too.

Note: The borough covers more than 70 sq miles and transport between its neighborhoods can be a challenge, so pick an area (ie northern or southern Brooklyn) that offers the best proximity to sights you're interested in seeing.

Lonely Planet's Top Choices

Crosby Street Hotel (p334)

Bowery Hotel (p335)

NoMad Hotel (p340)

Gramercy Park Hotel (p338)

Freehand New York (p338)

Best by Budget

$

Local (p345)

Harlem Flophouse (p343)

Carlton Arms (p337)

NY Moore Hostel (p343)

$$

Freehand New York (p338)

Boro Hotel (p345)

Arthouse Hotel NYC (p342)

Citizen M (p339)

TWA Hotel (p346)

At Home in Brooklyn (p344)

$$$

Greenwich Hotel (p333)

Gramercy Park Hotel (p338)

Knickerbocker (p341)

NoMad Hotel (p340)

Bowery Hotel (p335)

Wythe Hotel (p344)

Best Views

Standard (p337)

Four Seasons (p340)

Williamsburg Hotel (p345)

Z NYC Hotel (p346)

Best for Families

Hotel Beacon (p342)

Marram (p321)

Muse New York (p341)

Best Boutique Digs

Chatwal New York (p340)

Wythe Hotel (p344)

Ace Hotel (p339)

Broome (p334)

Best for Honeymooners

Plaza (p340)

Williamsburg Hotel (p345)

Andaz Fifth Avenue (p340)

Best for High Style

Gansevoort Meatpacking NYC (p336)

Hotel 50 Bowery (p334)

McCarren Hotel (p344)

Lowell (p341)

Best in Brooklyn

Henry Norman Hotel (p344)

Wythe Hotel (p344)

At Home in Brooklyn (p344)

The Brooklyn (p344)

NEED TO KNOW

Price Ranges

The following price ranges refer to rates for a standard double room regardless of the time of year.

$	less than $200
$$	$200 to $350
$$$	more than $350

Useful Websites

NYC (www.nycgo.com/hotels) Loads of listings from the NYC Official Guide.

Lonely Planet (lonelyplanet.com/usa/new-york-city/hotels) Accommodations reviews and recommendations.

Resort Fees

Some NYC hotels have introduced a 'resort fee' of between $20 and $35 a night, which hoteliers are using as a more palatable way of bundling previously ad-hoc additional charges for perks such as on-tap coffee and tea, gym access and wi-fi connectivity. Look at the fine print when browsing for accommodation (especially through aggregate booking sites).

Tipping

You should always tip the cleaner – leave $3 to $5 per night in an obvious location like on a pillow (sometimes envelopes are provided) or write a 'thank you' on hotel stationery nearby. Porters should receive a dollar or two, and service staff bringing items to your room should be tipped accordingly as well.

Where to Stay

NEIGHBORHOOD	FOR	AGAINST
Financial District & Lower Manhattan	Convenient to ferries and Tribeca's nightlife. Cheap weekend rates at business hotels.	The southernmost areas can feel impersonal, though Tribeca has great dining.
SoHo & Chinatown	Shopping right on your doorstep. Excellent dining options and a thriving nightlife scene.	Crowds (mostly tourists) swarm the commercial streets of SoHo almost any time of day. Expensive.
East Village & Lower East Side	Funky and fun, the area feels the most quintessentially 'New York'.	Options skew toward very pricey or bare-bones basic. Some locations are a long walk to the subway.
West Village, Chelsea & the Meatpacking District	Brilliantly close-to-everything feel in a part of town with an almost European flavor.	Prices soar for traditional hotels, B&Bs are reasonable.
Union Square, Flatiron District & Gramercy	Convenient subway access. Steps away from the Village and Midtown; good dining options and less touristy feel than Midtown.	Prices are high and there's not much in the way of neighborhood flavor.
Midtown	The postcard version of NYC: skyscrapers, museums, shopping and Broadway shows.	Expensive; expect small rooms. Can feel touristy and impersonal. Lacklustre midrange/budget dining.
Upper East Side	A stone's throw from top-notch museums and Central Park. Designer shops on Park Ave.	Fewer options and wallet-busting prices; not particularly central.
Upper West Side & Central Park	Convenient to Central Park, Lincoln Center and Museum of Natural History.	More family style than lively.
Harlem & Upper Manhattan	Great neighborhood vibe, better prices, close to Central Park. Stellar live music.	Long subway rides to the action downtown and in Brooklyn.
Brooklyn	Better prices; creative neighborhoods and less crowded attractions.	Long commute to Midtown and points farther north.
Queens	Cheaper, tourist-free and well located for world cuisines. Long Island City is a short subway ride from Midtown.	Locations farther out in Queens, particularly Flushing, are a long haul on the subway.

Financial District & Lower Manhattan

ANDAZ WALL ST BOUTIQUE HOTEL $$

Map p406 (☎212-590-1234; http://wallstreet.andaz.hyatt.com; 75 Wall St, at Water St, Financial District; r from $299; ❄@📶; Ⓢ2/3 to Wall St) A favorite of hip downtown business types, the 253-room Andaz takes sleek and handsome and gives it a relaxed, new-school vibe. Guests are checked-in on iPads and treated to complimentary wi-fi, local calls and minibar soda and snacks. Rooms are spacious, contemporary and elegantly restrained, with 7ft-high windows, oak floors and sublimely comfortable beds with 300-thread-count cotton sheets.

GILD HALL BOUTIQUE HOTEL $$

Map p406 (☎212-232-7700; www.thompsonhotels.com/hotels/gild-hall; 15 Gold St, at Platt St, Lower Manhattan; superior/deluxe from $300/340; ❄📶; Ⓢ2/3 to Fulton St) Boutique and brilliant, Gild Hall's entryway leads to a split-level, book- and sofa-stuffed lobby exuding a style best characterised as 'Wall St meets hunting lodge.' Rooms fuse Euro elegance and American comfort with high tin ceilings, Sferra linens and well-stocked minibars. King-size beds sport leather headboards, which work perfectly in their warmly hued, minimalist surroundings.

★**GREENWICH HOTEL** BOUTIQUE HOTEL $$$

Map p406 (☎212-941-8900; www.thegreenwichhotel.com; 377 Greenwich St, btwn N Moore & Franklin Sts, Tribeca; r from $650; ❄📶🏊; Ⓢ1 to Franklin St, A/C/E to Canal St) From the plush drawing room (complete with crackling fire and deep armchairs) to the lantern-lit pool inside a reconstructed 18th-century Japanese farmhouse, nothing about Robert De Niro's Greenwich Hotel is generic. Each of the 88 individually designed rooms features aged-wood floors, and bathrooms with opulent Carrara marble or Moroccan tiling. French windows open onto Tuscan-inspired inner courtyards in some rooms.

★**ROXY HOTEL** HOTEL $$$

Map p406 (☎212-519-6600; www.roxyhotelnyc.com; 2 Sixth Ave, at White St, Tribeca; r from $509; ❄📶🐾; Ⓢ1 to Franklin St, A/C/E to Canal St) The reimagined Tribeca Grand offers mid-century glamor, luxurious living, cinema, music, drinking and dining in one foxy package. Its 201 rooms, decked out with modern fittings in a retro brown-and-gold palette, surround a spacious central atrium with multiple bars, a boutique **art-house cinema** (Map p406; ☎212-519-6820; www.roxycinematribeca.com; 2 Sixth Ave, at White St, Tribeca; tickets $12; Ⓢ1 to Franklin St, A/C/E to Canal St) and jazz cellar **Django**. Regular events such as the annual **New Year's Surrealist Ball** heighten the fun.

AKA TRIBECA BOUTIQUE HOTEL $$$

Map p406 (☎212-587-7000; www.stayaka.com; 85 W Broadway, at Chambers St, Tribeca; r from $350; ❄📶; ⓈA/C, 1/2/3 to Chambers St) Newly acquired by AKA, this boutique hotel provides more than a whiff of Tribeca luxury. Modernist furniture, rugs and book-lined shelves give the Gachot-designed lobby a snug, chic, Scandinavian vibe, while the 100 soundproofed rooms are a soothing combo of charcoal carpets, walnut paneling and marble bathrooms with bountiful rain showers. The more expensive rooms have balconies with city views.

THE LOWDOWN ON APARTMENT RENTALS

Travelers browsing home-sharing websites will find hundreds of options in NYC, from rooms and studios to penthouse apartments. Private rooms and pocket-sized studios cost around $100 per night in Manhattan (multiroom apartments rise to several hundred dollars per night), or from $80 in Brooklyn 'hoods like Clinton Hill and Bed-Stuy. Before hitting 'book now', note that it's illegal under the Multiple Dwelling Law in NYC to rent out an apartment for fewer than 30 days, unless the host is also living there – but it's hosts, rather than guests, who could be hit with fines (from $1000 to $7500). As legal battles continue between NYC and Airbnb, travelers face a moral dilemma: if you snap up a desirable short-term apartment rental you may be contributing to the pressure cooker that is NYC's housing market, where rents are high and landlords are increasingly tempted to make fast cash from short-term guests.

CONRAD NEW YORK HOTEL $$$

Map p406 (☎212-945-0100; www.conradnewyork.com; 102 North End Ave, at Vesey St, Lower Manhattan; ste from $600; ❄📶; Ⓢ1/2/3, A/C to Chambers St) In Battery Park City, this well-heeled Hilton-group hotel is a top choice for business travelers. There's a trove of more than 2000 artworks to be discovered, including *Loopy Doopy*, a massive Sol LeWitt mural running up the wall of the 15-story atrium. The 463 suites are handsomely designed, featuring earthy tones and high-end furnishings. You'll find cheaper rates at weekends.

SoHo & Chinatown

BOWERY HOUSE HOSTEL $

Map p408 (☎212-837-2373; www.theboweryhouse.com; 220 Bowery, btwn Prince & Spring Sts, Nolita; s/d with shared bath from $80/130; ❄📶; ⓈR/W to Prince St) Across the street from the New Museum, this former 1920s-era flophouse has been resurrected as an upmarket hostel, its rooms decked out with Bowery-themed film posters and custom-made mattresses (ie shorter and narrower), while communal bathrooms feature rain showers. There's also a stylish lounge area with chesterfield sofas and chandeliers, a buzzing bar and a roof terrace.

Light sleepers may wish to avoid this place, which attracts a nightlife-loving crowd; earplugs come standard with every room.

HOTEL HUGO BOUTIQUE HOTEL $$

Map p408 (☎212-608-4848; www.hotelhugony.com; 525 Greenwich St, btwn Vandam & Spring Sts, SoHo; d from $240; 📶; Ⓢ1 to Houston St/Canal St, C/E to Spring St) It might not have the bells and whistles of some SoHo hotels, but Hotel Hugo is a quiet champion in this pricey 'hood. Rooms channel industrial style, there's a rooftop bar and suave restaurant-cafe. It's a 10- to 15-minute walk from central SoHo but that's A-OK when prices can be as low as $240 a night even in peak season.

NOMO SOHO BOUTIQUE HOTEL $$

Map p411 (☎646-218-6400; www.nomosoho.com; 9 Crosby St, btwn Howard & Grand Sts, SoHo; d from $316; ❄📶🐾; ⓈN/Q/R, J/Z, 6 to Canal St) Neobaroque playfulness underscores the plush, smallish rooms at this beautiful downtown property, where creamy whites and dreamy blues meet flouncy sconces and marble bathrooms. Upper-level rooms will leave you feeling like you're gazing out at Manhattan from a cloud. Note reception for the hotel is upstairs.

SOHO GRAND HOTEL BOUTIQUE HOTEL $$

Map p408 (☎212-965-3000; www.sohogrand.com; 310 W Broadway, SoHo; d $255-700; ❄@📶🐾; ⓈA/C/E to Canal St) The original boutique hotel of the 'hood still reigns, with its striking glass-and-cast-iron lobby stairway, and 353 rooms with cool, clean lines plus Frette linens, flat-screen TVs and bespoke grooming products. The lobby's Grand Bar & Lounge buzzes with scenesters and the occasional celebrity. Dogs are catered to, with amenities to match those of the human guests.

★BROOME BOUTIQUE HOTEL $$$

Map p408 (☎212-431-2929; www.thebroomenyc.com; 431 Broome St, at Crosby St, SoHo; d from $399; ❄📶; ⓈR/W to Prince St; 6 to Spring St) Occupying a handsomely restored, 19th-century building, the Broome feels far more intimate than most NYC hotels. Its 14 rooms are the epitome of simple elegance, each with locally sourced fittings. There's a hidden surprise here, too: a tranquil open-air internal patio with Parisian-style seating for relaxing with a coffee (which is complimentary, as is the farm-to-table breakfast). Service here is personable.

★CROSBY STREET HOTEL BOUTIQUE HOTEL $$$

Map p408 (☎212-226-6400; www.firmdalehotels.com; 79 Crosby St, btwn Spring & Prince Sts, SoHo; d from $725; 🚭❄📶; Ⓢ6 to Spring St; N/R to Prince St) The team behind this hotel have torn up the rule book in terms of interior design, and the results are sublime. Guest rooms all have oversized headboards with matching mannequins, but that's where the uniformity ends. Some are starkly black and white while others are as floral as an English garden; all are plush, refined and subtly playful.

★HOTEL 50 BOWERY BOUTIQUE HOTEL $$$

Map p411 (☎212-508-8000; www.jdvhotels.com; 50 Bowery; d from $469; ❄📶; ⓈB/D to Grand St; J/Z to Canal St) Smack in the heart of Chinatown is this newcomer boutique with sumptuously sleek rooms, bespoke bath products, luxe linens, robes emblazoned with red dragons and original works by NYC-based artists. A hip rooftop bar boasts unparalleled views of the city and its an ideal base for accessing Tribeca, SoHo, Lower East Side and Brooklyn (via the Manhattan bridge) on foot.

MERCER BOUTIQUE HOTEL $$$

Map p408 (☎212-966-6060; www.mercerhotel.com; 147 Mercer St, at Prince St, SoHo; d $695; ; S N/R to Prince St; B/D/F/M, 6 to Broadway and Lafayette) Right in the heart of SoHo's brick lanes, the decades-old Mercer is where stars sleep. Above a lobby full of fat, plush sofas, 74 rooms offer a slice of chic loft life in a century-old warehouse. Flat-screen TVs, dark hardwood floors and white-tiled bathrooms (some with soaking tubs) add a modern touch to the rooms.

JAMES NEW YORK BOUTIQUE HOTEL $$$

Map p408 (☎212-465-2000; www.jameshotels.com/new-york; 27 Grand St, btwn Sixth Ave & Thompson St, SoHo; d from $400; @; S A/C/E, 1 to Canal St) The James plays with a variety of architectural elements in each of its different spaces, and somehow they all work beautifully. The public areas blend abundant natural light with playful touches: check out the computer-key mural in the entrance foyer. Upstairs, the simple rooms have floor-to-ceiling windows, reclaimed timber floors, and a motorized screen separating each from its copper-hued bathroom.

Added sex appeal is provided by the petite rooftop plunge pool, complete with slinky bar Jimmy (p103) for see-and-be-seen cocktails. Prices can creep as low as $250 in low season.

East Village & Lower East Side

ST MARK'S HOTEL HOTEL $

Map p412 (☎212-674-0100; www.stmarkshotel.net; 2 St Marks Pl, at Third Ave, East Village; d from $119; ; S 6 to Astor Pl) This friendly place draws a young, nightlife-loving crowd who enjoy having one of the city's liveliest concentrations of bars and restaurants right outside the front door. With such low prices, it's best to lower your expectations, as the rooms are quite small. Street noise might be an issue for light sleepers. There's no lift.

LUDLOW HOTEL $$

Map p414 (☎212-432-1818; www.ludlowhotel.com; 180 Ludlow St, btwn E Houston & Stanton Sts, Lower East Side; d from $325; ; S F to 2nd Ave) This 175-room boutique hotel oozes New York style. Rooms are beautifully designed, with unique features such as huge golden-hued ceiling lights, nightstands made of petrified tree trunks, mosaic-tiled bathrooms and small balconies (although the cheapest rooms are quite small). There's a gorgeous lobby bar and patio, plus an acclaimed French bistro, **Dirty French**, open for breakfast, lunch and dinner.

SAGO HOTEL BOUTIQUE HOTEL $$

Map p414 (☎212-951-1112; www.sagohotel.com; 120 Allen St, btwn Rivington & Delancey Sts, Lower East Side; r from $200, studio from $320; ; S F, J/M/Z to Delancey-Essex Sts) No matter the weather in NYC, it always appears to be cool in the Sago Hotel. It's located in the bustling center of the Lower East Side and the rooms all bear the markings of the current vibe of the neighborhood: clean lines, gray brick and unfussy contemporary furniture. There are terraces on the upper floors that provide stunning city views.

BOWERY HOTEL BOUTIQUE HOTEL $$$

Map p412 (☎212-505-9100; www.theboweryhotel.com; 335 Bowery, btwn E 2nd & E 3rd Sts, East Village; r from $435; @; S F to 2nd Ave, 6 to Bleecker St) Pick up your red-tasselled gold room key in the hushed timber-lined lobby and admire the antique velvet chairs and faded Persian rugs. Walk over mosaic-tiled floors to your room with its huge factory windows and quality bed. Push aside the bowler-hatted 'bowery boy' teddy you'll find there, settle in and watch a movie on your 42in plasma TV.

STANDARD EAST VILLAGE HOTEL $$$

Map p412 (☎212-475-5700; www.standardhotels.com; 25 Cooper Sq/Third Ave, btwn E 5th & E 6th Sts, East Village; r $200-600; ; S R/W to 8th St-NYU, 4/6 to Bleecker St, 4/6 to Astor Pl) Rising incongruously above the low-rise East Village like an unfurled sail, Cooper Sq's gleaming white structure looms strikingly out of place. But the Standard's 144 rooms strike few jarring notes: stylish lines, Italian sheets, deep mattresses, picture windows and plenty of gadgets. The patio bars are great for warm-weather lounging, while the restaurant, **Narcissa**, cooks Californian (mains $22 to $38).

West Village, Chelsea & the Meatpacking District

JANE HOTEL HOTEL $

Map p416 (☎212-924-6700; www.thejanenyc.com; 113 Jane St, at West St, West Village; d with shared/private bath $135/295; P ❄ 📶; S A/C/E, L to 8th Ave-14th St, 1 to Christopher St-Sheridan Sq) The Jane's 50-sq-ft rooms are undeniably snug, but if you have the sea in your blood, check into this renovated red-brick gem, built for mariners in 1908 (*Titanic* survivors stayed here in 1912). The lobby is all pale-green antique tiles, stag's heads, peacocks and liveried bellboys, while the gorgeous ballroom-bar looks like it belongs in a five-star hotel.

The cheaper rooms have bunk beds and shared bathrooms, while the more expensive 'captain's cabins' come with private commodes.

CHELSEA INTERNATIONAL HOSTEL HOSTEL $

Map p420 (☎212-647-0010; www.chelseahostel.com; 251 W 20th St, btwn Seventh & Eighth Aves, Chelsea; dm $58, s from $81, d from $129; ❄ @ 📶; S 1, C/E to 23rd St; 1 to 18th St) Occupying some serious real estate in the desirable Chelsea neighborhood, this old bastion of backpackerdom is a good pick if location ranks at the top of your list.

It capitalizes on its convenience with somewhat steep prices considering the bare-bones furnishings, but it's kept clean and there's access to common rooms and kitchens where budget travelers meet and hang.

★MARLTON HOTEL HISTORIC HOTEL $$

Map p416 (☎212-321-0100; http://marltonhotel.com; 5 W 8th St, btwn Fifth Ave & MacDougal St, West Village; s/d from $275/295; 📶; S A/C/E, B/D/F/M to W 4th St-Washington Sq) Old-world Parisian style meets modern amenities at this stunning hotel located in a renovated historic building a block away from Washington Square Park. Each room features hand-selected furnishings and fixtures (think dark wood and polished brass), and a B&W checkered floor adds an elegant touch to even the most petite rooms.

Hotel-room sizes vary wildly, from typical NYC tiny to penthouse, but they all come with wi-fi, safes and fully stocked minibars.

TOWNHOUSE INN OF CHELSEA B&B $$

Map p420 (☎212-414-2323; www.townhouseinnchelsea.com; 131 W 23rd St, btwn Sixth & Seventh Aves, Chelsea; d $150-300; ❄ 📶; S 1, F/M to 23rd St) Housed in a lone 19th-century, five-story town house with exposed brick and wood floors, this 12-room B&B on busy 23rd St is a Chelsea gem. Bought in 1998 and extensively renovated (with an elevator installed), the rooms are big and welcoming, with fanciful fabrics on big brass or poster beds and TVs held in huge armoires.

There's an honor-system bar and wine and cheese from 4pm to 5pm on Fridays and Saturdays, plus a 2nd-floor, all-Victorian library that doubles as a breakfast room.

INCENTRA VILLAGE HOUSE B&B $$

Map p416 (☎212-206-0007; www.incentravillage.com; 32 Eighth Ave, btwn 12th & Jane Sts, West Village; d from $249; ❄ 📶; S A/C/E, L to 8th Ave-14th St) Boasting a great location in the West Village, these two red-brick, landmark town houses were built in 1841 and later became the city's first gay inn. Today, the 11 rooms get booked way in advance by many queer travelers; call early to get in on its gorgeous Victorian parlor and antique-filled, serious-Americana rooms.

The Garden Suite is especially picturesque as it has access to a small garden out back. The hotel advertises wi-fi that reaches all the rooms, but it's not always reliable. It does have a computer in the parlor that is free for guests to use.

CHELSEA PINES INN B&B $$

Map p416 (☎212-929-1023, 888-546-2700; www.chelseapinesinn.com; 317 W 14th St, btwn Eighth & Ninth Aves, Chelsea; s/d from $229/269; ❄ 📶; S A/C/E, L to 8th Ave-14th St) With its five walk-up floors coded to the rainbow flag, the 26-room Chelsea Pines is serious gay-and-lesbian central, but guests of all stripes are welcome. It helps to be up on your Hitchcock beauties, as vintage movie posters not only plaster the walls but rooms are named for starlets, such as Kim Novak, Doris Day and Ann-Margret.

The small lounge downstairs opens to a tiny courtyard out back, and breakfast is included in the rates.

GANSEVOORT MEATPACKING NYC HOTEL $$$

Map p416 (☎212-206-6700; www.hotelgansevoort.com; 18 Ninth Ave, at 13th St, Meatpacking District; d $365; ❄ 📶 🏊 🐾; S A/C/E, L to 8th

Ave-14th St) Coated in zinc-colored panels, the 14-floor Gansevoort has been a swank pioneer of the Meatpacking District since it opened in 2004. All 186 rooms and 21 suites are luscious and airy, with purple suede headboards, plasma-screen TVs and illuminated bathroom doors. On the rooftop are chic bar B. On Top and a skinny pool (heated and open year-round) overlooking the Hudson River.

★STANDARD BOUTIQUE HOTEL **$$$**

Map p416 (☎212-645-4646; www.standardhotels.com; 848 Washington St, at W 13th St, Meatpacking District; d from $383; ❄📶; Ⓢ A/C/E, L to 8th Ave-14th St) Straddling the High Line, this unique hotel welcomes guests with an upside-down sign, a canary-yellow revolving door and a giant gumball machine in the lobby, signalling the offbeat design within. Each of the 338 rooms has sweeping views of Manhattan and the Hudson and is filled with sunlight, making the glossy, wood-framed beds and marbled bathrooms glow.

The amenities are first rate, with a buzzing German beer garden and brasserie at street level, an ice rink in winter, and a plush nightclub on the top floor. The location is also unbeatable, with the best of NYC right outside. There's a hypermodern sister hotel (p335) in the East Village.

★HIGH LINE HOTEL HOTEL **$$$**

Map p420 (☎212-929-3888; www.thehighlinehotel.com; 180 Tenth Ave, at W 20th St, Chelsea; d from $379; Ⓢ 1, C/E to 23rd St) Serenity is assured during a stay at this neo-Gothic building, built in 1885 as the General Theological Seminary (which is still functioning in a building around the corner). The hotel's 60 rooms have solid hardwood floors, enormous beds and tastefully unique furniture, and the location is perfect for taking in the galleries of Chelsea or strolling the leafy High Line.

There's a fine lobby bar and restaurant, **Ingo's** (mains $29), while the front courtyard is a lovely place to unwind, particularly with a warm beverage from the **Intelligentsia** counter in the lobby. Guests can also borrow an elegant Shinola bicycle for a spin around town.

MARITIME HOTEL BOUTIQUE HOTEL **$$$**

Map p420 (☎212-242-4300; www.themaritimehotel.com; 363 W 16th St, at Ninth Ave, Chelsea; d $225-475; ❄📶; Ⓢ A/C/E, L to 8th Ave-14th St) This porthole-dotted white tower has been transformed into a high-end marine-themed inn by a hip team of architects. It feels like a plush *Love Boat* inside, as its 126 rooms, each with its own round window, are compact and teak paneled, with modern luxury in the form of superb beds, flat-screen TVs and rain showers in the en suites.

The low-ceilinged lobby, compartmentalized by deep couches and low bookshelves stacked with art-and-design titles, leads to a tiled bar-restaurant fronting Ninth Ave; below is Asian restaurant Tao Downtown (mains $39 to $45). Suites feature outdoor showers, access to a private terrace and sweeping Hudson views. The building was originally the site of the National Maritime Union headquarters (and then a shelter for homeless teens).

Union Square, the Flatiron District & Gramercy

MARCEL AT GRAMERCY BOUTIQUE HOTEL **$**

Map p422 (☎212-696-3800; www.themarcelatgramercy.com; 201 E 24th St, at Third Ave, Gramercy; d from $139; ❄@📶; Ⓢ 6 to 23rd St) The minimalist, 97-room Marcel is a poor-person's chic boutique, and that's not a bad thing. Rooms are simple yet modern (standard ones are walk-in-closet size), their gray-and-beige color scheme shaken up by bold, canary-yellow chesterfield bedheads. Bathrooms are uninspired but clean, while rooms on the avenue have decent views. Downstairs, the sleek lounge makes for a nifty place to unwind.

CARLTON ARMS HOTEL **$**

Map p422 (☎212-679-0680; www.carltonarms.com; 160 E 25th St, at Third Ave, Gramercy; s/d with shared bath $90/130, with private bath $130/160; ❄📶; Ⓢ 6 to 23rd St or 28th St) At this divey art hotel, every inch of the interior is a canvas scrawled with artists' musings. Murals crawl up the five flights of stairs and into each of the uniquely decorated guest rooms, ranging from fantastical to downright horrifying (the helpful staff will let you pick your room). Rooms with shared bathrooms still have a small sink.

Rooms are comfy enough and attract an eclectic mix of guests, who don't mind the rustic accommodations in exchange for big savings. There's no elevator, so prepare to work those legs. Rates drop significantly for winter travel between January and mid-March, but beware: the ancient heating system means some rooms swelter while others feel the chill at that time of year.

The Carlton Arms has gone through many incarnations during its 100 years as a hotel, from nights of subterfuge (the lobby was a speakeasy during Prohibition) to days of dereliction (as a refuge for addicts and prostitutes in the 1960s).

★**FREEHAND NEW YORK** BOUTIQUE HOTEL $$
Map p422 (☎212-475-1920; www.freehandhotels.com/new-york; 23 Lexington Ave, btwn E 23rd & E 24th Sts, Gramercy; d, tr & q from $220; ❄📶; Ⓢ6 to 23rd St) Budget-conscious style hunters will feel right at home at Freehand, hailed a New York hotel game-changer thanks to its combination of sensible pricing, group-friendly (bunk) and solo room options, and design-led common areas. The aesthetic is mid-century modern, while rooms also feature unobtrusive art murals and frills such as slippers, robes, Argan toiletries and free fruit. Note: prices can double in summer.

Rooms – all with bath – are comfortable, though nothing special: it's all the other trappings that put the icing on the cake. The 1st-floor **Studio** is a gorgeous retro-inspired space for morning coffee, breakfast or drinks. The semi-enclosed rooftop bar, **Broken Shaker** (accessed by a separate elevator), has live DJs, and there's also an upmarket **restaurant and artisan coffee shop** on the ground floor.

HOTEL HENRI HOTEL $$
Map p422 (☎844-277-9123; www.hotelhenrinyc.com; 37 W 24th St, btwn Fifth & Sixth Aves, Flatiron District; r from $247; ❄📶; ⓈF/M, N/R to 23rd St) Nearly equidistant from Chelsea and Union Square, Hotel Henri was once a serviceable but dull hotel in a great location. Its small rooms boast chic interior design (slate-gray walls, 1960s-inspired wood styling) in addition to the great service and amenities, including K-cup coffee machines and HDTVs.

★**GRAMERCY PARK HOTEL** BOUTIQUE HOTEL $$$
Map p422 (☎212-920-3300; www.gramercyparkhotel.com; 2 Lexington Ave, at 21st St, Gramercy; r from $330, ste from $1000; ❄📶; Ⓢ6, R/W to 23rd St) More than $50 million in contemporary art decorates the lounge of this stylish hotel, setting a tone of quiet opulence. Dark-wood paneling and sumptuous sofas greet guests in the lobby, with an open fire in winter, and the signature rose-and-jade color scheme is rich and alluring. Some rooms overlook the park (p168), and guests have private access.

W NEW YORK UNION SQUARE HOTEL $$$
Map p422 (☎212-253-9119; www.wnewyorkunionsquare.com; 201 Park Ave S, at 17th St, Union Square; r from $330; ❄📶🐾; ⓈL, N/Q/R, 4/5/6 to 14th St-Union Sq) Set in a 1911 one-time insurance building, the ultra-hip W demands a black wardrobe and a credit card. Boldly accented in hues of deep blue and vibrant orange, standard rooms aren't big, but they benefit from high ceilings and have all the modern bells and whistles, from 42in flat-screens to mood lighting and abstract headboards showing the Manhattan street grid.

HOTEL GIRAFFE BOUTIQUE HOTEL $$$
Map p422 (☎212-685-7700; www.hotelgiraffe.com; 365 Park Ave S, at 26th St, Gramercy; r from $289; ❄📶; ⓈR/W, 6 to 23rd St) It mightn't be particularly cool or cutting edge, but the affable, 12-floor Giraffe earns its stripes – or spots – with clean, modern rooms, complimentary continental breakfast, and free wine and cheese between 5pm and 8pm. Most of the 72 rooms have small balconies but there's also a petite rooftop garden. All rooms come with flat-screen TVs; corner suites add a living room with pull-out sofa.

Midtown

HOTEL 31 HOTEL $
Map p424 (☎212-685-3060; www.hotel31.com; 120 E 31st St, btwn Lexington & Park Aves, Midtown East; d with private/shared bathroom from $175/130; ❄📶; Ⓢ6 to 28th St) A lo-fi budget option in Midtown East, Hotel 31 has no public area or breakfast. What it does offer are simple, carpeted, homey rooms with basic cable TV, a choice of private or shared bathroom, and the ability to slumber in Midtown without breaking the bank.

KIXBY HOTEL HOTEL $
Map p424 (☎212-947-2500; www.kixby.com; 45 W 35th St, btwn Fifth & Sixth Aves, Midtown East; r $154-264; ❄@📶; ⓈN/Q/R, B/D/F/M to 34th St-Herald Sq) Amidst a new rebranding at research time, the 13-floor Kixby (formerly the Metro) offers a mix of rooms: the Pre-

mier Plus have been refurbished entirely in dignified monochrome palettes, while the older, less-expensive rooms are somewhat plain but undeniably comfortable. All have flat-screen TVs, pod-coffee makers, free wi-fi and more space than most hotels for this price. There's a small fitness room and a slick new **rooftop bar** with impressive views of the Empire State Building.

ACE HOTEL BOUTIQUE HOTEL **$$**
Map p424 (☎212-679-2222; www.acehotel.com/newyork; 20 W 29th St, btwn Broadway & Fifth Ave, Midtown West; r from $299; ❄📶; ⓈR/W to 28th St) A hit with cashed-up creatives, the Ace's standard and deluxe rooms recall upscale bachelor pads – plaid bedspreads, quirky wall stencils, leather furnishings and fridges. Some even have Gibson guitars and turntables. For cool kids with more cred than coins, there are 'mini' and 'bunk' rooms (with bunk beds), both of which can slip under $200 in winter.

The Ace vibe is upbeat and fun, with a cool-kid-packed lobby serving up live bands and DJs, superlative espresso bar Stumptown Coffee Roasters (p201) and meat-centric restaurant **Breslin** (Map p424; ☎212-679-1939; www.thebreslin.com; 16 W 29th St, btwn Broadway & Fifth Ave; lunch mains $17-29, dinner mains $29-39; ⏲7am-11pm Sun-Wed, to midnight Thu-Sat; ⓈR/W to 28th St). If you want your hotel to feel like a retreat from the chaos of Midtown, go elsewhere.

CITIZEN M HOTEL **$$**
Map p428 (☎212-461-3638; www.citizenm.com; 218 W 50th St, btwn Broadway & Eighth Ave, Midtown West; r from $250; ❄📶; Ⓢ1, C/E to 50th St) Steps from Times Square, Citizen M is a true Millennial. Communal areas are upbeat, contemporary and buzzing, and rooms are space-agey and compact. A tablet in each controls lighting, blinds and room temperature, and the plush mattresses, free movies and soothing rain showers keep guests purring. On-site perks include a gym, 24-hour canteen and flash **rooftop bar with terrace**.

YOTEL HOTEL **$$**
Map p428 (☎646-449-7700; www.yotel.com; 570 Tenth Ave, btwn 42nd & 41st Sts, Midtown West; r from $230; ❄📶; ⓈA/C/E to 42nd St-Port Authority Bus Terminal) Part futuristic spaceport, part *Austin Powers* set, this cool 713-room hotel bases its rooms on airplane classes: premium cabin (economy), first cabin (business) and suite (first) – some come with terraces and outdoor tubs. Yotel's design trademarks include adjustable beds and color-changing mood walls. Small but cleverly configured, all 'cabins' feature floor-to-ceiling windows with killer views, USB ports and device-streaming tech.

Hidden away on the 4th floor, the main hotel lobby feels like a city within a city, with an espresso bar, full-service restaurant, covered terrace bar with heaters – even an Off-Broadway entertainment space called the Green Room (ask staff about buying tickets for shows). The highlight is the city's largest outdoor hotel terrace, with a stunning skyscraper backdrop (naturally). The only downside is the grungy location, though you're still just a few blocks' walk from Times Square and Broadway.

6 COLUMBUS BOUTIQUE HOTEL **$$**
Map p428 (☎212-204-3000; www.sixtyhotels.com/6-columbus; 308 W 58th St, Midtown West; r from $238; ❄📶; ⓈA/C, B/D, 1 to 59th St-Columbus Circle) The details are nice here, like spherical moss sculptures outside the door and other touches crafted by NYC interior-designer Steven Sclaroff. Rooms are small but satisfying, with retro-cool detailing, Guy Bourdin artwork and flat-screen TVs. Luxury bedsheets and CO Bigelow toiletries crank up the luxe factor, while the intimate **rooftop bar** (5pm to midnight) begs for a romantic twilight toast.

NIGHT BOUTIQUE HOTEL **$$**
Map p428 (☎212-835-9600; www.nighthotels.com/theatre-district; 132 W 45th St, btwn Sixth & Seventh Aves, Midtown West; r from $250; ❄📶; ⓈB/D/F/M to 47th-50th Sts-Rockefeller Center) Sleeping at dark, decadent and delicious Night feels like stepping into an Anne Rice novel. From the black-and-white-only library behind the reception desk to the sleek and sexy black-and-white rooms (complete with Gothic lettering on the carpets), the stark, two-toned establishment stands out all the more in the Technicolor glare of Times Square's screens. Rooms are small but comfy.

AMERITANIA HOTEL HOTEL **$$**
Map p428 (☎212-247-5000; www.ameritanianyc.com; 230 W 54th St, at Broadway, Midtown West; r from $249; ❄📶; ⓈB/D, E to Seventh Ave, N/Q/R to 57th St-Seventh Ave) Steps away from the Theater District, this 223-room establishment delivers Midtown convenience at

midrange prices. The look is smart and modern, with mid-century accents in the lobby (like floating disc lights and retro-esque sofas), and deco-inspired patterns, lamps and armchairs in the small-yet-comfy rooms. Bathrooms are smallish but stylish, and the beds nothing short of fabulous.

Light sleepers may find the street noise a little challenging. Free wi-fi in lobby only; in the rooms, it's part of the $20-per-day 'residence fee.'

POD 51 HOTEL **$$**

Map p424 (☎212-355-0300; www.thepodhotel.com/pod-51; 230 E 51st St, btwn Second & Third Aves, Midtown East; r from $295; ❄📶; Ⓢ6 to 51st St; E/M to Lexington Ave-53rd St) A dream come true for folks who would like to live inside a cocoon – this affordable hot spot has a range of room types, most barely big enough for the bed. 'Pods' have bright bedding, tight workspaces, flat-screen TVs, iPod docking stations and 'raindrop' showerheads. In the warmer months, sip a drink on the perky rooftop deck.

★NOMAD HOTEL BOUTIQUE HOTEL **$$$**

Map p428 (☎212-796-1500; www.thenomadhotel.com; 1170 Broadway, at W 28th St, Midtown West; r/ste from $500/800; ❄📶; ⓈN/R to 28th St) 🍃 Crowned by a copper cupola, this beaux-arts dream is one of the city's hottest addresses. Rooms channel a nostalgic NYC-meets-Paris aesthetic, in which recycled hardwood floors, leather-steam-trunk minibars and Victorian clawfoot tubs mix with flat-screen TVs and high-tech LED lighting. The in-house NoMad (p198) restaurant is a coveted hangout and its bar is consistently on the World's 50 Best Bars list.

★ANDAZ FIFTH AVENUE BOUTIQUE HOTEL **$$$**

Map p424 (☎212-601-1234; https://newyork5thavenue.andaz.hyatt.com; 485 Fifth Ave, at E 41st St, Midtown East; r from $450; ❄📶; ⓈS, 4/5/6 to Grand Central-42nd St; 7 to 5th Ave; B/D/F/M to 42nd St-Bryant Park) Youthful, chic Andaz ditches stuffy reception desks for hip, mobile staff who check you in on laptops in the art-laced lobby. The hotel's 184 rooms are svelte and contemporary, with NYC-inspired details like 'Fashion District' rolling racks and subway-inspired lamps. Rooms are big for New York (from 320 sq ft), and quiet considering its location opposite New York Public Library. Minibars stock locally made treats.

★CHATWAL NEW YORK HOTEL **$$$**

Map p428 (☎212-764-6200; www.thechatwalny.com; 130 W 44th St, btwn Sixth Ave & Broadway, Midtown West; r from $595; ❄📶🏊; ⓈB/D/F/M to 42 St-Bryant Park, N/Q/R, S, 1/2/3, 7 to Times Sq-42nd St) A restored art deco jewel in the heart of Theater District, the Chatwal is as atmospheric as it is historic; the likes of Fred Astaire and Irving Berlin supped, sipped and sang in the thespian Lambs Club that once occupied this building. Luxe rooms have closets inspired by steamer cabin trunks and vintage Broadway posters on the walls, but also mod-cons like TVs in bathroom mirrors and iPad room controls.

★QUIN HOTEL **$$$**

Map p428 (☎212-245-7846; www.thequinhotel.com; 101 W 57th St, at Sixth Ave, Midtown West; d from $469; ❄📶; ⓈF to 57th St; N/Q/R/W to 57th St-7th Ave) The Quin is an opulent, modern hotel with the bones of a grand old dame. In the 1920s it was the storied Buckingham, which hosted musicians and artists like Georgia O'Keefe and Marc Chagall. Today it keeps the artistic connection alive with rotating exhibitions from artists-in-residence and a 15ft video wall showcasing installations. Rooms are exceedingly comfortable and elegantly restrained.

FOUR SEASONS HOTEL **$$$**

Map p424 (☎212-758-5700; www.fourseasons.com/newyork; 57 E 57th St, btwn Madison & Park Aves, Midtown East; r from $1195; ❄@📶; ⓈN/W/R to 5th Ave-59th St; 4/5 to Lexington Ave & 59th St) Housed in a 52-floor tower designed by IM Pei, the five-star Four Seasons delivers seamless luxury. Even the smallest of the neutrally hued rooms are generously sized, with spacious closets and HD TVs in the Tuscan-marble bathrooms. The views over Central Park from the 'Park View' rooms are practically unfair, with *oohs* and *aahs* also induced by the hotel's esteemed spa.

PLAZA HOTEL **$$$**

Map p424 (☎888-240-7775, 212-759-3000; www.theplazany.com; 768 5th Ave, at Central Park S; r from $840; ❄📶; ⓈN/R to Fifth Ave-59th St) Set in a landmark French Renaissance-style building, the iconic Plaza's 282 guest rooms are a regal affair, with sumptuous Louis XV–style furniture and 24-carat gold-plated bathroom faucets. On-site drawcards include the **Guerlain Spa** and fabled **Palm**

Court, the latter famed for its stained-glass ceiling and afternoon tea. (Less enticing is the hotel's daily $14.95 wi-fi surcharge.)

IBEROSTAR 70 PARK HOTEL $$$

Map p424 (212-973-2400; www.iberostar.com; 70 Park Ave, at E 38th St, Midtown East; r from $339; ; S, 4/5/6, 7 to Grand Central-42nd St) Beyond the plush and cozy lobby lounge, adorned with a limestone fireplace, this slumber number offers 205 gleaming rooms with comfy plush beds (featuring Frette linens) and a palate of rich golds and greys. Adjoining rooms can be turned into large suites for families. Pets are welcome, staff are friendly and spa treatments are offered in-room. Bliss.

KNICKERBOCKER BOUTIQUE HOTEL $$$

Map p428 (212-204-4980; www.theknickerbocker.com; 6 Times Sq, at W 42nd St; d from $367; ; A/C/E, N/Q/R/W, S, 1/2/3, 7 to Times Sq-42nd St) Originally opened in 1906 by John Jacob Astor, the 330-room Knickerbocker exudes a restrained, monochromatic elegance. Rooms are dashingly chic, hushed and modern, decked out with adjustable 55in flat-screen TV, bedside tablet and USB charging ports, as well as Carrara-marble bathrooms. Triple-glazed windows keep it wonderfully serene inside, but the Times Square location means perpetual chaos right outside the front door.

INK48 BOUTIQUE HOTEL $$$

Map p428 (212-757-0088; www.ink48.com; 653 Eleventh Ave, at W 48th St, Midtown West; r from $350; ; C/E to 50th St) The Kimpton hotel group has braved Midtown's wild far west with Ink48, perched on the subway-starved edge of Manhattan. Occupying a converted printing house, the compensation is sweet: stellar skyline and Hudson River views, chic contemporary rooms, a boutique spa and restaurant, and a stunning rooftop bar. Topping it off is easy walking access to Hell's Kitchen's thriving restaurant scene.

Dog owners will appreciate the free bowl of kibble and water that's just outside the lobby (pets stay for free). The hotel's daily $30 amenities fee includes wi-fi, free phone calls and a $10 daily food credit for room service or the in-house restaurant.

MUSE NEW YORK BOUTIQUE HOTEL $$$

Map p428 (212-485-2400; www.themusehotel.com; 130 W 46th St, btwn Sixth & Seventh Aves, Midtown West; d from $333; ; B/D/F/M to 47th-50th Sts-Rockefeller Center) Very near the theater district, the Muse is a shimmering 200-room high-rise brought to you by the Kimpton group, which is famed for its boutique hotels.

A recent refurb has their rooms done up in bold blacks with colorful pop-art touches and Frette linens. Staff are generally helpful and added perks include evening wine reception, complimentary bike usage and in-room spa services.

The daily $30 amenities fee includes wi-fi and a $10 credit at the hotel bar.

Upper East Side

★**LOWELL** BOUTIQUE HOTEL $$$

Map p430 (212-838-1400; www.lowellhotel.com; 28 East 63rd St, at Madison Ave; d/ste from $915/2020; ; N/R/W to 5th Ave) On a tree-lined residential street off Madison Ave, this refined boutique hotel feels much smaller than its 74 rooms might suggest. It was opened as an apart-hotel in 1927 and modernized in 2017 by Obama White House designer Michael Smith: intimacy now prevails. Rooms feel like small getaways dressed in muted grey and beige with contemporary marble-tiled bathrooms and (some) with working fireplaces.

A profound scent of nest bamboo pervades throughout. Most folks prefer the 4th floor, with windows in direct sight of the 63rd St treeline. Beyond the elegant library and sexy bar (Jacques), the classic French fine-dining Majorelle has received a kick in the kitchen by upstart Belgium chef Emmanuel Niess and is well worth a sophisticated evening out (two/three/five courses $105/122/155). The Lowell has hogged *Travel+Leisure* World's Best Awards for top reader-voted hotel in New York City two years running.

★**MARK** DESIGN HOTEL $$$

Map p430 (212-744-4300; www.themarkhotel.com; 25 E 77th St, at Madison Ave; d/ste from $895/1275; ; 6 to 77th St) French designer Jacques Grange left his artful mark on the Mark, with bold geometric shapes and rich, playful forms that greet visitors in the lobby (the zebra-striped marble floor, which carries on to the room bathrooms, is pure eye candy). Upstairs, lavishly renovated rooms and multi-bedroom suites are equally stylish, boasting the likes of custom-made furnishings and luxury local linen.

LOEWS REGENCY HOTEL HOTEL $$$

Map p430 (212-759-4100; www.loewshotels.com/regency-hotel; 540 Park Ave, btwn E 61st & 62nd Sts; d $300-600, ste $500-4000; ; N/R, 4/5/6 to Lexington Ave-59th St, F, Q to Lexington Ave-63rd St) This fabled hotel is prime territory for Park Ave shoppers. Guests even get 15% off at nearby Bloomingdales (25% during the holidays!). Inside, the hotel is designed to feel like an Upper East Side apartment block. Its 379 rooms – standard clock in huge at 325 to 375-sq-ft – come with roomy desks and elegant marble bathrooms with pro-style hair-dryers. Some rooms have balconies.

Upper West Side

HOSTELLING INTERNATIONAL NEW YORK HOSTEL $

Map p432 (HI; 212-932-2300; www.hinewyork.org; 891 Amsterdam Ave, at W 103rd St; dm $49-99; ; 1 to 103rd St) This red-brick mansion from the 1880s houses HI's 734 well-scrubbed and maintained bunks. It's rather 19th-century industrial, but benefits include good public areas, a backyard (that sees barbecue action in the summer), a communal kitchen, a cafe and environmentally friendly initiatives throughout. There are loads of activities on offer, from walking tours to club nights. It's short-staffed, however, and reception staff can be stubborn.

There are three attractive private rooms with private bathrooms, too. The hostel is alcohol-free.

YMCA HOSTEL $

Map p432 (212-912-2625; www.ymcanyc.org; 5 W 63rd St, at Central Park West; s/d/tr/q without bath from $90/115/125/150, d from $125; ; A/C, B/D, 1 to 59th St-Columbus Circle) Just steps from Central Park, this grand art deco building has several floors – 8th to the 13th – of basic but clean rooms, most with shared facilities. Some renovated doubles on floors 12 and 13 have en suites. Guests can access a large, old-school gym with racquetball courts, a pool and a sauna.

Four other YMCAs in town offer accommodation, including branches in Midtown, the Upper East Side and Harlem.

★ARTHOUSE HOTEL NYC BOUTIQUE HOTEL $$

Map p432 (212-362-1100; www.arthousehotelnyc.com; 2178 Broadway, at W 77th St; d/ste from $250/350; ; 1 to 79th St) This art-focused boutique hotel mixes vintage furnishings with contemporary industrial design. The dapper lounge and bar areas on the ground floor are stylish spaces to decamp after a day spent exploring. Above, 291 airy rooms benefit from lots of natural light and restrained decor. Flickers of mid-century design are complemented by contemporary amenities like coffeemakers, flat-screen TVs and marble bathrooms.

The penthouse suites have furnished private terraces and extravagant Manhattan views, but if you can't afford that, there's also a public outdoor terrace on the 16th floor, which hosts seasonal pop-up bars. Its latest renovation will see the hotel lobby's Warhols and Basquiats mingle with the wares of Upper West Side artists.

HOTEL BEACON HOTEL $$

Map p432 (212-787-1100, reservations 800-572-4969; www.beaconhotel.com; 2130 Broadway, btwn W 74th & 75th Sts; d from $250; ; 1/2/3 to 72nd St) Adjacent to the Beacon Theatre, this family favorite offers a winning mix of attentive service, comfortable rooms and convenient location. The Beacon has 278 rooms (some of which are multibedroom suites) decorated in muted shades of Pottery Barn green. The units are well maintained and quite roomy; all come with coffeemakers and kitchenettes. Amenities include a bar, a gym, outsourced cycling classes and a self-service laundry.

Upper stories on the east side of the building have views of Central Park in the distance. It's a good deal, and steep discounts can be found off-season.

HOTEL BELLECLAIRE HOTEL $$

Map p432 (212-362-7700; www.hotelbelleclaire.com; 250 W 77th St, at Broadway; d from $200; ; 1 to 79th St) This landmark beaux-arts building, designed by architect Emory Roth in 1903, houses a 249-room hotel that offers good value for the location. Contemporary rooms with pops of color and modern furnishings come in a variety of sizes and configurations, with some units bigger or with better daylight than others; beds sizes range from full (double) to king. Note that some rooms face interior alleyways.

EMPIRE HOTEL HOTEL $$$

Map p432 (212-265-7400; www.empirehotelnyc.com; 44 W 63rd St, at Broadway; d from $340; ; S1 to 66th St-Lincoln Center) The bones are all that remain of the original Empire, just across the street from Lincoln Center.

Wholesale renovations have dressed this hotel in earthy tones and contemporary stylings complete with a canopied pool deck, a huge Empire Rooftop bar (p239) and a sexy two-story lobby lounge with a sweeping staircase and floor-to-ceiling drapes. Its 420 rooms feature brightly hued walls with plush dark-leather furnishings.

Harlem & Upper Manhattan

★HARLEM FLOPHOUSE GUESTHOUSE $

Map p434 (347-632-1960; www.harlemflophouse.com; 242 W 123rd St, btwn Adam Clayton Powell Jr & Frederick Douglass Blvds, Harlem; d with shared bath $99-150; ; SA/B/C/D, 2/3 to 125th St) Rekindle Harlem's Jazz Age in this atmospheric 1890s town house, its four nostalgic rooms decked out with brass beds and vintage radios. It feels like a step back in time, which also means shared bathrooms, no air-con and no TVs. One of the downstairs lounges doubles as a music room that sometimes hosts intimate concerts.

Last but not least is friendly house cat Phoebe, who completes the homely, welcoming vibe. For longer stays, the owner also rents out a spacious basement suite (per night $175) with double and single bed plus an ensuite bathroom – contact directly to enquire.

ALOFT HARLEM HOTEL $$

Map p434 (212-749-4000; www.aloftharlem.com; 2296 Frederick Douglass Blvd, btwn 123rd & 124th Sts, Harlem; d from $249; ; SA/C, B/D, 2/3 to 125th St) Designed for younger travelers, Aloft channels a luxury vibe but at accessible prices. Guest rooms are snug (285 sq ft) but chic, with crisp white linens, fluffy comforters and colorful striped bolsters. The modern bathrooms are small (no tubs) but highly functional and feature amenities courtesy of Bliss, the upscale spa chain.

The basement lounge with pool tables can get boisterous, but it'll be stumbling distance to your room. All around, Aloft is convenient (the Apollo Theater and the bustling 125th St commercial district are nearby) and a good deal.

Brooklyn

LEFFERTS MANOR BED & BREAKFAST B&B $

Map p440 (347-351-9065; www.leffertsmanorbedandbreakfast.com; 80 Rutland Rd, btwn Flatbush & Bedford Aves, Prospect Lefferts Gardens; r $119-189; ; SB, Q to Prospect Park) Six sunny rooms in this classic Brooklyn brownstone feature tiled closed fireplaces, subtle color palettes and historically styled decor. Five rooms share two gleaming-white bathrooms, while the Parlor Suite has a private toilet and a clawfoot tub. Minimum stays usually apply but get in touch as one-night visits may be possible ($30 fee). Optional continental breakfast. Adult guests only.

The owners also have rooms available in two similar properties nearby, as well as two apartments with full kitchens in Fort Greene.

Downtown Manhattan is only 30 minutes away by subway.

NY MOORE HOSTEL HOSTEL $

Map p436 (347 227 8634; https://nymoorehostel.com; 179 Moore St; dm $40-46, tr $128; ; SL to Morgan Ave, J, M to Flushing Ave) Splashed with murals inside and out, NY Moore blends right in to this edgy corner of East Williamsburg. Clean dorm rooms come in a variety of sizes, including women-only dorms and private triples. The baroque-style lounge and business center are perks, and there's a sizeable kitchen. The 24-hour reception and personable staff make it feel secure as well as friendly.

POD BROOKLYN HOTEL HOTEL $

Map p436 (844-763-7666; www.thepodhotel.com/pod-brooklyn; 247 Metropolitan Ave, btwn Bedford & Driggs Aves, Williamsburg; d from $139; ; SL to Bedford Ave) Rooms are dinky, but in this well-designed hotel amenities are packed into tight spaces: safes beneath beds, retractable clothes hooks, and wet-room shower-toilets. Superb for solo travelers and couples who just want a contemporary crash pad; less enjoyable for anyone tall. For elbow room, head to the rooftop bar or simply step outside to central Williamsburg's bars and restaurants.

THE L HOTEL
HOTEL $

Map p440 (☑718-788-1801; www.choicehotels. com; 135 32nd St, btwn Third & Fourth Aves, Greenwood Heights; d from $119; ※⌖; ⑤D, N/R to 36th St) Soundproofing could be better and the decor's a little dated, but the well-kept compact rooms at The L Hotel benefit from comfy beds, complimentary breakfast, writing desks and showers with good water pressure, as well as responsive reception staff. For a reasonably priced room within a five-minute walk of the subway, The L won't make your trip but it ain't half bad.

HENRY NORMAN HOTEL
BOUTIQUE HOTEL $$

(☑718-989-1574; www.henrynormanhotel.com; 251 N Henry St, btwn Norman & Meserole Aves, Greenpoint; loft/apt from $237/360; ※⌖; ☐B48 to Nassau Ave/Monitor St, ⑤G to Nassau Ave) Set in a former 19th-century warehouse, this striking brick building (once home to artists' lofts) is styled like a love letter to Brooklyn. High-ceilinged rooms feel bohemian but debonair, with hardwood floors, dove-gray sofas, brass lamps and vivid artwork throughout – all of it made by the same Brooklyn artist.

Scour the website for advance discounted rates.

MCCARREN HOTEL & POOL
BOUTIQUE HOTEL $$

Map p436 (☑718-218-7500; www.mccarrenhotel.com; 160 N 12th St, btwn Bedford Ave & Berry St, Williamsburg; d from $286; ※⌖⌖; ⑤L to Bedford Ave, G to Nassau Ave) The tropical-style pool area, where patrons armed with cocktails drape themselves across loungers, is the prime lure of this swish, mural-clad hotel. Rooms (most with balconies) are attired like a hip friend's lounge – velvety sofas, vinyl, the odd guitar – while a rooftop vegan restaurant and jazz bar mean you can kick off your evening on-site. Note: the pool's summer only.

WYTHE HOTEL
BOUTIQUE HOTEL $$

Map p436 (☑718-460-8000; www.wythehotel. com; 80 Wythe Ave, at N 11th St, Williamsburg; d from $329; ※⌖; ⑤L to Bedford Ave, G to Nassau Ave) Set in a converted 1901 factory, the red-brick Wythe (pronounced 'white') Hotel brings a dash of high design to Williamsburg. Exposed brick and 13ft timber ceilings allow the building's history to breathe. Meanwhile beds fashioned from reclaimed wood and a faintly nautical theme conspire with nostalgic paisley, leather and custom-made wallpaper to create a space that feels rough-hewn but elegant.

AT HOME IN BROOKLYN
B&B $$

Map p440 (☑718-622-5292; www.athomein brooklyn.com; 15 Prospect Park West, btwn President & Carroll Sts, Park Slope; d with shared bath $175-325; ※⌖; ⑤2/3 Grand Army Plaza) Inside a swanky Brooklyn address is a guesthouse of great sophistication. Each room is elegantly furnished with painted armoires, wicker chairs and rugs, plus quality double- and king-sized mattresses. Common areas are lined with books, and a chivalrous host ushers in guests and prepares a superb continental breakfast spread. In a soothing location on the northwestern fringe of Prospect Park.

THE BROOKLYN
BOUTIQUE HOTEL $$

(☑718-789-1500; www.thebrooklynny.com; 1199 Atlantic Ave, btwn Bedford & Nostrand Aves, Bed-Stuy; d from $180; ※⌖; ⑤A/C to Franklin Ave) For travelers unperturbed by the dreary location next to a roaring main road, The Brooklyn is a smart, boutique hotel offering considerable luxury for the price tag. Rooms are large with tasteful bare-brick, high ceilings and feature walls paying homage to Brooklyn industry. Spacious, spa-style bathrooms have high-pressure showers and the beds offer cloud-like comfort. Book ahead online for great savings.

EVEN HOTEL
BOUTIQUE HOTEL $$

Map p443 (☑718-552-3800; www.evenhotels. com; 46 Nevins St, at Schermerhorn St, Downtown Brooklyn; d from $240; ※⌖; ⑤2/3, 4/5 to Nevins St, A/C, G to Hoyt-Schermerhorn) From the lemon-mint infused water at reception to the fitness equipment in every room, EVEN aims to leave guests refreshed. Each of the rooms has a yoga mat, stability ball, mood-changing colored lights and workout routines on video. The wellness theme continues with a 24-hour gym and nutritionally sound breakfasts like avocado-egg wraps (from $10).

The central location in Downtown Brooklyn is super convenient for subway stops.

NU HOTEL
HOTEL $$

Map p443 (☑718-852-8585; www.nuhotelbrook lyn.com; 85 Smith St, at Atlantic Ave, Boerum Hill; d from $209; Ⓟ※@⌖; ⑤F, G to Bergen

St) Brooklyn-themed adornments, upcycled teak furnishings and occasionally eyebrow-raising artwork bestow industrial style on rooms at NU. The location, on the border of Boerum Hill and Downtown, is handy and free bikes are a convenient perk. Groups of four can consider the 'Bunkbed' suite, with a queen and twin bunks, while art lovers will appreciate the mural-washed 'NU Perspective' rooms.

WYNDHAM GARDEN BROOKLYN SUNSET PARK BUSINESS HOTEL **$$**

Map p440 (718-972-0900; www.wyndhamhotels.com; 457 39th St, btwn Fourth & Fifth Aves, Sunset Park; d from $269; ; S D, N to 36th St) Positioned between two leafy-green neighborhood highlights, Sunset Park (p270) and Green-Wood Cemetery (p271), this likeable chain hotel has comfortable, contemporary rooms and helpful reception staff. Flashes of moss green and frosted glass give lodgings a soothing air, and pricier 'executive' rooms peep out towards the Manhattan skyline. Early-bird and online rates slash the price considerably, so book ahead.

WILLIAMSBURG HOTEL BOUTIQUE HOTEL **$$$**

Map p436 (718-362-8100; www.thewilliamsburghotel.com; 96 Wythe Ave, at N 10th St, Williamsburg; d from $396; ; S L to Bedford Ave) Just two blocks from the water, this eight-story, industrial-chic hotel is blessed with spectacular river and Manhattan views. It's worth paying extra for one of the 'terrace' rooms on the north side, which give you an unbroken view of the Empire State Building, the Chrysler Building and the Upper East Side from your artificial-grass-carpeted balcony (some have swing chairs).

Floor-to-ceiling windows and glassed-in showers with bright subway tiles make the smallish rooms feel more open. Minibars, leather headboards, safes and essential-oil amenities by local maker Apotheke all come standard. There's a rooftop bar in the shape of a classic NYC water tower (open 6pm to 4am Wednesday to Saturday) and an outdoor rooftop swimming pool, plus free pushbikes for cruising Williamsburg.

ALOFT NEW YORK BROOKLYN BOUTIQUE HOTEL **$$$**

Map p443 (718-256-3833; www.aloftnewyorkbrooklyn.com; 216 Duffield St, btwn Willoughby & Fulton Sts, Downtown Brooklyn; d $200-490; ; S 2/3 to Hoyt St; A/C, F to Jay St-MetroTech) Beyond the steely grey industrial-style lobby, rooms at Aloft are nicely soundproofed with flat-screen TVs, good beds, leatherette seats and old-school pictures of Brooklyn ornamenting the walls. Everything's pint-sized, from the rooftop lounge to the breakfast bar (complete with cold brew on tap), but comfortable and contemporary.

It's walking distance from the restaurants and bars of Cobble Hill and Fort Greene. There's offsite parking ($55) available.

Queens

★LOCAL HOSTEL **$**

Map p446 (347-738-5251; www.thelocalny.com; 13-02 44th Ave, btwn 11th & 21st Sts, Long Island City; dm/d $50/159; ; S E/M to Court Sq-23rd St) With clean-cut, comfortable en-suite doubles and dorms (male, female and mixed, all with under-bed storage) and common areas, the Local is a great budget base. The cafe morphs into a bar at night, quirky art is shown next to reception, the kitchen is properly equipped and there's usually an evening event (movie nights, live music, pub quizzes).

Friendly staff are helpful in highlighting some of NYC's lesser-known gems. Don't miss the view from the rooftop, which hosts DJ parties in summer.

BORO HOTEL DESIGN HOTEL **$**

Map p446 (718-433-1375; www.borohotel.com; 38-28 27th St, btwn 38th & 39th Aves, Long Island City; d from $199; P ; S N/Q to 39th Ave, W, 7 to Queensboro Plaza) The Boro offers minimalist city luxe (quality linens, plush robes, tubs in the suites) for far less than you'd pay in Manhattan – with the benefit of glittering skyline views from the floor-to-ceiling windows. Rooms have high ceilings and hardwood floors; some standards have patio nooks. There's a fitness room, and the better-than-average continental breakfasts feature flaky croissants and Greek yogurt.

Q4 HOSTEL **$**

Map p446 (718-706-7700; www.q4hotel.com; 29-09 Queens Plaza N, Long Island City; dm/d from $33/130; ; S 7, N/Q to Queensboro Plaza, E/M/R to Queens Plaza) Cheap, clean and steps from the subway station – it's hard to argue with this no-frills hostel splattered with Keith Haring–inspired murals. It has no phone (very millennial!) and rooms can be a little rattly from the elevated train going by out front. Dorms have between two beds (fine) and eight (cramped); private queen rooms are an option.

★TWA HOTEL BOUTIQUE HOTEL **$$**

(☎212-806-9000; www.twahotel.com; JFK Airport, access from Terminal 5; d from $249; P ❄ 📶 🏊; S A to Howard Beach, E, J/Z to Sutphin Blvd-Archer Ave then Airtrain) 🍃 Far be it from us to suggest that you come to NYC and stay at JFK (but that's just what we're going to do!). Superstar neo-futuristic architect Eero Saarinen's landmark 1962 TWA Flight Center has been revamped into a unique, LEED-certified time capsule of a hotel that screams Gilded Age of Travel.

Highlights and details are too numerous to comprehensively list. From one of NYC's coolest pools (a rooftop plane-spotter paradise overlooking runways 4L and 22R; public day passes $25 to $50) to Connie (a 1958 Lockheed Constellation propeller-driven, four-engine airliner that once ran drugs to Colombia but is now an imaginative cocktail bar), this is retro-hipster-traveler madness at its finest. It doubles as a virtual museum: original Solari split-flaps display flight info; several exhibits present vintage TWA paraphernalia; Saarinen's womb chairs, tulip lights and tables are everywhere; and minibars tempt with 1960s-era products (Sugar Daddies, TAB sodas, mini Etch A Sketches). Intelligentsia coffee, Jean-Georges Vongerichten's Paris Café and the world's largest hotel fitness center (not to mention Saarinen's incredible right angle-less building itself) round out this step back in time.

Book a night or go for a time slot (7am to 11am, 10am to 4pm, noon to 6pm for $149; 8am to 8pm for $209). The rooms? Who cares!

CAMP ROCKAWAY CAMPGROUND **$$**

(☎347-916-6199; www.camprockaway.com; 157 Rockaway Beach Blvd, Jacob Riis Park, Rockaway; tents weekday/weekend $195/245; ⏲Memorial Day-Oct 15; 📶; 🚌Q35 & Q22 to Jacob Riis Park, ⛴Sat, Sun & holidays from Pier 11 (Wall St) to Riis Landing (Rockaway)) This seasonal pop-up glampground is an idyllic beach escape from the Big Apple sitting on Riis Beach (p307) in the courtyard of the Jacob Riis bathhouse from Memorial Day to October 15. The safari-style canvas tents sit on raised wood platforms that extend to provide a deck and two chairs. Facilities include a picnic area, a camp store, hammocks, games and a communal fire pit.

THE COLLECTIVE PAPER FACTORY HOTEL **$$**

Map p446 (☎718-392-7200; www.thecollective.com/locations/paper-factory; 37-06 36th St, at 37th Ave, Long Island City; d $239-299; ❄ 📶 🐾; S M, R to 36th St) Originally a radio factory (paper came later), this five-story building in semi-industrial Long Island City now houses a whimsical gem of a hotel that underwent a complete revamp throughout 2021.

There's a hint of sophistication in the industrial-chic rooms that boast a vintage aesthetic without sacrificing comfort, including modern beds, good showers and antique film props from the previous owner's personal collection.

Z NYC HOTEL HOTEL **$$$**

Map p446 (☎877-256-5556, 212-319-7000; www.zhotelny.com; 11-01 43rd Ave, at 11th St, Long Island City; d $350-450; ❄ 📶; S F to 21st-Queensbridge, E/M to Court Sq-23rd St) In the industrial streets beneath the iconic Silvercup Studios sign, this design-savvy tower delivers cozy accommodation and jaw-dropping views of Manhattan. The 100 renovated rooms are snug but stylish, in dark, purple accents, and the heated bathroom floors and oversized showerheads are nice extras. There's a cellar cocktail bar with a basic menu and discounted rooms can be found online.

An additional mandatory 'Experience Fee' of $30 entitles guests to free Manhattan transport (perhaps changing to the subway station only in the future), upgraded continental breakfast, free international phone calls, wi-fi, and bike rental in good weather.

Understand New York City

History

This is the tale of a city that never sleeps, of a kingdom where tycoons and world leaders converge. From its original inhabitants, the Lenape people, to the difficult birth of the modern city, NYC has seen the highest highs and the most devastating lows. Yet through it all, it continues to reach for the sky (both figuratively and literally).

Living Off The Land

Long before the days of European conquest, the swath that would eventually become NYC belonged to Native Americans known as the Lenape (Original People), who resided in a series of seasonal campsites. They lived up and down the eastern seaboard, along the signature shoreline, and on hills and in valleys sculpted by glaciers after the Ice Age left New York with glacial debris (now called Hamilton Heights and Bay Ridge). Glaciers scoured off soft rock, leaving behind Manhattan's stark rock foundations of gneiss and schist. Around 11,000 years before the first Europeans sailed through the Narrows, the Lenape people foraged, hunted and fished the regional bounty. Spear points, arrowheads, bone heaps and shell mounds testify to their presence. Some of their pathways still lie beneath streets such as Broadway. In the Lenape language of Munsee, the term *Manhattan* may have translated as 'hilly island.' Others trace the meaning to a more colorful phrase: 'place of general inebriation.'

A Rude Awakening

The Lenape people lived here undisturbed until European explorers muscled in, firstly via French vessel *La Dauphine*, piloted by Florentine Giovanni da Verrazzano. He explored the Upper Bay in 1524, deemed it a 'very beautiful lake' and, while anchored at Staten Island, attempted to kidnap some of the Native Americans he encountered. This began several decades of European explorers raiding Lenape villages, and cultivated the Lenape's deep mistrust of outsiders. By the time the Dutch West India Company employee Henry Hudson arrived in 1609, encounters with Native Americans were often dichotomized into two crude stories that alternated between 'delightful primitives' and 'brutal savages.'

TIMELINE

c CE 1500

About 15,000 Native Americans, including the feuding Iroquois and Algonquins, live in 80 sites around the island; their history can be traced to several millennia earlier.

1625–26

The population grows to 200 at the settlement of New Amsterdam, and the Dutch West India Company imports slaves from Africa to work in the fur trade and construction.

1646

The Dutch found the village of Breuckelen on the East River shore of Long Island, naming it after Breukelen in the Netherlands; it remains an independent city until 1898.

Buying Manhattan

The Dutch West India Company sent 110 settlers to begin a trading post here in 1624. They settled in Lower Manhattan and called their colony New Amsterdam, touching off bloody battles with the unshakable Lenape. It all came to a head in 1626, when the colony's first governor, Peter Minuit, became the city's first – but certainly not the last – unscrupulous property developer, by purchasing Manhattan's 14,000 acres from the Lenape for 60 guilders ($24), some beads and various European tools. There are various theories about the Lenape perspective: some historians argue that the sale was an attempt at a strategic alliance, others suggest that the deal was an attempt to retain a stake in Manhattan (it may have been brokered by a band of Lenape who lived further north).

Peg Leg, Iron Fist

Following the purchase of Manhattan in 1626, the colony quickly fell into disrepair under the governance of Willem Kieft. Peter Stuyvesant stepped in and busily set about fixing the demoralized settlement, making peace with the Lenape, establishing markets and a night watch, repairing the fort, digging a canal (under the current Canal St) and authorizing a municipal wharf. His vision of an orderly and prosperous trading port was partially derived from his previous experience as governor of Curaçao. The burgeoning sugar economy in the Caribbean inspired an investment in slave trading that soon boosted New Amsterdam's slave workforce to 20% of the population. After long service, some were partially freed and given 'Negroe Lots' near today's Greenwich Village, the Lower East Side and City Hall.

The Dutch West India Company encouraged the fruitful connection to plantation economies on the islands, and issued advertisements and offered privileges to attract merchants to the growing port. Although these 'liberties' did not at first extend to the Jews who fled the Spanish Inquisition, the Dutch West India Company turned Stuyvesant's intolerance around. By the 1650s, warehouses, workshops and gabled houses were spreading back from the dense establishments at the river's edge on Pearl St.

By 1664, the English showed up in battleships, ready for a fight. Stuyvesant was tired, though, and avoided bloodshed by surrendering without a shot. King Charles II promptly renamed the colony after his brother, the Duke of York. New York became a prosperous British port with a population of 11,000 by the mid-1700s. The city grew in prominence as the change point for the exchange of slaves and goods between worlds. This period of prominence was short lived.

NYC Names & Their Dutch Origins

Gramercy: Krom Moerasje ('crooked lake')

Coney Island: Konijneneiland ('rabbits island')

Yonkers: jonk heer ('young gentleman')

Bowery: bouwerij (old-fashioned word for 'farm')

Bronx: named for Jonas Bronck

Brooklyn: after Dutch town Breukelen

1664

New Amsterdam is ceded to England and renamed New York; it will be regained by the Dutch and returned to England a decade later.

1754

The first institution of higher learning, King's College, is founded by royal charter from George II. After the American Revolution, it's reborn as Columbia University.

1776

American colonies sign the *Declaration of Independence* on July 4. Figures who help create this document include John Hancock, Samuel Adams and Benjamin Franklin.

1784

Alexander Hamilton founds the Bank of New York, with holdings of $500,000. Almost a decade later, it will become the first corporate stock to be traded on the NYSE.

Press Freedom & the Great Negro Plot

Rising tensions were evident in the colonial press, as John Peter Zenger's *New York Weekly Journal* flayed the king and royal governor so regularly that the authorities tried to convict Zenger for seditious libel in 1733. He was acquitted and that was the beginning of what we know today as 'freedom of the press.'

New York City was the first capital of the United States – George Washington took his first presidential oath at Federal Hall in 1789.

In 1741, a spate of fires occurred across the city, including one at Fort George, then home of Lieutenant Governor George Clarke. The blazes were widely blamed on African-American slaves, and rumors quickly spread of a plan by rebellious blacks and poorer white settlers to burn down New York City. Despite contradictory accounts and a lack of solid evidence, the so-called Great Negro Plot led to the arrest and execution of numerous slaves and their alleged co-conspirators.

Revolution & War

Patriots clashed in public spaces with Tories, who were loyal to the king, while Lieutenant Colonel Alexander Hamilton, an intellectual, became a fierce anti-British organizer. Citizens fled the city, sensing the oncoming war, and revolutionary battle began in August of 1776, when General George Washington's army lost about a quarter of its men in just a couple of days. He retreated, and fire encompassed much of the colony. But soon the British left and Washington's army reclaimed their city. After a series of celebrations, banquets and fireworks at Bowling Green, General Washington bade farewell to his officers at what is now the Fraunces Tavern Museum and retired as commander in chief.

However in 1789 the retired general found himself addressing crowds at Federal Hall, gathered to witness his presidential inauguration. Alexander Hamilton, meanwhile, began rebuilding New York and became Washington's secretary of the treasury, working to establish the New York Stock Exchange. But people distrusted a capitol located adjacent to the financial power of Wall St merchants, and New Yorkers lost the seat of the presidency to Philadelphia shortly thereafter.

Population Bust, Infrastructure Boom

The 19th century brought with it plenty of setbacks: the Great Fire of 1835, the bloody Draft Riots of 1863, massive cholera epidemics, rising tensions among 'old' and new immigrants, and the serious poverty and crime of Five Points, the city's first slum, located where Chinatown now lies. Eventually, though, the city became prosperous again and found resources to build mighty public works. The great Croton Aqueduct system relieved the thirst of city-dwellers and helped to stamp out the cholera and yellow fever epidemics that were sweeping the town. In a

1789

Following a seven-day procession from his home in Mount Vernon, George Washington is inaugurated at Federal Hall as the country's first president.

1811

Manhattan's grid plan is developed by Mayor DeWitt Clinton, which leads to reshaping the city by leveling hills, filling in swamps and laying out plans for future streets.

1853

The State Legislature authorizes the allotment of public lands, which removes 17,000 potential building sites from the real-estate market for what will later become Central Park.

1863

The Civil War Draft Riots erupt in New York, the days of violence ending only when President Lincoln dispatches combat troops from the Federal Army to restore order.

bold and expensive endeavor, Irish immigrants helped dig a 363-mile 'ditch' – the Erie Canal – linking the Hudson River with Lake Erie. The canal's chief backer, Mayor DeWitt Clinton (and source of the project's nickname, 'Clinton's Folly') celebrated the waterway by ceremonially pouring a barrel of Erie water into the sea. Clinton was also the mastermind behind the modern-day grid system of Manhattan's street layout – a plan created by his commission to organize the city in the face of an oncoming population explosion.

And there was yet another grand project afoot – one to boost the health of the people crammed into tiny tenement apartments – in the form of an 843-acre public park. Begun in 1855 in an area so far uptown that some immigrants kept pigs, sheep and goats there, Central Park was both a vision of green reform and a boon to real-estate speculation.

Another vision was realized by German-born engineer John Roebling, who sought a solution to a series of winter freezes that had shut down the ferry system connecting downtown Manhattan to Brooklyn, then an independent city. He designed a soaring symphony of spun wire and Gothic arches to span the East River, and his Brooklyn Bridge accelerated the fusion of the neighboring cities.

By the turn of the 20th century, elevated trains carried one million people a day in and out of the city. Rapid transit opened up areas of the Bronx and Upper Manhattan, spurring mini building booms in areas near the lines. At this point, the city was simply overflowing with the masses of immigrants arriving from southern Italy and Eastern Europe, who had boosted the metropolis's population to around three million. The journey from immigrant landing stations at Castle Garden and Ellis Island led straight to the Lower East Side. There, streets reflected these myriad origins with shop signs in Yiddish, Italian, German and Chinese.

Class Lessons

All sorts of folks were living in squalor by the late 19th century, when the immigration processing center at Ellis Island opened, welcoming one million newcomers in just its first year. They crammed into packed tenements, shivered in soup lines and shoveled snow for nickels. Meanwhile, newly wealthy folks – boosted by an economy jump-started by financier JP Morgan, who bailed out sinking railroads and turned the city into the headquarters of Standard Oil and US Steel – began to build increasingly splendid mansions on Fifth Ave modeled on European chateaux. Reporter and photographer Jacob Riis illuminated the widening gap between the classes by writing about it in the *New York Tribune* and in his now-classic 1890 book, *How the Other Half Lives,* eventually forcing the city to pass much-needed housing reforms.

On December 16, 1835, a gas line broke in a dry-goods store near Hanover Square, causing a massive fire to quickly spread south down Stone St and northeast toward Wall St. Raging for over a day, it destroyed much of what remained of the original Dutch and British colonial city.

1882

Thomas Edison switches on the country's first commercial power plant, Pearl Street, instantly bringing light to more than 80 Manhattan addresses.

1883

The Brooklyn Bridge, built at a cost of $15.5 million (and at least 27 lives) opens; 150,000 people walk across its span at the inaugural celebration.

1886

The Statue of Liberty's pedestal is completed, allowing the large lady to be presented to New York at a dedication ceremony that takes place before thousands of citizens.

1898

The *Charter of New York* is ratified and the five boroughs of Brooklyn, Staten Island, Queens, the Bronx and Manhattan unite to become the largest city in America.

Factory Tragedy, Women's Rights

Wretched factory conditions in the early 20th century – low pay, long hours, abusive employers – were highlighted by a tragic event in 1911. The infamous Triangle Shirtwaist Company fire saw rapidly spreading flames catch onto the factory's piles of fabrics, killing 146 of 500 female workers who were trapped behind locked doors. The event led to sweeping labor reforms after 20,000 female garment workers marched to City Hall. At the same time, suffragists held street-corner rallies to obtain the vote for women. Nurse and midwife Margaret Sanger opened the first birth-control clinic in Brooklyn, where 'purity police' promptly arrested her. After her release from jail in 1921 she formed the American Birth Control League (now Planned Parenthood), which provided services for young women and researched methods of safe birth control.

New York City has around 660 miles of subway tracks used for passenger services. Counting railyards and other nonpassenger-service tracks, the figure exceeds 840 miles.

The Jazz Age

The 1920s saw the dawning of the Jazz Age, when Prohibition outlawed the sale of alcohol, encouraging bootlegging and speakeasies, as well as organized crime. Congenial mayor James Walker was elected in 1925, Babe Ruth reigned at Yankee Stadium and the Great Migration from the South led to the Harlem Renaissance, when the neighborhood became a center of African American culture and society. It produced poetry, music, painting and an innovative attitude that continues to influence and inspire. Harlem's daring nightlife in the 1920s and '30s attracted the flappers and gin-soaked revelers who marked the complete failure of Prohibition, and provided a foretaste of the liberated nightlife New Yorkers enjoy today. But the fun could not last forever – economic collapse was looming.

NYC's Tallest Buildings

Woolworth Building (792ft; 1913–1930)

Chrysler Building (1046ft; 1930–31)

Empire State Building (1454ft; 1931–1971 & 2001–2013)

World Trade Center (1368ft; 1971–2001)

One World Trade Center (1776ft; 2013–present)

Hard Times

The stock market crashed in 1929, beginning the Great Depression of the 1930s, which the city dealt with through a combination of grit, endurance, rent parties, militancy and a slew of public-works projects. The once-grand Central Park blossomed with shacks, derisively called Hoovervilles, after the president who refused to help the needy. But Mayor Fiorello La Guardia found a friend in President Franklin Roosevelt, and worked his Washington connections to great effect to bring relief money – and subsequent prosperity – home.

WWII brought troops galore to the city, ready to party down to their last dollar in Times Square, before being shipped off to Europe. Converted to war industries, the local factories hummed, staffed by women and African American workers who had rarely had access to good, unionized jobs. The explosion of wartime activity led to a huge housing crunch that

1903

Luna Park in Coney Island opens, followed by Dreamland amusement park. Meanwhile, the IRT subway carries 150,000 passengers on its very first day of operation.

1919

The Yankees acquire slugger Babe Ruth from Boston, which helps them win their first championship.

1931

The Empire State Building (1454ft tall) supersedes the Chrysler Building as the world's tallest skyscraper; the World Trade Center's north tower steals the crown in 1970.

1941

Duke Ellington's band leader Billy Strayhorn, inspired by the subway line that leads to Harlem, composes 'Take the A Train,' which becomes the band's signature song.

brought New York its much-imitated, tenant-protecting Rent Control Law. There were few evident controls on business, as Midtown bulked up with skyscrapers after the war. The financial center marched north, while banker David Rockefeller and his brother, Governor Nelson Rockefeller, dreamed up the Twin Towers to revitalize downtown.

New York's Brooklyn Bridge opened with suitable fanfare on May 24, 1883. After New York mayor Franklin Edson and Brooklyn mayor Seth Low led President Chester Arthur and Governor Grover Cleveland across the structure, more than 150,000 members of the public followed suit, each paying a penny for the honor.

Enter Robert Moses

Working with Mayor La Guardia to usher the city into the modern age was Robert Moses, an urban planner who would influence the physical shape of the city more than anyone else in the 20th century – either wonderfully or tragically, depending on whom you ask. He was the mastermind behind the Triborough Bridge (now the Robert F Kennedy Bridge), Jones Beach State Park, the Verrazzano-Narrows Bridge, the West Side Hwy and the Long Island parkway system – not to mention endless highways, tunnels and bridges. His vision was one of doing away with intimate neighborhoods of brownstones and town houses, and of creating sweeping parks and soaring towers. The approach got preservationists fired up and their efforts to stop him from bulldozing neighborhoods led to the Landmarks Preservation Commission being formed in 1965.

Move to the Beats

The 1950s and '60s ushered in an era of legendary creativity and anti-establishment expression, with many of its creators centered in Greenwich Village. One movement was abstract expressionism, a large-scale outbreak of American painters – Mark Rothko, Jackson Pollock and Helen Frankenthaler among them – who offended and intrigued with incomprehensible squiggles, blotches and exuberant energy. Then there were the writers, such as Beat poets Allen Ginsberg and Jack Kerouac and novelist/playwright Jane Bowles. They gathered in Village coffeehouses to exchange ideas and find inspiration, which was often found in the form of folk music from burgeoning big names, such as Bob Dylan.

'Drop Dead'

By the early 1970s, deficits had created a serious fiscal crisis, effectively demoting the elected mayor Abraham Beame to a figurehead, turning over the city's real financial power to Governor Carey and his appointees. President Ford's refusal to lend federal aid – summed up nicely by the *Daily News* headline 'Ford to City, Drop Dead' – marked the nadir of the relationship between the US and the city it loved to hate. As massive layoffs decimated the city's working class, untended bridges, roads and parks reeked of hard times.

1945

The United Nations, headquartered on Manhattan's east side, is established after representatives of 50 countries meet in San Francisco to agree on a charter.

1963

The original Penn Station is demolished to build Madison Square Garden; outcry leads to the foundation of the Landmarks Preservation Commission.

1969

On June 28, eight police officers raid the gay-friendly Stonewall Inn. Patrons revolt, sparking days of rioting and the birth of the modern gay-rights movement.

1977

Following a lightning strike at a power substation, a summer blackout leaves New Yorkers in the dark for more than 24 sweltering hours, which leads to rioting around the city.

Top Historical Sights

Ellis Island & Statue of Liberty (New York Harbor)

Tenement Museum (Lower East Side)

Merchant's House Museum (NoHo)

Historic Richmond Town (Staten Island)

Jane's Carousel (Brooklyn)

Gracie Mansion (Upper East Side)

The traumatic '70s – which reached a low point in 1977 with a citywide blackout and terrorizing serial killer David Berkowitz – saw rents fall, which helped nourish an exciting alternative culture that staged performances in abandoned schools, opened galleries in unused storefronts and breathed new life into the hair-dye industry with the advent of the punk-rock aesthetic. The fees from shooting the movie *Fame* at PS 122 at 9th St and First Ave, for example, helped pay for the renovation of the still-popular performance space. Ramones-loving punks turned former warehouses into pulsing meccas of nightlife, transforming the former industrial precincts of SoHo and Tribeca. Immortalized in Nan Goldin's famous photographic performance piece *The Ballad of Sexual Dependency*, this renaissance challenged gender roles and turned the East Village into America's center of tattooing and independent filmmaking.

Out of the Ashes

During the 1970s a wave of arson attacks reduced blocks of apartment houses in the South Bronx to cinders. Amid the smoke, an influential hip-hop culture was born, fueled by the percussive rhythms of Puerto Rican salsa. Rock Steady Crew, led by 'Crazy Legs' Richie Colón, pioneered athletic, competitive break dancing. DJ Kool Herc spun vinyl for break beat all-night dance parties. Afrika Bambaataa, another founding hip-hop DJ, formed Zulu Nation, bringing DJs, break dancers and graffiti writers together to end violence.

Daring examples of graffiti dazzled the public with train-long graphics. The best-known 'masterpiece' belied the graf writers' reputation as vandals: Lee 163, with the Fab 5 crew, painted a whole car of trains with the message 'Merry Christmas, New York.' Some of these maestros of the spray can infiltrated the art world, most notably Jean-Michel Basquiat. Some of the money snagged in the booming stock markets of the 1980s was spent on art, but even more was blown up the noses of young traders. While Manhattan neighborhoods struggled with the spread of crack cocaine, the city reeled from the impact of addiction, citywide crime and an AIDS epidemic that cut through communities.

Dot-Com Days

A *Time* magazine cover in 1990 sported a feature story on New York: 'The Rotting of the Big Apple.' Still convalescing from the real-estate crash at the end of the 1980s, the city faced crumbling bridges and roads, jobs leaking south and Fortune 500 companies hopping the rivers to suburbia. And then the dot-com market roared in, turning geeks into millionaires and the New York Stock Exchange into a speculator's

1988

Squatters, who turned the East Village's Tompkins Square Park into a massive homeless encampment, riot when cops attempt to remove them from their de facto home.

1993

On February 26, terrorists detonate a bomb below the North Tower of the World Trade Center. The explosion kills six people and injures more than 1000.

2001

On September 11, terrorist hijackers fly two planes into the Twin Towers, destroying the World Trade Center and killing nearly 3000 people.

2002

Gambino crime-family boss John Gotti (the Dapper Don) dies of cancer in prison while serving a sentence for murder, racketeering, tax evasion and other charges.

fun park. Buoyed by tax receipts from IPO (initial public offering) profits, the city launched a frenzy of building, boutique-ing and partying unparalleled since the 1920s.

With pro-business Rudy Giuliani as mayor, the dingy and the destitute were swept from Manhattan's yuppified streets to the outer boroughs, leaving room for Generation X to score digs and live the high life. Mayor Giuliani grabbed headlines with his campaign to stamp out crime, even kicking the sex shops off notoriously seedy 42nd St. The energetic mayor succeeded in making New York America's safest big city, by targeting high-crime areas and using statistics to focus police presence. Crime dropped, restaurants boomed, real-estate prices sizzled, and *Sex & the City* beamed a vision of sophisticated singles in Manolos around the world. Still, things were faltering in New York at the dawn of the new millennium and, when that fateful day came in 2001, it forever changed the perspective of both the city and the world.

September 11

On September 11, 2001, terrorists flew two hijacked planes into the World Trade Center's Twin Towers, turning the whole complex to dust and rubble and killing nearly 3000 people. Downtown Manhattan took months to recover from the ghastly fumes wafting from the ruins as forlorn missing-person posters grew ragged on brick walls. While the city mourned its dead and recovery crews coughed their way through the debris, residents braved constant terrorist alerts and an anthrax scare. Shock and grief drew people together, uniting the oft-fractious citizenry in a determined effort not to succumb to despair.

The September 11 terrorist attacks caused an estimated $3.3 trillion in damage. The destruction of the World Trade Center site, the subway system and surrounding buildings cost up to $60 billion, but the wider economic impact (homeland security, economic impact) cost hundreds of billions more.

Protests, Storms & Political Change

The decade after September 11 was a period of rebuilding – both physically and emotionally. In 2002, then-mayor Michael Bloomberg began the unenviable task of picking up the pieces of a shattered city that had thrust all of its support behind his predecessor, Mayor Giuliani, whose popularity rose in the wake of September 11.

Much to Bloomberg's pleasure, New York saw much renovation and reconstruction, especially after the city hit its stride with spiking tourist numbers in 2005. In 2008, however, the economy buckled under its own weight, in what has largely become known as the Global Financial Crisis. Anger toward the perceived recklessness of America's financial institutions saw thousands take to the Financial District's Zuccotti Park on September 17, 2011, in a stand against the nation's unfair division of personal wealth. Known as Occupy Wall Street, the protest subsequently spread to hundreds of other cities across the world.

2008–09

The stock market crashes due to mismanagement by major American financial institutions. The Global Financial Crisis spreads worldwide.

2009

On January 15, US Airways Flight 1549 plunges in the Hudson River after losing engine power. All 155 aboard are successfully evacuated.

2012

Superstorm Sandy hits NYC in October, causing major flooding and property damage, cutting power and shutting down the New York Stock Exchange for two days.

2013

Bill de Blasio wins the NYC mayoral election, defeating opponent Joseph J Lhota and becoming the city's first Democratic mayor in almost 20 years.

Fury of the meteorological kind hit New York in 2012, in the form of superstorm Hurricane Sandy. While a prestorm surge on October 28 turned parts of Brooklyn and New Jersey into a New World Venice, Sandy saved her ultimate blow for the following day. Cyclonic winds and drenching rain pounded the city, causing severe flooding and property damage, including to the NYC subway system, Hugh L Carey Tunnel and the World Trade Center site. A major power blackout plunged much of Lower Manhattan into surreal darkness, while trading at the New York Stock Exchange was suspended for two days.

The winds of political change swept through the city in November 2013, when Bill de Blasio became the city's first Democrat mayor elected since 1989. The self-proclaimed 'progressive' also became the first white mayor of NYC married to an African American woman, political adviser Chirlane McCray.

Forgotten-NY.com is Queens native Kevin Walsh's compendium of historical NYC, with not-found-elsewhere tales about everything from old subway stations to cemeteries.

The World Turned Upside Down

News that a mysterious pneumonia-like virus was killing scores of people in central China hardly made a ripple among New Yorkers in early 2020, but soon the COVID-19 pandemic would hit town, and hit hard. Lockdown began in mid-March: theaters and bars closed, trains and buses emptied, restaurants shut their dining rooms and thousands of office workers moved away or toughed it out working from home. Healthcare workers battled bravely against the disease, which pushed hospitals to the limit and saw 5000 daily new cases at the peak of the city's first wave. New Yorkers of color bore the brunt of the pandemic, as the majority of 'essential workers' here – delivery cyclists, public transit workers and staff at supermarkets, drug stores and restaurant kitchens – are Black, Hispanic- and Asian American, while the richest (overwhelmingly white) New Yorkers decamped to rural second homes. COVID life improved over summer as cases subsided, outdoor dining sprouted up and people flocked to parks and closed-off streets for impromptu block parties, but afterwards came a long, dreary lockdown winter. In the first year of the pandemic, NYC lost over 33,000 lives to the virus.

In early 2021, the vaccine rollout began, and by mid-summer over half of New Yorkers had been fully immunized. City life began opening up again with COVID-safe protocols in place – and anything that could be done out-of-doors boomed in popularity. June's primary election saw Brooklyn Borough President Eric Adams clinch the Democratic Party nomination, an office he's heavily favored to win in the November general election. But with the COVID delta variant spreading, hundreds of retail storefronts still shuttered, returning office workers battling rent surges and small business owners struggling to survive, the resiliency of New York City will continue to be tested.

2014

The World Trade Center redevelopment nears completion when the National September 11 Memorial Museum and One World Trade Center open.

2017

After creating universal pre-kindergarten, lowering unemployment and raising the minimum wage for city workers, Bill de Blasio wins his second term as mayor by a landslide.

2020

NYC goes into severe lockdown in mid-March as the COVID-19 pandemic hits. The virus will end up killing more than 30,000 New Yorkers over the next year.

2021

Ranked-choice voting makes its debut, allowing voters to choose multiple candidates by preference. Eric Adams becomes the Democratic Party mayoral candidate.

The NYC Table

Unlike California or the South, New York doesn't have one defining cuisine. Ask for some 'New York food' and you'll wind up with anything from brick-oven pizza in Brooklyn to vegan soul food in Harlem. Cuisine in the multicultural city is global by definition, a testament to the immigrants who have unpacked their bags and recipes on its streets. And just like the city itself, it's a scene that's constantly evolving, driven by insatiable ambition.

Urban Farm to Table

Whether it's upstate triple-cream Kunik at Bedford Cheese Shop (p174) or seasonal mushrooms at fine-dining Craft (p171), New York City's passion for all things local and artisanal continues unabated. The city itself has become an unlikely food bowl, with an ever-growing number of rooftops, backyards and community gardens finding new purpose as urban farms.

The urban harvest makes smart use of space, with organic tomatoes grown at Upper East Side delis and beehives on East Village tenement rooftops. There are more expansive spaces, too, like Brooklyn Grange (www.brooklyngrangefarm.com), an organic farm covering three rooftops in Long Island City and the Brooklyn Navy Yards. At almost 5.5 acres, it produces over 80,000lb of organically cultivated goodness annually, from eggs to carrots, chard and heirloom tomatoes. Another Brooklyn producer is **Whole Foods** (Map p440; ☎718-907-3622; www.wholefoodsmarket.com; 214 3rd St, btwn Third Ave & Gowanus Canal, Gowanus; ⌚8am-11pm; 📶✍; Ⓢ R to Union St, F, G to 4th Ave-9th St), whose commercial-scale greenhouse farm covers some 20,000 sq ft, making use of a high-efficiency irrigation system to further reduce the produce's carbon footprint.

Bargain-savvy gastronomes love the biannual NYC Restaurant Week. Taking place in January to February and July to August, it sees many of the city's restaurants, including some of its very best, serve up two-course lunches for $26, or three-course dinners for $42. Check www.nycgo.com/restaurantweek for details and reservations.

Food Specialties

Bagels

Bagels may have been invented in Europe, but they were perfected around the turn of the 19th century in NYC – and once you've had one here, you'll have a hard time enjoying one anywhere else. It's a straightforward masterpiece: a ring of plain-yeast dough that's first boiled and then baked, either left plain or topped with various finishing touches, from sesame seeds to chocolate chips. 'Bagels' made in other parts of the country are often just baked and not boiled, which makes them nothing more than a roll with a hole. And even if they do get boiled elsewhere, bagel-makers here claim that it's the New York water that adds an elusive sweetness never to be found anywhere else. Which baker creates the 'best' bagel in New York is a matter of (hotly contested) opinion, but most agree that Manhattan's Ess-a-Bagel (p195) and Queens' Brooklyn Bagel & Coffee Company (p312) rank pretty high. The most traditionally New York way to order one is by asking for a 'bagel and a schmear,' which will yield you said bagel with a small but thick swipe of cream cheese. Or splurge and add some lox – thinly sliced smoked salmon – as was originally sold from pushcarts on the Lower East Side by Jewish immigrants back in the early 1900s.

Pizza

Pizza is certainly not indigenous to Gotham. But New York–style pizza is a very particular item, and the first pizzeria in America was Lombardi's in Manhattan's Little Italy, which opened in 1905.

While Chicago–style pizza is 'deep dish' and Californian tends to be light and doughy, New York prides itself on pizza with a thin crust, an even thinner layer of sauce and triangular slices (unless they're Sicilian-style, in which case they're rectangular). Pizza made its way over to New York in the 1900s through Italian immigrants and its regional style soon developed, the thin crust allowing for faster cooking time in a city where everyone is always in a hurry.

Today there are pizza parlors about every 10 blocks, especially in Manhattan and most of Brooklyn, where you'll find standard slices for $3. The style at each place varies slightly – some places touting cracker-thin crust, others offering slightly thicker and chewier versions, and plenty of nouveau styles throwing everything from shrimp to cherries on top. The city's booming locavore movement has also made its mark, with hip pizzerias like Roberta's (p287) in Brooklyn peddling wood-fired pies topped with sustainable, local produce.

City Harvest (www.cityharvest.org) is a nonprofit organization that distributes unused food to around 1.2 million struggling New Yorkers each year. A whopping 64 million pounds of food is rescued from city restaurants, bakeries and catering companies over the course of a year. Individuals wanting to make a monetary donation can do so via the City Harvest website.

Hot Dogs

The hot dog made its way to New York via various European butchers in the 1800s. One, Charles Feltman of Germany, was apparently the first to sell them from pushcarts along the Coney Island seashore. Nathan Handwerker, originally an employee of Feltman's, opened his own shop across the street, offering hot dogs at half the price of those at Feltman's, which put his former employer out of business. Today, the original and legendary Nathan's (p287) still stands in Coney Island, while its empire has expanded on an international scale. There is barely a New York neighborhood that does not have at least a few hot-dog vendors on its street corners, although some locals would never touch one of those 'dirty-water dogs,' preferring the new wave of chichi hot-dog shops that can be found all over town. Enjoy yours, wherever it's from, with 'the works': smothered with spicy brown mustard, relish, sauerkraut and onions.

Egg Creams

Now don't go expecting eggs or cream in this frothy, old-school beverage – just milk, seltzer water and plenty of chocolate syrup (preferably the classic Fox's U-Bet brand, made in Brooklyn). When Louis Auster of Brooklyn, who owned soda fountains on the Lower East Side, invented the treat back in 1890, the syrup he used was indeed made from eggs, with added cream to thicken the concoction. The name stuck, even though the ingredients were modified, and soon they were a staple of every soda fountain in New York. While Mr Auster sold them for 3¢ apiece, today they'll cost you anywhere from $2.50 to $5, depending on where you find one – which could be from old-school institutions such as Katz's Delicatessen (p122) in the Lower East Side or Tom's Restaurant (p248) in Brooklyn.

New York–Style Cheesecake

In one form or another, cheesecake has been around for quite a while. Look back 2400 years and you'll notice that Greek historian Thucydides and his posse were already kneading honey into fresh feta and baking it over hot coals for a sweet treat. Centuries later, the Romans adopted it, tweaking the concept by incorporating spelt flour for a more 'cake-like' form. This would be followed by countless more tweaks across the continent and centuries.

It would, however, take the error of a 19th-century New York farmer to create the key ingredient in New York–style cheesecake: cream cheese. A botched attempt at making French Neufchâtel cheese resulted in a curious product with the texture of polyethylene plastic. Enter James Kraft, founder of Kraft Foods, who picked it up in 1912, reformulated it, wrapped it in foil and introduced the country to the wonder of cream cheese.

Classic New York cheesecake would be immortalized by Lindy's restaurant in Midtown. Opened by Leo Lindemann in 1921, the particular type of confection served there – made of cream cheese, heavy cream, a dash of vanilla and a cookie crust – became wildly popular in the '40s. Today, this calorific local masterpiece is a staple on countless dessert menus, whether you're at a Greek diner or haute-cuisine hot spot. The most famous (and arguably best) cheesecake in town is that from Brooklyn stalwart **Junior's** (Map p443; ☎718-852-5257; www.juniorscheesecake.com; 386 Flatbush Ave, at DeKalb Ave, Downtown Brooklyn; mains from $11; ⏰6:30am-midnight Sun-Thu, to 1am Fri & Sat; Ⓢ B, Q/R to DeKalb Ave, 2/3 to Hoyt St, A/C, G to Hoyt-Schermerhorn), whose well-known fans include Barack Obama.

There's a plethora of books about NYC's culinary history. Top reads include William Grimes' *Appetite City: A Culinary History of New York*, Arthur Schwartz's *New York City Food: An Opinionated History and More Than 100 Legendary Recipes*, and *Gastropolis: Food & New York City*, edited by Annie Hauck-Lawson and Jonathan Deutsch.

Drink Specialties

Cocktails

New York City is a master of mixed libations. After all, this is the home of Manhattans, legendary speakeasies and cosmo-clutching columnists with a passion for fashion. Legend has it that the city's namesake drink, the Manhattan – a blend of whiskey, sweet vermouth and bitters – began life on the southeastern corner of 26th St and Madison Ave, at the long-gone Manhattan Club. The occasion was a party in 1874, allegedly thrown by Jennie Churchill (mother of British prime minister Winston) to celebrate Samuel J Tilden's victory in the New York gubernatorial election. One of the barmen decided to create a drink to mark the occasion, naming it in honor of the bar.

Another New York classic was born that very year – the summer-centric Tom Collins. A mix of dry gin, sugar, lemon juice and club soda, the long drink's name stems from an elaborate hoax in which hundreds of locals were informed that a certain Tom Collins had been sullying their good names. While many set out to track him down, clued-in bartenders relished the joke by making the drink and naming it for the fictitious troublemaker. When the aggrieved stormed into the bars looking for a Tom Collins, they were served the drink to cool their tempers.

These days, NYC's kicking cocktail scene is big on rediscovered recipes, historical anecdotes and vintage speakeasy style. Once, obscure bartenders such as Harry Johnson and Jerry Thomas are now born-again legends, their vintage concoctions revived by a new generation of braces-clad mixologists. Historic ingredients such as Crème de Violette, Old Tom gin and Batavia Arrack are back in vogue. In the Financial District, cocktail bar Dead Rabbit (p81) has gone one further, reintroducing

NYC Master Chef Cookbooks

Daniel: My French Cuisine (Daniel Boulud & Sylvie Bigar)

The Babbo Cookbook (Mario Batali)

A Girl and Her Greens (April Bloomfield)

Momofuku (David Chang & Peter Meehan)

the 17th-century practice of pop-inns, drinks that fuse ale, liqueurs, spices and botanicals.

Other establishments give a single spirit prominence on their menus, among them whiskey-versed Ward III (p83) and self-explanatory Brandy Library (p81), both in Tribeca, Rum House (p204) in Midtown, and, in Brooklyn, craft bourbon creators Kings County Distillery (p269) and whisky-worshipping Moonlight Mile (p292). There's even a drinking den devoted to Moonshine – Wayland (p123) – in the East Village.

Borough Brews

Beer brewing was once a thriving industry in the city – by the 1870s, Brooklyn boasted a belly-swelling 48 breweries. Most of these were based in Williamsburg, Bushwick and Greenpoint, neighborhoods packed with German immigrants with extensive brewing know-how. By the eve of Prohibition in 1919, the borough was one of the country's leading beer peddlers, as famous for kids carrying growlers (beer jugs) as for its bridges. By the end of Prohibition in 1933, most breweries had shut shop. And while the industry rose from the ashes in WWII, local flavor gave in to big-gun Midwestern brands.

The first public brewery in America was established by colonial governor Peter Minuit (1580–1638) at the Market (Marckvelt) field in what is now known as the Financial District in Lower Manhattan. Minuit is remembered for 'purchasing' Manhattan from the native Lenape people in May 1626.

Fast-forward to today and Brooklyn is once more a catchword for a decent brewski as a handful of craft breweries put integrity back on tap. Head of the pack is Brooklyn Brewery (p274), brewing IPAs, lagers, non-alcoholic beers plus limited-release offerings like raspberry sour ale. The brewery's comrades-in-craft include SixPoint Craft Ales (www.sixpoint.com), Threes Brewing (www.threesbrewing.com), Other Half Brewing Co (www.otherhalfbrewing.com) and Transmitter Brewing (www.transmitterbrewing.com).

In Queens, the dominant player remains SingleCut Beersmiths (www.singlecut.com); its launch in 2012 saw Queens welcome its first brewery since Prohibition. Its offerings include unusual takes on lager, among them the summery, orange zesty Jan Alpine White Lager. The borough is also home to beach-born Rockaway Brewing Company (www.rockawaybrewco.com). Further north, the Bronx lays claim to Bronx Brewery (p254) and Gun Hill Brewing Co (www.gunhillbrewing.com), the latter making waves with its Void of Light, a jet-black, roastalicious stout.

The Arts Scene

The spectacles of Broadway, the gleaming white-box galleries of Chelsea, joints playing jazz, music halls blaring moody indie rock and opera houses that bellow melodramatic tales – for more than a century, New York City has been America's capital of cultural production. And while gentrification has pushed many artists out to the city's fringes and beyond, New York nonetheless remains a nerve center for the visual arts, music, theater, dance and literature.

Dynamo of the Art World

That New York claims some of the world's mightiest art museums attests to its enviable artistic pedigree. From Pollock and Rothko to Warhol and Rauschenberg, the city has nourished many of America's greatest artists and artistic movements.

Birth of an Arts Hub

In almost all facets of the arts, New York really got its sea legs in the early 20th century, when the city attracted and retained a critical mass of thinkers, artists, writers and poets. It was at this time that the homegrown art scene began to take shape. In 1905, photographer (and husband of Georgia O'Keeffe) Alfred Stieglitz opened 'Gallery 291,' a Fifth Ave space that provided a vital platform for American artists and helped establish photography as a credible art form.

In the 1940s, an influx of cultural figures fleeing the carnage of WWII saturated the city with fresh ideas – and New York became an important cultural hub. Peggy Guggenheim established the Art of this Century gallery on 57th St, a space that helped launch the careers of painters such as Jackson Pollock, Willem de Kooning and Robert Motherwell. These Manhattan-based artists, along with other leading artists such as Elaine de Kooning, Joan Mitchell and Helen Frankenthaler, came to form the core of the abstract-expressionist movement (also known as the New York School), creating an explosive and rugged form of painting that changed the course of modern art as we know it.

American Avant-Garde

The abstract expressionists helped establish New York as a global arts center. Another generation of artists then carried the baton. In the 1950s and '60s, Robert Rauschenberg, Jasper Johns and Lee Bontecou turned paintings into off-the-wall sculptural constructions that included everything from welded steel to taxidermy goats. By the mid-1960s, pop art – a movement that utilized the imagery and production techniques of popular culture – had taken hold, with Andy Warhol at the helm.

On any given week, New York is home to countless art exhibits, installations and performances. Get a comprehensive listing of happenings at www.nyartbeat.com.

By the '60s and '70s, when New York's economy was in the dumps and much of SoHo lay in a state of decay, the city became a hotbed of conceptual and performance art. Gordon Matta-Clark sliced up abandoned buildings with chainsaws and the artists of Fluxus staged happenings on downtown streets. Carolee Schneemann organized performances that utilized the human body. At one famous 1964 event, she had a crew of nude dancers roll around in an unappetizing mix of paint, sausages and dead fish in the theater of a Greenwich Village church.

New York's Art World Today

Today, the arts scene is mixed and wide-ranging. The major institutions – the Metropolitan Museum of Art, the Museum of Modern Art, the Whitney Museum of American Art, the Guggenheim Museum, the Met Breuer and the Brooklyn Museum – deliver major retrospectives covering everything from Renaissance portraiture to contemporary installation. The New Museum of Contemporary Art (p110), on the Lower East Side, is more daring, while countless smaller institutions, among them the excellent Bronx Museum (p254), El Museo del Barrio (p251) and the Studio Museum in Harlem (p249), focus on more precise slices of art history.

New York remains the world's gallery capital, with well over 1000 spaces showcasing all kinds of art all over the city. The blue-chip dealers can be found clustered in Chelsea and the Upper East Side. Galleries that showcase emerging and midcareer artists dot the Lower East Side, while prohibitive rents have pushed the city's more emerging and experimental scenes further out, with current hot spots including Harlem and the Brooklyn neighborhoods of Bushwick, Greenpoint, Clinton Hill and Bedford-Stuyvesant (Bed-Stuy).

In January 2018 the Metropolitan Museum of Art (p214) started charging admission to out-of-state visitors for the first time since 1970. The decision was controversial: while many recognized the museum's financial bind – only 8% of its budget is government funded – others mourned the loss of the open-door policy that allowed universal access to a world-class art collection.

Graffiti & Street Art

Public art has come a long way since Emma Stebbins' sculpture *Angel of the Waters* (1873) was planted in Central Park. Contemporary graffiti as we know it was cultivated in NYC. In the 1970s, the graffiti-covered subway train became a potent symbol of the city and work by figures such as Dondi, Blade and Lady Pink became known around the world. In addition, fine artists such as Jean-Michel Basquiat, Kenny Scharf and Keith Haring began incorporating elements of graffiti into their work.

The movement received new life in the late 1990s when a new generation of artists – many with art-school pedigrees – began using materials such as cut paper and sculptural elements. Well-known New York City artists working in this vein include John Fekner, Stephen 'ESPO' Powers, Swoon, and the twin-brother duo Skewville and Shepard Fairey, who later went on to create the Obama 'Hope' poster. The city's diverse canvas has also been enlivened by the large-scale works of Tokyo-born artist Lady Aiko, crocheted installations by Olek, and Alice Mizrachi's murals.

Less celebratory was the 2013 closure of the iconic 5Pointz, a cluster of Long Island City warehouses dripping with Technicolor graffiti. Not even a plea from legendary British artist Banksy could save the veritable gallery, condemned to demolition. These days, spray-can and stencil hot spots include the Brooklyn side of the Williamsburg Bridge and the corner of Troutman St and St Nicholas Ave in Bushwick, also in Brooklyn. In Astoria, Queens, explore the Technicolor artworks around Welling Ct and 30th Ave.

Musical Metropolis

This is the city where jazz players such as Ornette Coleman, Miles Davis and John Coltrane pushed the limits of improvisation in the 1950s. It's where various Latin sounds – from cha-cha-cha to rumba to mambo – came together to form the hybrid we now call salsa, where folk singers such as Bob Dylan and Joan Baez crooned protest songs in coffeehouses, and where bands such as the New York Dolls and the Ramones tore up the stage in Manhattan's gritty downtown. It was the nerve center of disco. And it was the cultural crucible where hip-hop was nurtured and grew – and then exploded.

Village Vanguard (p158)

The city remains a magnet for musicians. The local indie-rock scene is especially vibrant: groups including the Yeah Yeah Yeahs, LCD Soundsystem and Animal Collective all emerged in NYC. Williamsburg is at the heart of the action, packed with clubs and bars, as well as indie record labels and internet radio stations. The best venues for rock include the Music Hall of Williamsburg (p298) and Manhattan's Bowery Ballroom (p129).

And All That Jazz

Jazz remains a juggernaut – from the traditional to the experimental. The best bets for jazz are the Village Vanguard (p158) in the West Village and the **Jazz Standard** (Map p424; 212-576-2232; www.jazzstandard.com; 116 E 27th St, btwn Lexington & Park Aves; cover $25-40; shows 7:30pm & 9:30pm; S 6 to 28th St) near Madison Square Park. For more highbrow programming, there's Midtown's Jazz at Lincoln Center (p204), which is run by trumpeter Wynton Marsalis and features a wide array of solo outings by important musicians, as well as tribute concerts to figures such as Dizzy Gillespie and Thelonious Monk.

Classical & Opera

The classics are alive and well at Lincoln Center (p232). Here, the Metropolitan Opera (p241) delivers a wide array of celebrated operas, from Verdi's *Aida* to Mozart's *Don Giovanni*. The New York Philharmonic (p242) (the symphony that was once directed by one of the 20th century's great maestros, Leonard Bernstein) is also based here out of the newly refurbished David Geffen Hall. Carnegie Hall (p204), the **Merkin Concert Hall** (Map p432; 212-501-3330; www.kaufman-center.org/mch; 129 W 67th St, btwn Amsterdam Ave & Broadway; box office noon-7pm Sun-Thu, to 4:30pm Fri, 1hr before performances Sat; S 1 to 66th St-Lincoln Center)

World-Changing Women

You know Pollock, de Kooning and Rothko – but what about the women who shaped 20th-century abstract painting? In *Ninth Street Women* (2018), Mary Gabriel reveals how five female artists, including Lee Krasner and Grace Hartigan, worked their way to the top of the NYC art world.

Joyce Theater (p159)

and the Frick Collection (p224) also offer wonderful – and more intimate – spaces to enjoy great classical music.

For more avant-garde fare, try the Center for Contemporary Opera (http://centerforcontemporaryopera.org) and the Brooklyn Academy of Music (p294) – the latter is one of the city's vital opera and classical-music hubs. Other excellent venues, featuring highly experimental work, are St Ann's Warehouse (p294) and National Sawdust (p294), both in Brooklyn. If you like your performances *outré,* keep an eye on their calendars.

On Broadway & Beyond

In the early 20th century, clusters of theaters settled into the area around Times Square and began producing popular plays and suggestive comedies – a movement that had its roots in early vaudeville. By the 1920s, these messy works had evolved into on-stage spectacles like *Show Boat,* an all-out Oscar Hammerstein production about the lives of performers on a Mississippi steamboat. In 1943, Broadway had its first runaway hit – *Oklahoma!* – that remained on stage for a record 2212 performances.

Brooklyn has a hopping indie-music scene, with local bands performing regularly in Williamsburg and Bushwick. To hear the latest sounds, log on to www.newtownradio.com.

Today, Broadway musicals are shown in one of 41 official Broadway theaters, lavish early-20th-century jewels that surround Times Square, and are a major component of cultural life in New York. If you're on a budget, look for off-Broadway productions. These tend to be more intimate, inexpensive and often just as good.

NYC bursts with theatrical offerings beyond Broadway, from Shakespeare to David Mamet to rising experimental playwrights including Young Jean Lee. In addition to Midtown staples such as Playwrights Horizons (p206) and Second Stage Theatre (p208), the Lincoln Center theaters (p232) and smaller companies like Soho Rep (p83) are important hubs for works by modern and contemporary playwrights.

Across the East River, Brooklyn Academy of Music (p294) and St Ann's Warehouse (p294) offer edgy programming. Numerous festivals, such as BAM's epic Next Wave Festival (p294) and the biennial **Performa** (www.performa-arts.org; ⊙Nov), offer brilliant opportunities to catch new work.

For comprehensive theater listings, news and reviews (both glowing and scathing), visit www.nytimes.com/section/theater. You'll also find listings, synopses and industry news at www.playbill.com.

Bust a Move: Dance in NYC

For nearly 100 years, New York City has been at the center of American dance. It is here that the American Ballet Theatre (ABT) – founded by Lucia Chase and Richard Pleasant – was founded in 1939. The company promoted the idea of cultivating American talent, hiring native-born dancers and putting on works by choreographers such as Jerome Robbins, Twyla Tharp and Alvin Ailey. The company continues to perform in New York and around the world.

But NYC is perhaps best known for nurturing a generation of modern-dance choreographers – figures such as Martha Graham, who challenged traditional notions of dance with boxy, industrial movements on bare, almost abstract sets. The boundaries were pushed ever further by Merce Cunningham, who disassociated dance from music. Today, companies such as STREB (http://streb.org) are still pushing dance to its limits.

Lincoln Center (p232) and Brooklyn Academy of Music (p294) host regular performances, while up-and-coming acts feature at spaces including Chelsea's Kitchen (p159), Joyce Theater (p159) and New York Live Arts (p158), as well as Midtown's Baryshnikov Arts Center (http://bacnyc.org).

New York in Letters

The city that is home to the country's biggest publishing houses has also been home to some of its best-known writers. In the 19th century, Herman Melville *(Moby Dick)*, Edith Wharton *(The House of Mirth)* and Walt Whitman *(Leaves of Grass)* all congregated here. But literary life became even more exciting in the early part of the 20th century. There were the liquor-fueled literary salons of poet-communist John Reed in the 1910s, the acerbic wisecracks of the Algonquin Round Table in the 1920s and the thinly veiled novels of Dawn Powell in the '40s, whose work often critiqued New York's media establishment.

The 1950s and '60s saw the rise of writers who began to question the status quo. Poet Langston Hughes examined the condition of African Americans in Harlem and Beat poets such as Allen Ginsberg rejected traditional rhyme in favor of free-flowing musings. The last few decades of the 20th century offered a wide gamut to choose from, including Jay McInerney, chronicler of the greed and coke-fueled '80s, to new voices from under-represented corners of the city such as Puerto Rican-Cuban writer Piri Thomas and Audre Lorde, a ground-breaking feminist poet and civil rights activist.

NYC scribes continue to cover a vast array of realities in their work, from the immigrant experience (Imbolo Mbue) and the Manhattan music business (Jennifer Egan), to the crazy impossibility that is New York in Michael Chabon's Pulitzer-winning *The Amazing Adventures of Kavalier & Clay*. Among the latest crop of Gotham-based talent is award-winning Ben Lerner, whose metafiction novel *10:04* is as much about the city's visceral intensity as it is about its neurotic protagonist with a heart condition.

Both Brooklyn Academy of Music (p294) and the New York Public Library (p191) host widely attended lectures and readings. Neighborhood book stores often have packed calendars of events, too.

The City Skyline

New York's architectural history is a layer cake of ideas and styles – one that is literally written on the city's streets. There are the revivals (Greek, Gothic, Romanesque and Renaissance) and the unadorned forms of the International style. But if there is one style associated with New York beyond all others it is art deco, which was fused onto the cityscape in the 1930s. Today, icons like the Chrysler and Empire State are decadent reminders of that defining era.

Above: Federal Hall (p72)

Colonial Foundations

New York's architectural roots are modest. Early Dutch-colonial farmhouses were all about function: clapboard-wood homes with shingled, gambrel roofs were positioned to take advantage of daylight and retain heat in winter. A number of these have somehow survived to the present. The most remarkable is the Pieter Claesen Wyckoff House (p271) in East Flatbush, Brooklyn. Originally built in 1652 (with additions made over the years), it is the oldest house in the entire city.

After the Dutch colony of New Amsterdam became the British colony of New York in 1664, architectural styles moved to Georgian. Boxy, brick and stone structures with hipped roofs began to materialize. In the northern Manhattan district of Inwood, the Morris-Jumel Mansion (p253) from 1765 is an altered example of this: the home was built in the Georgian style by Roger Morris, then purchased by Stephen Jumel, who added a neoclassical facade in the 19th century. Another British-colonial building of interest is the Fraunces Tavern (p72), where George Washington bid an emotional farewell to the officers who had accompanied him throughout the American Revolution. Today the structure contains a museum and restaurant.

On the ceremonial end is St Paul's Chapel (p72), south of City Hall Park. Built in the 1760s, it is the oldest surviving church in the city. Its design was inspired by the much bigger St Martin-in-the-Fields church in London.

Architecture in the New Republic

In the early 1800s, architecture grew lighter and more refined. The so-called Federal style employed classical touches – slim, columned entrances, triangular pediments at the roofline and rounded fanlights over doors and windows. Some of the best surviving examples are tied to municipal government. City Hall (p78), built in 1812, owes its French form to émigré architect Joseph François Mangin and its Federal detailing to American-born John McComb Jr. The interior contains an airy rotunda and curved cantilevered stairway.

Uptown on the Upper East Side, the 1799 Gracie Mansion (p219) is the official residence of New York City's mayor since 1942 It's a fine example of a Federal residence, with its broad, river-view porch and leaded glass sidelights. This stretch of riverfront was once lined with buildings of the sort – a sight that impressed Alexis de Tocqueville during his tour of the United States in the early 19th century.

Other Federal-style specimens include the 1793 James Watson House at 7 State St across from Battery Park, and the 1832 Merchant's House Museum (p91), in NoHo. The latter still contains its intact interiors.

Must-See Buildings

Chrysler Building (Midtown)

Grand Central Terminal (Midtown)

Morris-Jumel Mansion (Washington Heights)

Empire State Building (Midtown)

Temple Emanu-El (Upper East Side)

Guggenheim Museum (Upper East Side)

Greek, Gothic & Romanesque: The Revivals

Following the publication of an important treatise on Greek architecture in the late 1700s, architects began to show a renewed interest in pure, classical forms. By the 1830s, becolumned Greek Revival structures were going up all over New York. Manhattan contains a bevy of these buildings, including the gray granite St Peter's Church (1838) and the white-marble Federal Hall (p72; 1842).

Starting in the late 1830s, the simple Georgian and Federalist styles started to give way to more ornate structures that employed Gothic and Romanesque elements. An early example was the Church of the Ascension (1841) in Greenwich Village – an imposing brownstone structure studded with pointed arches and a crenelated tower. The same architect – Richard Upjohn – also designed downtown Manhattan's Trinity Church (p72; 1846) in the same style.

By the 1860s, places of worship were growing in size and scale. Among the most resplendent are St Patrick's Cathedral (p193; 1858–1879), which took over an entire city block at Fifth Ave and 51st St, and the perpetually under-construction Cathedral Church of St John the Divine (p247; since 1911), in Morningside Heights. Indeed, the style was so popular that one of the city's most important icons – the Brooklyn Bridge (p262;

Palace Hotel

1870–83) – was constructed à la Gothic Revival by John Roebling and his son Washington, and later by the latter's wife, Emily Roebling.

Romanesque elements (such as curved arches) can be spotted on structures all over the city. Some of the most famous include the Joseph Papp Public Theater (formerly the Astor Library) in Greenwich Village, built between 1853 and 1881, and the breathtaking Temple Emanu-El (p219; 1929) on Fifth Ave on the Upper East Side.

Beaux-Arts Blockbusters

At the turn of the 20th century, New York entered a gilded age. Robber barons such as JP Morgan, Henry Clay Frick and John D Rockefeller – awash in steel and oil money – built themselves lavish manses. Public buildings grew ever more extravagant in scale and ornamentation. Architects, many of whom trained in France, came back with European design ideals. Gleaming white limestone began to replace all the brownstone, first stories were elevated to allow for dramatic staircase entrances, and buildings were adorned with sculptured keystones and Corinthian columns.

AIA Guide to New York (5th edition; 2010) is a comprehensive guide to the most significant buildings in the city.

Game-changing architectural firm McKim, Mead and White's Villard Houses, from 1884 (now the Palace Hotel), show the movement's early roots. Loosely based on Rome's Palazzo della Cancelleria, they channeled the symmetry and elegance of the Italian Renaissance. Other classics include the central branch of the New York Public Library (p191; 1911), designed by Carrère and Hastings; the 1902 extension of the Metropolitan Museum of Art (p214), by Richard Morris Hunt; and Warren and Wetmore's stunning Grand Central Terminal (p184; 1913), which is capped by a statue of Mercury, the god of commerce.

Woolworth Building (p78)

Reaching Skyward

By the time New York settled into the 20th century, elevators and steel-frame engineering had allowed the city to grow up – literally. This period saw a building boom of skyscrapers, starting with Cass Gilbert's neo-Gothic 60-story Woolworth Building (p78; 1913), which was the world's tallest building for almost two decades.

Others soon followed. In 1930, the Chrysler Building (p186), the 77-story art-deco masterpiece designed by William Van Alen, trumped the Woolworth as the world's tallest structure. The following year, the record was broken by the Empire State Building (p180), a clean-lined moderne monolith crafted from Indiana limestone with a beautiful art-deco interior. Its spire was meant to be used as a mooring mast for dirigibles (airships) – an idea that made for good publicity, but which proved to be impractical and unfeasible.

The influx of displaced European architects and other thinkers who had resettled in New York by the end of WWII fostered a lively dialogue between American and European architects. This was a period when urban planner Robert Moses furiously rebuilt vast swaths of New York – to the detriment of many neighborhoods – and designers and artists became obsessed with the clean, unadorned lines of the International style.

One of the earliest projects in this vein were the UN buildings (1948–52), the combined effort of a committee of architects, including the Swiss-born Le Corbusier, Brazil's Oscar Niemeyer and USA's Wallace K Harrison. The Secretariat employed New York's first glass curtain wall – which looms over the ski-slope curve of the General Assembly. The city's greatest emblem of this architectural era is the controversial inverted ziggurat of the Guggenheim Museum (p213), which was completed in 1959 but conceived more than a decade earlier.

The New Guard

By the late 20th century, numerous architects began to rebel against the hard-edged, unornamented nature of modernist design. Among them was Philip Johnson. His pink-granite 550 Madison Ave building (1984), formerly the AT&T Building and later the Sony Tower, is topped by a scrolled, neo-Georgian pediment – a postmodern icon of the Midtown skyline.

Esteemed New York architecture critic Ada Louise Huxtable gathers some of her most important essays in the book *On Architecture: Collected Reflections on a Century of Change.*

What never became an icon was Daniel Libeskind's twisting, angular design for the One World Trade Center (p70) tower (2013), replaced by a boxier architecture-by-committee glass obelisk. On the same site, budget blowouts led to tweaks of Santiago Calatrava's luminous design for the World Trade Center Transportation Hub (2016). According to critics, what should have looked like a dove in flight now resembles a winged dinosaur. An ongoing WTC site controversy involves Two World Trade Center, its original Sir Norman Foster design scrapped for one by Danish firm Bjarke Ingels Group (BIG). According to the chief operating officer of 21st Century Fox, James Murdoch, Foster's design was too conventional for what will become the media company's new base. BIG responded with its trademark unconventionalism: a tower of giant, differently sized boxes, soaring playfully into the sky (estimated completion date: 2022–23).

Not that Sir Foster can't do cutting-edge style. The British architect's Hearst Tower (p192; 2006) – a glass skyscraper zigzagging its way out of a 1920s sandstone structure – remains a Midtown trailblazer. The building is one of numerous daring 21st-century additions to the city's architectural portfolio, among them Brooklyn's sci-fi arena Barclays Center (p296; 2012), Thom Mayne's folded-and-slashed 41 Cooper Square (2009) in the East Village, and Frank Gehry's rippling, 76-storey apartment tower New York by Gehry (2011) in the Financial District.

Starchitects on the Line

Frank Gehry's IAC Building (2007) – a billowing, white-glass structure often compared to a wedding cake – is one of a growing number of starchitect creations appearing around railway-turned-urban-park, the High Line (p134). The most prolific of these is Renzo Piano's Whitney Museum (p136; 2015). Dramatically asymmetrical and clad in blue-gray steel, the building has received significant praise for melding seamlessly with the elevated park.

In 2017 the area welcomed Dame Zaha Hadid's apartment complex at 520 West 28th St. Rising 11 stories, the luxury structure was the Iraqi-British architect's first residential project in the city, its voluptuous, sci-fi curves complimented by a 2500-sq-ft sculpture deck showcasing art presented by Friends of the High Line. Sadly the Pritzker Prize–winning architect wasn't able to see its completion; Hadid died aged 65 in 2016.

Public Art: New York by Jean Parker Phifer, with photos by Francis Dzikowski, is an informative guide to the city's public monuments.

The redevelopment of the Hudson Yards area (p194) has revitalized the riverside skyline. The final extension of the High Line loops around the Hudson Yards, ending at 34th St. At the heart of the development, a huge public space is anchored by the Vessel (p195; 2019) – an Escher-like steel structure by Heatherwick Studio rising skywards. Its 2500 steps are fashioned into a series of interlocking walkways and staircases designed for climbing; locals have nicknamed it 'the shawarma.' Also newly minted in 2019 is The Shed (p207), an arts center with a 500-seat theater and retractable shell, designed by Diller Scofidio + Renfro in collaboration with the Rockwell Group. An outdoor observation deck on the 100th floor of 30 Hudson Yards opened to vertigo-immune visitors in 2019; at 1100ft above ground, it's the highest of its kind in the Western Hemisphere.

Queer City: From Stonewall to Marriage Equality

New York City is out and damn proud. It was here that the Stonewall Riots took place, that the modern gay-rights movement bloomed and that America's first Pride march hit the streets. Yet even before the days of 'Gay Lib,' the city had a knack for all things queer and fabulous, from Bowery sex saloons and Village Sapphic poetry to drag balls in Harlem. It hasn't always been smooth sailing, but it's always been one hell of a ride.

Before Stonewall

Subversion in the Villages

By the 1890s, New York City's rough-and-ready Lower East Side had established quite a reputation for scandalous 'resorts' – dancing halls, saloons and brothels – frequented by the city's 'inverts' and 'fairies.' From Paresis Hall at 5th St and Bowery to Slide at 157 Bleecker St, these venues offered everything from cross-dressing spectaculars and dancing to back rooms for same-sex encounters. For closeted middle-class men, these dens were a secret thrill – places reached undercover on trains for a fix of camaraderie, understanding and uninhibited fun. For curious middle-class straights, they were just as enticing – salacious destinations on voyeuristic 'slumming tours.'

As New York strode into the 20th century, writers and bohemians began stepping into Greenwich Village, lured by the area's cheap rents and romantically crooked streets. The unconventionality and free thinking the area became known for turned the Village into an Emerald City for gays and lesbians, a place with no shortage of bachelor pads, more tolerant attitudes and – with the arrival of Prohibition – an anything-goes speakeasy scene. A number of gay-owned businesses lined MacDougal St, among them the legendary Eve's Hangout at number 129, a tearoom run by Polish Jewish immigrant Eva Kotchever (Eve Addams). Police raided the place in June 1926, charging Eve with 'obscenity' for penning her *Lesbian Love* anthology, and deporting her back to Europe, where she ran a bookstore and club in Paris, fought in the Spanish Civil War and was eventually imprisoned and murdered in Auschwitz. Playwright Barbara Kahn wrote *Unreachable Eden* about Kotchever's life.

America's first gay-rights rally was held in New York City in 1964. Organized by the Homosexual League of New York and the League for Sexual Freedom, the picket took place outside the Army Induction Center on Whitehall St, where protestors demanded an end to the military's anti-gay policies.

Divas, Drag & Harlem

While Times Square had developed a reputation for attracting gay men (many of them working in the district's theaters, restaurants and speakeasy bars), the hottest gay scene in the 1920s was found further north, in Harlem. The neighborhood's flourishing music scene included numerous gay and lesbian performers, among them Gladys Bentley, who was as famous for her tuxedos and girlfriends as she was for her singing.

Queer NYC on Screen

- *Torch Song Trilogy* (1988)
- *The Boys in the Band* (1970)
- *Paris Is Burning* (1990)
- *Angels in America* (2003)
- *Jeffrey* (1995)
- *The Normal Heart* (2014)

Even more famous were Harlem's drag balls, which became a hit with both gay and straight New Yorkers in the roaring '20s. The biggest of the lot was the Hamilton Lodge Ball, organized by Lodge #710 of the Grand United Order of Odd Fellows and held annually at the swank Rockland Palace on 155th St. Commonly dubbed the Faggots Ball, it was a chance for both gay men and women to (legally) cross-dress and steal a same-sex dance, and for fashionable 'normals' to indulge in a little voyeuristic titillation. The evening's star attraction was the beauty pageant, which saw the drag-clad competitors vie for the title of 'Queen of the Ball.' Langston Hughes proclaimed it the 'spectacles of color' and the gay writer was one of many members of New York's literati to attend the ball. It was attended by everyone from sex workers to high-society families. Even the papers covered the extravaganza; its outrageous frocks were the talk of the town.

The Stonewall Revolution

The relative transgression of the early 20th century was replaced with a new conservatism in the following decades, as the Great Depression, WWII and the Cold War took their toll. Conservatism was helped along by Senator Joseph 'Joe' McCarthy, who declared that homosexuals in the State Department threatened America's security and children. Tougher policing aimed to eradicate queer visibility in the public sphere, forcing the scene further underground in the 1940s and '50s. Although crackdowns on gay venues had always occurred, they became increasingly common.

Yet on June 28, 1969, when police officers raided the Stonewall Inn – a gay-friendly watering hole in Greenwich Village – patrons did the unthinkable: they revolted. Fed up with both the harassment and corrupt officers receiving payoffs from the bars' owners (who were mostly organized-crime figures), they began bombarding the officers with coins, bottles, bricks and chants of 'gay power' and 'we shall overcome.' They were also met by a line of high-kicking drag queens and their now-legendary chant: 'We are the Stonewall girls, we wear our hair in curls, we wear no underwear, we show our pubic hair, we wear our dungarees, above our nelly knees...' Their collective anger and solidarity was a turning point, igniting intense and passionate debate about discrimination and forming the catalyst for the modern gay-rights movement, not just in New York, but across the US and in countries from the Netherlands to Australia. On the one-year anniversary of the riots, the day was marked by the US's first LGBTIQ+ Pride march.

LGBTIQ+ Reads

- *Dancer from the Dance* (Andrew Holleran)
- *Last Exit to Brooklyn* (Hubert Selby)
- *Another Country* (James Baldwin)
- *City Boy* (Edmund White)
- *People in Trouble* (Sarah Schulman)
- *The House of Impossible Beauties* (Joseph Cassara)

In the Shadow of AIDS

LGBTIQ+ activism intensified as HIV and AIDS hit world headlines in the early 1980s. Faced with ignorance, fear and the moral indignation of those who saw AIDS as a 'gay cancer,' activists such as writer Larry Kramer set about tackling what was quickly becoming an epidemic. Out of his efforts was born ACT UP (AIDS Coalition to Unleash Power) in 1987, an advocacy group set up to fight the perceived homophobia and indifference of then-president Ronald Reagan, as well as to end the price gouging of AIDS drugs by pharmaceutical companies. One of its boldest protests took place on September 14, 1989, when seven ACT UP protesters chained themselves to the VIP balcony of the New York Stock Exchange, demanding pharmaceutical company Burroughs Wellcome lower the price of AIDS drug AZT from a prohibitive $10,000 per patient per annum. Within days, the price was slashed to $6400 per patient.

The epidemic itself had a significant impact on New York's artistic community. Among its most high-profile victims were artist Keith Haring, photographer Robert Mapplethorpe and fashion designer Halston. Out of this loss grew a tide of powerful AIDS-related plays and musicals that would not only win broad international acclaim but would become part of America's mainstream cultural canon. Among these are Tony Kushner's political epic *Angels in America* and Jonathan Larson's rock musical *Rent*. Both works would win Tony Awards and the Pulitzer Prize.

Marriage & the New Millennium

The LGBTIQ+ fight for complete equality took two massive steps forward in 2011. On September 20, a federal law banning LGBTIQ+ military personnel from serving openly – the so-called 'Don't Ask, Don't Tell' policy – was repealed after years of intense lobbying. Three months earlier persistence had led to an even greater victory – the right to marry. On June 15, the New York State Assembly passed the Marriage Equality Act. On June 24, the very eve of New York City Gay Pride, the bill was signed into law by New York Governor Andrew Cuomo. State victory became a national one on June 26, 2015, when the US Supreme Court ruled that same-sex marriage is a legal right across the country, striking down the remaining marriage bans in 13 US states.

In the same year, organizers of New York City's St Patrick's Parade lifted their long-standing ban on LGBTIQ+ groups, allowing Out@NBCUniversal – a group consisting of gay, lesbian, bisexual and transgender people working for NBCUniversal – to join the parade. The lifting of the ban no doubt met the approval of New York City mayor Bill de Blasio, who had famously boycotted the event in protest.

Despite these significant triumphs, New York City is not immune to intolerance and prejudice. In 2013, New Yorkers reeled when a Brooklyn man, Mark Carson, was fatally shot in Greenwich Village, one of Manhattan's most historically tolerant neighborhoods. Carson and a friend had been walking along 8th St in the early hours of May 18 when, after a short altercation with a group of men hurling homophobic abuse, the 32-year-old was shot at point-blank range. The attack was a sobering reminder that even in liberal New York City, not everyone is happy to live and let live.

When President Trump took office in 2017, New York's annual Gay Pride march gained new purpose in the face of perceived anti-LGBTIQ+ sentiment from within the Trump administration. NYC Pride 2019, marking the 50th anniversary of the Stonewall Riots, brought together 150,000 marchers – double the usual number – for the largest procession in the event's history.

LGBTIQ+ HISTORY

1927

New York State amends a public-obscenity code to include a ban on the appearance or discussion of gay people on stage in reaction to the increasing visibility of gays on Broadway.

1969

Police officers raid the Stonewall Inn in Greenwich Village on June 28, sparking a riot that lasts several days and gives birth to the modern gay rights movement.

1987

ACT UP is founded to challenge the US government's slow response in dealing with AIDS. The activist group stages its first major demonstration on March 24 on Wall St.

2011

New York's Marriage Equality Act comes into effect at 12.01am on July 24. A lesbian couple from Buffalo take their vows just seconds after midnight in Niagara Falls.

2016

President Barack Obama declares a swath of the West Village, including the iconic Christopher Park, a US National Monument, the first such designation honoring the LGBTIQ+ civil rights movement.

2019

The 50th anniversary of the Stonewall riots brings five million attendees to NYC's Pride events.

NYC on Screen

New York City has a long and storied life on screen. It was on these streets that a bumbling Woody Allen fell for Diane Keaton in *Annie Hall,* that Meg Ryan faked her orgasm in *When Harry Met Sally,* and that Sarah Jessica Parker philosophized about the finer points of dating and Jimmy Choos in *Sex & the City.* To fans, traversing the city can feel like one big déjà vu of memorable scenes, characters and one-liners.

Hollywood Roots & Rivals

Believe it or not, America's film industry is an East Coast native. Fox, Universal, Metro, Selznick and Goldwyn all originated here in the early 20th century, and long before Westerns were shot in California and Colorado, they were filmed in the (now former) wilds of New Jersey. Even after Hollywood's year-round sunshine lured the bulk of the business west by the 1920s, 'Lights, Camera, Action' remained a common call in Gotham.

Combined, the city's TV and film industries spend more than $8.7 billion (and rising) on production annually and support 130,000 jobs. More than a third of professional actors in the US are based here.

The Kaufman Astoria Legacy

The heart of the local scene was Queens' still-kicking Kaufman Astoria Studios. Founded by Jesse Lasky and Adolph Zukor in 1916 as a one-stop-shop for their Famous Players–Lasky Corporation, the complex would produce a string of silent-era hits, among them *The Sheik* (1921) and *Monsieur Beaucaire* (1924), both starring Italian-born heartthrob Rudolph Valentino, as well as *Manhandled* (1924), starring early silver-screen diva Gloria Swanson. Renamed Paramount Pictures in 1927, the studios became known for turning Broadway stars into big-screen icons, among them the Marx Brothers, Fred Astaire and Ginger Rogers, the latter making her feature-film debut as a flapper in *Young Man of Manhattan* (1930).

Despite Paramount moving all of its feature film shoots to Hollywood in 1932, the complex – renamed Eastern Services Studio – remained the home of Paramount's newsreel division. Throughout the 1930s, it was also known for its 'shorts,' which launched the careers of homegrown talents including George Burns, Bob Hope and Danny Kaye. After a stint making propaganda and training films for the US Army between WWII and 1970, what had become known as the US Signal Corps Photographic Center was renamed the Kaufman Astoria Studios by George S Kaufman (the real-estate magnate, not the playwright) in 1983. Modernized and expanded, the studio has gone on to make a string of flicks, including *All that Jazz* (1979), *Brighton Beach Memoirs* (1986) and *The Stepford Wives* (2004). It was here that the Huxtables lived out their middle-class Brooklyn lives in the '80s TV sitcom *The Cosby Show,* where the heroine of *Nurse Jackie* juggled addictions and work, and the inmates of Litchfield Penitentiary battled their demons in *Orange is the New Black*. It's still here that small-screen favorite *Sesame Street* is taped.

Beyond Astoria

Slap-bang in the historic Brooklyn Navy Yard, the 760,000-sq-ft Steiner Studios is the largest studio complex east of LA. Its film credits to date include *The Producers* (2005), *Revolutionary Road* (2008), *Sex & the City* 1 and 2 (2008, 2010), and *The Wolf of Wall Street* (2013). The studios have also been used for numerous TV shows, among them Martin Scorsese's critically acclaimed gangster drama *Boardwalk Empire* and fellow HBO series *Vinyl*, a rock drama by Scorsese, Mick Jagger and Terence Winter.

Back in Queens you'll find the city's other big gun, Silvercup Studios. Its list of features include NYC classics such as Francis Ford Coppola's *The Godfather: Part III* (1990) and Woody Allen's *Broadway Danny Rose* (1984) and *The Purple Rose of Cairo* (1985), plus TV gems such as mafia drama *The Sopranos* and the equally lauded comedy *30 Rock,* starring Tina Fey as a TV sketch writer and Alec Baldwin as a network executive at the Rockefeller Center. In reality, the Rockefeller Center is home to the NBC TV network, its long-running variety show *Saturday Night Live* the real inspiration behind Fey's *30 Rock* project.

Other media networks dotted across Manhattan include the Food and Oxygen Networks, both housed in the Chelsea Market, as well as Robert De Niro's Tribeca Productions, based in the Tribeca Film Center.

Beyond the studios and headquarters are some of the top film schools: New York University's Tisch Film School, the New York Film Academy, the School of Visual Arts, Columbia University and the New School. But you don't have to be a student to learn, with both the Museum of the Moving Image (p306) in Astoria, Queens, and the Paley Center for Media (p193) in Midtown Manhattan acting as major showcases for screenings and seminars about productions both past and present.

Landmarks on Screen

Downtown Drama to Midtown Romance

It's not surprising that NYC feels strangely familiar to many first-time visitors – the city itself has racked up more screen time than most Hollywood divas put together and many of its landmarks are as much a part of American screen culture as its red-carpet celebrities. In Brooklyn, the brownstone buildings of Fort Greene were the setting for Spike Lee's cosmopolitan comedy-drama *She's Gotta Have It* (1986). Then there's the Staten Island Ferry, which takes bullied secretary Melanie Griffith from suburbia to Wall St in *Working Girl* (1988); Battery Park, where Madonna bewitches Aidan Quinn and Rosanna Arquette in *Desperately Seeking Susan* (1985); or the New York County Courthouse, where villains get their just desserts in *Wall Street* (1987) and *Goodfellas* (1990). Then there are small-screen classics such as *Cagney & Lacey*, *NYPD Blue* and *Law & Order*. The latter show, famous for showcasing New York and its characters, is honored with its own road – Law & Order Way – that leads to Pier 62 at Chelsea Piers. More recently, the Marvel series *Jessica Jones* and *Luke Cage* capitalized on the moody atmospheres of their filming locations (respectively, Brooklyn and Harlem).

LOCATION TOURS

Movie- and TV-location guided tours such as On Location Tours (p385) are a good way to visit some of the spots where your screen favorites were shot, including *The Devil Wears Prada, Spider-Man, How I Met Your Mother, Jessica Jones, The Sopranos* and more. Alternatively, you can do it yourself after visiting the comprehensive On the Set of New York website (www.onthesetofnewyork.com), which offers free downloadable location maps covering much of Manhattan.

Few landmarks can claim as much screen time as the Empire State Building, famed for its spire-clinging ape in *King Kong* (1933, 2005), as well as for the countless romantic encounters on its observation decks. One of its most famous scenes is Meg Ryan and Tom Hanks' after-hours encounter in *Sleepless in Seattle* (1993). The sequence – which uses the real lobby but a studio-replica deck – is a tribute of sorts to *An Affair to Remember* (1957), which sees Cary Grant and Deborah Kerr make a pact to meet and (hopefully) seal their love atop the skyscraper.

Sarah Jessica Parker is less lucky in *Sex & the City* (2008), when a nervous Mr Big jilts her and her Vivienne Westwood wedding dress at the New York Public Library. Perhaps he'd seen *Ghostbusters* (1984) a few too many times, its opening scenes featuring the haunted library's iconic marble lions and Rose Main Reading Room. The library's foyer sneakily stands in for the Metropolitan Museum of Art in *The Thomas Crown Affair* (1999), in which thieving playboy Pierce Brosnan meets his match in sultry detective Rene Russo. It's at the fountain in adjacent Bryant Park that DIY sleuth Diane Keaton debriefs husband Woody Allen about their supposedly bloodthirsty elderly neighbor in *Manhattan Murder Mystery* (1993). True to form, Allen uses the film to showcase a slew of New York locales, among them the National Arts Club in Gramercy Park and one of his own former hangouts, Elaine's at 1703 Second Ave. It's at this since-closed Upper East Side restaurant that Keaton explains her crime theory to Allen and dinner companions Alan Alda and Ron Rifkin. The restaurant was a regular in Allen's films, also appearing in *Manhattan* (1979) and *Celebrity* (1998).

More than 70 TV shows are filmed in NYC, from hit series such as *Law & Order: Special Victims Unit* and *The Good Fight* and quirky comedies like *The Marvelous Mrs Maisel*, to long-standing classics including *The Tonight Show Starring Jimmy Fallon* and *Saturday Night Live*.

Across Central Park – whose own countless scenes include Barbra Streisand and Robert Redford rowing on its lake in clutch-a-Kleenex *The Way We Were* (1973) – stands the Dakota Building, used in the classic thriller *Rosemary's Baby* (1968) and once the home of Judy Garland. The Upper West Side is also where you'll find Tom's Restaurant, the facade of which was used regularly in *Seinfeld*. Another neighborhood star is the elegant Lincoln Center, where Natalie Portman slowly loses her mind in the psychological thriller *Black Swan* (2010), and where love-struck Brooklynites Cher and Nicolas Cage meet for a date in *Moonstruck* (1987). The Center sits on what had previously been a rundown district of tenements, captured in Oscar-winning gangland musical *West Side Story* (1961).

The Oscar-winner *Birdman* (2014) shines the spotlight on Midtown's glittering Theater District, in which a long-suffering Michael Keaton tries to stage a Broadway adaptation at the St James Theatre on W44th St. Locked out of the building, a mortified Keaton fronts Times Square in nothing but his underwear. A few blocks further east, he spars over his play with Lindsay Duncan at historic drinking den Rum House. Locations in Manhattan, as well as Harlem and Brooklyn, form a much crueller backdrop in *Joker* (2019), which makes effective use of the graffiti-scarred subway to evoke the unforgiving city as it nudges the alienated protagonist towards violence.

Dancing in the Street

Knives make way for leotards in the cult musical *Fame* (1980), in which New York High School of Performing Arts students do little for the city's traffic woes by dancing on Midtown's streets. The film's graphic content was too much for the city's Board of Education, who banned shooting at the real High School of Performing Arts, then located at 120 W 46th St. Consequently, filmmakers used the doorway of a disused church on the opposite side of the street for the school's entrance, and Haaren Hall (Tenth Ave and 59th St) for interior scenes.

STARRING NYC

It would take volumes to cover all the films tied to Gotham, so fire up your imagination with the following celluloid hits:

Taxi Driver (Martin Scorsese, 1976) Starring Robert De Niro, Cybill Shepherd and Jodie Foster. De Niro is a mentally unstable Vietnam War vet whose violent urges are heightened by the city's tensions. It's a funny, depressing, brilliant classic that's a potent reminder of how much grittier this place used to be.

Desperately Seeking Susan (Susan Seidelman, 1985) Starring Madonna, Rosanna Arquette and Aidan Quinn. A case of mistaken identity leads a bored New Jersey housewife on a wild adventure through Manhattan's subcultural wonderland. Relive mid-80s East Village and long-gone nightclub Danceteria.

Summer of Sam (Spike Lee, 1999) Starring John Leguizamo, Mira Sorvino and Jennifer Esposito. Spike Lee puts NYC's summer of 1977 in historical context by weaving together the Son of Sam murders, the blackout, racial tensions and the misadventures of one disco-dancing Brooklyn couple, including scenes at CBGB and Studio 54.

Angels in America (Mike Nichols, 2003) Starring Al Pacino, Meryl Streep and Jeffrey Wright. This movie version of Tony Kushner's Broadway play recalls 1985 Manhattan: crumbling relationships, out-of-control AIDS and a closeted Roy Cohn – advisor to President Ronald Reagan – doing nothing about it except falling ill himself. Follow characters from Brooklyn to Lower Manhattan to Central Park.

Party Monster (Fenton Bailey, 2003) Starring Seth Green and Macaulay Culkin, who plays the famed, murderous club kid Michael Alig, this is a disturbing look into the drug-fueled downtown clubbing culture of the late '80s. The former Limelight club is featured prominently.

Precious (Lee Daniels, 2009) Starring Gabourey Sidibe and Mo'Nique. Based on the novel *Push* by Sapphire, this unflinching tale of an illiterate teenager abused by her parents takes place in Harlem, its gritty streets a the backdrop to stellar performances.

Birdman (Alejandro G Iñárritu, 2014) Oscar-winning black-comedy/drama starring Michael Keaton and featuring Zach Galifianakis, Edward Norton, Andrea Riseborough, Amy Ryan, Emma Stone and Naomi Watts. *Birdman* documents the struggles of a has-been Hollywood actor trying to mount a Broadway show.

Ghostbusters (Paul Feig, 2016) The reboot of the original 1984 film stars four female ghost hunters (comedy stars Melissa McCarthy, Kristen Wiig, Kate McKinnon and Leslie Jones) who light up NYC during their encounters with ghoulish creatures. Though it received mixed reviews, the film broke new ground with its all-female leads.

The Greatest Showman (Michael Gracey, 2017) Musical starring Hugh Jackman, Michelle Williams and Zac Efron. Inspired by the story of PT Barnum, who established the first circus and freak show in 19th-century Manhattan. This film tackles New York society tensions and class divide as low-born Barnum (Hugh Jackman) strives to establish himself and his tribe of New York misfits as respectable performers.

Fame is not alone in turning Gotham into a pop-up dance floor. In *On the Town* (1949), starstruck sailors Frank Sinatra, Gene Kelly and Jules Munshin look straight off a Pride float as they skip, hop and sing their way across this 'wonderful town,' from the base of Lady Liberty to Rockefeller Plaza and the Brooklyn Bridge. Another wave of campness hits the bridge when Diana Ross and Michael Jackson cross it in *The Wiz* (1978), a bizarre take on *The Wizard of Oz,* complete with munchkins in Flushing Meadows Corona Park and an Emerald City at the base of the WTC Twin Towers. Topping them all, however, is the closing scene in Terry Gilliam's *The Fisher King* (1991), which sees Grand Central Terminal's Main Concourse turned into a ballroom of waltzing commuters.

VALESTOCK/SHUTTERSTOCK ©

Above: Hook & Ladder Company 8's firehouse, home to the *Ghost-busters* crew (p376)
Left: Tom's Restaurant (p248), which appeared as Monk's Diner in *Seinfeld*

Survival Guide

Transportation

ARRIVING IN NEW YORK CITY

With three busy airports, two main train stations and a monolithic bus terminal, New York City rolls out the welcome mat for millions of visitors each year.

Direct flights are possible from most major American and international cities. Figure 5½ hours from Los Angeles, seven hours from London and Amsterdam, and 14 hours from Tokyo. Consider getting here by train instead of car or plane to enjoy a mix of bucolic and urban scenery en route, without traffic hassles, security checks and excess carbon emissions.

Flights, cars and tours can be booked online at lonelyplanet.com/bookings.

John F Kennedy International Airport

Fifteen miles from Midtown in southeastern Queens, **John F Kennedy International Airport** (JFK; ☎718-244-4444; www.jfkairport.com; S A to Howard Beach, E, J/Z to Sutphin Blvd-Archer Ave then Airtrain) has six working terminals, serves more than 59 million passengers annually and hosts flights coming and going from all corners of the globe. You can use the AirTrain (free within the airport) to move between terminals.

A massive overhaul of the airport was approved in early 2017, its costs ballooning to $13 billion by 2018. At the time of research, various phases of construction were expected to be completed in 2023 and 2025.

Taxi

A yellow taxi from Manhattan to the airport will use the meter; prices (often about $60) depend on traffic. Expect the ride to take 45 to 60 minutes. From JFK, taxis charge a flat rate of $52 to any destination in Manhattan (not including tolls or tip); it can take 45 to 60 minutes for most destinations in Manhattan. To/from a destination in Brooklyn, the metered fare should be up to $47 (Coney Island) to $64 (downtown Brooklyn). Note that the Williamsburg, Manhattan, Brooklyn and Queensboro–59th St Bridges have no toll either way, while the Queens–Midtown Tunnel and the Hugh L Carey Tunnel (aka the Brooklyn–Battery Tunnel) cost $9.50 going into Manhattan.

Fares for ride-sharing apps like Lyft and Uber are often substantially lower but change depending on the time of day.

Shuttle & Car Service

Shared vans, like those run by Super Shuttle Manhattan (www.supershuttle.com), cost from $26 per person, depending on the destination. They're a good option for budget travelers and solo travelers, though be aware that you may have to wait 30 to 45 minutes for a pick-up from the airport once you check in for your ride after baggage reclaim. Car services traveling to the airport from NYC have set fares from around $50.

Express Bus

The NYC Express Bus (formerly called the NYC Airporter bus; www.nycairporter.com) runs to Grand Central Terminal or the Port Authority Bus Terminal from JFK between 11am and 7pm. The one-way fare is $19.

Subway

The subway is the cheapest but slowest way of reaching Manhattan. From the airport, hop on the AirTrain ($5, payable as you exit) to Sutphin Blvd-Archer Ave (Jamaica Station) to reach the E, J or Z line (or the Long Island Rail Road). To take the A line instead, ride the AirTrain to Howard Beach station. The E train to Midtown has the fewest stops. Expect the journey to take a little over an hour to Midtown.

Long Island Rail Road (LIRR)

This is by far the most relaxing way to arrive in the city.

CLIMATE CHANGE & TRAVEL

Every form of transport that relies on carbon-based fuel generates CO_2, the main cause of human-induced climate change. Modern travel is dependent on airplanes, which might use less fuel per mile per person than most cars but travel much greater distances. The altitude at which aircraft emit gases (including CO_2) and particles also contributes to their climate change impact. Many websites offer 'carbon calculators' that allow people to estimate the carbon emissions generated by their journey and, for those who wish to do so, to offset the impact of the greenhouse gases emitted with contributions to portfolios of climate-friendly initiatives throughout the world. Lonely Planet offsets the carbon footprint of all staff and author travel.

From the airport, take the AirTrain ($5, as you exit) to Jamaica Station. From there, LIRR trains go frequently to Penn Station in Manhattan or to Atlantic Terminal in Brooklyn (near Fort Greene, Boerum Hill and the Barclay Center). It's about a 20-minute journey from station to station. One-way fares to either Penn Station or Atlantic Terminal cost $10.75 ($7.75 at off-peak times).

LaGuardia Airport

Used mainly for domestic flights, **LaGuardia** (LGA; ☎718-533-3400; www.laguardiaairport.com; 🚌M60, Q70) is smaller than JFK but only 8 miles from midtown Manhattan; it sees about 29 million passengers per year.

Much maligned by politicians and ordinary travelers alike, the airport is set to receive a much-needed $8 billion overhaul of its terminal facilities, along with better public transport links. The upgrade is due for completion in 2022.

Taxi

A taxi to/from Manhattan costs about $42 for the approximately half-hour ride; it's metered, no set fare. The meter should read $3 at the start of the journey. Fares for ride-hailing apps like Lyft and Uber vary.

Car Service

A car service to LaGuardia costs from $40. The airport's website lists companies that ply this route.

Express Bus

The NYC Express Bus (formerly the NYC Airporter Bus; www.nycairporter.com) costs $16 and goes to/from Grand Central and the Port Authority Bus Terminal.

Subway & Bus

It's less convenient to get to LaGuardia by public transportation than the other airports. The best subway link is the 74 St-Broadway station (7 line, or the E, F, M and R lines at the connecting Jackson Heights-Roosevelt Ave station) in Queens, where you can pick up the Q70 Express Bus to the airport (about 10 minutes to the airport). Or you can catch the M60 bus from several subway stops in upper Manhattan and Harlem or from the Astoria Blvd station (Hoyt Ave at 31st St) on the N/W subway lines.

Newark Liberty International Airport

Don't write off New Jersey when looking for airfares to New York. About the same distance from Midtown as JFK (16 miles), **Newark** (EWR; ☎973-961-6000; www.newarkairport.com) is used by many New Yorkers (some 46 million passengers traveled through in 2018) and is a hub for United Airlines. A $2.7 billion redevelopment to replace aging Terminal A is scheduled to be completed by the end of 2022.

Car Service

A car service runs about $50 to $70 for the 45-minute ride from Midtown; a taxi is roughly the same. You'll have to pay a whopping $15 to get into NYC through the Lincoln (at 42nd St) and Holland (at Canal St) Tunnels and, further north, the George Washington Bridge, though there's no charge going back through to NJ. There are a couple of cheap tolls on New Jersey highways too, unless you ask your driver to take Hwy 1 or 9.

Subway & Train

NJ Transit (www.njtransit.com) runs a rail service (with a $5.50 AirTrain connection) between Newark airport (EWR) and New York's Penn Station for $13 each way ($9 for children). The trip takes 25 minutes and runs every 20 or 30 minutes from 4:50am to about 2:20am. Hold onto your ticket, which you must show upon exiting at the airport.

Express Bus

The Newark Liberty Airport Express (www.newarkairportexpress.com) has a bus service between the airport and Port Authority Bus Terminal, Bryant Park and Grand Central Terminal in Midtown ($18 one way).

The 45-minute ride operates every 20 minutes between 9am and 11pm, and every half hour between 4:15am and 9am, and between 11pm and 2:20am.

Port Authority Bus Terminal

For long-distance bus trips, you'll arrive and depart from the world's busiest bus station, the **Port Authority Bus Terminal** (Map p428; ☎212-502-2200, bus information 212-564-8484; www.panynj.gov/bus-terminals; 625 Eighth Ave, btwn W 41st & W 42nd Sts, Midtown; 24hr; SA/C/E to 42nd St-Port Authority Bus Terminal), which sees 66 million passengers each year. Efforts to replace the aging and less-than-salubrious station are always on the agenda.

Bus companies leaving from here include the following:

Greyhound (www.greyhound.com) Connects New York with major cities across the country. Has free wi-fi and power outlets on board.

Peter Pan Trailways (www.peterpanbus.com) Daily express services to Boston, Washington, DC, Philadelphia and more.

Short Line Bus (www.shortlinebus.com) Serves northern New Jersey, upstate New York and Pennsylvania, focusing on college towns such as Ithaca; part of Coach USA.

Trailways (www.trailwaysny.com) Bus service to upstate New York, including Albany, Ithaca, Syracuse and the Adirondack Mountains, as well as Montréal, Canada.

Budget Bus Lines

A number of budget bus lines operate from locations on the west side of Midtown:

BoltBus (Map p428; ☎877-265-8287; www.boltbus.com; W 36th St, btwn Seventh & Eighth Aves, Midtown;) Services from New York to Philadelphia, Boston, Baltimore and Washington, DC. The earlier you purchase tickets, the better the deal. Notable for its free wi-fi, which occasionally actually works.

Megabus (Map p428; ☎877-462-6342; https://us.megabus.com; 34th St, btwn 11th & 12th Aves, Midtown; ; S7 to 34th St-Hudson Yards) Travels from New York to Boston, Washington, DC, and Toronto, among other destinations. Free (sometimes functioning) wi-fi. Departures leave from 34th St between Eleventh and Twelfth Aves and incoming arrivals stop at 27th St and Seventh Ave.

Vamoose (Map p428; ☎212-695-6766; www.vamoosebus.com; cnr Seventh Ave & W 30th St, Midtown; from $20; S1 to 28th St; A/C/E, 1/2/3 to 34th St-Penn Station) Buses head to Bethesda, Maryland, and Arlington, Virginia, both near Washington, DC (one way from $20), leaving from the northwest corner of Seventh Ave and W 30th St. There's a luggage storage service at the New York bus stop office (10am to 7pm; per luggage item $5).

Penn Station

Penn Station (W 33rd St, btwn Seventh & Eighth Aves, Midtown; S1/2/3, A/C/E to 34th St-Penn Station), not to be confused with the Penn Station in Newark, NJ, is the oft-maligned departure point for all Amtrak (www.amtrak.com) trains, including the Acela Express services to Boston (four hours) and Washington, DC (three hours). Fares vary, based on the day of the week and the time you want to travel. There's no baggage-storage facility. The station, a confusing underground retail warren, is also a hub for NJ Transit, the Long Island Railroad and various subway lines. Work is underway to create a new train hall opposite the station, but the planned changes are expected to take years.

Long Island Rail Road (www.mta.info/lirr) Serves more than 90 million riders each year, with services from Penn Station to points in Brooklyn and Queens, and on Long Island. Prices are broken down by zones. A peak-hour ride from Penn Station to Jamaica Station (en route to JFK via AirTrain) costs $10.50 if you buy it at the station (buying LIRR tickets on board adds a fee of between $5.75 and $6.50 to the fare!).

NJ Transit (www.njtransit.com) Also operates trains from Penn Station, with services to the New Jersey suburbs and the Jersey Shore.

New Jersey PATH (www.panynj.gov/path) An option for getting into NJ's northern points, such as Hoboken and Newark. Trains ($2.75) run from Penn Station along the length of Sixth Ave, with stops at 33rd, 23rd, 14th, 9th and Christopher Sts, as well as at the reopened World Trade Center site.**Metro-North Railroad** (www.mta.info/mnr) The last line departing from the magnificent Grand Central Terminal serves Connecticut, Westchester County and the Hudson Valley.

GETTING AROUND

Once you've arrived in NYC, getting around is fairly easy. The 660-mile subway system is cheap and (reasonably) efficient and can whisk you to nearly every corner of the city. There are also buses, ferries, trains, bicycles and those ubiquitous yellow taxis. The sidewalks of New York, however, are the real stars – this city is made for walking.

Subway

The New York subway system, run by the Metropolitan Transportation Authority (www.mta.info), is iconic, cheap ($2.75 per ride, regardless of the distance traveled), round-the-clock and often the fastest and most reliable way to get around the city. It's also safer and (a bit) cleaner than it used to be. The downside is the signage is often not very intuitive for first-time visitors and service schedules can baffle even locals.

Grab a free map from the kiosk attendant when you enter, or download a useful smartphone app (like the free Citymapper) for trip planners, subway maps and alerts of service outages (free wi-fi is available in all stations). When in doubt, ask MTA staff for advice. Some platforms also have info points where you can call someone. Avoid headphones while riding, as you might miss an important announcement about track changes or skipped stops.

Taxi

Hailing and riding in a cab, once a rite of passage in New York, is being replaced by the ubiquity of ride-hailing app services like Lyft and Uber. Most taxis in NYC are clean and, compared with those in many international cities, reasonably priced. Don't forget to buckle up for safety.

Taxi & Limousine Commission (TLC; www.nyc.gov/html/tlc/html/home/home.shtml) The taxis' governing body has set fares for rides (which can be paid with credit or debit card). It's $2.50 for the initial charge (first one-fifth of a mile), 50¢ for each additional one-fifth mile as well as per 60 seconds in slow/non-moving traffic, $1 peak surcharge (weekdays 4pm to 8pm), and a 50¢ night surcharge (8pm to 6am), plus an MTA State surcharge of 50¢ per ride. Passengers must pay all bridge and tunnel toll charges. Tips are expected to be 10% to 15%, but give less if you feel in any way mistreated; be sure to ask for a receipt and use it to note the driver's license number.

Passenger rights The TLC keeps a Passenger's Bill of Rights, which gives you the right to tell the driver which route you'd like to take, or ask your driver to turn off an annoying radio station. Also, the driver does not have the right to refuse you a ride based on where you are going. Tip: get in first, then say where you're going.

SUBWAY CHEAT SHEET

A few tips for understanding the madness of the New York subway:

Numbers, letters, colors Color-coded subway lines are named by a letter or number; most carry a collection of two to four trains on their tracks.

Express & local lines Each color-coded line is shared by local trains and express trains; the latter make only select stops in Manhattan (indicated by a white circle on subway maps). For example, the 2 and 3 lines are express, while the slower, local 1 makes every stop. If you're covering a greater distance – say from the Upper West Side to Wall St – transfer to the express train (usually just across the platform from the local) to save time.

Getting in the right station Many stations have separate entrances for 'downtown' or 'uptown' lines (read the entrance sign carefully). If you swipe in at the wrong one, you'll either need to ride the subway to a station where you can transfer for free, or just lose the $2.75 and re-enter the other side (usually across the street). Also look for the green and red lamps above the stairs at each station entrance; green means that it's always open, while red means that particular entrance will be closed at certain hours, usually late at night.

Weekends All the rules switch on weekends, when some lines combine with others, some get suspended, some stations get passed, others get reached. Check www.mta.info for weekend schedules. Sometimes posted signs aren't visible until after you reach the platform.

Private car These services are a common taxi alternative in the outer boroughs. Fares differ depending on the neighborhood and length of ride, and must be determined beforehand, as they have no meters. These 'black cars' are quite common in Brooklyn and Queens, but it's illegal if a driver simply stops to offer you a ride – no matter what borough you're in. A couple of car services in Brooklyn include Northside (www.northsidecarservice.com, 718-387-2222) in Williamsburg and Arecibo (www.arecibocc.com, 718-783-6465) in Park Slope.

Boro Taxis Green Boro Taxis operate in the outer boroughs and Upper Manhattan. These allow folks to hail a taxi on the street in neighborhoods where yellow taxis rarely roam. They have the same fares and features as yellow cabs, and are a good way to get around the outer boroughs (from, say, Astoria to Williamsburg, or Park Slope to Red Hook). Drivers are reluctant (but legally obligated) to take passengers into Manhattan as they aren't legally allowed to take fares going out of Manhattan south of 96th St.

Ride-sharing App-based car-hailing services have taken over the streets of the five boroughs. They're convenient and indispensable for some, but are of course adding to the already terrible traffic problem. Tipping is highly encouraged.

Ferry

NYC Ferry (www.ferry.nyc; one-way $2.75) Operating in the East River since May 2017 (it replaced the former East River Ferry service), these boats link Manhattan, Brooklyn, Queens and the Bronx. At only $2.75 a ride ($1 more to bring a bicycle on board) and with charging stations and mini convenience stores on board, it's an altogether more pleasurable commute than being stuck underground on the subway. It has become a popular and scenic way to reach beach spots in Rockaway, Queens.

NY Water Taxi (www.nywatertaxi.com) Has a fleet of zippy yellow boats that provide hop-on, hop-off services with four stops around Manhattan (Pier 83 at W 42nd St; Battery Park; Pier 16 near Wall St) and Brooklyn (Pier 1 in Dumbo). At $37 for an all-day pass, though, it's priced more like a sightseeing cruise than practical transport.

Staten Island Ferry (Map p406; www.siferry.com; Whitehall Terminal, 4 Whitehall St, at South St, Lower Manhattan; 24hr; S 1 to South Ferry, R/W to Whitehall St, 4/5 to Bowling Green) FREE Bright orange and large, this free commuter-oriented ferry to Staten Island makes constant journeys across New York Harbor. Even if you simply turn around to reboard in Staten Island, the views of lower Manhattan and the Statue of Liberty make this a great sightseeing experience and one of the cheapest dates in the city.

Bus

Part of the Metropolitan Transportation Authority (www.mta.info), buses can be a handy way to cross town or to cover short distances. Rides cost the same as the subway ($2.75 per ride), and you can use your MetroCard or pay in cash (exact change in coins required) when entering the bus. If you pay with a MetroCard, you get one free transfer between bus and subway (either direction) or bus to bus within a two-hour window. If you pay in cash, ask for a transfer (good only for a bus-to-bus transfer) from the bus driver when paying. You'll find the route indicated on the small display box mounted on the pole of the bus stop.

Bicycle

Hundreds of miles of designated bike lanes have been installed over the past decade. Add to this the excellent bike-sharing network Citi Bike (www.citibikenyc.com), and you have the makings of a surprisingly bike-friendly city. There are around 750 Citi Bike stations spread across Manhattan, parts of Brooklyn, Queens and Jersey City, housing the bright-blue and sturdy bicycles. Rates are reasonable for short-term users and there are an estimated 12,000 bikes in the system.

Tourists can either pay for a single ride ($3), or buy a pass (24-hour/three-day passes $12/24 including tax) at any Citi Bike station. You will then be given a five-digit code to unlock a bike. Return the bike to any station within 30 minutes to avoid incurring extra fees. Reinsert your credit card (you won't be charged) and follow the prompts to check out a bike again. If you buy a pass, you can make an unlimited number of 30-minute checkouts during the time period you've paid for.

You'll need to bring your own helmet. They aren't required by law for adults, but are strongly recommended. They are a legal requirement for children 13 and under. City parks like Central Park, the Brooklyn Waterfront Greenway and Prospect Park in Brooklyn are good places to test out your comfort level on wheels in less stressful environments than the chaotic city streets. And most importantly, for your safety and that of others, obey traffic laws.

You'll find routes and bike lanes for every borough on NYC Bike Maps (www.nycbikemaps.com). For downloadable maps and information on NYC cycling laws, visit NYC DOT (www.nyc.gov/

html/dot/html/bicyclists/bikemaps.shtml). Free bike maps are also available at most bike shops.

Train

Long Island Rail Road (www.mta.info/lirr), NJ Transit (www.njtransit.com), New Jersey PATH (www.panynj.gov/path) and Metro-North Railroad (www.mta.info/mnr) all offer useful services for getting around NYC and surrounds.

TOURS

Big Apple Greeter (☎212-669-8159; www.bigapplegreeter.org) For an inside take on NYC, book a walking tour in the neighborhood of your choice led by an enthusiastic local volunteer. You'll be matched with a guide who will suit your needs, or knowing whether that means speaking Spanish, knowing American Sign Language, or where to find the best wheelchair-accessible spots in the city. Reserve at least four weeks in advance.

Big Onion Walking Tours (☎888-606-9255; www.bigonion.com; tours $25) Attention to fine detail makes the award-winning Big Onion stand apart. Choose from nearly 30 tours, including Brooklyn Bridge and Brooklyn Heights, historic Harlem, Chelsea and the High Line, and a 'Gangs of New York' themed walk. There's also an eating tour ($32) of the Lower East Side's global cuisines.

Bike the Big Apple (☎212-749-4444; https://bikethebigapple.com; tours incl bike & helmet from $95) Bike the Big Apple offers eight set tours – including evening rides – each lasting four to seven hours. With a gentle pace and tour leaders keeping watch at both ends of the group, they're well suited to travelers who feel timid about cycling in the city but are eager to cover more ground than a walking tour.

Circle Line Boat Tours (Map p428; ☎212-563-3200; www.circleline.com; Pier 83, W 42nd St at Twelfth Ave; cruises from adult/child $31/26; 🚌westbound M42 or M50 to 12th Ave, Ⓢ A/C/E to 42nd St-Port Authority) The classic Circle Line guides you through all the big sights of Manhattan Island on a variety of boat cruises. Options include a 2½-hour full-island cruise, a shorter (90-minute) 'Landmarks' journey and a two-hour evening tour. From May through September, the outfit also operates adrenaline-fueled cruises aboard the high-speed *Beast*. See the website for schedules.

Foods of New York (☎inquiries 9am-5pm Mon-Fri, to 3pm Sat & Sun 917-408-9539; www.foodsofny.com; tours adult/child from $54/35) The official foodie tour of NYC & Company offers various three-hour tours that help you eat your way through gourmet shops, markets and restaurants in either the West Village, Chelsea, Chinatown, Nolita or Brooklyn. It's a moving feast of French bread, fresh Italian pasta, hot dogs, real New York pizza, Chinese and Polish dumplings, and divine chocolate. Advance booking essential.

Museum Hack (☎347-282-5001; www.museumhack.com; 2hr tour from $59) For a fascinating, alternative perspective of the Met, sign up for a tour with Museum Hack. Knowledgeable but delightfully irreverent guides take on topics like 'Badass Bitches' (a look at paradigm-shifting feminist artists) and lead night tours that include wine. Museum Hack also runs tours in the Museum of Natural History. Check online to see if tours have resumed.

New York City Audubon (Map p422; ☎212-691-7483; www.nycaudubon.org; 71 W 23rd St, Suite 1523, at Sixth Ave, Flatiron District; tours & classes free-$170; Ⓢ F/M to 23rd St) Throughout the year, this society runs bird-watching field trips (including seal- and waterbird-spotting on New York Harbor and eagle-watching in the Hudson Valley), plus lectures and beginners' birding classes. Its 'bird walks' in Central Park and Prospect Park are popular, so book ahead on the website.

Nosh Walks (☎212-222-2243; http://noshwalks.com; 3/4hr tours from $54/60) Deeply knowledgeable foodie Myra Alperson leads food-themed walks all over the NYC area, with special attention given to the ethnically rich hoods of Queens and Brooklyn.

On Location Tours (☎212-913-9780; www.onlocationtours.com; tours from $31) Face it: you want to sit on Carrie Bradshaw's apartment stoop and recreate kick-ass scenes from *Jessica Jones*. This company offers various tours – themed around superheroes and TV and movie locations – as well as deep dives into filming locations for *Gossip Girl*, *Sex and the City*, *The Sopranos* and the *Real Housewives of NYC*.

Wildman Steve Brill (☎914-835-2153; www.wildmanstevebrill.com; suggested donation adult/child $20/10) New York's best-known naturalist has been leading folks on foraging expeditions through city parks for more than 30 years. He'll trek with you through Central Park, Prospect Park, Inwood Park and many more, teaching you to identify natural riches including sassafras, chickweed, ginkgo nuts, garlic and wild mushrooms along the way. It's wild.

Directory A–Z

Accessible Travel

Much of the city is accessible, with curb cuts for wheelchair users. All the major sites (like the Met museum, the Guggenheim, the 9/11 Memorial and Museum, and the Lincoln Center) are also accessible. Some, but not all, Broadway venues have provisions for theater-goers with disabilities, from listening devices to wheelchair seating; consult http://theatre access.nyc.

Unfortunately, only about 100 of New York's 468 subway stations are fully wheelchair accessible. In general, the bigger stations have access, such as 14th St-Union Sq, 34th St-Penn Station, 42nd St-Port Authority Terminal, 59th St-Columbus Circle, and 66th St-Lincoln Center. For a complete list of accessible subway stations, visit http://web.mta.info/accessibility/stations.htm. Also visit www.nycgo.com/accessibility.

On the plus side, all of NYC's MTA buses are wheelchair accessible, and are often a better option than negotiating cramped subway stations. Taxis suitable to travelers with mobility aids are available through Accessible Dispatch (646-599-9999; http://accessibledispatch.org); there's also an app that allows you to request the nearest available service.

Another excellent resource is the **Big Apple Greeter** (☎212-669-8159; www.bigapplegreeter.org) FREE program, which is staffed by more than 50 volunteers with various disabilities who are happy to show off their corner of the city.

Restrooms can be found in most department stores and the NYC parks website (www.nycgovparks.org/facilities/bathrooms) is a good source of info regarding bathrooms – some of them wheelchair accessible – across the city's green spaces.

The city also provides paratransit buses for getting around town for the same price as a subway fare, though this service – called Access-a-Ride (https://access.nyc.gov/programs/access-a-ride) – isn't very practical for tourists; you'll need to attend an assessment appointment and fill in mailed paperwork before eligibility for the service can be confirmed (which can take up to 21 days). Visit the website for more info.

Download Lonely Planet's free Accessible Travel guides from https://shop.lonelyplanet.com/categories/accessible-travel.com.

Customs Regulations

US Customs allows each person over the age of 21 to bring 1L of liquor (provided it isn't absinthe...yes, really!) and 200 cigarettes into the US duty free. Agricultural items including meat, fruits, vegetables, plants and soil are prohibited. US citizens are allowed to import gifts duty free, usually up to $800 worth, while non-US citizens are allowed to import $100 worth. If you're carrying more than $10,000 in US and foreign cash, traveler's checks or money orders, you need to declare the excess amount. There is no legal restriction on the amount that may be imported, but undeclared sums in excess of $10,000 will probably be subject to investigation. If you're bringing prescription drugs, make sure they're in clearly marked containers. Obviously, leave the illegal narcotics at home. For updates, check www.cbp.gov.

Discount Cards

If you plan on blitzing the major sights, consider one of the numerous multi-attraction passes (see www.nycgo.com/attraction-passes). Getting one of these discount cards will save you a wad of cash. Go online to find out more or to purchase a pass.

New York CityPASS (www.citypass.com) Buys you admission to six major attractions (including the Empire State Building) for $132 ($108 for kids), saving you more than 40% than if purchased separately.

The New York Pass (www.newyorkpass.com) This pass gives you one-day access to some 100 different sites, including the Empire State Building, for $134 (or $99 for children). Multiday passes also available (from two to 10 days).

Go City (www.gocity.com) This pass lets you choose between three and 10 attractions for discounted admission. You pick the sites from among more than 90 options, including the MoMA, the 9/11 Memorial and Museum, the Top of the Rock and activities like Central Park bike rental and walking tours. Prices start at $94 for three sites and go up to $270 for 10 sites.

Electricity

The US electric current is 110V to 115V, 60Hz AC. Outlets are made for flat two-prong plugs (which often have a third, rounded prong for grounding). If your appliance is made for another electrical system (eg 220V), you'll need a step-down converter, which can be bought at hardware stores and drugstores. Most electronic devices (laptops, camera-battery chargers etc) are built for dual-voltage use, however, and will only need a plug adapter.

Type A
120V/60Hz

Type B
120V/60Hz

Emergency & Important Numbers

Local directory	☎411
Municipal offices & NYC information	☎311
Fire, police & ambulance	☎911

Internet Access

Most public parks in the city now offer free wi-fi. Some prominent Manhattan spots include the High Line, Bryant Park, Battery Park, City Hall Park, Madison Square Park and Tompkins Square Park. Brooklyn has many free wi-fi spots, including Prospect Park and Brooklyn Bridge Park; Queens also has locations though they're more thinly dispersed. Note that connectivity may be poor in some locations. See a map of wi-fi spots on www.nycgovparks.org/facilities/wifi.

Museums also often offer free wi-fi, as do underground subway stations and libraries. LinkNYC (www.link.nyc), rolled out in 2016 to replace anachronistic pay phones (once iconic symbols of the city in which Superman changed into his suit), has installed free internet-connected kiosks (funded by advertising), replete with charging stations and wi-fi access. The network aims to install some 7500 of these structures throughout the five boroughs.

It's rare to find accommodations in New York City that don't offer free wi-fi these days. Most cafes offer wi-fi for customers (though they may not always advertise it), as do the ubiquitous Starbucks around town.

Legal Matters

If you're arrested, you have the right to remain silent. There is no legal reason to speak to a police officer if you don't wish to – especially since anything you say 'can and will be used against you' – but never walk away from an officer until given permission (politely ask if you are free to leave). All persons who are arrested have the legal right to make one phone call. If you don't have a lawyer or family member to help you, call your consulate. The police will give you the number upon request.

Medical Services

Before traveling, contact your health-insurance provider to find out what types of medical care will be covered outside your hometown (or home country). Overseas visitors should acquire travel insurance that covers medical situations in the US, as nonemergency care for uninsured patients can be very expensive. For nonemergency appointments at hospitals, you'll need proof of insurance or cash. Even with insurance, you'll most likely have to pay up front for nonemergency care and

PRACTICALITIES

Newspapers & Magazines

New York Post (www.nypost.com) The *Post* is known for screaming headlines, conservative political views and its popular Page Six gossip column.

New York Times (www.nytimes.com) 'The gray lady' is far from staid, with hard-hitting political coverage, and sections on technology, arts and dining out.

Wall Street Journal (www.wallstreetjournal.com) This intellectual daily focuses on finance, though media mogul Rupert Murdoch has ratcheted up the general coverage.

New York Magazine (www.nymag.com) A biweekly magazine with feature stories and great listings about anything and everything in NYC, plus an indispensable website.

New Yorker (www.newyorker.com) This highbrow weekly covers politics and culture through its famously lengthy works of reportage; it also publishes fiction and poetry.

Time Out New York (www.timeout.com/newyork) A weekly magazine with event listings and restaurant and nightlife roundups.

Gothamist (https://gothamist.com) Light-hearted coverage of local news, arts and gossip.

Radio

NYC has some excellent radio options beyond commercial pop-music stations. An excellent programming guide can be found in the *New York Times* Entertainment section on Sunday. Our top pick is WNYC (820AM and 93.9FM; www.wnyc.org), NYC's public radio station that is the local NPR (National Public Radio) affiliate and offers a blend of national and local talk and interview shows.

Die-hard sports fans tune in to call-in shows on WFAN (660AM and 101FM; https://wfan.radio.com) throughout the day. Yankees and Mets fanatics tend to be the most obsessive callers, usually unwilling to give any credit to their rivals.

Smoking

Smoking is strictly forbidden in any location that's considered a public place, including subway stations, restaurants, bars, taxis and parks. A few hotels have smoking rooms, but the majority are entirely smoke-free.

then wrangle with your insurance company afterward in order to get your money reimbursed.

Travel MD (212-737-1212; www.travelmd.com) offers 24-hour medical advice for visitors to NYC, and has a doctor that will do home visits to patients' hotels.

Emergency Rooms & Hospitals

Emergency services can be stress-inducing and slow (unless your medical condition is absolutely dire); a visit should be avoided if other medical services can be accessed to mitigate the situation. In a genuine health emergency, dial ☎911.

New York-Presbyterian/Columbia Hospital (☎212-305-2500; www.nyp.org/locations/newyork-presbyterian-columbia-university-medical-center; 630 W 168th St, at Ft Washington Ave; Ⓢ A/C, 1 to 168th St) Reputable hospital.

Bellevue Hospital Center (☎212-562-4141; www.nychealthandhospitals.org/bellevue; 462 First Ave, at 27th St, Midtown East; Ⓢ 6 to 28th St) Major public hospital with emergency room and trauma center.

Tisch Hospital (New York University Langone Medical Center;☎212-263-5800; www.nyulangone.org/locations/tisch-hospital; 550 First Ave, Midtown East; ⏲24hr) Large, state-of-the-art facility with highly regarded departments in every critical care specialty.

Callen-Lorde Community Health Center (☎212-271-7200; www.callen-lorde.org; 356 W 18th St, btwn Eighth & Ninth Aves; ⏲8am-8:15pm Mon-Thu, 9:45am-4:45pm Fri, 8:15am-3:15pm Sat; Ⓢ A/C/E, L to 8th Ave-14th St) This medical center, dedicated to the LGBTIQ+ community and people living with HIV/AIDS, serves people regardless of their ability to pay.

Lenox Hill Hospital (☎212-434-2000; www.northwell.edu/find-care/locations/lenox-hill-hospital; 100 E 77th St, at Lexington Ave; ⏲24hr; Ⓢ 6 to 77th St) A good hospital with a 24-hour emergency room and multilingual translators in the Upper East Side.

Mount Sinai Hospital (☎212-241-6500; www.mountsinai.org/locations/mount-sinai; 1468 Madison Ave, at E 101st St; ⏰24hr; Ⓢ6 to 103rd St) An excellent hospital in the Upper East Side.

NYU Langone Health Cobble Hill (☎646-754-7900; https://nyulangone.org; 83 Amity St, at Hicks St, Cobble Hill; Ⓢ2, 3, 4, 5 to Borough Hall) Emergency-care specialist based in Brooklyn.

Planned Parenthood (Margaret Sanger Center; ☎212-965-7000; www.plannedparenthood.org; 26 Bleecker St, btwn Mott & Elizabeth Sts, NoHo; ⏰8am-8:30pm Mon-Thu, to 6:30pm Fri, to 5:30pm Sat; ⓈB/D/F/V to Broadway-Lafayette St; 6 to Bleecker St) Provides birth control, STD screenings and gynecological care.

Pharmacies

New York is bursting with 24-hour 'drug stores,' which are handy all-purpose stores where you can buy over-the-counter medications anytime; the pharmaceutical prescription counters have more limited hours. Major drug store chains include CVS, Duane Reade, Rite Aid and Walgreens.

Money

ATMs widely available; credit cards accepted at most hotels, stores and restaurants. Farmers markets and some food trucks, restaurants and bars are cash-only.

ATM

ATMs are on practically every corner. You can either use your card at banks – usually in a 24-hour-access lobby, filled with up to a dozen monitors at major branches – or you can opt for the lone wolves, which sit in delis, restaurants, bars and grocery stores, charging fierce service fees that average $4 but can go higher than $5.

Most New York banks are linked by the New York Cash Exchange (NYCE) system, and you can use local bank cards interchangeably at ATMs – for an extra fee if you're banking outside your system.

Changing Money

Banks and money changers, found all over New York City (including all three major airports), will give you US currency based on the current exchange rate, often with a fee. Travelex has a branch in Times Square but considerable fees apply.

Credit Cards

Major credit cards are accepted at most hotels, restaurants and shops throughout New York City. In fact, you'll find it difficult to perform certain transactions, such as purchasing tickets to performances and renting a car, without one.

Stack your deck with a Visa, MasterCard or American Express, as these are the cards of choice here. Places that accept Visa and MasterCard also accept debit cards. Be sure to check with your bank to confirm that your debit card will be accepted in other states or countries – debit cards from large commercial banks can often be used worldwide.

If your cards are lost or stolen, contact the company immediately.

Opening Hours

Standard business hours are as follows:

Banks 9am–6pm Monday–Friday, some also 9am–noon Saturday

Bars 5pm–4am

Businesses 9am–5pm Monday–Friday

Clubs 10pm–4am

Restaurants Breakfast 6am–11am, lunch noon to around 3pm, and dinner 5pm–11pm. Weekend brunch 10am–4pm.

Shops 10am to around 7pm weekdays, 11am to around 8pm Saturday; Sunday can be variable – some stores stay closed while others keep weekday hours. Stores tend to stay open later in the neighborhoods downtown, such as SoHo.

Post

Visit the US Postal Service (www.usps.com) website for up-to-date information about postage prices and branch locations throughout the city.

Public Holidays

New Year's Day January 1

Martin Luther King Day Third Monday in January

Presidents' Day Third Monday in February

Memorial Day Late May

Independence Day July 4

Labor Day First Monday in September

Veterans Day November 11

Thanksgiving Fourth Thursday in November

Christmas Day December 25

Safe Travel

NYC is one of the USA's safest cities – in 2018 homicides fell to 289, a record low not seen since the early 1950s. Overall violent-crime statistics have declined for the 28th straight year. Still, keep your wits about you.

➡ Don't walk alone at night in unfamiliar, sparsely populated areas.

➡ Beware pickpockets, particularly in mobbed areas like Times Square or Penn Station.

➡ While it's generally safe to ride the subway after midnight, you may want to take a taxi, especially when alone (ride in the back).

➡ Avoid pressure sales for show tickets and cruises; book online or at official vendors.

Telephone

Phone numbers within the US consist of a three-digit area code followed by a seven-digit local number. In NYC, dial 1 + the three-digit area code + the seven-digit number. To make an international call from NYC, call ☎011 + country code + area code + number. When calling Canada, there is no need to use the 011.

Time

New York City is in the Eastern Standard Time (EST) zone – five hours behind Greenwich Mean Time (London) and three hours ahead of Pacific Standard Time (California). Almost all of the USA observes daylight-saving time: clocks go forward one hour on the second Sunday in March and are turned back one hour on the first Sunday in November. Devices connected to the internet update automatically but it's easy to remember by the phrase 'spring ahead, fall back.'

Toilets

Considering the number of pedestrians, there aren't nearly enough public restrooms around the city. You'll find spots to relieve yourself in Grand Central Terminal, Penn Station and Port Authority Bus Terminal, and in parks, including Madison Square Park, Bryant Park, Battery Park, Tompkins Square Park, Washington Square Park and Columbus Park in Chinatown, plus several places scattered around Central Park – check www.nycgovparks.org/facilities/bathrooms for a full list of locations. Automated coin-operated public toilets are popping up in locations including Madison Square Park and Grand Army Plaza (Brooklyn). A good bet, though, is to pop into a Starbucks (there's one about every three blocks), or a department store (Macy's, Century 21, Bloomingdale's or, in Brooklyn, Empire Stores).

Tourist Information

NYC Information Center (Map p428; ☎212-484-1222; www.nycgo.com; Macy's, 151 W 34th St, at Broadway; ⏲10am-10pm Mon-Sat, to 9pm Sun; Ⓢ B/D/F/M, N/Q/R/W to 34th St-Herald Sq) NYC's official tourist information kiosk is inside Macy's department store, with free maps and brochures and helpful, bilingual staff (languages spoken include Spanish, French, Mandarin Chinese, Portuguese and Italian; availability varies). It's located at the back on the 1st-floor mezzanine level. Tourists are also eligible for 10% store-discount vouchers (bring ID).

Visas

Visa Waiver Program

The US Visa Waiver Program (VWP) allows nationals from 38 countries to enter the US without a visa for up to 90 days, provided you are carrying a machine-readable passport. For the up-to-date list of countries included in the program and current requirements, see the US Department of State (https://travel.state.gov) website.

Citizens of VWP countries need to register with the US Department of Homeland Security and fill out an ESTA application (Electronic System for Travel Authorization; www.cbp.gov/travel/international-visitors/esta) before arrival. There is a $14 fee for registration; when approved, the registration is valid for two years or until your passport expires, whichever comes first (unless your name, gender or citizenship changes).

Visas Required

You must obtain a visa from a US embassy or consulate in your home country if:

➡ You do not currently hold a passport from a VWP country.

➡ You are from a VWP country, but don't have a machine-readable passport.

➡ You are planning to stay longer than 90 days.

➡ You are planning to work or study in the US.

Volunteering

There are numerous volunteer opportunities in NYC. You can help mentor struggling students, assist in cleaning up the parks, plant and harvest in urban farms, play Bingo with seniors or lend a hand serving food in a soup kitchen (a place where homeless or low-income residents can get a free meal). A few places where you can sign up to help include the following organizations:

New York Cares (www.newyorkcares.org)

NYC Service (www.nycservice.org)

Street Project (www.streetproject.org)

VolunteerMatch (www.volunteermatch.org)

Behind the Scenes

SEND US YOUR FEEDBACK

We love to hear from travelers – your comments keep us on our toes and help make our books better. Our well-traveled team reads every word on what you loved or loathed about this book. Although we cannot reply individually to your submissions, we always guarantee that your feedback goes straight to the appropriate authors, in time for the next edition. Each person who sends us information is thanked in the next edition – the most useful submissions are rewarded with a selection of digital PDF chapters.

Visit **lonelyplanet.com/contact** to submit your updates and suggestions or to ask for help. Our award-winning website also features inspirational travel stories, news and discussions.

Note: We may edit, reproduce and incorporate your comments in Lonely Planet products such as guidebooks, websites and digital products, so let us know if you don't want your comments reproduced or your name acknowledged. For a copy of our privacy policy visit lonelyplanet.com/privacy.

WRITER THANKS

Ali Lemer

Thanks to Trisha Ping and Lauren Keith, to Dawn Hopper at Dutchess Tourism and Stacey-Ann Hosang at the Empire State Building, and to my co-authors, especially Anita Isalska and MaSovaida Morgan. Thanks also to Mark Batt and to Michael and Ellen Korney for their love and support. My chapters are dedicated to the memories of my two favorite New Yorkers, Toni Halbreich and Albert Lemer.

Anita Isalska

Big thanks to Lauren Keith for the opportunity and clear guidance, an enormous thank you to Ali Lemer for local insights, and to Normal Matt for being game to hit Williamsburg so hard.

MaSovaida Morgan

Deepest thanks to the wonderful folks who made my return to this beloved, sweltering beast of a city for this summer research trip a success: Travis Williams and Alfie de Longchamp, Hailey Mahan, Patrick Salami, Tracy Gilmore and Rich Timbol, Floris Billiet and Charles Mussche, Lauren Weber, Mark Toslu, Travis Levius, Oneika Raymond, Matthew Downing, Benno, and Dana Givens. Finally, big thanks to Lauren Keith for rallying me, and to my dream team of co-writers, Kevin, Ali and Anita.

Kevin Raub

Thanks to Lauren Keith and all my fellow partners in crime at Lonely Planet. On the road, Tommy and Shelley Martin for the life-saving Upper West Side digs and Discover Long Island, Sian Perry and Jo Webb for the helping hand. Alice Brignani, Brian and Jennifer Patterson, Charles Runnette and Nathan Lump, Isabel Sinistore, Emily Munro, Kathleen O'Connor, Sharon Nieuwenhuis, Margeret Anne-Logan, Michelle Perlin, Alex Wittenberg, Lisbeth Cassaday, Susan Galardi and Helen Harrison.

ACKNOWLEDGEMENTS

Cover photograph: Empire State Building, Midtown, New York City, Michele Falzone/AWL Images ©
Illustration pp230-1 by Javier Zarracina

THIS BOOK

This 12th edition of Lonely Planet's *New York City* guidebook was researched and written by Ali Lemer, Anita Isalska, MaSovaida Morgan and Kevin Raub. This guidebook was produced by the following:

Destination Editors Lauren Keith, assisted by Bailey Freeman

Senior Product Editors Daniel Bolger, Grace Dobell, Martine Power

Regional Senior Cartographers Mark Griffiths, Alison Lyall

Product Editors Pete Cruttenden, Alison Ridgway

Book Designers Hannah Blackie, Fergal Condon

Assisting Editors Hannah Cartmel, Melanie Dankel, Kellie Langdon, Jodie Martire, Kristin Odijk, Monique Perrin, Mani Ramaswamy, Fionnuala Twomey, Maja Vatrić

Assisting Cartographers Corey Hutchison, Anthony Phelan, Julie Sheridan, Diana von Holdt

Cover Researcher Meri Blazevski

Thanks to Bruce Evans, Andi Jones, Femi Pai, Andrea Pizzuto, Greta, Dania and Robert Rauer, Vicky Smith, Gabrielle Stefanos ,Yosef Yeroshalmi

See also separate subindexes for:

- **EATING P397**
- **DRINKING & NIGHTLIFE P399**
- **ENTERTAINMENT P400**
- **SHOPPING P401**
- **SPORTS & ACTIVITIES P402**
- **SLEEPING P402**

Index

Sights 000
Map Pages **000**
Photo Pages **000**

Sights 000
Map Pages **000**
Photo Pages **000**

EATING

INDEX EATING

DRINKING & NIGHTLIFE

☆ ENTERTAINMENT

Sights 000
Map Pages **000**
Photo Pages **000**

Sights 000
Map Pages **000**
Photo Pages **000**

New York City Maps

Sights

- Beach
- Bird Sanctuary
- Buddhist
- Castle/Palace
- Christian
- Confucian
- Hindu
- Islamic
- Jain
- Jewish
- Monument
- Museum/Gallery/Historic Building
- Ruin
- Shinto
- Sikh
- Taoist
- Winery/Vineyard
- Zoo/Wildlife Sanctuary
- Other Sight

Activities, Courses & Tours

- Bodysurfing
- Diving
- Canoeing/Kayaking
- Course/Tour
- Sento Hot Baths/Onsen
- Skiing
- Snorkeling
- Surfing
- Swimming/Pool
- Walking
- Windsurfing
- Other Activity

Sleeping

- Sleeping
- Camping
- Hut/Shelter

Eating

- Eating

Drinking & Nightlife

- Drinking & Nightlife
- Cafe

Entertainment

- Entertainment

Shopping

- Shopping

Information

- Bank
- Embassy/Consulate
- Hospital/Medical
- Internet
- Police
- Post Office
- Telephone
- Toilet
- Tourist Information
- Other Information

Geographic

- Beach
- Gate
- Hut/Shelter
- Lighthouse
- Lookout
- Mountain/Volcano
- Oasis
- Park
- Pass
- Picnic Area
- Waterfall

Population

- Capital (National)
- Capital (State/Province)
- City/Large Town
- Town/Village

Transport

- Airport
- BART station
- Border crossing
- Boston T station
- Bus
- Cable car/Funicular
- Cycling
- Ferry
- Metro/Muni station
- Monorail
- Parking
- Petrol station
- Subway/SkyTrain station
- Taxi
- Train station/Railway
- Tram
- Underground station
- Other Transport

Routes

- Tollway
- Freeway
- Primary
- Secondary
- Tertiary
- Lane
- Unsealed road
- Road under construction
- Plaza/Mall
- Steps
- Tunnel
- Pedestrian overpass
- Walking Tour
- Walking Tour detour
- Path/Walking Trail

Boundaries

- International
- State/Province
- Disputed
- Regional/Suburb
- Marine Park
- Cliff
- Wall

Hydrography

- River, Creek
- Intermittent River
- Canal
- Water
- Dry/Salt/Intermittent Lake
- Reef

Areas

- Airport/Runway
- Beach/Desert
- Cemetery (Christian)
- Cemetery (Other)
- Glacier
- Mudflat
- Park/Forest
- Sight (Building)
- Sportsground
- Swamp/Mangrove

Note: Not all symbols displayed above appear on the maps in this book

0 5 km
0 2.5 miles
Hudson River
BRONX
CROTONA PARK
MORRISANIA
WEEHAWKEN
HARLEM
LONGWOOD
HUNTS POINT
East River
Randalls Island
Rikers Island
UNION CITY
Central Park
ASTORIA
LONG ISLAND CITY
JACKSON HEIGHTS
MANHATTAN
SUNNYSIDE
FLUSHING
HOBOKEN
QUEENS
East River
GREENPOINT
MASPETH
JERSEY CITY
WILLIAMSBURG
RIDGEWOOD
GLENDALE
BUSHWICK
Ellis Island
DUMBO
BROOKLYN HEIGHTS
DOWNTOWN BROOKLYN
Liberty Island
Governors Island
BROOKLYN
RED HOOK
GOWANUS
PROSPECT HEIGHTS
NEW LOTS
Upper New York Bay
PROSPECT PARK
GREENWOOD HEIGHTS
18 Coney Island & Brighton Beach (4.5mi)
1
2
3
4
5
6
7
8
9
10
11
12
13
14
15
16
17
19
20

MAP INDEX

LOWER MANHATTAN & THE FINANCIAL DISTRICT *Map on p406*

Top Experiences (p64)

1 Ellis Island ... B8
2 National September 11 Memorial & Museum ... C5
3 One World Trade Center ... B4
4 Statue of Liberty ... C8

Sights (p72)

5 African Burial Ground National Monument ... D3
6 Battery Park ... C7
7 Bowling Green ... C7
8 Castle Clinton ... C7
9 City Hall ... D4
10 Federal Hall ... D6
11 Fraunces Tavern Museum ... D7
12 Museum of Jewish Heritage ... B7
13 National Museum of the American Indian ... D7
14 National September 11 Memorial ... B5
15 New York Stock Exchange ... D6
One World Observatory ... (see 3)
16 Pier 17 ... F5
17 SeaGlass Carousel ... D8
18 Skyscraper Museum ... C7
19 South Street Seaport District ... F4
20 South Street Seaport Museum ... E5
21 St Paul's Chapel ... C4
22 Trinity Church ... C6
23 USCGC Lilac ... A2
24 Woolworth Building ... C4

Eating (p78)

25 Augustine ... D4
26 Bâtard ... C2
27 Brookfield Place ... B5
28 Da Mikele ... C2
29 Gotan ... C2
30 Grand Banks ... A3
Hudson Eats ... (see 27)
Le District ... (see 27)
Locanda Verde ... (see 67)
31 Luchadores NYC ... E5
32 Maman ... C2
33 Paris Cafe ... F5
34 Tiny's & the Bar Upstairs ... C3
35 Two Hands ... C2
36 Van Leeuwen ... F5

Drinking & Nightlife (p81)

37 Bluestone Lane ... D6
38 Brandy Library ... C2
39 Cowgirl SeaHorse ... F4
40 Dead Rabbit ... D7
41 La Colombe ... C1
42 Macao Trading Co ... C1
43 Pier A Harbor House ... C7
44 Smith & Mills ... B2
45 Terroir Tribeca ... B2
46 Ward III ... C3
47 Weather Up ... C3

Entertainment (p83)

48 City Vineyard ... A2
49 Flea Theater ... C3
Roxy Tribeca Cinema ... (see 68)
50 Soho Rep ... C1

Shopping (p84)

51 Best Made Company ... C2
52 Bowne & Co Stationers ... E5
53 Century 21 ... C5
54 CityStore ... D3
55 Mysterious Bookshop ... C3
56 Pasanella & Son ... F5
57 Pearl River Mart ... D2
58 Philip Williams Posters ... C3
59 Shinola ... B2

Sports & Activities (p85)

60 Downtown Boathouse ... A2
61 Institute of Culinary Education ... B5
Pioneer ... (see 20)
62 Staten Island Ferry ... D8
WO Decker ... (see 20)

Sleeping (p333)

63 AKA Tribeca ... C3
64 Andaz Wall St ... E6
65 Conrad New York ... A4
66 Gild Hall ... D5
67 Greenwich Hotel ... B2
68 Roxy Hotel ... C2

LOWER MANHATTAN & THE FINANCIAL DISTRICT

0 500 m
0 0.25 miles

Key on p405

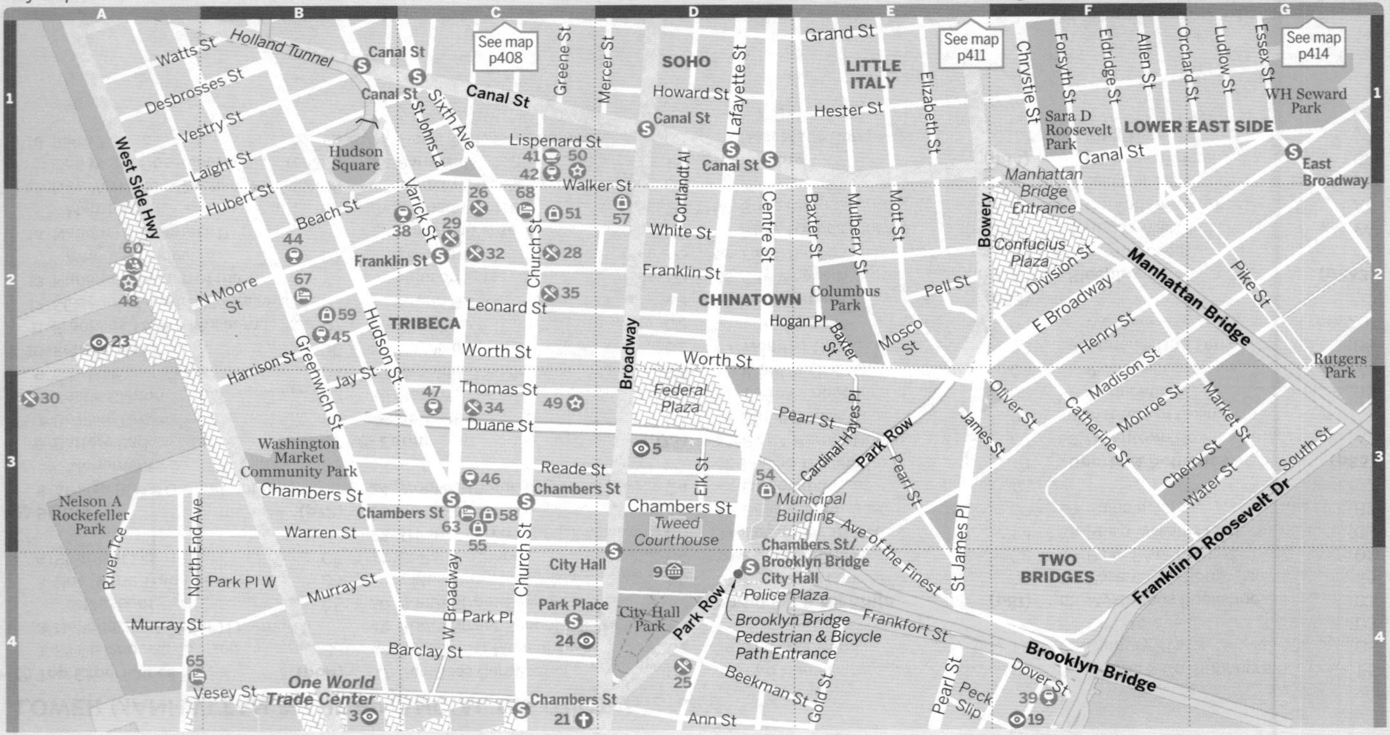

LOWER MANHATTAN & THE FINANCIAL DISTRICT

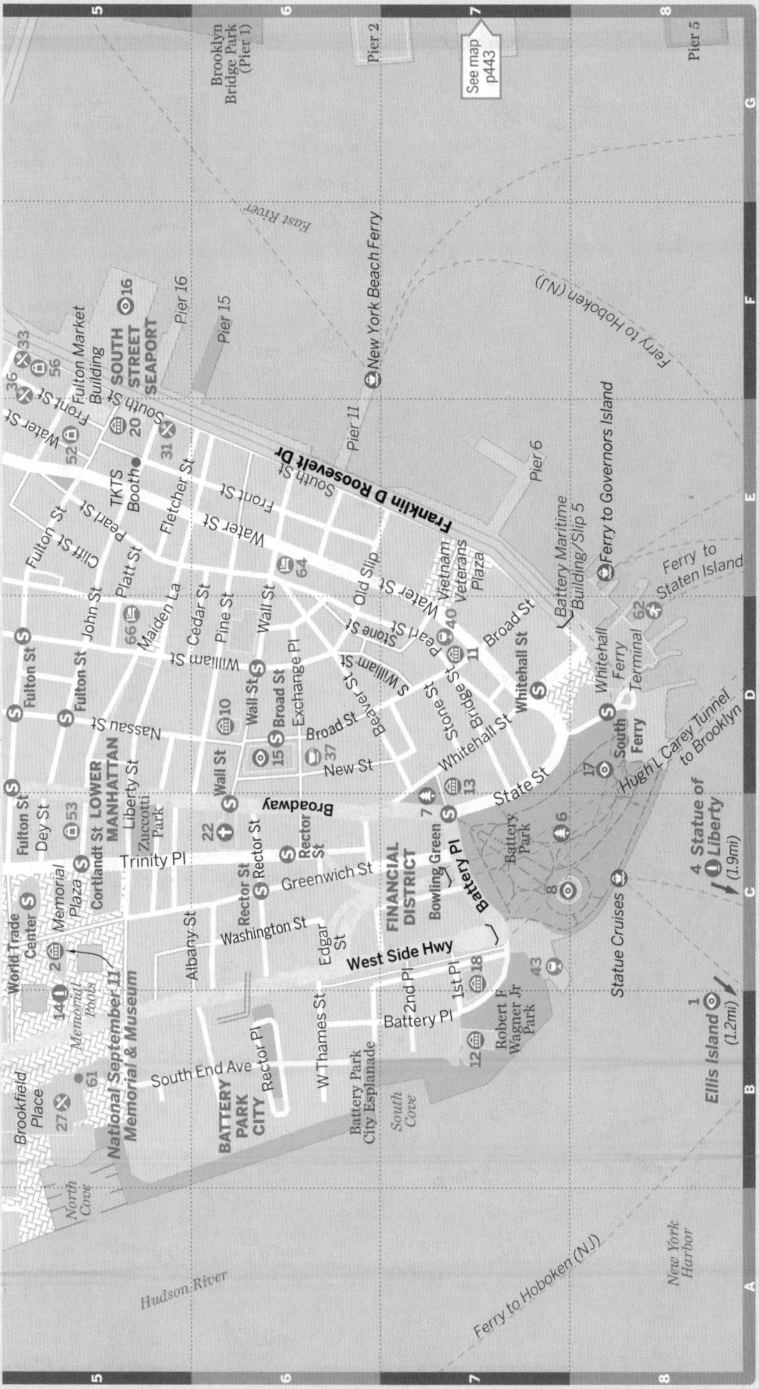

Key on p410

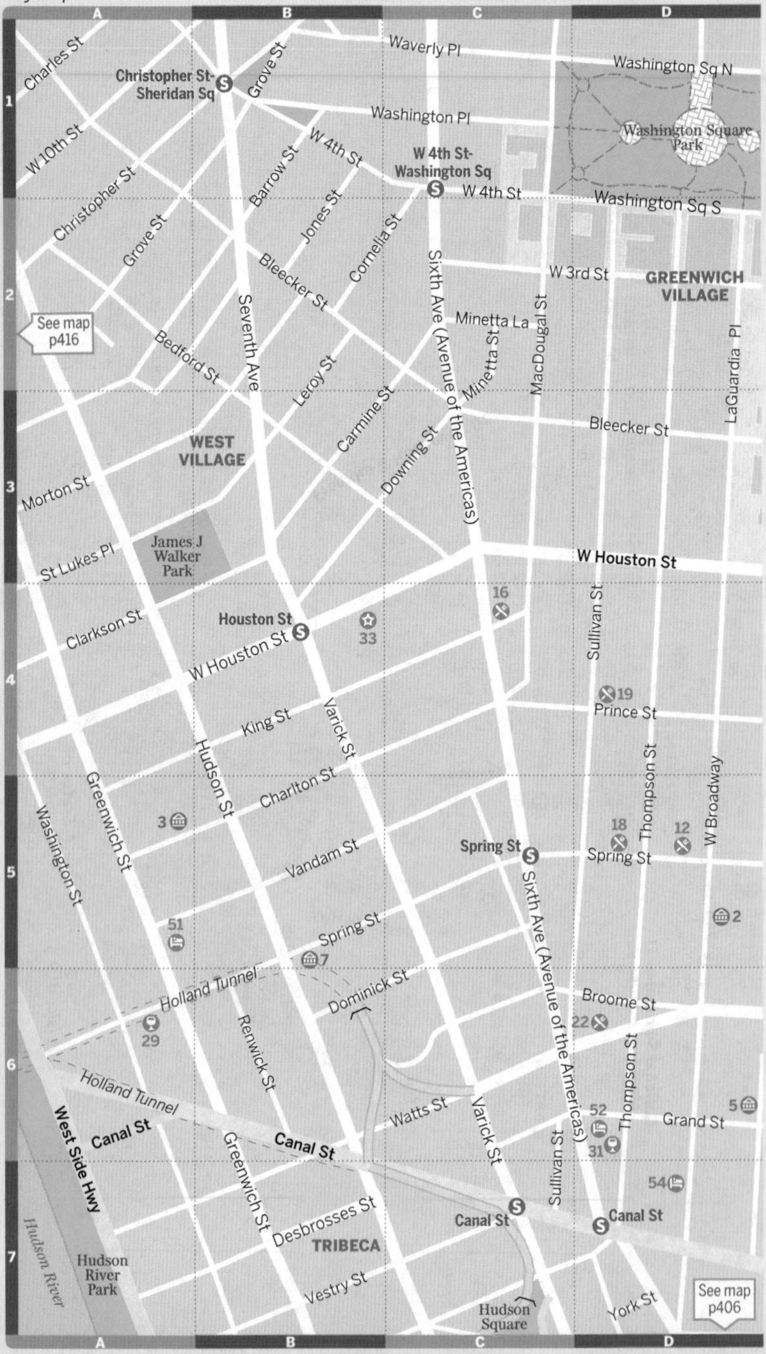
A
B
C
D
1
2
3
4
5
6
7
Charles St
Christopher St-Sheridan Sq
Grove St
Waverly Pl
Washington Sq N
Washington Pl
Washington Square Park
W 10th St
W 4th St
Barrow St
W 4th St-Washington Sq
W 4th St
Washington Sq S
Christopher St
Jones St
Grove St
Cornelia St
Bleecker St
Sixth Ave (Avenue of the Americas)
W 3rd St
GREENWICH VILLAGE
See map p416
Seventh Ave
MacDougal St
Minetta La
Bedford St
Minetta St
LaGuardia Pl
Leroy St
Carmine St
Bleecker St
WEST VILLAGE
Downing St
Morton St
James J Walker Park
St Lukes Pl
W Houston St
16
Sullivan St
Clarkson St
Houston St
33
W Houston St
19
Prince St
King St
Varick St
Hudson St
Charlton St
Greenwich St
Thompson St
Washington St
3
18
12
W Broadway
Spring St
Spring St
Vandam St
2
51
Spring St
7
Holland Tunnel
Dominick St
Broome St
22
29
Renwick St
Thompson St
Holland Tunnel
Varick St
West Side Hwy
Watts St
52
5
Canal St
Grand St
Canal St
Greenwich St
Sullivan St
31
54
Canal St
Canal St
Desbrosses St
TRIBECA
Hudson River
Hudson River Park
Vestry St
Hudson Square
York St
See map p406

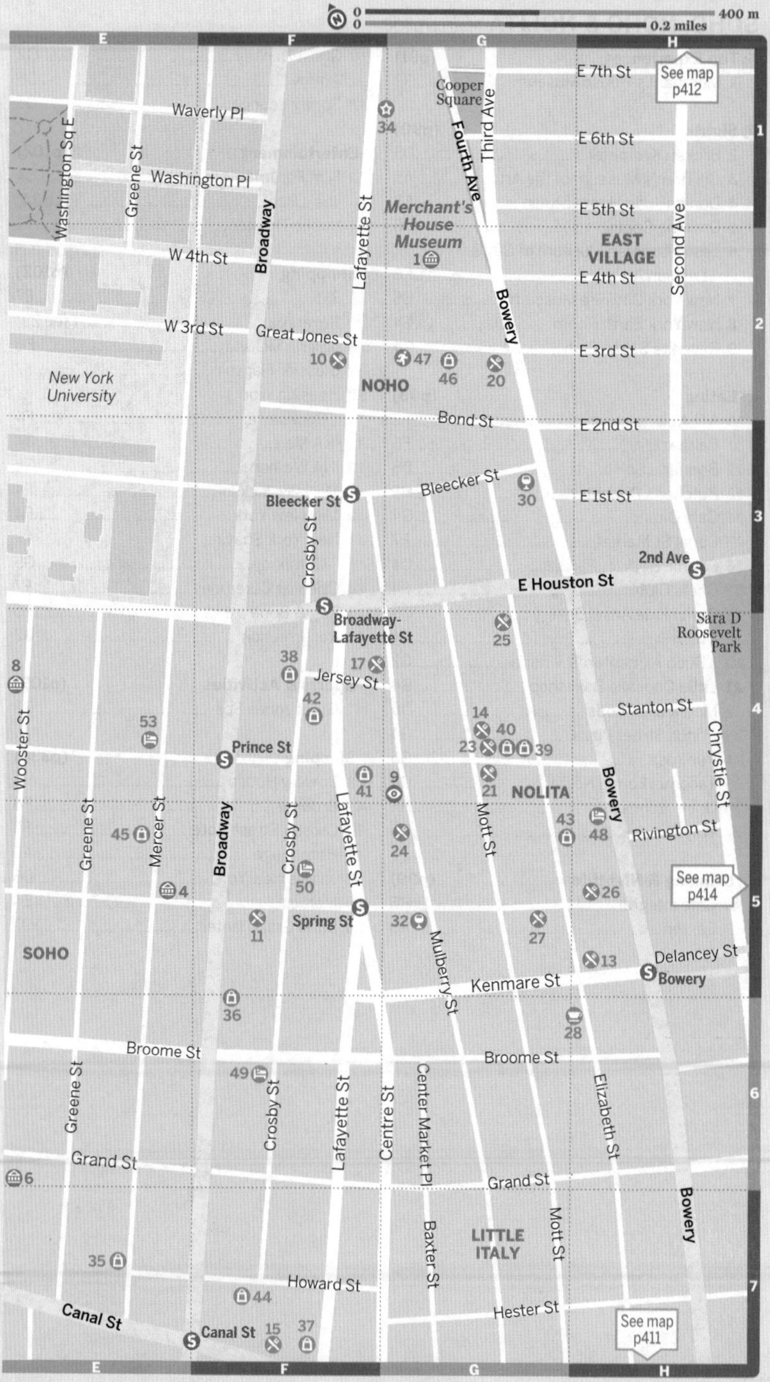
0 400 m
0 0.2 miles
E
F
G
H
1
2
3
4
5
6
7
SOHO, NOHO & NOLITA
See map p412
E 7th St
Cooper Square
Waverly Pl
34
E 6th St
Washington Sq E
Greene St
Washington Pl
Fourth Ave
Third Ave
Merchant's House Museum
1
E 5th St
EAST VILLAGE
W 4th St
Broadway
Lafayette St
E 4th St
Second Ave
Bowery
W 3rd St
Great Jones St
E 3rd St
10
47
46
20
NOHO
New York University
Bond St
E 2nd St
Bleecker St
30
E 1st St
Bleecker St
Crosby St
2nd Ave
E Houston St
Broadway-Lafayette St
Sara D Roosevelt Park
25
38
17
Jersey St
8
42
Stanton St
Chrystie St
14
40
53
Wooster St
23
39
Prince St
41
9
21
NOLITA
Bowery
Greene St
Mercer St
Broadway
Crosby St
Lafayette St
Mott St
43
45
48
Rivington St
24
50
4
See map p414
26
Spring St
32
11
27
Mulberry St
SOHO
13
Delancey St
Bowery
Kenmare St
36
28
Broome St
Broome St
49
Greene St
Crosby St
Lafayette St
Centre St
Center Market Pl
Elizabeth St
Grand St
Grand St
6
Bowery
Baxter St
LITTLE ITALY
Mott St
35
Howard St
44
Hester St
Canal St
Canal St
15
37
See map p411

SOHO, NOHO & NOLITA *Map on p408*

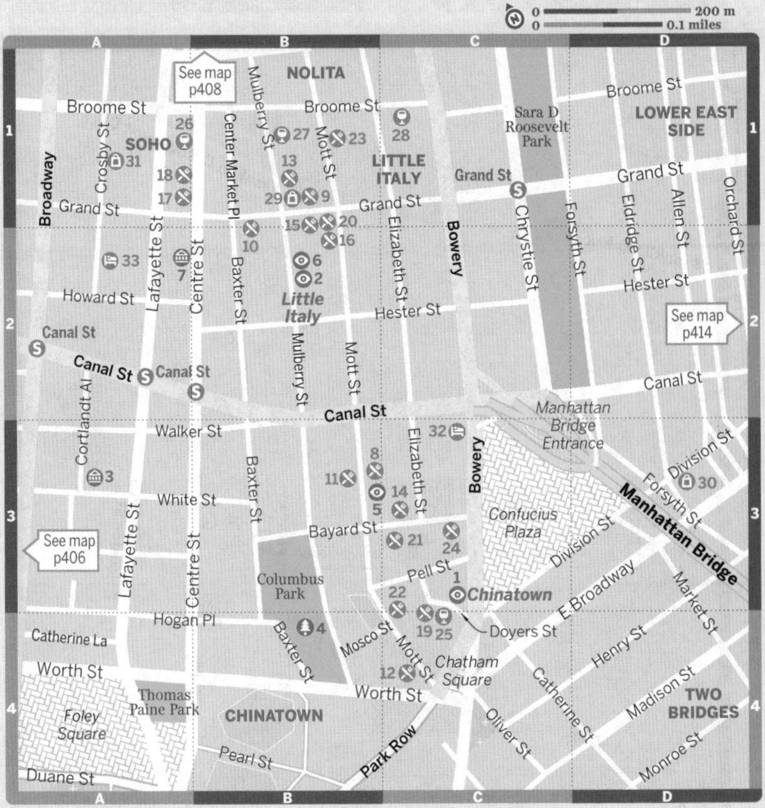

Top Experiences **(p88)**
1 Chinatown C3
2 Little Italy B2

Sights **(p91)**
3 Artists Space A3
4 Columbus Park B4
5 Eastern States Buddhist Temple B3
6 Mulberry Street B2
7 Museum of Chinese in America A2

Eating **(p98)**
8 Amazing 66 B3
9 Bánh Mì Saigon Bakery B1
10 Baz Bagels B2
11 Big Wong B3
12 Buddha Bodai C4
13 Da Nico B1
14 Deluxe Green Bo C3
15 Ferrara Cafe & Bakery B1
16 Golden Steamer B2
17 Lan Larb A1
18 Marché Maman A1
19 Nom Wah Tea Parlor C4
20 Nyonya B1
21 Original Chinatown Ice Cream Factory C3
22 Peking Duck House C3
23 Two Hands B1
24 Xi'an Famous Foods C3

Drinking & Nightlife **(p99)**
25 Apothéke C4
26 La Compagnie des Vins Surnaturels A1
27 Mulberry Street Bar B1
28 Randolph C1

Shopping **(p102)**
29 Alleva B1
30 Fong On D3
31 Saturdays A1

Sleeping **(p334)**
32 Hotel 50 Bowery C3
33 Nomo SoHo A2

EAST VILLAGE

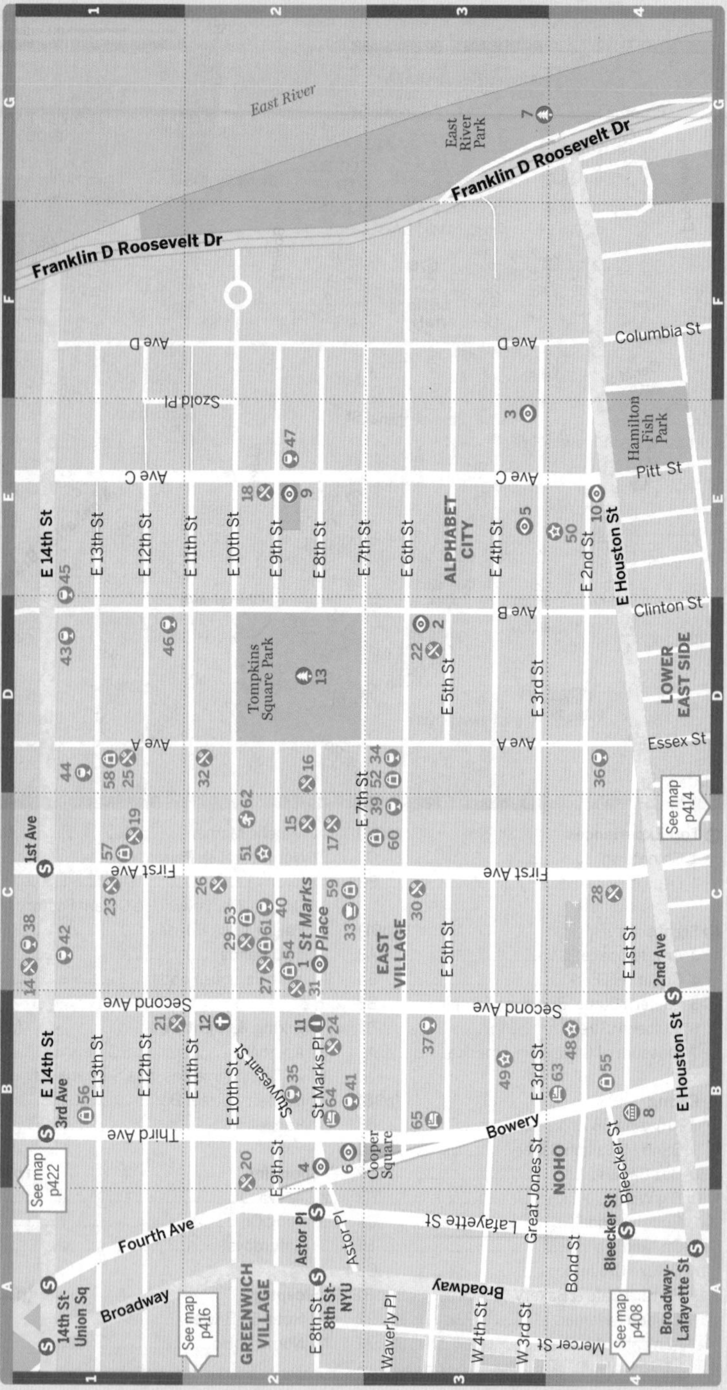

EAST VILLAGE

Top Experiences **(p112)**
1 St Marks Place ... C2

Sights **(p114)**
2 6th & B Garden ... D3
3 All People's Garden ... E3
4 Astor Place ... B2
5 Brisas del Caribe ... E3
6 Cooper Union Building ... B2
7 East River Park ... G3
8 Hole ... B4
9 La Plaza Cultural de Armando Perez Community Garden ... E2
10 Le Petit Versailles ... E4
11 Mosaic Trail ... B2
12 St Mark's Church in-the-Bowery ... B2
13 Tompkins Square Park ... D2

Eating **(p115)**
14 Artichoke Pizza ... C1
15 Cafe Mogador ... C2
16 Crif Dogs ... D2
17 Dun-Well Doughnuts ... C2
18 Esperanto ... E2
19 Hearth ... C1
20 Ippudo NY ... B2
21 Kanoyama ... B1
22 Lavagna ... D3
23 Luzzo's ... C1
24 Mamoun's ... B2
25 Mikey Likes It ... D1
26 Momofuku Noodle Bar ... C2
27 MUD Spot ... C2
28 Prune ... C4
29 Rai Rai Ken ... C2
30 Upstate ... C3
31 Veselka ... C2
32 Westville East ... D2

Drinking & Nightlife **(p123)**
33 Abraço ... C2
34 Amor y Amargo ... D3
35 Angel's Share ... B2
36 Berlin ... D4
37 Cock ... B3
38 Crocodile Lounge ... C1
39 Death & Co ... C3
40 Immigrant ... C2
41 McSorley's Old Ale House ... B2
42 Nowhere ... C1
43 Otto's Shrunken Head ... D1
PDT ... (see 16)
44 Phoenix ... D1
45 Pouring Ribbons ... E1
Proletariat ... (see 17)
46 Rue B ... D1
47 Wayland ... E2

Entertainment **(p128)**
48 Anyway Café ... B4
49 La MaMa ETC ... B3
50 Nuyorican Poets Café ... E4
51 Performance Space New York ... C2

Shopping **(p129)**
52 A-1 Records ... D3
53 Consigliere ... C2
54 Dinosaur Hill ... C2
55 John Varvatos ... B4
56 Kiehl's ... B1
57 No Relation Vintage ... C1
58 Obscura Antiques ... D1
59 Tokio 7 ... C2
60 Trash & Vaudeville ... C3
61 Verameat ... C2

Sports & Activities **(p128)**
62 Russian & Turkish Baths ... C2

Sleeping **(p335)**
63 Bowery Hotel ... B4
64 St Mark's Hotel ... B2
65 Standard East Village ... B3

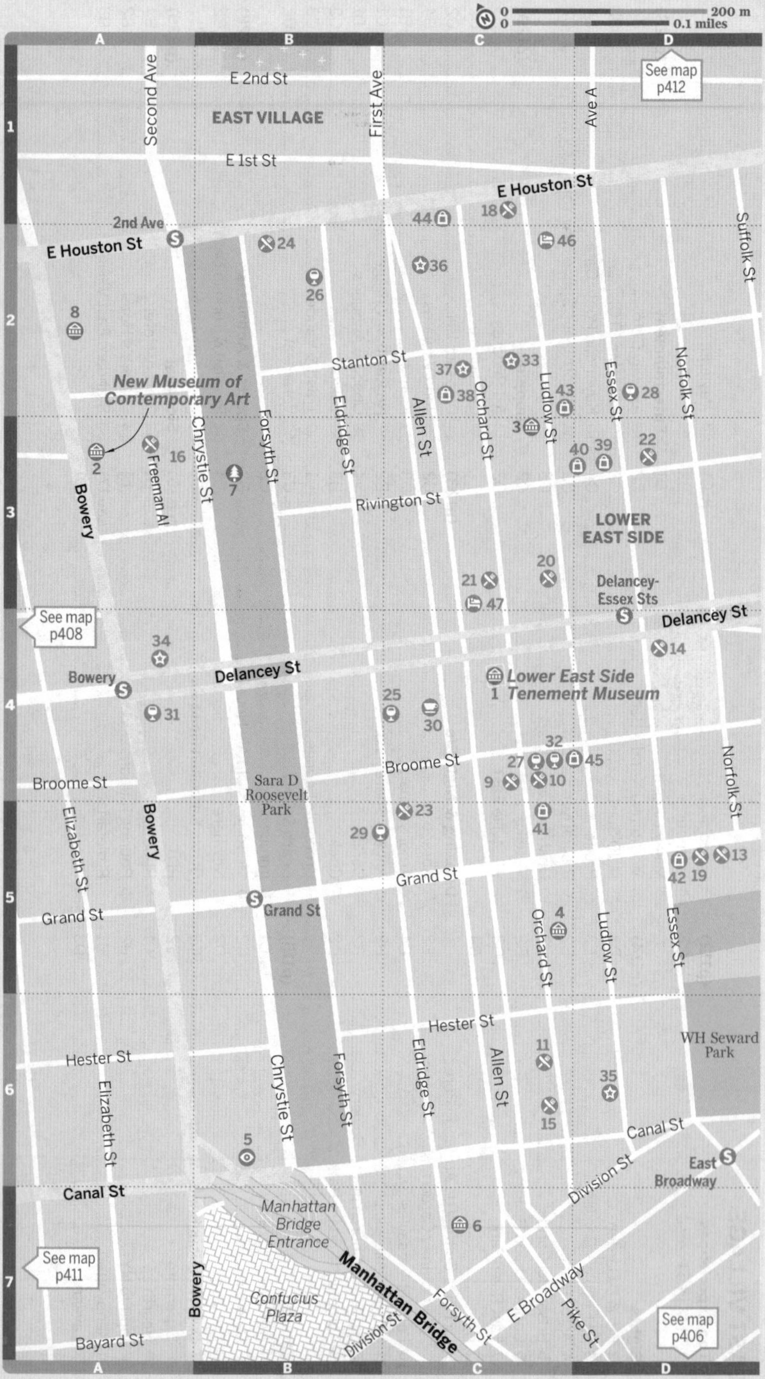
0 200 m
0 0.1 miles
A
B
C
D
1
2
3
4
5
6
7
See map p412
See map p408
See map p411
See map p406
E 2nd St
EAST VILLAGE
Second Ave
First Ave
Ave A
E 1st St
E Houston St
2nd Ave
E Houston St
Suffolk St
Stanton St
New Museum of Contemporary Art
Chrystie St
Forsyth St
Eldridge St
Allen St
Orchard St
Ludlow St
Essex St
Norfolk St
Freeman Al
Bowery
Rivington St
LOWER EAST SIDE
Delancey-Essex Sts
Delancey St
Bowery
Delancey St
Lower East Side Tenement Museum
Broome St
Broome St
Sara D Roosevelt Park
Elizabeth St
Bowery
Grand St
Grand St
Grand St
Orchard St
Ludlow St
Essex St
Norfolk St
Hester St
Hester St
WH Seward Park
Chrystie St
Forsyth St
Eldridge St
Allen St
Elizabeth St
Canal St
Canal St
Division St
East Broadway
Manhattan Bridge Entrance
Manhattan Bridge
Confucius Plaza
Bowery
Division St
Forsyth St
E Broadway
Pike St
Bayard St
1
2
3
4
5
6
7
8
9
10
11
13
14
15
16
18
19
20
21
22
23
24
25
26
27
28
29
30
31
32
33
34
35
36
37
38
39
40
41
42
43
44
45
46
47

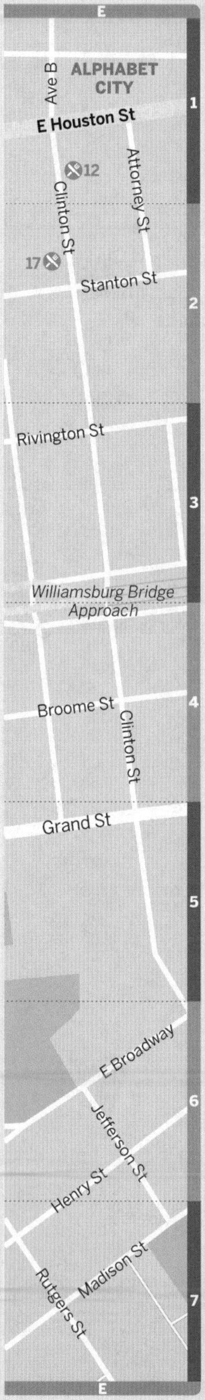

Top Experiences (p109)

1 Lower East Side Tenement Museum C4
2 New Museum of Contemporary Art A3

Sights (p114)

3 Anastasia Photo C3
4 Lesley Heller C5
5 Mahayana Temple B6
6 Museum at Eldridge Street Synagogue C7
7 Sara D Roosevelt Park B3
8 Sperone Westwater A2

Eating (p119)

9 An Choi C4
10 Casa Mezcal C4
11 Cheeky Sandwiches C6
12 Clinton Street Baking Company E1
13 Doughnut Plant D5
14 Essex Market D4
15 Fat Radish C6
16 Freemans A3
17 Ivan Ramen E2
18 Katz's Delicatessen C1
19 Kossar's Bagels & Bialys D5
20 Kuma Inn C3
21 Russ & Daughters Cafe C3
22 Supermoon Bakehouse D3
23 Vanessa's Dumpling House C5
24 Yonah Schimmel Knish Bakery B2

Drinking & Nightlife (p127)

25 Attaboy C4
26 Bar Goto B2
27 Barrio Chino C4
28 Beauty & Essex D2
29 Flower Shop B5
30 Round K C4
31 Sel Rrose A4
32 Ten Bells C4

Entertainment (p128)

33 Arlene's Grocery C2
34 Bowery Ballroom A4
35 Metrograph D6
36 Rockwood Music Hall C2
37 Slipper Room C2

Shopping (p130)

38 Bluestockings C2
39 Economy Candy D3
40 Edith Machinist D3
41 Moo Shoes C5
42 Pickle Guys D5
43 Reformation C2
44 Russ & Daughters C1
45 Top Hat D4

Sleeping (p335)

46 Ludlow C2
47 Sago Hotel C3

Key on p418

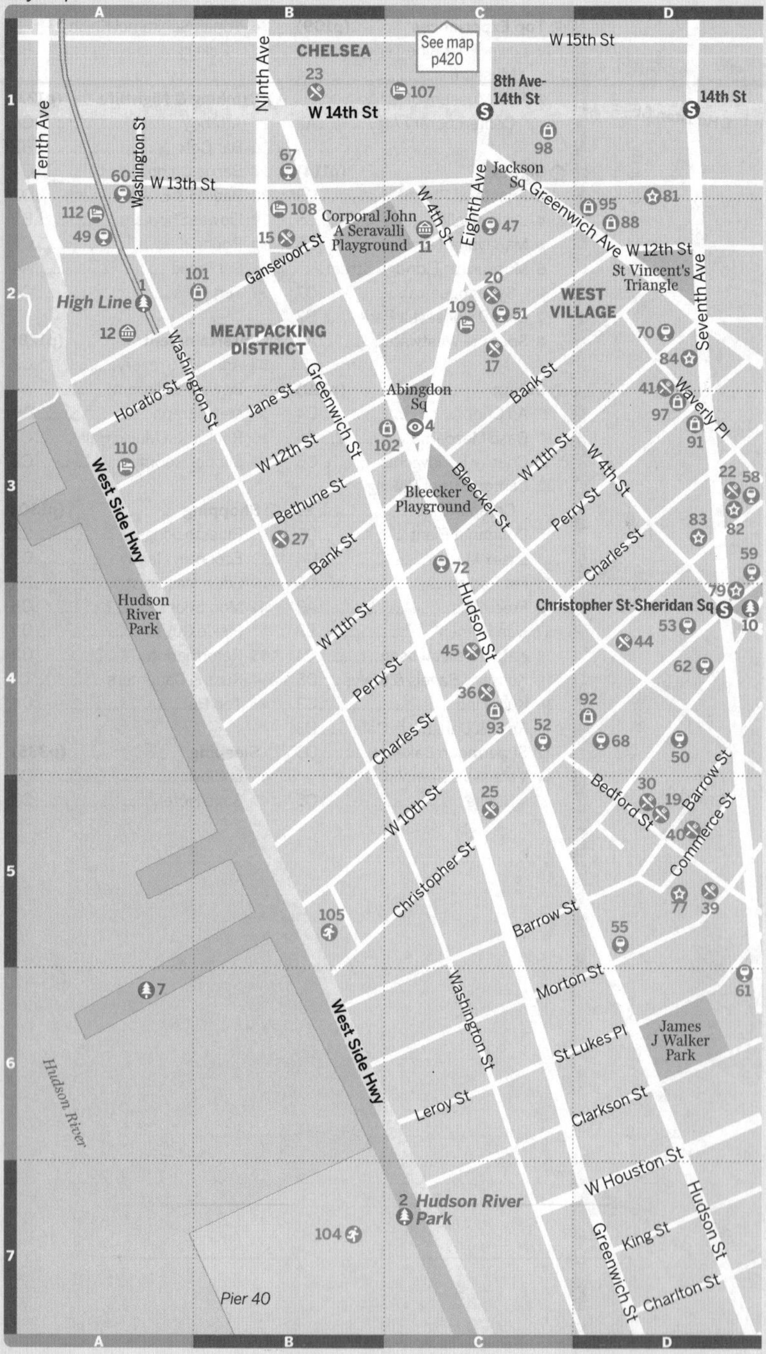
A
B
C
D
1
2
3
4
5
6
7
See map p420
W 15th St
CHELSEA
Ninth Ave
23
107
8th Ave-14th St
14th St
W 14th St
Tenth Ave
Washington St
98
67
Jackson Sq
60
W 13th St
Eighth Ave
Greenwich Ave
95
81
112
108
Corporal John A Seravalli Playground
W 4th St
88
49
15
Gansevoort St
11
47
W 12th St
St Vincent's Triangle
101
20
WEST VILLAGE
Seventh Ave
1
High Line
109
51
12
MEATPACKING DISTRICT
70
Washington St
17
84
Horatio St
Jane St
Greenwich St
Abingdon Sq
Bank St
41
Waverly Pl
97
110
102
4
91
W 12th St
W 11th St
W 4th St
West Side Hwy
Bleecker St
22
58
Bethune St
Bleecker Playground
Perry St
82
83
27
Bank St
Charles St
59
72
Hudson River Park
Hudson St
79
Christopher St-Sheridan Sq
10
53
W 11th St
44
45
62
Perry St
36
92
93
52
68
50
Charles St
Bedford St
Barrow St
30
25
19
W 10th St
40
Commerce St
Christopher St
77
39
105
Barrow St
55
7
Morton St
61
Washington St
West Side Hwy
James J Walker Park
St Lukes Pl
Hudson River
Leroy St
Clarkson St
W Houston St
2
Hudson River Park
104
King St
Hudson St
Greenwich St
Pier 40
Charlton St

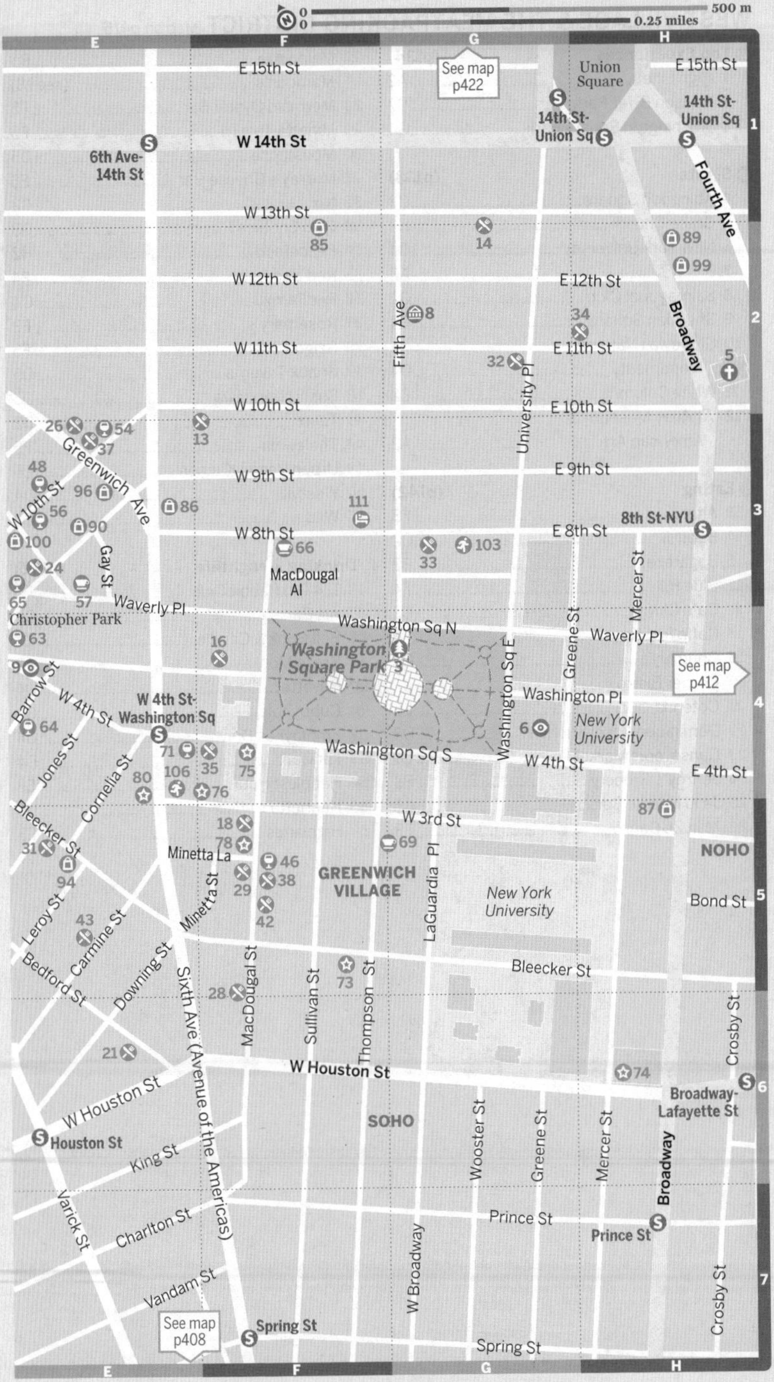
0 500 m
0 0.25 miles
E
F
G
H
E 15th St
See map p422
Union Square
14th St-Union Sq
W 14th St
6th Ave-14th St
Fourth Ave
W 13th St
85
14
89
99
W 12th St
E 12th St
Fifth Ave
8
34
Broadway
W 11th St
E 11th St
32
5
University Pl
W 10th St
E 10th St
26
54
37
13
Greenwich Ave
48
W 10th St
96
W 9th St
E 9th St
56
86
111
90
8th St-NYU
100
W 8th St
E 8th St
66
33
103
24
Gay St
MacDougal Al
Mercer St
65
57
Waverly Pl
Christopher Park
Washington Sq N
Greene St
Waverly Pl
63
16
Washington Square Park
3
Washington Sq E
See map p412
9
Barrow St
W 4th St
W 4th St-Washington Sq
Washington Pl
64
6
New York University
Jones St
71
35
75
Washington Sq S
W 4th St
E 4th St
Cornelia St
80
106
75
76
Bleecker St
18
W 3rd St
87
31
78
69
Minetta La
46
NOHO
94
29
38
GREENWICH VILLAGE
LaGuardia Pl
Minetta St
New York University
Bond St
Leroy St
42
43
Carmine St
Bedford St
Downing St
Bleecker St
Sixth Ave (Avenue of the Americas)
MacDougal St
73
28
Sullivan St
Thompson St
Crosby St
21
W Houston St
74
W Houston St
Broadway-Lafayette St
SOHO
Wooster St
Greene St
Mercer St
Houston St
King St
Broadway
Varick St
Charlton St
Prince St
Prince St
W Broadway
Vandam St
Crosby St
See map p408
Spring St
Spring St
1
2
3
4
5
6
7
WEST VILLAGE & THE MEATPACKING DISTRICT

WEST VILLAGE & THE MEATPACKING DISTRICT *Map on p416*

57 Joe Coffee Company E3
58 Julius' D3
59 Kettle of Fish D3
60 Le Bain A1
61 Little Branch D6
62 Marie's Crisis D4
63 Monster E4
64 One If By Land, Two If By Sea E4
65 Stonewall Inn E3
66 Stumptown Coffee Roasters F3
Top of the Standard .... (see 112)
67 Troy Liquor Bar B1
68 Ty's D4
69 Uncommons G5
70 Vin Sur Vingt D2
71 Vol de Nuit E4
72 White Horse Tavern C3

Entertainment **(p157)**

73 (Le) Poisson Rouge F5
55 Bar .... (see 65)
74 Angelika Film Center H6
75 Bar Next Door F4
76 Blue Note F4
77 Cherry Lane Theatre D5
78 Comedy Cellar F5
79 Duplex D4
80 IFC Center E4
81 LGBT Community Center D1
82 Mezzrow D3
83 Smalls D3
84 Village Vanguard D2

Shopping **(p160)**

85 Beacon's Closet F2
86 CO Bigelow Chemists E3
87 Evolution Nature Store H5
88 Flight 001 .... D2
89 Forbidden Planet H2
90 Greenwich Letterpress E3
91 Idlewild Books D3
92 McNulty's Tea & Coffee Co, Inc D4
93 Meadow C4
94 Murray's Cheese E5
95 Odin D2
96 Personnel of New York E3
97 Saturdays D3
98 Screaming Mimis C1
99 Strand Book Store H2
100 Three Lives & Company E3
101 Trina Turk B2
102 Yoya C3

Sports & Activities **(p163)**

103 MNDFL G3
104 New York Trapeze School B7
105 Waterfront Bicycle Shop B5
106 West 4th Street Basketball Courts E4

Sleeping **(p336)**

107 Chelsea Pines Inn C1
108 Gansevoort Meatpacking NYC B2
109 Incentra Village House C2
110 Jane Hotel A3
111 Marlton Hotel F3
112 Standard A2

CHELSEA

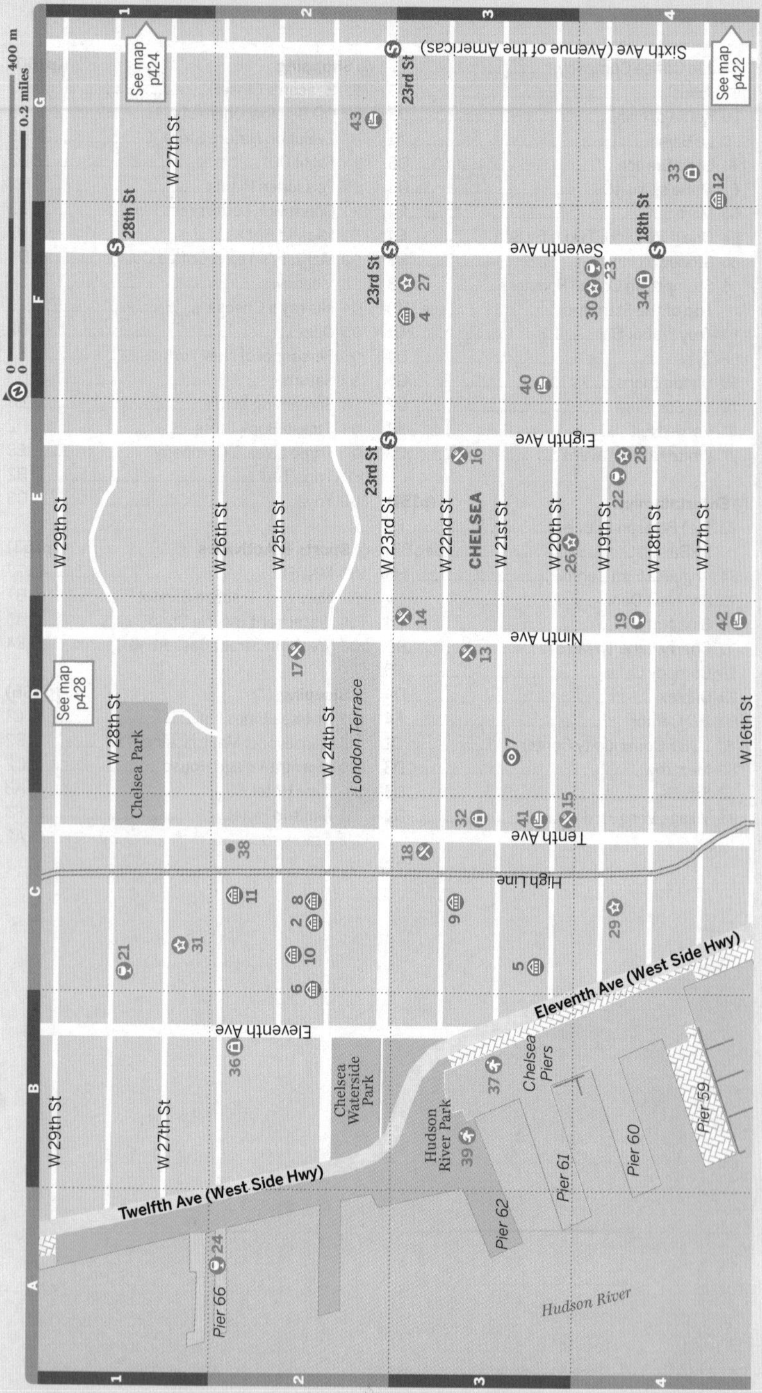
400 m
0.2 miles
See map p424
See map p422
See map p428
Sixth Ave (Avenue of the Americas)
Seventh Ave
Eighth Ave
Ninth Ave
Tenth Ave
Eleventh Ave
Eleventh Ave (West Side Hwy)
Twelfth Ave (West Side Hwy)
High Line
23rd St
28th St
18th St
W 29th St
W 28th St
W 27th St
W 26th St
W 25th St
W 24th St
W 23rd St
W 22nd St
W 21st St
W 20th St
W 19th St
W 18th St
W 17th St
W 16th St
CHELSEA
Chelsea Park
London Terrace
Chelsea Waterside Park
Hudson River Park
Chelsea Piers
Pier 66
Pier 62
Pier 61
Pier 60
Pier 59
Hudson River

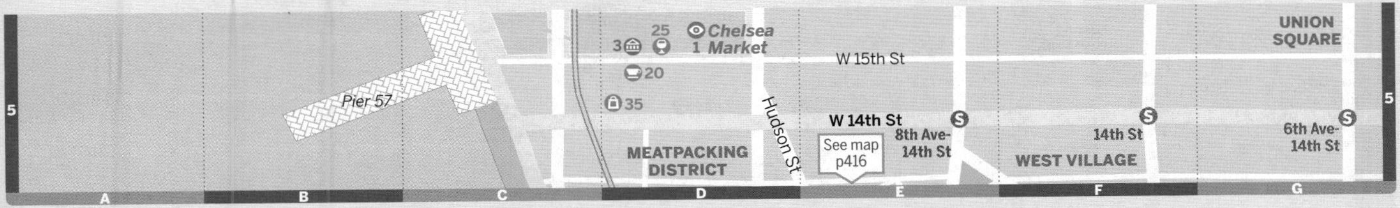
UNION SQUARE
Chelsea 1 Market
25
3
20
35
W 15th St
Pier 57
Hudson St
W 14th St
8th Ave-14th St
14th St
6th Ave-14th St
See map p416
MEATPACKING DISTRICT
WEST VILLAGE
A
B
C
D
E
F
G
5

UNION SQUARE, THE FLATIRON DISTRICT & GRAMERCY PARK

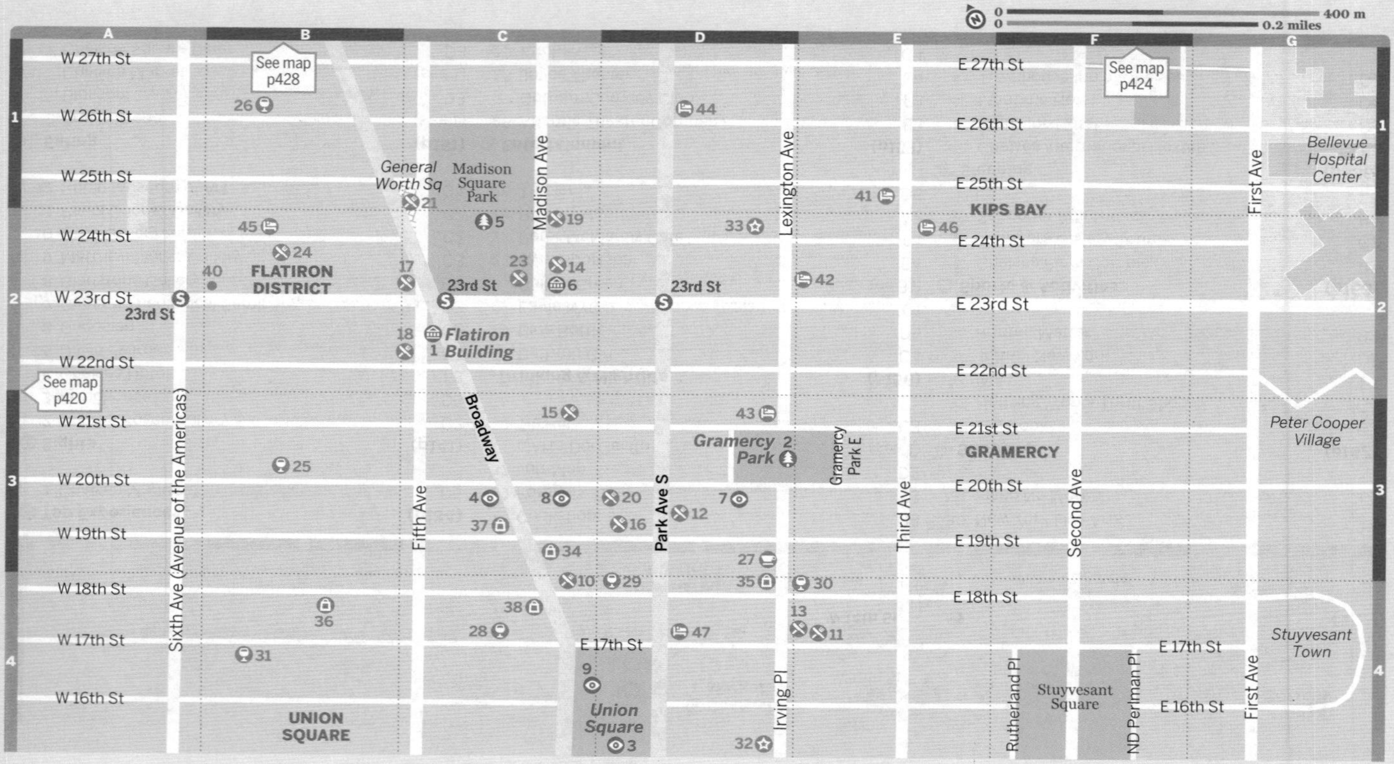

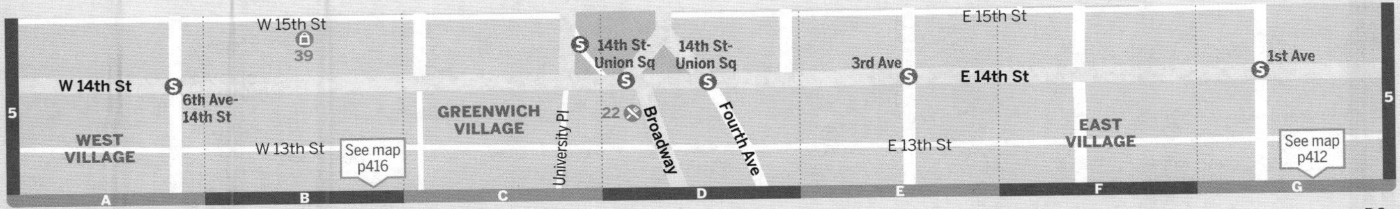

Top Experiences **(p166)**
1 Flatiron Building C2
2 Gramercy Park D3
3 Union Square D4

Sights **(p167)**
4 Lord & Taylor Building C3
5 Madison Square Park C2
6 Metropolitan Life Tower C2
7 National Arts Club D3
8 Theodore Roosevelt Birthplace C3
9 Union Square Greenmarket C4

Eating **(p169)**
10 ABC Kitchen C4
11 Bar Jamón E4
12 Big Daddy's D3
13 Casa Mono E4
14 Clocktower C2
15 Cosme C3
16 Craft D3
17 Eataly C2
18 Eisenberg's Sandwich Shop C2
19 Eleven Madison Park C2
20 Gramercy Tavern D3
21 Mad Sq Eats C1
Maialino .... (see 43)
22 Max Brenner D5
23 Shake Shack C2
24 Tacombi Café El Presidente B2

Drinking & Nightlife **(p172)**
25 Boxers NYC B3
26 Flatiron Room B1
27 Irving Farm Roasters D3
28 Lillie's Victorian Establishment C4
29 Old Town Bar & Restaurant D4
30 Pete's Tavern E4
31 Raines Law Room B4
Serra .... (see 17)

Entertainment **(p173)**
32 Irving Plaza D4
33 Peoples Improv Theater D2

Shopping **(p173)**
34 ABC Carpet & Home C3
35 Bedford Cheese Shop D4
36 Books of Wonder B4
37 Fishs Eddy C3
38 Paragon Sporting Goods C4
39 Rent the Runway B5

Sports & Activities **(p174)**
40 New York City Audubon B2

Sleeping **(p337)**
41 Carlton Arms E1
42 Freehand New York E2
43 Gramercy Park Hotel D3
44 Hotel Giraffe D1
45 Hotel Henri B2
46 Marcel at Gramercy E2
47 W New York Union Square D4

MIDTOWN EAST & FIFTH AVENUE

MIDTOWN EAST & FIFTH AVENUE

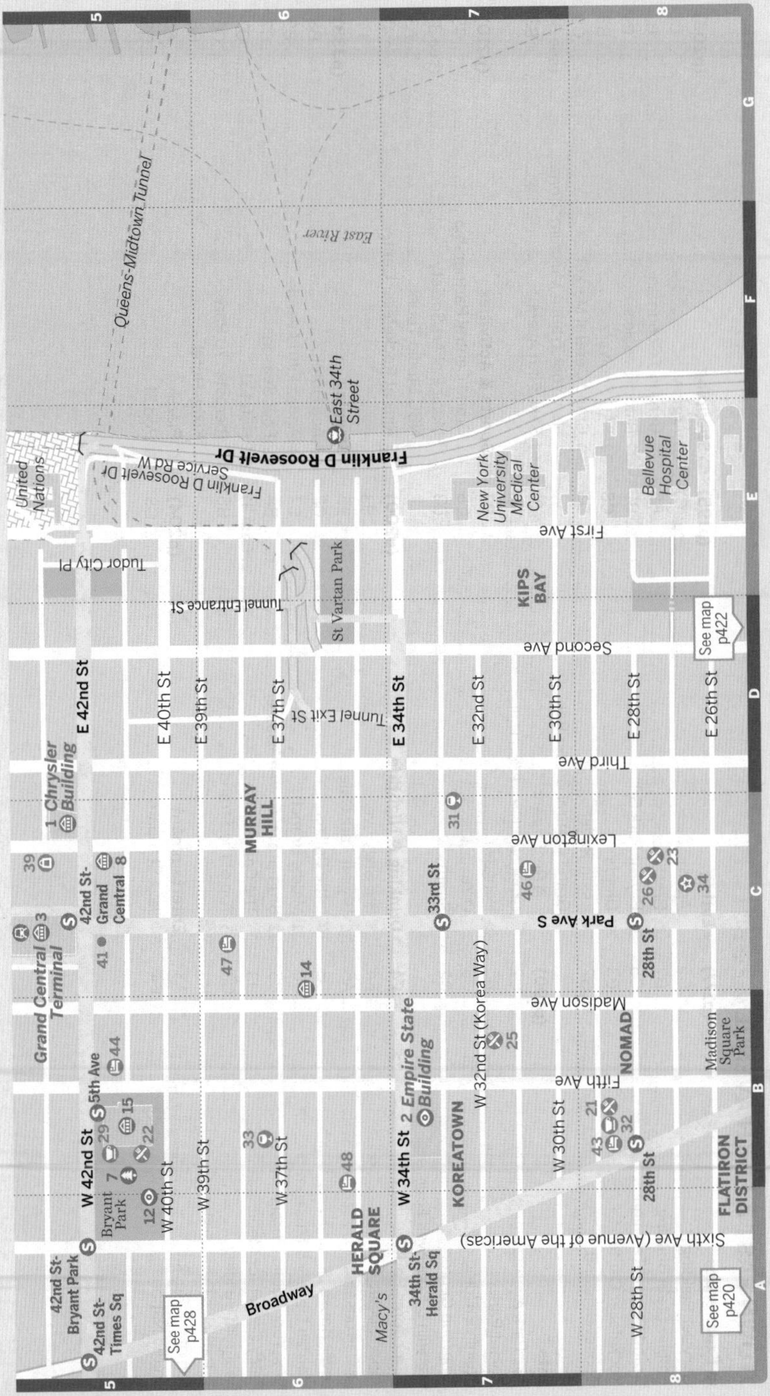

꞉TOWN EAST & FIFTH AVENUE *Map on p424*

ɪp Experiences **(p177)**

- Chrysler Building C5
- Empire State Building B7
- Grand Central Terminal C5
- Rockefeller Center B3
- Roosevelt Island G2

ghts **(p190)**

- 432 Park Avenue C2
- Bryant Park B5
- Chanin Building C5
- Citigroup Center C2
- Franklin D Roosevelt Four Freedoms Park F4
- Japan Society E4
- Le Carrousel A5
- Lever House C2
- Morgan Library & Museum C6
- New York Public Library B5
- Paley Center for Media B3
- Seagram Building C3
- St Patrick's Cathedral B3
- Top of the Rock A3
- United Nations E4

Eating **(p195)**

- Agern ...... (see 3)
- 21 Breslin B8
- 22 Bryant Park Grill B5
- 23 Dhaba C8
- 24 Ess-a-Bagel D3
- Grand Central Oyster Bar & Restaurant ...... (see 3)
- Great Northern Food Hall ...... (see 3)
- 25 Hangawi B7
- 26 O Ya C8
- 27 Smith D3

Drinking & Nightlife **(p200)**

- 28 Bar SixtyFive B3
- 29 Bryant Park Cafe B5
- 30 Little Collins C2
- 31 Middle Branch C7
- 32 Stumptown Coffee Roasters B8
- The Campbell ...... (see 3)
- 33 Top of the Strand B6

Entertainment **(p204)**

- 34 Jazz Standard C8

Shopping **(p208)**

- 35 Argosy C1
- 36 Bergdorf Goodman B1
- 37 Bloomingdale's C1
- 38 FAO Schwarz B3
- 39 Grand Central Market C5
- New York Transit Museum Store ...... (see 3)
- 40 Saks Fifth Avenue B3

Sports & Activities **(p210)**

- 41 Grand Central Partnership C5
- Municipal Art Society ...... (see 3)
- 42 NBC Studio Tours A3
- Rink at Rockefeller Center ...... (see 4)

Sleeping **(p338)**

- 43 Ace Hotel B8
- 44 Andaz Fifth Avenue B5
- 45 Four Seasons C2
- 46 Hotel 31 ...... C7
- 47 Iberostar 70 Park C6
- 48 Kixby Hotel B6
- 49 Plaza B1
- 50 Pod 51 ...... D3

MIDTOWN WEST & TIMES SQUARE *Map on p428*

Top Experiences **(p177)**

1 Museum of Modern Art G2
2 Radio City Music Hall F3
3 Times Square E5

Sights **(p193)**

4 Bank of America Tower F5
5 Brill Building E3
6 Hearst Tower E2
7 Hudson Yards C7
8 Intrepid Sea, Air & Space Museum A4
9 Museum at FIT E8
10 Museum of Arts & Design E1
11 Vessel (TKA) C7

Eating **(p196)**

12 Burger Joint F2
Cafe 2 .... (see 1)
13 Danji D3
14 Don Antonio D3
15 Fournos Theophilos G4
16 Le Bernardin F3
17 Margon F4
18 Mercado Little Spain C7
Modern .... (see 1)
19 NoMad G8
20 Pennsy Food Hall E7
21 Souvlaki GR E2
22 Taboon C3
Terrace Café .... (see 1)
23 Totto Ramen D3
24 Virgil's Real Barbecue F4

Drinking & Nightlife **(p200)**

25 Bar Centrale D4
26 Boxers NYC D3
27 Flaming Saddles D2
28 Industry D3
29 Jimmy's Corner F4
30 R Lounge E4
Robert .... (see 10)
31 Rudy's Bar & Grill D4
32 Rum House E4
33 Therapy D3
34 Waylon C3

Entertainment **(p204)**

35 Ambassador Theatre E3
36 August Wilson Theater E3
37 Birdland D4
38 Carnegie Hall E2
39 Caroline's on Broadway E3
40 CBS Broadcast Center C2
41 Don't Tell Mama D4
42 Ed Sullivan Theater E2
43 Eugene O'Neill Theatre E3
44 Gershwin Theatre E3
45 Hardware C4
46 Jazz at Lincoln Center D1
47 Lyceum Theatre E4
48 Lyric Theatre E5
49 Madison Square Garden E7
50 Minskoff Theatre E4
51 New Amsterdam Theatre E5
52 New Victory Theater E5
53 New York City Center F2
54 Playwrights Horizons D5
55 Richard Rodgers Theatre E4
56 Roundabout Theatre Company F4
57 Second Stage Theater D5
58 Signature Theatre C5
59 The Daily Show with Trevor Noah B3
60 The Shed C7
61 Upright Citizens Brigade Theatre B5

Shopping **(p209)**

62 B&H Photo Video D7
63 Fine & Dandy C3
64 Macy's F7
MoMA Museum & Design Stores .... (see 1)
65 Nepenthes New York D6
66 Shops & Restaurants at Hudson Yards C7

Sports & Activities **(p210)**

67 Circle Line Boat Tours A5
68 Lucky Strike B5
69 Manhattan Community Boathouse A2

Sleeping **(p338)**

70 6 Columbus D1
71 Ameritania Hotel E2
72 Chatwal New York F4
73 Citizen M E3
74 Ink48 .... B4
75 Knickerbocker F5
76 Muse New York F4
77 Night F4
NoMad Hotel .... (see 19)
78 Quin F1
79 Yotel C5

MIDTOWN WEST & TIMES SQUARE

Key on p427

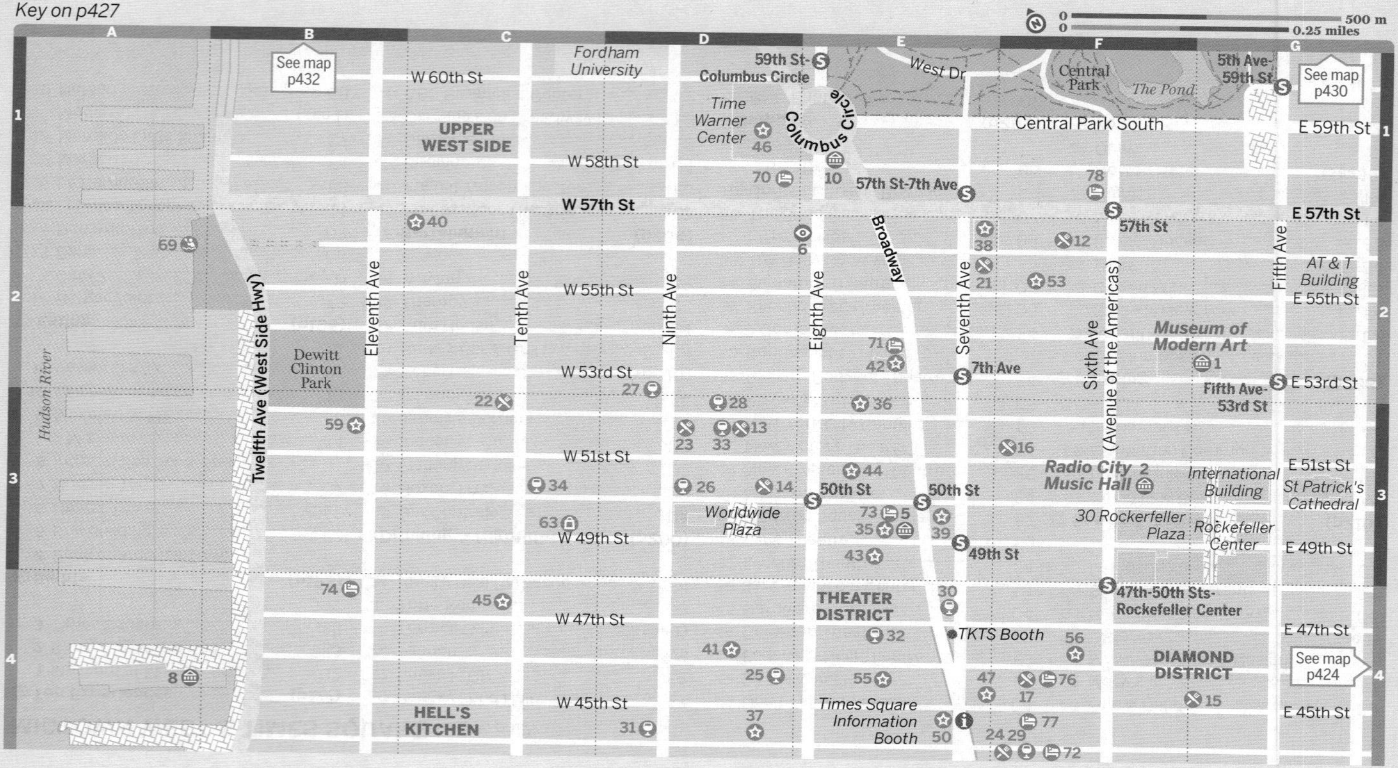

MIDTOWN WEST & TIMES SQUARE

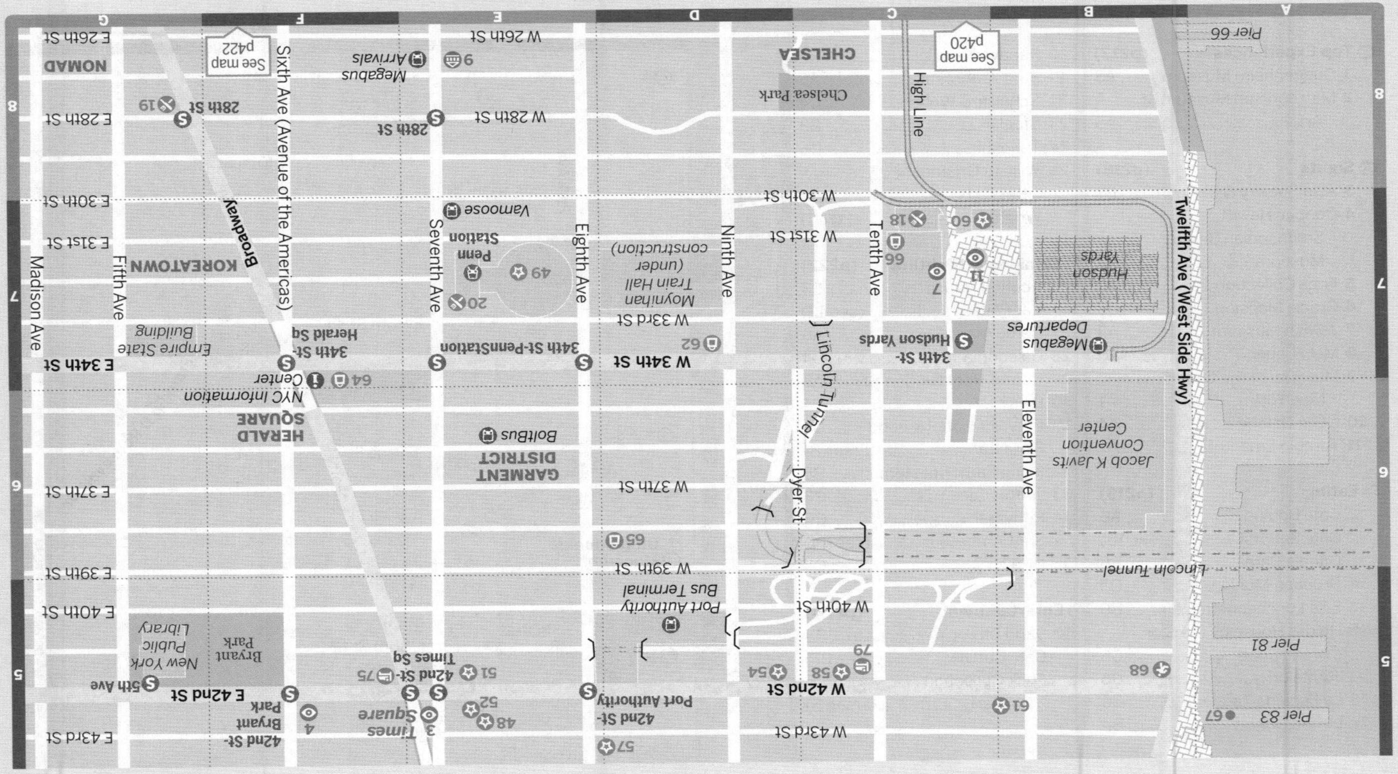

UPPER EAST SIDE

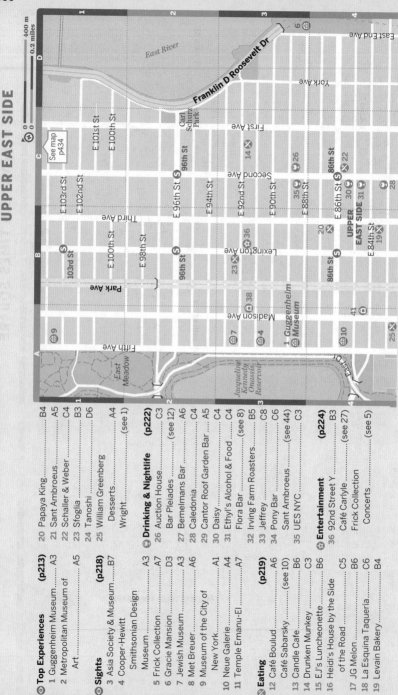

Top Experiences (p213)
1 Guggenheim Museum......... A3
2 Metropolitan Museum of Art.......... A5

Sights (p218)
3 Asia Society & Museum.......B7
4 Cooper-Hewitt Smithsonian Design Museum.......... A3
5 Frick Collection..........A7
6 Gracie Mansion.......... D3
7 Jewish Museum.......... A3
8 Met Breuer.......... A6
9 Museum of the City of New York.......... A1
10 Neue Galerie.......... A4
11 Temple Emanu-El..........A7

Eating (p219)
12 Café Boulud.......... A6
Café Sabarsky..........(see 10)
13 Candle Cafe.......... B6
14 Drunken Munkey.......... C3
15 EJ's Luncheonette.......... B6
16 Heidi's House by the Side of the Road.......... C5
17 JG Melon.......... B6
18 La Esquina Taquería.......... C6
19 Levain Bakery.......... B4
20 Papaya King.......... B4
21 Sant Ambroeus.......... A5
22 Schaller & Weber.......... C4
23 Sfoglia.......... B3
24 Tanoshi.......... D6
25 William Greenberg Desserts.......... A4
Wright..........(see 1)

Drinking & Nightlife (p222)
26 Auction House.......... C3
Bar Pleiades..........(see 12)
27 Bemelmans Bar.......... A6
28 Caledonia.......... C4
29 Cantor Roof Garden Bar..... A5
30 Daisy.......... C4
31 Ethyl's Alcohol & Food........ C4
Flora Bar..........(see 8)
32 Irving Farm Roasters.......... B5
33 Jeffrey.......... C8
34 Pony Bar.......... C6
Sant Ambroeus..........(see 44)
35 UES NYC.......... C3

Entertainment (p224)
36 92nd Street Y.......... B3
Café Carlyle..........(see 27)
Frick Collection Concerts..........(see 5)

Shopping **(p225)**

Sleeping **(p341)**

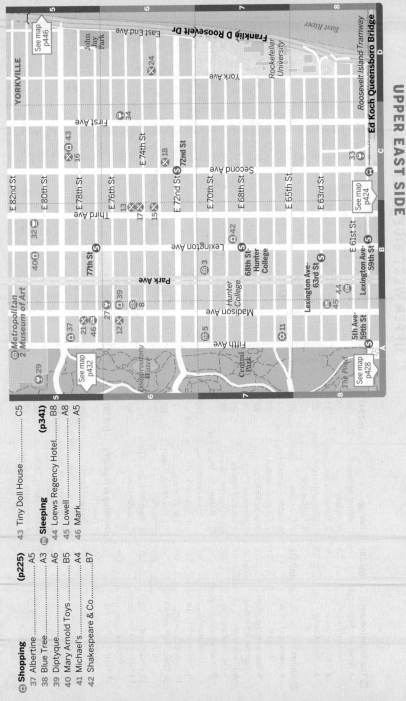

UPPER WEST SIDE & CENTRAL PARK

Top Experiences (p228)

1 American Museum of Natural History C5
2 Central Park D5
3 Lincoln Center B7

Sights (p233)

4 American Folk Art Museum C7
5 Bethesda Fountain D6
Bethesda Terrace .... (see 5)
6 Blockhouse C1
7 Central Park Zoo D7
8 Children's Museum of Manhattan B5
9 Conservatory Garden D2
10 Dakota Building C6
11 David Rubenstein Atrium B8
12 Great Lawn D5
13 New-York Historical Society C6
14 Nicholas Roerich Museum A1
15 Ramble D6
16 Riverside Park A1
17 Straus Park B1
18 Strawberry Fields C6
19 The Mall D7

Eating (p234)

20 Absolute Bagels B1
21 Awadh B3
22 Barney Greengrass B4
23 Blossom on Columbus C5
24 Boulud Sud C7
25 Cafe Lalo B5
26 Cafe Luxembourg B7
27 Épicerie Boulud C7
28 Gray's Papaya B6
29 Hummus Place B6
30 Jacob's Pickles B5
31 Jin Ramen B5
32 Lakeside Restaurant at Loeb Boathouse D6
Peacefood Cafe .... (see 31)
33 Pier i Café A7
34 Silver Moon Bakery B2
35 Smith C7
36 West 79th Street Boat Basin Café A5

Drinking & Nightlife (p239)

37 Dead Poet B5
Empire Rooftop .... (see 64)
38 Gebhard's Beer Culture B6
39 Irving Farm Roasters B5
40 Owl's Tail B6
41 Plowshares Coffee B2
42 Prohibition B5

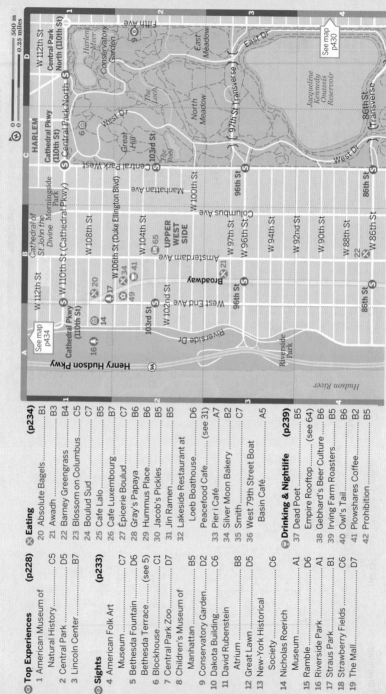

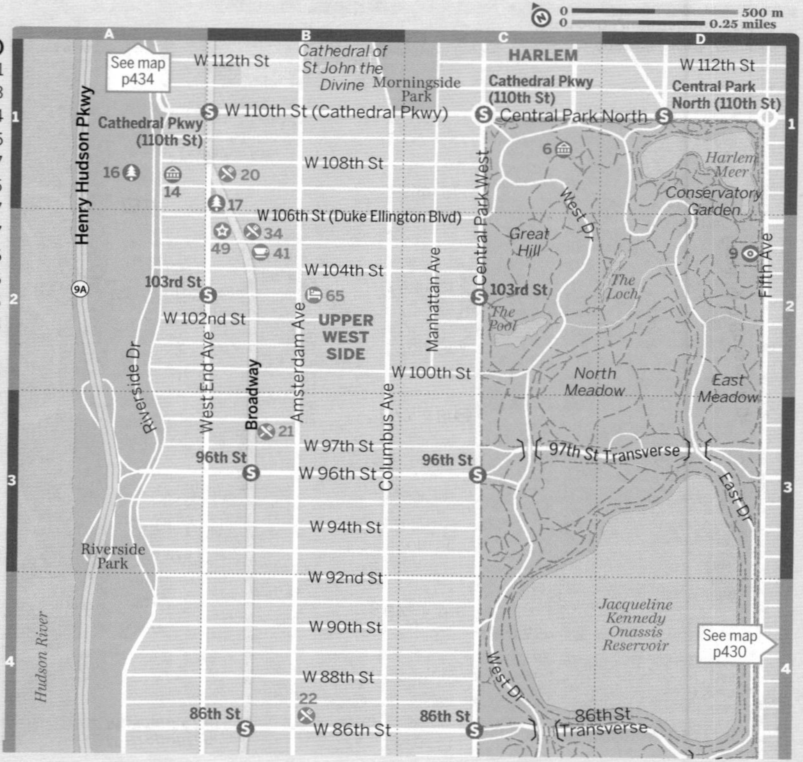

Entertainment (p241)

American Ballet Theatre...........(see 3)
43 Beacon Theatre B6
44 Delacorte Theater........C5
45 Elinor Bunin Munroe Film Center B7
Film at Lincoln Center..(see 3)
46 Merkin Concert Hall........B7
Metropolitan Opera House ....(see 3)
47 New York City Ballet........B8
48 New York Philharmonic........B7
49 Smoke B2
50 Walter Reade Theater........B7

Shopping (p242)

51 Book Culture B5
52 Grand Bazaar NYC B6
53 Icon Style B7
54 Magpie........B5
55 T2........B7
West Side Kids ....(see 54)
56 Westsider Books........B5
57 Westsider Records........B6
58 Zabar's B5

Sports & Activities (p244)

59 Belvedere Castle........C5
60 Central Park Bike Tours........C8
Loeb Boathouse........(see 32)
61 Toga Bike Shop........B7
62 Wollman Skating Rink........D8

Sleeping (p342)

63 Arthouse Hotel NYC........B6
64 Empire Hotel B8
65 Hostelling International New York........B2
Hotel Beacon........(see 43)
66 Hotel Belleclaire........B6
67 YMCA........C7

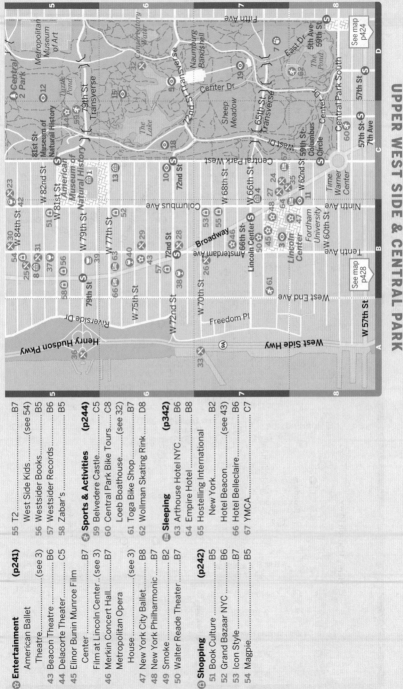

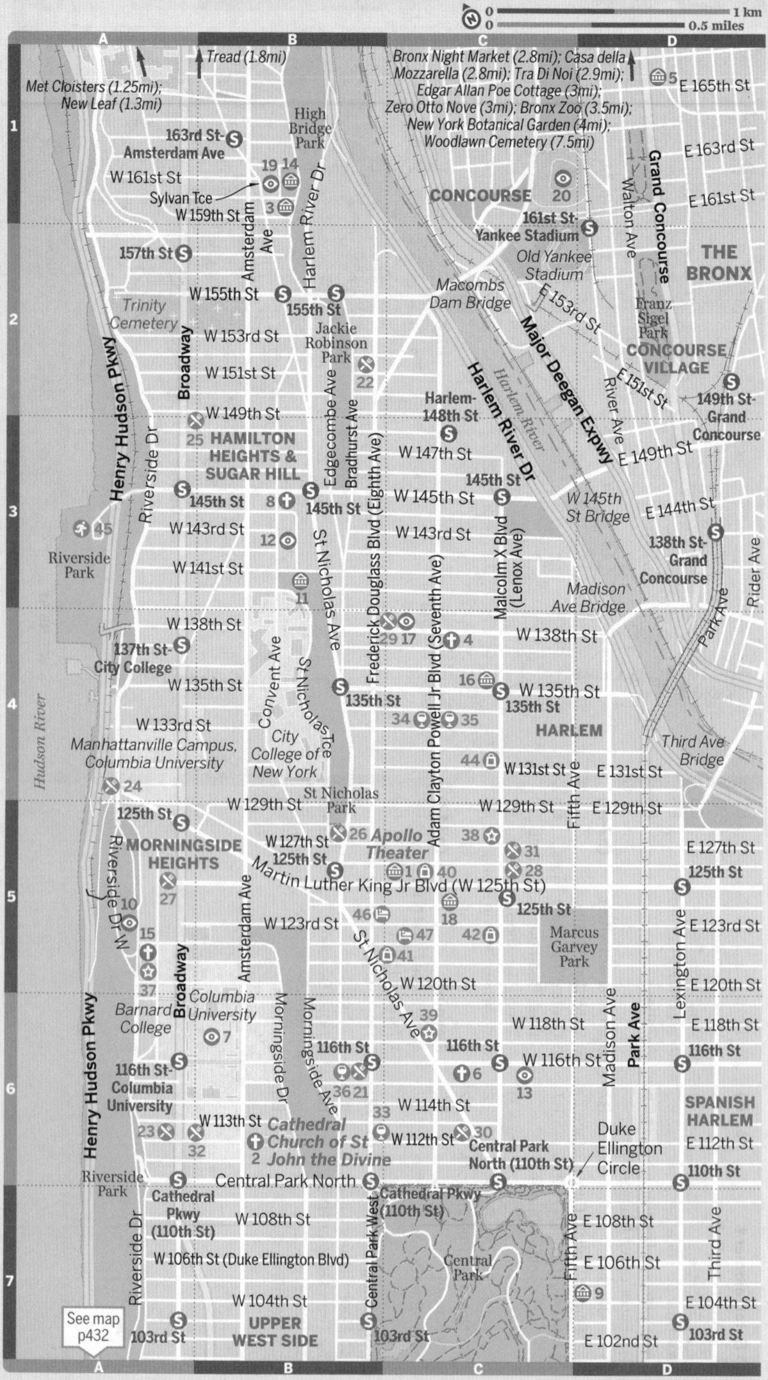

0 1 km
0 0.5 miles
A B C D
1 2 3 4 5 6 7
Tread (1.8mi)
Met Cloisters (1.25mi); New Leaf (1.3mi)
Bronx Night Market (2.8mi); Casa della Mozzarella (2.8mi); Tra Di Noi (2.9mi); Edgar Allan Poe Cottage (3mi); Zero Otto Nove (3mi); Bronx Zoo (3.5mi); New York Botanical Garden (4mi); Woodlawn Cemetery (7.5mi)
High Bridge Park
163rd St-Amsterdam Ave
W 161st St
Sylvan Tce
W 159th St
Amsterdam Ave
Harlem River Dr
CONCOURSE
161st St-Yankee Stadium
Old Yankee Stadium
Walton Ave
Grand Concourse
E 165th St
E 163rd St
E 161st St
THE BRONX
157th St
W 155th St
155th St
Macombs Dam Bridge
E 153rd St
Major Deegan Expwy
Franz Sigel Park
CONCOURSE VILLAGE
Trinity Cemetery
W 153rd St
Jackie Robinson Park
Broadway
W 151st St
Henry Hudson Pkwy
W 149th St
Edgecombe Ave
Bradhurst Ave
Harlem-148th St
Harlem River Dr
Harlem River
River Ave
E 151st St
149th St-Grand Concourse
E 149th St
HAMILTON HEIGHTS & SUGAR HILL
Riverside Dr
Frederick Douglass Blvd (Eighth Ave)
W 147th St
145th St
W 145th St
W 145th St Bridge
E 144th St
W 143rd St
St Nicholas Ave
Malcolm X Blvd (Lenox Ave)
Adam Clayton Powell Jr Blvd (Seventh Ave)
138th St-Grand Concourse
Rider Ave
Riverside Park
W 141st St
Madison Ave Bridge
Park Ave
W 138th St
137th St-City College
Convent Ave
St Nicholas Tce
W 135th St
135th St
HARLEM
Hudson River
W 133rd St
Manhattanville Campus, Columbia University
City College of New York
Third Ave Bridge
W 131st St
E 131st St
W 129th St
St Nicholas Park
Fifth Ave
E 129th St
125th St
MORNINGSIDE HEIGHTS
W 127th St
Apollo Theater
E 127th St
Martin Luther King Jr Blvd (W 125th St)
Riverside Dr W
W 123rd St
Marcus Garvey Park
E 123rd St
Lexington Ave
W 120th St
E 120th St
Columbia University
Barnard College
Morningside Dr
Morningside Ave
W 118th St
Madison Ave
Park Ave
E 118th St
116th St
W 116th St
116th St-Columbia University
W 114th St
SPANISH HARLEM
W 113th St
Cathedral Church of St John the Divine
W 112th St
Central Park North (110th St)
Duke Ellington Circle
E 112th St
110th St
Riverside Park
Central Park North
Cathedral Pkwy (110th St)
W 108th St
Central Park West
E 108th St
W 106th St (Duke Ellington Blvd)
Central Park
E 106th St
Third Ave
W 104th St
E 104th St
See map p432
103rd St
UPPER WEST SIDE
E 102nd St
1 2 3 4 5 6 7 8 9 10 11 12 13 14 15 16 17 18 19 20 21 22 23 24 25 26 27 28 29 30 31 32 33 34 35 36 37 38 39 40 41 42 44 45 46 47

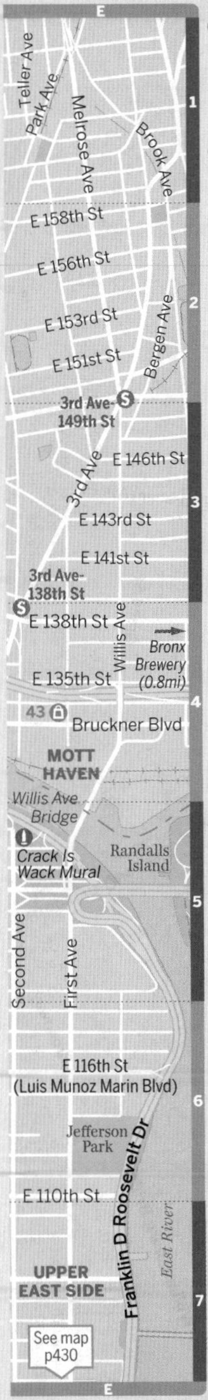

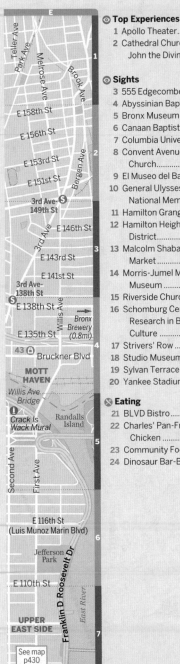

Top Experiences (p247)
1 Apollo Theater C5
2 Cathedral Church of St John the Divine B6

Sights (p251)
3 555 Edgecombe Ave B1
4 Abyssinian Baptist Church. C4
5 Bronx Museum D1
6 Canaan Baptist Church C6
7 Columbia University B6
8 Convent Avenue Baptist Church B3
9 El Museo del Barrio D7
10 General Ulysses S Grant National Memorial A5
11 Hamilton Grange B3
12 Hamilton Heights Historic District B3
13 Malcolm Shabazz Harlem Market C6
14 Morris-Jumel Mansion Museum B1
15 Riverside Church A5
16 Schomburg Center for Research in Black Culture C4
17 Strivers' Row C4
18 Studio Museum in Harlem ... C5
19 Sylvan Terrace B1
20 Yankee Stadium C1

Eating (p255)
21 BLVD Bistro B6
22 Charles' Pan-Fried Chicken B2
23 Community Food & Juice A6
24 Dinosaur Bar-B-Que A4
25 Harlem Public A3
26 Maison Harlem B5
27 Pisticci A5
28 Red Rooster C5
29 Reverence C4
30 Seasoned Vegan C6
31 Sylvia's C5
32 Tom's Restaurant B6

Drinking & Nightlife (p258)
33 67 Orange Street B6
Ginny's Supper Club .. (see 28)
34 Harlem Hops C4
35 Shrine C4
36 Silvana B6
The Chipped Cup .... (see 25)

Entertainment (p258)
37 Amore Opera A5
Marjorie Eliot's Parlor Jazz .... (see 3)
38 Maysles Documentary Center C5
39 Minton's C6

Shopping (p259)
40 Atmos C5
41 Flamekeepers Hat Club C5
42 Harlem Haberdashery C5
43 Lit. Bar E4
44 Revolution Books C4

Sports & Activities (p259)
45 Riverbank State Park A3

Sleeping (p343)
46 Aloft Harlem B5
47 Harlem Flophouse C5

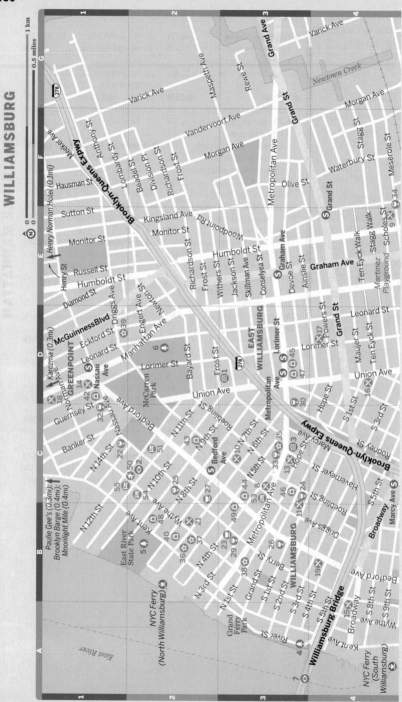

WILLIAMSBURG

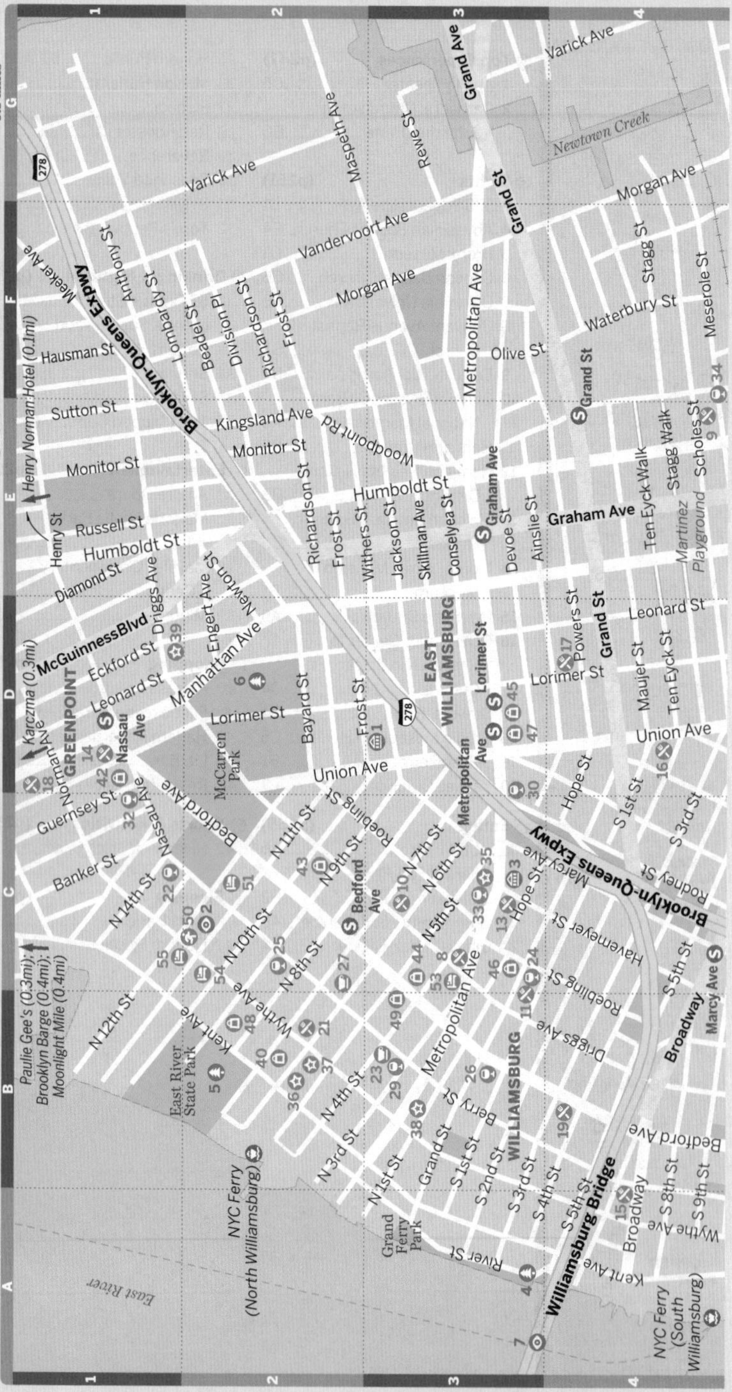

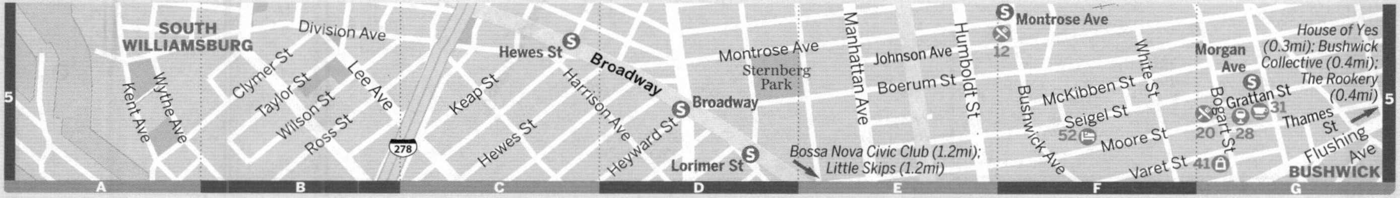

Sights (p273)
1 Brooklyn Art Library ... D3
2 Brooklyn Brewery ... C2
3 City Reliquary ... C3
4 Domino Park ... A3
5 East River State Park ... B2
6 McCarren Park ... D2
7 Williamsburg Bridge ... A3

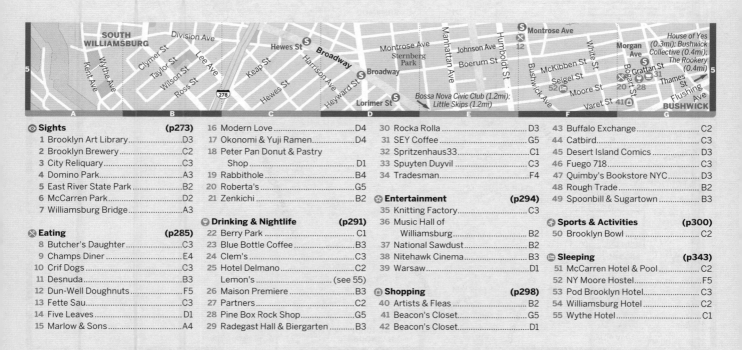

Eating (p285)
8 Butcher's Daughter ... C3
9 Champs Diner ... E4
10 Crif Dogs ... C3
11 Desnuda ... B3
12 Dun-Well Doughnuts ... F5
13 Fette Sau ... C3
14 Five Leaves ... D1
15 Marlow & Sons ... A4
16 Modern Love ... D4
17 Okonomi & Yuji Ramen ... D4
18 Peter Pan Donut & Pastry Shop ... D1
19 Rabbithole ... B4
20 Roberta's ... G5
21 Zenkichi ... B2

Drinking & Nightlife (p291)
22 Berry Park ... C1
23 Blue Bottle Coffee ... B3
24 Clem's ... C3
25 Hotel Delmano ... C2
Lemon's ... (see 55)
26 Maison Premiere ... B3
27 Partners ... C2
28 Pine Box Rock Shop ... G5
29 Radegast Hall & Biergarten ... B3
30 Rocka Rolla ... D3
31 SEY Coffee ... G5
32 Spritzenhaus33 ... C1
33 Spuyten Duyvil ... C3
34 Tradesman ... F4

Entertainment (p294)
35 Knitting Factory ... C3
36 Music Hall of Williamsburg ... B2
37 National Sawdust ... B2
38 Nitehawk Cinema ... B3
39 Warsaw ... D1

Shopping (p298)
40 Artists & Fleas ... B2
41 Beacon's Closet ... G5
42 Beacon's Closet ... D1
43 Buffalo Exchange ... C2
44 Catbird ... C3
45 Desert Island Comics ... D3
46 Fuego 718 ... C3
47 Quimby's Bookstore NYC ... D3
48 Rough Trade ... B2
49 Spoonbill & Sugartown ... B3

Sports & Activities (p300)
50 Brooklyn Bowl ... C2

Sleeping (p343)
51 McCarren Hotel & Pool ... C2
52 NY Moore Hostel ... F5
53 Pod Brooklyn Hotel ... C3
54 Williamsburg Hotel ... C2
55 Wythe Hotel ... C1

BOERUM HILL, CARROLL GARDENS, COBBLE HILL, FORT GREENE & RED HOOK

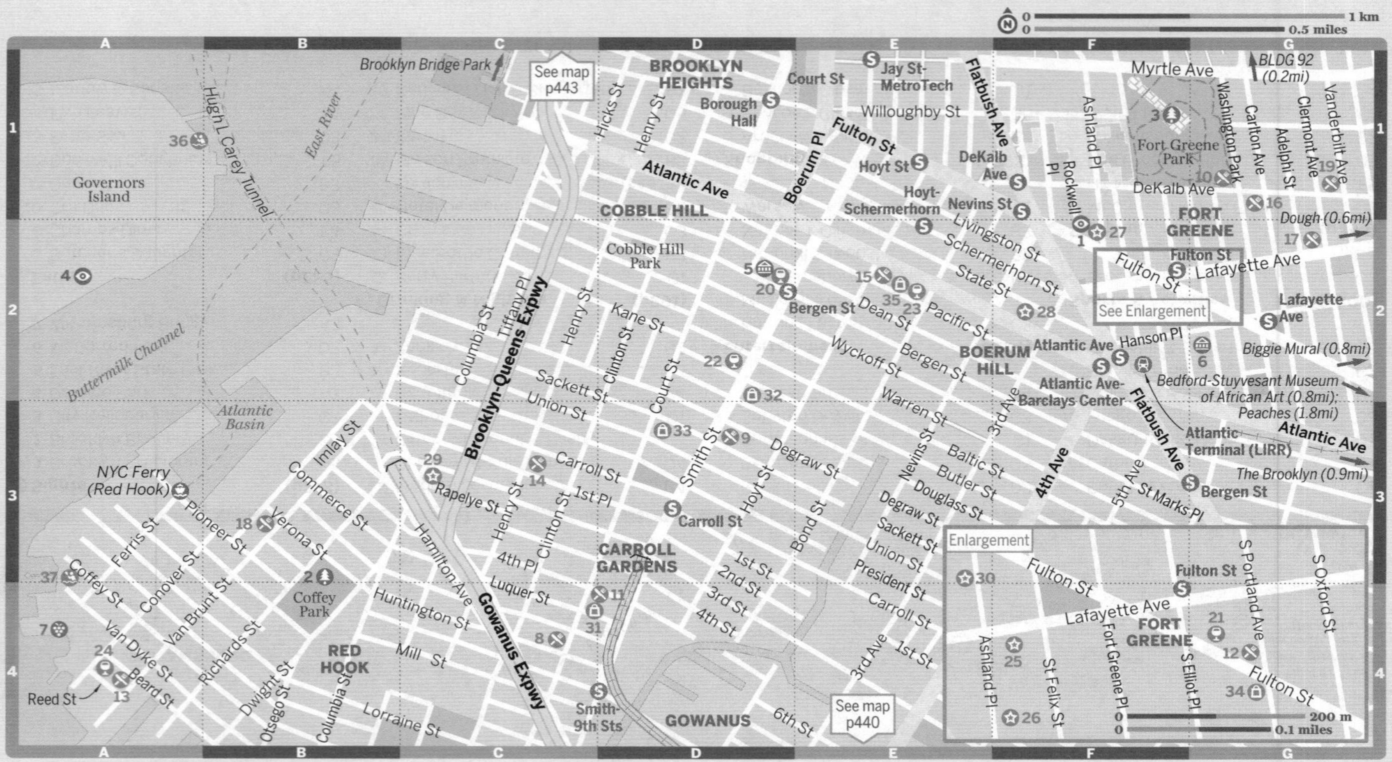

BOERUM HILL, CARROLL GARDENS, COBBLE HILL, FORT GREENE & RED HOOK

Sights **(p267)**

1 BRIC House ... F2
2 Coffey Park ... B3
3 Fort Greene Park ... F1
4 Governors Island ... A2
5 Invisible Dog ... D2
6 Museum of Contemporary African Diasporan Arts ... G2
7 Red Hook Winery ... A4

Eating **(p280)**

8 Buttermilk Channel ... C4
9 FOB ... D3
10 Fort Greene Greenmarket ... G1
11 Frankies 457 Spuntino ... D4
12 Green Grape Annex ... G4
13 Hometown Bar-B-Que ... A4
14 Lucali ... C3
15 Mile End ... E2
16 Miss Ada ... G1
17 Olea ... G2
18 Red Hook Lobster Pound ... B3
19 Roman's ... G1

Drinking & Nightlife **(p289)**

20 61 Local ... D2
21 Black Forest Brooklyn ... G4
22 Clover Club ... D2
23 Robert Bar ... E2
24 Sunny's ... A4

Entertainment **(p294)**

25 BAM Café ... F4
26 BAM Fisher Building ... F4
BAM Howard Gilman Opera House ... (see 25)
BAM Rose Cinemas ... (see 25)
27 BAM Strong ... F2
Brooklyn Academy of Music ... (see 25)
28 Eastville Comedy Club ... F2
29 Jalopy ... C3
30 Theater for a New Audience ... E3

Shopping **(p296)**

31 Black Gold Records ... C4
32 Books Are Magic ... D2
33 Brooklyn Strategist ... D3
34 Greenlight Bookstore ... G4
35 Twisted Lily ... E2

Sports & Activities **(p300)**

36 Governors Island Pier 101 ... A1
37 Red Hook Boaters ... A3

PARK SLOPE & PROSPECT PARK

Key on p442

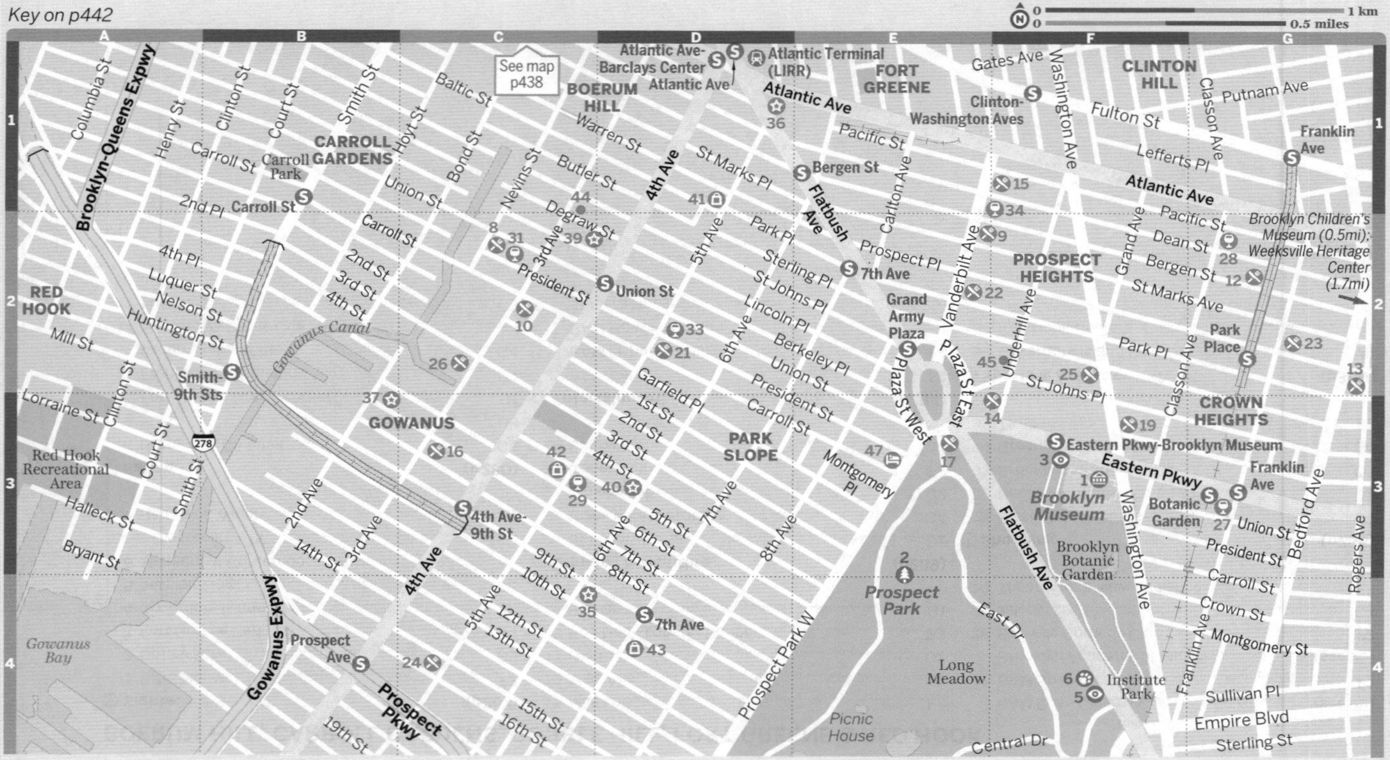

PARK SLOPE & PROSPECT PARK

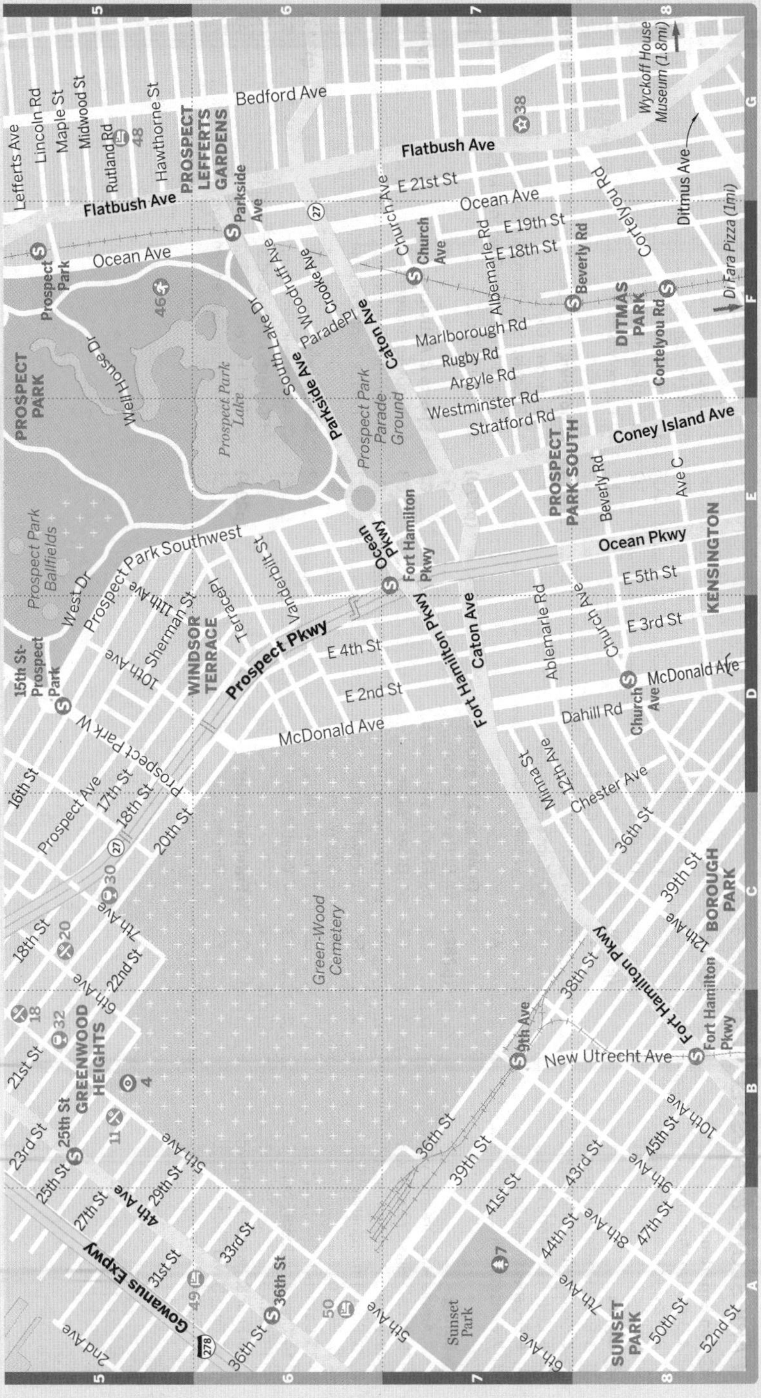

PARK SLOPE & PROSPECT PARK *Map on p440*

Top Experiences (p262)
1 Brooklyn Museum ... F3
2 Prospect Park ... E3

Sights (p270)
3 Brooklyn Botanic Garden ... F3
4 Green-Wood Cemetery ... B5
5 Lefferts Historic House ... F4
6 Prospect Park Zoo ... F4
7 Sunset Park ... A7

Eating (p282)
8 Ample Hills Creamery ... C2
9 Ample Hills Creamery ... E2
10 Baba's Pierogies ... C2
11 Baked in Brooklyn ... B5
12 Berg'n ... G2
13 Catfish ... G2
14 Cheryl's Global Soul ... F3
15 Chuko ... F1
16 Four & Twenty Blackbirds ... C3
17 King David Tacos ... E3
18 Korzo ... B5
19 Lincoln Station ... F3
20 Lot 2 ... C5
21 Luke's Lobster ... D2
22 Olmsted ... E2
23 Screamer's Pizza ... G2
24 Sidecar ... C4
25 Tom's Restaurant ... F2
26 Whole Foods ... C2

Drinking & Nightlife (p290)
27 Butter & Scotch ... G3
28 Friends and Lovers ... G2
29 Ginger's Bar ... C3
30 Greenwood Park ... C5
31 Royal Palms ... C2
32 Sea Witch ... B5
33 Union Hall ... D2
34 Weather Up ... F1

Entertainment (p294)
35 Barbès ... C4
36 Barclays Center ... D1
37 Bell House ... B3
38 Kings Theatre ... G7
39 Littlefield ... C2
40 Puppetworks ... D3

Shopping (p298)
41 Beacon's Closet ... D1
42 Brooklyn Superhero Supply Co ... C3
Grand Army Plaza Greenmarket ... (see 17)
43 Leroy's Place ... D4

Sports & Activities (p300)
44 Brooklyn Boulders ... C1
45 Brooklyn Brainery ... F2
46 LeFrak Center at Lakeside ... F5

Sleeping (p343)
47 At Home in Brooklyn ... E3
48 Lefferts Manor Bed & Breakfast ... G5
49 The L Hotel ... A6
50 Wyndham Garden Brooklyn Sunset Park ... A6

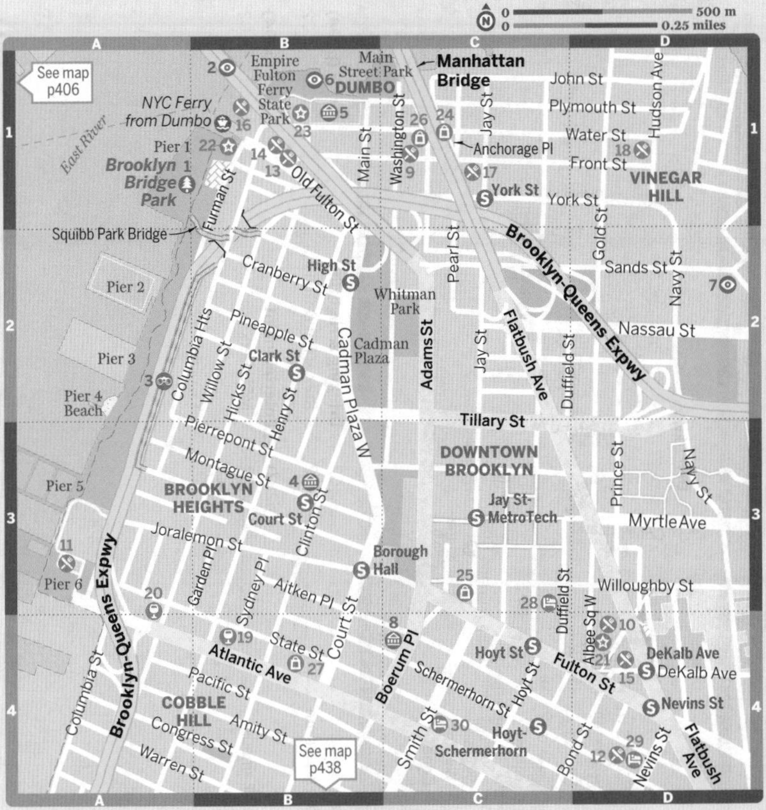

Top Experiences (p262)
1 Brooklyn Bridge Park ... A1

Sights (p266)
2 Brooklyn Bridge ... B1
3 Brooklyn Heights Promenade ... A2
4 Brooklyn Historical Society ... B3
5 Empire Stores ... B1
6 Jane's Carousel ... B1
7 Kings County Distillery ... D2
8 New York Transit Museum ... C4

Eating (p278)
9 AlMar ... C1
10 DeKalb Market Hall ... D4
11 Fornino at Pier 6 ... A3
12 Govinda's Vegetarian Lunch ... D4
13 Grimaldi's ... B1
14 Juliana's ... B1
15 Junior's Restaurant & Bakery ... D4
16 River Cafe ... B1
17 Superfine ... C1
18 Vinegar Hill House ... D1

Drinking & Nightlife (p289)
19 Floyd ... B4
20 Montero Bar & Grill ... A3

Entertainment (p294)
21 Alamo Drafthouse ... D4
22 Bargemusic ... B1
23 St Ann's Warehouse ... B1

Shopping (p297)
24 Brooklyn Flea ... C1
25 Fulton Mall ... C3
26 Powerhouse Arena ... C1
27 Sahadi's ... B4

Sleeping (p343)
28 Aloft New York Brooklyn ... C3
29 EVEN Hotel ... D4
30 NU Hotel ... C4

CONEY ISLAND & BRIGHTON BEACH

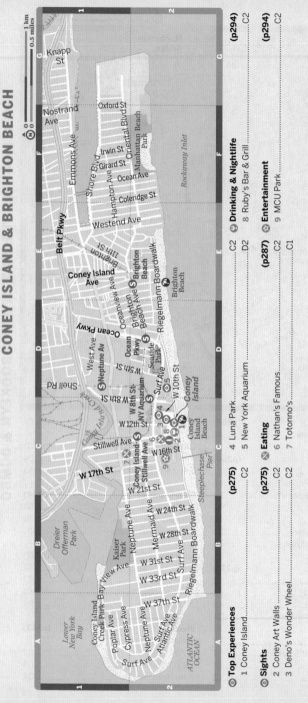

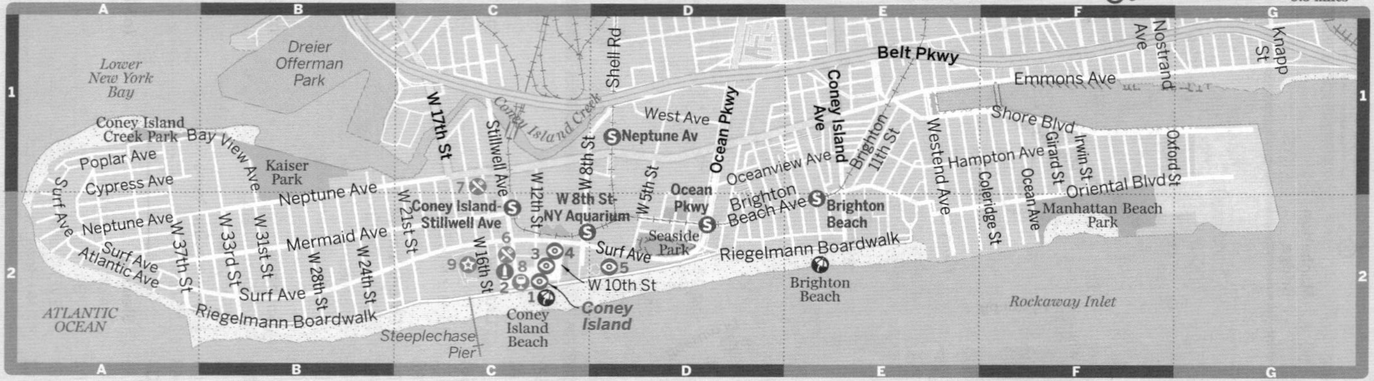

Top Experiences (p275)
1 Coney Island C2

Sights (p275)
2 Coney Art Walls C2
3 Deno's Wonder Wheel C2
4 Luna Park C2
5 New York Aquarium D2

Eating (p287)
6 Nathan's Famous C2
7 Totonno's C1

Drinking & Nightlife (p294)
8 Ruby's Bar & Grill C2

Entertainment (p294)
9 MCU Park C2

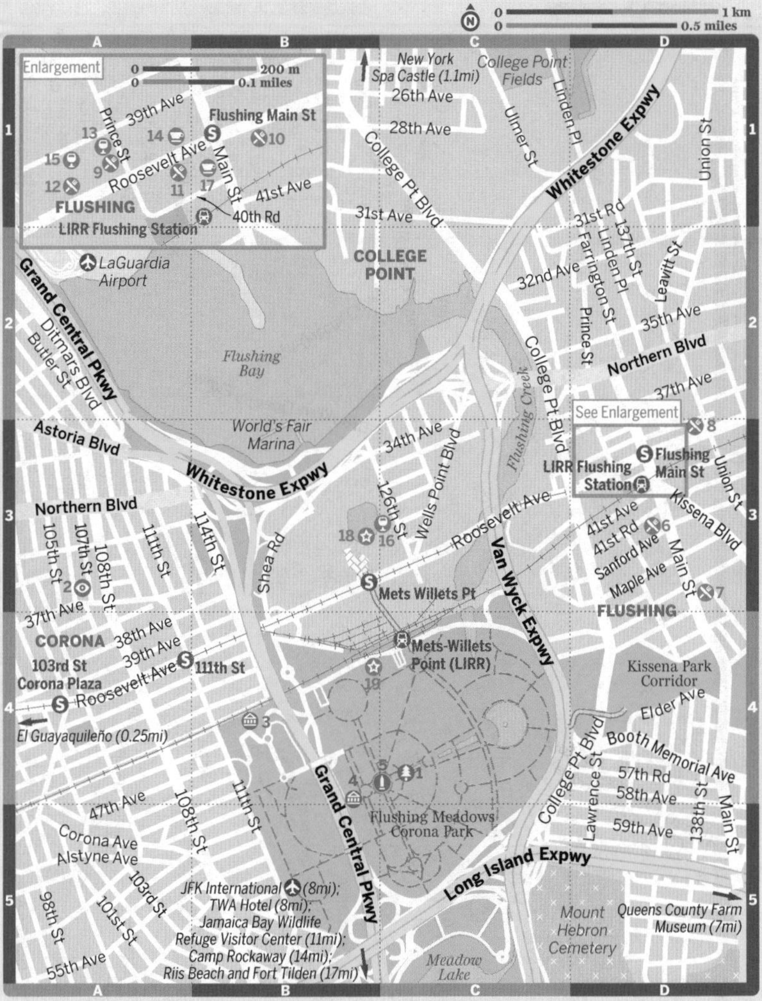

Sights (p306)

1 Flushing Meadows Corona Park............C4
2 Louis Armstrong House............A3
3 New York Hall of Science............B4
4 Queens Museum............B4
5 Unisphere............C4

Eating (p313)

6 Golden Shopping Mall............D3
7 Hunan Kitchen of Grand Sichuan............D3
8 Liuyishou Hotpot............D3
9 Nan Xiang Xiao Long Bao............A1
10 New World Food Court............B1
11 Soy Bean Chen Flower Shop............A1
12 Szechuan House............A1

Drinking & Nightlife (p316)

13 COOP............A1
14 Fang Gourmet Tea............A1
15 Leaf Bar & Lounge............A1
16 Mikkeller NYC............C3
17 Tiger Sugar............B1

Entertainment (p316)

18 Citi Field............B3
19 USTA Billie Jean King National Tennis Center............B4

ASTORIA

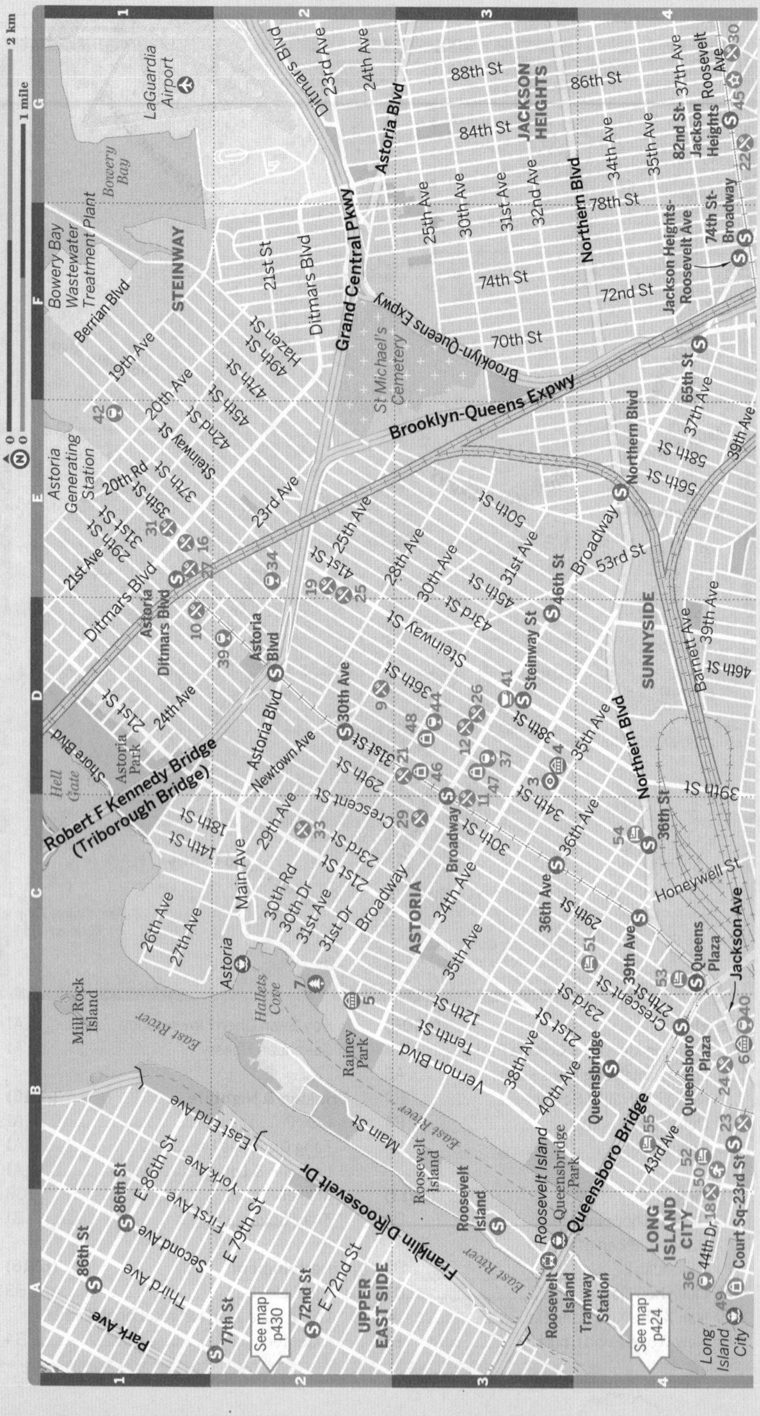

ASTORIA
1 mile
2 km
LaGuardia Airport
Bowery Bay
Bowery Bay Wastewater Treatment Plant
Astoria Generating Station
STEINWAY
JACKSON HEIGHTS
ASTORIA
SUNNYSIDE
LONG ISLAND CITY
UPPER EAST SIDE
Mill Rock Island
Hell Gate
Astoria Park
Hallets Cove
Rainey Park
Roosevelt Island
St Michael's Cemetery
Queensbridge Park
East River
Robert F Kennedy Bridge (Triborough Bridge)
Queensboro Bridge
Grand Central Pkwy
Brooklyn-Queens Expwy
Astoria Blvd
Ditmars Blvd
Northern Blvd
Broadway
Steinway St
Shore Blvd
Berrian Blvd
Newtown Ave
Main Ave
Vernon Blvd
Crescent St
Franklin D Roosevelt Dr
East End Ave
York Ave
First Ave
Second Ave
Third Ave
Park Ave
E 86th St
E 79th St
E 72nd St
Main St
Hazen St
Honeywell St
Barnett Ave
Jackson Ave
Roosevelt Ave
Astoria-Ditmars Blvd
Astoria Blvd
30th Ave
Broadway
36th Ave
39th Ave
Queensboro Plaza
Queens Plaza
Court Sq-23rd St
44th Dr
Long Island City
Queensbridge
Roosevelt Island
Roosevelt Island Tramway Station
46th St
Steinway St
Northern Blvd
65th St
36th St
Jackson Heights-Roosevelt Ave
74th St-Broadway
82nd St-Jackson Heights
86th St
77th St
72nd St
See map p430
See map p424

Top Experiences (p303)
1 MoMA PS1 ... B5

Sights (p306)
2 Gantry Plaza State Park ... A5
3 Kaufman Arts District ... D3
4 Museum of the Moving Image ... D3
5 Noguchi Museum ... B2
6 SculptureCenter ... B4
7 Socrates Sculpture Park ... C2

Eating (p311)
8 Addā ... C5
9 Ample Hills Creamery ... D2
10 Artopolis ... D1
11 Bahari Estiatorio ... C3
12 Brooklyn Bagel & Coffee Company ... D3
13 Cannelle Patisserie ... A5
14 Casa Enrique ... A5
15 Cyclo ... A5
16 HinoMaru ... E1
17 HK Food Court ... G5
18 John Brown Smokehouse ... A4
19 Kabab Cafe ... E2
20 Khao Kang ... G5
21 King Souvlaki ... D3
22 La Esquina del Camarón ... G4
23 LIC Market ... B4
24 M Wells Steakhouse ... B4
Mina's ... (see 1)
25 Mombar ... E2
26 Pye Boat Noodle ... D3
27 Rosario's ... E1
28 Sripraphai ... F5
29 Strand Smokehouse ... C3
30 Taco Veloz ... G4
31 Taverna Kyclades ... E1
32 Tournesol ... A5
33 Vesta Trattoria & Wine Bar ... C2

Drinking & Nightlife (p315)
34 Albatross ... E2
35 Alewife ... A5
36 Anable Basin Sailing Bar & Grill ... A4
37 Astoria Bier & Cheese ... D3
38 Bierocracy ... A5
39 Bohemian Hall & Beer Garden ... D2
40 Dutch Kills ... B4
41 Kinship Coffee ... D3
42 SingleCut Beersmiths ... E1
43 Sweetleaf ... A5
44 Vite Vinosteria ... D3

Entertainment (p316)
Creek & the Cave ... (see 43)
45 Terraza 7 ... G4

Shopping (p317)
Artbook ... (see 1)
46 Astoria Bookshop ... D3
47 Lockwood ... D3
48 LoveDay 31 ... D3
49 Mimi & Mo ... A4

Sports & Activities (p318)
50 Cliffs ... B4

Sleeping (p345)
51 Boro Hotel ... C4
52 Local ... B4
53 Q4 ... C4
54 The Collective Paper Factory ... C4
55 Z NYC Hotel ... B4

Our Story

A beat-up old car, a few dollars in the pocket and a sense of adventure. In 1972 that's all Tony and Maureen Wheeler needed for the trip of a lifetime – across Europe and Asia overland to Australia. It took several months, and at the end – broke but inspired – they sat at their kitchen table writing and stapling together their first travel guide, *Across Asia on the Cheap*. Within a week they'd sold 1500 copies. Lonely Planet was born.

Today, Lonely Planet has offices in the US, Ireland and China, with a network of over 2000 contributors in every corner of the globe. We share Tony's belief that 'a great guidebook should do three things: inform, educate and amuse'.

Our Writers

Ali Lemer

Ali has been a Lonely Planet writer and editor since 2007, and has authored guidebooks and articles on Russia, Germany, NYC, Chicago, Los Angeles, Melbourne, Bali, Hawaii, Japan and Scotland, among others. A native New Yorker, Ali has also lived in Melbourne, Chicago, Prague and the UK, and has traveled extensively around Europe, North America, Oceania and Asia.

Anita Isalska

Anita Isalska is a travel journalist, editor and copywriter. After several merry years as a staff writer and editor – a few of them in Lonely Planet's London office – Anita now works freelance between San Francisco, the UK and any Baltic bolthole with good wi-fi. Anita specialises in Eastern and Central Europe, Southeast Asia, France and off-beat travel. Read her stuff on www.anitaisalska.com.

MaSovaida Morgan

MaSovaida is a travel journalist whose wayfaring tendencies have taken her to more than 50 countries across all seven continents. As a Lonely Planet author, she contributes to guidebooks on destinations throughout Southeast Asia, the Middle East, Europe and the Americas. Prior to going freelance in 2018, MaSovaida spent four years in-house at Lonely Planet's Nashville office as a Destination Editor, where she oversaw all of the company's content on South America and Antarctica. Follow her on Instagram @MaSovaida.

Kevin Raub

Atlanta native Kevin Raub started his career as a music journalist in New York, working for *Men's Journal* and *Rolling Stone* magazines. He ditched the rock 'n' roll lifestyle for travel writing and has written more than 95 Lonely Planet guides, focused mainly on Brazil, Chile, Colombia, USA, India, Italy and Portugal. Raub also contributes to a variety of travel magazines in both the USA and UK. Along the way, the self-confessed hophead is in constant search of wildly high IBUs in local beers. Find him at www.kevinraub.net or follow on Twitter and Instagram (@RaubOnTheRoad).

Published by Lonely Planet Global Limited
CRN 554153
12th edition – January 2022
ISBN 978 1 78701 601 9

10 9 8 7 6 5 4 3 2 1
Printed in China